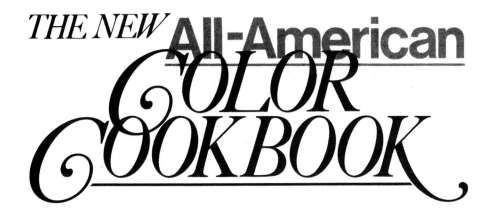

THE NEW All-American COLOR COOKBOOK

THE NEW All-American COLOR COOKBOOK

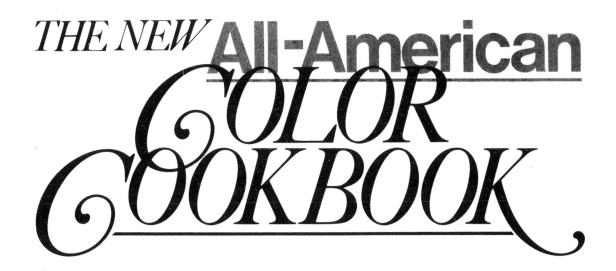

Exeter Books

NEW YORK

Editor: Mary Lambert

This edition published in the USA 1988 by Exeter Books
Distributed by Bookthrift
Exeter is a trademark of Bookthrift Marketing Inc.
Bookthrift is a registered trademark of
Bookthrift Marketing,
New York, New York

ISBN 0-671-09218-9

Printed and bound in Italy by New Interlitho SpA

CONTENTS

SOUPS AND APPETIZERS

Soups	6
Pâtés and mousses	24
Fish and seafood	37
Cheese and egg dishes	54
Vegetable appetizers	70
Meat dishes	78

MAIN COURSES

Pork	86
Beef and veal	100
Lamb	115
Poultry	127
Fish and seafood	144
Offal	159

DELIGHTFUL DESSERTS

Fruity desserts	166
Cakes, pies and flans	180
Light and creamy desserts	197
Ice creams and sherbets	215
Favorites and quick desserts	228

QUICK 'N' EASY COOKING

Salads and vegetables	246
Soups and snacks	259
Quick main meals	273
Pasta 'n' rice	291
Egg 'n' cheese dishes	304
Sandwiches	317

VEGETABLE DISHES

Appetizers	326
Soups	339
Salads	350
Tasty main courses	362
Accompanying dishes	378
Spicy vegetables	393

PARTY COOKING

International cooking	406
Special occasions	428
Family meals	445
Cheap 'n' easy cooking	462
Entertaining friends	474

INTRODUCTION

Eating is one of life's great pleasures, but when it actually comes to preparing and cooking food for family and friends it can often be difficult to plan a varied and appetizing meal which does not take too long to cook or, more importantly, cost too much.

The New All-American Color Cookbook will solve your problems. It is a book which covers all aspects of cooking in one volume. There are over 450 easy-to-follow recipes to suit all occasions – and they won't cost you a fortune! There are soups and appetizers, main courses and desserts plus extra sections on quick 'n' easy cooking for the person with very little time to spare; vegetable dishes for the vegetarian or vegetable lover and party cooking for those who do a lot of entertaining. Now you will easily be able to choose a simple supper snack, plan a mid-week meal or maybe a more elaborate dinner. Try the *Caribbean-Style Dinner* menu in "Party Cooking". It is a full three course meal and also has recipes for cocktails to suit the mood of the evening. Suggestions on drinks to accompany some of the meals are also given in other menus in the "Party Cooking" section. Make sangria for the Spanish Evening and have light, red wine to drink with the French dinner party.

All the recipes are illustrated in full color so that you can see from the start how the dish will turn out. Every recipe also contains comprehensive "Cook's Tips" which give you the timing of each dish, how many calories it contains and buying ideas. Suggestions are also made for alternative fillings to make the dish more economic or perhaps more exotic.

The New All-American Color Cookbook is an invaluable guide to everyday cooking and it is a title you will use time and time again.

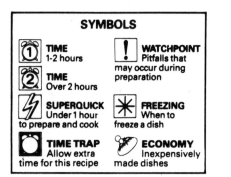

SYMBOLS

TIME
1-2 hours

TIME
Over 2 hours

SUPERQUICK
Under 1 hour
to prepare and cook

TIME TRAP
Allow extra
time for this recipe

WATCHPOINT
Pitfalls that
may occur during
preparation

FREEZING
When to
freeze a dish

ECONOMY
Inexpensively
made dishes

SOUPS AND APPETIZERS

Planning a balanced menu for a dinner party or a pleasant family meal is never easy and often it can be very difficult to find that right first course. This section on soups and appetizers gives you a wide range of inexpensive and quick recipes to choose from.

You can make a warm filling soup, a tasty pâté or maybe a more exotic seafood appetizer, often using some ingredients you will already have on the pantry shelf. There are also a good selection of meat and vegetable recipes to give you that extra variety.

SOUPS

Frankfurter and vegetable soup

SERVES 4

¼ lb frankfurters, cut into ¼-inch slices
2 tablespoons vegetable oil
⅓ lb carrots cut into ½-inch dice
1 celery stalk, thinly sliced
½ lb turnips, cut into ½-inch dice
1 onion, chopped
1 clove garlic, crushed (optional)
3 cups beef broth
1 can (about 14 oz) tomatoes, chopped
salt and freshly ground black pepper
¾ cup shredded green cabbage
1 tablespoon pasta (see Buying guide)
½ cup grated Cheddar cheese

1 Heat the oil in a heavy-based saucepan, add the carrots, celery, turnips, onion and garlic, if using, and cook for 7 minutes, stirring.
2 Remove from the heat and stir in the broth and tomatoes with juice. Season to taste with salt and pepper.
3 Return the pan to the heat and bring to a boil. Lower the heat, cover the pan and simmer for 20 minutes.
4 Add the cabbage and pasta, then cover again and simmer for a further 10 minutes until the pasta is soft.
5 Stir in the frankfurters, taste and adjust seasoning, and cook for a further 3 minutes.
6 Ladle into warmed individual bowls or a soup tureen and serve at once. Hand the grated cheese in a separate bowl for sprinkling on top of the soup.

Cook's Notes

TIME
Preparation takes 20 minutes, cooking 45 minutes.

BUYING GUIDE
Soup pasta, or pastina, as the Italians call it, comes in tiny star and circle shapes. If it is not available, use small pasta shapes or quick-cook pasta broken into ½-inch lengths.

VARIATION
Use potatoes or rutabagas in place of turnips.

FREEZING
Transfer to a rigid container, cool quickly, then seal, label and freeze for up to 6 months. To serve: Thaw at room temperature for 2-3 hours, then reheat thoroughly until bubbling.
Add a little more broth if necessary.

SERVING IDEAS
Serve this hearty soup with toast or whole wheat bread for a meal in itself.

● 250 calories per portion

Quick meat and potato soup

SERVES 4

1½ lb potatoes, diced
1 tablespoon vegetable oil
1 large onion, finely chopped
2½ cups chicken broth
salt and freshly ground black pepper
1 can (about 7 oz) corned beef, diced
1 can (about 7½ oz) whole kernel corn, drained
1 tablespoon chopped parsley

1 Heat the oil in a large saucepan, add the onion and cook gently for 2-3 minutes. Add the potatoes and cook for a further 1-2 minutes, stirring with a wooden spoon.

2 Stir the broth into the pan, season lightly with salt and pepper and bring to a boil. Lower the heat, cover and simmer for 10 minutes.

3 Add the corned beef and the corn, bring back to a boil, then lower the heat again and simmer for a further 10 minutes.

4 Stir in parsley, taste and adjust seasoning, then pour into warmed soup bowls. Serve at once.

Cook's Notes

TIME
This pantry-shelf meal-in-one soup is extremely quick to make: It can be ready to serve within 30 minutes.

VARIATIONS
Drained canned lima beans could be used instead of, or in addition to, the corn. Children like baked beans in this soup.

SERVING IDEAS
Serve with hot pita bread, wholewheat rolls or French bread.

BUYING GUIDE
Choose firm, waxy potatoes such as the Idaho type for this soup. Floury potatoes would not be suitable, as they tend to disintegrate.

● 350 calories per portion

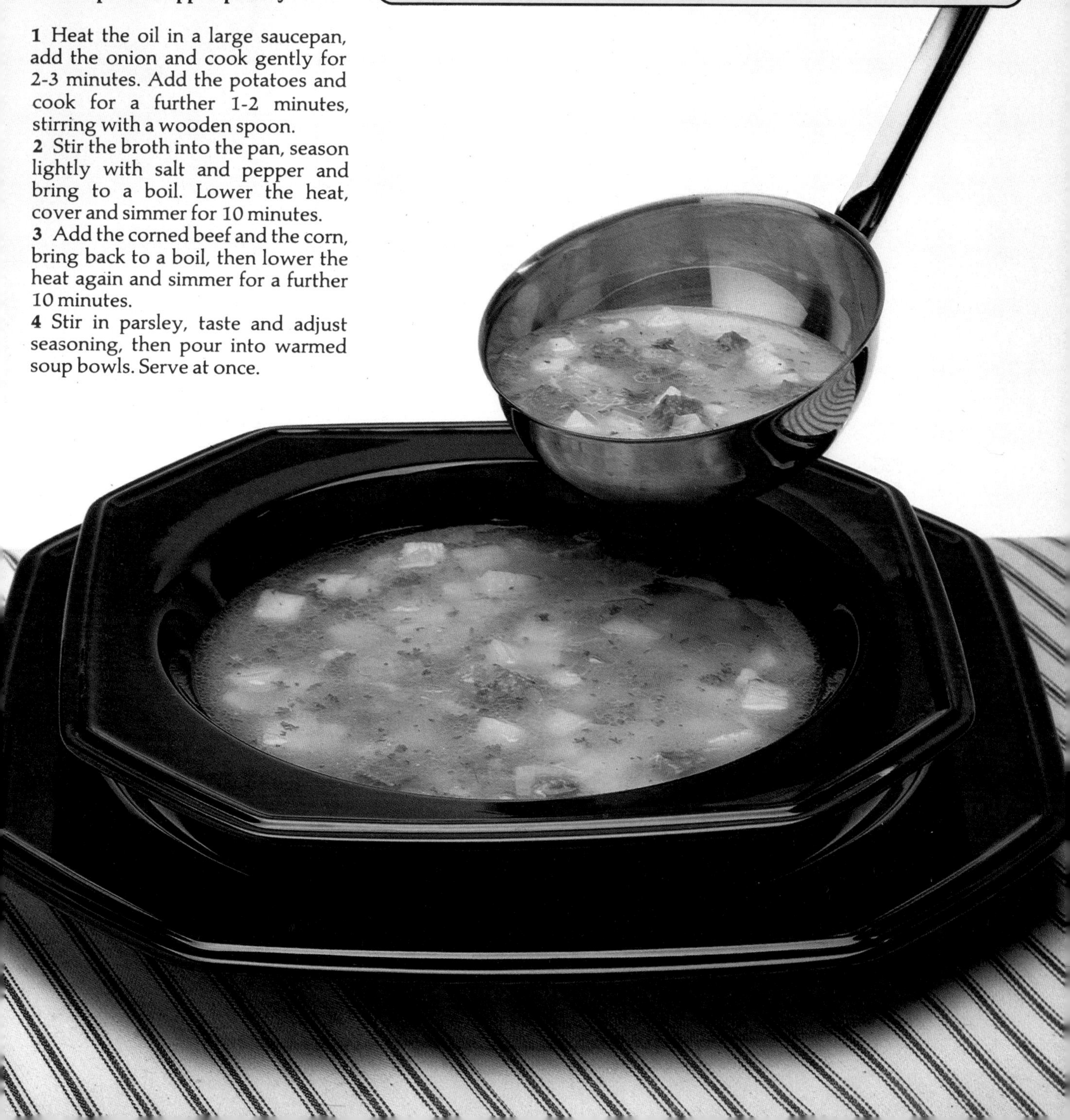

Salami and tomato soup

SERVES 4

⅓ cup sliced, skinned and roughly
  chopped salami
1 tablespoon butter
¾ cup diced potatoes
¾ cup diced carrots
1 onion, roughly chopped
1 teaspoon paprika
1 can (about 8 oz) tomatoes, chopped
⅔ cup tomato juice
2 cups chicken broth
¼ teaspoon dried rosemary
salt and freshly ground white
  pepper
1 can (about 14 oz) navy beans
1 tablespoon chopped fresh parsley

SESAME CROUTONS

2 tablespoons butter, softened
1 tablespoon sesame seeds
1 teaspoon Dijon-style mustard
4 thick slices white bread, crusts
  removed

1 Melt the butter in a saucepan, add
the potatoes, carrots, onion and
paprika and cook gently for 5
minutes until the onions are soft.

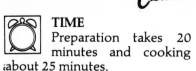

Cook's Notes

 TIME
Preparation takes 20
minutes and cooking
about 25 minutes.

 VARIATIONS
Use ham or garlic
sausage instead of the
salami. Red kidney beans or
butter or lima beans could be
used instead of navy beans.

ECONOMY
Use any left-over cook-
ed meat such as pork or
chicken for this recipe.

 FOR CHILDREN
Use sliced frankfurters
or cooked pork sausages
instead of the salami.

FREEZING
Cool completely, then
transfer to a rigid con-
tainer. Seal, label and freeze for
up to 3 months. To serve:
Reheat from frozen, then stir in
the beans and cook for a further
5 minutes while making the
sesame croutons.

● 330 calories per portion

2 Stir in the tomatoes and their
juice, the tomato juice and broth
then bring to a boil. Lower the heat,
stir in the rosemary and season with
salt and pepper. Cover and simmer
for 20 minutes until the vegetables
are tender.

3 Remove from the heat and leave
to cool slightly, then purée in a
blender or work through a sieve.

4 Make the croutons: Put the butter
in a bowl and beat in the sesame
seeds and mustard. Spread on one
side of each slice of bread. Cut the

bread into ¾-inch cubes and put
them in a skillet. Cook gently for 5
minutes or until they are golden,
turning frequently.

5 Return the soup to the rinsed-out
pan and stir in the salami. ✳ Add
the beans and heat through gently
for 5 minutes, then taste and adjust
the seasoning if necessary.

6 Ladle the soup into warmed
individual bowls or a soup tureen,
top with the sesame croutons and
then sprinkle over the chopped
parsley. Serve the soup at once.

Spinach and liver pâté soup

SERVES 4

1 can (about 1 lb 12 oz) cream of chicken soup
½ lb chopped frozen spinach, thawed, or canned spinach, drained
¼ lb liver pâté (see Buying guide)
a little milk (optional)
2 teaspoons lemon juice
salt and freshly ground black pepper

TO GARNISH

2 tablespoons butter or margarine
4 slices bacon, chopped
2 slices white bread, crusts removed and cut into small dice

1 Make up the garnish: Melt the butter in a skillet. Add the bacon and cook briskly for 2-3 minutes to release any fat. Add the diced bread and cook over moderate to high heat until both bacon and bread are lightly browned and crisp. Drain the bacon and croutons well on paper towels and keep hot until serving.

2 Pour the soup into a large saucepan, add the spinach and heat very gently until the mixture is just simmering.

3 Using a wire whisk, gradually beat the liver pâté into the soup. If the soup seems too thick, add a small amount of milk. Add the lemon juice and season carefully with salt and pepper.

4 Serve the soup piping hot in warmed individual soup bowls, sprinkled with the crispy bacon pieces and the croutons.

Cook's Notes

TIME
Preparation takes about 20 minutes.

BUYING GUIDE
Canned liver pâté is an ideal choice for this soup. A can of pâté is handy for instant snacks. Or use it in savory sauces.

SERVING IDEAS
With its interesting flavor and attractive green color this soup is also perfect for a warming snack, served with crusty French bread. It is not meant to be a complete meal in itself.

● 370 calories per portion

Country soup

SERVES 4
1 potato, diced
1 large onion, sliced
1 small head celery, sliced
¼ head firm cabbage, shredded
1 can (about 8 oz) tomatoes with juice
3¾ cups beef or ham broth
1 can (about 8 oz) kidney beans, drained
1 large or 2 medium frankfurter sausages
⅓ cup diced garlic sausage or salami
⅓ cup diced smoked sausage
salt and freshly ground black pepper
1 tablespoon finely chopped fresh parsley

1 Put the potato, onion, celery and cabbage in a large saucepan. Add the tomatoes with their juice, breaking them up against the sides of the pan with a wooden spoon.

2 Add the broth to the pan and bring quickly to a boil. Lower the heat to moderate, cover and simmer for 40 minutes.

3 Add the kidney beans, cover and cook for a further 20 minutes.

4 Meanwhile, bring a pan of water to a boil. Put the frankfurters into it and heat them through for 2 minutes. Remove with a slotted spoon and slice.

5 Add the garlic and smoked sausage and the frankfurters to the soup. Simmer over low heat for 15 minutes. Taste and adjust seasoning, [!] then pour into warmed individual soup bowls and sprinkle with chopped parsley. Serve at once.

Beefy soup

SERVES 4-6
1 lb lean ground beef
3 tablespoons shortening
2 onions, finely chopped
1 large potato, cut into ½-inch
    dice
1 large green pepper, seeded and cut
    into chunks
2 teaspoons paprika
2 tablespoons tomato paste
3¾ cups beef broth (see Cook's tip)
1 can (about 7 oz) whole kernel corn,
    drained
salt and freshly ground black
    pepper
⅔ cup dairy sour cream
1 tablespoon chopped chives

1 Melt shortening in a large saucepan, add the onions and potato and cook gently for about 5 minutes. Add the green pepper and cook for a further 10 minutes, stirring the vegetables occasionally to prevent them from sticking.
2 Sprinkle the paprika into the pan and cook for 1-2 minutes. Add the tomato paste and cooked beef, stirring with a wooden spoon to remove any lumps. Cook for 5 minutes, then pour in the beef broth and bring to a boil. Lower the heat and simmer for about 15 minutes, until the potatoes are tender.
3 Stir in the drained corn, heat through for 1-2 minutes, then taste and adjust seasoning if necessary.
4 Pour into warmed individual soup bowls. Top each serving with a swirl of sour cream, sprinkle with the chives and serve at once.

Mexican chili soup

SERVES 4
⅓-½ lb lean ground beef
1 tablespoon corn oil
1 large onion, chopped
½ teaspoon ground cumin
1½ tablespoons all-purpose flour
1 can (about 8 oz) tomatoes
½ teaspoon hot-pepper sauce (see
    Variations)
3¾ cups beef broth
salt and freshly ground black pepper
1 can (about 15 oz) red kidney beans,
    drained (see Variations)
fresh coriander or flat-leaved
    parsley, to garnish (optional)

1 Heat the oil in a saucepan and add the onion, ground beef and cumin. Cook over high heat until the meat is evenly browned, stirring with a wooden spoon to remove any lumps and mix thoroughly.
2 Sprinkle in the flour and stir well, then add the tomatoes with their juice, the pepper sauce and broth.
3 Bring to a boil, stirring. Season to taste with salt and pepper and simmer, uncovered, for 25 minutes.
4 Add the drained beans, stir them in and cook for a further 5 minutes or until heated through. Transfer to a warmed serving dish, sprinkle with coriander, if liked, then serve the soup at once (see Serving ideas).

Cook's Notes

 TIME
Preparation time is about 5 minutes and cooking is about 35 minutes.

VARIATIONS
This amount of hot-pepper sauce gives piquancy. If unavailable, use chili powder.
    Drained canned butter beans or navy beans can be used here instead of red kidney beans and a small red pepper, thinly sliced, can be added with the onion.

SERVING IDEAS
This soup is also ideal for lunch or supper, served with whole wheat, granary or hot pita bread or warmed whole wheat rolls.

FOR CHILDREN
Add 1 can (about 8 oz) baked beans in tomato sauce instead of the kidney beans and add only a drop of hot-pepper sauce or omit it.

● 210 calories per portion

Autumn soup

SERVES 4-6

1 large onion, chopped
2 carrots, cut into ½-inch dice
1 small rutabaga, peeled and cut into
   ½-inch dice
½ green pepper, seeded and thinly
   sliced
3 tablespoons vegetable oil
1 tablespoon tomato paste
3¾ cups beef broth
⅓ cup red lentils
salt and freshly ground black pepper
⅓ lb pork sausagemeat
½ cup fresh white bread crumbs
½ teaspoon chopped fresh
   rosemary, or 1 teaspoon dried
   rosemary
1 green apple
1 large potato, cut into ½-inch
   dice
chopped chives, to garnish

1 Heat the oil in a large flameproof casserole. Add the onion, carrots, rutabaga and green pepper and cook gently for 3 minutes until the vegetables are soft but not colored.
2 Stir in the tomato paste, broth and lentils, and season to taste with salt and pepper.
3 Bring to a boil, then lower the heat, cover and simmer for 20 minutes until the vegetables are just tender.
4 Meanwhile, put the sausagemeat, bread crumbs and rosemary in a bowl. Mix thoroughly with your hands, then shape into 12 small balls.
5 Pare and core the apple, then cut it into ½-inch dice. Add to the soup with the potato and sausage-meat balls and simmer for a further 25 minutes until all the vegetables are tender.
6 Taste and adjust seasoning, then serve hot, sprinkled with chives.

Cook's Notes

TIME
Preparation takes 20 minutes, cooking 50 minutes.

SERVING IDEAS
Serve with crusty bread or rolls as a main-meal soup for lunch. Sprinkle with grated cheese, if liked.

VARIATIONS
In place of the sausage-meat balls, dice ¼ lb skinned garlic sausage or salami and stir into the soup 10 minutes before the end of cooking. Pearl barley can be used instead of lentils, but you will need to allow at least another 30 minutes cooking time before adding the sausage-meat balls.

COOK'S TIP
To give the sausage-meat balls a golden-brown color cook them separately in a little oil, then add to the soup just before serving.

● 380 calories per portion

Mussel soup

SERVES 4

4½ pints fresh mussels (see Buying guide and Preparation)
2 tablespoons vegetable oil
2 tablespoons butter
1 large onion, finely chopped
1 clove garlic, crushed (optional)
3 tablespoons finely chopped fresh coriander (see Variation)
3 cups water
⅔ cup white wine
1 can (about 8 oz) tomatoes, drained and chopped
salt and freshly ground black pepper

1 Heat the oil and butter in a large heavy-based saucepan, add the onion, the garlic, if using, and the coriander and cook gently for about 5 minutes until the onion is soft and lightly colored.
2 Pour in the water and wine and add the tomatoes. Season to taste with salt and pepper.

Cook's Notes

TIME
Preparing and cooking the soup takes about 30 minutes. Allow extra time for preparing the mussels.

PREPARATION
Check that the mussels are fresh: Tap any open ones against a work surface and discard if they do not shut. Pull away any beards (pieces of seaweed) gripped between the shells of mussels. Scrub the mussles under cold running water, then scrape away the encrustations with a sharp knife. Soak the mussels in fresh cold water to cover for 2-3 hours, changing the water several times during this period.

BUYING GUIDE
Fresh mussels are available from October-March. Always buy them the day you are going to eat them. Look for closed mussels with unbroken shells. Frozen shelled mussels, which are available all year round, can be used instead.

VARIATION
Use parsley or chervil instead of coriander.

SERVING IDEAS
The mussels can be eaten with the fingers so provide napkins and a large dish to put the empty shells in.

● 255 calories per portion

3 Add the mussels and bring to a boil. Cover the pan, lower the heat and simmer gently for about 10 minutes or until the mussel shells have opened. Discard any mussels that do not open during cooking.
4 Spoon the mussels and soup into a warmed soup tureen or individual soup bowls and serve at once (see Serving ideas).

Fish and vegetable soup

SERVES 4

½ lb cod steaks, thawed if frozen, bones and skin removed and cut into ¾-inch pieces
1 tablespoon vegetable oil
1 small onion, chopped
2 potatoes, cut into ½-inch dice (see Buying guide)
2 carrots, cut into ½-inch dice
3 tablespoons all-purpose flour
1¼ cups warm milk
2½ cups warm chicken broth
1 bay leaf
salt and freshly ground black pepper
¼ cup shelled shrimp
½ bunch watercress, stalks removed, to garnish

1 Heat the oil in a large saucepan, add the onion, potatoes and carrots and cook over gentle heat, stirring, for 3 minutes. ⚠️
2 Sprinkle in the flour, stir for 1 minute, then remove from heat and gradually stir in the milk and broth.
3 Return the pan to the heat and bring to boil, stirring. Lower heat, add bay leaf and salt and pepper to taste. Simmer for 15 minutes.
4 Add the cod to the pan and simmer for a further 10 minutes.

5 Discard the bay leaf, stir the shrimp into the soup and heat through for 5 minutes. ✳️ Taste and adjust seasoning, then pour into warmed individual soup bowls and garnish with the watercress. Serve the soup at once.

Cook's Notes

TIME
Preparation takes 20 minutes and cooking about 35 minutes.

FREEZING
Make the soup without adding the watercress. Cool quickly, then freeze in a plastic bag or rigid container for up to 3 months. Reheat from frozen, adding a little extra milk or broth if liked.

VARIATIONS
Any white fish may be used instead of cod.
Use 2 tablespoons chopped parsley or chopped chives in-stead of the watercress.
Swirl 1 tablespoon cream on top of each bowl just before serving.

WATCHPOINT
Do not allow the vege-tables to brown, or the soup will be light brown instead of pale and creamy.

BUYING GUIDE
Choose floury potatoes such as Idaho. Waxy potatoes are not suitable for this soup, as they do not dis-integrate so easily.

● 250 calories per portion

Corn and tuna chowder

SERVES 4-6

1 can (about 12 oz) whole kernel corn
1 can (about 7 oz) tuna
2 tablespoons butter or margarine
1 large onion, finely chopped
2 tablespoons all-purpose flour
2 teaspoons paprika
pinch of cayenne pepper
3¾ cups milk
pinch of salt
grated rind of ½ lemon

TO FINISH
½ cup finely grated Cheddar cheese
4 tablespoons chopped parsley

1 Drain the corn kernels, reserving the juice. Drain off the oil from the tuna fish and discard. Place the tuna on paper towels to remove excess oil. Flake all the tuna into a bowl.

2 Melt the butter in a saucepan, add the onion and cook gently until soft but not colored.
3 Stir in the flour, paprika and cayenne pepper and cook for 1 minute, stirring constantly with a wooden spoon. Gradually stir in 1½ cups milk and reserved corn juice and bring to a boil, stirring.
4 Stir in the remaining milk and bring the mixture to simmering

point. Add the salt and the grated lemon rind.
5 Add the corn and then simmer the soup, uncovered, for 5 minutes. Add the tuna fish and simmer for a further 5 minutes until heated through.
6 To finish: Taste and adjust seasoning, then pour into warmed individual soup bowls. Sprinkle with the cheese and parsley and serve at once.

Cook's Notes

TIME
The soup takes 30 minutes to prepare and cook.

COOK'S TIP
To make the soup in advance, prepare it up to the end of stage 4, leave to cool, then refrigerate. To finish: Reheat until bubbling, stirring constantly, then continue from stage 5.

! WATCHPOINT
It is important to remove as much oil as possible from the tuna so that the chowder is not greasy.
Always add the cheese just before serving, when the soup is still hot enough for it to melt. Do not bring back to a boil after adding the cheese or the soup will be stringy.

● 410 calories per portion

Provencal fish chowder

SERVES 4-6

1½ lb firm white fish fillets, skinned
    and cut into 1½-inch pieces (see
    Variation)
3 tablespoons vegetable oil
1 lb onions, grated
1 can (about 2 lb) tomatoes
bouquet garni
2 potatoes, cut into small ½-inch
    cubes
24 small black olives, halved and
    pitted
2 tablespoons capers, drained
1¼ cups tomato juice
2½ cups vegetable broth (see
    Preparation)
salt and freshly ground black pepper
3 tablespoons finely chopped fresh
    parsley

1 Heat the oil in a large saucepan,
add the onions and cook gently for
5 minutes until soft and lightly
colored. Add the tomatoes, with
their juice, and the bouquet garni.
Bring to a boil, then lower the heat
and simmer for 5 minutes, stirring
and breaking up the tomatoes with
a wooden spoon.
2 Add all the remaining ingredients
except the parsley and simmer uncovered, for 10-15 minutes, or until
the potato is cooked (see Cook's tip).
3 Add the fish to the pan and
simmer gently, uncovered, for
about 5 minutes, or until the fish is
tender but not breaking up. Remove
the bouquet garni, stir in the
parsley, then taste and adjust
seasoning. Transfer to a warmed
serving bowl and serve at once.

Cook's Notes

 TIME
Total preparation and
cooking time is about
50 minutes.

PREPARATION
For vegetable broth,
save the liquid from
cooked vegetables such as
carrots and cabbage. Alternatively, use a vegetable bouillon
cube, from health food shops.

 SPECIAL OCCASION
This soup is a filling
appetizer and can also
make a lunch or supper party
dish. Give it a real Mediterranean flavor by adding a
crushed clove of garlic.

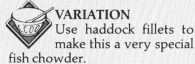 **VARIATION**
Use haddock fillets to
make this a very special
fish chowder.

COOK'S TIP
You can prepare the
chowder up to the end
of stage 2 the day before, then
add the fish and complete the
cooking just before serving.

SERVING IDEAS
Serve with toasted
French bread and butter.

● 395 calories per portion

Pea soup with cheese toast

SERVES 4

1 large can (about 1lb 3oz) green peas
1 tablespoon dried onion flakes
2 tablespoons boiling water
1¼ cups chicken broth
½ teaspoon dried thyme
3 tablespoons instant potato powder (see Cook's tip)
1-2 teaspoons lemon juice
2-3 tablespoons evaporated milk or light cream
salt and freshly ground black pepper
1 tablespoon finely chopped fresh parsley

TOAST

4 small thick slices whole wheat bread
½ cup grated Cheddar cheese
2 tablespoons evaporated milk
¼ teaspoon prepared English mustard

1 Put the dried onion flakes into a cup, pour over the boiling water and leave to stand for at least 15 minutes.
2 Put the peas with their liquid in the pitcher of a blender with the onion mixture and blend until smooth. Work through a strainer. Put into a saucepan with the broth and thyme and bring to a boil over moderate heat.
3 Lower the heat and sprinkle in the potato powder. Stir for 1-2 minutes then remove from heat and stir in the lemon juice and milk. Season to taste with salt and pepper. Return to the heat and simmer gently while you prepare the toast.
4 Preheat the broiler to high, and toast the bread on both sides. Remove from the broiler.
5 Mix the cheese with the milk, mustard and salt and pepper.
6 Spread the cheese mixture on the toast, return to the broiler and cook until the cheese mixture browns.
7 Ladle the soup into warmed individual bowls. Cut each slice of toast into 4 and top with parsley.

Celery and peanut soup

SERVES 4

4 large celery stalks, chopped (see Economy)
6 tablespoons crunchy peanut butter
1 tablespoon butter or margarine
1 tablespoon vegetable oil
1 onion, chopped
3 cups light broth
salt and freshly ground black pepper
4 tablespoons light cream, to serve
chopped celery leaves, to garnish

1 Heat the butter and oil in a saucepan, add the celery and onion and cook gently for 5 minutes until the onion is soft and lightly colored.

2 Add the broth and bring to a boil. Lower the heat, cover and simmer gently for about 30 minutes until the celery is tender.

3 Cool the mixture a little, then work in a blender for a few seconds until smooth.

4 Return to the rinsed-out pan, place over low heat, then beat in the peanut butter. Heat through until just boiling. ✳ Taste and then adjust seasoning.

5 Ladle the soup into 4 warmed individual bowls. Stir 1 tablespoon cream into each, then wait for a few seconds for the cream to rise to the surface. Sprinkle the chopped celery leaves in the center of the bowls and serve at once.

Cheesy potato soup

SERVES 4

1½ lb potatoes, pared and cut into even-sized pieces
salt
2 tablespoons butter or margarine
1 large onion, finely chopped
2 large cloves garlic, finely chopped (optional)
3 celery stalks, finely chopped
1 large carrot, diced small
¼ small rutabaga (weighing about ⅛ lb), diced small
1¼ cup chicken or vegetable broth (see Cook's tip)
⅔ cup milk
½ teaspoon dried thyme or marjoram
½ teaspoon celery salt
freshly ground black pepper
¾ cup grated Cheddar cheese
3 tablespoons chopped parsley

1 Cook the potatoes in enough boiling salted water to cover for about 15 minutes or until tender.
2 When the potatoes are cooked, leave them to cool slightly in the water, then transfer both potatoes and water to a blender and blend until smooth. (If you do not have a blender, pass them through a sieve.) Return the purée to the rinsed-out pan.
3 Melt the butter in a large skillet, add the onion and garlic, if using, and cook over moderate heat until beginning to soften. Add the remaining vegetables to the pan and cook, stirring occasionally, for about 10 minutes, until just beginning to color.
4 Mix the vegetables with the potato purée in the saucepan, then stir in the broth, milk, thyme and celery salt. Add pepper to taste.
5 Bring to a boil, lower the heat and simmer gently for about 15 minutes or until the vegetables are just soft. [!] Stir in the cheese, reserving 2 tablespoons, and simmer for a further 2-3 minutes. Taste and adjust seasoning.
6 Pour into a warmed soup tureen. Sprinkle with the chopped parsley and the remaining cheese and serve at once.

Cook's Notes

TIME
This very filling soup takes just under 1 hour to prepare and cook.

ECONOMY
Stretch the soup to 6 servings and give it a slightly different flavor by adding a small can of corn.

SERVING IDEAS
Serve the soup with hot buttered toast.

WATCHPOINT
Thick soups sometimes stick to the bottom of the saucepan, so it is best to stand the pan on something like wire mesh if you are using a gas stove.

COOK'S TIP
If possible, use home-made broth for a fuller flavor.

● 335 calories per portion

Leek and barley soup

SERVES 4
4 leeks, sliced
¼ cup pearl barley
1 tablespoon vegetable oil
1 small onion, chopped
2 carrots, sliced
1 can (about 14 oz) tomatoes
2½ cups vegetable broth or water
  (see Cook's tip)
½ teaspoon dried mixed herbs
1 bay leaf
salt and freshly ground black pepper
1 can (about 7 oz) butter or lima
  beans, drained

CHEESY BREAD
4 round slices French bread, ¾-inch
  thick
3 tablespoons butter, for cooking
1 clove garlic, cut in half (optional)
1 cup grated Cheddar cheese

1 Heat the oil in a large saucepan, add the onion, leeks and carrots and cook gently for 3-4 minutes.
2 Add the tomatoes with their juice, the broth and the barley, herbs and bay leaf. Season to taste with salt and pepper. Bring to a boil, stirring, then lower the heat, cover and simmer for 50 minutes. Stir occasionally during this time.
3 Meanwhile, make the cheesy bread: Melt the butter in a skillet and when it sizzles add the slices of French bread. Cook over fairly high heat, turning once, until the bread is crisp and golden brown on both sides. Remove from the pan, drain on paper towels and leave to cool.
4 Rub each side of fried bread with the cut sides of the garlic, if using. Press the grated cheese evenly onto the slices of bread, dividing it equally between them. Preheat the broiler to high.
5 Remove the bay leaf from the soup, stir in the drained beans and heat through. Adjust seasoning.
6 Toast the cheese-topped slices of bread until the cheese starts to bubble.
7 Ladle the soup into 4 warmed individual soup bowls and top each one with a slice of cheesy bread. Serve at once.

Chilled zucchini and cheese soup

SERVES 6

1 lb zucchini, cut into 1-inch lengths
3¾ cups chicken broth
1 mint sprig
2 tablespoons butter or margarine
1 onion, chopped
1 clove garlic, crushed (optional)
⅓ lb cream or Boursin cheese (see Economy)
⅔ cup milk
salt and freshly ground black pepper

TO SERVE
6 ice cubes
2 tablespoons heavy cream (see Economy)
extra mint sprigs, to garnish

1 Put the zucchini into a large pan with the broth and mint sprig. Bring to a boil, then lower the heat and simmer for 10 minutes.
2 Meanwhile, melt the butter in a small pan, add the onion and garlic, if using, and cook gently for 5 minutes until the onion is soft and lightly colored.
3 Remove the zucchini from the heat and stir in the onion and garlic. Allow to cool slightly, then pour the zucchini mixture into a blender and work to a purée.
4 In a large bowl, blend the cheese with the milk a little at a time, then beat with a wooden spoon until smooth and creamy. Stir in the zucchini purée.
5 Pour the soup into a clean large bowl or soup tureen, cover and refrigerate for about 4 hours or overnight.
6 To serve: Season the soup to taste with salt and pepper (see Cook's tip). Add ice cubes, swirl over the cream and sprinkle with sprigs of mint. Serve at once.

Cook's Notes

TIME
15 minutes preparation, cooking time 10 minutes, then chill for 4 hours or overnight.

VARIATION
Instead of zucchini, use 1 large cucumber cut into ¾-inch lengths.

ECONOMY
For a less expensive soup lower in calories, use a curd cheese instead of full-fat cheese and plain yoghurt instead of the heavy cream.

COOK'S TIP
Wait until the soup has chilled and the flavors have developed before adding the seasoning.

SERVING IDEAS
Served just with fresh rolls or crusty bread and butter, this soup makes a delicious lunch for a hot day.

● 180 calories per portion

Chilled carrot and orange soup

SERVES 4
1 lb carrots, thinly sliced
1 tablespoon vegetable oil
1 onion, finely chopped
2 tablespoons medium-dry sherry
  (optional)
2½ cups chicken broth
salt and freshly ground black pepper
grated rind of 1 orange
juice of 3 large oranges
1 small carrot, grated, to garnish

1 Heat the oil in a saucepan, add the onion and cook gently for 5 minutes until soft and lightly colored. Add the sherry, if using, and bring to a boil

2 Add the sliced carrots and broth to the pan and season to taste.

3 Bring to a boil, stirring, then lower the heat, cover and simmer gently for 45 minutes until the carrots are very tender. Leave to cool.

4 Pass the soup through a strainer or purée in a blender. Pour the soup into a bowl, cover and refrigerate

for at least 2 hours or overnight.

5 Just before serving, stir the orange rind and juice into the soup, then taste and adjust seasoning. Pour into 4 chilled individual soup bowls, sprinkle a little grated carrot onto each bowl and serve at once.

Cook's Notes

TIME
15 minutes preparation, 45 minutes cooking, plus 2 hours chilling time.

VARIATION
¼ cup unsweetened concentrated orange juice may be substituted for the fresh orange juice.

SERVING IDEAS
If serving the soup at a summer dinner party, give it a special garnish. Cut half an orange into 4 very thin slices. Remove the rind and pith. Float 1 orange slice on top of each bowl of chilled soup and arrange a little grated carrot on top of the slices.

The soup can also be served hot: Prepare to stage 3 but do not cool, reduce to a purée at once and reheat gently with the orange rind and juice.

● 130 calories per portion

PATES AND MOUSSES

Mixed fish pâté

SERVES 4
1 can (about 6 oz) tuna fish in oil
1 can (about 4½ oz) mackerel fillets
 in oil
¼ cup butter, melted and cooled
grated rind of 1 lemon
1 tablespoon lemon juice
1 clove garlic, crushed (optional)
salt and freshly ground black pepper
1 tablespoon light cream (optional)

TO GARNISH
few lemon slices
1-2 parsley sprigs

1 Place the tuna and mackerel, with their oil, in a blender or food processor. Pour over the melted butter and add the lemon rind and juice and the garlic, if using.
2 Blend to a smooth purée. Season well and stir in the cream, if using.
3 Spoon into individual dishes, cover and refrigerate for 2 hours.
4 Garnish with lemon slices and parsley. Served chilled with toast.

Cook's Notes

TIME
10 minutes preparation, plus 2 hours chilling.

COOK'S TIPS
The beauty of this pâté is that it can be made in superquick time, from pantry-shelf ingredients. This makes it ideal for an impromptu appetizer or snack.

VARIATION
Large supermarkets stock cans of tuna with vegetables in a curry sauce. If this is used instead of plain tuna in oil, it will make the pâté more exotic, with just a hint of curry.

● 270 calories per portion

Quick sardine pâté

SERVES 4

1 can (about 15 oz) sardines in tomato sauce (see Cook's tip)
3 tablespoons heavy cream
½ teaspoon Worcestershire sauce
few drops of hot-pepper sauce
2 teaspoons lemon juice
2 tablespoons finely chopped dill pickles
salt and freshly ground black pepper

TO GARNISH

1 tablespoon chopped fresh parsley or flat-leaved parsley sprigs
4 dill pickle fans

1 Drain the sardines and reserve 1 tablespoon of the tomato sauce. Cut the sardines in half

Cook's Notes

TIME
Preparation takes about 5 minutes and chilling takes 30 minutes.

SERVING IDEAS
Serve with slices of warm pita bread or crackers and butter. As a more substantial appetizer, serve with a seasonal salad.

● 180 calories per portion

COOK'S TIP
If preferred, the can of sardines can be refrigerated unopened for 1 hour before making the paté — then there is no need to chill the paté after it is made.

VARIATIONS
This paté can also be made with pilchards in tomato sauce or with canned mackerel in tomato sauce.

2 Place the fish in a bowl with the reserved tomato sauce, the cream, Worcestershire sauce, pepper-sauce, lemon juice and pickles. Beat together thoroughly with a fork and season to taste with salt and pepper.

3 Spoon the mixture into a serving bowl or 4 individual bowls, cover with plastic wrap and then refrigerate for 30 minutes.

4 To serve: Garnish the sardine paté with finely chopped parsley or parsley sprigs and the prepared pickle fans and serve chilled (see Serving ideas).

Egg pâté

SERVES 4

½ lb cream cheese
4 hard-boiled eggs, shelled and
    roughly chopped (see Cook's tip)
1 tablespoon finely chopped chives
salt and freshly ground black pepper
stuffed olives, sliced, to garnish

1 Put the cheese into a bowl and beat until soft. Beat in the chopped eggs and chives and season well with salt and pepper.
2 Spoon into 4 individual dishes. Smooth the top of each with a round-bladed knife, cover with plastic wrap and refrigerate for 30 minutes.
3 To serve: Garnish with the olive slices and serve at once.

Cook's Notes

TIME
Preparation (including hard-boiling the eggs) takes about 30 minutes, but allow another 30 minutes for chilling.

VARIATIONS
Use a full-fat soft cheese flavored with chives, herbs, garlic or crushed peppercorns, and omit the chives and/or the black pepper. For an extra "tangy" flavor, add 1 teaspoon good mustard or Worcestershire sauce or a dash of hot-pepper sauce.

COOK'S TIP
Hard-boiled eggs can be kept, unshelled, in a plastic bag in the refrigerator for 3-4 days.

SERVING IDEAS
Serve as a dinner party appetizer or snack with toast fingers or bread rolls.

● 305 calories per portion

Vegetable terrine

SERVES 4

12 cabbage leaves (see Buying guide), central midribs removed
salt
1 carrot (about ¼ lb), cut into matchstick lengths
1 zucchini (about ¼ lb), cut into matchstick lengths
1 can (about 7 oz) corn and pimiento, drained
2 eggs, plus 1 egg yolk
⅔ cup milk
3 tablespoons heavy cream
¼ teaspoon ground nutmeg
freshly ground black pepper
vegetable oil, for brushing

TOMATO SAUCE

½ lb tomatoes, roughly chopped
3 tablespoons plain yoghurt
1 teaspoon Dijon-style mustard
1 teaspoon Worcestershire sauce
1 teaspoon tomato catsup
pinch of sugar

1 Preheat the oven to 325°.
2 Bring a saucepan of salted water to a boil and blanch the cabbage leaves for 2 minutes. Drain and dry on a clean dish towel.
3 Bring a saucepan of salted water to a boil and put the carrot and zucchini matchsticks in to simmer for 5 minutes. Drain and refresh under cold water, drain again.
4 Brush a 8½ × 4½ × 2½ inch loaf pan with oil. Line the loaf pan with 3 or 4 of the largest cabbage leaves and chop the remainder fairly finely.
5 Put half the carrot and zucchini mixture into the lined loaf pan, add about half the corn and pimiento, then half the chopped cabbage. Repeat the layering to make 6 layers in all.
6 Beat the eggs lightly with the extra yolk, milk, cream and nutmeg. Season with salt and pepper. Carefully pour the egg mixture into the loaf pan, gently easing the vegetables apart in several places with a round-bladed knife, to make sure the egg mixture is evenly distributed through the pan and goes right to the bottom. Fold any protruding cabbage leaves over the

filling. Cover the pan with foil.
7 Set the loaf pan in a roasting pan. Pour in hot water to come three-quarters up the sides of the loaf pan and cook for 1½-2 hours, until the custard is set and firm to the touch. Remove the loaf pan from the roasting pan and cool. Chill overnight in the refrigerator.
8 To make the sauce: Put the tomatoes in a blender for a few seconds until liquidized, then strain to remove the skins and seeds.
9 Mix the tomato purée with the remaining sauce ingredients, stirring to make sure they are well combined. Season to taste with salt and pepper. Cover with plastic wrap and chill for at least 2 hours.
10 To serve: Allow the terrine to stand at room temperature for about 10 minutes. Run a knife around the sides of the terrine, invert a serving plate on top and shake gently to unmold. Serve cut in slices (see Cook's tips) with the tomato sauce.

Cook's Notes

TIME
Preparing the terrine takes 45-60 minutes, cooking 1½-2 hours. Preparing the sauce takes about 5 minutes. Allow for overnight chilling.

SERVING IDEAS
This terrine is an attractive addition to a cold buffet and also makes a lovely fresh appetizer for a dinner party. It can also be served as a summer supper with salad.

BUYING GUIDE
Large-leaved, dark green cabbages — such as Savoy or summer cabbage — are better for this terrine than hard cabbages with closely packed leaves.

COOK'S TIP
Do not peel off the cabbage leaves used for lining — cut through to serve.

● 195 calories per portion

Three-tier pâté

SERVES 4
½ lb liver sausage
5 tablespoons butter, softened
¼ cup blanched almonds, finely
　chopped
a few black peppercorns, finely
　crushed
1 teaspoon medium sherry
salt
1 cup grated Cheddar cheese
2 teaspoons chopped chives
2 teaspoons finely chopped fresh
　parsley
1 cup cream cheese
2 teaspoons tomato paste
good pinch of paprika

1 Line the base of a freezerproof rigid container, which is approximately 4 inches square and 3 inches deep, with foil or alternatively waxed paper.

2 Using 1 tablespoon of the butter, thoroughly grease the base and sides of the container, then coat with the chopped almonds.
3 Mix together the liver sausage, black peppercorns, sherry and salt to taste. Spoon this mixture into the prepared container and press down firmly. Smooth the surface with a wet round-bladed knife.
4 In a bowl, beat together the remaining butter, the Cheddar cheese, chives, parsley and salt to taste. Spread this mixture over the liver sausage.
5 Beat the cream cheese in a separate bowl with the tomato paste, paprika and salt to taste. Spoon into the container and spread evenly on top of the Cheddar cheese mixture.
6 Cover and refrigerate for 1-2 hours.
7 To serve: Carefully run a knife around the sides of the container, then invert a serving plate on top. Invert the container onto the plate, remove the container and foil.

Meat terrine

SERVES 6

½ lb chicken livers
½ lb boneless fresh bacon with some fat
1 small onion, cut into chunks
½ lb ground beef
1 tablespoon tomato paste
½ teaspoon dried oregano
1 clove garlic, crushed (optional)
3 tablespoons red wine (see Economy)
salt and freshly ground black pepper
¼ lb stuffed olives
3 bay leaves
1 tablespoon chopped parsley, to garnish

1 Preheat the oven to 350°.
2 Wash and trim the livers, removing any discolored parts with a sharp knife.
3 Mince the livers, pork and onion finely in a mincer or chop finely in a food processor (see Cook's tip). Place in a large bowl and stir in the ground beef, tomato paste, oregano, garlic, if using, and wine. Mix thoroughly and season generously with salt and pepper.
4 Reserve 3 of the olives for garnish, then halve the rest. Spoon half of the terrine mixture into a 9 × 5 × 3 inch loaf pan or dish. Arrange the halved olives in the dish (see Preparation).
5 Carefully spoon the remaining terrine mixture on top of the olives and arrange the bay leaves on top. Tap the base of dish a few times on a work surface so the mixture fills the gaps between the olives. Cover the dish loosely with foil.
6 Put the dish into a roasting pan, pour in boiling water to come halfway up the sides of the dish and cook in the oven for about 1½ hours. To test for doneness, tilt the dish and if the juices run clear the terrine is cooked. Remove the dish from the roasting pan and cover the surface of the terrine with foil. Put heavy weights on top, leave to cool, then refrigerate overnight.
7 To serve: Turn the terrine out onto a platter. Slice the reserved olives and arrange them down the center of the terrine. Sprinkle a row of chopped parsley either side.

Pâté puffs

SERVES 4

¼ lb smoked bacon slices, rinds removed and finely diced
1 tablespoon butter or margarine
¾ cup finely chopped mushrooms (about 2 oz)
1 tablespoon chopped fresh parsley
celery or garlic salt (optional)
freshly ground black pepper
1 sheet (½ of 17 oz package) frozen puff pastry, thawed
¼ lb liver pâté (see Buying guide)
1 egg, beaten
1-2 tablespoons sesame seeds

TO GARNISH (optional)
lettuce
tomato slices

1 Melt the butter in a skillet over moderate heat, add the bacon and cook for 2-3 minutes. Add the mushrooms and cook for about 5 minutes. Stir in the parsley and season to taste with celery salt, if using, and pepper. [!] Set aside to cool slightly.
2 Preheat the oven to 400°.
3 Roll out the puff pastry on a floured surface to a square measuring about 12 inches. Trim the edges to straighten them, then cut it into 16 squares about 3 inches each.
4 Mash the pâté with a fork to soften it then divide it between the 16 squares spreading it roughly in the center of each one. Top with the bacon and mushroom mixture.
5 Brush the beaten egg around the edges of each pastry square. Carefully fold over the pastry to make a triangle, keeping the filling away from the edges. Press the edges of the pastry together firmly to seal them. [!] Brush with beaten egg.
6 Put the triangles on a large dampened cookie sheet and sprinkle over the sesame seeds.
7 Bake for about 10-15 minutes until the pastry is puffy and golden. Lift the puffs off the cookie sheet at once and cool slightly on a wire rack. Arrange the hot puffs on a plate garnished with lettuce and tomato, if using.

Chicken liver and walnut pâté

SERVES 12

1 lb chicken livers
¼ lb walnuts or pecans, chopped
¼ lb butter
1 small onion, finely chopped
1-2 cloves garlic, crushed (optional)
2 bay leaves
¼ lb bacon slices
2 tablespoons dry or medium sherry
1 tablespoon brandy
2 large eggs, beaten
pinch of freshly ground nutmeg
salt and freshly ground black
　　pepper

1 Melt the butter in a saucepan, add the chicken livers, onion, garlic, if using, bay leaves and bacon. Simmer gently for 10 minutes, stirring from time to time. Remove from the heat and leave to cool for about 30 minutes.
2 Preheat the oven to 325°.
3 Remove the bay leaves from the liver mixture and put the mixture

through a mincer or chop finely. Stir in the remaining ingredients with salt and pepper to taste. Mix thoroughly.
4 Transfer the mixture to a 7-inch terrine or loaf pan or a 1-quart round or oval ovenproof dish.
5 Place the dish in a roasting pan and pour in enough water to come halfway up the dish. Bake in the

oven for 1½ hours or until firm to the touch. [!] Leave until cold then cover and refrigerate overnight.
6 Serve straight from the dish, or run a knife around the edge of the dish, then invert a serving plate on top of the dish. Hold the mold and plate firmly together and invert them giving a sharp shake halfway around. Serve cut into slices.

Cook's Notes

TIME
20 minutes preparation, plus about 30 minutes standing and 1½ hours cooking. Chill overnight in the refrigerator before serving.

FREEZING
Open freeze the pâté in the dish until solid, then turn out and wrap in foil. Seal, label and return to the freezer for up to 1 month. Thaw in the refrigerator overnight then unwrap and serve as for fresh pâté, garnished with walnuts.

WATCHPOINT
Cover the top of the pâté with a piece of foil if it begins to brown too quickly; this will prevent over-browning and drying out.

SERVING IDEAS
Garnish the finished pâté with whole walnuts and large bay leaves. Serve with a mixed salad and crisp rolls. Alternatively, serve as a appetizer for 12 people with fingers of hot toast.

● 315 calories per portion

Quick tuna pâté

SERVES 4
1 can (about 7 oz) tuna, drained and
  flaked
4 tablespoons thick mayonnaise
4 tablespoons butter, melted
few drops of hot-pepper sauce
2 teaspoons lemon juice
2 teaspoons capers, drained and
  chopped
salt and freshly ground black
  pepper
4 black olives, pitted and sliced
  (optional)
4 tablespoons consommé (see
  Cook's tip)

1 Mix the tuna, mayonnaise, butter,
pepper sauce and lemon juice in a
bowl until well blended. Stir in
the capers and season the mixture

with both salt and pepper to taste.
2 Spoon the mixture into 4 individual serving dishes. Smooth the
surfaces and arrange the olive slices
on top, if using.

3 Gently heat the consommé in a
saucepan and spoon 1 tablespoon
over each pâté. Refrigerate for 10
minutes, until the consommé has set
(see Serving ideas).

Cook's Notes

 TIME
This pâté takes only 10
minutes to prepare, plus
10 minutes chilling time in the
refrigerator.

SERVING IDEAS
This quickly made pâté
is ideal for impromptu
entertaining: Made from pantry-
shelf ingredients, it is really a
useful recipe to remember for
unexpected guests. Serve with
hot whole wheat or granary
toast and butter for an appetizer, or with French bread and a
mixed salad for a light lunch.

VARIATION
Use canned red salmon,
drained and flaked, in-
stead of the tuna.

COOK'S TIP
Consommé, which is a
useful pantry-shelf
item, is available in cans of
about 10 oz. Left-over consommé can be kept in refrigerator 4-5 days, dice and add to
chilled soups or dilute with
water and use as broth in sauces
and casseroles.

● 285 calories per portion

Quick pâté mousse

SERVES 4-6
2 cans (about 7 oz each) pork or
   chicken paté
⅓ lb cream cheese with
   chives
3 tablespoons chopped chives
2-3 tablespoons brandy
freshly ground black pepper
few stuffed olives and small dill
   pickles, to garnish

1 Put all the ingredients, except the
garnish, in a blender or food processor and work for several minutes
until smooth (see Cook's tip).
2 Spoon the mixture into individual
serving bowls, or 1 large bowl.
3 Cover and refrigerate for several
hours or overnight.
4 Remove from the refrigerator 30
minutes before serving to allow to
come to room temperature. Garnish
with stuffed olives and pickles.

Cook's Notes

TIME
The preparation only
takes 10 minutes, but
allow several hours chilling
time.

COOK'S TIP
If you do not have a
blender or food pro-
cessor, mash the ingredients
together with a fork. Add a little
cream if you find that the
mixture is very stiff.

VARIATIONS
Substitute fresh herbs of
your choice instead of
the chives. Whisky or an
orange-flavored liqueur may
be used instead of the brandy.
Decorate with black olives
instead of stuffed olives.

SERVING IDEAS
Serve with hot toast or
crisp crackers as an ap-
petizer or lunchtime or evening
snack, or as part of a cold buffet.

● 520 calories per portion

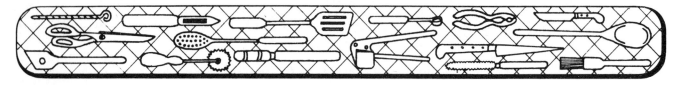

Salmon mousse

SERVES 4-6
1 can (about 7 oz) salmon, drained,
    with juice reserved
about 1 cup milk
2 tablespoons butter or margarine
4 tablespoons all-purpose
    flour
2 eggs, separated
2 envelopes unflavored gelatin
2 tablespoons lemon juice
2 tablespoons water
2 tablespoons tomato catsup
⅔ cup light cream
salt and freshly ground black pepper
sprigs of dill
cucumber slices, to garnish

1 Strain the juice from the salmon into a measuring jug and make up to 1¼ cups with milk.
2 Melt the butter in a small saucepan, sprinkle in the flour and stir over low heat for 1-2 minutes until straw-colored. Remove from the heat and gradually stir in the milk mixture. Return to the heat and simmer, stirring, until thick and smooth.
3 Remove from the heat and stir in the egg yolks.
4 Mash the fish roughly with a fork, discarding all skin and bones. Stir into the sauce, then work the mixture in a blender for a few seconds until smooth. Pour into a clean bowl and set aside to cool.
5 Sprinkle the gelatin over the lemon juice and water in a small flameproof bowl. Leave to soak for 5 minutes until spongy then stand the bowl in a pan of gently simmering water for 1-2 minutes, stirring occasionally, until the gelatin has dissolved.
6 Remove from the heat, leave to cool slightly, then stir into the salmon mixture with the tomato catsup and cream. Season to taste with salt and pepper. Cover and refrigerate for 2-3 hours, or until on the point of setting.
7 In a clean, dry bowl, beat the

egg whites until standing in stiff peaks, then fold into salmon mixture with a large metal spoon.
8 Line base of an oiled 3-cup tube pan with dill sprigs. Spoon salmon mixture carefully on top. Refrigerate overnight.
9 Dip base of pan in hot water for 10 seconds, then turn mousse out onto a serving plate. Serve chilled, garnished with cucumber.

Egg and cucumber mousse

SERVES 6

4 hard-boiled eggs, shelled and
   chopped
½ lb cucumber, quartered
   lengthwise
1 teaspoon salt
3 large scallions
   (including green tops), finely
   chopped
4 tablespoons chopped fresh
   parsley
2 teaspoons unflavored gelatin
3 tablespoons water
⅔ cup thick mayonnaise
⅓ cup plain yogurt
freshly ground black pepper
1 egg white

1 Scrape out the cucumber seeds
with a teaspoon and chop the
cucumber finely. Spread it out on a
plate and sprinkle with salt. Put
another plate over the cucumber

and place heavy weights on top.
Leave for 30 minutes, then drain
thoroughly.
2 Put the hard-boiled eggs, cucumber, onions and parsley into a bowl
and mix well.
3 Sprinkle the gelatin over the
water in a small flameproof bowl
and leave to soak for 5 minutes, until
spongy. Stand the bowl in a pan of
gently simmering water and leave
for 1-2 minutes, stirring occasionally, until gelatin has dissolved.
4 In a large bowl, blend the
mayonnaise with the yogurt.
Allow the gelatin liquid to cool
slightly, then stir it briskly into the
mayonnaise mixture. Stir in the egg
mixture and pepper to taste. Cover
and refrigerate for 30-40 minutes,
until beginning to set.
5 In a clean dry bowl, beat the egg
white until standing in stiff peaks,
then fold it into the egg mixture
with a large metal spoon. Turn the
mousse into a 4-cup serving dish,
cover and refrigerate for about 2
hours, until set. Serve chilled (see
Serving ideas).

Zucchini and tomato mousse

SERVES 4-6

½ lb zucchini, sliced about
   ½-inch thick
2 tablespoons butter or margarine
⅔ cup thick mayonnaise
⅔ cup cold chicken broth
2 eggs, separated
3 tablespoons water
4 teaspoons unflavored gelatin
2 tablespoons chopped chives
few drops hot-pepper sauce
   (optional)
salt and freshly ground black pepper
½ lb tomatoes, peeled,
   seeded and diced
   (see Cook's tip)

TO GARNISH
tomato slices
1 tablespoon chopped chives

1 Melt the butter in a large skillet over low heat, add the zucchini and cook gently for about 15 minutes until soft, stirring so that the zucchini do not brown.
2 Place the zucchini with the mayonnaise, chicken broth and egg yolks in a blender or food processor and blend to a purée.
3 Put the water in a bowl, sprinkle over the gelatin and leave to soak until spongy. Then stand the bowl in a pan of hot water and stir until the gelatin is dissolved and the liquid is clear.
4 Turn the purée into a large bowl and stir in the chives and the pepper sauce, if using. Taste and season. Then stir in the dissolved gelatin. Leave in the refrigerator for about 30 minutes until just setting.
5 Stir the purée until smooth then stir in the diced tomato. Beat the egg whites until they stand in stiff peaks and then carefully fold into the purée.

6 Turn the mixture into a 5-cup soufflé dish and chill for about 1½ hours or until set.
7 Serve garnished with tomato slices and chopped chives.

Cook's Notes

TIME
The mousse takes about 30 minutes to prepare, allow 30 minutes for the mixture to come to setting point in the refrigerator, plus the chilling time.

COOK'S TIP
When seeding the tomatoes, cut out the hard white piece of core under the stalk as it is rather dry and tough to eat and will spoil the texture of the mousse.

● 355 calories per portion

FISH AND SEAFOOD

Fish gratin

SERVES 4

4 frozen cod steaks, total weight
    about 1 lb
⅔ cup water
1 small onion, sliced
1 bay leaf
salt and freshly ground black pepper
3 tablespoons butter or margarine
2 tablespoons all-purpose flour
⅔ cup milk
1 cup grated Cheddar cheese
1 cup fresh white bread crumbs
butter, for greasing

1 Grease 4 scallop shells or individual ovenproof dishes.

2 Put the frozen fish steaks into a heavy-based skillet. Pour over the water, then add the onion and bay leaf and season to taste with salt and pepper. Bring to a boil, then lower the heat, cover and simmer for 15 minutes.

3 With a slotted spatula, lift the fish and onion from the liquid. Strain the liquid and reserve.

4 Leave the fish until cool enough to handle, then flake the flesh. Divide the fish between the prepared dishes and set aside.

5 Preheat the broiler to medium.

6 Melt 2 tablespoons of the butter in a small saucepan, sprinkle in the flour and stir over low heat for 1-2 minutes until straw-colored. Then remove from the heat and gradually stir in the reserved fish liquid and then the milk. Return to the heat and simmer, stirring, until thick and smooth. Remove from the heat and stir in half the grated cheese. Stir vigorously until the cheese has melted, then season to taste.

7 Spoon the cheese sauce over the fish in each shell, dividing it equally between them. Mix the bread crumbs with the remaining cheese and sprinkle over the sauce in each shell. Dot with rest of butter.

8 Broil until golden brown and heated through and serve at once.

Cook's Notes

 TIME
Preparing and cooking take 40 minutes.

 **VARIATIONS**
Any white fish fillets such as haddock or whiting may be used instead of the cod steaks. If using fresh fish, simmer 10 minutes.

● 330 calories per portion

SPECIAL OCCASION
Pipe a border of mashed potatoes, to which some beaten egg has been added, around the edge of each shell before broiling.

Instead of cod, use monkfish, which tastes rather like lobster, and then add ¼ lb cooked shrimp in stage 4.

Replace the water with white wine.

Spicy fish

SERVES 4

¾ lb flounder or tilefish, bones
    removed, cut into 4 × ½-inch
    strips
    (see Buying guide)
1½ cups fresh white bread crumbs
½ cup shredded coconut
¼ teaspoon chili powder
½ teaspoon ground coriander
½ teaspoon ground cumin
salt and freshly ground black
    pepper
3 tablespoons all-purpose flour
2 eggs, beaten
¼ cucumber, pared and chopped
2 tablespoons chopped dill pickles
⅓ cup thick mayonnaise
vegetable oil, for deep-frying
lemon and tomato, to garnish

1 Put the bread crumbs in a bowl
and stir in the coconut, chili,
coriander and cumin. Season with
salt and black pepper to taste.

2 Spread the flour out on a large flat
plate and season with salt and
pepper. Beat the eggs in a shallow
bowl. Dip the fish strips in the flour,
turning to coat thoroughly, then in
the egg, and then in the bread crumb
mixture until evenly coated.

3 Lay the strips on a cookie sheet or
tray and refrigerate for 10 minutes.

4 Meanwhile, mix the cucumber
and pickles into the mayonnaise and
spoon into a small serving jug.
Preheat the oven to 225°.

5 Pour enough oil into a deep-fat
fryer with a basket to come halfway
up the sides. Heat the oil to 375°, or
until a stale bread cube turns golden
in 50 seconds. Fry the fish strips a
few at a time ⚠ for 5-7 minutes
until they are golden brown and
crisp.

6 Drain on paper towels and keep
warm in oven while frying remaining batches. Serve the fish strips at
once garnished with thin wedges of
lemon and tomato halves and with
the cucumber and pickle sauce
handed separately.

Cook's Notes

TIME
20 minutes to prepare,
plus 15-20 minutes
cooking time.

BUYING GUIDE
Flounder (or alterna-
tively you can use file-
fish) is a good firm-fleshed fish
which is normally available
from most fishstores. Both fish
are ideal for this recipe as they
can easily be cut into strips.

WATCHPOINT
Do not put too many
fish strips into the fat at
one time as the coconut tends to
make the fat bubble. It is best to
fry in 3 or 4 batches.

SERVING IDEAS
For a substantial meal,
serve with fried potatoes.

● 405 calories per portion

Dressed smoked mackerel

SERVES 4

1 lb smoked mackerel fillets,
cut in half lengthwise if large
(see Buying guide)
¼ cup thick mayonnaise, (preferably
homemade)
2 tablespoons plain yogurt
¼ teaspoon Dijon-style mustard
salt and freshly ground black pepper
3 celery stalks, chopped
¾ cup green grapes, halved and
pitted
¼ lb radishes, thinly sliced
4 large lettuce leaves

GARNISH
mustard and garden cress
1 lemon, cut into wedges

1 In a bowl, mix together the mayonnaise, yogurt and mustard and season to taste with salt and pepper. Stir in the celery, grapes and radishes.

2 Put the lettuce leaves on a serving dish. Arrange the mackerel fillets over them, slightly overlapping.

3 Spoon the salad mixture in a line on top of the mackerel. Garnish with the mustard and cress and lemon wedges.

Cook's Notes

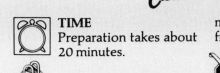

TIME
Preparation takes about 20 minutes.

BUYING GUIDE
Ready-cooked whole smoked mackerel can be bought from good fishstores and delicatessens and are easily filleted. Frozen, vacuum-packed, or canned smoked mackerel fillets are available from supermarkets.

SERVING IDEAS
For an even more substantial dish, serve with plain cooked rice to which some chopped nuts have been added.

● 425 calories per portion

Baked stuffed kippers

SERVES 4

4 kippered herrings, bones removed
  (see Preparation)
¼ cup butter or margarine
3 eggs, hard-boiled and chopped
  while hot
2 tablespoons chopped parsley
grated rind and juice of ½ lemon
freshly ground black pepper
12 slices lemon and a few small
  parsley sprigs, to garnish

1 Preheat the oven to 400°.
2 Cream the butter in a bowl with a wooden spoon and gradually work in the chopped eggs and parsley. Add the lemon rind and juice and season to taste with pepper. (Kippers can be salty so do not add salt.)
3 Cut 4 pieces of foil, each big enough to enclose a kipper.
4 Place a kipper on each piece of foil and spoon an equal amount of stuffing over the half of each kipper. Fold the kipper over the stuffing and wrap the foil into a loose parcel, turning in the ends of the foil to seal them tightly, so that the juices do not run out during cooking.
5 Place the parcels on a cookie sheet and cook in oven for 15-20 minutes.
6 Fold back the foil around the kippers, then carefully remove the skin from the top side, leaving on the heads and tails. Lay 3 lemon slices along each kipper and place a sprig of parsley in the center of each one.
7 Serve the kippers hot in the foil with their juices. If you prefer, use paper towels to drain away some of the juices first.

Cook's Notes

TIME
Preparation 20 minutes (including boning the kippers), cooking 15-20 minutes.

PREPARATION
Slide a sharp knife under the backbone and remove it with as many of the small bones as possible.

COOK'S TIP
If the kippers look dry, they can be made more succulent before cooking by placing them in a shallow dish and pouring over boiling water. Soak for 5 minutes, then dry thoroughly on paper towels.

SERVING IDEAS
Chunks of French or granary bread are perfect for mopping up the kipper juices.
  A tomato and cucumber salad provides a refreshing contrast to the rich flavor of kippers.

VARIATIONS
Smoked mackerel can be substituted for the kippers. If kipper fillets are easier to obtain than whole kippers, use 2 per person and sandwich them together with the filling in between.

● 380 calories per portion

Creamy cod appetizer

SERVES 4
½ lb cod fillets, skinned
1¼ cups milk
2 tablespoons butter
2 tablespoons all-purpose flour
¼ lb frozen shelled shrimp thawed
2 tablespoons chopped fresh
    parsley

POTATO TOPPING
1¼ lb potatoes, cooked and
    mashed
2 tablespoons butter
2 tablespoons milk
pinch of freshly ground nutmeg
salt and freshly ground black pepper

TO GARNISH
shelled cooked shrimp
parsley sprigs

1 Pour the milk into a saucepan and heat until simmering. Add the cod and cover the pan. Simmer for 15 minutes or until the fish is cooked. Using a slotted spatula, transfer the cod to a plate, then flake the flesh with a fork, discarding any bones. Strain the broth into a jug and set aside.
2 Make the potato topping: Put the mashed potato in a bowl, then stir in the butter, milk ⚠ and nutmeg. Beat until smooth. Season to taste with salt and pepper, then spoon into a large pastry bag fitted with a medium-sized nozzle. Set aside.
3 Melt the butter in a saucepan, sprinkle in the flour and stir over low heat for 1-2 minutes until straw-colored. Remove from the heat and gradually stir in reserved broth. Return to the heat and simmer, stirring, until thick and smooth.
4 Stir in cod, shrimp and parsley. Simmer gently for 5 minutes and season with salt and pepper.
5 Preheat the broiler to high.
6 Divide the fish mixture equally between 4 small shallow flameproof pots or dishes. Pipe a border of potato around the edge of each pot, then put under the broiler for 3-4 minutes, until the potato border has browned a little.
7 Garnish each pot with a shrimp and a sprig of parsley. Serve at once.

Fish rolls

SERVES 4
2 flounder, divided into 8 fillets
¼ lb Cheddar cheese in 1 piece
2 large eggs, beaten
4 cups fresh white bread crumbs
vegetable oil, for deep frying

1 Skin and wash the fillets, then dry them on paper towels.
2 Cut the cheese into 8 pieces, each long enough to fit just across the width of a fish fillet. Place a piece of cheese on each fillet and roll it up, starting from the tail end.
3 Pour the beaten eggs onto a shallow dish and put the bread crumbs on a plate. Coat each fish roll all over in egg, then in bread crumbs. Repeat, so that the rolls are coated twice, pressing the second coating of bread crumbs on thoroughly.
4 Pour enough oil into a deep-fat fryer to cover the fish rolls and heat to 325° (see Cook's tips).

Carefully lower the fish rolls into the hot oil and cook for about 7 minutes until they are golden brown and crisp (fry the rolls in 2 batches if necessary). Remove with a spoon and drain on paper towels. Serve at once, with tartar sauce.

Cook's Notes

TIME
Preparation and cooking 30-45 minutes.

COOK'S TIPS
If you do not have a cooking thermometer or deep-fat fryer with its own thermostat, test the heat of the oil by dropping in a 1-inch cube of bread: this should brown in 75 seconds at a temperature of 325°.

 WATCHPOINT
It is very important to coat the rolls thoroughly in egg and bread crumbs, or the cheese will melt and it will bubble out.

● 510 calories per portion

Selsey soused herrings

SERVES 4

4 large herrings, each weighing about ½ lb, boned but left in 1 piece (see Buying guide)
salt and freshly ground black pepper
1 small onion, sliced
⅔ cup white wine vinegar
½ cup water
4 bay leaves
8 whole black peppercorns
1-inch stick cinnamon

TO SERVE

2 teaspoons creamed horseradish sauce
pinch of dry mustard
⅔ cup heavy cream
lemon and beet wedges, to garnish (optional)

1 Preheat the oven to 325°.
2 Season the herrings with salt and pepper and roll them up, starting from head end, with skin on outside and secure with toothpicks if necessary. Arrange them in a single layer in a casserole just large enough to hold them comfortably.
3 Add the onion, vinegar and water. Push the bay leaves, peppercorns and cinnamon between the herring rolls. Cover with a lid or foil and bake in the oven for 1 hour. Leave to cool in the cooking liquid for at least 8 hours.
4 Drain the herrings, reserving 4 tablespoons cooking liquid, and place on a serving dish.
5 Put the reserved liquid into a bowl with the horseradish sauce, mustard powder and cream and whisk until standing in soft peaks.
6 Spoon a little sauce over each herring and garnish with lemon and beet wedges, if liked. Serve cold, with the remaining cream sauce handed separately.

Cook's Notes

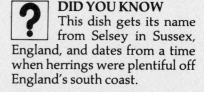

TIME
This recipe takes 10 minutes to prepare and 1 hour to cook, but allow a further 8 hours for cooling.

BUYING GUIDE
Ask your fishstore to bone the fish and cut off the head.

STORAGE
The flavor of soused herrings is best after they have been left for 24 hours, but they can be left in the refrigerator for up to 3-4 days.

SERVING IDEAS
Halve the herrings lengthwise before serving as an appetizer. Alternatively, for a complete meal, serve with potato salad and lettuce tossed in an oil and vinegar dressing.

DID YOU KNOW
This dish gets its name from Selsey in Sussex, England, and dates from a time when herrings were plentiful off England's south coast.

● 370 calories per portion

Salmon and macaroni layer

SERVES 4

1 can (about 7½ oz) salmon, drained
   with juice reserved, flaked
   (see Economy)
salt
1 cup elbow macaroni
2 tablespoons butter or margarine
2 tablespoons all-purpose flour
1¼ cups milk
2 hard-boiled eggs, chopped
1 tablespoon chopped fresh parsley
pinch of ground mace
freshly ground black pepper
¾ cup grated Cheddar cheese
tomato wedges and watercress,
   to garnish

1 Bring a large pan of salted water
to a boil, add the macaroni and cook
for 10 minutes until tender but firm
to the bite (*al dente*).
2 Meanwhile, melt the butter in a
saucepan, sprinkle in the flour and
stir over low heat for 1-2 minutes
until straw-colored. Remove from
the heat and gradually stir in the
milk and reserved salmon juice.
Return to the heat and simmer,
stirring, until thick and smooth.
3 Remove the sauce from the heat
and gently fold in the eggs and
salmon with the parsley and mace.
Season to taste with salt and pepper,
then spoon into a flameproof dish
(see Serving ideas).
4 Drain the macaroni thoroughly
and turn into a bowl. Add half the
cheese and toss to coat well. Spoon
the macaroni over the salmon mixture. Sprinkle over the remaining
cheese. Broil for 5 minutes until the
cheese is golden and bubbling. Garnish with tomato and watercress.
Serve at once, straight from dish.

Herring salad

SERVES 4
½ lb salt herring fillets, drained
    (see Buying guide)
2 large waxy potatoes, cooked
    (see Watchpoint)
1 large beet, cooked (see Buying
    guide)
1 large dill pickle
1 large crisp green apple
2 tablespoons mayonnaise
6 tablespoons plain yogurt or dairy
    sour cream

1 Cut the herring fillets, potatoes, beet and the pickle into small dice and place in a large bowl (see Preparation). Pare and core the apple and cut it into small dice. Add to the bowl (see Serving ideas).
2 Mix the mayonnaise and yogurt together until well blended and smooth. Pour over the chopped

ingredients in the bowl and mix thoroughly until everything is well coated.

3 Cover the bowl with plastic wrap and refrigerate for several hours, ideally overnight, before serving.

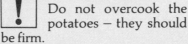

Cook's Notes

TIME
Preparation, including boiling the potatoes and beet, takes 1½ hours, plus chilling time.

BUYING GUIDE
Any salt herring is suitable for this salad. Pickled rollmops in jars, or herrings canned in wine are available from delicatessens and good supermarkets.
    Buy a ready-cooked beet from the supermarket, to cut down on preparation time.

WATCHPOINT
Do not overcook the potatoes – they should be firm.

PREPARATION
Make sure the ingredients are cut into small dice for this salad – the flavors will mingle more easily.

SERVING IDEAS
You can serve as a main course, with a green salad and French bread.
    Salt herring fillets have a strong, distinctive flavor, and you may prefer not to mix them into the salad. Combine the other diced ingredients as in stages 1 and 2, then roll the drained fillets up tightly and arrange around the dish, as in the picture.

● 365 calories per portion

Creamy pasta with tuna

SERVES 4
¾ lb pasta shapes (see Buying guide)
salt
6 tablespoons butter or margarine
1 small onion, chopped
1 clove garlic, crushed (optional)
2 tablespoons all-purpose flour
1¼ cups chicken broth
⅔ cups dairy sour cream (see Variations)
freshly ground black pepper
2 cups (about ¼ lb) button mushrooms, quartered
1 can (about 14 oz) tomatoes, drained and roughly chopped (see Economy)
1 cup grated Cheddar cheese
1 can (about 7 oz) tuna, drained and flaked

SAVORY BUTTER
6 tablespoons butter
2 tablespoons grated Parmesan cheese
2 tablespoons finely chopped parsley

1 Preheat the oven to 375°. Set a large saucepan of salted water over high heat to boil.
2 Make the savory butter: Cream the butter with the Parmesan cheese and parsley. Put the savory butter inside a piece of folded waxed paper and shape into a cylinder. Pat the ends to flatten and neaten and twist the ends of the waxed paper. Chill in

the refrigerator while you prepare the pasta.
3 Add the pasta to the pan of boiling water and cook for 10-12 minutes, or according to package directions, until tender yet firm to the bite. Drain well.
4 While the pasta is cooking, melt 4 tablespoons of the butter in a saucepan, add the onion and garlic, if using, and cook over gentle heat until soft but not colored. Sprinkle in the flour and stir over low heat for 2 minutes until straw-colored. Remove from the heat and gradually stir in the chicken broth.
5 Return the pan to the heat and simmer, stirring, until thick and

smooth. Reduce the heat and stir in the dairy sour cream. Remove from heat and season to taste with salt and pepper. Cover and set aside.
6 Melt the remaining butter in a small saucepan, add the mushrooms and cook for 2-3 minutes.
7 Add the tomatoes to the sauce with the mushrooms and grated cheese. Stir in the cooked pasta. Put the tuna fish in the base of a large ovenproof dish. Spoon the pasta over the tuna.
8 Cut the chilled savory butter into 8 slices and arrange them over the top of the pasta. Cook in the oven for about 15-20 minutes until the dish is piping hot.

Cook's Notes

TIME
Preparation about 45 minutes, cooking in the oven 15-20 minutes.

VARIATIONS
If sour cream is not available you can use ⅔ cup natural yogurt instead, or light cream with 1 teaspoon lemon juice added.

FREEZING
The dish can be made up to the end of stage 7 and frozen for 1 month without the savory butter. To serve: Defrost at room temperature, add the savory butter and cover with foil.

Reheat in the oven preheated to 400° for 20 minutes, remove the foil and continue cooking for a further 20 minutes or until heated through.

BUYING GUIDE
Choose pasta shapes such as shells that will hold the sauce readily. Pasta rings would not be suitable for this dish.

ECONOMY
Reserve the juice from the tomatoes for use in another dish, such as a beef casserole.

● 925 calories per portion

Crab-stuffed tomatoes

SERVES 4

8 large tomatoes
about ¾ lb canned or frozen crabmeat (see Buying guide)
grated rind of 2 lemons
¼ cup lemon juice
2 tablespoons thick mayonnaise
4 tablespoons cottage cheese, sieved
1 bunch of watercress, chopped with stems removed
salt and freshly ground black pepper
few drops of hot-pepper sauce

1 Slice off the top of each tomato and set aside. Using a grapefruit knife or teaspoon, gently scoop out the flesh and seeds, taking care not to pierce the tomato shells (see Economy). Turn them upside down on paper towels and leave them to drain while you prepare the crab filling.
2 In a bowl, mix together the crabmeat, lemon rind and juice, mayonnaise and sieved cottage cheese (see Cook's tip). Lightly stir in the watercress and season to taste with salt, pepper and the pepper-sauce. Cover the bowl and chill the mixture in the refrigerator for 1-2 hours.

3 Spoon the crab mixture into the tomato shells, filling them as full as possible without letting the mixture run down the sides of the tomatoes. Carefully replace the tomato tops on the crab stuffing and serve the tomatoes at once.

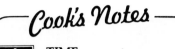

Cook's Notes

TIME
Preparation takes 30 minutes. Allow 1-2 hours for chilling the stuffing.

SERVING IDEAS
These stuffed tomatoes are very versatile: They make an unusual appetizer for a dinner party, or may be served as a main meal with a mixed salad and French bread. For a tasty supper dish, serve the tomatoes on circles of fried or toasted bread, garnished with watercress.

BUYING GUIDE
Canned and frozen crabmeat is sold in varying weights according to individual brands. Exact weight of crabmeat is not critical for this recipe as the size of the tomatoes will vary as well.

ECONOMY
Discard the seeds and use the scooped-out tomato flesh for sandwiches.

COOK'S TIP
If you find the flavor of crab rather strong, use less crabmeat and add more cottage cheese when you are mixing the filling.

VARIATION
Tomatoes may be stuffed with all sorts of mixtures. Substitute drained, mashed tuna fish for the crabmeat in this recipe. Or try mixing equal quantities of cream cheese with sieved cottage cheese and adding some chopped shrimp or chopped walnuts. You can also try lime juice instead of lemon juice.

● 140 calories per portion

Roes on toast

SERVES 4

1 lb soft cod roes (milt), thawed if frozen (see Buying guide)
⅓ cup butter or margarine
1 tablespoon lemon juice
1 tablespoon chopped parsley
salt and freshly ground white pepper (see Cook's tip)
4 large slices bread, crusts removed

TO GARNISH
lemon slices, halved
parsley sprigs

1 Drain the cod roes on paper towels.
2 Melt the butter in a skillet, add the roes and cook fairly briskly for 3-4 minutes, turning the roes several times to brown. ⚠
3 Add the lemon juice and parsley and season with salt and pepper.
4 While the roes are cooking toast the bread, cut and arrange the slices on a warmed serving dish. Spoon a portion of roes with the buttery juices onto each slice of toast (see Serving ideas).
5 Garnish the top of each serving with lemon slices and parsley sprigs. Serve at once.

Cook's Notes

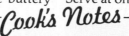

TIME
This dish takes only 10 minutes to prepare.

COOK'S TIP
Use white pepper in pale-colored dishes: Black pepper spoils the color of the finished dish.

WATCHPOINT
Soft roes break up easily and need careful cooking in a non-stick pan.

SERVING IDEAS
Broiled rolled slices of bacon may be served with the roes.

BUYING GUIDE
You can buy canned fish roes which are already cooked: Simply turn them very briefly in some melted butter or margarine with the lemon juice added.

● 285 calories per portion

Oriental seafood salad

SERVES 6
½ lb beansprouts
4 scallions, chopped
1 celery stalk, finely sliced
1 red pepper, seeded and cut into
¼-inch strips (optional)
¼ lb shelled shrimp, thawed if
frozen (see Economy)
1 can (about 6 oz) crab meat, drained
and flaked
6 Chinese cabbage leaves or lettuce
scallion tassels, to garnish

DRESSING
⅔ cup plain yogurt
6 tablespoons thick mayonnaise
finely grated rind of 1 lemon
1 tablespoon lemon juice
1 teaspoon ground ginger
a little salt and freshly ground
black pepper

1 Combine the beansprouts, scallions and celery in a bowl with the red pepper, if using.
3 Make the dressing: Put the yogurt in a bowl with the mayonnaise, lemon rind and juice and ginger. Mix together and season with salt and pepper to taste.
3 Add the dressing to the bean-

sprouts mixture and toss to coat well, then fold the shrimp and crabmeat into the salad. Cover with plastic wrap and refrigerate the salad for about 15-30 minutes.
4 Arrange the Chinese cabbage on a serving plate and spoon the salad on top. Garnish with scallion tassels and serve at once.

Mussel omelet

MAKES 4

2 jars (about 5 oz each) mussels in their own juice, drained, with juice reserved (see Variations)
½ cup butter
1 onion, finely chopped
2 celery stalks, finely chopped
4 tablespoons all-purpose flour
3 tablespoons dry or medium white wine
8 eggs
salt and freshly ground black pepper
2-3 tablespoons heavy cream
1 tablespoon finely chopped fresh parsley

1 Melt half of the butter in a saucepan. Add the onion and celery and cook very gently, stirring with a wooden spoon, for about 10 minutes until soft.
2 Sprinkle in the flour and stir for 1-2 minutes. Gradually stir in ⅓ cup reserved mussel juice and the wine and simmer, stirring, until thick and smooth, then stir in the mussels and enough cream to make a thick sauce (see Cook's tip). Season to taste with salt and pepper, being cautious with the salt, and stir in the chopped parsley. Leave the sauce on very low heat, stirring occasionally, while you make the omelets.
3 Lightly beat 2 eggs and season sparingly with salt and pepper. Melt 1 tablespoon butter in a skillet. When it sizzles, pour in the eggs, and cook for 2-3 minutes, drawing the edges towards the center with a fork as they cook. The omelet is ready when the center is still slightly runny.
4 Spoon one-quarter of the mussel sauce onto one-half of the omelet in the pan and fold the omelet over. Carefully slide it out onto a warmed individual serving plate and serve at once. Make the other 3 omelets in the same way serving each as soon as it is made.

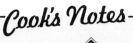

Cook's Notes

TIME
These omelets take only 30 minutes to prepare and cook.

COOK'S TIP
The mussel mixture is very thick. Add the cream gradually until you have the sauce consistency to suit your taste.

VARIATIONS
Use ½ lb shelled frozen mussels, thawed, and substitute milk for the mussel juice. Mussels or clams in brine can be used. They should be drained and milk used in place of the brine to prevent the sauce from becoming salty.

● 453 calories per portion

Devilled prawns and eggs

simmer, uncovered, for 10 minutes.
4 Meanwhile, cook the eggs in gently simmering water for 7-8 minutes until hard-boiled.
5 Stir the shrimp into the tomato sauce and cook for a further 5

minutes. Season to taste with salt and pepper.
6 Peel and halve the eggs and place in a warmed serving dish. Spoon the tomato and shrimp mixture over them. Serve at once.

SERVES 4
⅓ lb frozen shrimp
4 eggs
1 can (about 14 oz) tomatoes
1 tablespoon tomato paste
2 tablespoons light brown sugar
2 tablespoons wine vinegar
1 tablespoon Worcestershire sauce
salt and freshly ground black pepper

1 Put the tomatoes in a saucepan with half the juice from the can, the tomato paste, sugar, vinegar, and Worcestershire sauce. Reserve the remaining tomato juice for future use in a casserole.
2 Bring to a boil, stirring well to break up the tomatoes.
3 Reduce the heat a little and

Crab and cheese florentines

SERVES 4

1 can (about 6 oz) crab meat, drained and flaked, or the same weight of frozen crab meat, thawed
3 tablespoons vegetable oil
1 tablespoon white wine vinegar
juice of 1 lemon
salt and freshly ground black pepper
¼ lb raw spinach, trimmed, shredded
⅔ cup plain yogurt
finely grated rind of ½ lemon
1 tablespoon chopped chives
½ lb cottage cheese

TO GARNISH (OPTIONAL)
cayenne pepper
radish waterlilies (see Preparation)

1 Put the oil, vinegar and half the lemon juice into a large bowl and season well with salt and pepper. Beat together with a fork, then add the spinach and toss it with 2 forks until thoroughly coated. Use it to line 4 individual dishes.
2 Put the yogurt, lemon rind and the chives into a bowl with the remaining lemon juice and salt and pepper to taste. Mix thoroughly.
3 In a separate bowl, fork together the cottage cheese and crab meat. Fold in the yogurt and spoon onto the spinach.
4 Sprinkle with cayenne pepper, if liked, then garnish with radish waterlilies. Serve at once.

Cook's Notes

 TIME
Preparation time is about 25 minutes, but remember to allow time for radishes to soak if using them.

VARIATIONS
Use shrimp or other shellfish in place of the crab. For a milder garnish, use paprika, not cayenne.

 DID YOU KNOW
Spinach is a rich source of iron and vitamins and is even more nutritious when eaten raw as suggested here.

PREPARATION
To make radish water-lilies:

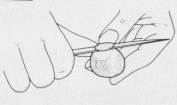

1 Slice off the stalk and root ends, then with the stalk end downwards, cut 5 shallow petal shapes, cutting almost to the base.

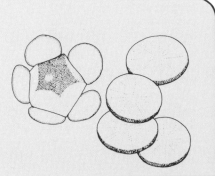

2 Place in ice-cold water for at least 30 minutes for the petals to open. Then arrange the radish on a circle of very thin radish slices.

● 225 calories per portion

Slimmers' crab dip with crudités

SERVES 4
1 can (about 6 oz) crab meat
⅔ cup plain yogurt
1 tablespoon chopped chives
salt
few drops of hot-pepper sauce

CRUDITES
1 red pepper
1 cucumber
3 celery stalks
2 carrots
1½ cups button mushrooms

1 Drain the crab meat and flake it into a bowl. Beat in the yogurt and chives and season to taste with salt and pepper sauce. Chill the dip while preparing the vegetables.
2 Seed the pepper and cut into strips about 2-inches long and ½-inch thick.

3 Pare the cucumber and cut into sticks the same size as the pepper. Cut the celery and carrots into the same size sticks. Halve the button mushrooms lengthwise.

4 Beat the dip again and spoon into a serving bowl. Put the bowl on a large platter and surround with the prepared vegetables. Serve at once (see Cook's tip and Serving ideas).

Cook's Notes

 TIME
Preparation takes about 15 minutes, including the chilling time.

COOK'S TIP
The dip will separate if it is left to stand — if this happens, beat it vigorously until evenly blended again. If a smoother dip is preferred, work the dip in an electric blender before serving.

VARIATION
Canned tuna fish or pink salmon can be used instead of the crab but they are more fattening. A 6 oz can crab meat, drained, is 145 calories; the same weight of tuna in brine, drained, is 185 calories; tuna in oil, drained, 370 calories; and pink salmon 270 calories.

 SERVING IDEAS
For an attractive display, spoon the dip into a crab shell and arrange the crudités in separate bowls.
Use savory crackers and chips instead of the vegetables, but remember that the calorie count will be higher.

● 85 calories per portion

CHEESE AND EGG DISHES

Fruit and cheese kabobs

SERVES 4
⅓ cup cream cheese
3 tablespoons seedless raisins, chopped
2 tablespoons walnuts or unsalted peanuts, finely chopped
2 oz Danish blue cheese
2 oz smoked cheese
2 oz sharp Cheddar cheese in 1 piece
1 large red apple
juice of 1 lemon
1 can (about 11 oz) mandarin orange segments, well drained, or 2 fresh mandarin oranges, peeled and divided into segments
1 can (about 8 oz) pineapple chunks, well drained
1 cup black or green grapes, washed and dried
6 lettuce leaves, shredded, to serve

1 Put the cream cheese into a bowl with the raisins and mix well. Roll into 8 small even-sized balls.

2 Spread the chopped nuts out on a flat plate and roll the balls in them. Transfer to a plate and refrigerate while you prepare the other ingredients.
3 Cut the Danish blue cheese into 8 even-sized cubes. Repeat with both the smoked cheese and the sharp Cheddar cheese.
4 Quarter and core the apple, but do not pare it. Cut in even-sized slices and immediately squeeze the lemon juice over them to prevent discoloration.
5 On 8 individual skewers, spear 1 cream cheese ball and 1 cube each of Danish blue, smoked and Cheddar cheeses, interspersed with apple slices, mandarin orange segments, pineapple chunks and grapes. Serve 2 skewers per person on a bed of shredded lettuce.

Cook's Notes

TIME
Total preparation time is about 20 minutes.

SERVING IDEAS
These kabobs make an interesting and refreshing snack or an unusual, fresh-tasting dinner party appetizer. Slices of whole wheat bread and butter go well with them, or they can be served inside whole wheat pita bread.

● 355 calories per kabob

VARIATIONS
You can vary the ingredients according to the cheese, nuts and fruit you prefer and have available; you can also add salad ingredients such as red or green pepper, chunks of cucumber, radishes or tiny tomatoes.

ECONOMY
If you have any fruit left over, tip it into a bowl and add a can of guavas for a quick fruit salad.

Cottage cheese crepes

MAKES 12
⅔ cup cottage cheese
4 tablespoons all-purpose flour
½ teaspoon salt
2 tablespoons butter, melted
3 eggs, separated
vegetable oil, for greasing

1 Preheat the oven to 225°.
2 Sift the flour and salt into a bowl, then add the cottage cheese, butter and egg yolks and mix well.
3 In a clean, dry bowl, beat the egg whites until they form soft peaks. With a metal spoon, fold 3 tablespoons of the egg whites into the cottage cheese mixture and then carefully fold in the remainder. [!]
4 Heat a little oil in a heavy-based skillet. Drop about 6 table-spoons of the mixture into the pan, spacing them well apart, and cook over moderate heat for 2-3 minutes on each side until they are golden brown.
5 Remove the crepes with a spatula and keep hot in the oven while cooking the second batch. Serve at once (see Serving ideas).

Cook's Notes

 TIME
The crêpes take less than 1 hour to make.

 WATCHPOINT
The air trapped in the beaten egg whites makes the mixture light, so fold them into the cottage cheese mixture very gently to avoid losing the air and making the crêpes heavy.

 SERVING IDEAS
Spread the crêpes with smoked cod's roe pâté (taramosalata), available in tubs from specialty stores and deli-catessens, or with cream cheese mixed to a spread with tomato paste, chopped chives and salt and pepper to taste.

● 65 calories per crêpe

Cottage cheese and ham cocottes

SERVES 4

1 cup cottage cheese
1 tablespoon vegetable oil
  1 small onion, finely chopped
2 cups chopped mushrooms
2 eggs, lightly beaten
⅓ cup diced ham
pinch of freshly ground nutmeg
salt and freshly ground black pepper
2 tablespoons butter, melted
parsley sprigs, to garnish

1 Preheat the oven to 400°.
2 Heat the oil in a small saucepan, add the onion and cook gently until it is soft.
3 Add the mushrooms and cook for 1-2 minutes only, stirring constantly. Remove the saucepan from the heat and cool.
4 Sieve the cottage cheese into a bowl and beat in the beaten eggs, a little at a time.
5 Add the diced ham to the cheese mixture with the onion and mushrooms. Add the nutmeg, then season to taste with salt and pepper.
6 Brush 4 ramekins or cocottes with the melted butter and divide the mixture between them.
7 Place on a cookie sheet and bake for about 20-25 minutes or until well risen, and brown and bubbly on top. Serve immediately, garnished with sprigs of parsley.

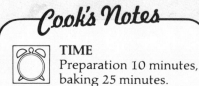

Cook's Notes

TIME
Preparation 10 minutes, baking 25 minutes.

VARIATION
Replace the ham with ⅔ cup shelled shrimp and the mushrooms with a small amount of canned or frozen whole kernel corn.

● 210 calories per portion

Crunchy Camembert

SERVES 4
4 Camembert triangle portions
2 tablespoons all-purpose flour
salt and freshly ground black pepper
1 large egg
3-4 tablespoons fresh white bread crumbs
¼ cup, blanched almonds, finely chopped

FRUITY SALAD
2 oranges
1 grapefruit
2 teaspoons superfine sugar
4 tomatoes, each cut into 6 wedges
1 tablespoon olive oil
1 teaspoon chopped fresh parsley
vegetable oil, for deep frying

1 Chill the cheese portions in the freezer or freezing compartment of the refrigerator for 30 minutes
2 Put the flour in a large plastic bag; season with salt and pepper.
3 Lightly beat the egg in a shallow dish. Mix together the bread crumbs and almonds and spread out on a flat plate.
4 Add the cheeses to the flour and shake until well coated. Dip them into the egg and then into the bread crumbs. Coat the portions in the egg and bread crumbs again until evenly coated. Put on a plate and refrigerate for 30 minutes.
5 Meanwhile, make the salad: Divide the fruit into segments making sure that all white pith and any pips are removed then put the segments into a bowl and mix together with the sugar. Add the tomato wedges and mix well.
6 Drain off any liquid then divide the salad mixture between 4 serving plates. Spoon over the olive oil and sprinkle with parsley.
7 Pour enough oil into a deep-fat fryer to cover the cheeses. Heat to 350°, or until a stale bread cube browns in 60 seconds.
8 Using a slotted spoon, lower the cheeses into the hot oil and deep-fry for 30-60 seconds until the coating begins to turn golden. Drain on paper towels and serve at once, with the salad (see Cook's tips).

Cook's Notes

TIME
15 minutes preparation plus a total of 1 hour chilling time and 30-60 seconds cooking time.

COOK'S TIPS
The cheese must be very cold before cooking or it will melt before the bread crumbs turn golden.
Serve the cheeses immediately they come out of the oil while their centers are still hot and the coating is crisp.

SERVING IDEAS
For a dinner-party appetizer, serve only with cranberry sauce or jelly. Alternatively serve the cheese with the fruity salad, serve with a green salad and crusty French bread. Prepare them in advance and refrigerate until just before you are ready to cook them.

● 300 calories per portion

Parsley cheese bites

SERVES 4
⅓ cup cream cheese
1 cup grated Cheddar cheese
½ cup Danish Blue cheese, at room temperature
freshly ground black pepper
4-5 tablespoons finely chopped fresh parsley
2-3 tablespoons all-purpose flour

1 Work the cheeses together with a fork to form a smooth paste. Add pepper to taste.
2 Put the chopped parsley and flour on separate flat plates. Dip your hands in the flour, shaking off any excess, then shape the cheese mixture into 20 small balls, reflouring your hands as necessary. Roll each ball in chopped parsley.
3 Transfer to a serving plate and refrigerate for 30 minutes before serving. Serve chilled.

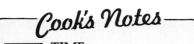

Cook's Notes

 TIME
Total preparation time is only 10-15 minutes but allow a further 30 minutes for chilling.

VARIATIONS
Any mixture of cheese can be used and it is fun to experiment with different flavors, but the base must always be made from full-fat soft cheese to make the bites cling together. Try soft cheese flavored with chives and instead of Cheddar, use a grated hard cheese. A Roquefort or Italian Dolcelatte or Gorgonzola can be used in place of Danish Blue.

SERVING IDEAS
Serve on cocktail sticks, with sticks of celery and Melba toast as an appetizer or snack or add them to a cheeseboard to end a meal.

● 250 calories per ball

Dutch fondue

SERVES 4

½ lb flat mushrooms with their stalks, finely chopped
2½ cups chicken broth
4 tablespoons cornstarch
⅔ cup milk
½ lb Gouda cheese, finely grated (see Variations)
1 tablespoon finely chopped fresh parsley
1 teaspoon Worcestershire sauce
salt and freshly ground black pepper
mushroom slices, to garnish

TO SERVE

1 small loaf French bread, cut into 1-inch cubes
1 lb pork sausages, fried and thickly sliced

1 Put the chopped mushrooms in a saucepan with the broth and bring to a boil. Lower the heat, cover

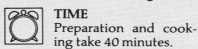
and simmer gently for 10 minutes.
2 In a small bowl, blend the cornstarch to a smooth paste with a little of the milk. Stir into the mushroom broth, then add the remaining milk. Bring to a boil, lower the heat and simmer for 2 minutes, stirring all the time.
3 Turn the heat under the pan to the lowest setting. Add the grated cheese to the pan, 2 tablespoons at a time, stirring well until all the

cheese has melted. Do not allow the mixture to simmer. [!]
4 Remove the pan from the heat and stir in the fresh parsley and Worcestershire sauce, with salt and pepper to taste. Pour the fondue into a warmed serving bowl, [!] or 4 individual bowls, garnish with mushroom slices and serve at once. Hand the bread cubes and sliced fried sausages separately. Provide forks for dipping.

Tomato, cheese and basil flan

SERVES 6-8

6 oz pie crust mix. Make up according to package directions.
4 large tomatoes (about ½ lb), sliced
1¼ cups milk
3 large eggs
1½ teaspoons dried basil (see Did you know)
¾ cup grated sharp Cheddar cheese
salt
freshly ground black pepper
a few tomato slices, to garnish (optional)

1 Preheat the oven to 375°.
2 Roll out the pastry on a floured surface and then use to line an 8-inch plain flan ring set out on a cookie sheet.
3 Arrange the tomato slices overlapping in the flan case. In a bowl, beat together the milk, eggs, basil, ½ cup of the cheese and salt and pepper to taste.
4 Pour the mixture into the flan case and sprinkle over the remaining cheese. Bake in the oven for 40-45 minutes until the filling is set and golden brown on top.
5 Allow the flan to cool for 5 minutes, then carefully remove the flan ring. Transfer the flan to a serving dish, then arrange the remaining tomato slices as a garnish, if preferred.

Cook's Notes

TIME
Preparation takes about 20 minutes, baking 40-45 minutes.

DID YOU KNOW
The flavor of sweet basil perfectly complements tomato, and this is a classic combination in many dishes, particularly those of Italian origin.

Fresh herbs are always preferable in cooking, but fresh basil is not readily available, though it can sometimes be found in specialist garden shops during the summer months.

Remember, if you want to grow basil, that it is an annual and so you will need to buy a new plant each year. It likes a sunny, sheltered spot.

There are two main kinds, with which you can experiment. Sweet basil has largish, shiny dark green leaves and white flowers. Bush basil has many small pale green leaves and tiny white flowers. Bush and sweet basil have an equally good flavor.

The strong, aromatic flavor of basil is delicious in egg, mushroom and pasta dishes, as well as with tomatoes.

SERVING IDEAS
The flan is equally good served warm or cold. It serves 6-8 as an appetizer for either a lunch or supper party. Try accompanying it with a spicy tomato relish. This tasty flan also makes perfect picnic food.

●385 calories per portion

Stilton quiche

SERVES 5-6

6 oz pie crust mix. Make up
   according to package directions.
1 cup Stilton cheese, grated
⅔ cup milk
⅔ cup heavy cream
3 large eggs
2 tablespoons chopped parsley
¼ cup Stilton cheese, crumbled, to
   garnish (optional)

1 Preheat the oven to 400°.

2 Roll out the pastry on a floured surface and use to line an 8-inch flan ring placed on a cookie sheet. Refrigerate for 30 minutes.

3 Put the 1 cup grated Stilton, the milk, cream, eggs and parsley in a bowl and beat together, using a fork, until well blended. Pour the mixture into the prepared flan ring and bake in the oven for 40-45 minutes, until the filling has set.

4 Carefully remove the flan ring and transfer the quiche to a serving dish. Serve hot or cold, garnished with crumbled cheese if liked.

Cook's Notes

TIME
If using ready-made pastry, the quiche takes 15 minutes to prepare. Allow 30 minutes for chilling the unbaked pastry case. Baking takes 40-45 minutes.

SERVING IDEAS
Serve the quiche with a crisp green salad.

● 550 calories per portion

Eggs Florentine

SERVES 4
1 lb fresh spinach
4 large eggs, hard-boiled and sliced
salt
3 tablespoons butter or margarine
1 small onion, grated
3 tablespoons all-purpose flour
1¼ cups milk
⅔ cup grated Colby cheese
½ teaspoon Dijon-style mustard
freshly ground black pepper
½ cup grated sharp Cheddar cheese
   (see Buying guide)

1 Wash the spinach in several changes of water to remove all the grit. Remove the stalks and mid-ribs and discard. Put the spinach in a large saucepan with just the water that adheres to the leaves after washing. Sprinkle with salt.

2 Cook the spinach over moderate heat for about 15 minutes, stirring occasionally with a wooden spoon. Turn the cooked spinach into a colander and drain thoroughly, pressing with a large spoon or a saucer to extract as much moisture as possible. Keep hot.

3 Meanwhile melt the butter in a pan, add the onion and cook gently for about 5 minutes until soft and lightly colored. Sprinkle in the flour and stir over low heat for 1-2 minutes. Remove from the heat and gradually stir in the milk. Return to the heat and simmer, stirring, until thick and smooth. Mix in Colby cheese and the mustard, season to taste with salt and pepper and remove from the heat.

4 Preheat the broiler to high.

5 Divide the spinach between 4 individual gratin dishes. Arrange a row of egg slices on top of the spinach. Pour sauce over, covering the surface as much as possible. Sprinkle the sharp Cheddar cheese

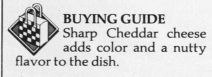
on top of the rows of egg slices.
6 Place under the broiler for about 5 minutes or until the cheese has melted. Serve hot. (See Serving ideas.)

Egg and spinach nests

SERVES 4
½ lb spinach, stalks and large
   midribs removed, shredded
2 tablespoons butter or margarine
salt and freshly ground black pepper
4 eggs
4 tablespoons heavy cream
cayenne, to garnish
butter for greasing

1 Preheat the oven to 375°. Grease
4 individual ovenproof dishes or
ramekins.
2 Melt the butter in a saucepan, add
the spinach and cook gently for 8
minutes, or until soft. Season to
taste with salt and pepper.
3 Divide the spinach between the
prepared dishes. Break 1 egg into
each dish on top of the cooked
spinach mixture.
4 Place the dishes on a cookie sheet
and bake in oven for 10 minutes,
until the egg whites begin to set.
Remove from the oven and spoon 1
tablespoon cream over each egg.
Return to the oven and cook for a
further 5 minutes. Sprinkle a little
cayenne over each egg and serve at
once (see Serving ideas).

Cook's Notes

TIME
Preparation 20 minutes,
cooking 15 minutes.

SERVING IDEAS
Ideal as a first course for
a dinner party or serve
with whole wheat toast for a
light lunch or supper.

DID YOU KNOW
In France the nests are
served in cocotte dishes
– small dishes with a handle.
Cocotte dishes hold one egg.

VARIATIONS
Place 4 tablespoons
chopped cooked mush-
rooms or asparagus in the dish
in place of the spinach.

● 195 calories per portion

Chinese egg rolls

SERVES 4

- ⅓ lb cooked chicken cut into 1-inch strips (about 1½ cups)
- ½ teaspoon cornstarch
- 3-4 tablespoons vegetable oil
- 2 tablespoons soy sauce
- 1 teaspoon sherry
- 3 celery stalks, sliced
- 8-10 scallions, sliced
- 1 cup beansprouts, well drained if canned
- 6 eggs, beaten
- 1 tablespoon water
- salt
- freshly ground black pepper

1 Put the chicken on a plate and sprinkle with the cornstarch.

2 Pour 2 tablespoons of the oil into a heavy skillet or wok. Stir in the soy sauce and sherry and heat over high heat until very hot.

3 Add the celery and scallions and toss for 2 minutes, either by lifting and shaking the pan, or using a large flat spoon.

4 Add the chicken to the pan with the beansprouts. Toss over high heat for about 1 minute, ⚠ then transfer to a plate and keep warm.

5 Put the eggs and water into a bowl with salt and pepper to taste and beat until thoroughly mixed.

6 Clean the skillet with several sheets of paper towel. Add 1 tablespoon vegetable oil and heat over moderate heat. Pour in a quarter of the egg mixture, tilting the pan so that it spreads over the surface to make a thin crêpe, cook until egg sets.

7 Keep warm. Slide crêpe out onto a piece of waxed paper and place a quarter of the chicken and beansprout mixture in the middle of the crêpe. Fold in the sides and then roll up into a parcel (see Preparation).

8 Repeat with the remaining egg and chicken mixture to make 3 more egg rolls, adding more oil to the pan if necessary. Serve at once.

Cook's Notes

TIME
This nutritious appetizer takes less than 20 minutes to prepare and cook.

ECONOMY
Instead of sherry, use a little more soy sauce. Any kind of left-over cooked meat can be cut into strips and used in this recipe.

WATCHPOINT
Do not cook the beansprouts for too long or they will go limp and lose their vitamin C content.

PREPARATION
To make the egg roll parcels:

● 295 calories per roll

Small corn quiches

MAKES 12

1 can (about 11 oz) whole kernel
  corn, drained
6 oz pie crust mix. Make up
  according to package directions.
¼ lb bacon slices cut into ½-inch
  strips
1 egg
⅓ cup light cream
salt and freshly ground black pepper
1 tablespoon fresh or dried parsley

1 Preheat the oven to 375°.
2 Roll out the pastry on a lightly
floured surface to a circle ¼ inch
thick. Cut into rounds with a 3-inch
cutter. Roll out the trimmings to
make 12 rounds altogether. Press
the rounds lightly into a muffin tin,
then refrigerate while making the
filling.

3 Put the bacon into a non-stick
skillet (see Cook's tip) and cook over
moderate heat for 3-5 minutes.
Drain on paper towels.
4 Mix the bacon with the drained
corn kernels and spoon into the
prepared pastry cases.

5 Beat the egg with the cream.
Season with salt and pepper to taste,
then stir in the parsley. Spoon
carefully over the corn mixture. ☐
6 Bake in the oven for 20-25
minutes until the pastry is golden
and the filling firm.

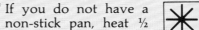

Cook's Notes

TIME
The quiches take 20
minutes to prepare and
about 25 minutes to cook.

COOK'S TIP
If you do not have a
non-stick pan, heat ½
teaspoon vegetable oil in a pan
and cook the bacon.

 WATCHPOINT
Make sure that the
mixture does not spill
over the edge of the pastry or
the quiches will stick.

SERVING IDEAS
Serve as a snack, or as
part of a buffet. Or
double the quantities and serve
with a salad as a main meal.

FREEZING
Cool quickly, open
freeze until solid, then
pack into a rigid container.
To serve: Thaw at room
temperature for 6 hours, then
refresh in a 375° oven for 10
minutes.

● 85 calories per quiche

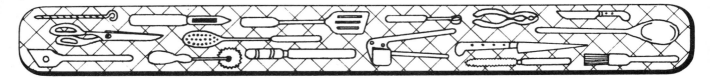

Egg mousse

SERVES 4
**3 hard-boiled eggs, yolks and whites
  separated**
4 teaspoons unflavored gelatin
⅔ cup chicken broth
**1¼ cups thick mayonnaise,
  preferably homemade**
**1-2 teaspoons curry paste (see Did
  you know)**
few drops of Worcestershire sauce
salt and freshly ground black pepper
1 egg white
parsley sprigs, to garnish

1 Sprinkle the gelatin over the broth in a small pan and leave for 1-2 minutes to soften and become spongy. Set the pan over very gentle heat without allowing it to boil, until the gelatin is completely dissolved ⚠ (the liquid should be absolutely clear).
2 Leave the gelatin to cool, then beat it slowly into the mayonnaise in a bowl until smooth.

3 Sieve the egg yolks and stir into the mayonnaise mixture with the curry paste and Worcestershire sauce. Chop the egg whites and fold two-thirds of them into the mixture. Season carefully with salt and pepper.
4 Beat the egg white stiffly and

fold it into the mixture with a large metal spoon until evenly incorporated. Pour into an 2-pint soufflé dish (see Serving ideas).
5 Refrigerate for about 3 hours or until set. Just before serving, garnish with the remaining chopped egg white and the parsley sprigs.

Cook's Notes

TIME
Preparation takes about 30 minutes including hard-boiling the eggs; allow 3 hours for the mousse to set.

DID YOU KNOW
Curry paste is a blend of curry powder, oil and vinegar. It is very handy for adding to sauces and liquid mixtures, as it dissolves more readily than curry powder.

WATCHPOINT
If soaked gelatin is allowed to boil, it will lose its setting power. As an extra precaution, you can dis-

solve gelatin in a bowl set over a pan of simmering water, but this is not absolutely necessary.

SERVING IDEAS
An attractive way to serve this mousse, and one that is ideal for a dinner party appetizer, is to set the mixture in 4 custard cups and accompany with toast.
To serve the mousse turned out, rinse inside of dish with cold water before putting in mixture: When set, run knife around edge before unmolding onto inverted plate.

● 555 calories per portion

Cauliflower and salami soufflés

SERVES 4

1 small cauliflower, broken into very small flowerets
⅓ cup skinned and chopped salami (about 2 oz)
3 tablespoons butter or margarine
salt
3 tablespoons all-purpose flour
1¼ cups milk
pinch of freshly ground nutmeg
freshly ground white pepper
2 large eggs, separated

1 Preheat the oven to 400°. Use 1 tablespoon of the butter to grease four custard cups or ovenproof dishes.
2 Bring a pan of salted water to a boil and add the cauliflower. Simmer for 4-5 minutes, or until the cauliflower is just cooked.
3 Meanwhile, melt the remaining butter in a small saucepan, sprinkle in the flour and stir over low heat for

1-2 minutes until straw-colored. Remove from the heat and gradually stir in the milk. Return to the heat and simmer, stirring, until thick and smooth. Add the nutmeg and salt and pepper to taste, remove from the heat and leave to cool for a few minutes, then stir in the egg yolks.
4 Drain cauliflower and set aside.

5 In a clean, dry bowl, beat the egg whites until standing in stiff peaks. Using a metal spoon, fold into the sauce with the salami.
6 Arrange the cauliflower in the prepared dishes and spoon the soufflé mixture on top. Bake in the oven for 30 minutes until well risen and golden. Remove from the oven and serve at once. [!]

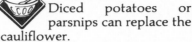

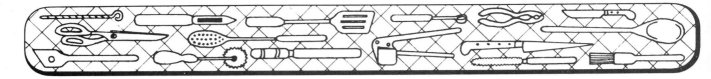

Cheese and chive soufflé

SERVES 4

**1 cup finely grated Cheddar
cheese**
4 tablespoons butter or margarine
1 small onion, finely chopped
4 tablespoons all-purpose flour
pinch of dry mustard
pinch of cayenne
1 cup milk
4 large eggs, separated
1 tablespoon chopped chives
salt and freshly ground black pepper
melted butter, for greasing

1 Brush the inside of a 2-pint soufflé dish with melted butter. Preheat the oven to 350°.
2 Melt the butter in a saucepan, add the onion and cook gently for about 5 minutes until soft and lightly colored but not browned.
3 Sprinkle the flour, mustard and cayenne into the pan and stir over low heat for 2 minutes.
4 Remove from the heat and gradually stir in the milk. Return to the heat and simmer, stirring, until thick and smooth.
5 Remove the pan from heat, stir in the cheese, then leave the sauce to cool slightly. Beat the egg yolks, then stir them into the cheese sauce with the chives. Season well with pepper, and salt if necessary.
6 Beat the egg whites until stiff but not dry. Fold them into the cheese mixture with a large metal spoon, in a figure-of-eight motion, using the edges of the spoon to cut through the mixture.
7 Pour the mixture into the pre-pared soufflé dish. Run a round-bladed knife through the mixture, to make an attractive "crown" effect (see Preparation).
8 Bake in the oven for 50 minutes or until the soufflé is well-risen and golden. When lightly shaken, it should only wobble slightly. Serve at once straight from the dish.

Cook's Notes

TIME
Preparation takes about 30 minutes, cooking in the oven about 50 minutes.

PREPARATION
To give the soufflé a "crown" effect:

Draw a spatula or round-bladed palette knife through the top of the mixture in a circle, about 1½ inches in from the edge.

● 405 calories per portion

Eggs in potato nests

SERVES 4
4 large eggs
1½ lb potatoes
1 tablespoon vegetable oil
1 large egg yolk
2 tablespoons butter or
margarine
about ⅓ cup half and half
¼ lb mushrooms, finely chopped
(about 1½ cups)
1 small onion, finely chopped
½ cup cooked ham, diced
1 teaspoon tomato paste
salt and freshly ground black pepper
1 small egg, beaten, to glaze
1 tablespoon chopped parsley
butter, for greasing

1 Cook the potatoes in boiling salted water until tender. Drain well and press them through a strainer.

Beat in the egg yolk, half the butter and just enough of the half and half to make a firm mixture.

2 Put the creamed potato into a pastry bag fitted with a large star nozzle and pipe 4 "nests" onto a greased cookie sheet. To form the nests: Using a spiral motion, make a flat round of potato about 5 inches in diameter, then pipe a wall about 2 inches high round the outer edge. Or shape the mixture with a teaspoon.

3 Preheat the oven to 350°. Heat the oil in a skillet. Add the mushrooms and onion and cook gently until soft. Stir in the ham and the tomato paste with salt and pepper to taste, then mix well. Remove from the heat.

4 Brush the potato nests with beaten egg to glaze and spoon in the mushroom and ham mixture, dividing it equally between the nests.

5 Break 1 egg at a time into a cup and slide the eggs into the potato nests.

6 Spoon a little half and half on top of each egg to cover the yolk and

dot with the remaining butter to protect the yolk during cooking.

7 Bake nests in the oven for 10-15 minutes until the whites of the eggs have just set and the yolks are still soft. With a metal spatula, carefully remove the nests from the baking sheet without breaking the egg yolks, then place them on warmed serving plates or individual dishes. Sprinkle with chopped parsley and serve at once.

Cook's Notes

TIME
Total preparation and cooking time, including boiling the potatoes, is about 1 hour.

SERVING IDEAS
Broiled tomatoes and/or chopped spinach could be served as accompaniments.

● 390 calories per portion

VEGETABLE APPETIZERS

Cheese-stuffed zucchini

SERVES 4
4 large zucchini
salt
1 tablespoon vegetable oil
1 onion, chopped
1 cup cottage cheese, sieved
¼ cup grated Parmesan cheese
1 egg, beaten
1 tablespoon finely chopped
  parsley
freshly ground black pepper
4 tablespoons day-old soft white
  bread crumbs
½ cup grated Cheddar cheese
2 tablespoons butter or margarine
  melted
butter, for greasing

1 Preheat the oven to 400°.
2 Bring a large saucepan of salted water to a boil, add the zucchini, bring back to a boil, reduce the heat and simmer for about 10 minutes until barely tender. [!] Drain and refresh under cold running water for 1 minute. Drain again.

3 Cut the zucchini into half lengthwise and with a teaspoon or grapefruit knife carefully scrape out the core and seeds from the center, leaving a good shell. Reserve the scooped-out flesh and seeds (see Cook's tip). Sprinkle the inside of the zucchini with salt, place upside down on paper towels and leave to drain for 5-10 minutes.
4 Meanwhile, chop the reserved zucchini flesh. Heat the oil in a skillet add the onion and zucchini flesh and cook over moderate heat for about 10 minutes until the onion is just beginning to brown. Transfer to a bowl and leave to cool.
5 Mix the cottage cheese with the onion and zucchini mixture. Stir in the Parmesan cheese, egg and parsley and season to taste with salt and pepper. The mixture should hold its shape: If it is too soft, add a few of the bread crumbs.
6 Grease a large shallow ovenproof dish and stand the zucchini halves in it in a single layer, skin side down. Using a teaspoon, fill the zucchini with the stuffing, heaping it in a mound on each half.
7 Mix together the bread crumbs and grated Cheddar cheese and

sprinkle evenly over the zucchini. Drizzle the melted butter over the top and bake in the oven for 25-30 minutes until golden and bubbling. Serve hot.

Cook's Notes

TIME
Preparation and cooking take 55 minutes.

WATCHPOINT
Do not overcook the zucchini at this stage: They should still be firm or they will disintegrate when baked.

SERVING IDEAS
Serve for a tasty appetizer accompanied by rolls and butter.

COOK'S TIP
There is no need to discard the zucchini seeds: When mixed and cooked with the other stuffing ingredients they will not be noticeable.

● 330 calories per portion

Egg and avocado bake

SERVES 6

6 eggs, separated
1 large avocado
6 tablespoons browned bread
  crumbs (see Preparation)
3 tablespoons vegetable oil
1 onion, finely chopped
1 clove garlic, crushed (optional)
4 tablespoons finely chopped fresh
  parsley
salt and freshly ground black pepper
¾ cup grated Cheddar cheese
melted butter or margarine for
  greasing

1 Preheat the oven to 400°. Brush 6 individual ovenproof dishes with melted butter, then coat them evenly with 4 tablespoons of the bread crumbs. Set aside.

2 Heat the oil in a skillet, add the onion and garlic, if using, and cook gently for 3-4 minutes until the onion is soft but not colored. Set aside to cool for about 5 minutes.

3 Cut the avocado in half. Remove the seed, scoop out the flesh into a bowl, then mash with a fork to a purée. Beat in the egg yolks and parsley, then the cooled onion and salt and pepper to taste.

4 Beat the egg whites until standing in stiff peaks, then fold them into the avocado mixture. Pile into the dishes, scatter remaining crumbs on top and bake in the oven for 20 minutes.

5 Sprinkle the top of the rising mixture with the cheese, then return dishes to the oven for a further 15 minutes until they are well risen and golden. Serve at once.

Cook's Notes

TIME
Preparation takes about 30 minutes, plus 30 minutes for making bread crumbs, cooking 35 minutes.

PREPARATION
To make the quantity of browned bread crumbs needed for this recipe: Toast 3-4 slices of day-old white bread in a 350° oven for 20 minutes until golden. Cool, then put in a plastic bag and crush with a rolling pin.

SERVING IDEAS
Serve with French bread and a salad.

● 330 calories per portion

Salad kabobs

SERVES 4

½ small cauliflower, divided into
flowerets (see Watchpoint)

1 can (about 12 oz) luncheon meat,
cut into 1-inch cubes (see Cook's
tips)

⅓ lb Edam cheese, rind removed and
cut into ¾-inch cubes (about 1½
cups)

1 tablespoon olive oil

1 teaspoon wine vinegar

1 teaspoon chopped fresh parsley

1 red apple

2 teaspoons lemon juice

½ teaspoon superfine sugar

SAUCE

4 tablespoons thick mayonnaise,
preferably homemade

2 tablespoons dairy sour cream

1 teaspoon tomato paste

½ teaspoon Dijon-style mustard

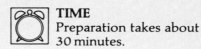

1 Beat the olive oil, vinegar and
parsley together in a bowl. Add the
cauliflower, mix well and leave to
stand for 5-10 minutes.

2 Meanwhile, leaving the skin on,
cut the apple into 8 wedges and
remove the core. Mix the lemon
juice and sugar together and toss
the apple in this mixture.

3 Thread the cauliflower, apple,
luncheon meat and cheese alternately onto 4 long kabob skewers.
Transfer to a serving plate and, if
liked, use remaining pieces of apple
or cauliflower to garnish.

4 Make the sauce: Beat the sauce
ingredients together, then transfer
to a small bowl. Serve the kabobs
(see Cook's tips) with the sauce
handed separately.

Spinach and Brie puffs

SERVES 4

½ lb frozen spinach, thawed and well drained (see Cook's tip)
2 oz Brie, thinly sliced (see Buying guide)
1 egg, beaten
¼ teaspoon freshly ground nutmeg
salt and freshly ground black pepper
1 sheet (½ of 17 oz package) frozen puff pastry, thawed
1 tablespoon grated Parmesan cheese

1 Preheat the oven to 425°.
2 Put the spinach in a bowl, stir in half the beaten egg and the nutmeg. Season to taste with salt and pepper.
3 Roll out the pastry on a lightly floured surface. Trim it to a 12-inch square, then cut into four 6-inch squares.
4 Divide the spinach equally between the squares, spreading it diagonally over one-half of each and leaving a ½-inch border. Top the squares with Brie slices, dividing them equally between the 4 squares.
5 Brush the edges of the pastry with beaten egg, then fold the pastry over to form a triangle and enclose the filling. Press the edges firmly together to seal them, then knock up with a knife and flute. Brush the tops with beaten egg, then use a sharp knife to make 2 small slits to allow the steam to escape. Sprinkle over the Parmesan cheese.
6 Dampen a cookie sheet and carefully transfer the triangles to it.
7 Bake in the oven for about 10 minutes, until the pastry is golden. Serve the puffs hot or cold.

Cook's Notes

TIME
The puffs take about 20 minutes to prepare and 10 minutes to cook.

SERVING IDEAS
Make the puffs smaller (cut 3-inch squares) for an unusual appetizer or snack to serve with drinks.

COOK'S TIP
Put the spinach into a colander or sieve and drain thoroughly, pressing the spinach with a large spoon or a saucer to extract as much moisture as possible.

BUYING GUIDE
Look for Brie that is not too ripe. If it is quite soft, put it in the freezer or freezing compartment of the refrigerator for about 30 minutes before making the puffs.

● 320 calories per puff

Gingered eggplant dip

SERVES 4

2 lb firm eggplant, stems removed
¾ cup plain yogurt
1 clove garlic, crushed (optional)
1 tablespoon light brown sugar
1 teaspoon grated fresh ginger
½ teaspoon cumin powder
a little salt and freshly ground black pepper
fresh coriander or parsley sprigs, to garnish (optional)

1 Preheat the oven to 400°. Prick the eggplant all over with a fork, then put them into a roasting pan and bake in the oven for 45-60 minutes, until they feel really soft when they are pressed with the back of a spoon.

Cook's Notes

TIME
Preparing and cooking 1¼ hours, plus chilling.

SERVING IDEAS
Serve the dip with small pieces of toasted pita bread and raw vegetable, such as carrot and cucumber sticks, strips of red and green pepper, tomato wedges, lengths of celery and cauliflower flowerets.

● 65 calories per portion

PREPARATION
To extract the eggplant juices:

Hold the halved eggplant over a dish and squeeze gently in your hand so that the juices run out.

2 Remove the eggplant from the oven and leave until cool enough to handle. Cut them in half lengthwise, and squeeze gently in your hand to drain off the bitter juices (see Preparation). Scoop out flesh and leave until cold.

3 Put eggplant flesh in a blender with the yogurt, the garlic, if using, sugar, ginger, cumin and salt and pepper to taste. Blend until smooth. Transfer to 1 large or 4 small serving dishes. Refrigerate for 2-3 hours to allow dip to firm up.

4 Just before serving, garnish with coriander or parsley sprigs, if liked.

Avocado and apple grill

SERVES 4

2 ripe avocados
4 crisp green apples
2 tablespoons butter
2 tablespoons all-purpose flour
1 cup milk
¾ cup grated Cheddar cheese
2 teaspoons Dijon-style mustard
salt and freshly ground black pepper
juice of ½ lemon
4 tablespoons fresh whole wheat
    bread crumbs

1 Preheat the broiler to high.
2 Make the sauce: Melt the butter in a small saucepan, sprinkle in the flour and stir over a low heat for 1-2 minutes until it is straw-colored. Remove from the heat and gradually stir in the milk. Return to the heat and simmer, stirring, until thick and smooth. Stir in ½ cup of the cheese and the mustard and season to taste with salt and pepper. Stir until the cheese has melted, then remove the pan from the heat.
3 Peel the avocados, cut in half and remove the seeds. ⚠️ Cut lengthwise into thin slices. Pare, quarter and core the apples. Cut into thin slices. Arrange the slices of avocado and apple in layers in 1 large or 4 individual shallow gratin dishes (see Serving ideas). Squeeze the lemon juice over them immediately to prevent discoloration.
4 Pour the sauce over the avocado and apple. Mix together the remaining cheese and the bread crumbs and sprinkle evenly over the top.
5 Place under the broiler for about 5 minutes until golden brown and bubbling. Serve at once.

Cook's Notes

TIME
Preparation and cooking take about 20 minutes.

⚠️ **WATCHPOINT**
Prepare the avocados just before they are needed as their flesh quickly turns black if exposed to the air when left to stand.

SERVING IDEAS
Serve in individual gratin dishes, this makes a most delicious first course for a dinner party. The number of servings can be easily adjusted up or down by allowing ½ an avocado and 1 apple per person — the quantity of cheese sauce remains the same for up to 8 servings.

Swiss or Emmenthal cheese and a combination of half milk and half dry white wine would make a richer sauce for special occasions.

● 455 calories per portion

Stuffed cucumber salad

SERVES 4

1 large cucumber, cut into 24 even slices (see Buying guide)
1 head Boston lettuce, leaves separated (see Buying guide)
¾ lb carrots, finely grated
3 tablespoons golden raisins
small parsley sprigs and a few chopped walnuts, to garnish

FILLING

½ lb cream cheese
⅔ cup shelled chopped walnuts
2 teaspoons finely chopped fresh parsley
2 teaspoons chopped fresh chives or finely chopped scallion
½ teaspoon paprika
salt and freshly ground black pepper

DRESSING

5 tablespoons vegetable oil
2 tablespoons white wine or cider vinegar
large pinch of dry mustard
pinch of sugar

1 Make the filling: Put all the filling ingredients in a bowl, season with salt and pepper and mix well with a fork.
2 Remove the seeds from each slice of cucumber with an apple corer or a small sharp knife. Season on both sides with salt and pepper and set out on a flat plate.
3 Divide the filling between the cucumber slices, pressing it into the central hole and piling it up on top.
4 Make the dressing: Put all the dressing ingredients in a small screw-top jar, season with salt and pepper then shake the jar well to mix together.
5 Arrange the lettuce leaves on 4 individual plates and drizzle a teaspoonful of the dressing over each serving. Carefully transfer 6 cucumber slices to each plate, arranging them in a ring.
6 Mix the grated carrots with the golden raisins in a bowl. Add the remaining dressing. Toss to coat thoroughly, then pile into the center of the rings of stuffed cucumber slices. Garnish 3 cucumber slices on each plate with a parsley sprig and 3 slices with a few chopped walnuts. Serve at once.

Cook's Notes

TIME
Preparation time is about 45 minutes.

BUYING GUIDE
Choose a straight cucumber so that it will be easy to slice evenly.
A curly, soft-leaved lettuce is best for this recipe because it gives an added attraction, but any soft-leaved lettuce will do.

SERVING IDEAS
Serve the stuffed cucumber slices, with the lettuce as a garnish, as a tasty starter or with drinks. As an alternative suggestion, the salad could be accompanied by cold, sliced meat to make a much more filling supper or lunch.

VARIATION
Use chopped muscatel raisins instead of golden raisins.

● 410 calories per portion

Eggplants on waffles

SERVES 4

2 large eggplant, cut into cubes
salt
2 tablespoons vegetable oil
1¼ cups beef broth
4 teaspoons tomato paste
2 cloves garlic, crushed (optional)
½ teaspoon dark brown sugar
freshly ground black pepper
4 waffles
¾ cup grated Cheddar cheese
coriander sprigs or parsley, to
**   garnish**

1 Layer the eggplant cubes in a colander, sprinkling each layer with salt. Put a plate on top and weight down. Leave to drain for about 30 minutes to remove the bitter juices. Rinse under cold running water, pat dry with paper towels or a clean dish cloth and set aside.

2 Heat the oil in a large skillet, add the eggplant, broth, tomato paste, garlic, if using, and sugar. Season with salt and pepper.

3 Bring to a boil, then lower the heat, cover the pan and simmer for 8-10 minutes, stirring frequently, until the liquid is absorbed and the eggplant cubes are tender.

4 Meanwhile, preheat the broiler to high and toast the waffles for 4 minutes on each side or cook as directed on the package.

5 Place the waffles in a flameproof dish, pile the eggplant mixture on top and sprinkle over the grated cheese. Broil for 1-2 minutes (see Cook's tip).

6 Garnish waffles with coriander sprigs or parsley and serve at once.

MEAT DISHES

Bacon and onion crispies

SERVES 4

4 slices lean bacon, chopped or diced
1 small onion, chopped
3 tablespoons butter or margarine
3 tablespoons all-purpose flour
⅔ cup milk
1 teaspoon dried mixed herbs
1 egg, lightly beaten
1 cup fresh white bread crumbs
vegetable oil, for deep-frying

1 Melt the butter in a small saucepan, add the bacon and onion and cook them over moderate heat for 3-4 minutes.

2 Sprinkle in the flour and stir over low heat for 1-2 minutes until straw-colored. Remove from the heat and gradually stir in the milk.

3 Return the pan to the heat and cook for 2-3 minutes, stirring all the time until very thick and creamy. Remove from the heat and leave to cool.

4 Stir the herbs into the mixture, divide into 8 equal portions, then form each portion into a ball (see Preparation). Put the egg and bread crumbs in separate shallow dishes.

5 Roll each ball in the egg, then coat with the bread crumbs.

6 Heat enough oil to cover the balls in a deep-fat fryer to 350° or until a stale bread cube browns in 60 seconds. Add the balls to the oil a few at a time and deep-fry for 2-3 minutes until golden brown on all sides.

7 Drain the crispies on paper towels and serve at once.

Saucy ham and shrimp rolls

SERVES 4

8 slices cooked ham (½ lb)
¼ lb package parsley and thyme stuffing mix
½ cup shelled, chopped shrimp, thawed if frozen
parsley sprigs, to garnish

CHEESE SAUCE
¾ cup grated Cheddar cheese
2 tablespoons butter or margarine
2 tablespoons all-purpose flour
1 cup milk
pinch of freshly ground nutmeg
½ teaspoon prepared English mustard
salt and freshly ground black pepper

1 Preheat the oven to 400°.
2 Make the stuffing according to package directions. Allow to cool slightly and mix in the shrimp.

3 Divide the stuffing between the ham slices, spooning it in a strip about 1½ inches from each edge. Starting at the edge nearest the stuffing, carefully roll up each slice of ham. Place the shrimp-filled ham rolls, with the join side down, in a shallow ovenproof dish, large enough to hold them in one layer.
4 Make the sauce: Melt the butter in a saucepan, sprinkle in the flour and stir over low heat for 1-2 minutes until straw-colored. Remove from heat and gradually stir in the milk. Add the nutmeg and mustard and season to taste with salt and pepper. Return to the heat and simmer, stirring, until thick and smooth. Remove the pan from the heat and stir in half the grated Cheddar cheese.
5 Pour the sauce over the ham rolls and sprinkle with the remaining cheese. Bake in the oven for 20 minutes until the sauce is golden and bubbling. Garnish with parsley and serve at once straight from the dish (see Serving ideas).

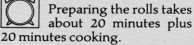

Cook's Notes

TIME
Preparing the rolls takes about 20 minutes plus 20 minutes cooking.

VARIATIONS
Use slices of roast pork instead of the ham.
If preferred, make your own stuffing with ¾ cup cooked rice (you will need ¼ cup raw rice), chopped celery, green pepper and mushrooms.
For a stronger-flavored sauce use Swiss cheese instead of Cheddar.

SERVING IDEAS
To make a substantial supper dish, serve with a green vegetable such as green beans or broccoli and crusty bread and butter.

● 380 calories per portion

Bacon kabobs with peanut dip

SERVES 4
¾ lb bacon in one piece, trimmed
   and then cut into ¾-1 inch
   cubes
3 tablespoons crunchy peanut
   butter
⅓ cup shredded coconut
⅔ cup water
salt and freshly ground black pepper
coriander leaves, to garnish

MARINADE
2 tablespoons vegetable oil
2 teaspoons curry paste
2 teaspoons lemon juice
½ teaspoon ground coriander
¼ teaspoon ground turmeric

1 Make the marinade: Blend the marinade ingredients in a bowl.
2 Add the meat cubes and coat thoroughly in the marinade. Cover and leave to stand for 30 minutes.
3 Preheat the broiler to moderate.

4 Remove the meat cubes from the marinade with a slotted spoon. Reserve marinade. Thread the bacon pieces onto each of 12 wooden toothpicks (see Cook's tip).
5 Broil the kabobs for 10 minutes, turning occasionally, until cooked.
6 Meanwhile, pour the reserved marinade into a saucepan and add peanut butter, coconut and water. Season to taste with salt and pepper and heat through gently, stirring constantly until well mixed.
7 Arrange the bacon kabobs on a warmed serving plate and garnish with coriander. Serve at once with the dip handed separately in a warmed bowl (see Serving ideas).

Chicken fritters

SERVES 4

1 cup boneless cooked, skinned and
    finely chopped chicken
2 tablespoons butter
3 tablespoons all-purpose flour
⅔ cup milk
1 egg yolk
⅓ cup cooked, finely chopped ham
4 button mushrooms, finely
    chopped
½ teaspoon dried oregano
salt
freshly ground black
    pepper
¼ lb package batter mix
6 slices of bacon
vegetable oil, for deep frying

1 Make the sauce: Melt the butter in a saucepan, sprinkle in 2 tablespoons flour and stir over heat for 1-2 minutes until straw-colored. Remove from heat and gradually stir in the milk and the egg yolk. Return to heat and simmer, stirring, until thick and smooth.

2 Stir in the chicken, ham, mushrooms and oregano and season to taste with salt and pepper. Pour the mixture onto a large plate, spread it out with a knife and leave until completely cool, about 15-20 minutes.

3 Make up the batter according to the package directions. [!]

4 Stretch each of the bacon slices with the back of a knife and then cut them in half.

5 Divide the chicken mixture into 12, then roll each piece into a ball, and shape it into a roll. Wrap each roll with bacon.

6 Spread out the remaining tablespoon flour on a flat plate and season with salt and pepper. Dip each roll in the flour until evenly coated.

7 Heat the oil in a deep-fat fryer to 375° or until a day-old bread cube browns in 50 seconds.

8 Dip the rolls one at a time into the batter, then drop into the hot oil and deep fry 6 at a time for about 6 minutes until golden and crispy.

9 Drain on paper towels and keep warm while cooking the second batch. Serve at once.

Curried chicken salad

SERVES 4

1 lb boneless cooked chicken,
  skinned and cut into 4-inch
  strips
⅔ cup thick mayonnaise, preferably
  homemade
⅔ cup plain yogurt
1 teaspoon curry paste (see Cook's
  tip)
juice of ½-1 lemon
2 red apples
4 celery stalks, chopped
4 scallions or 1 small onion, finely
  chopped
¾ cup green grapes, halved and
  pitted
½ cup shelled, coarsely chopped
  walnuts
salt and freshly ground black pepper
1 small lettuce, shredded

1 In a bowl, mix together the mayonnaise and yogurt. Mix the curry paste with the juice of half a lemon and fold into the mayonnaise mixture.

2 Core and slice but do not pare the apples and mix them into the mayonnaise mixture with the celery, onions, grapes and walnuts.

3 Add the chicken strips to the mixture turning them to coat evenly with the mayonnaise. Taste and season with salt and pepper if necessary, and add more lemon juice if liked.

4 Arrange the lettuce in individual dishes. Pile the salad on top and serve at once.

Peanut drumsticks

SERVES 4
8 chicken drumsticks, skinned (see
    Preparation)
⅓ cup smooth peanut butter
1 egg, beaten
⅓ cup milk
salt and freshly ground black pepper
about ½ lb plain potato chips
½ cup all-purpose flour
vegetable oil, for greasing

1 Preheat the oven to 375°. Brush a cookie sheet with oil.
2 Put the peanut butter into a bowl and beat in the egg with a wooden spoon. Gradually beat in the milk, then season to taste with salt and pepper. Pour the mixture into a shallow bowl.

3 Put the potato chips into a plastic bag and crush with a rolling pin. Spread out on a flat plate.
4 Spread the flour out on a separate plate.
5 Coat each chicken drumstick in flour, then in the peanut mixture

followed by the crushed chips. Make sure that each layer is evenly covered.
6 Place the coated drumsticks on the prepared cookie sheet and bake in the oven for 45-50 minutes, or until crisp and lightly browned. Serve hot or cold.

Cook's Notes

TIME
Total preparation and cooking time is about 1 hour.

VARIATIONS
Crunchy peanut butter can be used instead of smooth. Dried bread crumbs or crushed cornflakes can replace the crushed potato chips.

● 590 calories per portion

PREPARATION
To skin the drumsticks, cut through the skin lengthwise with a sharp knife or scissors, then pull the skin away with a sharp tug.

SERVING IDEAS
Serve hot with buttered noodles or baked potatoes, or cold with an endive and cress salad or as part of a finger buffet with a relish.

Savory bacon fritters

SERVES 4

about ½ lb lean bacon slices, (see
  Buying guide)
1 cup all-purpose flour
2 teaspoons dry mustard
large pinch of celery salt
large pinch of paprika
freshly ground black pepper
2 eggs, separated
½-⅔ cup beer
1 tablespoon vegetable oil
1 onion, finely chopped
½ green pepper, seeded and
  chopped
vegetable oil, for deep-frying
tomato wedges, to serve

1 Sift the flour into a bowl with the
dry mustard, celery salt, paprika and
pepper to taste. Make a well in the
center, add the egg yolks and beat
to mix thoroughly, gradually working the dry ingredients into the
center. Beat in enough beer to make
a batter with a thick coating
consistency.

2 Cover the bowl with plastic wrap,
then set aside in a cool place for 2
hours (see Time).

3 Broil the bacon until cooked but
not crisp. Drain on paper towels,
then cut into 1-inch lengths.

4 Heat a little oil in a skillet. Add
the onion and pepper and cook
gently for 5 minutes until the onion
is soft and lightly colored. Remove
with a slotted spoon and add to the
bacon.

5 Pour enough oil into a deep-fat
fryer to come halfway up the sides.
Heat the oil gently to 375°, or until a
stale bread cube turns golden in 50
seconds.

6 Meanwhile, in a clean dry bowl,
beat the egg whites until they are
standing in stiff peaks. Using a large
metal spoon, carefully fold the egg
whites into the batter with the
bacon, onion and green pepper.

7 Drop a few tablespoonfuls of
batter into the hot oil and deep-fry
for 3-4 minutes, until puffed and
golden brown. Drain well on paper
towels and keep hot while frying
the remainder, but remember to
reheat the oil between each batch.

8 Serve with tomato wedges.

Cook's Notes

 TIME
Preparation, 20 minutes,
cooking 15 minutes,
and 2 hours for batter to rest. To
save time, use milk instead of
beer and rest it 30 minutes.

BUYING GUIDE
Collar slices are lean
and less expensive than
back bacon; they are ideal for
this recipe.

SERVING IDEAS
Serve with a selection of
relishes, and with a
colorful white and red cabbage
coleslaw.

● 595 calories per portion

MAIN COURSES

The highlight of any meal is the main course, but it is often hard to achieve the variety of dishes that you would like without spending too much money. This section contains a balanced selection of Pork, Beef and Veal, Lamb, Poultry, Fish and Seafood and Variety Meat dishes to suit all palates – and they don't take ages to make. There are nearly 80 recipes including a mixture of casseroles, dishes with joints of meat and more spicy dishes like *Stir-fried beef with cashews* or *Chicken paprikash*. If you prefer the more traditional dishes you can make *Pot-roasted leg of lamb* or perhaps the tasty *Family fish pie*.

PORK

Pork scallops with plums

SERVES 4

8 pork scallops, each weighing 2 oz
1 can (about 1 lb) red plums, drained (see Buying guide)
2 tablespoons vegetable oil
2 tablespoons butter or margarine
1 onion, finely chopped
⅔ cup apple juice or dry white wine
1 teaspoon ground cinnamon
½ teaspoon ground coriander
salt and freshly ground black pepper

1 Carefully remove the pits from the plums, keeping them as whole as possible if using canned ones.

2 Make the sauce: Heat half the oil and half the butter in a pan, add the onion, cook gently 10 minutes until softened. Pour in the juice and bring to a boil. Add the spices and salt and pepper to taste. Stir well, then lower the heat, cover and cook the sauce gently for 5 minutes.

3 Add the plums to the sauce, cover and simmer very gently a further 5 minutes, taking care not to break up the plums. Taste and adjust seasoning.

4 Meanwhile, divide the remaining oil and butter beween 2 large skillets and heat gently. Add the pork scallops and cook over high heat 3 minutes on each side, until browned. ⚠

5 To serve, arrange the scallops on a warmed serving dish and spoon over the sauce. Serve at once.

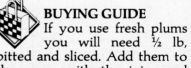

Marinated pork chops

SERVES 4

**8 thin pork chops, or 4 thicker
   chops**

MARINADE

4 tablespoons soy sauce
2 tablespoons orange juice
2 tablespoons olive oil or corn oil
2 tablespoons tomato catsup
**2 tablespoons light soft brown
   sugar**
1 teaspoon ground ginger
grated rind of 1 orange
**salt and freshly ground black
   pepper**
**small bunch scallions, thinly
   sliced**

1 Make the marinade: Mix all the ingredients together, including the scallions, making sure the sugar dissolves.

2 Put 4 of the chops in a dish so they do not overlap one another. Spoon over half the marinade, putting a few pieces of scallion on each chop.

3 Put the remaining chops on top and spoon the rest of the marinade over them. Cover with plastic wrap and refrigerate at least 6 hours, basting occasionally.

4 Remove chops from the marinade and broil under high heat about 4 minutes on each side. (Thicker chops will need about 7-8 minutes each side.) Spoon the marinade with the scallions onto the chops when you turn them, so that the scallions become brown and crispy. Serve at once on a warmed serving plate.

Mediterranean pork casserole

SERVES 4

1½-1¾ lb pork loin rib chops, trimmed of bone and fat and cut into small cubes
1 tablespoon vegetable oil
1 onion, sliced
1 clove garlic, crushed (optional)
1-2 teaspoons paprika
¼ teaspoon dried thyme
salt and freshly ground black pepper
1 large green pepper, seeded and cut into strips
1 can (about 14 oz) tomatoes
¼ lb button mushrooms, quartered
2 teaspoons cornstarch

1 Heat the oil in a large flameproof casserole and cook the pork cubes over brisk heat about 5 minutes, stirring continuously. Lower the heat, add the onion and garlic, if using, and cook about 5 minutes until the onion is soft and translucent.

2 Sprinkle over the paprika and thyme and season to taste. Stir in the green pepper, tomatoes and mushrooms and bring to a boil. Lower the heat, cover the pan and simmer gently 1 hour or until the pork is tender, stirring occasionally.

3 Mix the cornstarch to a smooth paste with a little cold water, stir in a spoonful of the hot liquid from the pork, then stir this mixture back into the pork. Bring to a boil, stirring, then simmer 1-2 minutes until thickened. Taste and adjust seasoning. Serve at once, straight from the casserole.

Cook's Notes

TIME
Preparation takes about 30 minutes and cooking just over 1 hour.

COOK'S TIP
This casserole improves in flavor if made a day in advance. It can be kept, covered, in the refrigerator overnight.

BUYING GUIDE
Use lean rib chops for this dish, not the fatter ribs used in Chinese cooking.

VARIATION
If you prefer a slightly spicier flavor, simply add more paprika according to taste.

SERVING IDEAS
Boiled noodles or potatoes plus a bright-colored vegetable such as carrots or broccoli, are good accompaniments to this casserole.

FREEZING
Allow the cooked casserole to cool and then remove the excess fat from the surface. Freeze in a rigid container up to 3 months. Thaw overnight in the refrigerator, then heat through until bubbling.

● 525 calories per portion

Pork ragoût

SERVES 4

1¾ lb fresh belly pork, or side of pork trimmed of excess fat, cut into strips 1 inch long and ¾ inch wide
2 tablespoons vegetable oil
1 large onion, chopped
6 tablespoons all-purpose flour
2½ cups chicken broth
4 large carrots, cut into thin slices
thinly pared rind of 1 lemon, cut into strips
¼ lb black-eyed beans, soaked overnight in cold water, drained
½ teaspoon ground coriander
½ teaspoon ground turmeric
¼ teaspoon ground ginger
freshly ground black pepper
salt
strips of lemon rind and chopped parsley to garnish

1 Preheat the oven to 325°.

2 Heat three-quarters of the oil in a flameproof casserole, add the pork and cook 3-4 minutes until lightly browned and sealed on both sides. Remove with a slotted spoon and drain on paper towels.

3 Heat the remaining oil in the casserole, add the onion and cook gently 5 minutes until soft and lightly colored. Sprinkle in the flour and stir over low heat 1-2 minutes. Gradually stir in broth. Bring to a boil and then simmer, stirring, until thick.

4 Add the carrots, lemon strips, beans and spices, and season to taste with ground black pepper. Bring back to a boil and then boil 10 minutes. Return the meat to the casserole, cover and cook in the oven about 2 hours.

5 Before serving, add salt and black pepper to taste, and garnish with the strips of lemon rind and the chopped parsley. Serve at once.

Stir-fried pork and cucumber

SERVES 4–6
2 lb fresh streaky pork belly slices
1 medium cucumber
2 tablespoons cornstarch
2 tablespoons dry sherry
2 tablespoons soy sauce
1¼ cups chicken broth
2 tablespoons vegetable oil
1 clove garlic, finely chopped
1 large onion, finely chopped
1 teaspoon ground ginger, or ½ teaspoon finely chopped fresh root ginger.

1 Trim the slices of pork of any excess fat. Cut the slices into thin strips about 2 inches long.
2 Wipe but do not pare the cucumber, then cut into quarters lengthwise, trimming off the ends. Scoop out the seeds with a teaspoon. Cut the quarters lengthwise again and cut the pieces into 1-inch lengths.
3 Mix the cornstarch to a paste in a

bowl, with a little of the sherry or soy sauce, then stir in the remainder with the broth.
4 Put the oil and garlic into a skillet and set over high heat until the garlic sizzles.
5 Add the pork and cook over high heat about 15 minutes until all the pieces are crisp and well browned, stirring briskly all the time.
6 Pour all but about 1 tablespoon of the fat from skillet and then

set the pan back over low heat.
7 Stir in the cucumber, onion and ginger and cook, stirring, about 5 minutes until the onion is translucent.
8 Give the cornstarch mixture a stir and pour it into the pan. Increase the heat and bring the mixture to a boil. Cook over high heat 3 minutes until a thick, translucent sauce is formed.
9 Transfer to a warmed serving dish and serve at once.

Baked honey ribs

SERVES 4

3 lb pork spare ribs, Chinese style (see Buying guide)
4 tablespoons clear honey
3 tablespoons light brown sugar
1 tablespoon Worcestershire sauce
2 tablespoons tomato catsup
1 tablespoon Dijon-style mustard
2 tablespoons red wine vinegar
salt and freshly ground black pepper

1 Preheat the oven to 400°.
2 If necessary, cut through the ribs to separate them. Put them in a single layer in 1 large or 2 small roasting pans.
3 Combine the remaining ingredients in a small saucepan and season well with salt and pepper.

Heat gently over low heat until just simmering.
4 Brush the ribs with the sauce on both sides, using a pastry or similar kitchen brush, then pour over any remaining syrup, making sure the ribs are well coated.

5 Bake in the oven uncovered, 1 hour, basting and turning the ribs frequently then turn the oven down to low, and bake 30 minutes more, or until the flesh is well cooked and the ribs thoroughly coated in syrupy sauce. Serve at once.

Cook's Notes

TIME
Preparation 15 minutes. Cooking 1½ hours.

BUYING GUIDE
Most butchers will supply sheets of Chinese-style spare ribs, but some need a few days notice. Ordinary spare rib chops will not make a satisfactory substitute.

● 310 calories per portion

COOK'S TIP
Marinate the ribs in the sauce ingredients for a few hours, before barbecuing them, basting with the sauce.

SERVING IDEAS
Eat the ribs with your fingers (making sure you have plenty of napkins on hand). Excellent accompaniments for these honey ribs are hot Greek pita bread and fresh green salad.

Pork fillet in puff pastry

SERVES 4-6

2 pieces pork fillet (tenderloin), each weighing about ¾ lb
1 tablespoon vegetable oil
1 sheet (½ of 17 oz package) frozen puff pastry, thawed
⅓ cup button mushrooms, sliced
1 dessert apple

STUFFING

½ cup fresh white bread crumbs
1 tablespoon vegetable shortening
1 small onion, grated
1 teaspoon dried sage
salt and freshly ground black pepper
1 egg, beaten

1 Preheat the oven to 400°.
2 Slit the pork fillets ready for stuffing (see Preparation).
3 Heat the oil in a large skillet and cook the fillets over moderate heat until they are lightly browned. Remove from the skillet and drain on paper towels.
4 To make the stuffing: Put the bread crumbs in a bowl with the shortening, onion and sage, and season with salt and pepper. Add enough egg to bind the mixture, reserving the remaining egg for sealing and glazing the pastry.
5 Roll out the pastry thinly on a floured surface to make a rectangle measuring about 16 × 12 inches. Trim edges of the pastry and reserve for decorating. Place the pastry on a dampened cookie sheet.
6 Place 1 pork fillet in the center of the pastry and sprinkle the mushrooms over it. Pare, core and grate the apple and sprinkle over the mushrooms Place the second pork fillet on top of mushroom and apple layer and spread the stuffing mixture over this.
7 Fold over the ends of the pastry then the sides, so that the meat is enclosed in a pastry parcel with the join on the top. Seal the edges with some of the reserved egg.
8 Decorate along the seam of the parcel with pastry leaves made from the trimmings. Brush with the remaining beaten egg and bake in the oven 40 minutes until the pastry has risen and is golden. Transfer to a warmed serving dish and serve at once.

Cook's Notes

TIME
Total preparation and cooking time is 50 minutes.

SERVING IDEAS
Serve with broccoli, or Brussels sprouts sprinkled with ground mace and mushroom sauce.

PREPARATION
To cut the pork fillet so that it is ready for the stuffing:

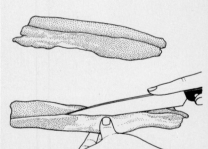

1 Carefully slit each piece of pork fillet (tenderloin) without cutting right through. Open out each piece flat so that there are 2 rectangular pieces of meat, each about 20 cm/8 inches long and 13 cm/5 inches wide.

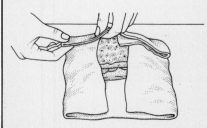

2 Make a pastry parcel around the meat and stuffing to enclose it completely.

●805 calories/3375 kj per portion

Roast pork with peaches

SERVES 4

2½ lb boned pork roast (see Buying guide)
salt
1 tablespoon vegetable oil

STUFFED PEACHES

4 ripe fresh peaches, peeled (see Preparation)
2 tablespoons lemon juice
2 tablespoons butter or margarine
⅓ cup fresh white bread crumbs
1 onion, finely chopped
2 celery stalks, finely chopped
1 teaspoon dried sage
½ teaspoon grated lemon rind
freshly ground black pepper
1 teaspoon grated Parmesan cheese

1 Preheat the oven to 375°.
2 Using a sharp knife, score the skin of the pork at ¼-inch intervals, cutting into the fat below the skin but not into the meat.
3 Wipe the pork dry with paper towels. Sprinkle skin liberally with salt and rub it in with the oil.
4 Place the pork in a small roasting pan and roast in the oven 1 hour.
5 Meanwhile, prepare the stuffed peaches. Halve the peaches, remove the pits and sprinkle the cut sides of fruit with a little lemon juice.
6 Melt the butter in a small saucepan, add the bread crumbs, onion and celery and cook gently 4-5 minutes, stirring constantly to prevent sticking. Remove from the heat and add the sage, lemon rind and 1 tablespoon lemon juice. Mix the ingredients together and season well with salt and pepper.
7 Place 1 tablespoonful of the stuffing in the hollow of each peach and smooth over with a knife. Sprinkle lightly with the Parmesan cheese.
8 When the pork has cooked 1 hour, remove the roasting pan from the oven, and place the stuffed peaches around the pork. Return to the oven a further 30 minutes or until the pork is tender, basting once with the drippings in the pan. Transfer the pork to a warmed serving platter and surround with the stuffed peaches. Serve at once.

Cook's Notes

TIME
Preparation of pork, 5 minutes, then 30 minutes to prepare the stuffed peaches once the pork is in the oven. Cooking 1½ hours.

BUYING GUIDE
Cuts suitable for this recipe are: Any boned rolled roast from the loin, leg, shoulder, belly or spareribs.

Ask your butcher to bone the joint for you and to tie it into a neat shape.

PREPARATION
To peel the peaches, immerse in very hot water for 1 minutes. Drain then nick the skin near the stem and peel away the skin.

● 740 calories per portion

Hawaiian pork parcels

SERVES 4

4 thick pork loin rib chops weighing about ⅓-½ lb.
1 can (about 1 lb) pineapple rings in natural juice, drained with juice reserved (see Economy)
1 tablespoon butter or margarine
1 small onion, chopped
1 cup fresh whole wheat bread crumbs
1 teaspoon cider vinegar
1 tablespoon finely chopped fresh parsley
dash of hot-pepper sauce
salt and freshly ground black pepper
parsley sprigs, to garnish

SAUCE
1 tablespoon cornstarch
⅔ cup chicken broth
1 teaspoon Worcestershire sauce
1 teaspoon cider vinegar

1 Cut 4 squares of foil each large enough to contain a chop easily.
2 Using a sharp knife, slit each pork chop horizontally, from the fatty outside edge to the bone, without cutting all the way through, to make a small pocket.

3 Make the stuffing (see Cook's tips): Chop 1 pineapple ring finely. Melt the butter in a skillet, add the onion and cook gently 5 minutes until soft and lightly colored. In a bowl combine the onion mixture with the chopped pineapple, bread crumbs, vinegar, 1 tablespoon pineapple juice, the parsley and pepper sauce. Season thoroughly with salt and pepper.
4 Preheat the broiler to moderate. Preheat the oven to 375°.
5 Divide the stuffing mixture into 4 portions. Using a teaspoon, spoon a portion of stuffing into the pocket of each chop. Broil the chops about 5 minutes on each side, until lightly browned (see Cook's tips).
6 Place a chop on each piece of foil and top each with a pineapple ring. Fold over the edges of the foil to make a loose parcel, then seal the edges tightly.
7 Arrange the parcels in a large, shallow roasting pan and bake in the oven about 50 minutes, or until the juices run clear when the meat is pierced with a fine skewer.
8 About 5 minutes before the end of cooking time, make the sauce: Measure out ⅔ cups of the reserved pineapple juice into a saucepan. In a cup, blend the cornstarch with a little of the measured pineapple juice stirring all the time to make a

smooth paste. Stir the mixture into the pineapple juice with the broth, Worcestershire sauce and vinegar, and season to taste with salt and pepper. Bring slowly to a boil, stirring, until the sauce is thickened and smooth.
9 Remove the Hawaiian pork chops from their foil parcels and place them on a warmed serving plate. Garnish each pork chop with a sprig of parsley placed in the center of the pineapple ring. Pass the sauce in a warmed gravyboat.

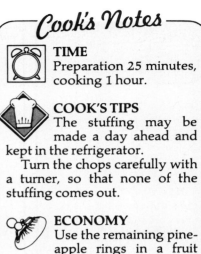

Cook's Notes

TIME
Preparation 25 minutes, cooking 1 hour.

COOK'S TIPS
The stuffing may be made a day ahead and kept in the refrigerator.
Turn the chops carefully with a turner, so that none of the stuffing comes out.

ECONOMY
Use the remaining pineapple rings in a fruit salad or with ice cream.

● 445 calories per portion

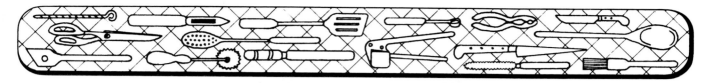

Pork and pears

SERVES 4
4 pork loin rib chops, trimmed of fat and rind
2 tablespoons butter or margarine
salt and freshly ground black pepper
1 can (about 15 oz) pear halves
1 tablespoon chopped fresh marjoram, or 1½ teaspoons dried marjoram
1 tablespoon lemon juice

1 Preheat the oven to 375°.
2 Melt the butter in a large skillet. Add the chops and cook for 3-4 minutes on each side until golden brown.
3 Remove with a slotted spoon and place in a single layer in an oven-proof dish. Sprinkle with salt and pepper to taste. Drain the pears,

reserving the juice, and cook in the hot fat about 10 minutes until brown. Place on top of the chops in the dish.
4 Pour the reserved pear juice into the pan and stir with a wooden spoon to dislodge any sediment at the bottom. Add the marjoram and lemon juice, and raise the heat.

Bring to a boil and boil rapidly, stirring frequently, for about 5 minutes until reduced by about half.
⚠ Pour over the chops and pears, then cover the dish.
5 Bake in the oven for 25 minutes or until the chops are tender. Transfer to a warmed serving dish and serve at once.

Cook's Notes

TIME
25 minutes preparation, 25 minutes to cook.

VARIATION
Try canned apricot halves, or pineapple rings instead of pears.

WATCHPOINT
When reducing the pear juice, do not boil for longer than 5 minutes or it will

become too thick and syrupy at this stage and not coat the chops and pears. It will reduce further during baking in the oven.

SERVING
Good accompaniments are cauliflower or leeks, lightly boiled then drained and tossed with butter and about ¼ cup chopped flaked almonds.

● 490 calories per portion

Quick Portuguese pork

SERVES 4

**1½ lb pork fillets
(tenderloin), sliced into thin
strips**

1 large grapefruit (see Cook's tip)

2 teaspoons ground coriander

salt and freshly ground black pepper

3 tablespoons olive oil

4 tablespoons dry white wine

**1 can (about 6 oz) pimientos, drained
and cut into strips (see Buying
guide)**

1 Grate the rind from the grapefruit
and reserve. Remove all the remaining rind and pith, then divide the
flesh into segments, cutting away all
membranes.

2 Put the strips of pork in a bowl,
sprinkle with the ground coriander,
the reserved grated rind of the
grapefruit and salt and pepper to

taste and turn the meat over until
thoroughly coated.

3 Heat the oil in a skillet until very
hot. Add the pork and cook briskly
turning from time to time until
evenly browned on all sides. Lower
the heat.

4 Pour the juice from a quarter of
the grapefruit segments through a
strainer. Add to the skillet and stir in
the wine and pimientos. Cook 3-4
minutes until the pork is tender,
stirring all the time.

5 Transfer the pork and pimientos
to a warmed serving dish with a
slotted spoon. Keep hot in the
lowest possible oven.

6 Bring the liquid in the pan to a
boil and boil rapidly until reduced
slightly. Lower the heat, add the
remaining grapefruit segments and
heat through.

7 Remove the grapefruit segments
from the pan with a slotted spoon
and reserve. Pour the pan juices
over the pork and pimientos, then
garnish with the reserved grapefruit
segments. Serve at once.

Cook's Notes

TIME
10 minutes preparation,
15 minutes to cook.

BUYING GUIDE
Canned red pimientos
are available from most
supermarkets. They are small,
sweet peppers, and the fact that
they are ready-skinned and
sliced makes them a handy
pantry shelf item. If you prefer
to use a fresh red pepper for this
dish, cut it into strips, discarding
the white membrane and seeds.
Plunge into boiling water 2–3
minutes then refresh under cold
running water.

COOK'S TIP
All citrus friuts are
easier to grate if they
have been thoroughly chilled.

● 400 calories per portion

Dynasty pork

SERVES 4

1½ lb lean stewing pork, trimmed and cut into 1-inch cubes
4 tablespoons all-purpose flour
salt and freshly ground black pepper
2 tablespoons vegetable oil
2 tablespoons butter or margarine
1 onion, chopped
1 green pepper, seeded and sliced
1 clove garlic, crushed (optional)
1¼ cups chicken broth
1 can (about 11 oz) mandarin orange segments, drained, with syrup reserved
1 tablespoon wine vinegar
1 tablespoon soy sauce
2 tomatoes, peeled and chopped

1 Put the flour in a plastic bag and season with salt and pepper. Place the pork in the bag and shake until the meat is well coated with flour.

Reserve any flour remaining in the bag.

2 Heat the oil and butter in a flameproof casserole, add the onion, green pepper and garlic, if using, and cook over gentle heat 5 minutes until the onion is soft and lightly colored. Remove with a slotted spoon and set aside.

3 Add the pork to the pan together with any flour remaining in the bag. Cook over brisk heat 4–5 minutes, turning constantly until browned on all sides.

4 Gradually blend in the chicken broth, mandarin orange syrup, vinegar and soy sauce. Return the cooked vegetables to the pan, bring to a boil and simmer 2-3 minutes, stirring constantly. Add salt and pepper to taste.

5 Lower the heat, cover the pan and simmer very gently for about 1½ hours or until the pork is tender. Add the orange segments and chopped tomatoes and cook a further 5 minutes. Taste and adjust seasoning, then transfer to a warmed serving dish. Serve hot.

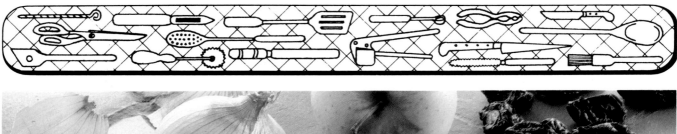

Fruity stuffed pork chops

SERVES 4
4 thick pork loin chops (see Buying guide)
2 tablespoons vegetable oil

STUFFING
1 tablespoon butter or margarine
1 small onion chopped
⅓ cup prunes, soaked overnight, pits removed and finely chopped
1 small dessert apple, pared, cored and grated
½ cup walnuts, roughly chopped
½ cup soft day-old white bread crumbs
salt and freshly ground black pepper
1 small egg, beaten

1 Preheat the oven to 375°.
2 Make the stuffing: Melt the butter in a skillet, add the onion and cook gently 5 minutes until soft and lightly colored. Put the prunes in a bowl with the apple, walnuts and bread crumbs and stir in the onion. Season with salt and pepper and stir in the egg to bind.
3 Using a sharp knife, slit each pork chop horizontally, from the fatty outside edge to the bone, without cutting all the way through. Fill the chops with the stuffing mixture and secure the slit edges with wooden toothpicks.
4 Brush a baking or roasting pan with half the oil. Put in the chops and brush with the remaining oil.
5 Cook the chops in the oven about 20 minutes, then cover the dish with foil and return to the oven 30-40 minutes longer until cooked through. Remove toothpicks to serve.

Pork and peas

SERVES 4

2 lb boneless shoulder of pork, trimmed and cut into ½-inch cubes
1¾ cups shelled fresh peas
salt
1 tablespoon vegetable shortening
1 large onion, finely chopped
1 clove garlic, finely chopped (optional)
2 teaspoons paprika
¼ teaspoons cayenne
½ cup hot chicken broth
⅓ cup dry white wine
2 tablespoons chopped fresh parsley

1 Cook the peas in boiling salted water 10 minutes.

2 Meanwhile, melt the shortening in a large skillet, add the pork and cook over brisk heat 5 minutes until browned on all sides. Remove from the pan with a slotted spoon and set aside.

3 Lower the heat and stir in the onion, garlic, if using, paprika and cayenne. Raise the heat to moderate and cook 5 minutes until the onion is soft.

4 Drain the peas, then add to pan with the pork. Stir well, pour in broth and wine. Bring to a boil.

5 Lower the heat, then cover the pan and simmer 40 minutes or until the pork is tender. ✳

6 Taste and adjust seasoning and the parsley then transfer the pork and peas to a warmed serving dish and serve at once, while piping hot.

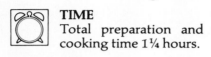

Cook's Notes

TIME
Total preparation and cooking time 1¼ hours.

✳ FREEZING
Transfer the pork and peas to a rigid container, cool quickly, then seal, label and freeze up to 2 months. To serve: Reheat from frozen until heated through and bubbling. Stir frequently and add a little broth or water if the mixture sticks.

COOK'S TIP
To use frozen peas, do not thaw, simply stir into pan in last 10 minutes.

PRESSURE COOKING
Heat the shortening in the base of cooker, cook the onion, then remove and drain. Cook pork and, if very fatty, drain off excess fat. Return onion and pork to pressure cooker, add liquid (½ cup chicken broth and ⅓ cup white wine) and bring to a boil. Skim liquid if necessary, then bring to high (H) pressure and cook 12 minutes. Reduce pressure quickly, add peas. Bring back to high (H) pressure and cook a further 3 minutes. Reduce pressure quickly.

● 700 calories per portion

BEEF AND VEAL

Stilton steak

SERVES 4

**4 rump steaks, each weighing ½ lb
 (see Buying guide)**
1 tablespoon finely chopped onion
1 tablespoon Worcestershire sauce
⅓ cup vegetable oil
¼ cup port or sweet sherry
freshly ground black pepper
1 bay leaf, crumbled
⅔ cup grated Blue Stilton cheese
**watercress sprigs and tomato slices,
 to garnish**

1 Put the steaks in a large shallow
dish. Combine the onion, Worcestershire sauce, oil, port, pepper and
bay leaf and pour over the steaks.
Cover and leave to marinate at least
3 hours at room temperature,
turning the steaks several times.
2 Line broiler pan with foil, and
preheat the broiler to moderate.
3 Using a turner lift the steaks from

the marinade and arrange them on
the broiler rack. Broil 5-8 minutes,
depending on whether you like
your steak medium or well done,
basting from time to time with the
marinade. Turn the steaks and broil
another 2-5 minutes.
4 Sprinkle the Stilton over each

steak, dividing it equally between
them and pressing down with the
back of the spoon. Broil a further 3
minutes until the Stilton topping is
melted and bubbling.
5 Transfer the steaks to a warmed
serving dish, garnish with watercress and tomato and serve at once.

Cook's Notes

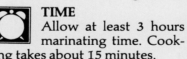

TIME
Allow at least 3 hours
marinating time. Cook-
ing takes about 15 minutes.

BUYING GUIDE
Rump steak is cut from
the lower part of the
sirloin. Choose rump steaks that
have a slightly purplish tinge
which shows that they have
been well aged and will be
tender. Some supermarkets sell
smallish pieces of rump steak in
special economy packs: These
would be ideal.
 Chuck steaks which are much

cheaper than rump steak, may
be used instead; they will need
to be cooked for slightly longer.

COOK'S TIP
If steaks are marinated
there is no need to beat
the meat to tenderize it. The
alcohol in the marinade will
break down fibers of the meat.

SERVING IDEAS
Serve the steaks with
baked or new potatoes
and a green salad.

● 380 calories per portion

Steak and parsnip pie

SERVES 4

1½ lb chuck steak, cut into bite-
   sized pieces
2 tablespoons vegetable oil
1 large onion, sliced
4 tablespoons all-purpose flour
1 can (about 14 oz) tomatoes
1 chicken bouillon cube
bouquet garni
salt and freshly ground black pepper
½lb parsnips, cut into chunky pieces
1 sheet (½ of 17 oz package) frozen
   puff pastry, thawed
a little beaten egg, to glaze

1 Preheat the oven to 350°.
2 Heat the oil in a flameproof casserole, add the meat and onion and cook until the onion is soft and the meat is browned on all sides. Sprinkle in the flour, then cook 1-2 minutes, stirring constantly.
3 Stir in the tomatoes and their juice, crumble in the bouillon cube

Cook's Notes

TIME
Preparation time is 15 minutes. Cooking time is 2¾ hours but remember to allow time for the pastry to thaw.

● 675 calories per portion

VARIATIONS
You could use shoulder or stewing steak, in which case the meat will need longer to cook. Turnips, carrots or rutabagas can be used instead of the parsnips or try using a mixture of root vegetables.

and stir well to mix. Add the bouquet garni and season to taste with salt and pepper. Bring to a boil, stirring, then cover and transfer to the oven. Cook 1½ hours or until the meat is just tender.
4 Stir in the parsnips and cook a further 45 minutes.
5 Meanwhile, roll out the pastry on a floured surface to a shape slightly larger than the circumference of a deep pie dish or baking dish. Cut off a long narrow strip of pastry all around the edge. Reserve this and other trimmings.
6 Transfer the meat and parsnip mixture to the pie dish, then discard the bouquet garni and taste and adjust seasoning. Increase the oven

temperature to 425°. Brush the rim of the pie dish with water, then press the narrow strip of pastry all around the rim. Brush the strip with a little more water, then place the large piece of pastry on top. Trim the edge of the pastry, then knock up and flute.
7 Make leaves or other shapes with the pastry trimmings, then place on top of the pie, brushing the under-neath with water so that they do not come off during baking. Make a small hole in the center of the pie for the steam to escape, then brush all over the pastry with beaten egg.
8 Bake the pie in the oven 25—30 minutes until the pastry is well risen and golden brown. Serve hot.

minutes or until just tender. Drain well and mix with the potatoes in a bowl. While the vegetables are still warm, pour over 2 tablespoons of the marinade from the beef and gently, turn them with a fork, without breaking them up, to coat thoroughly with the marinade. Cover and chill in the refrigerator 1 hour.

6 When ready to serve, mix the grated carrots and the tomatoes with the potatoes and beans. Remove the meat slices from the marinade, draining off any excess marinade from the slices. Remove the onions from the marinade with a slotted spoon and mix them into the mixed vegetables.

7 Pile the vegetable salad into the center of a serving platter and arrange the marinated beef slices around it. Garnish the platter with black olives and chopped parsley. Serve at once.

Marinated summer beef

SERVES 4
1½-2 lb roasting beef (see Buying guide)
⅓ cup vegetable oil
⅔ cup dry white wine
1 teaspoon mild Dijon-style mustard
1 teaspoon dried thyme
1 tablespoon lemon juice
1 clove garlic, crushed (optional)
salt and freshly ground black pepper
1 small onion, finely sliced

SALAD
2 potatoes
¼ lb green beans, fresh or frozen
2 carrots, grated
2 tomatoes, quartered

GARNISH
8-10 black olives
1 tablespoon chopped fresh parsley

1 Preheat the oven to 350°.

2 Wrap the beef in foil and place in a roasting pan. Roast in the oven about 1 hour (see Cook's tips). Remove from the oven and leave the beef, still wrapped in foil, to cool about 45 minutes.

3 Make the marinade: Put the oil, wine, mustard, thyme, lemon juice and garlic, if using, in a bowl or in a blender. Season with salt and pepper and beat well with a fork, or process in the blender for 30 seconds.

4 Slice the cooled beef into even, neat slices and arrange them in a shallow dish. Arrange the onion slices on top of the beef and pour over the marinade. Cover the dish of beef with plastic wrap and refrigerate at least 5-6 hours or overnight if possible.

5 Make the salad: Cook the potatoes in boiling salted water 15—20 minutes or until just tender. Drain, cool slightly and cut into bite-sized chunks. Meanwhile, cook the beans in boiling salted water 5-10

Tasty hamburgers

SERVES 4
1½ lb lean ground beef
1 small onion, finely grated
1 tablespoon tomato catsup
**salt and freshly ground black
    pepper**
⅔ cup mashed Danish Blue cheese
2 tablespoons vegetable oil

1 In a large bowl, mix together the
ground beef, onion and tomato
catsup and season well with salt and
pepper. ✳ Cover the mixture and
refrigerate 1 hour.
2 Divide the mashed cheese into 4
portions. Shape each portion into a
ball and flatten slightly. Divide the
chilled beef mixture into 4 portions
and mold 1 portion around each ball
of cheese. Shape into a fairly thick
hamburger, making sure that the

cheese is completely enclosed by
the meat mixture.
3 Heat the oil in a large skillet, add
the hamburgers and cook about 5-8
minutes on each side, until they are

done to your liking.
4 Remove the hamburgers from the
pan with a turner, drain quickly on
paper towels and serve at once (see
Serving ideas).

Cook's Notes

TIME
Preparation takes 10
minutes but allow 1
hour chilling time. Cooking
then takes 10-15 minutes.

FREEZING
Shape beef mixture
around the cheese as in
stage 2. Open freeze ham-
burgers until solid, then wrap
individually in foil and pack
together in a freezer bag. Seal,
label and return to the freezer up
to 3 months. To serve: Thaw at
room temperature, then pro-
ceed from the beginning of
stage 3.

VARIATIONS
Grated sharp Cheddar
cheese or finely shred-
ded mozzarella may be substituted for the Danish Blue.
    Add a few drops of hot-
pepper sauce to the ground beef
mixture, for a more piquant taste.

SERVING IDEAS
Serve in the traditional
sesame bun with let-
tuce, sliced tomato and various
relishes or mustard. Alternatively, serve with French fried
potatoes, without the bun.

● 415 calories per portion

Pot roast brisket

SERVES 4

**2 lb fresh brisket of beef, rolled and
tied (see Buying guide)**
2 tablespoons butter or margarine
1 onion, quartered
2 large carrots, sliced
2 celery stalks, sliced
2 cups beef broth
½ teaspoon dried thyme
½ teaspoon dried marjoram
1 tablespoon soy sauce
freshly ground black pepper
4 teaspoons cornstarch
salt

1 Melt the butter in a large
flameproof casserole and cook the
brisket over high heat until
browned on all sides. Transfer to a
plate.
2 Add the onion, carrots and celery
to the pan, lower the heat and cook
gently 5 minutes, stirring. Return
the meat to the pan and add the
broth, thyme, marjoram, soy sauce
and freshly ground black pepper to
taste.
3 Bring to a boil, then lower the
heat, cover and simmer gently 2½

hours, turning the meat over every
30 minutes. ⚠
4 When tender, remove the meat
from the pan and keep warm.
5 Blend the cornstarch to a paste
with a little cold water, stir into the
pan and bring to a boil. Lower the
heat and simmer 2-3 minutes,
stirring constantly, then mash the

onions, carrots and celery into the
gravy in the pan with a potato
masher. Taste and adjust seasoning.
6 Place the meat on a warmed serving platter, cutting a few thin slices
from one end, if wished. Pour over a
little of the gravy, then serve at
once, with the remaining gravy
passed separately in a gravy boat.

Cook's Notes

TIME
20 minutes preparation;
2½ hours cooking turn-
ing the meat every 30 minutes.
Allow an extra 5-10 minutes to
finish the gravy and slice the
meat.

BUYING GUIDE
Make sure you buy a
fresh brisket, not a
salted one. Look for a good, lean
piece.

PRESSURE COOKING
Calculate the cooking
time at 12 minutes per
1 lb meat. Remove the trivet
from the pressure cooker pan.
Brown the meat and vege-
tables in the pan as described,
then add the broth and flavor-

ings. Cover with the lid, bring
up to pressure according to
manufacturer's instructions,
then cook at high (H) pressure
for the calculated cooking time
(about 50 minutes). Reduce
pressure with cold water, lift out
the meat and thicken the gravy
as described.

WATCHPOINT
To turn the brisket over
without splashing or
burning yourself, use 2 large
kitchen forks, or a fork and a
wooden spoon. Make sure you
have a firm grip on the meat
before you lift it; if it slips back
into the pan the hot broth will
splash dangerously.

●505 calories per portion

Flemish beef casserole

SERVES 4

1½ lb chuck steak, trimmed and cut into 1-inch cubes
3 tablespoons vegetable oil
3 medium onions, sliced
¼ lb smoked streaky bacon, chopped
1 clove garlic, crushed (optional)
2 tablespoons all-purpose flour
½ pint beer or ale
⅓ cup beef broth
1 tablespoon red wine vinegar
1 tablespoon light brown sugar
bouquet garni (parsley, thyme, bay leaf)
salt and freshly ground black pepper
1 tablespoon finely chopped parsley, to garnish

MUSTARD CROUTONS

2 large slices white bread, crusts removed, each cut into 4 triangles or squares
2 teaspoons prepared English mustard
vegetable oil, for frying

1 In a large saucepan or flameproof casserole, heat the oil over fairly high heat, and cook the meat, a few pieces at a time, until evenly brown all over. Remove with a slotted spoon to a plate and keep warm.

2 Reduce the heat and cook the onions and bacon, stirring occasionally, 5-7 minutes until softened and beginning to color. Add the garlic, if using, and cook 1 minute.

3 Add the flour and stir, scraping the crusty bits off the bottom of the pan. Cook until it begins to brown. Stir in the beer and broth and bring to a boil, stirring. Return the meat to the pan, then add the remaining ingredients, except the parsley. Stir well, reduce the heat, cover and simmer gently over low heat 1¾-2 hours until the meat is tender.

4 Spread both sides of the bread triangles or squares with mustard.

5 Heat oil in a skillet and cook the croutons for a few seconds until evenly browned on all sides.

6 Drain on paper towels.

7 When the meat is tender, check and adjust seasoning. ✳ Serve hot, garnished with parsley and the mustard croutons.

Cook's Notes

TIME
Preparation 25 minutes, cooking 2 hours.

BUYING GUIDE
Ready-made bouquet garnis are available from most good supermarkets and delicatessens. Remember to remove before serving.

FREEZING
Cool quickly, remove any excess solidified fat and pack in a rigid container or heavy-duty freezer bag. Seal, label and freeze up to 3 months. To use, thaw gently over low heat, bring to boiling point and cook about 20 minutes until thoroughly heated.

COOK'S TIPS
This casserole can be cooked in the oven at 350° for the same length of time.
Like most casseroles, the flavor is improved if it is made one day, cooled, then reheated thoroughly the next day.

ECONOMY
If you use a cheaper cut of stewing steak, such as shin beef, the dish will be less expensive, but remember to trim away all the fat and gristle. Shin beef is tougher than chuck and will need to cook at least an hour longer.

● 620 calories per portion

Mexican beef

SERVES 4

1 lb ground beef (see Buying
   guide)
1-2 tablespoons vegetable oil
1 small onion, finely chopped
3-4 teaspoons chili seasoning
2 tablespoons quick-cooking
   oatmeal
1¼ cups beef broth
1 tablespoon tomato paste
pinch of freshly ground nutmeg
salt and freshly ground black pepper
1 can (about 12 oz) whole kernel
   corn with sweet peppers, drained
1 large or 2 medium avocados
1 tablespoon lemon juice
¼ lb Cheddar cheese, cut into 1-inch
   cubes

1 Heat 1 tablespoon oil in a heavy-based saucepan. Add the beef and cook over moderate heat 3 minutes, stirring constantly until all the beef has browned, breaking up any lumps with a wooden spoon. Remove the beef with a slotted spoon. Add the onion to the pan and cook 5 minutes until soft and lightly colored, adding a further tablespoon oil if necessary, to prevent overbrowning.
2 Return the beef to the pan, stir in 3 teaspoons chili seasoning, then the oatmeal, broth, tomato paste, nutmeg, salt to taste and add a light sprinkling of pepper.
3 Bring to a boil, stirring, then reduce the heat, cover and simmer gently 40–45 minutes or until the oatmeal is soft and the meat cooked.
4 Stir the drained corn and peppers into the beef mixture and continue to cook, uncovered, 5 minutes, or until most of the excess liquid has evaporated. Taste and adjust seasoning, adding more chili if slightly hotter flavor is liked.
5 Just before serving, cut the avocado in half lengthwise and discard the pit. Cut into quarters lengthwise and peel away the skin, then cut the flesh into neat thin slices lengthwise. Brush with the lemon juice to prevent discoloration.
6 Stir the cheese into the beef until just beginning to melt, then spoon the mixture into a warmed serving dish and arrange the avocado slices around the edge. Serve at once.

Cook's Notes

TIME
Preparation 30 minutes, cooking 45 minutes.

BUYING GUIDE
Various grades of ground beef are available, but for this dish choose a good-quality, lean beef and use it on the day of purchase.
   Cheaper grades of ground beef will require longer cooking and any excess fat should be skimmed from the top before serving.

VARIATION
If you do not have any chili seasoning (available in jars from most supermarkets), use the same quantity of mild curry powder; this will season the beef, but will not be sufficient to give a strong curry flavor. Chili powder can be used, but as it is hotter than chili seasoning, add a little at a time to the required strength.

PRESSURE COOKING
Pre-brown the beef and onion in the base of the pressure cooker, then add all the other ingredients, except for the corn, avocado, lemon juice and cheese. Bring to high (H) pressure and cook 7 minutes. Reduce the pressure quickly, then add the corn. Bring to a boil, uncovered, remove from the heat and stir in the cheese. Garnish with avocado slices.

●555 calories per portion

Beef curry

SERVES 4

1½ lb stewing steak, trimmed of excess fat and cut into ½-inch cubes
1 teaspoon ground coriander
1 teaspoon ground turmeric
1 teaspoon chili powder
½ teaspoon ground ginger
2 tablespoons vegetable oil
1 onion, sliced
1 clove garlic, crushed (optional)
1½ cups beef broth
1 tablespoon shredded coconut
1 tablespoon lemon juice
salt

1 Put the coriander, turmeric, chili and ginger in a bowl and gradually add a little water, stirring all the time until a smooth paste is formed. Set aside.

2 Heat the oil in a large flameproof casserole, add the onion and garlic, if using, and cook for 5 minutes until the onion is soft and lightly colored.

3 Stir in the spicy paste and cook a further 3-4 minutes, stirring all the time.

4 Add the meat and cook a further 3-4 minutes, stirring to cook on all sides in the spices. Stir in the broth and bring to a boil, then lower the heat and stir in the coconut, lemon juice and salt to taste. Cover and simmer gently 2 hours ✳ until the meat is tender.

5 Taste and adjust seasoning (see Cook's tips) then serve hot, straight from the casserole.

Cook's Notes

TIME
15 minutes initial preparation, then 2 hours cooking time.

COOK'S TIPS
All curries have an infinitely better flavor if left to go cold overnight and are reheated the following day.
For extra "bite", add more lemon juice before serving.

● 405 calories per portion

Stir-fried beef with cashews

SERVES 4

1 lb rump steak or flash-fry steak, cut ½ inch thick and all fat removed (see Cook's tip)
3 tablespoons vegetable oil
1 clove garlic, crushed (optional)
4 scallions, cut into 1-inch pieces
1 large onion, chopped
½ cup unsalted cashew nuts
1 small green or red pepper, seeded and cut into thin strips
1 teaspoon ground ginger
1 tablespoon cornstarch
⅔ cup chicken broth
2 teaspoons medium sherry
2 teaspoons soy sauce
salt and freshly ground black pepper

1 Dry the beef on paper towels. Place it between 2 sheets of waxed paper and beat to flatten, with a wooden rolling pin. Using kitchen scissors, snip the beef into thin strips about 2 inches long.

2 Heat 1 tablespoon of oil in a large skillet or wok, add half the beef strips, stir about 1 minute until browned on all sides, ☐! remove from the pan with a slotted spoon and reserve. Heat 1 more tablespoon of oil in the pan, add the remaining beef strips, stir-fry in the same way and reserve.

3 Heat the remaining oil in the pan add the garlic, if using, scallions, onion, cashew nuts and pepper strips and cook gently 3-4 minutes, stirring, until the vegetables are tender and the nuts lightly browned. Remove the pan from the heat and stir in the ginger.

4 Blend the cornstarch with the chicken broth, sherry and soy sauce to make a smooth paste, and stir into the pan.

5 Return to the heat, bring to a boil, lower heat and simmer gently 1 minute, stirring constantly. Season to taste with salt and pepper.

6 Return the reserved cooked beef strips to the pan and stir over gentle heat until heated through. Serve at once in individual bowls.

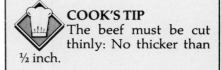

Beef goulash

SERVES 4

1 lb chuck steak, cubed
½ lb stewing veal, cubed
2 tablespoons butter or margarine
2 tablespoons vegetable oil
2 large onions, finely chopped
2 teaspoons paprika
1 can (about 14 oz) tomatoes,
    drained
⅓ lb button mushrooms
¼ cup beef broth or water
1 tablespoon tomato paste
salt and freshly ground black
    pepper
⅔ cup dairy sour cream
1 tablespoon chopped parsley

1 Preheat the oven to 325°.
2 Heat the butter and half the oil in a skillet, add the onions and cook without browning over low heat. Drain and remove to a casserole.
3 Add the remaining oil to the pan and cook the meat over high heat until evenly browned. Sprinkle the paprika over, cook 1-2 minutes and remove to the casserole.
4 Chop the tomatoes, lay them on top of the meat, and add the whole mushrooms, broth and tomato paste. Season with salt and pepper. Cover and cook in the oven, until the meat is tender about 2-2½ hours. Taste and adjust seasoning.
✳ Before serving, stir in half the sour cream and pour the rest over the top. Sprinkle with chopped parsley. Serve at once.

Cook's Notes

TIME
Preparation will take 25-30 minutes. Cook the goulash 2-2½ hours, until the meat is tender when tested with a fork.

● 530 calories per portion

SERVING IDEAS
Small new boiled potatoes are nicest with goulash, but you can also serve mashed potatoes, macaroni or noodles with a crisp green vegetable such as broccoli or green beans.

 FREEZING
Freeze in casserole. Tip out, wrap in foil, and replace in freezer. When ready to use, turn back into the casserole which was used for cooking. Cover and reheat until the goulash is bubbling.

Serbian beef

SERVES 4

2 lb stewing beef, trimmed and cut
  into bite-sized pieces
2 tablespoons vegetable oil
2 large onions, sliced
1 tablespoon paprika
1 celery stalk, chopped
2 cloves garlic, crushed (optional)
1 bay leaf
1 tablespoon chopped parsley
salt and freshly ground black pepper
⅔ cup red wine vinegar (see Cook's
  tip)
4 potatoes, thinly sliced
vegetable oil, for brushing

1 Preheat the oven to 300° and
lightly brush a large ovenproof dish
with oil.
2 Heat half the oil in a heavy
flameproof casserole over high heat
and cook the meat in batches, if
necessary, until crisp and golden on
all sides. Transfer the meat with a
slotted spoon to a plate.
3 Add the remaining oil to the pan
and cook the onions gently about 5
minutes until soft and translucent.
4 Return the meat and any juices to
the pan. Add the paprika and stir
over low heat for 2 minutes.
5 Add the celery, garlic, if using,
bay leaf, parsley, salt and pepper to
taste and the wine vinegar. Bring to
a boil, remove from the heat and
then allow to cool down for a few
minutes.
6 Put half the potatoes in a layer on
the bottom of the oiled ovenproof
dish, cover with the meat mixture
and then add the remaining
potatoes in a neat layer on top.
Cover tightly with a top or foil and
cook in the oven about 2½ hours
until the meat is tender.
7 Brush the potatoes with oil and
place the casserole under a high
broiler 5 minutes until the potatoes
are browned. Serve hot straight
from the dish.

Apple-stuffed veal chops

SERVES 4

4 veal chops, each weighing about ½ lb, trimmed of excess fat (see Buying guide)
2 large green apples
juice of ½ lemon
2 tablespoons golden raisins
1½ teaspoons ground cloves
salt and freshly ground black pepper
1 tablespoon vegetable oil
2 tablespoons butter or margarine
2 tablespoons golden raisins, soaked in 1 tablespoon sherry, to garnish

1 Using a very sharp knife, make a pocket in each chop: Slit horizontally, from the outside edge to the bone, cutting through to within ½ inch of the edge.
2 Quarter, pare and core 1 apple. Cut into ¼-inch slices and put into a bowl with the lemon juice. Toss the apple slices in the lemon juice, then add the golden raisins and 1 teaspoon of ground cloves. Mix together well.
3 Spoon the apple mixture into the pocket of each chop, dividing it equally between them. Secure the slit edges with wooden toothpicks. Sprinkle the chops with the remaining ground cloves and season well with salt and freshly ground black pepper.
4 Heat the oil and butter in a large skillet, add the veal chops and cook them over high heat 2-3 minutes on each side, to brown and seal. Lower the heat and cook 10-15 minutes on each side, until cooked through and the juices run clear when the meat is pierced.
5 Pare and core the remaining apple. Slice into rings. Using a turner transfer chops to a warmed serving platter and keep warm. Add the apple rings to the skillet and cook gently, turning carefully so that the rings do not break up, until golden brown.
6 Arrange the cooked apple rings on top of the chops, spoon the golden raisins into the center of the apple rings and serve the apple-stuffed veal chops at once (see Serving ideas).

Cook's Notes

TIME
Preparing and cooking the veal chops takes only 30 minutes.

BUYING GUIDE
Veal chops are cut from the loin. As the loin is usually sold in one piece for roasting, veal chops may have to be ordered in advance from the butcher.

ECONOMY
Use 4 thick pork chops, in place of the veal chops used here.

SERVING IDEAS
Serve the veal chops with an apple juice sauce, if liked. Pour off excess fat from the skillet after cooking the apples. Pour in ⅔ cup apple juice, then bring slowly to a boil, stirring and scraping the sediment from the bottom of the pan with a wooden spoon. Remove from the heat and stir in 3 tablespoons heavy cream. Season to taste with salt and pepper. Spoon the sauce over the apples and veal to serve.

●305 calories per portion

Italian veal rolls

SERVES 4

1 lb veal topside or rump, cut across the grain of the meat into 8 equal-sized pieces
4 thin square slices cooked ham, halved
1 tablespoon Dijon-style mustard (optional)
¼ lb Edam or Gouda cheese cut into 8 sticks 2 × ½ inch (see Watchpoint)
2 tablespoons butter
2 tablespoons vegetable oil
1 onion, chopped
1 clove garlic, crushed (optional)
¼ lb mushrooms sliced
1 can, (about 14 oz) tomatoes, drained and chopped
⅓ cup chicken broth
½ teaspoon dried oregano
1 bay leaf
salt and freshly ground black pepper
chopped chives, to garnish

1 Place the veal pieces between 2 sheets of waxed paper and pound with a wooden rolling pin or mallet, to flatten to the same size as the halved ham slices. Spread the ham slices with the mustard, if using.

2 Place a slice of ham on each piece of veal, mustard side down if used. Place a cheese stick at one end, then roll the veal and ham up around the cheese. Tie the rolls at both ends with fine string (see Preparation).

3 Heat the butter with the oil in a large skillet. When sizzling, add the veal rolls and cook over moderate heat about 6 minutes to brown on all sides. Remove the rolls from the pan with a slotted spoon or kitchen tongs and leave to drain on paper towels.

4 Add the onion and garlic, if using, to the pan and cook 5 minutes over gentle heat until soft and lightly colored. Add the mushrooms to the pan and cook a further 3 minutes.

5 Stir the tomatoes, broth and oregano into the pan, add the bay leaf and season to taste with salt and pepper. Bring to a boil. Return the veal rolls to the pan and turn in the sauce.

6 Lower the heat, cover the pan and cook gently 10 minutes. Uncover and cook a further 10 minutes or until the veal is tender and the sauce has reduced by about one-half.

7 Remove the rolls from the pan and carefully remove the string. Place the rolls in a warmed serving dish and keep hot. Discard the bay leaf from the sauce and taste and adjust seasoning.

8 Spoon the sauce over the veal rolls and sprinkle with chives. Serve.

Cook's Notes

TIME
Preparation takes about 45 minutes, cooking 35-40 minutes.

PREPARATION
Make the veal rolls in the following way:

1 *Place the cheese stick at one end of the ham and roll up.*

2 *Tie the rolls at either end with fine string as shown.*

WATCHPOINT
The cheese sticks must not protrude from the ends of the rolls, or the cheese will ooze out during cooking.

SPECIAL OCCASION
Use Swiss cheese, Parma ham, and dry white wine or vermouth instead of chicken broth.

● 415 calories per portion

Ratatouille veal

SERVES 4
3–3½ lb boned breast of veal (boned weight)
1 teaspoon chopped fresh basil or ½ teaspoon dried basil
¼ cup vegetable oil

RATATOUILLE STUFFING
3 tablespoons olive oil
1 onion finely chopped
1 eggplant, weighing about ½ lb, peeled and cut into ½-inch cubes, salted, drained, rinsed and dried
1 small green pepper, seeded and finely chopped
2 large tomatoes, peeled and chopped
1 teaspoon chopped fresh basil or ½ teaspoon dried basil
salt and freshly ground black pepper

1 Make the stuffing: Heat the oil in a saucepan, add the onion and cook gently 5 minutes until soft and lightly colored. Add the remaining stuffing ingredients with salt and pepper to taste and cook gently 15 minutes, stirring from time to time. Remove the stuffing from the heat and leave to cool.

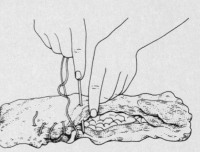

TIME
Preparation takes about 30 minutes, cooking about 1½ hours.

PREPARATION
To stuff the veal with ratatouille:

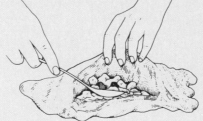

Spoon the ratatouille into the pocket, packing it in well.

Sew up the opening in the veal with trussing thread.

SERVING IDEAS
This tasty and unusual dish may be accompanied with croquette potatoes and, if liked, a green salad.

● 760 calories per portion

2 Preheat the oven to 375°.
3 Pat the veal dry with paper towels. With a very sharp knife make a pocket in the veal by slitting horizontally through one long edge to within 1 inch of other 3 edges. Spoon the cooled ratatouille into the pocket (see Preparation). Using a trussing needle and fine string, sew up the opening (see Preparation).
4 Place the ratatouille-stuffed veal in a roasting pan. Sprinkle with the basil, season with salt and pepper and brush with the oil. Cover the veal with foil and then roast in the oven ¾ hour, basting often. Remove foil and roast a further ¾ hour, basting often, until the veal is tender (the juices run clear when the meat is pierced with a fine skewer).
5 Remove from oven and cut away trussing string. Transfer veal to a warmed serving dish and serve at once, cut into slices.

Veal with Stilton and walnuts

SERVES 4-6
**3-3½ lb boned shoulder of
  veal**
1 tablespoon vegetable oil
1 tablespoon butter
2 cups chicken broth
bouquet garni
⅓ lb mushrooms, sliced
2 teaspoons cornstarch
2 teaspoons water
walnut halves, to garnish

STUFFING
¼ lb Stilton cheese
½ cup shelled walnuts, chopped
**3 tablespoons parsley and thyme
  package stuffing mix**
salt and freshly ground black pepper
1 egg
2 tablespoons water

1 Preheat the oven to 350°.
2 Make the stuffing: Put the Stilton into a bowl and mash it with a fork. Stir in the walnuts and the stuffing mix. Season with salt and pepper. Beat the egg with the water and stir into the mixture.

3 Lay the veal skin side down on a board or work surface. Spread the stuffing mixture over it. Roll the veal up from one short end, then tie securely with string in several places to neaten the roll.

4 Heat the oil and butter in a large flameproof casserole. Add the veal and cook over brisk heat, turning, to brown and seal the meat. Drain any excess fat from the casserole and pour the broth around the veal. Add the bouquet garni. Cover with foil, then with the top and cook in the oven 1 hour (see Cook's tip).

5 Add the mushrooms to the casserole, cover again with the foil and top and cook a further 30 minutes, or until the veal is cooked through and the juices run clear when the meat is pierced with a skewer.

6 Place the veal on a warmed serving dish and remove the string. Keep the veal warm in the oven turned to its lowest setting while making the sauce.

7 Transfer the casserole to the top of the range and bring the cooking liquid to a boil. Blend the cornstarch to a smooth paste with the water in a small bowl, stir in a little of the hot cooking liquid, then stir this mixture back into the casserole. Cook, stirring, 1-2 minutes until the sauce thickens, then taste and adjust seasoning.

8 Carve veal into neat slices, then garnish with walnuts. Pour over a little sauce and pass the rest separately in a warmed gravyboat.

Cook's Notes

TIME
Preparation takes about 20 minutes. Cooking in the oven takes 1½ hours, making the sauce takes only about 5 minutes.

COOK'S TIP
Veal is best braised in liquid rather than dry roasted: Braising helps prevent the meat, on which there is little fat, from becoming dry.

● 703 calories per portion

LAMB

Pot-roasted leg of lamb

SERVES 4-6

3 lb leg of lamb
(see Buying guide)
⅔ cup red wine
⅔ cup water
1 tablespoon white wine vinegar
1 medium onion, finely chopped
1 teaspoon dried oregano
2 tablespoons vegetable oil
2 tablespoons tomato paste
pinch of sugar
salt and freshly ground black pepper
chopped parsley, to garnish

1 Put the lamb into a large bowl. Mix together the wine, water, vinegar, onion and oregano and pour over the lamb. Cover and leave to marinate in the refrigerator several hours, preferably overnight. Turn the lamb in the marinade from time to time.

2 Remove the lamb and reserve the marinade. Pat the lamb all over with paper towels until dry.

3 Heat the oil in a large flameproof casserole, add the lamb and cook over moderate heat until browned on all sides. Pour over the reserved marinade and cover the casserole with a tight fitting top. Cook over low heat 1½-2 hours or until the meat is cooked to your liking.

4 Remove the lamb and keep hot. Skim off any fat from the cooking liquid with a slotted spoon, then stir in the tomato paste and sugar. Bring to a boil, add salt and pepper to taste, then lower the heat and return the lamb to the casserole. Simmer gently a further 5 minutes.

5 To serve: Transfer the lamb to a warmed serving dish, pour over the sauce and sprinkle with parsley. Serve at once.

Cook's Notes

TIME
Preparation takes only a few minutes, but the lamb needs several hours to marinate. Cooking time is 1½-2 hours.

SERVING IDEAS
A pot roast makes a welcome, often more succulent, change to the traditional roast meal on a Sunday, but it can still be served with all the traditional accompaniments to a roast.

BUYING GUIDE
Ask for the chump end of a large leg of lamb. Not only is it the meatiest part of the leg, it is also neater in shape and therefore easier to fit into a casserole dish.

ECONOMY
For a more economical dish, use 1¼ cups well-flavored broth instead of the wine and water.

● 655 calories per portion

Breast of lamb and apple rounds

SERVES 4

2 breasts of lamb, each weighing 1¼ lb
1 small onion, halved
1 small carrot, roughly chopped
1 celery stalk, roughly chopped
1 tablespoon chopped celery leaves (optional)
1 teaspoon whole cloves
3-inch piece stick cinnamon
2 bay leaves
1 sprig each fresh rosemary and thyme or pinch each dried rosemary and thyme
2 tablespoons cider vinegar or white wine vinegar
1 teaspoon black peppercorns
1 teaspoon salt

APPLE FILLING
2 large green apples, pared, cored and chopped
6 tablespoons cider vinegar
4 whole cloves

1 Put the vegetables, spices, herbs and vinegar in a large saucepan with the peppercorns and salt. Pour in enough water to cover the lamb — but do not add the lamb at this stage. Bring to a boil, then lower the heat and simmer 10 minutes.

2 Add the lamb, cover the pan and bring back to a boil. Lower the heat and simmer 1½ hours or until the meat is tender.

3 Let the lamb cool in the liquid in the pan.

4 Meanwhile, make the apple filling: Put the apples into a saucepan with the vinegar and cloves. Cover and cook over low heat 15 minutes or until the apple is very soft. Remove the cloves and, using a wooden spoon, mash the apples to a purée.

5 When the lamb is cool enough to handle, lift out of the liquid and remove the bones and as much of the skin and the fat as possible (see Preparation).

6 Spread the lamb breasts with the apple purée then roll them up and tie with kitchen string. Leave in a cool place at least 4 hours to set into shape.

7 Preheat the broiler to high.

8 Bring the breasts of lamb to room temperature, then cut each roll into 4 thick slices, leaving the string in place.

9 Broil the rounds of lamb until they are brown and crisp on both sides (10-15 minutes in all). Remove the string and serve at once.

Lamb chops and peppers

SERVES 4

4 large loin lamb chops, trimmed
4 tablespoons vegetable oil
2 medium onions, thinly sliced
1 clove garlic, chopped (optional)
1 lb tomatoes, peeled, seeded and chopped
2 green peppers, seeded and cut into strips
1 red pepper, seeded and cut into strips
1 teaspoon crushed coriander seeds (optional)
salt and freshly ground black pepper
⅔ cup dry white wine
1 tablespoon tomato paste

1 Heat the oil in a large skillet over high heat. Brown the chops on both sides, cooking in 2 batches if necessary.

2 With all the chops in the pan, lower the heat, put in onions and garlic, if using, and cover pan. Cook about 10 minutes until the onions and garlic are soft and beginning to color.

3 Add the tomatoes, peppers, coriander and salt and pepper to taste. Cover the pan again and cook a further 15 minutes or until the chops are tender.

4 Remove chops from pan and keep hot. Raise the heat and stir the wine into the pan. Cook rapidly, uncovered, until the liquid in the pan is reduced by half, stirring the sauce constantly.

5 Stir in the tomato paste and simmer, uncovered, 5 minutes. Taste and adjust seasoning. ✳

6 Place the chops on a warmed serving platter, then spoon the sauce over them. Serve at once.

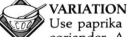

Roast lamb with zucchini sauce

SERVES 4

½ shoulder lamb, weighing about 2 lb
1 clove garlic (optional), cut into thin slices
grated rind of ½ lemon
1½ teaspoons clear honey

SAUCE
2 tablespoons butter or margarine
1 small onion, finely chopped
½ lb zucchini, grated
juice of ½ lemon
1¼ cups chicken broth
1 teaspoon superfine sugar
salt and freshly ground black pepper

1 Preheat the oven to 400°.
2 Place the lamb in a roasting pan skin side up. Score the surface with a sharp knife to make a trellis pattern. Make a series of small slits within the trellis squares; press a garlic sliver, if using, into each.
3 Sprinkle the surface of the lamb with the lemon rind, then spread thinly with the honey.

4 Roast the lamb about 1¼ hours (see Cook's tip), until the juices run clear when the thickest part of the meat is pierced with a sharp knife or skewer.
5 Meanwhile, make the sauce: Melt the butter in a skillet, add the onion and cook gently about 5 minutes until soft and lightly colored. Stir in the grated zucchini, and cook stirring for a further 2-3 minutes, then stir in the lemon juice and broth. Bring the sauce slowly to a boil, add the sugar and season to taste with salt and pepper. Remove from the heat and leave to cool slightly, then pour into a blender and work to a smooth purée. Reheat gently, if necessary, to serve.
6 Remove the lamb from the oven and transfer to a warmed serving platter. Carve a few slices and pour over a little of the sauce. Serve at once, with the remaining sauce passed separately in a warmed gravyboat.

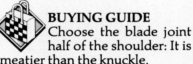

Cook's Notes

TIME
Preparing the lamb and making the sauce takes 30 minutes. Roasting in the oven takes about 1¼ hours.

COOK'S TIP
The total cooking time for shoulder of lamb is calculated at 25 minutes per 1 lb, plus 25 minutes.

BUYING GUIDE
Choose the blade joint half of the shoulder: It is meatier than the knuckle.

PRESSURE COOKING
Make sure the lamb fits comfortably in the cooker and that there is enough headroom. Pre-brown the lamb in hot fat, then drain. Put the trivet into the base of the cooker, place the lamb on it and pour in 1¼ cups broth. Cook at high (H) pressure 24 minutes. Release pressure quickly. Crisp the lamb in a 400° oven 10-12 minutes, while making the sauce.

● 470 calories per portion

Egg and almond lamb

SERVES 4

1 lb boneless lean lamb, ground (see
    Economy)
4 slices white bread, torn into pieces
1¼ cups milk
1 tablespoon vegetable oil
1 large onion, finely chopped
2 teaspoons curry powder
2 teaspoons sugar
2 teaspoons lemon juice
⅓ cup packed golden raisins
½ teaspoon salt
2 eggs, beaten
¼ cup flaked almonds

1 Preheat the oven to 375°.
2 Put the bread into a bowl and
pour over the milk. Leave to soak.
3 Meanwhile heat the oil in a
large skillet, add the onion and
cook gently until soft. Stir in the
curry powder, sugar and lemon juice
and cook 1-2 minutes, stirring.
4 Squeeze the milk from the bread,
reserving the milk. Beat the bread
with a fork to break it up.
5 Add the meat and bread to the
onion mixture and cook until the
meat is well browned. Stir in the
raisins and salt; remove from heat.
6 Add a quarter of the beaten eggs
to meat mixture and pour into a
greased ovenproof dish. Level the
surface, then bake 30 minutes.
7 Meanwhile, beat the reserved
milk into the remaining eggs.
8 Lower the oven heat to 350°.
Drain away fat from the lamb, then
pour over the egg mixture. Scatter
the almonds on top and cook 30
minutes.

Cook's Notes

TIME
Preparation 30 minutes,
cooking 1 hour.

ECONOMY
Shoulder of lamb is
probably the most eco-
nomical cut to use for this
recipe, but you will have to trim
it well before cooking or the
finished dish may be too fatty.
This recipe is also an excellent
way to use up left-over lamb
from the weekend roast. Grind
or chop it finely, then follow the
method above, omitting the
initial 30 minutes baking.

? DID YOU KNOW
Almonds are one of the
world's most popular
nuts. They are often mentioned
in the Old Testament and were
known by the Romans as "the
Greek nut". They were also
eaten before meals in medieval
times, in the belief this would
prevent drunkenness.

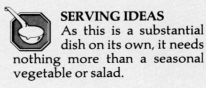

SERVING IDEAS
As this is a substantial
dish on its own, it needs
nothing more than a seasonal
vegetable or salad.

● 620 calories per portion

Indian skewered lamb

SERVES 4

1½ lb lean lamb (preferably cut from
   the fillet or top end of the leg) cut
   into 1-inch cubes, trimmed of
   excess fat
1¼ cups plain yogurt
1 onion, finely grated
1 teaspoon ground ginger
2 tablespoons garam masala (see
   Buying guide)
½ teaspoon chili powder
salt
1 large green pepper, seeded and cut
   into 1 inch-squares
1 large red pepper, seeded and cut
   into 1 inch-squares
24 button mushrooms, trimmed
vegetable oil, for greasing

1 In large bowl, mix together the
yogurt, onion, ginger, garam
masala, chili powder and salt to
taste. Add the cubes of lamb to the
mixture, turning them over so that
each piece is well-coated. Cover
with plastic wrap and leave to
marinate in a cool place (not in the
refrigerator) overnight.

2 Preheat the oven to 375°.

3 Remove the lamb from the
marinade but do not wipe off the
yogurt coating. Thread the meat,
the red and green peppers and
mushrooms alternately onto 8 oiled
kabob skewers.

4 Brush the inside of a large
roasting pan with oil and place the
skewers in it side-by-side (see
Cook's tips). Brush the meat with a
little oil, then cook in the oven
about 1 hour, until the meat is
tender, turning the skewers and
brushing them with more oil every
15 minutes. Transfer the skewers to
a bed of plain rice and serve
at once, with the tasty juices from
the roasting pan spooned carefully
over the kabobs.

Cook's Notes

TIME
10 minutes initial pre-
paration, then over-
night marinating. To prepare
ingredients and thread skewers
about 30 minutes, then about 1
hour cooking.

BUYING GUIDE
Garam masala — an
aromatic spice mix — is
available from Indian shops,
supermarkets and delicatessens.

COOK'S TIPS
For this quantity of
meat and vegetables,
you will need skewers 10 inches
long.
   Alternatively, you can cook
the kabobs for an outdoor meal
over a barbecue.

●365 calories per portion

Lamb and asparagus casserole

SERVES 4

2½ lb half shoulder of lamb, boned, excess fat removed, cut into 1-inch cubes (see Buying guide)
1 tablespoon all-purpose flour
1 tablespoon chopped fresh thyme, or 1 teaspoon dried thyme
salt and freshly ground black pepper
1 tablespoon vegetable oil
2 shallots, chopped
1 clove garlic, crushed (optional)
1¼ cups water
⅓ cup medium white wine
1 lb fresh or frozen asparagus (see Preparation)
¼ lb mushrooms, sliced
2 tablespoons heavy cream and asparagus spears, to finish

1 Preheat the oven to 325°.
2 Put the flour in a large plastic bag, add half the thyme and salt and pepper to taste. Add lamb cubes and shake to coat well. Reserve any excess seasoned flour.
3 Heat the oil in a large flameproof casserole, add the lamb cubes and cook quickly over brisk heat to brown and seal on all sides. Remove from the pan with a slotted spoon and leave to drain thoroughly on paper towels.
4 Add the shallots to the casserole with the garlic, if using, and cook gently 5 minutes until soft and lightly colored. Sprinkle in any excess seasoned flour, stir in the water and wine and season to taste with salt and pepper. Bring to a boil, then return the lamb cubes to the casserole 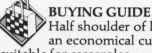 and stir in the remaining thyme.
5 Cover and cook in the oven about 1½ hours.
6 Add the blanched asparagus and the mushrooms to the casserole and cook a further 30 minutes, until the lamb is cooked through and tender when pierced with a sharp knife. Swirl over the cream, garnish with asparagus spears. Serve at once, straight from the casserole.

Cook's Notes

TIME
Preparation 30 minutes, cooking 2 hours.

PREPARATION
Fresh asparagus needs to be blanched: Trim off woody bases of stems and cut stems into 2-3 inch lengths. Simmer 5 minutes in salted water, drain. Add frozen asparagus straight to casserole.

FREEZING
Cook the casserole in a foil container, cool quickly, then seal, label and freeze up to 3 months. To serve: Thaw overnight in the refrigerator, then reheat in a 350° oven 30-40 minutes until bubbling.

BUYING GUIDE
Half shoulder of lamb is an economical cut, very suitable for casseroles.

The asparagus season is short, so it is worth making the most of it while home-grown asparagus is least expensive. Choose thick-stemmed asparagus, usually sold in bundles, for this recipe: The less expensive, thin-stemmed asparagus is unsuitable.

● 590 calories per portion

Lamb ratatouille

SERVES 4

4 large loin or sirloin lamb chops,
   trimmed of fat
3 tablespoons olive or corn oil
1 onion roughly chopped
1 can (about 12 oz) tomatoes, peeled
   and roughly chopped
1 eggplant, peeled, cut into 1-inch
   cubes
2 zucchini, cut into 1-inch slices
1 green pepper, seeded and
   chopped
1-2 garlic cloves, crushed with ½
   teaspoon salt
1 teaspoon dried basil
salt and freshly ground black
   pepper

1 Heat the oil in a heavy-based deep saucepan, add the onion and cook gently about 5 minutes until soft and lightly colored.
2 Stir in the tomatoes, then the eggplant, the zucchini, green pepper, garlic and basil. Bring the mixture to a boil, then lower the heat, cover and simmer about 30 minutes until the eggplant cubes are soft when pressed with a spoon. Stir the mixture frequently during this time.
3 Preheat the broiler to high.
4 Uncover the pan of ratatouille, increase the heat and boil rapidly until most of the liquid has evaporated. Taste and season with salt and pepper, then cover the pan again and keep the ratatouille warm on the lowest possible flame, stirring occasionally.
5 Lay the chops on the hot broiler rack and broil about 7 minutes on each side until browned and cooked through.
6 Spoon half the ratatouille into a warmed serving dish, arrange the chops in a single layer on top, then top each with a spoonful of the remaining ratatouille. Serve at once.

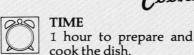

Cook's Notes

TIME
1 hour to prepare and cook the dish.

DID YOU KNOW
Ratatouille is best described as a French vegetable stew. Native to Provence in the south of France, it is made there with the best of the summer vegetables — eggplant, zucchini, peppers, tomatoes, onions and garlic.

SERVING IDEAS
Serve with spaghetti, pasta shells or spirals, or boiled or steamed rice.

FREEZING
Ratatouille freezes very successfully, and is a useful vegetable dish to keep in the freezer to serve with any roast or broiled meats. Transfer to a rigid container, cool quickly, then seal, label and store in the freezer up to 3 months. To serve: Reheat from frozen in a heavy-based saucepan, stirring frequently until bubbling. Take care not to overcook the vegetables or they will be mushy. Taste and adjust seasoning before serving.

● 750 calories per portion

Lamb with plums

SERVES 4
2½ lb lamb rib rack of lamb
  in one piece, boned
  (see Buying guide)
1 lb dark cooking plums
1 tablespoon butter or margarine
1 small onion, finely chopped
1 tablespoon chopped fresh parsley
2 teaspoons dried mixed herbs
⅔ cup whole wheat bread crumbs
2 tablespoons hot chicken broth
salt and freshly ground black pepper

SAUCE
1 tablespoon butter or margarine
1 small onion, finely chopped
2 teaspoons all-purpose flour
1¼ cups hot chicken broth
bouquet garni
4 tablespoons dry white wine
few drops of red food coloring
  (optional)

1 Preheat the oven to 350°.
2 Make a slit across the width of the thick end of the lamb, to make a pocket for the stuffing. Make the slit about 1½ inches deep, but do not cut right through.
3 Reserve 2 whole plums for the garnish. Pit and chop the rest.
4 To make the stuffing: Melt the butter in a small skillet, add the onion and cook gently 5 minutes until soft and lightly colored.
5 Remove the pan from the heat and stir in the parsley, herbs, bread crumbs and one-third of the chopped plums. Gradually add the broth and stir well. Season with salt and pepper to taste.
6 Place the lamb skin side down on a flat surface and spread the stuffing over it, and also push it into the slit. Roll the lamb and tie it with trussing thread or fine string in several places. Place the lamb in a roasting pan and roast in the oven 45 minutes.
7 Turn the lamb over and roast a further 45 minutes or until cooked to your liking. Meanwhile, make the sauce: Melt the butter in a small saucepan, add the onion and cook gently 5 minutes until soft and lightly colored. Sprinkle in the

flour and stir over low heat 1-2 minutes. Gradually stir in the broth, bring to a boil, then add the remaining chopped plums, the bouquet garni and salt and pepper to taste. Lower the heat, cover and simmer 30 minutes, stirring occasionally.
8 Remove the bouquet garni from the sauce, then push the sauce through a strainer, pressing hard with a wooden spoon to extract as much liquid as possible. Set the sauce aside. Halve, pit and slice the 2 remaining plums.
9 When the lamb is cooked, lift it out of the roasting pan and keep hot with any loose stuffing from the pan.
10 Pour off all the fat from the roasting pan and place the pan on top of the stove. Pour in the wine and bring to a boil, scraping up all the sediment from the sides and bottom of the pan with a wooden spoon.
11 Stir in the sauce, lower the heat

and simmer 1 minute, then strain to remove any black specks if necessary. If liked, stir in food coloring to make the sauce pink. Taste and adjust seasoning. Keep hot.
12 Carve the lamb into 8 thick slices and arrange on a warmed serving platter. Spoon a little sauce over each slice. Garnish with the sliced plums. Serve at once with the remaining sauce passed separately.

Cook's Notes

TIME
Preparation 35 minutes, cooking takes 1¾ hours.

BUYING GUIDE
Ask you butcher to bone the lamb for you.

● 560 calories per portion

Summer lamb

SERVES 4
½ leg of lamb, weighing about 2 lb
(see Buying guide)
2 sprigs fresh rosemary
2 bay leaves
salt and freshly ground black pepper
2 tablespoons vegetable oil

TUNA MAYONNAISE
1 can (about 7 oz) tuna, drained and
flaked
3 tablespoons thick
mayonnaise
⅔ cup plain yogurt
2 teaspoons anchovy paste
grated rind of 1 lemon
1 tablespoon lemon juice

TO GARNISH
1 small red pepper, seeded and cut
into strips
12 black olives

1 Preheat the oven to 375°.
2 Place the lamb on a large sheet of foil, and tuck the sprigs of rosemary and the bay leaves into the meat. Sprinkle with salt and pepper and brush with the oil. Wrap the foil around the meat and place in a roasting pan. Roast in the oven 1¼ hours or until the meat is tender (the juices run clear when the meat is pierced with a skewer).
3 Remove from the oven and leave the meat to cool overnight in its wrappings (see Cook's tips).
4 Make the tuna mayonnaise: Put the tuna in a blender with the mayonnaise, yogurt, anchovy paste, lemon rind and juice. Blend until the mixture is smooth. Alternatively, if you do not have a blender, mash the ingredients with a fork until well combined.
5 Pour into a bowl, then taste and add salt and pepper if necessary.
Cover with plastic wrap and refrigerate until ready to serve.
6 Plunge the strips of pepper into boiling water 1 minute to blanch them, then drain and refresh under cold running water. Drain thoroughly.
7 Carve the cold lamb into thin slices. Lay the slices in a single layer on a serving dish and cover with the tuna mayonnaise (see Cook's tips). Arrange the strips of pepper in a lattice pattern over the mayonnaise and place the olives in the squares. Serve cold.

Cook's Notes

TIME
Cooking time for the lamb is 1¼ hours, but remember to allow it to cool overnight in a cold place.
Preparation of the tuna mayonnaise takes 10-15 minutes, and allow 10 minutes to finish.

COOK'S TIPS
You can use left-over lamb for this dish, but meat cooked and left to cool in the piece has a better flavor and is also more moist.
If the slices of lamb will not fit in the dish in a single layer, make 2 layers and separate them with a layer of half the mayonnaise mixture.
If you have any tuna mayonnaise left over it will make a delicious snack or appetizer served the following day spooned over halved hard-boiled eggs or a bed of shredded lettuce.

BUYING GUIDE
The frozen lamb joints sold in supermarkets are ideal for this recipe. If you are using frozen lamb make sure the joint is thoroughly thawed before cooking.

● 565 calories per portion

Lamb bake

SERVES 4
1 lb cooked lamb, cut into small cubes
¼ cup butter or margarine
1 tablespoon all-purpose flour
½ teaspoon dry mustard
1¼ cups canned beef consommé, undiluted
⅔ cup light cream
1 teaspoon Worcestershire sauce
2 hard-boiled eggs, quartered
¼ lb mushrooms, sliced
salt and freshly ground black pepper
½ cup fresh whole wheat bread crumbs
1 tablespoon chopped parsley

1 Preheat the oven to 350°.
2 Over low heat, gently melt half the butter in a flameproof casserole. Stir in the flour and mustard, mix well, raise the heat and cook about 1 minute, stirring constantly. Add the consommé and bring to a boil, stirring briskly. Continue to boil 2-3 minutes until sauce is cooked.
3 Lower the heat and add the cream, Worcestershire sauce, hard-boiled eggs, sliced mushrooms and the cooked lamb. Fold gently to mix, taking care not to break the eggs. Taste and adjust seasoning.
4 Melt the remaining butter in a separate pan and mix with the bread crumbs and parsley. Sprinkle on top of the casserole.
5 Bake uncovered in the heated oven about 30 minutes until the casserole is golden on top, and the meat heated through. Serve at once.

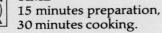 Cook's Notes

 TIME
15 minutes preparation, 30 minutes cooking.

ECONOMY
This is an excellent way of using up leftover roast lamb.

SERVING IDEAS
Serve with golden brown sautéed potatoes (potatoes boiled until nearly cooked, then sliced and fried in hot oil), and a green vegetable.

VARIATIONS
Use 2-4 tablespoons red wine in place of some of the consommé for a richer flavor.
For a sharper taste, use plain yogurt in place of some or all of the light cream.

COOK'S TIP
To hard-boil eggs: Put eggs in a pan, cover with cold water and bring to a boil. Simmer 7-8 minutes only, then drain and immediately plunge into cold water. Remove shells and keep in cold water to prevent a black ring forming around yolks.

●655 calories per portion

Spinach-stuffed lamb

SERVES 8

**3-3½ lb shoulder of lamb, blade
    bone removed
    (see Buying guide)**
all-purpose flour, for dusting
3 tablespoons vegetable oil

SPINACH STUFFING
¼ cup butter or margarine
1 onion, finely chopped
2 celery stalks, finely chopped
½ lb frozen chopped spinach
½ lb pork sausagemeat
1 egg, beaten
**1 tablespoon finely chopped fresh
    mint, or 1 teaspoon dried mint**
**good pinch of freshly ground
    nutmeg**
salt and freshly ground black pepper

1 Make the stuffing: Melt the butter in a saucepan, add the onion and celery and cook gently about 5 minutes until the vegetables are soft and lightly colored but not browned.

2 Meanwhile, cook the spinach in a separate pan about 4 minutes, stirring occasionally. Drain through a fine strainer, pressing with the back of a spoon to remove as much liquid from it as possible.

3 Mix the spinach into the cooked onion mixture and cook gently 1 minute, stirring constantly.

4 Mash the sausagemeat in a bowl. Add spinach mixture and stir well. Stir in the egg, mint and nutmeg. Season well with salt and pepper and mix thoroughly. Cover and refrigerate for 30 minutes.

5 Meanwhile preheat the oven to 325°.

6 With a sharp knife, carefully enlarge pocket left in the lamb by removal of the bone. Pack in prepared stuffing, pressing it down well. Draw edges of pocket together and secure with a meat skewer (see Cook's tip).

7 Cut a piece of foil nearly large enough to enclose the lamb. Line a roasting pan with the foil, then put the lamb, skin side up, in the pan. Season with salt and pepper and dust with flour. Pour the oil evenly over the surface of the lamb.

8 Bring the foil up closely around the sides of the lamb but do not cover the surface.

9 Roast the lamb in the oven 2 hours, basting occasionally with the juices in the foil.

10 Increase oven heat to 400°, open out foil and cook a further 30 minutes until the skin is crisp and browned and the meat is cooked through (the juices run clear when the lamb is pierced with a fine meat skewer).

11 Remove skewer and transfer lamb to a warmed carving dish. Return to oven turned to lowest setting 10-15 minutes for meat to "rest" so that it is easier to carve, then slice and serve.

POULTRY

Chicken in lychee sauce

SERVES 4

3 chicken breasts, each weighing
⅓ lb, skinned
3 tablespoons cornstarch
3 tablespoons vegetable oil
1 onion, thinly sliced
1 chicken bouillon cube
2 tablespoons boiling water
2 tablespoons tomato catsup
2 teaspoons soy sauce
1 can (about 11 oz) lychees, drained
and quartered, with syrup
reserved
2 large tomatoes, peeled and
roughly chopped
2 tablespoons chopped chives or
chopped scallions
1-2 tablespoons lemon juice
freshly ground black pepper

1 Cut away any bones from the chicken with a sharp knife. Discard any fat. Cut the chicken into ½-inch cubes.
2 Put the cornstarch into a plastic bag then add the chicken cubes and shake until well coated.
3 Heat the oil in a large skillet, add the onion and cook gently 5 minutes until soft and lightly colored.
4 Raise the heat, add the chicken and cook about 5 minutes, turning frequently until lightly browned all over. Remove the pan from the heat.
5 In a bowl, dissolve the bouillon cube in the boiling water. Stir in the tomato catsup and soy sauce, then stir this mixture into the chicken together with the quartered lychees and reserved syrup, the tomatoes and half the chives. Mix well.
6 Return to the heat, bring to a boil, then simmer 1 minute, stirring constantly. Cover with a top or foil and simmer gently a further 5 minutes, or until the chicken is tender and cooked through. Stir in lemon juice and pepper to taste, then transfer to a warmed serving dish. Sprinkle with remaining chives. Serve at once.

Cook's Notes

 TIME
40 minutes to prepare and cook.

SERVING IDEAS
Serve with fresh peas and fried, fresh bean-sprouts or boiled Chinese noodles.

 DID YOU KNOW
Lychees are a small fruit with a pit, of Chinese origin. When bought fresh, they have a hard, parchment-like skin which is reddish-brown in color. The flesh is firm and slippery, with a slightly perfumed taste.

VARIATION
Use a diced pepper instead of tomatoes.

PRESSURE COOKING
Without coating in cornstarch, pre-brown the chicken in the cooker, then add the rest of the ingredients, except for the lychees. Bring the pressure to high (H) and cook 5 minutes. Reduce the pressure quickly, add the cornstarch mixed with a little water, and simmer uncovered 2 minutes. Add lychees, heat through, stir in lemon juice.

● 325 calories per portion

Spanish stuffed chicken

SERVES 4-6
3-3½ lb roasting chicken
vegetable oil, for brushing

STUFFING
2 tablespoons butter or margarine
1 small onion, chopped
⅓ cup soft white bread crumbs
¼ cup blanched almonds, chopped
1 canned red pimiento, chopped
8 green olives, pitted and
   quartered
1 large tomato, peeled and
   chopped
½ teaspoon salt
freshly ground black pepper

1 Preheat the oven to 350°.
2 Make the stuffing: Melt the butter in a skillet, add the onion and cook gently 5 minutes until soft and lightly colored. Remove the pan from the heat.
3 Add the remaining stuffing ingredients to the pan and mix well.
4 Wash the chicken and pat dry with paper towels. Using a small sharp knife, remove the wishbone from the neck end of the chicken by cutting away the flesh around it (see Cook's tip). Break off the bone at the joints and lift it out.
5 Fill the neck cavity with the stuffing, fold the neck skin back into position, then fold the wing tips over it. Secure with a metal skewer. Carefully truss the drumsticks with string, if necessary.
6 Lightly oil a roasting pan. Place the chicken in the pan, brush with oil and season with salt and pepper.
7 Roast the chicken in the oven 1½ hours until cooked (the juices run clear when the thigh is pierced with a skewer). Remove skewer and any string and, if serving hot, transfer to a warmed serving dish (see Serving ideas).

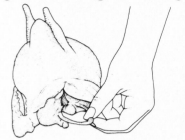

Chicken curry

SERVES 4

4 chicken pieces, each weighing ¾ lb
2 tablespoons butter or margarine
2 onions, chopped
1 clove garlic, crushed (optional)
1 tablespoon all-purpose flour
1 tablespoon curry powder
3 tomatoes, peeled and roughly
　chopped
2 celery stalks, chopped
2 bananas, thickly sliced
1 dessert apple, roughly chopped
½ cup chicken broth
salt and freshly ground black
　pepper
1 cup yogurt or dairy sour cream
1½ tablespoons toasted flaked
　almonds, to garnish

1 Melt the butter in a large skillet and cook the chicken pieces over moderate heat until browned on both sides. Remove from the pan with a slotted spoon and set aside.
2 Add the onions to the pan with the garlic, if using, and cook 5 minutes until the onion is trans-
lucent. Stir in the flour and curry powder and cook 2-3 minutes, then stir in all the remaining ingredients except the salt, pepper and yogurt.
3 Bring to a boil, stirring constantly, then return the chicken pieces to the pan and season to taste with salt and pepper. Lower the heat, cover and cook gently about 45 minutes or until the chicken is tender when pierced with a skewer (see Cook's tips). ✳
4 Remove the chicken from the pan and keep hot on a serving plate. Boil the sauce until thick, then remove the pan from the heat and stir in the yogurt.
5 Taste and adjust seasoning (see Cook's tips), pour over the chicken and sprinkle with the flaked almonds. Serve at once.

Cook's Notes

TIME
The curry takes 20 minutes preparation plus 45 minutes cooking.

SERVING IDEAS
Serve with rice, chapati, or poppadoms and prepare separate bowls of mango chutney and sliced onion or cucumber.

COOK'S TIPS
The flavor of the dish will improve if it is left overnight. If you intend to do this, reduce the cooking time by 10 minutes and insure the meat is thoroughly heated before serving the next day. If, at the end of the cooking the flavor is too hot for your taste, add a little more yogurt or sour cream.

 FREEZING
Transfer to a rigid container, cool quickly, then seal, label and freeze up to 3 months. To serve: Thaw in refrigerator overnight, then reheat until the chicken is heated through and the sauce is bubbling. Stir in a little chicken broth or water if the sauce is too thick. Continue from the beginning of stage 4.

● 460 calories per portion

Rosé chicken

SERVES 4
3-3½ lb broiler/fryer
salt and freshly ground black pepper
2 tablespoons butter or margarine
2 sprigs fresh tarragon, chopped, or
   1 teaspoon dried tarragon
1 small onion, halved
⅔ cup rosé vermouth
2 good pinches paprika
2 teaspoons tomato paste
1 tablespoon cornstarch
¼ cup milk
⅔ cup chicken broth
1-2 teaspoons lemon juice,
   according to taste

1 Preheat the oven to 375°.
2 Pat the chicken dry with paper towels, then sprinkle inside and out with salt and pepper.
3 Place half the butter inside the chicken with half the tarragon and the onion halves. Truss with thread or fine string.
4 Place the chicken in an ovenproof dish [!] and spread with the remaining butter. Sprinkle over the remaining tarragon, then pour the vermouth around the chicken.
5 Roast in the oven 1¼ hours or until the chicken is tender and the juices run clear when the thickest part of the thigh is pierced with a skewer. Baste occasionally during the cooking time.
6 Remove the chicken from the dish and discard the trussing thread. Place the chicken on a warmed serving platter and keep hot in the lowest possible oven.
7 To make the sauce: Pour the juices from the chicken into a saucepan. Stir in a pinch of paprika and the tomato paste. In a bowl, blend the cornstarch to a paste with the milk, gradually stir in the chicken broth and add to the pan. Stir well to combine, bring to a boil, then simmer 2 minutes, stirring constantly. Taste and adjust seasoning, then add lemon juice to taste, for a sharper flavor. ✳
8 Pour a little of the sauce over the chicken and sprinkle with the remaining paprika. Serve at once, with the remaining sauce passed separately.

Cook's Notes

TIME
Preparation 10 minutes and cooking time 1¼ hours. Last-minute finishing touches, 10 minutes.

WATCH POINT
Choose an ovenproof dish just large enough to take the chicken. The vermouth will evaporate too quickly if a large space is left around the bird.

FREEZING
Cut the chicken into portions, arrange in a freezer container and cover completely with the sauce. Cool quickly, then seal, label and freeze up to 6 months. To serve: reheat from frozen in a 400° oven about 1 hour, or until thawed.

PRESSURE COOKING
Weigh the chicken and calculate exact cooking time at 7 minutes per 1 lb. Pre-brown the chicken, drain, then stand on the trivet, rimside down. Pour vermouth and 1¼ cups broth into base of cooker. Bring to high (H) pressure, then cook for calculated time. Release pressure quickly. Make the sauce using liquid in base of cooker.

●395 calories per portion

Crunchy chicken salad

SERVES 4

1¾ cups boneless cooked
  chicken
1 cup brown rice
2½ cups chicken broth
1 large red pepper, seeded and finely
  chopped
1 bunch scallions, chopped
¼ lb frozen peas, cooked and
  cooled
½ cup grated carrot
¾ cup walnuts, roughly
  chopped
¾ cup mayonnaise
1 tablespoon tomato paste
generous pinch of sugar
1 tablespoon chopped parsley
  (optional)

DRESSING

2 tablespoons olive or salad oil
1 tablespoon lemon juice
2 teaspoons wine vinegar or dry
  white wine
pinch of dry mustard
salt and freshly ground black pepper

1 Cook the brown rice in the chicken broth about 45 minutes until tender. If necessary, top up the pan with boiling water during the latter part of the cooking time.

2 Meanwhile, make the dressing: Combine all the ingredients in a screw-top jar and shake well to mix.

3 Drain any excess liquid from the rice, then mix in the red pepper, scallions, peas and carrot.

4 While the rice is still warm, fork the dressing through the mixture. Cover the bowl with plastic wrap and chill in the refrigerator at least 1 hour.

5 When ready to serve, add the walnuts to the rice and mix thoroughly. Spoon into a serving dish and arrange the cooked chicken on top of the rice.

6 Mix the mayonnaise with the tomato paste and sugar. It should be the consistency of a coating sauce; if it is too thick, stir in a little hot water.

7 Carefully spoon the mayonnaise on top of the cooked chicken, then sprinkle the top with chopped parsley, if liked.

TIME
The rice will take 45 minutes to cook and 1 hour to chill, during which time the other preparations can be completed.

COOK'S TIP
Brown rice takes longer to cook than long-grain white rice, but has a lovely, nutty flavor. It will absorb the dressing better if you fork it through while the rice is still quite warm.

ECONOMY
Cut down the cooking time for the rice by soaking it for 2 hours in cold water before cooking.

VARIATIONS
Add finely chopped celery, green peppers, drained canned whole kernel corn, chopped green beans or any other suitable crisp vegetable to the salad.

● 865 calories per portion

Chicken paprikash

SERVES 4
4 chicken pieces, skinned
1 tablespoon butter or margarine
1 lb onions, finely chopped
1 clove garlic, crushed (optional)
1 tablespoon paprika
salt and freshly ground black
    pepper
about ⅔ cup hot chicken broth
½ cup dairy sour cream
chopped chives, to garnish

1 Preheat the oven to 350°.
2 Melt the butter in a large, shallow flameproof casserole big enough to take the chicken pieces in a single layer (see Cook's tip). Add onions and garlic, if using, cover and cook gently abut 45 minutes until a soft, golden brown purée is formed.
3 Raise the heat slightly, then sprinkle in the paprika and salt and pepper to taste. Add the chicken

and spoon over the onion mixture.
4 Cover the casserole and bake in the oven 45 minutes or until the juices run clear when the thickest part of the chicken flesh is pierced with a skewer. Check the casserole contents regularly and add a little

broth from time to time if the chicken appears to be becoming a little too dry.
5 Heat the sour cream in a pan; do not boil, or it will curdle. Pour over the chicken; sprinkle with chives and serve at once.

Cook's Notes

TIME
Preparation 10 minutes, total cooking time about 1½ hours.

COOK'S TIP
If you do not have a casserole big enough to take the chicken in 1 layer use a large, lidded skillet and cook the complete dish on the top of the range.

! WATCHPOINT
Be careful that the purée does not become too liquid — it should be thick enough to coat the chicken without forming a sauce.

SERVING IDEAS
Serve with savory rice made by adding some cooked chopped mushrooms and cooked chopped green pepper and onion to plain boiled rice.

✳ FREEZING
Cool quickly, then freeze in a rigid container up to 2 months. To serve: Thaw overnight in the refrigerator, pour in ⅔ cup hot chicken broth, reheat in oven at 375° 40 minutes or until bubbling. Continue from stage 5.

● 290 calories per portion

Chicken lasagne

SERVES 4
6 strips lasagne (see Buying guide)
salt
1 teaspoon vegetable oil
freshly ground black pepper
1 cup grated Cheddar cheese
butter, for greasing

CHICKEN SAUCE
3 tablespoons vegetable oil
1 large onion, sliced
¼ lb streaky bacon, chopped
4 tablespoons all-purpose flour
1¼ cups chicken broth
1 can (about 8 oz) tomatoes
1⅔ cups boneless cooked chicken,
**   chopped (see Buying**
**   guide)**
1 tablespoon tomato paste

WHITE SAUCE
2 tablespoons butter or margarine
4 tablespoons all purpose flour
pinch of freshly ground nutmeg
1¼ cups milk

1 Preheat the oven to 350° and then thoroughly grease a shallow ovenproof dish.
2 Make the chicken sauce: Heat the oil in a skillet, add the onion and cook gently until soft and lightly colored. Add the bacon and cook 1 minute.
3 Sprinkle in the flour and cook 1 minute, stirring, until straw-colored. Remove from the heat and gradually stir in broth, tomatoes, chicken and tomato paste.
4 Return to the heat and bring to a boil, stirring constantly, then lower the heat and simmer 3 minutes. Remove from the heat and set aside.
5 Bring a large pan of salted water to a boil and cook the lasagne with the oil 10 minutes.
6 Meanwhile, make the white sauce: Melt the butter in a saucepan, sprinkle in the flour and nutmeg and stir over low heat 2 minutes until straw-colored. Remove from the heat and gradually stir in the milk, return to the heat again and simmer, stirring, until thick and smooth. Set aside.
7 Drain the lasagne and pat dry with paper towels.

8 Spread half the chicken sauce in the bottom of the greased ovenproof dish and sprinkle with salt and pepper. Place 3 strips of lasagne on top.
9 Spread the remaining chicken sauce over the lasagne, sprinkle with more salt and pepper and cover with a second layer of lasagne. Pour the white sauce over the lasagne and sprinkle with salt and pepper.
10 Sprinkle the grated cheese over the top of the white sauce, then bake in the oven 1 hour until bubbling and golden. If the topping is not golden at the end of the cooking time, preheat the broiler to high and transfer the lasagne to the broiler 2-3 minutes to brown the cheese. Serve hot, straight from the dish.

Cook's Notes

TIME
Preparation 35 minutes, cooking 1 hour.

BUYING GUIDE
Lasagne varies in width, from one manufacturer to another—"strips" of lasagne are narrow; "sheets" are wider.
For 1⅔ cups boneless chicken, buy 2 large chicken breasts and cook, skin and bone them before using, or buy half a roasted chicken and simply remove the meat.

FREEZING
Do not pre-cook the lasagne strips. Arrange them over the chicken sauce in layers as in stage 8. Cook the lasagne in a foil freezer container, cool quickly, then seal, label and freeze. Store up to 1 month. To serve: Reheat from frozen, uncovered, in the foil container in a 400° oven 1½ hours until bubbling.

●655 calories per portion

Chicken polka pie

SERVES 4

2 cups boneless cooked chicken, cut into bite-sized pieces (see Buying guide)
2 lb potatoes
salt
¼ lb frozen mixed vegetables with whole kernel corn
1¼ cups package parsley sauce mix
1¼ cups milk
1 teaspoon Worcestershire sauce
pinch of freshly ground nutmeg
freshly ground black pepper
3 hard-boiled eggs, chopped (see Freezing)
3 tablespoons butter or margarine
¾ cup grated Cheddar cheese
¼ cup flaked almonds (optional)

1 Cook the potatoes in boiling salted water about 15 minutes until tender but still firm. At the same time, cook the frozen vegetables according to package directions.

2 While the potatoes and vegetables are cooking, make up the parsley sauce with the milk according to package directions. Stir in the Worcestershire sauce, nutmeg and salt and pepper to taste.

3 Drain the frozen vegetables and fold into the sauce with the chicken and hard-boiled eggs. Simmer over very gentle heat until the chicken is thoroughly heated through, stirring occasionally.

4 Meanwhile, drain the potatoes and, when cool enough to handle, slice thickly. Grease a shallow flame-proof dish with 1 tablespoon butter. Preheat the broiler to high.

5 Pour the chicken mixture into the dish and level the surface. Place the potato slices on top, overlapping them so they cover the chicken mixture completely. Dot with the remaining butter and sprinkle with the cheese.

6 Place under the heated broiler 7-10 minutes until crisp and golden brown. Sprinkle the flaked almonds over the top, if using, and replace under the broiler until the almonds are lightly toasted.  Serve at once, straight from the dish.

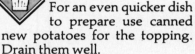
 TIME
Preparation and cooking about 1 hour; broiling 7-10 minutes.

 FREEZING
If freezing this dish, leave out the hard-boiled eggs because they become rubbery in the freezer. Make the pie up to the end of stage 6 in a freezerproof casserole dish instead of the flame-proof dish. Leave until cold, then seal, label and freeze up to 6 months. To serve: Cook from frozen, uncovered, in a 400° oven about 1 hour or until heated through and golden brown.

SERVING IDEAS
As the dish already contains potatoes and vegetables, serve with a contrasting, crisp salad of lettuce and watercress. Sliced tomatoes can be used as a garnish in place of the almonds.

VARIATION
Use cheese or onion sauce mix instead of parsley.

COOK'S TIP
For an even quicker dish to prepare use canned new potatoes for the topping. Drain them well.

WATCHPOINT
Keep a strict eye on the dish at this stage, the almonds can easily burn and spoil the flavor.

BUYING GUIDE
Left-over cooked chicken can be used for this dish, but if you are buying ready-cooked chicken pieces, you will need 3 with a total weight of about 1¼ lb in order to have 2 cups meat when all the skin and bones have been removed.

● 620 calories per portion

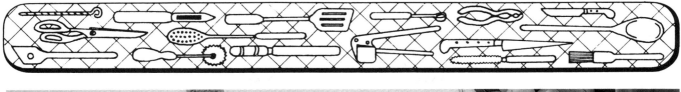

Turkey parcels

SERVES 4
8 turkey scallops (see Buying guide)
1 cup dried apricots, soaked overnight and drained
⅓ cup ground almonds
¼ cup butter or margarine
½ cup dry white wine
salt and freshly ground black pepper
watercress, to garnish
butter, for greasing

1 Preheat the oven to 375°. Cut 8 pieces of foil, large enough to enclose the turkey scallops, and then lightly grease them with butter.
2 Roughly chop two-thirds of the apricots and mix in a bowl with the ground almonds. Spread equal portions of this mixture on one half of each scallop and then fold the other half over to make a sandwich.
3 Place each stuffed scallop on a piece of greased foil. Fold up the sides of the foil without sealing, put a knob of butter on each scallop and then pour 1 tablespoon wine over each. Season well with salt and pepper and loosely fold the foil to enclose the stuffed scallop.

Seal and place the parcels on a cookie sheet and cook in the oven about 30 minutes.
4 To serve the scallops: Remove the foil and transfer the meat to a warmed serving platter, pour over the juices, then garnish with the remaining apricot halves and top with the watercress.

Cook's Notes

TIME
Allow 30 minutes for preparation and 30 minutes for cooking.

VARIATIONS
Use pork scallops or chicken breasts instead of the turkey. Replace the dried apricots with ½ cup of thick apple sauce flavored with ground nutmeg, or use 1½ tablespoons of plain yogurt in each parcel instead of the butter and wine.

SERVING IDEAS
Serve with croquette potatoes, green beans or a crisp fennel and zucchini salad.

BUYING GUIDE
Turkey scallops, thin slices of meat cut from the breasts, are available in packages at large supermarkets. You will need 2 scallop parcels per person.

● 420 calories per portion

Creamy almond turkey

SERVES 4
1 lb turkey fillets/scallops
2 tablespoons butter
2 teaspoons all-purpose flour
1¼ cups chicken broth
2 teaspoons tomato paste
2 tablespoons ground almonds
salt and freshly ground black pepper
¼ cup flaked almonds
⅓ cup light cream

1 Preheat the oven to 350°.
2 Melt the butter in a shallow flameproof casserole. Add the turkey fillets and cook over moderate heat 2-3 minutes on each side until lightly colored. Remove from the casserole with a slotted spoon and reserve.
3 Sprinkle the flour into the hot butter in the casserole and stir over low heat 1-2 minutes until straw-colored. Gradually stir in the chicken broth, then simmer, stirring, until thick and smooth.
4 Stir in the tomato paste and ground almonds and mix well. Season to taste with salt and pepper. Return the turkey fillets to the casserole. Cover and bake in the oven 30 minutes.
5 Meanwhile, brown the flaked almonds: Put them into a heated, ungreased, skillet and shake the pan over the heat until the almonds are light brown all over. [!]
6 Add the cream to the cooked turkey and stir it into the sauce. Sprinkle over the browned almonds and serve at once.

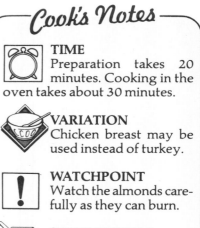

Cook's Notes

TIME
Preparation takes 20 minutes. Cooking in the oven takes about 30 minutes.

VARIATION
Chicken breast may be used instead of turkey.

WATCHPOINT
Watch the almonds carefully as they can burn.

SERVING IDEAS
For a pretty color contrast with the pink sauce, serve with green pasta and spinach or broccoli.

● 285 calories per portion

Macaroni turkey

SERVES 4

1½ lb boneless turkey meat,
    cut into 1-inch cubes (see Buying
    guide)
1 tablespoon vegetable oil
¼ cup butter or margarine
1 large onion, chopped
2 celery stalks, chopped
2 teaspoons all-purpose flour
1 can (about 10 oz) condensed cream
    of chicken soup
1¼ cups chicken broth
salt and freshly ground black pepper
2 teaspoons Dijon-style mustard
1⅓ cups whole wheat macaroni
½ lb mushrooms, sliced
2 tablespoons chopped parsley
½ cup fresh white bread crumbs
tomato slices, to garnish

1 Heat oil and half the butter in a large skillet. Add the onion and celery and cook gently 1-2 minutes. Add the turkey and cook briskly a further 3-4 minutes, stirring often, to brown on all sides.
2 Sprinkle the flour into the skillet and stir over low heat 1-2 minutes. Remove from the heat and stir in the soup and the chicken broth. Return to heat and bring to a boil, stirring. Season to taste. Lower the heat, add the mustard and simmer for about 20 minutes.
3 Preheat the oven to 400°.
4 Meanwhile, bring a large pan of salted water to a boil and cook the macaroni for 10 minutes. Drain well. Melt the remaining butter in the rinsed-out pan, add the macaroni and stir it well to coat thoroughly.
5 Spoon the macaroni over the base of a large ovenproof dish.
6 Stir the sliced mushrooms into

the turkey mixture and spoon over macaroni. Sprinkle with the parsley and bread crumbs and bake 20 minutes. Serve hot, straight from the dish, garnished with tomato slices.

Turkey in breadcrumbs

SERVES 4

4 turkey fillets/scallops, each weighing about ¼ lb, thoroughly thawed if frozen

2 tablespoons all-purpose flour

salt and freshly ground black pepper

⅓ cup fresh white bread crumbs

2 eggs

vegetable oil, for cooking

tomato wedges and parsley sprigs, to garnish

SAUCE

1 tablespoon butter

2 tomatoes peeled and chopped

½ lb frozen whole kernel corn (see Cook's tip)

2 tablespoons heavy cream

1 Place the turkey fillets between 2 large sheets of waxed paper and beat with a rolling pin or mallet until they are very thin and twice their original size.

2 Preheat the oven to 225°.

3 Spread the flour out on a flat plate and season with salt and pepper. Spread the bread crumbs out on a separate flat plate. Beat the eggs in a shallow dish.

4 Dip the turkey scallops into the flour, then into beaten egg, and then into bread crumbs, to coat evenly.

5 Pour oil into a large skillet to a depth of about ¼ inch. Heat the oil, add 2 turkey scallops and cook over brisk heat about 3 minutes on each side, until golden brown and crisp.

6 Drain the scallops on both sides on paper towels. Transfer to a warmed serving dish and keep warm in the oven while cooking the remaining scallops in same way.

7 While the last 2 scallops are cooking, make the sauce: Melt the butter in a small saucepan, add the tomatoes and cook 1-2 minutes until very soft. Stir in the corn and cook 3 minutes, then stir in the cream and heat through gently. Season with salt and pepper.

8 Drain the last 2 turkey scallops on both sides on paper towels and transfer to the serving dish.

Garnish with tomato wedges and parsley sprigs and serve at once, with the sauce passed separately in a warmed gravyboat.

Cook's Notes

TIME
Preparation takes about 25 minutes. Cooking, including making the sauce, takes 15 minutes.

SERVING IDEAS
Serve with sautéed potatoes and peas cooked in the French way with tiny onions, shredded lettuce and diced bacon.

COOK'S TIP
The corn does not need to be thawed: Just stir into the pan and heat thoroughly without overcooking, as this will toughen it.

● 435 calories per portion

Farmhouse turkey and ham pie

SERVES 4

1 package (17 oz) frozen puff pastry, thawed
2 cups cooked turkey, chopped
1½ cups cooked ham, chopped
2 hard-boiled eggs, quartered
a little beaten egg, to glaze

SAUCE
2 tablespoons butter or margarine
4 tablespoons flour
1¼ cups milk
finely grated rind and juice of ½ lemon
1 tablespoon chopped fresh parsley
salt and freshly ground black pepper

1 Preheat the oven to 425°.
2 Roll out the pastry on a lightly floured surface to a shape slightly larger than the circumference of a deep pie dish. Cut off a long narrow strip all around edge. Reserve with other trimmings.
3 Mix the turkey and ham together in the pie dish and arrange the quartered eggs on top.
4 Make the sauce: Melt the butter in a small saucepan, sprinkle in the flour and stir over low heat 1-2 minutes until straw-colored. Remove from the heat and gradually stir in the milk. Return to the heat and simmer, stirring, until it is thick and smooth.
5 Remove from the heat and stir in the lemon rind and juice, and the parsley. Season to taste with salt and pepper and allow to cool. Pour evenly over the turkey and ham in the pie dish.
6 Brush the rim of the pie dish with water, and then press the narrow strip of pastry all around the rim. Brush the strip with a little more water, then place the large piece of pastry on top. Trim the edge of the pastry, then knock up the flute.
7 Make leaves with the pastry trimmings, brush the undersides with water and place on top of the pie. Brush with beaten egg and make a small hole in the center of the pastry top.
8 Bake in the oven 25-30 minutes until the pastry is well risen and golden brown. Serve hot or cold.

Cook's Notes

TIME
Preparation takes about 20 minutes, baking in the oven 25-30 minutes.

SPECIAL OCCASION
Add 1 tablespoon dry white wine instead of the lemon juice to the sauce.

FREEZING
Omit the hard-boiled eggs in stage 3, then prepare the pie to stage 7, but do not brush with beaten egg. Open freeze until solid, then wrap in a freezer bag. Seal, label and return to the freezer up to 2 months. To serve: Remove from bag, thaw overnight in the refrigerator, then brush with beaten egg and make a hole in the top. Bake in a 425° oven for about 30 minutes.

SERVING IDEAS
A green salad is the best accompaniment to the turkey and ham pie.

● 825 calories per portion

Stuffed turkey drumsticks

SERVES 4

4 turkey drumsticks, unskinned
¼ lb streaky bacon slices, chopped
1 onion, finely chopped
1 red pepper, seeded and finely
    chopped
½ cup button mushrooms, finely
    chopped
½ cup fresh white bread crumbs
3 tablespoons finely chopped fresh
    parsley
1 egg, beaten
salt and freshly ground black
    pepper
vegetable oil, for brushing

1 Preheat oven to 350°.
2 Bone the drumsticks: With a sharp knife cut through the tendons at each end of the bone, then starting at the thigh end work the flesh down towards the knuckle and ease the flesh over the narrow end, to expose the bone.
3 Place the blade of the knife across the bone at the knuckle. Bang the knife sharply with a rolling pin to cut through the bone, so that only a small piece is left inside the flesh. ⚠
4 Put the bacon in a skillet and cook over gentle heat until the fat runs (see Cook's tips). Add the onion and red pepper and cook gently 5 minutes until softened. Stir in the mushrooms and cook 2 minutes.
5 Put the cooked bacon and vegetables in a bowl and combine with the bread crumbs, parsley and egg, stirring well to mix. Season with salt and pepper.
6 Allow the stuffing mixture to cool, then pack it into the drumsticks. Secure the ends with wooden toothpicks and place drumsticks in a small roasting pan. Brush with oil and sprinkle with salt (see Cook's tips).
7 Bake in the oven 45-50 minutes, until golden. Remove the toothpicks and serve hot or cold.

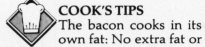

Cook's Notes

TIME
Preparation, including boning the drumsticks, making the stuffing and stuffing the drumsticks takes about 1 hour. Cooking in the oven takes about 50 minutes.

FREEZING
Cool quickly, open freeze until solid, then pack in a freezer bag. Seal, label and return to the freezer up to 6 months. To serve: Thaw at room temperature 3-4 hours, then serve cold (the drumsticks tend to go dry if reheated after freezing.

WATCHPOINT
During the boning process be careful not to split the skin.

COOK'S TIPS
The bacon cooks in its own fat: No extra fat or oil for cooking is needed.
Sprinkling with salt makes the skin deliciously crisp.

● 275 calories per portion

Roast duck with grapes

SERVES 4
1 duck, weighing 4½-5 lb, giblets
reserved
salt
1 small onion, quartered
bouquet garni
freshly ground black pepper
2 cups water
grapes and watercress, to garnish

SAUCE
1 onion, very finely chopped
4 tablespoons all-purpose flour
1¼ cups duck giblet stock
⅔ cups dry white wine
¼ lb each green and black grapes,
quartered and pitted
2 tablespoons heavy cream

1 Preheat the oven to 350°.
2 Pat the duck dry inside and out with paper towels. Prick the skin all over and sprinkle with salt.
3 Weigh the duck and calculate the roasting time at 30 minutes per 1 lb. Place the duck breast side up, on a broiler rack or trivet in a roasting pan. Roast, without basting, in the oven for the calculated cooking time, until the skin is brown and crisp, and the juices run clear when thigh is pierced with a fine skewer.

4 Meanwhile, rinse the giblets in cold water and place in a saucepan together with the quartered onion and bouquet garni. Season with salt and pepper and cover with the water. Bring to a boil, then lower heat and simmer gently 1 hour. Strain and set aside.
5 Drain the cooked duck well, saving 2 tablespoons drippings (see Economy). Place the duck on a warmed serving dish and keep hot in the oven turned down to 225°, while making sauce.
6 Pour the 2 tablespoons of hot duck drippings into a small sauce-pan. Add the chopped onion, cover

the pan and cook gently 10 minutes, shaking the pan from time to time until the onion is soft and golden brown. Sprinkle in the flour and stir over low heat 1-2 minutes then gradually stir in 1¼ cups of the strained giblet stock and the wine. Bring to a boil, and simmer 2 minutes, stirring, until thickened.
7 Add the grapes and heat through gently a further 2 minutes. Remove from the heat and stir in the cream. Pour into a warmed bowl or gravy boat and pass separately with the roast duck (see Cook's tip), garnished with grapes and water-cress.

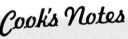

Cook's Notes

TIME
Preparation takes about 25 minutes, cooking 2¼-2½ hours, including roasting the duck, preparing the stock and making the sauce.

SERVING
This makes a perfect Christmas dinner for 4 people and a more suitable alternative to turkey, which is best for serving larger numbers.

COOK'S TIP
For easier serving, cut the duck in half

lengthwise, using sharp kitchen scissors to cut down the breast-bone and along backbone. Then cut each half into 2 even portions.
    Arrange the 4 portions on a warmed serving dish.

ECONOMY
Strain the remaining drippings from the duck into a bowl. Cover and keep in the refrigerator for roasting po-tatoes. Duck drippings can also be used for roasting parsnips.

● 490 calories per portion

Honey duck salad

SERVES 4
4½ lb duck, thawed if frozen
salt
2 tablespoons clear honey
1 tablespoon hot water

SALAD GARNISH
2 heads endive leaves, separated
1 bunch watercress, divided into small sprigs
2 oranges, divided into segments

DRESSING
4 tablespoons vegetable oil
1 tablespoon tarragon vinegar
1 tablespoon fresh orange juice
pinch of sugar
½ teaspoon Dijon-style mustard
salt and freshly ground black pepper

1 Preheat the oven to 350°.
2 Pat the duck dry inside and out with paper towels. Prick the skin all over with a fork and sprinkle evenly with salt.
3 Place the duck breast side up, on a rack in a roasting pan. Roast in the oven 1 hour, then drain off the fat from the pan. Blend the honey with the hot water and brush the duck all over with the mixture.
4 Return the honey duck to the oven and roast a further 1¼ hours, basting 2-3 times to glaze and brown. Drain the duck over the pan, transfer to a plate and leave until completely cold (3-4 hours).
5 Divide the duck into 4 (see Preparation). Arrange on a serving dish. Garnish with endive leaves, watercress sprigs and orange segments.
6 Place ingredients for dressing in a screw-top jar, with salt and pepper to taste, and shake well together. Sprinkle over the salad just before serving.

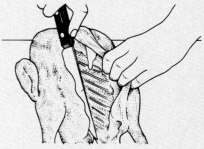

Duck 'n' beans

SERVES 4

4 duck pieces, each weighing about ¾ lb, thawed if frozen (see Buying guide)
salt and freshly ground black pepper
1 onion, chopped
1 clove garlic, crushed (optional)
2 cups chicken broth
1 tablespoon medium sherry
1 can (about 15 oz) baked beans in tomato sauce
1 tablespoon tomato catsup
⅓ lb spicy garlic sausage, chopped
1 teaspoon dried thyme
1 bay leaf

TOPPING

4 tablespoons chopped fresh parsley
1 cup fresh white bread crumbs

1 Preheat the oven to 375°.
2 Prick the duck pieces all over with a fork, season with salt and pepper and place on a rack in a roasting pan. Roast 1¼ hours, until the duck pieces are cooked through (the juices run clear when the meat is pierced with a fine skewer). Remove the duck pieces from the pan, drain on paper towels and place in a large casserole. Turn the oven down to 350°.
3 Drain off all but 1 tablespoon fat from the pan and transfer the pan to the top of the stove. Add the onion and garlic, if using, and cook gently 2 minutes.
4 Gradually stir in the broth and sherry and bring to a boil, stirring constantly. Stir in the baked beans in their sauce, the tomato catsup, garlic sausage, thyme and bay leaf. Season to taste with salt and freshly ground black pepper.
5 Pour the mixture over the duck pieces in the casserole. Cover and cook the casserole in the oven 30 minutes.

Cook's Notes

TIME
Preparation takes about 20 minutes, cooking about 2¼ hours.

BUYING GUIDE
Duck pieces, consisting of the breast and wing, are available from high-quality butchers, large supermarkets and freezer centers.

SERVING IDEAS
Serve with jacket-baked potatoes and a salad

● 840 calories per portion

6 Increase the oven heat to 425°. Mix the parsley and bread crumbs together and sprinkle evenly over the surface of the casserole. Return to the oven and cook a further 15 minutes, uncovered, to brown the topping. Serve hot.

FISH AND SEAFOOD

Spiced fried herrings

SERVES 4

**8 herrings, each weighing about
¼ lb, heads removed, cleaned,
boned and roes reserved
(optional)**
1 egg yolk
1 tablespoon milk
3 tablespoons all-purpose flour
½ teaspoon paprika
salt and freshly ground black pepper
vegetable oil, for cooking
lemon and lime wedges and
coriander or parsley sprigs, to
garnish

SPICE MIXTURE
**3 tablespoons finely chopped fresh
coriander or parsley**
**2 tablespoons olive or sunflower
oil**
1 tablespoon ground cumin
1 teaspoon paprika
½ teaspoon cayenne
½ teaspoon ground cinnamon
¼ teaspoon salt

1 Combine all ingredients for the spice mixture in a small bowl and mix well together. Open out the herrings and lay them flat, skin side down, on the board or work surface. Spread with spice mixture, then close the herrings up, cover and set aside in a cool place and leave for at least 3 hours.
2 Beat the egg yolk with the milk in a small bowl. Spread the flour out on a large flat plate and season with the paprika and salt and pepper to taste. Brush the herrings with the egg yolk mixture, then turn in the flour to coat evenly. Shake off the excess flour and reserve for the herring roes, if using.
3 Heat enough oil in a large skillet just to cover the base. Add 4 of the herrings and cook over moderate heat 4-5 minutes on each side until cooked through (the flesh should be opaque). Using a turner, transfer the cooked herrings to

a warmed serving dish and keep warm. Heat a little more oil in the pan, add the remaining herrings and cook in the same way.
4 Turn the reserved roes, if using, in the remaining flour to coat evenly. Add to pan and cook 2-3 minutes, turning once, until just cooked. Remove and drain on paper towels.
5 Arrange the herrings with roes, if using, on serving dish. Garnish with lemon and lime wedges and coriander or parsley sprigs.

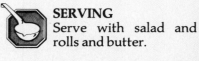

Breton steaks

SERVES 4
½ lb cod or halibut steaks
salt and freshly ground black
   pepper
2 fl oz sweet vermouth

SAUCE
6 tablespoons butter
2 celery stalks, thinly sliced
2 small leeks, thinly sliced
1 small onion, thinly sliced
¼ lb mushrooms, thinly sliced
6 tablespoons all-purpose flour
⅔ cup milk

1 Preheat the oven to 350°.
2 Season the fish steaks well with salt and pepper. Arrange in the base of a casserole and pour over the vermouth. Cover and bake in the oven 30 minutes until the fish is tender and the flesh flakes easily when pierced with a knife.
3 Meanwhile, make the sauce: Melt

Cook's Notes

TIME
This dish takes 1 hour to prepare and cook.

SERVING IDEAS
Serve with boiled new potatoes and broccoli or snow peas, and chilled white wine. Traditionally these fish steaks are garnished with small crescents of flaky pastry known as *fleurons*. To make *fleurons:* Cut out crescent shapes of puff pastry, using a metal cutter, and put them on a cookie sheet. At stage 4 remove fish steaks from the oven and keep warm. Increase heat to 400° and bake the *fleurons* 10 minutes.

DID YOU KNOW
In French cookery the term *à la bretonne*, when applied to fish, indicates that the dish is served with a sauce made with leeks, onions, celery and mushrooms.

● 405 calories per portion

half the butter in a large skillet, add the celery, leeks, onion and mushrooms and cook gently 5-6 minutes until soft. Set aside.
4 Using a turner, transfer the fish steaks to a warmed serving dish and keep warm in the oven turned to its lowest setting. Reserve the fish cooking juices.
5 In a small pan, melt remaining butter, sprinkle in the flour and stir over low heat 1-2 minutes until it is light straw-colored. Remove from the heat and gradually stir in the milk and the fish juices. Return to the heat and simmer, stirring, until thick and smooth.
6 Stir in the vegetables and heat through gently about 5 minutes. Pour the sauce over the fish steaks and serve the dish at once, while still piping hot (see Serving ideas).

Peanut flounder

SERVES 4
8 flounder fillets, each weighing
about ¼ lb, skinned
1 large egg
2 tablespoons light cream
2 teaspoons lemon juice
salt and freshly ground black
pepper
⅓ cup toasted bread crumbs
(see Preparation)
3¼ cups peanuts, finely chopped
(see Cook's tip)
1 tablespoon vegetable oil
2 tablespoons butter or margarine
lemon wedges, to serve

1 Put the egg, cream and lemon
juice in a shallow bowl with salt and
pepper to taste. Beat well to mix
2 Mix the bread crumbs and peanuts together on a plate.

3 Dip the fillets one by one into the
egg mixture, lift by the tail to drain
off the surplus egg, then coat in the
bread crumb and peanut mixture.
Press the crumbs into the fish and
make sure each fillet is well coated
on both sides.
4 Heat the oil and butter together
in a large skillet until the mixture is
foaming. Cook the fish, in 2 batches
if necessary, 4-5 minutes on each
side until they are all light golden in
color. Then keep hot on paper
towels until all are cooked, serve at
once with wedges of lemon.

Cook's Notes

TIME
Preparation takes 20-25
minutes, cooking 10
minutes.

COOK'S TIP
Use ordinary raw pea-
nuts, not the roasted
or salted varieties, for this
recipe. You can leave the skins
on or remove them, before
chopping, by rubbing them
between your fingers. The
peanuts can be chopped in a
coffee grinder, blender or food
processor, but do not chop too
finely or the coating will not be
crunchy.

PREPARATION
To make ¾ cup toasted
bread crumbs, toast 4
thin slices of bread until golden
on each side. Cut off the
crusts, then work for a few
seconds in a blender or food
processor until reduced to
crumbs.

● 430 calories per portion

Halibut special

(see Buying guide)

SERVES 4

4 × ⅓ lb halibut steaks, skinned
   (see Buying guide)
⅔ cup white wine
1 tablespoon cornstarch
1 tablespoon cold water
fresh thyme, to garnish

TOPPING

2 tablespoons butter
1 onion, chopped
2 celery stalks, chopped
3 tomatoes peeled and chopped
¼ lb mushrooms, chopped
1 teaspoon chopped fresh thyme or
   ½ teaspoon dried thyme
salt and freshly ground black pepper

1 Preheat the oven to 325°.
2 Make the topping: Melt the butter in a saucepan. Add the onion and cook gently 5 minutes until soft and lightly colored. Add celery, tomatoes and mushrooms and cook 1 more minute, stirring once or twice. Add the thyme, season well with salt and pepper and set aside.
3 Arrange the halibut steaks in a single layer in a large shallow ovenproof dish. Spoon the vegetable mixture evenly over the halibut and pour around the white wine. Cover the dish with foil and bake in the oven about 40 minutes, until the halibut is cooked through and flakes easily when pierced with a sharp knife. Transfer the halibut steaks to a warmed serving dish.
4 Pour the cooking liquid into a small saucepan. Blend the cornstarch with the water to make a smooth paste and stir into the liquid. Bring to a boil, stirring constantly. Taste and adjust the seasoning if necessary, then pour over the halibut. Garnish with thyme and serve the halibut at once (see Serving ideas).

Cook's Notes

TIME
Preparation takes about 15 minutes, cooking in the oven about 40 minutes.

SERVING IDEAS
Serve simply with minted garden peas and potatoes gratin dauphinois (sliced and baked with cheese).

BUYING GUIDE
Halibut has a delicious delicate flavor, but is a more expensive white fish than cod or tilefish, which can be used instead. Some freezer centers sell economy packs of halibut.

● 230 calories per portion

Celery-stuffed trout

SERVES 4

**4 rainbow trout, each weighing
    10-12 oz, cleaned with heads and
    tails left on**
butter, for greasing
celery leaves, to garnish

CELERY STUFFING
2 tablespoons butter or margarine
1 tablespoon vegetable oil
1 small onion, finely chopped
**2 large celery stalks, finely
    chopped**
**⅔ cup fresh whole wheat bread
    crumbs**
finely grated rind of 1 orange
finely grated rind of ½ lemon
1 teaspoon dried basil
1 teaspoon mustard powder
1 egg, beaten
2-3 tablespoons fresh orange juice
salt and freshly ground black pepper

1 Preheat the oven to 375°. Cut out
and grease 4 foil squares each large
enough to contain a whole rainbow
trout.

2 Make celery stuffing: Heat the
butter and oil in a saucepan,
add the onion and cook gently 5
minutes until soft and lightly
colored. Add celery and cook a
further 2-3 minutes, stirring the
mixture once or twice.
3 Remove from the heat and stir
in the bread crumbs, orange and
lemon rinds, the basil and mustard.
Stir in the egg and enough orange
juice just to bind. Season to taste
with salt and pepper.
4 Spoon the stuffing into the trout

cavities, dividing it equally between
them. Place each trout on a piece of
greased foil and seal tightly to make
neat parcels (see Cook's tips).
5 Place the parcels on a cookie sheet
and cook in the oven 25-30 minutes
(see Cook's tips) until the fish
is cooked through and the flesh
flakes very easily when pierced with
a sharp knife.
6 Open up the foil parcels and
carefully transfer the trout to a
warmed serving plate. Garnish with
celery leaves and serve at once.

Cook's Notes

TIME
Preparation, including
making the stuffing,
takes 35 minutes. Cooking the
trout in the oven takes about
25-30 minutes.

SERVING IDEAS
Top the fish with pats
of herb butter if liked or
garnish with thin orange and
lemon slices or a sprinkling of
herbs. Serve with potatoes
boiled in their skins and oven-
baked tomatoes.

COOK'S TIPS
The trout may be pre-
pared in advance up to
the end of stage 4, then refrigerated up to 4 hours until ready
to cook.
   To brown the fish: Turn back
the foil for last 10 minutes.

VARIATION
Use fennel instead of
celery and use the
feathery leaves as a garnish.

● 505 calories per portion

Family fish pie

SERVES 4

1 lb cod or tilefish fillets
2 cups milk
1 small onion, quartered
2 bay leaves
4 cloves
6 whole black peppercorns
2 lb potatoes
salt
½ lb package frozen mixed
    vegetables
5 tablespoons butter or margarine
5 tablespoons milk
4 tablespoons chopped chives or
    finely chopped scallion tops
2 hard-boiled eggs, chopped
2 tablespoon chopped parsley
freshly ground black pepper
6 tablespoons all-purpose flour
1 tablespoon tomato paste
3 tomatoes, sliced to finish

1 Preheat the oven to 350°.

2 Put the fish in an ovenproof dish and cover with the milk. Add the onion quarters, bay leaves, cloves and peppercorns. Cover with foil or parchment paper and bake in the oven about 20 minutes until the fish flakes easily.

3 Meanwhile, cook the potatoes in boiling salted water 20 minutes until tender. Cook the frozen vegetables as directed on the package then drain.

4 When the fish is cooked, remove it from the dish and strain the cooking liquid into a cup or bowl. Increase the oven heat to 375°.

5 Drain the potatoes and mash with 2 tablespoons butter and the milk. Beat in the chives.

6 Flake the fish into a bowl, removing any skin and bones. Stir in the mixed vegetables, the hard-boiled eggs and the parsley. Season well with salt and pepper. Put the mixture in a large saucepan.

7 Melt the remaining 3 tablespoons butter gently in a separate saucepan and sprinkle in the flour. Stir over low heat 2 minutes until straw-colored, then remove from the heat and gradually stir in the reserved cooking liquid from the fish. Return to the heat, stir in the tomato paste and simmer, stirring

TIME
Preparing and cooking the fish and potatoes takes about 1 hour. Heating through the finished pie takes 20-30 minutes.

COOK'S TIP
This pie is a meal in itself, and is well worth the time it takes to prepare because you do not need to serve an accompanying vegetable with it.

ECONOMY
Any economical white fish may be used instead of cod.

SPECIAL OCCASION
Substitute a few frozen or canned shrimp, or canned mussels, for the mixed vegetables and mash the potatoes with light cream.

FREEZING
Make the pie without hard-boiled eggs and freeze after stage 9. Freeze up to 2 months. To serve: Thaw the pie overnight in the refrigerator then top with the tomatoes and give the pie slightly longer in the oven to heat through completely.

● 635 calories per portion

constantly until the sauce is thick and smooth.

8 Pour the sauce into the fish mixture and fold gently to mix over low heat until heated through. Taste and adjust seasoning.

9 Turn the fish mixture into a buttered ovenproof dish. Spoon the mashed potato evenly over the top,

level the surface and mark with a fork in a criss-cross pattern. ❋

10 Bake the fish in the oven 20-30 minutes until heated through. Arrange the sliced tomatoes on the top, then place the pie under a heated broiler 5 minutes, to brown the topping. Serve very hot, straight from the dish.

Salmon parcels

SERVES 4

4 × ½ lb salmon steaks, skinned and
    bones removed, thawed if frozen
    (see Buying guide)
3 tablespoons butter, softened
1 tablespoon finely chopped fresh
    parsley
½ teaspoon chopped fresh thyme, or
    ¼ teaspoon dried thyme
pinch of paprika
salt and freshly ground black
    pepper
2 sheets (17 oz package) frozen puff
    pastry, thawed
4 teaspoons lemon juice
little beaten egg, to glaze
4 lemon slices sprinkled with
    paprika, to garnish

1 Preheat the oven to 400°.
2 Put the butter in a small bowl with parsley, thyme and paprika. Season well with salt and pepper and beat with a wooden spoon until the herbs and spices are thoroughly blended with the butter.
3 Divide the pastry into 4 equal pieces. Roll each piece out on a lightly floured board into a circle about 8 inches in diameter, or large enough to enclose a salmon steak.
4 Spread each salmon steak with a quarter of prepared butter and place, buttered side up, on one-half of a pastry circle. Sprinkle the salmon steak with a little lemon juice and season lightly with salt and freshly ground black pepper.
5 Moisten edges of each pastry circle with water, then fold over to cover salmon and seal firmly to make neat parcels. ⚠ Make diagonal cuts on top and decorate with pastry trimming, if wished.
6 Dampen a cookie sheet and place the pastry parcels on it. Brush the parcels with beaten egg to glaze.
7 Bake just above center of the oven 20 minutes, then lower the heat to 350° and cook a further 15 minutes or until the pastry is well risen and golden brown. Serve the salmon parcels hot or cold, garnished with lemon slices dusted with paprika (see Serving ideas).

Cook's Notes

TIME
Preparation and cooking take about 1 hour.

BUYING GUIDE
Fresh salmon is at its best from May to July and many large supermarkets now sell trimmed steaks in their refrigerated cabinets. Frozen salmon steaks are available most of the year from large supermarkets and freezer centers.

! WATCHPOINT
Do not try to make too tight a parcel or it may break open during baking. But be sure to seal parcels firmly.

SERVING IDEAS
Serve hot with new potatoes, garden peas and dairy sour cream dressing
Serve cold with potato salad, sliced cucumber and lettuce salad and mayonnaise. Or, for picnics, wrap each parcel carefully in foil, then pack in a rigid container.

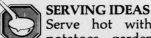

VARIATION
Omit the seasoned butter and spread each salmon steak with 1 teaspoon of dairy sour cream with chives before wrapping in pastry.

● 865 calories per portion

Tilefish thermidor

SERVES 6
1½ lb tilefish steaks
½ bay leaf
1 small carrot, sliced
½ small onion, sliced
4 black peppercorns (optional)
salt
½ cup butter or margarine
½ cup all-purpose flour
2½ cups milk
½ teaspoon dry mustard
pinch of cayenne
½ lb mushrooms, sliced
2 tablespoons dry sherry (optional)
⅓ cup grated Parmesan cheese
butter or margarine, for greasing
lemon slices, to garnish

1 Preheat the oven to 425°. Lightly grease an ovenproof baking dish.

2 Put the fish steaks in a wide shallow skillet in 1 layer, and scatter over the bay leaf, carrot, onion, peppercorns and salt. Add water to cover and bring to a boil. Lower the heat and cook gently until the fish flakes easily when tested with a fork, about 10 minutes. With a slotted spoon, or turner remove the fish carefully and keep warm.

3 Meanwhile, make the sauce: Melt ¼ cup butter in a small saucepan, sprinkle in the flour and stir over low heat 1-2 minutes until straw-colored. Remove from the heat and gradually stir in the milk. Return to the heat and simmer, stirring, until thick and smooth. Add the mustard powder, cayenne and salt to taste. Remove saucepan from the heat.

4 Melt the remaining butter in a skillet and cook the mushrooms about 3 minutes, stirring. Mix into the sauce with the sherry, if using.

5 Cut the fish into bite-sized pieces and carefully combine with the sauce. ✳

6 Pour the fish and sauce into the greased baking dish, sprinkle the Parmesan over the top and bake in the oven about 15 minutes until the top is golden brown and bubbling. Serve hot, straight from the dish, garnished with lemon.

Herby fish kabobs

SERVES 4
1½ lb boneless cod or tilefish steaks,
   skinned
2 tablespoons lemon juice
1 tablespoon vegetable oil
1 teaspoon Worcestershire sauce
1 tablespoon chopped mixed fresh
   herbs, or 1 teaspoon dried basil
good pinch of fresh chopped dill or
   dried chopped dillweed
salt and freshly ground black pepper
1 large green pepper, seeded
4 small tomatoes, halved
vegetable oil, for greasing

1 Cut the fish into 32 cubes and
place on a large plate. In a bowl mix
together the lemon juice, oil,
Worcestershire sauce and herbs.
Season well with salt and pepper
and pour over the fish. Leave to
stand for 5 minutes, turning the
cubes of fish in the marinade from
time to time.
2 Put the green pepper in a bowl
and cover with boiling water. Leave
to stand 5 minutes. Drain well, then
cut into chunky pieces big enough
to thread onto skewers.
3 Preheat the broiler to moderate.
Slide alternative pieces of fish and
green pepper onto 8 oiled skewers,
10 inches long. Complete each
skewer with a halved tomato.
4 Place the skewers in a broiler
pan and cook under the broiler 15-
20 minutes, turning as necessary
and basting with juices from the
pan [!] until the fish is cooked
through and lightly browned. Serve
at once.

Cook's Notes

TIME
Preparation 15 minutes,
cooking 15-20 minutes.

WATCHPOINT
The basting is necessary
to avoid the fish becom-
ing dry during cooking.

SERVING IDEAS
Prepare 4 portions of
creamed potato and
spread evenly over a shallow
flameproof serving dish. Sprinkle with a little grated cheese
and place under the hot broiler
until golden brown. Keep hot
below the broiler pan while
cooking the fish. Arrange the
fish kabobs on top of the
browned potato and garnish
with lemon slices and watercress. Serve with mayonnaise or
tartar sauce.

In summer, cook the fish on
skewers over the barbecue, and
serve on a bed of shredded and
chopped fresh salad ingredients.

VARIATIONS
Use raw cucumber in-
stead of blanched green
pepper. Add 1 tablespoon dry
vermouth to the marinade.

● 180 calories per portion

Smoked fish and spinach roll

SERVES 4

1 lb smoked fish fillets
1¼ cups milk
2 bay leaves
1 lemon
½ lb frozen spinach
4 eggs, separated
3 hard-boiled eggs, finely chopped
¼ nutmeg, freshly ground
salt and freshly ground black pepper
3 tablespoons butter or margarine
2 tablespoons all-purpose flour
vegetable oil, for greasing

TO GARNISH
few tomato slices (optional)
parsley sprigs (optional)

1 Preheat the oven 350°.

2 Put the fish in an ovenproof dish and add the milk and bay leaves. Grate the rind from the lemon and reserve. Cut 2 slices from the lemon and put them on top of the fish. Cover the surface of the dish with aluminum foil and bake in the oven 15-20 minutes, until the flesh flakes easily.

3 Cook the spinach according to package directions, then drain thoroughly in a strainer pressing out all excess moisture with the back of a spoon.

4 Grease a 13½ × 9½ × 1 inch baking pan and line it with waxed paper. Grease the paper well (see Cook's tip).

5 Lift the fish from the pan with a slotted spoon and reserve the cooking liquid. Flake the flesh into a bowl, discarding all skin and bones. Mash the flesh well with a fork, then stir in the lemon rind.

6 Increase the oven temperature to 400°.

7 Beat the egg yolks and stir them into the fish. Beat the egg whites until stiff and standing in peaks, then fold into the fish. Turn the mixture out of the bowl into the jelly roll pan and spread it evenly over the base with a knife. Place in the oven and bake 10-12 minutes until the mixture is firm to the touch and beginning to brown.

8 Place the drained spinach in a saucepan with 1 tablespoon butter.

Stir in the chopped egg, nutmeg and a little salt ⚠ and pepper to taste. Reserve, keeping warm.

9 Meanwhile, melt the remaining butter in a small saucepan, sprinkle in the flour and stir over low heat for 2 minutes until straw-colored. Remove from the heat and gradually strain in the reserved cooking liquid. Return to the heat and simmer, stirring, until thick and smooth. Keep warm.

10 Remove the fish from the oven and turn it out of the jelly roll pan

onto a clean sheet of waxed paper. Gently ease the fish away from the lining paper. ⚠

11 Spread the warm spinach mixture over the surface of the fish, then roll it up like a jelly roll, using the waxed paper to help you roll the fish. Slide the roll onto a warmed serving dish, join side down, and garnish the top with tomato slices and parsley sprigs, if liked. Cut a few slices off the roll and serve at once with the sauce passed separately.

Cook's Notes

TIME
This dish takes 1¼ hours to prepare and cook.

COOK'S TIP
To help avoid the fish mixture sticking to the aluminum foil during baking, brush the foil liberally with oil, or use a silicone paper or non-stick baking parchment, available from large supermarkets and hardware stores.

! WATCHPOINTS
Add salt sparingly because the smoked fish has a salty flavor.
If the foil needs a little coaxing to come away from the fish mixture — run a knife carefully between them.

● 405 calories per portion

Squid salad

SERVES 4

1½ lb squid (see Buying guide)
7 tablespoons olive oil
1 clove garlic, crushed
   (optional)
2 scallions, finely chopped
3 tomatoes, peeled, seeded and
   chopped
1 small green and 1 small red
   pepper, seeded and roughly
   chopped
¼ lb shelled shrimp, thawed and
   drained if frozen
juice of ½ lemon
salt and freshly ground black
   pepper

1 Clean the squid and slice the flesh thinly into rings.

Cook's Notes

TIME
Total preparation takes about 45 minutes, including cleaning the squid. Allow 1 hour chilling time.

SERVING IDEAS
Serve with potato salad and a salad of lettuce and cucumber. Accompany with chunks of French bread and butter, and a glass of dry white wine.

BUYING GUIDE
Many fishstores now sell squid and it is becoming increasingly popular, as it represents good value for money. Small squid (no more than 4 inches long) are the most tender.

Ready-prepared, skinned and cleaned squid is sometimes sold, but it is more expensive.

● 375 calories per portion

2 Heat 3 tablespoons of the oil in a skillet, add squid and garlic, if using, and cook, stirring often, about 10 minutes or until the squid is tender. Drain on paper towels and then set aside until the squid is completely cold.

3 Put the squid, scallions, tomatoes, peppers and shrimp into a serving dish. Blend the remaining oil with the lemon juice and season with salt and pepper. Pour the dressing over the squid salad, then, using two forks, gently toss until coated in dressing. Cover the salad and refrigerate 1 hour.

Seafood macaroni bake

SERVES 4

¾ lb fresh or frozen cod or halibut
    fillets, skinned (see Cook's
    tips)
2½ cups milk
1 lemon (see Preparation)
1 bay leaf
3 whole black peppercorns
salt
¼ cup butter or margarine
½ lb mushrooms, thinly sliced
½ lb elbow macaroni, boiled,
    drained and rinsed (see
    Watchpoint)
1 jar (about 5 oz) mussels, drained
6 tablespoons all-purpose flour
½ lb shelled shrimp (see Cook's
    tips).
pinch of freshly grated nutmeg
freshly ground black pepper
butter, for greasing
extra lemon slices and unshelled
    fresh shrimp, to garnish

1 Put the fish in a large skillet with a lid and pour in enough of the milk to just cover. Add 2 slices of lemon, the bay leaf, peppercorns and a good pinch of salt. Bring gradually to a boil, then cover and turn off the heat under the pan. Leave to stand 5 minutes, then remove the fish with a turner. Flake the flesh into 1½-inch pieces, discarding any bones. Strain all the cooking liquid and reserve.

2 Melt 1½ tablespoons butter in the rinsed-out skillet, add the sliced mushrooms and cook 2-3 minutes. Stir in the lemon juice and remove from heat.

3 Preheat the oven to 350°.

4 Put the macaroni into a greased large ovenproof dish with the fish, mushrooms and mussels. Stir carefully to mix, without breaking up the fish.

5 Melt the remaining butter in a saucepan, sprinkle in the flour and stir over low heat 1-2 minutes until straw-colored. Remove from the heat and gradually stir in rest of milk and reserved cooking liquid. Return to the heat and simmer, stirring, until thick and smooth. Remove from heat, stir in the shrimp, nutmeg and salt and pepper to taste, then pour evenly over macaroni and fish mixture. Cook in the oven 20 minutes.

6 Garnish with lemon slices and unshelled shrimp, if liked, and serve hot, straight from the dish.

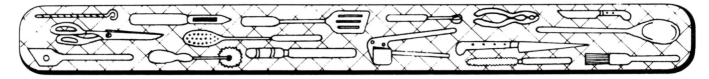

Mussel and shrimp pie

SERVES 4

1 sheet (½ of 17 oz package) frozen puff pastry, thawed
lightly beaten egg white, for glazing
lemon wedges, to garnish

FILLING
1 jar (about 1 lb) mussels in brine, drained
½ cup frozen shrimp, thawed
3 tablespoons butter or margarine
1 small onion, chopped
4 tablespoons all-purpose flour
1 cup less 2 tablespoons milk
⅓ cup dry white wine
salt and freshly ground black pepper
1 tablespoon chopped fresh parsley

1 On a lightly floured surface, roll out the pastry to 1½ inches larger all around than the top of an oven-proof pie dish. Invert the pie dish on the rolled out pastry and cut around the edge with a sharp knife to make a top. Then cut a strip the same width as the rim of the pie dish, from the outer edge.
2 Use the trimmings for decorations and refrigerate with the pastry.
3 Make the filling: Melt butter in a heavy-based saucepan, add the onion and cook gently about 5 minutes until it is soft and lightly colored. Sprinkle in the flour and stir over low heat 1-2 minutes. Remove from heat and gradually stir in milk. Return to heat and simmer, until thick.
4 Stir in the wine, mussels and shrimp and season to taste with salt and pepper. Simmer 2 minutes, then stir in the parsley. Pour the mixture into the pie dish and leave until cold (see Cook's tip).
5 Preheat the oven to 425°.
6 Dampen the rim of the dish with water. Place the pastry strip on the rim and press down lightly. Brush the strip with egg white, place pastry top on top of dish and press around the edge to seal. Trim any surplus pastry, then flute the edge.

Brush pastry decorations with egg white and stick onto pastry top. Brush top with egg white.
7 Bake in the oven 20 minutes, then lower oven temperature to 375° and bake a further 15 minutes until the pastry is puffed up and golden. Serve the pie hot (see Serving ideas) with lemon wedges.

Kedgeree special

SERVES 4-6

1 lb smoked fish fillets, thawed if
   frozen (see Did you know)
1¼ cups white or brown rice
2 tablespoons butter or margarine
1 onion, chopped
½ lb frozen mixed vegetables,
   thawed
½ cup plain yogurt
juice of ½ lemon
1 can (about 4 oz) smoked mussels,
   drained
¼ lb shelled shrimp, thawed if
   frozen
2 hard-boiled eggs roughly
   chopped
2 tablespoons finely chopped fresh
   parsley
salt and freshly ground black
   pepper
thick lemon wedges, to garnish
   (optional)

1 Put the smoked fish in a large saucepan, cover with cold water and bring to a boil. Lower the heat, cover the pan, and simmer gently 10 minutes, until the fish flakes

Cook's Notes

TIME
Preparation of fish and cooking take about 1 hour.

DID YOU KNOW
Smoking is actually one of the oldest methods of preserving food. Nowadays, however, the process is used more for the unique flavor it imparts.

There are 2 ways of smoking fish: Hot-smoking and cold-smoking. The first produces cooked fish that is ready to eat. Salmon, trout and mackerel can be hot-smoked. Cold-smoking is done at a much lower temperature and the fish needs to be cooked before eating (e.g. cod, haddock and kippers).

● 500 calories per portion

easily when pierced with a sharp knife.

2 Remove the fish with a slotted spoon, reserving the poaching liquid in the pan. Leave the fish until cool enough to handle, then flake the flesh into small pieces, discarding the skin and any remaining bones.

3 Make the fish poaching liquid up to 4½ cups with water. Bring to a boil, add the rice, cover and simmer 15 to 40 minutes until tender. Turn into a strainer and leave to drain.

4 Meanwhile, melt the butter in a separate large saucepan, add the onion and cook gently 5 minutes

until soft and lightly colored. Stir in the mixed vegetables and cover the pan. Continue cooking over low heat 5 minutes, shaking the pan from time to time.

5 Add the flaked fish and drained rice to the vegetables, with the yogurt, lemon juice, mussels, shrimp, hard-boiled eggs and parsley. Season to taste with salt and pepper. Taking care not to break up the ingredients, fork through lightly over gentle heat until well mixed and heated through.

6 Pile the kedgeree into a warmed serving dish, garnish the ends of the dish with lemon wedges, if liked and serve at once.

Seafood and orange kabobs

SERVES 4
1 lb tilefish fillet, skinned and cut into 1-inch cubes
½ lb unshelled shrimp
4 large oranges
watercress sprigs, to garnish

MARINADE
¼ cup vegetable oil
¼ cup lemon juice
½ teaspoon dried marjoram
1 large clove garlic, crushed (optional)
salt and freshly ground black pepper

1 Combine all the marinade ingredients in a large shallow dish. Add the tilefish cubes and shrimp and turn to coat (see Cook's tip). Leave to marinate 30 minutes at room temperature.
2 Meanwhile, peel and segment the

oranges over the marinade, so that any juice drips into it. Set the orange segments aside on a plate.
3 Line the broiler pan with a piece of foil. Preheat the broiler to moderate.
4 Remove the tilefish cubes and shrimp from the marinade and thread them and the orange segments onto 4 oiled long kabob skewers (see Preparation).

5 Place the kabobs on the broiler pan and brush well with some of the marinade. Broil about 5 minutes, then turn the kabobs and broil a further 5 minutes, brushing once or twice with more marinade. [!]
6 Arrange the cooked kabobs on a warmed large serving plate. Brush with marinade, garnish with watercress sprigs and serve at once.

VARIETY MEAT

Kidney and orange simmer

SERVES 4
1 lb lamb kidneys, skinned and chopped, with cores removed (see Buying guide)
1 tablespoon vegetable oil
1 onion, chopped
1 clove garlic, crushed (optional)
1¼ cups chicken broth
1 tablespoon white wine vinegar
pinch of dry mustard
pinch of cayenne
2 teaspoons chopped fresh tarragon
finely grated rind of 1 orange
1 tablespoon orange juice
¼ lb mushrooms, sliced
salt and freshly ground black pepper

TO GARNISH
1 tablespoon chopped fresh parsley
orange slices

1 Heat the oil in a large skillet with a top, add the onion and garlic, if using, and cook over moderate heat 1-2 minutes. Add the kidneys to the pan and cook a further 2-3 minutes, stirring all the time.
2 Stir the broth, vinegar, mustard, cayenne and tarragon into the pan, with the grated orange rind and juice. Add the mushrooms, stir well and season to taste with salt and pepper.
3 Bring to a boil, then lower the heat, cover the pan and simmer for 15 minutes until the kidneys are tender.
4 Transfer to a warmed serving dish, sprinkle with parsley and garnish with orange slices. Serve at once, piping hot.

Cook's Notes

TIME
Preparation takes 10 minutes, cooking about 20 minutes.

BUYING GUIDE
Kidneys go "off" very quickly and must be eaten the day they are bought. Frozen kidneys may be used but must be thawed completely before using.

SPECIAL OCCASION
Stir in 2 tablespoons light cream just before serving.

SERVING IDEAS
Serve with plain boiled white rice. This is a rich dish, which is best served with a simple green salad.

● 150 calories per portion

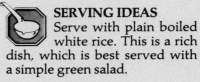

Kidney and pork medley

SERVES 4

4 lamb kidneys, halved and cores removed
½ lb lean pork fillet, cut into 1-inch cubes
2 tablespoons vegetable oil
1 onion, chopped
1 can (about 12 oz) tomatoes, peeled and quartered
3 tablespoons sweet red vermouth
½ teaspoon dried oregano
salt and freshly ground black pepper
⅔ cup plain yogurt

1 Heat the oil in a large saucepan, then add the onion and cook very gently 5 minutes until soft and lightly colored.
2 Add the pork to the pan and cook turning from time to time, 10 minutes until lightly browned.
3 Cut each kidney half into 4 pieces. Add to the pan and cook, stirring frequently, 5 minutes,
4 Stir in the tomatoes, vermouth and oregano, and season to taste with salt and pepper. Cover and cook 10 minutes, then remove the top and cook a further 5 minutes until the pork is tender when pierced with a sharp knife.
5 Remove from the heat, taste and adjust seasoning, then swirl in the yogurt. Turn into a warmed serving dish and serve at once.

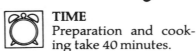

Liver loaf

SERVES 6

1 lb lamb liver, trimmed and sliced
1 tablespoon vegetable oil
½ lb pork sausagemeat
⅔ cup fresh white bread crumbs
1 large onion, grated
1 tablespoon Worcestershire sauce
2 small eggs, beaten
1 teaspoon dried thyme
salt and freshly ground black
    pepper

TOMATO SAUCE

1 tablespoon vegetable oil
1 small onion, finely chopped
1 clove garlic, crushed (optional)
1 can (about 14 oz) tomatoes
⅔ cup water
1 teaspoon tomato paste
½ teaspoon sugar
½ teaspoon dried sweet basil

TO GARNISH

1-2 tomatoes, sliced
parsley sprigs

1 Preheat the oven to 350°.
2 Grease an 8½ × 4½ × 2½ inch loaf pan. Heat the oil in a skillet, add the liver and cook over brisk heat until browned on all sides. Remove with a slotted spoon. Drain and cool on paper towels, then grind.
3 Mix in the ground liver with all the remaining ingredients, adding salt and pepper to taste. Make sure that all the ingredients are combined.
4 Spoon the mixture into the prepared pan pressing it down firmly. Cover with foil, then place the loaf pan in a roasting pan half filled with hot water.
5 Bake in the oven about 1 hour or until the juices run clear when the loaf is pierced in the center with a knife.
6 Meanwhile, make the tomato sauce: Heat the oil in a saucepan, add the onion and garlic (if using) and cook gently until soft. Add the remaining sauce ingredients with salt and pepper to taste, then bring to a boil, stirring constantly to break up the tomatoes.
7 Lower the heat, half cover with a top and simmer gently about 20 minutes, stirring from time to time.

Remove from the heat, leave to cool for a few minutes, then purée in a blender or work through a strainer. Return to the pan, taste and adjust seasoning, then simmer gently on top of the stove until cooked.
8 Remove the cooked liver loaf from the roasting pan, leave to stand 5 minutes, ⚠ then pour off any fat and juices from the pan.
9 Turn the loaf out onto a warmed serving platter then pour a little of the hot tomato sauce over the top (see Variation). Serve at once, with the remaining sauce passed separately in a gravyboat.

Cook's Notes

TIME
25 minutes preparation, plus about 1 hour baking. Allow an extra 5-10 minutes for turning out.

FREEZING
Leave until cold, then unmold, wrap in plastic wrap and overwrap in a freezer bag. Seal, label and freeze up to 3 months, Thaw in wrappings overnight in the refrigerator.

● 385 calories per portion

VARIATION
Use about ¼ cup instant mashed potato mix made according to package directions, to cover the loaf. Pipe it over, or use a fork to mark it decoratively. Garnish with tomatoes and parsley.

WATCHPOINT
The loaf must be left to stand in the pan for at least 5 minutes after cooking to allow the mixture to settle. If the loaf is turned out immediately it will be difficult to slice neatly.

Liver and bacon hotpot

SERVES 4

1 lb lamb, calves or pig liver, cut into 16 small slices
1 tablespoon vegetable oil
2 tablespoons butter or margarine
2 medium onions, sliced into thin rings
4 bacon slices
1 green apple, pared, cored and sliced
salt and freshly ground black pepper
few drops Worcestershire sauce
1¼ cups hot beef broth
1 teaspoon cornstarch

1 Preheat the oven to 350°.
2 Heat oil and butter in a large skillet and cook the liver slices over moderate heat until brown on both sides. Remove with a slotted spoon and transfer to a plate.
3 Lower the heat and cook the onion rings 5 to 10 minutes. Spread the onion evenly over the base of an ovenproof serving dish.
4 Sandwich ½ slice of bacon between 2 apple slices and 2 liver slices. Turn the liver sandwiches on their sides and arrange in rows on top of the onions. Sprinkle with salt and pepper.
5 Add a few drops of Worcestershire sauce to the broth. Blend the cornstarch to a paste in a small saucepan with a little cold water, then gradually stir in the broth. Bring to a boil stirring constantly, then lower the heat and simmer gently until thickened. Pour over the liver.
6 Cover and bake in the oven about 30 minutes. [!] Serve hot, straight from the serving dish.

Cook's Notes

TIME
An easy dish taking less than an hour.

COOK'S TIP
If using pig liver, soak it in a little milk for about an hour to remove the strong flavor. Drain and dry it before cooking.

! WATCHPOINT
Always use liver on the day it is bought, or within 24 hours if kept well wrapped in a refrigerator. Do not be tempted to leave the liver in the oven for longer than 30 minutes — overcooked liver is tough and leathery, and the apple slices will disintegrate.

SERVING IDEAS
Serve with creamy mashed potatoes — made extra special with a large knob of butter, a few tablespoons of cream and a beaten egg. Beat them well until soft and fluffy.

● 365 calories per portion

Liver cobbler

SERVES 4
¾ lb lamb liver, cut into bite-sized pieces
1¼ cups milk
1 tablespoon all-purpose flour
salt and freshly ground black pepper
¼ cup butter or margarine
6 streaky bacon slices, cut into thin strips
2 large onions, sliced
1 can (about 8 oz) tomatoes
½ teaspoon dried mixed herbs

TOPPING
2 cups self-rising flour
pinch of salt
¼ cup butter or margarine, diced
½ teaspoon dried mixed herbs
⅔ cup milk
a little milk, to glaze

1 Put the liver pieces in a shallow dish, pour over the milk and leave to marinate at room temperature 1 hour (see Cook's tip).
2 Remove the liver from the milk and dry on paper towels. Spread out the flour on a flat plate and season with salt and pepper. Dip the liver strips in the seasoned flour, turning them to coat thoroughly.
3 Melt the butter in a skillet add the bacon and onions and cook gently 5 minutes until soft. Remove with a slotted spoon and put in a round 9 inch diameter deep casserole dish.
4 Add the liver to the skillet and cook 1-2 minutes, turning the pieces to seal.
5 Gradually stir the milk into the pan and bring to a boil, stirring. Cook 2-3 minutes.
6 Using a slotted spoon, transfer the liver to the casserole with the onions and bacon. Pour in the milk and stir in the tomatoes with their juice and herbs. Season to taste with salt and pepper.
7 Preheat the oven to 425°.
8 Make the cobbler topping: Sift the flour and salt into a bowl. Add the butter and cut it into the flour with the fingertips until the mixture resembles fine bread crumbs. Add the herbs and gradually mix in the milk to form a soft dough.

9 Turn the dough onto a lightly floured surface and knead gently until smooth. Roll out to about ½-inch thickness. Cut into rounds, using a 2½-inch cutter.
10 Arrange the rounds of dough overlapping in a circle on top of the liver mixture in the casserole. Brush the dough topping with a little milk to glaze.
11 Bake the cobbler in the oven 20-25 minutes until the topping is well risen and golden brown. Serve at once, straight from the casserole.

Cook's Notes

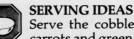

TIME
Preparation, including pre-cooking, takes about 30 minutes. Cooking in the oven takes 20-25 minutes, but allow 1 hour for the liver to marinate in the milk.

COOK'S TIP
Marinating the liver in milk makes it beautifully tender, and the milk also gives a deliciously creamy sauce.

VARIATION
Add 1 can (about 7½ oz) mushrooms drained, to the liver mixture.

SERVING IDEAS
Serve the cobbler with carrots and green beans. The topping is starchy, so there is no need for a potato accompaniment.

● 770 calories per portion

Chinese-style liver

SERVES 4-5

½ lb lamb or calves liver,
   trimmed and thinly sliced
   (see Preparation)
4 tablespoons vegetable oil
12 large scallions, cut
   into ½-inch lengths
   (see Preparation)
¼ lb mushrooms, sliced
2 tablespoons dry or medium
   sherry
1-2 tablespoons soy sauce
1 tablespoon wine vinegar
1 teaspoon sugar
½ teaspoon ground ginger
2 tablespoons cornstarch
2 cups water
thin carrot strips, to garnish

MARINADE

1 teaspoon salt
½ teaspoon freshly ground black
   pepper
4 teaspoons cornstarch
4 teaspoons dry sherry
4 teaspoons vegetable oil

1 To make the marinade: Mix the marinade ingredients together in a large bowl. Add the sliced liver, stir well and leave 10 minutes.

2 Heat 3 tablespoons oil in a large saucepan over moderate heat. Drain the liver and add to the pan. Stir-fry (see Did you know) over high heat 2-3 minutes only, until the liver is browned all over. Remove from the pan with a slotted spoon, and reserve.

3 Heat the remaining tablespoon oil in the pan, add the scallions and mushrooms and stir-fry over high heat 1 minute.

4 Remove the pan from the heat and stir in the sherry, soy sauce, wine vinegar, sugar and ginger.

5 In a large bowl, mix the cornstarch to a paste with a little of the water. Gradually stir in remaining water.

6 Return the pan to the heat and bring to a boil, scraping up all the sediment from the sides and bottom of the pan with a wooden spoon.

7 Stir in the cornstarch mixture, add the liver and bring to a boil, stirring. Simmer gently 2 minutes. Transfer the mixture to a warmed serving dish (see Serving ideas). Garnish with carrot strips and serve at once.

DELIGHTFUL DESSERTS

A delicious dessert can be the ideal and fitting end to an enjoyable meal. This section contains a tantilising choice of different types of hot and cold desserts, some of which are fruity, others light and creamy, plus the always popular ice creams and the more filling cakes, pies and flans. The recipes are ideal for the busy cook as they are easy to follow and quick to make. There is also a selection of extremely quick desserts for those occasions when time is really at a premium. The family's favorites are also included – those dishes like apple crumble and chocolate pudding that you are asked to make time and time again.

FRUITY DESSERTS

Pineapple bread

SERVES 4
4 medium eggs
3 tablespoons superfine sugar
1 can (13 oz) crushed pineapple
1 teaspoon ground allspice
6 tablespoons butter, melted
4 thick slices bread, crusts removed,
    cut into ½-inch cubes

TO DECORATE
4 rings canned pineapple
4 candied cherries

1 Put the eggs and sugar into a 1-quart ovenproof dish and beat lightly with a fork until the sugar has dissolved.
2 Stir in the crushed pineapple with its syrup, the allspice and butter. Fold in the bread cubes.
3 Press down the bread cubes lightly to level the surface, then cover the dish. Leave to soak in the refrigerator overnight.
4 The next day, when ready to cook, preheat the oven to 325°.
5 Uncover the dish and bake the dessert for 40-45 minutes or until the top is golden brown. Decorate the bread with pineapple rings and candied cherries.

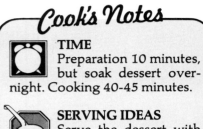

Chilled cherry compote

SERVES 4

2 cans (1 lb each) pitted cherries, drained, with syrup reserved (see Buying guide)

2-inch piece stick cinnamon, or large pinch of ground cinnamon

2-inch strip lemon rind (see Cook's tips)

1 teaspoon lemon juice

about 2 tablespoons red currant jelly, or to taste

2 teaspoons arrowroot

2 tablespoons water

TO SERVE

4 tablespoons plain yogurt

8 ratafias (see Did you know)

1 Put the cherries into a large bowl and set aside.

2 Pour the reserved cherry syrup into a medium heavy-bottomed saucepan. Add the cinnamon, lemon rind and juice and 2 tablespoons red currant jelly. Stir over low heat to dissolve the jelly, then bring to a boil and simmer for 1 minute. Remove from the heat.

3 Blend the arrowroot with the water, then stir into the syrup. Return to the heat and bring to a boil, stirring. Simmer for 1-2 minutes, stirring constantly, until the syrup thickens slightly and is clear. Taste and stir in more red currant jelly to sweeten, if necessary.

4 Strain the syrup through a nylon strainer over the cherries. Mix well, then leave to cool. Cover and refrigerate the compote for 1-2 hours (see Cook's tips).

5 To serve: Spoon the cherries and syrup into 4 individual glass dishes. Top each with 1 tablespoon yogurt and 2 ratafias. (Stand the ratafias upright and at a slight angle, like butterfly wings.)

Spiced banana dumplings

MAKES 16

1 package (17 oz) frozen puff pastry, thawed
4 large firm bananas
1-2 tablespoons lemon juice
1 cup superfine sugar
1 teaspoon ground allspice
1 egg, beaten

1 Preheat the oven to 425°. Brush a cookie sheet with water.
2 On a floured board, roll out sheets of pastry into rectangles, 20 × 10 inches. [!] Trim the edges with a knife to straighten them. Let the pastry rest for 5-10 minutes, then cut into 16 squares about 5 inches each.
3 Cut each banana into quarters crosswise and toss in lemon juice to prevent discoloration. Place 1 banana quarter diagonally in the center of each pastry square. Mix the sugar and allspice, then sprinkle 1 teaspoon over each banana piece.
4 Brush the edges of 1 dough square with some of the beaten egg, then wrap the banana (see Preparation). Repeat for each dumpling.
5 Brush the dumplings with the remaining beaten egg and sprinkle over the remaining spiced sugar. Arrange the dumplings on the cookie sheet, then bake in the oven for 15-20 minutes or until the pastry is puffed up and golden brown.
6 Carefully lift the dumplings with a spatula. Serve warm.

Cook's Notes

TIME
Preparation time 30 minutes, cooking time 15-20 minutes.

PREPARATION
Roll up the spiced banana dumplings as shown below:

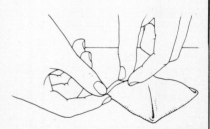

1 *Bring the 2 opposite corners of the pastry together across the length of the banana. Overlap the ends of the dough over the top of the banana and press firmly to seal.*

2 *Bring the other 2 corners to the center and overlap them on top of the first 2 corners. Press firmly to seal.*

3 *Fold over the open edges slightly and press to seal.*

WATCHPOINT
Do not stretch pastry or it will shrink during baking. To prevent this, let the dough rest for 5-10 minutes after rolling out.

● 170 calories each

168

Oranges in Cointreau

SERVES 4
8 small oranges
½ cup superfine sugar
¼ cup water
¼ cup Cointreau (see Buying guide)

1 Using a small sharp knife, pare the rind from oranges, then cut the rind into shreds (see Cook's tip).

2 Put the sugar and water in a large heavy-bottomed saucepan. Stir over very low heat until the sugar has dissolved, then bring to a boil.

3 Add the orange shreds and boil for 1 minute, then remove with a slotted spoon and pat them dry on paper towels. Transfer to a saucer, cover and refrigerate until required. Leave syrup to cool.

4 Pare the oranges with a sharp knife, removing every scrap of white pith and taking care not to damage the orange flesh.

5 Cut the oranges across into thin slices, then stack the slices (see Preparation), to reshape each orange. Spear together with cocktail sticks and carefully transfer to a serving dish.

6 Add the Cointreau to the cooled syrup, then pour over the oranges. Refrigerate for at least 1 hour, spooning the juice over the oranges from time to time.

7 To serve: Sprinkle the oranges with the chilled shreds and serve at once.

Mango spoon sweet

SERVES 4-6

2 ripe mangos, total weight about 1½ lb (see Preparation)
1 can (about 8 oz) pineapple rings in natural juice, drained with ½ cup juice reserved
¼ lb green grapes, halved and pitted
¼ lb black grapes, halved and pitted

1 Put the mangos in a blender with their juice and the measured pineapple juice. Work to a purée, then pour into a large bowl.
2 Cut each pineapple ring into 6 pieces and add to the mango purée together with the grapes. Cover and refrigerate for 30 minutes.
3 Spoon the mixture into 4-6 small dishes. Serve chilled.

Cook's Notes

TIME
Total preparation time (including chilling) is about 1 hour.

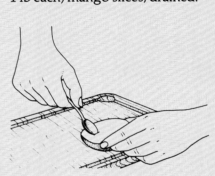

VARIATION
When fresh mangos are scarce, use 2 cans (about 1 lb each) mango slices, drained.

PREPARATION
Prepare each mango as follows:

1 *Using a sharp knife, make 2 cuts across the mango, each about ½ inch from the center, to make 3 sections. The middle section contains the large central pit.*

2 *Using a teaspoon, scoop out the flesh from both side sections. Save any juice and add to flesh. Remove skin from central section then cut flesh from pit.*

● 135 calories per portion

Plum and banana compote

SERVES 4
1 lb plums (see Buying guide)
1¼ cups water
⅓ cup sugar
**¼ cup red wine or orange
   juice**
2 small bananas
¼ cup flaked almonds

1 Wash and wipe the plums, then halve them and remove the pits (see Preparation).
2 Put the water and sugar into a heavy-bottomed saucepan and heat very gently until the sugar has dissolved, stirring occasionally. Bring the syrup slowly to a boil, without stirring, then boil for 2-3 minutes.
3 Carefully add the plums to the hot syrup; allow it to bubble up over them, then reduce the heat and cook the plums gently until they are just tender when pierced with a fine skewer. ⚠
4 Using a slotted spoon, transfer the plums to a serving bowl.
5 Add the wine to the syrup and boil rapidly until thickened and reduced by about half. Remove from the heat and allow to cool for a few minutes, then pour over the plums. Leave until completely cold.

6 Just before serving, peel the bananas and cut diagonally into slices. Fold gently into the plums, then sprinkle the flaked almonds over the top. Serve at once or the bananas will discolor.

Cook's Notes

TIME
About 30 minutes preparation, plus a few hours cooling time.

BUYING GUIDE
Plums vary in size, color, juiciness, and flavor according to variety. Dark, purple-skinned plums are best for this dish, but you can use another variety if preferred. If the fruit is very large, cut it into quarters rather than halves.

When fresh plums are scarce or out of season, substitute frozen plums and thaw them before cooking. Alternatively, use drained, canned plums and do not cook them; use the syrup and boil it with the red wine.

PREPARATION
To pit plums, cut around them along the indentation from the stalk end, then twist the halves in opposite directions to separate them.

Ease out the pit with your fingers or the tip of a knife.

WATCHPOINT
Cooking time depends on the variety of plum used. It is important that the plums retain their shape for this dish, so take care not to overcook them or they will become mushy and the appearance of the dessert will be spoiled.

● 175 calories per portion

Harvest dessert

SERVES 4-6

½ lb plums, halved and pitted
1 lb cooking apples, pared, cored
   and sliced
1 cup sugar
½ pint fresh or frozen
   blackberries
1 sponge layer (½ package) cut into
   thin strips
softly whipped cream, to serve
   (optional)

1 Put the plums, apples and the sugar into a heavy-bottomed saucepan. Cover and cook gently for 10 minutes, stirring occasionally. Add the blackberries and remaining sugar, replace the lid and cook for a further 10 minutes, until all the fruit is very soft.

2 Turn the fruit into a strainer set over a bowl to drain off juice.

3 Arrange a few slices of sponge cake in the base of a 1½-quart pudding mold. Cover the sponge with a layer of fruit and sprinkle over about 1 tablespoon of the drained juice. Continue making layers in this way ⚠ until all the sponge and fruit are used, finishing with a layer of cake (see Economy).

4 Stand the basin on a plate, then cover pudding with plastic wrap. Put a small plate or lid which fits just inside the rim of the basin on top of the pudding. Weight the plate down, then leave the pudding in the refrigerator overnight.

5 To serve: Run a round-bladed knife around the sides of the dessert to loosen it, then invert a serving plate on top. Hold the plate and basin firmly and invert, giving a sharp shake halfway around. Carefully lift off the basin. Serve the dessert chilled, with cream, if liked.

Gooseberry and apple amber

SERVES 4

½ pint gooseberries, topped and tailed if fresh, thawed if frozen
½ lb cooking apples, pared, quartered, cored and sliced
1 tablespoon water
2 tablespoons butter or margarine
2-4 tablespoons sugar
¼ cup fresh cake or bread crumbs (see Cook's tip)
2 eggs, separated
¼ teaspoon ground cloves or allspice
½ cup superfine sugar

1 Preheat the oven to 350°.
2 Put the gooseberries, apples, water and butter into a heavy-bottomed pan. Cover and cook over moderate heat for about 10 minutes, until tender. Remove from the heat and beat in the sugar to taste, the crumbs, egg yolks and cloves.

3 Turn the mixture into four 1-cup ramekins and level the surface. Stand the dishes on a cookie sheet and bake in the oven for about 15 minutes, until just set.

4 Meanwhile, in a clean, dry bowl beat the egg whites until standing in stiff peaks. Beat in the superfine sugar, 1 tablespoon at a time, beating the mixture thoroughly after each addition and continue beating until the meringue is stiff and glossy. Swirl or pipe the meringue over the gooseberry mixture in the ramekins. ☐
5 Lower the heat to 275°; then return the dish to the oven for about 30 minutes, until the meringue is crisp on the outside and lightly browned. Serve hot or cold.

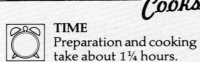

Cook's Notes

TIME
Preparation and cooking take about 1¼ hours.

VARIATIONS
For apple amber, omit the gooseberries and increase the apples to about 1 lb. Add the grated rind of 1 lemon with the cloves.

Use ground cinnamon or ground nutmeg instead of cloves.

COOK'S TIP
The crumbs absorb the fruit juices and prevent the mixture separating when the egg yolks are added.

WATCHPOINT
Take meringue right to the rim of each dish, otherwise it may "weep."

● 270 calories per portion

Fruit flambé

SERVES 6

1 can (about 1 lb) peach slices
1 can (about 1 lb) red cherries
1 can (about 14 oz) pear slices
1 can (about 8 oz) pineapple rings
¼ cup brandy or rum
¼ cup sweet butter (see Cook's tips)
¼ cup superfine sugar
1 teaspoon ground allspice
6 portions vanilla ice cream, to
   serve

1 Drain the fruits thoroughly, then blot dry on paper towels. Pit the cherries (see Preparation), and quarter the pineapple rings.
2 Pour the brandy into a cup and stand in a pan or bowl of hot water to warm through gently.
3 Melt the butter in a large, heavy-bottomed saucepan. Add the super-fine sugar and allspice and cook over low heat, stirring occasionally, until the sugar has dissolved. [!]

Cook's Notes

TIME
Preparation and cooking take about 20 minutes.

COOK'S TIPS
It is worth using sweet butter for this dish, otherwise the flavor will not be so good.
  Use a spatula and palette knife to turn the fruits gently so that they remain whole and do not break.

PREPARATION
A cherry pitter is useful when you have a lot of fruit to prepare. If you do not have one, slit the cherries down one side, then flick out the pits with the point of a knife.

WATCHPOINTS
Keep the heat low, so that the butter does not burn.
  Make sure that the excess liquid from the fruit has evaporated before you add the brandy—if the spirit is diluted too much it will not ignite.
  Hold the match just above the side of the pan and stand well back since the flames will shoot high for a few seconds and could be dangerous.

● 290 calories per portion

4 Add the fruit and turn carefully until evenly coated, (see Cook's tips), then cook gently to heat through.
5 Meanwhile, put the ice cream into 6 dessert bowls.
6 When the fruit is heated and all excess liquid has evaporated [!] turn off the heat. Pour the warmed brandy over the fruit and immediately set light to it. [!] Let the flames die completely, then spoon the fruit over the ice cream. Serve at once.

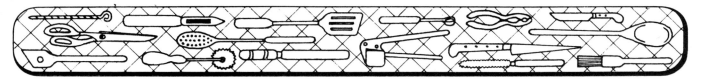

Gingered fruit cocktails

SERVES 4

3 unpared dessert apples, cored and sliced

2 large oranges, pared and chopped, with pits removed (see Preparation)

½ small melon, pared, seeded and cubed (see Buying guide)

2 tablespoons light brown sugar (optional)

⅔ cup dairy sour cream

8-10 gingernut cookies, coarsely crushed

1 Place the prepared fruit in a heavy-bottomed saucepan. Cover and cook gently until the apples and melon are tender but not mushy. Remove from the heat. Taste the fruit mixture and sweeten with brown sugar, if necessary, [!] then leave to cool.

2 Divide fruit mixture between 4 dessert glasses. Cover each glass with plastic wrap and refrigerate for 20-30 minutes.

3 To serve: Spoon the dairy sour cream over the fruit and sprinkle the crushed cookies on top. [!]

Fruit kabobs

SERVES 4
6 tablespoons butter
¼ teaspoon cinnamon
¼ cup white wine, or 3 tablespoons water mixed with 1 tablespoon lemon juice
2 tablespoons honey
2 dessert apples
1 large or 2 small ripe dessert pears
2 small bananas
8 whole dates, pitted
8 maraschino cherries
4 slices bread, crusts removed

1 Beat ¼ cup butter with the cinnamon and set aside.
2 Put the remaining butter into a small saucepan. Add the wine and honey and stir over low heat until melted and blended. Bring slowly to a boil and cook for 1-2 minutes until the sauce is slightly syrupy. Remove from the heat and set aside.

3 Pare and core the apples and pear, then cut into chunky pieces. Peel the bananas and cut each across into 8 pieces. Thread the apples, pears, bananas, dates and the maraschino cherries alternately on to eight 6-inch long skewers (see Preparation).
4 Lay foil over the broiler rack and preheat broiler to moderate.
5 Place the skewers on the foil, brush liberally with some of the sauce, then place as far as possible away from the heat and broil for 10 minutes, turning them over frequently and basting with more sauce.
6 Remove the kabobs and foil from the broiler pan and keep warm.
7 Increase the heat of the broiler to high, then toast the bread on 1 side only. Spread the untoasted side with the cinnamon butter, then broil until crisp at the edges.
8 Meanwhile, reheat any remaining sauce until bubbling. Place the toast on individual serving plates and place 2 kabobs on each. Pour over the hot sauce and serve at once.

Cook's Notes

TIME
These tasty kabobs take about 30 minutes to prepare and cook.

SERVING IDEAS
Whipped cream with a little sugar and liqueur added, if liked, can be served separately for "dunking" the fruit pieces.

Provide dessert forks and knives for eating. Use the prongs of the fork to slide the fruit off the skewers onto the hot toast.

PREPARATION
The apples and pears can be prepared up to 1 hour in advance and left to soak in the sauce to prevent them discoloring (Do not soak the bananas or they will become too soft to thread.)

If the apples have glossy unblemished skin, you can leave them unpared.

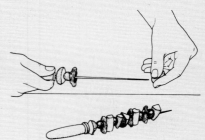

Threading alternate pieces of apple, pear and banana with whole dates and cherries.

VARIATIONS
Use canned fruit instead of fresh, as long as it is firm and well drained. Peaches, apricots and pears are the most suitable. Cooked and drained dried fruit such as apples, apricots and prunes can also be used. Candied cherries can replace maraschino cherries.

Finely chopped walnuts may be mixed with the butter and cinnamon to spread on the untoasted side of the bread.

● 360 calories per portion

Coupe Jacques

SERVES 6
¾ lb mixed fresh fruits, cut into
    small pieces (see Cook's tips)
3 tablespoons kirsch or orange-
    flavored liqueur (see Economy)
sugar, to taste
1 pint lemon sherbet
1 pint strawberry sherbet

1 Place 6 shallow bowls in the refrigerator to chill.
2 Put the fruits into a bowl and sprinkle with 2 tablespoons of the liqueur and add sugar to taste. Mix gently but thoroughly, then cover and refrigerate for at least 1 hour.
3 To serve: Put 1 scoop or large spoonful each of lemon and strawberry sherbet side by side in

each of the chilled bowls. Carefully drain off any excess juice from the mixed chilled fruits, then divide the fruits equally between

the bowls, spooning them in between and on top of the 2 sherbets. Sprinkle over the remaining liqueur and serve at once.

Cook's Notes

TIME
20-30 minutes preparation (depending on the fruits used), plus chilling time.

COOK'S TIP
You can use any combination of fruits. If using those which discolor when peeled (such as bananas or apples), turn the pieces in lemon juice before adding to the bowl.

ECONOMY
Use orange juice in place of the orange-flavored liqueur.

DID YOU KNOW
This is a classic French fruit salad which is always served with kirsch and lemon and strawberry sherbets. What is not known about the dish is who the original Jacques was!

VARIATIONS
Other flavored sherbets, or water ices, can be used. If you find the sherbets difficult to obtain, use vanilla and strawberry ice cream instead.

● 220 calories per portion

Grilled pineapple

SERVES 4
1 large pineapple
4 tablespoons dark brown sugar
2 tablespoons butter
¼ cup rum

1 Preheat the broiler to high.
2 Cut the pineapple lengthwise into quarters, slicing through the green crown. Cut out the core and loosen the flesh (see Preparation). Wrap foil around each crown.
3 Arrange the pineapple quarters in the broiler pan. Sprinkle each quarter with 1 tablespoon sugar and dot with butter. Broil for 4-5 minutes until the pineapple is heated through. Transfer to warmed dishes and remove the foil.
4 Put the rum into a small saucepan, heat it through gently, then remove from the heat and immediately set light to it. As soon as the flames subside, pour the rum over the pineapple together with any juice from the broiler pan. Serve at once.

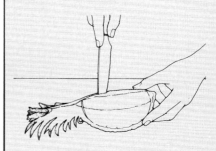
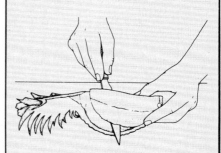

Date rice

SERVES 4
⅓ cup long grain rice
2½ cups milk
1 tablespoon butter or
    margarine
⅓ cup pressed dates, chopped (see
    Buying guide)
grated rind of 1 orange
melted butter, for greasing

1 Preheat the oven to 300°. Brush the inside of 1-quart ovenproof dish with melted butter.
2 Put the rice, milk and butter into a saucepan. Bring just to boiling point, then remove from the heat. Stir in the dates and orange rind. Pour into the prepared ovenproof dish and place the dish onto a cookie sheet.
3 Bake in oven for about 1 ½ hours, or until the rice is tender and most of the milk has been absorbed. Serve hot (see Serving ideas).

Cook's Notes

TIME
Preparation 20 minutes, cooking time 2 hours.

ECONOMY
If you are using the oven preheated to 325° for a main dish, the pudding may be baked on the bottom shelf.

VARIATIONS
Use other dried fruits, such as raisins or currants in place of some or all of the dates. For added flavor, sprinkle a little nutmeg over the top.

BUYING GUIDE
Buy dates that are already pitted — available from most supermarkets.

SERVING IDEAS
Serve hot, topped with chilled fresh orange segments, or drained canned mandarins.

COOK'S TIP
Heating the milk and rice first helps to keep baking time to a minimum.

● 220 calories per portion

CAKES, PIES AND FLANS

Ginger cream refrigerator cake

MAKES 8 SLICES
1 oblong ginger cake (see Buying guide)
1¼ cups heavy cream
¼ cup ginger marmalade
1 tablespoon Advocaat (optional)
candied fruit slices, to decorate

1 Remove the cake from its paper wrapper. Scrape off the remnants of cake sticking to the wrapper with a round-bladed knife, then crumble them between your fingers and reserve for decoration, if liked.
2 Cut the cake vertically into 4 equal slices, as shown in photograph.
3 Beat the cream until thick, then fold in the marmalade and Advocaat, if using. Sandwich the cake back together with about half of the cream mixture, then place on a narrow serving dish.

4 Spread the remaining cream mixture all over the cake to cover it completely. ✳
5 Decorate the top with candied fruit slices and sprinkle with the reserved cake crumbs, if using. Refrigerate the cake for 1-2 hours before serving.

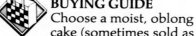

TIME
20 minutes preparation, plus 1-2 hours chilling.

BUYING GUIDE
Choose a moist, oblong cake (sometimes sold as "Jamaica" cake).

FREEZING
Make the cake up to the end of stage 4, assembling it on a freezer tray. Open freeze until solid, then place carefully in a rigid container. Seal, label and store in the freezer for up to 3 months. To serve: Remove from container and place on a serving dish; thaw at room temperature for 3 hours, then decorate.

VARIATIONS
Use an orange- or lemon-flavored cake and add orange or lemon jelly marmalade to the whipped cream. Drained mandarin segments or fresh orange slices can be used to decorate the top of the cake, if liked.

DID YOU KNOW
Advocaat is a thick and creamy, yellow Dutch liqueur; it is based on brandy and thickened with egg yolks and sugar.

● 335 calories per slice

Chocolate éclairs

MAKES 8

1 package (4 oz) choux pastry mix
(see Buying guide)
1 cup tepid water
vegetable oil and flour, for cookie
sheet

FILLING AND ICING
⅔ cup heavy cream
2 drops vanilla
1 tablespoon superfine sugar
2 squares (2 oz) semi-sweet
chocolate, broken into pieces
knob of butter
2-3 tablespoons water
1 cup confectioners' sugar

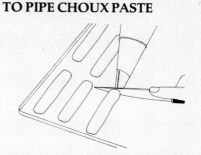
1 Preheat the oven to 400°. Prepare a large cookie sheet (see Preparation).
2 Put the pastry mix into a small bowl, add the water and beat with a rotary or hand-held electric mixer for 4 minutes. Put paste in pastry bag fitted with a ¾-inch plain nozzle, and pipe onto prepared cookie sheet (see Preparation).
3 Bake in the oven for 40 minutes, until puffed and golden. With a spatula, ease the éclairs off the cookie sheet and transfer to a wire rack. Split each one lengthwise in half with a sharp knife, then scrape out and discard any uncooked pastry from the inside with a teaspoon. Leave to cool completely.
4 Make the filling: Beat the cream until beginning to thicken, then add vanilla and superfine sugar and continue beating until thick but not stiff. Pipe or spoon the cream into the bottom half of each éclair, then replace the tops.
5 Put the chocolate, butter and 1 tablespoon water in a flameproof bowl set over a pan of hot water. Leave, stirring occasionally, until the chocolate has melted. Remove the bowl from the pan and beat in the sifted confectioners' sugar, a little at a time. If necessary, beat in 1-2 more tablespoons water to thin the icing.
6 Spoon or spread the icing over the tops of the éclairs, then leave in a cool place to set.

Cherry cream slices

MAKES 8 SLICES
**2 sheets (1 17 oz package) frozen
   puff pastry, thawed**

FILLING
**1 can (about 1 lb) pitted black
   cherries in syrup**
2 tablespoons cornstarch
2 tablespoons water
1¼ cups heavy cream
3 drops vanilla
2 tablespoons sugar

ICING
1½ cups confectioners' sugar, sifted
2-3 tablespoons warm water
**1 square (1 oz) semi-sweet
   chocolate, melted**

1 Preheat the oven to 450°. Dampen a large cookie sheet with water. Firmly roll out each sheet of puff pastry to a rectangle, about 14 × 6 inches. ⚠ Place on the prepared cookie sheet and prick well with a fork. Bake in the oven for 15 minutes, turning the pieces around halfway through the cooking time so that they become evenly browned. Transfer to a wire rack and leave to cool completely.
2 Meanwhile, make the filling:

Place the cherries, with their syrup, in a small saucepan and bring slowly to simmering point. Blend the cornstarch to a smooth paste with the water. Remove the pan from the heat and stir in the cornstarch mixture. Return to low heat and bring back to a boil, stirring constantly, then set aside to cool completely. ⚠
3 Make the icing: Blend the confectioners' sugar with enough warm water to give a thick coating consistency.
4 Turn one layer of pastry over and spread the icing over the surface (see Cook's tips).
5 Beat the cream until it begins to thicken; add the vanilla and sugar. Continue beating until the cream stands in stiff peaks.
6 Assemble the dessert: Spread the cold cherry mixture over the other layer of pastry, then cover with the whipped cream.
7 Put the iced layer of pastry on top of the cream, iced side up, then lift onto a wooden board and place in the refrigerator for 30 minutes, or the freezer for 20 minutes.
8 With a sharp serrated knife, and a sawing motion, carefully cut the pastry into 6 slices. Using a teaspoon, drizzle melted chocolate over the top of each slice in a zig-zag pattern. Return to the refrigerator for 10 minutes to set before serving.

Cook's Notes

TIME
About 4 hours total preparation and cooking time, including cooling the cherry mixture which can take as long as 2 hours.

WATCHPOINTS
When rolling the pastry, keep a good rectangular shape with neat edges.
Before filling, insure that the cherry mixture and the pastry are well cooled or the cream will melt. To speed up cooling of any mixture, place in a cool container and stand on a wire rack so the air can circulate freely.

COOK'S TIPS
Icing the flat underside of the layer, before turning it over, gives a better finished appearance.
Place the dessert in the refrigerator or freezer for a short time makes it easier to slice.

STORAGE
Keep covered in a large plastic container in the refrigerator for up to 2 days.

● 735 calories per slice

Frozen macaroon mold

SERVES 6-8

⅔ cup heavy cream
1 quart soft-scoop vanilla ice cream
  (see Buying guide)
¼ cup orange juice
¼ lb macaroons, crushed
¼ cup whole almonds, split and
  lightly toasted

SAUCE
¾ pint raspberries, thawed if
  frozen
¼ cup red currant jelly
1 teaspoon cornstarch
2 tablespoons water

1 Beat the cream until thick. Add the ice cream and orange juice and beat gently together until evenly combined. Quickly fold in the macaroons. Turn the mixture immediately into a 1½-quart freezerproof mold and level the surface. Cover tightly and freeze for at least 8 hours or overnight, until firm (see Cook's tip).

2 When the mixture is firm, make the sauce: Reserve some of the whole raspberries for decoration; sieve the remainder, then pour the purée into a saucepan and add the red currant jelly. Blend the cornstarch to a smooth paste with the water and stir into the pan. Bring slowly to a boil, stirring, and simmer for 2-3 minutes. Pour the sauce into a jug and cool. Cover and refrigerate. ✳

3 Turn the frozen mixture out of the mold onto a chilled, deep serving plate. ⚠ Pour the sauce over the dessert and spike with the almonds.

Cook's Notes

TIME
20 minutes preparation (including turning out and decorating), plus at least 8 hours freezing.

WATCHPOINT
When the dessert is turned out of the mold the mixture melts slightly, so have paper towels ready to mop up liquid from the base.

BUYING GUIDE
Use soft-scoop ice cream for this dessert, not the block variety which is too hard to blend in easily.

COOK'S TIP
You can make this dessert in the freezer compartment of the refrigerator. Turn the refrigerator to its coldest setting at least 1 hour beforehand, and pour the ice cream and macaroon mixture into a well-chilled metal mold.

FREEZING
The ice cream and macaroon mixture can be stored in the freezer for up to 3 months. Freeze the sauce separately; thaw before use.

● 400 calories per portion

Mocha meringue

SERVES 8
3 large egg whites
¾ cup light brown sugar,
    sifted
1 teaspoon instant coffee powder
vegetable oil, for greasing

FILLING
4 squares (4 oz) semi-sweet
    chocolate, broken into squares
¼ cup water
1¼ cups heavy cream
2 teaspoons instant coffee powder
grated chocolate, to finish

1 Preheat the oven to 300°. Line 3 cookie sheets with non-stick parchment paper or waxed paper (see Cook's tips). Mark each piece with a 7-inch circle. If using waxed paper, lightly brush each circle with oil.
2 Put the egg whites into a dry, grease-free large bowl. Beat until stiff and white and standing in firm peaks.
3 Add the sugar, 1 tablespoon at a time, beating well after each addition so that the meringue is firm and glossy. Beat in the instant coffee powder.

4 Spread the meringue mixture evenly over the marked circles on the cookie sheet linings. Bake in the oven for 1½ hours or until crisp and dry in the center. Swap the top and bottom sheets after 45 minutes to insure even cooking. Set aside to cool, then peel off lining paper.
5 Prepare the filling: Put the chocolate and water into a small bowl over a pan of simmering water and heat until the chocolate has melted. Stir, then set aside to cool for about 10 minutes or until the chocolate begins to thicken.
6 Beat the cream until stiff, then put half of it into another bowl. Stir the chocolate mixture into one half and the instant coffee powder into the other half.

7 To finish: Put 1 meringue round onto a serving plate and spread it with half the coffee cream. ⚠ Cover with another meringue round and spread with half the chocolate cream. Cover with the third meringue round. Spread the remaining coffee cream over the top and mark decoratively with a fork.
8 Lightly beat the remaining chocolate cream until stiff. Put the cream into a pastry bag fitted with a small nozzle. Pipe 8 rosettes around the edge of the cake. Sprinkle the rosettes with a little grated chocolate. Serve as soon as possible, or within 2 hours if kept in the refrigerator, otherwise the mocha meringue will lose its fresh crisp appearance.

Cook's Notes

TIME
Preparation time 20 minutes, cooking time 1½ hours. Allow another 15 minutes for decoration.

COOK'S TIPS
If you do not have 3 cookie sheets, use large flan dishes, or put 2 meringue rounds on 1 large sheet.
    If possible, use an electric mixer to beat the meringue.

WATCHPOINT
The cooked meringue is very brittle, so it must be handled with a great deal of care at this stage otherwise it may crack badly or break.

VARIATION
Stir ¼ lb thick fruit purée into the cream in place of the chocolate.

● 295 calories per portion

Chocolate cheesecake

SERVES 6-8
1¾ cups chocolate cookie crumbs
2 tablespoons sugar
6 tablespoons melted butter

FILLING
1 cup cottage cheese
½ lb cream cheese, softened
⅔ cup sugar
1 teaspoon vanilla
1 envelope unflavored gelatin
1 cup heavy cream
2 egg whites
1 bar (4 oz) cooking chocolate
1 tablespoon butter or margarine
2 tablespoons milk

1 Preheat oven to 350°. Mix crumbs, 2 tablespoons sugar and melted butter; press firmly onto bottom and up sides of greased 9-inch springform pan. Bake 10-12 minutes. Cool completely.
2 Whirl cottage cheese in blender until smooth; add cream cheese; blend until well combined. Pour into mixing bowl; stir in ⅔ cup sugar and vanilla.
3 Sprinkle gelatin over crean in small saucepan; place over low heat.

Cook's Notes

TIME
20 minutes preparation. Allow 30 minutes for chilling the cookie crust and 3 hours for the cheesecake filling to set.

FREEZING
Once the cheesecake has set, open freeze until solid, then remove from the pan and wrap in plastic wrap or foil. Store for up to 1 month. To serve, unwrap and then thaw overnight in the refrigerator. Decorate the top with fruit or chocolate just before serving.

WATCHPOINT
When swirling the chocolate into the cheese take the skewer right down the bottom to give a marble effect right through.

COOK'S TIP
To crush the bourbon cookies, put them whole into a strong plastic bag, and then roll them firmly with a rolling pin.

SERVING IDEAS
If liked, decorate the edge of the cheesecake with drained mandarin segments and dot with chocolate sprinkles or strands. Instead of fruit sprinkle coarsely grated chocolate around the edge.

● 635 calories per portion

Heat, stirring constantly, until gelatin is dissolved; cool. Blend into cheese mixture gradually.
4 Beat egg whites until stiff. Fold into cheese mixture. Refrigerate until mixture is thickened and mounds when dropped from a spoon.
5 Heat chocolate, butter and milk in small saucepan over low heat, stirring until smooth. then cool.

6 Measure 1 cup cheese mixture into separate bowl. Stir in melted chocolate mixture until blended.
7 Pour remaining cheese mixture over cheesecake; swirl with small flat-bladed knife to create marbled effect. Chill 4 hours until set.
8 To serve, run knife round edge of cake; remove side of pan carefully. Slide cake onto plate.

Spicy apple crunch

SERVES 4

1½ lb green apples (see Buying guide)
1 tablespoon light brown sugar
1 teaspoon cinnamon
2 tablespoons cold water
butter, for greasing

TOPPING
1 cup rolled oats
¼ cup light brown sugar
¼ cup whole wheat flour
¼ teaspoon salt
3 tablespoons butter or margarine, melted

1 Preheat the oven to 375°.
2 Grease a shallow 1¾-quart oven-proof dish thoroughly with butter (see Cook's tips). Pare, quarter and core the apples, then slice them thinly. Mix the sugar with the cinnamon. Layer the apple slices in the dish, sprinkling the spiced sugar

mixture in between. Sprinkle over the water.
3 Make the topping: Mix the oats, sugar, flour and salt in a bowl. Stir in the melted butter with a knife until thoroughly mixed.

4 Sprinkle the topping evenly over the apples. Bake in the oven for 50-60 minutes, until the apples are very tender and the topping is crisp and browned. Serve hot or warm, straight from the dish.

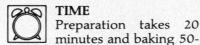

Cook's Notes

TIME
Preparation takes 20 minutes and baking 50-60 minutes.

SERVING IDEAS
This dessert is delicious served hot or warm with vanilla ice cream, chilled dairy sour cream or plain yogurt. It is also good cold.

VARIATIONS
You can use plain white flour instead of whole wheat flour, if preferred. Gooseberries (topped and tailed) or halved and pitted plums can replace the apples, but they will need an extra tablespoon of sugar; alternatively, you could use a mixture of apples and blackberries.

BUYING GUIDE
The best type of cooking apples to use are Winesaps, which reduce to a soft pulp when cooked.

COOK'S TIPS
This dessert is served straight from the dish, so choose an attractive one to bake it in. You can make the dish ahead and reheat it, if liked, in the oven at 325° for about 30 minutes.

● 335 calories per portion

Redcurrant jelly tart

MAKES 10 SLICES
1 lb red currant jelly
⅔ cup butter, softened
⅔ cup superfine sugar
few drops of vanilla
1 egg, lightly beaten
⅔ cup ground almonds
1½ cups all-purpose flour, sifted
confectioners' sugar, for dredging
lightly whipped cream, to serve
extra softened butter, for greasing

1 Preheat the oven to 350°. Butter an 8-inch springform cake pan (see Cook's tips).
2 Beat the butter and superfine sugar together until very pale and fluffy, then beat in the vanilla. Add the egg, a little at a time, beating thoroughly after each addition. Using a wooden spoon, gradually work in the almonds and flour.

3 Draw the mixture into a ball with your fingers, turn out onto a lightly floured surface and knead briefly until smooth (see Cook's tips).
4 Reserve one-quarter of the dough in a cool place. With your hand, gently press the remaining dough over the base and 1½ inches of the way up the sides of the prepared pan. Neaten the edges.
5 Spread the jelly evenly in the pastry case.
6 On a lightly floured surface, roll out the reserved dough to a 8½ × 2 inch strip. Trim edges with a sharp knife, then cut lengthwise into 6 narrow strips.
7 Dampen the ends of the pastry strips, then arrange over the jelly in a lattice pattern. Press the ends against the pastry edge to seal, then flute the rim of the pastry. Bake in the oven for 45 minutes, or until the pastry is cooked and browned.
8 Sift confectioners' sugar over the top of the hot tart, if liked. Leave to cool completely, then remove from the pan and transfer to a serving plate.

American chocolate pie

MAKES 6-8 SLICES
⅓ lb gingernut cookies, finely crushed
¼ cup butter or margarine, melted
butter or margarine, for greasing

FILLING AND TOPPING
1¼ cups milk
4 squares (4 oz) semi-sweet chocolate, broken into pieces
½ cup superfine sugar
3 tablespoons all-purpose flour
¼ cup butter or margarine
2 large egg yolks, lightly beaten
⅔ cup heavy cream
1 piece drained stem ginger, finely chopped, to decorate (optional)

1 Grease a 7-8 inch loose-based flan dish. Mix the finely crushed cookies with the melted butter until evenly coated.

2 Spoon the crumbs into the greased dish and press evenly over the base and up the sides with the back of a metal spoon (see Cook's tip). Cover and refrigerate for 30 minutes.

3 Meanwhile, make the chocolate filling: Put the milk and broken chocolate into a saucepan and heat gently, stirring frequently, until the chocolate has melted. [!] Remove from the heat.

4 Combine the sugar, flour, butter and beaten egg yolks in a bowl and mix together thoroughly with a fork. Stir in the hot chocolate milk, mixing well.

5 Return the mixture to the pan and bring slowly to a boil, stirring constantly. Reduce the heat and cook, still stirring, for about 5 minutes until the mixture is very thick and smooth.

6 Remove the pan from the heat and let the mixture cool for 5 minutes before pouring it into the cookie-lined dish. Leave for about 30 minutes until the chocolate filling is cold and set.

7 Carefully remove the pie from the dish and place on a serving plate. Beat the cream until thick, then spread over the chocolate filling. Decorate with the stem ginger, if liked. Refrigerate until required.

Cook's Notes

TIME
Preparation takes about 1 hour and setting about 30 minutes.

COOK'S TIP
For a really smooth finish, work an empty jam jar over the base and sides of the cookie case.

WATCHPOINT
Be sure to use a heavy-bottomed saucepan to avoid scorching the mixture.

VARIATIONS
For a richer chocolate flavor, use chocolate wafer cookies instead of gingernuts, and sprinkle the top with grated chocolate or orange rind rather than ginger. If preferred, a baked pie crust pastry case can be used instead of cookie crust — use ⅓ lb prepared pastry.

● 570 calories per slice

Nectarine tart

MAKES 6 SLICES
¼ lb cream cheese
   (see Cook's tip)
1 cup all-purpose flour, sifted
1 tablespoon superfine sugar

FILLING
4 nectarines
1¼ cups water
¼ cup sugar
1 tablespoon lemon juice
¼ cup red currant jelly or strained
   apricot jam, for glazing

1 Make the pastry: Beat the cream cheese with a wooden spoon until soft and smooth. Add the flour and sugar and continue beating until the mixture is evenly crumbly. Keep drawing the mixture together until it forms a soft dough.

2 Turn the dough out onto a lightly floured surface and knead briefly; wrap in plastic wrap and refrigerate for 1 hour (and up to 24 hours).

3 Preheat the oven to 400°.

4 On a lightly floured surface, roll out the pastry and use to line a loose-based, 8-inch fluted flan dish. Prick the base with a fork, then line with a large circle of waxed paper or foil and weight down with dried beans.

5 Bake in the oven for 10 minutes. Remove paper or foil and dried beans and return to the oven for a further 10-15 minutes until pastry is set and lightly colored. Remove the sides of the dish, slide the pastry case onto a wire rack and leave to cool completely.

6 Meanwhile, prepare the filling: Put the water into a heavy-bottomed saucepan with the sugar and lemon juice. Stir over low heat until the sugar has dissolved, then bring to a boil, without stirring, and simmer for 1-2 minutes.

7 Halve and pit the nectarines and lower into the syrup with a slotted spoon. Cover and poach gently for about 5 minutes until just tender. ⚠ Remove the pan from the heat. Lift nectarines out of the syrup with the slotted spoon and leave to cool completely. Reserve 1 tablespoon of syrup in the pan.

8 Assemble the tart: Place the pastry case on a serving plate. Peel nectarines, if liked, then cut into thick slices or leave the halves intact and arrange them carefully in the pastry case.

9 Add jelly or jam to reserved syrup and stir well over low heat until melted. Allow the glaze to cool until beginning to thicken, then brush over the nectarines. Leave to set before serving.

Cook's Notes

TIME
10-15 minutes, plus chilling the pastry, then 1¼ hours, plus setting.

WATCHPOINT
Do not overcook the nectarines: They must keep their shape or the whole look of the tart will be spoiled.

VARIATION
Firm peaches can be used instead. Do not use canned fruit for this recipe.

COOK'S TIP
Pastry made with cream cheese is richer and more crumbly than shortcrust. There are also fewer calories. It has a delicious flavor which goes beautifully with fresh nectarines, but plain pie crust can be used instead, if you prefer. When using ordinary shortcrust pastry, you will need ⅓ lb dough for an 8-inch fluted flan dish.

● 245 calories per slice

Raised plum pie

SERVES 6
1 package (11 oz) pie crust sticks,
prepared
milk and superfine sugar, for glazing

FILLING
1 tablespoon cornstarch
1 teaspoon cinnamon
¾ cup superfine sugar
1½ lb ripe plums (see Buying guide),
halved and pitted
pouring cream or custard, to serve

1 Preheat the oven to 375°.
2 On a lightly floured surface, roll out just under half of the pastry and use to line an 8-inch pie plate.
3 Place the cornstarch, cinnamon and sugar in a strong, large plastic bag, then add the plums and shake well until the fruit is coated with the sugar mixture.
4 Turn the plum and sugar mixture into the pastry-lined plate, mounding it slightly in the center. Brush the pastry edges with water.
5 On a lightly floured surface, roll out the remaining pastry to a 9½-inch circle and use to cover the pie. Brush the pastry lid with milk, then sprinkle with superfine sugar. Pierce the top with a skewer or fork to make a steam vent.
6 Bake in the oven for about 45 minutes, until the pastry is golden brown. Serve hot or warm.

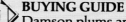
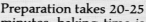

Raisin pie

MAKES 4-6 SLICES
1½ cups all-purpose flour
pinch of salt
2 tablespoons superfine sugar
6 tablespoons butter or margarine,
    diced
1 egg, beaten
a little milk, for brushing
superfine sugar, for sifting

FILLING
2 cups seedless raisins
grated rind and juice of 1 lemon
½ teaspoon cinnamon
¼ cup sugar
⅔ cup water
2 teaspoons cornstarch
2 teaspoons water

1 Sift the flour with the salt and sugar into a bowl. Add the diced butter and cut it into the flour until the mixture resembles fine bread crumbs. Add the beaten egg and mix to a stiff dough. Wrap in plastic wrap or foil and refrigerate.
2 Preheat the oven to 425°.
3 Prepare the filling: Put the raisins, lemon rind and juice, cinnamon, sugar and water into a saucepan and cook gently for 5 minutes. Mix the cornstarch to a smooth paste with the water, then stir into the raisin mixture. Bring to a boil, stirring all the time. Remove from the heat and leave to cool completely.
4 Cut off one-third of the pastry and set it aside. Roll out the remaining pastry and use to line an 8-inch loose-bottomed fluted flan dish or a flan ring set on a cookie sheet.
5 Spoon the cold raisin filling into the pastry-lined dish. [!] Roll out the reserved piece of pastry to a round large enough to cover the pie. Dampen the pastry rim with water, then place the pastry lid on top and press the edges together to seal. Brush the top of the pie with milk, then prick it with a fork. ✳
6 Bake the pie in the oven for 25-30 minutes. Remove the sides of the dish or the flan ring and return the pie to the oven for a further 5 minutes to brown the sides. Remove the pie from the oven and immediately sift over superfine sugar (see Serving ideas).

Cook's Notes

 TIME
40 minutes preparation, plus 30-35 minutes baking.

 WATCHPOINT
Make sure that the raisin filling is quite cold before it is put into the pastry-lined dish. If hot filling is put into raw pastry it will make the fat in the pastry melt and thus cause the pastry base to become soggy.

FREEZING
Prepare the pie up to the end of stage 5. Open freeze, then remove from the dish, or ring, and wrap in foil. Return to the freezer and store for up to 3 months. To serve: Unwrap and replace in the flan dish or ring; bake from frozen, allowing an extra 10 minutes.

SERVING IDEAS
This pie can be served hot, warm or cold, with vanilla ice cream, custard, whipped cream or plain yogurt.

STORAGE
The pastry and filling can be prepared and stored separately in the refrigerator for 2-3 days.

● 650 calories per slice

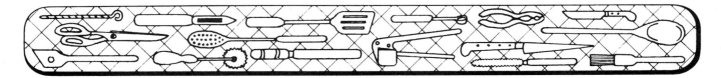

Frangipani tart

MAKES 6 SLICES
1 sheet (½ 17 oz package) frozen puff
pastry, thawed
6 canned apricot halves, drained and
finely chopped
½ teaspoon finely grated orange
rind
½ cup soft tub margarine
½ cup superfine sugar
2 eggs, lightly beaten
1 cup ground almonds
melted butter, for greasing

ICING
½ cup confectioners' sugar, sifted
2 tablespoons orange juice, warmed

1 Preheat the oven to 375°. Lightly grease an 8-inch flan or cake pan with a loose base.
2 Roll out the pastry on a lightly floured surface and use to line the pan. Mix the apricots and orange

rind together and sprinkle over the base of the pastry case.
3 Beat the margarine with the sugar until pale and fluffy. Beat in the eggs, a little at a time, then stir in the ground almonds. Spoon the mixture into the pastry case and level the surface.
4 Bake in the oven for about 40

minutes, until the filling is set and browned. Leave to cool in the pan ✳ for 10-15 minutes, remove from the pan and place on a serving dish.
5 Make the icing: Blend the confectioners' sugar and orange juice until smooth. Using a pastry brush, brush the icing over the top of the flan. Serve warm or cold.

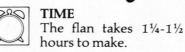

TIME
The flan takes 1¼-1½ hours to make.

VARIATIONS
Omit the apricots and orange rind and spread 3 tablespoons apricot jam over the base of the pastry case. Add 2 tablespoons chopped blanched almonds to the filling.

FREEZING
Cool completely, then remove from the pan. Do not ice. Wrap in a plastic

bag, seal, label and freeze for up to 1 month.
To serve: Thaw in wrappings at room temperature for 4-5 hours. Warm through in a 375° oven for 15 minutes, then ice the tart.

DID YOU KNOW
This aromatic tart is named after the frangipani, a tropical plant noted for its fragrancy; its oils are used to make perfume.

●505 calories per slice

Pineapple meringue pie

MAKES 6 SLICES
⅓ lb graham crackers, crushed

6 tablespoons butter, melted
FILLING
2 tablespoons cornstarch
2 tablespoons sugar
1 can (about 13 oz) crushed
    pineapple, well drained, with
    syrup reserved
¼ teaspoon vanilla
2 large eggs, separated
½ cup superfine sugar

1 Mix the cracker crumbs with the melted butter. Spoon into a loose-based 8-inch cake or flan dish and press evenly and firmly over the base and up the sides. Cover and refrigerate for at least 30 minutes.
2 Preheat the oven to 400°.

3 Make the filling: In a small, heavy-bottomed saucepan, mix together the cornstarch and sugar. Stir in a little of the reserved pineapple syrup to make a smooth paste, then blend in the remainder. Bring gently to a boil, stirring constantly, then remove from the heat.
4 Allow mixture to cool slightly, then beat in vanilla and egg yolks. Stir in the crushed pineapple. Spoon the pineapple mixture into the cracker case and level the surface.
5 In a spotlessly clean, dry bowl, beat the egg whites until they stand in stiff peaks. Beat in the superfine sugar, 1 tablespoon at a time, and continue beating until the meringue is stiff and glossy.
6 Pipe swirls of meringue over pie or spread with a spatula, then draw up into peaks. Bake in the oven for 10-15 minutes, until the meringue is golden brown. Leave to cool completely, [!] then remove from the dish and place on a serving plate. Serve at room temperature.

Cook's Notes

 TIME
30 minutes preparation, 10-15 minutes baking, plus at least 4 hours cooling.

! **WATCHPOINTS**
Use eggs at room temperature.
  Resist the temptation to remove the pie from the dish before it is completely cold as the cracker case may crumble.

 **STORAGE**
The wafer case will keep for up to 2 days in the refrigerator. Wrap it well in foil or place in a plastic bag and seal tightly. The baked pie will keep fresh overnight if left loosely covered in a cool place, but not the refrigerator.

● 400 calories per slice

Citrus apple flan

SERVES 4
RICH PIECRUST PASTRY
1½ cups all-purpose flour
pinch of salt
½ cup butter or margarine
2 tablespoons water, chilled

FILLING
6 tablespoons butter or margarine
⅓ cup superfine sugar
2 cups fresh white bread crumbs
grated rind of 1 orange
½ teaspoon ground allspice
¼ cup thick-cut marmalade
2 green apples
confectioners' sugar, to dust

1 To make the pastry: Sift the flour and salt into a large bowl. Cut the butter into ½-inch cubes and add it slowly to the flour until the mixture resembles coarse crumbs. Sprinkle over the water, then draw the mixture together to a firm dough. Wrap in plastic wrap and refrigerate for at least 30 minutes before using.

2 Preheat the oven to 400°.

3 Roll out the pastry on a floured surface and use to line an 8-inch loose-based cake pan or a plain or fluted flan ring placed on a cookie sheet. Prick lightly in several places with a fork.

4 In a saucepan, melt the butter over low heat. Remove from the heat and stir in the sugar, bread crumbs, orange rind and allspice.

5 Spread the marmalade over the base of the flan. Pare, core and slice the apples and arrange over the marmalade. Spoon the bread crumb mixture evenly over the top and press down lightly. ✳

6 Bake in the oven for 25 minutes, then reduce the heat to 350° and bake for a further 10-15 minutes until golden.

7 Remove from the pan (see Cook's tip), sift confectioners' sugar lightly and evenly over the top to dust and serve the flan hot.

Tropical flan

SERVES 6

10-inch sponge flan case
3 oranges
1 can (about 1 lb) pineapple rings in natural juice, drained with juice reserved
1 mango
1-2 tablespoons superfine sugar
2 teaspoons arrowroot (see Buying guide)
⅔ cup heavy whipping cream, to serve

1 Put the flan case on a flat serving dish.

2 Peel and slice the oranges over a bowl to reserve any juice. Remove any pits and the central pith and arrange around the edge of the sponge flan.

3 Cut the pineapple rings in half and arrange, overlapping, in a ring inside the ring of orange slices.

4 Again working over a bowl, score the skin of the mango lengthwise into several sections and remove the skin with a small sharp knife. Chop the mango flesh neatly and pile into the center of the flan. Squeeze the mango pit, which will have some flesh clinging to it, over the bowl to extract all the juice.

5 Strain the reserved orange, pineapple and mango juice into a measuring jug and make up to ⅔ cup with water. Stir in 1-2 tablespoons superfine sugar, to taste, and mix until dissolved.

6 Spoon ¼ cup of this juice over the sponge around the rim of the flan to moisten it.

7 Put the arrowroot into a bowl. Stir in a little of the fruit juice to make a smooth paste, then gradually stir in the remainder. Transfer to a small saucepan and bring to a boil over moderate heat, stirring constantly, until thick, smooth and clear.

8 Spoon the hot glaze over the fruit, allowing a little to run down the sides of the flan.

9 Leave in a cool place for 30 minutes, or up to 8 hours, then serve accompanied by the cream. (If liked the cream can be whipped until standing in soft peaks and piped around the edge instead.)

Cook's Notes

TIME
Preparation takes about 30 minutes, but allow another 30 minutes for the flan to cool.

BUYING GUIDE
Buy arrowroot powder at supermarkets and delicatessens. It looks like cornstarch, but has the advantage of giving a clear glaze when boiled, not a cloudy one.

VARIATIONS
A sliced banana, tossed in lemon juice to prevent discoloration, can be used in place of the mango. Or use fresh or canned apricots.

● 375 calories per portion

Latticed gooseberry tart

SERVES 4
1 package (about 11 oz) pie crust sticks, prepared
little beaten egg, for glazing
superfine sugar, for dredging
custard or cream, to serve

FILLING
½ pint gooseberries, topped and tailed if fresh, thawed and well drained if frozen
2 tablespoons fresh white bread crumbs (see Cook's tips)
2 tablespoons sugar
½ teaspoon finely chopped fresh mint (optional)

1 Preheat the oven to 400°.
2 Cut off one-third of the pastry and reserve. On a lightly floured surface, roll out the remaining pastry and use to line a 9-inch pie plate.
3 Mix the gooseberries with the bread crumbs, sugar and mint, if using. Spoon into the pastry-lined pie plate and spread evenly. Brush the edges of the pastry with water.

4 Use the reserved pastry to make a lattice decoration over the tart (see Preparation). Brush the pastry lattice with beaten egg.
5 Bake the tart in the oven, just above the center, for 20 minutes; then lower the heat to 375° and bake for about 15 minutes more, until the gooseberries are tender (see Cook's tips). Cover the top with waxed paper if the pastry is browning too quickly.
6 Remove the tart from the oven and sift superfine sugar thickly over the top. Serve hot, warm or cold, with custard or cream.

Cook's Notes

TIME
30 minutes preparation, plus about 35 minutes baking.

COOK'S TIPS
Bread crumbs absorb the juices produced by the filling during baking and help prevent the pastry becoming soggy.
Use a fine skewer to test that the gooseberries are tender.

VARIATIONS
Fresh mint gives a pleasant flavor to gooseberries, but you could use a little grated orange or lemon rind, or ¼ teaspoon ground allspice instead.

PREPARATION
A lattice is a very decorative way of topping a tart. If using a very soft or moist filling, make the lattice on waxed paper, then gently shake it onto the tart.
For a scalloped effect, the strips can be cut with a pastry lattice. A plain lattice is made as follows: Roll out the pastry to a rectangle, ½ inch larger than diameter of the pie plate. Cut in ½-inch wide strips. Place half the strips over the tart in parallel lines. Lay the remaining strips in parallel lines across the first set. Trim the edges and press to seal.

● 345 calories per portion

LIGHT AND CREAMY DESSERTS

Mediterranean rice dessert

SERVES 4
1 can (about 1 lb) creamed rice milk
   pudding
1 tablespoon cornstarch
⅔ cup milk
2 tablespoons sugar
1 large egg yolk
grated rind of 1 small lemon
grated chocolate, to decorate

1 Turn the creamed rice into a saucepan and set over low heat.
2 Blend the cornstarch with 2-3 tablespoons of milk, then stir in half the remaining milk. Add the cornstarch mixture to the rice together with the sugar. Bring slowly to a boil, stirring, and simmer for 2 minutes.
3 Beat the egg yolk with the remaining milk, then stir into the rice pudding. Add the lemon rind and simmer, stirring, for 2 minutes more.
4 Remove the pan from the heat and pour the pudding into 4 individual dessert bowls. Sprinkle a little grated chocolate over each pudding. Serve hot or chilled.

Cook's Notes

TIME
Preparation and cooking take about 10 minutes. Remember to allow chilling time if serving cold.

ECONOMY
This is a quick and easy way to stretch a can of rice pudding to serve 4.

? DID YOU KNOW
This type of pudding is popular in the Mediterranean, where it is often sprinkled with cinnamon.

● 185 calories per portion

Coffee mousse

SERVES 6

4 teaspoons instant coffee
¼ cup superfine sugar
3 tablespoons boiling water
1 envelope unflavored gelatin
3 tablespoons cold water
1¼ cups heavy cream
2 egg whites
small chocolate curls or chopped
    walnuts to decorate (see
    Preparation)

1 Dissolve the coffee and superfine sugar in the boiling water.
2 Sprinkle the gelatin over the cold water in a small flameproof bowl and leave to soak for 5 minutes, then stand the bowl in a pan of gently simmering water for 1-2 minutes until the gelatin has completely dissolved, stirring occasionally.
3 Pour the coffee into the gelatin liquid, stirring well to mix. Remove the bowl from the pan and leave the coffee mixture until tepid. [!]
4 Meanwhile, beat the cream until standing in soft peaks. Just before the coffee mixture is ready, beat the egg whites until stiff in a clean, dry bowl and using clean beaters.

5 Using a large metal spoon, quickly blend the coffee mixture into the cream, then fold in the egg whites. Divide the mixture equally between 6 small dishes. Cover and refrigerate for 2-3 hours, until set.
6 Just before serving, decorate each mousse with chocolate curls.

Cook's Notes

TIME
15 minutes preparation plus 2-3 hours chilling.

WATCHPOINT
You need to keep a close watch on the coffee mixture as it cools very quickly. Test the mixture frequently with a clean finger; it should feel just warm. Do not let it become too cool or it will set in threads as soon as it comes into contact with the whipped cream.

● 280 calories per mousse

PREPARATION
For a 2-tone effect, make curls from bars of white and milk chocolate.

Draw a swivel vegetable parer towards you, along the side of bar, to shave off small curls.

198

Rhubarb and orange cream

SERVES 4

1 can (about 1¼ lb) rhubarb
finely grated rind and juice of 1
   orange
1 tablespoon superfine sugar,
   or to taste
3 eggs
⅔ cup heavy whipping
   cream
sweet cookies, to serve

1 Put the rhubarb and 2 table-spoons juice from the can into a blender with the orange rind and juice and sugar. Blend at high speed until a smooth purée.
2 Beat the eggs together thoroughly in a flameproof bowl, then beat in the rhubarb purée.
3 Place the bowl over a saucepan of simmering water and cook for 10-15 minutes, beating constantly with a wire whisk until the mixture is thick and creamy. [!]
4 Remove the bowl from the heat, leave to cool, then chill in the refrigerator until absolutely cold. [!]
5 Beat the cream until it stands in soft peaks, then fold into the cooled rhubarb mixture. Cover and chill in the refrigerator for at least 6 hours (preferably overnight) before serving.
6 Serve chilled in individual dishes or glasses, with sweet cookies.

Cook's Notes

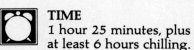

TIME
1 hour 25 minutes, plus at least 6 hours chilling.

VARIATIONS
Use fresh rhubarb when in season. Weigh 1 lb, trim and slice, then cook with sugar to taste until tender. Drain, reserving 2 tablespoons of the juice.
   Try using canned plums instead of rhubarb, but strain them after puréeing to remove the skins. Add a pinch of ground cinnamon to give a deliciously different flavor.

COOK'S TIPS
If you do not have a blender simply mash the rhubarb thoroughly until it is a smooth, creamy pulp.
   Use the finest part of the grater to grate the orange rind. Do not grate for too long in one place, but simply take off the rind, or the orange-colored part of the skin, because the pith underneath is rather bitter.

! **WATCHPOINT**
It is important the bowl containing the eggs and rhubarb purée should not come in contact with the water simmering in the pan. It should rest just above the surface of the water so the mixture does not boil and curdle or separate.
   The cooked mixture must be quite cold before you add the cream, or the cream will flop.

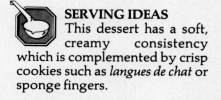

SERVING IDEAS
This dessert has a soft, creamy consistency which is complemented by crisp cookies such as *langues de chat* or sponge fingers.

● 250 calories per portion

Fruit mallow

SERVES 6

6 oz pink and white marshmallows (see Buying guide)
1 can (about 14 oz) fruit cocktail, well drained
1¼ cups heavy cream
2 tablespoons milk
extra marshmallows and fan wafers, to decorate (optional)

1 Snip the marshmallows into pieces (see Preparation) and put into a large bowl. Using a wooden spoon, gently stir in the fruit cocktail and mix until evenly blended.

2 In a separate bowl, beat the cream with the milk until standing in stiff peaks. Using a large metal spoon, fold the cream into the fruit and marshmallow mixture.

3 Spoon the mixture into 6 tall glasses. Cover each with plastic wrap and refrigerate for at least 8 hours, or overnight, to allow the flavors to blend and the texture to firm.

4 Remove the desserts from the fridge 15 minutes before serving to take chill off. Just before serving, decorate with marshmallows and wafers if liked.

Cook's Notes

TIME
Preparation takes only 15 minutes, but allow at least 8 hours chilling time. Decorating the desserts takes a few extra minutes.

BUYING GUIDE
Some supermarkets sell their own brand of marshmallow in 6 oz packages. They are also available in ¼ lb packages; in which case, buy 2 packages and use the extra to decorate the desserts. Tiny marshmallows are also available.

● 290 calories per portion

PREPARATION
Cut the marshmallows as follows:

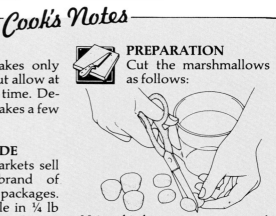

Using kitchen scissors, cut each marshmallow in half across, then cut each half into 3 pieces. Dip the scissors into hot water at frequent intervals — this will prevent the blades becoming too sticky.

Apple flummery

SERVES 4
2 large eggs, separated
¼ cup sugar
2½ cups milk
2 tablespoons semolina
pinch of salt
**1 large green apple, weighing about
    ¾ lb, pared, cored and puréed**
juice of ½ small lemon

TO SERVE
1 red-skinned dessert apple
few drops of lemon juice

1 Put the egg yolks and sugar in a bowl and beat together until creamy.
2 Put the milk into a large saucepan and warm it over moderate heat. Sprinkle in the semolina and bring to a boil, stirring. Add the salt and lower the heat, then simmer for 10 minutes, stirring constantly.
3 Gradually stir in the egg yolk and sugar mixture until well mixed, then continue cooking very gently for a further 2 minutes, stirring all the time. Do not allow the mixture to boil or it will stick to the bottom of the pan and may burn.
4 Remove the pan from the heat, then stir in the apple purée and lemon juice until well blended.
5 Beat the egg whites until stiff and fold into the mixture in the pan, using a metal spoon.
6 Carefully spoon the mixture into individual glasses and leave to cool for about 30 minutes.
7 To serve: Thinly slice the apple, discarding the core, but leaving the skin on. Sprinkle immediately with lemon juice to prevent discoloration. Place a few slices on each serving and serve at once.

Cook's Notes

TIME
About 50 minutes, including 15 minutes to prepare and purée the apple.

COOK'S TIP
The flummery is a particularly light and refreshing dessert — it separates slightly into a shallow layer of liquid at the bottom, topped with a fluffy mixture.

DID YOU KNOW
According to the dictionary, flummery is an old Welsh word of unknown derivation, but it refers to a traditional sweet dish (popular in the British Isles) which is milk and egg-based and always eaten cold.

● 250 calories per portion

Honeyed apricot whips

SERVES 4
¾ cup dried apricots
1¼ cups hot water
2 tablespoons honey
1¼ cups plain yogurt
2 egg whites
boudoir wafers, or chocolate fingers,
to serve

1 Put the apricots in a small bowl with the hot water and leave to soak for at least 4 hours or, if possible, overnight.

2 Turn the apricots and water into a heavy-bottomed saucepan. Add the honey, cover and simmer very gently for about 20 minutes, until the apricots are tender. Remove from the heat and leave to cool completely.

3 Purée the apricots with the cooking syrup and yogurt in a blender. Alternatively, press the apricots through a strainer, then stir in the cooking syrup and fold in the yogurt.

4 Beat the egg whites until they stand in soft peaks. Using a metal spoon, lightly stir 1 tablespoon of the beaten egg whites into the apricot purée mixture, then fold in the remainder.

5 Spoon the whip into stemmed glasses. Serve at once, or refrigerate until serving time. Serve with the wafers.

Cook's Notes

TIME
1¼ hours (including cooling time), but remember that the apricots need to be soaked for a minimum of 4 hours before they are ready to be cooked.

DID YOU KNOW
Yogurt is a high-protein, low-calorie food, and dried apricots are a good source of iron. This dessert is suitable for anyone on a low-fat diet.

● 135 calories per portion

Mango yoghurt foam

SERVES 4

1 orange
2 large, ripe mangos, sliced (see Preparation)
1 teaspoon unflavored gelatin
3 tablespoons cold water
1¼ cups plain yogurt
2-3 tablespoons superfine sugar
1 egg white

1 Using a vegetable parer, pare several strips of rind from the orange. ☐ With a small, sharp knife, shred the rind into matchstick sized strips.
2 Bring a small pan of water to a boil and blanch the strips for 2-3 minutes; drain and refresh under cold running water. Drain again, then pat dry on paper towels and set aside.

3 Squeeze the juice from the orange, then purée the prepared mangos and orange juice in a blender, or work the mangos through a strainer and stir in the orange juice.
4 Sprinkle the gelatin over the water in a small, heavy-bottomed pan. Leave to soak for 5 minutes, then set over very low heat for 1-2 minutes, until the gelatin is dissolved.
5 Stirring constantly with a wooden spoon, pour the dissolved gelatin in a thin stream onto the mango purée (see Cook's tip). Gradually beat in the yogurt, then sweeten to taste with superfine sugar.
6 In a spotlessly clean, dry bowl, beat the egg white until standing in stiff peaks. Using a large metal spoon, fold the egg white into the mango mixture. Taste and fold in more superfine sugar, if necessary.
7 Spoon the foam into 4 dessert dishes or stemmed glasses and decorate with the strips of orange rind. Serve within 2 hours.

Cook's Notes

⏰ **TIME**
30 minutes preparation, plus cooling and setting.

❗ **WATCHPOINT**
Be sure to use a nylon strainer; metal may taint or discolor the melon flesh.

SERVING IDEAS
Decorate with slices of kiwi fruit, or drained and chopped stem ginger; serve with crisp wafers.

COOK'S TIP
The mixture itself needs to be quite strongly colored, as the cream and egg whites will make it paler.

PREPARATION
Use a large metal spoon and a "figure of eight" action to fold the egg whites into the melon mixture.

● 145 calories per portion

Melon mousse

SERVES 6
½ large honeydew melon,
   weighing about 1½ lb,
   seeded and pared
1 rounded tablespoon (1 envelope)
   unflavored gelatin
1 tablespoon lemon juice
1 tablespoon water
¼ cup superfine sugar
few drops of green food coloring
2 pinches ground ginger (optional)
2 egg whites
⅔ cup heavy cream

1 Sprinkle the gelatin over the lemon juice and water in a flame-proof bowl and leave to soak for 5 minutes until spongy.
2 Meanwhile, cut the melon flesh into chunks and work through a strainer, ❗ or purée in a blender then strain to remove fibers.
3 Pour the purée into a saucepan. Add the sugar and heat gently, stirring constantly, until the sugar is dissolved. Remove from the heat.
4 Stand the bowl containing the gelatin in a pan of gently simmering water and heat gently for 1-2 minutes until the gelatin has dissolved, stirring occasionally.
5 Stir the dissolved gelatin into the melon mixture, then add enough coloring to tint it a fairly strong green. Stir in ginger, if using. For a streaky effect, lightly stir in a little extra coloring.
6 Pour the mixture into a bowl; cool, then cover and refrigerate until beginning to set.
7 In a clean, dry bowl, beat the egg whites until standing in stiff peaks. Beat the cream in a separate bowl until it will just hold its shape. Fold the cream and then the egg whites into the melon mixture (see Preparation).
8 Divide the mixture between 6 individual glasses or glass bowls, cover and refrigerate for 8 hours, or overnight, until set. Serve chilled (see Serving ideas).

Tangerine jelly

SERVES 6
8 tangerines
2 tablespoons superfine sugar
2 tablespoons lemon juice
2 tablespoons water
1 rounded tablespoon unflavored gelatin
½ cup heavy cream
1 tablespoon orange liqueur (optional)

1 Rinse out 1-quart metal gelatin or ring mold with cold water and place it in the refrigerator to chill.
2 Squeeze the juice from 4 of the tangerines and strain into a measuring jug. Stir in the sugar, adding a little more to taste if liked.
3 Mix the lemon juice and water in a small bowl; sprinkle gelatin on top and leave to soak for about 5 minutes, until opaque and spongy. Then stand the bowl in a pan of hot water and stir until the gelatin is dissolved and the liquid is clear.
4 Remove the bowl from the pan and cool slightly. Pour the gelatin solution in a thin stream onto the strained fruit juice, stirring constantly. Make up to 2½ cups with water and refrigerate for about 1 hour, until just beginning to set.
5 Using a sharp serrated knife, pare the remaining tangerines, taking care to remove every bit of bitter white pith. Divide the fruit into segments and remove any pits.
6 Fold the segments through the almost set gelatin ☐ and pour into the chilled mold. Refrigerate at least 4 hours, or overnight, until set.
7 Unmold the tangerine jelly carefully and allow to stand at room temperature for about 30 minutes to take the chill off the flavor. Lightly beat the cream and flavor with liqueur if liked. Use the cream to decorate the jelly or serve it in a separate bowl.

Chocolate mousse special

SERVES 4

4 squares (4 oz) semi-sweet
    chocolate, broken into pieces
1 tablespoon water
few drops of vanilla
3 eggs, separated
20–24 sponge finger wafers (see
    Cook's tip)
chocolate curls and orange slices, to
    decorate (optional)

1 Put the chocolate, water and vanilla into a flameproof bowl. Set the bowl over a pan half full of simmering water and leave, stirring occasionally, until the chocolate is melted. Set aside to cool slightly.
2 In a large bowl, beat the egg yolks until pale. Add the melted chocolate and continue beating until the mixture is thick.
3 In a clean, dry bowl and using clean beaters, beat the egg whites until standing in stiff peaks. Fold the egg whites into the chocolate mixture with a large metal spoon.
4 Use half the wafers to line the base of an oblong 1-quart serving dish. (Trim the wafers, if necessary, so they fit neatly.)
5 Pour the chocolate mixture over the wafers, then cover with plastic wrap; refrigerate at least 2 hours.
6 To serve: Arrange the remaining wafers, cut in half, on top of the mousse. Decorate with chocolate flakes and orange slices, if liked, and serve chilled.

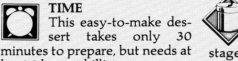

Cook's Notes

TIME
This easy-to-make dessert takes only 30 minutes to prepare, but needs at least 2 hours chilling.

STORAGE
The mousse can be prepared up to the end of stage 5 and kept, covered, in the refrigerator for up to 48 hours.

COOK'S TIP
The number of sponge fingers you need depends on the shape of your serving dish.

SERVING IDEAS
Serve with a dish of sliced oranges.

● 275 calories per portion

Rich caramel mold

SERVES 6-8
⅓ cup sugar
3 tablespoons cold water
1¼ cups milk
2 × 6 inch sponge layers, cut in half horizontally
¼ cup apricot jam
1¼ cups light cream
4 large eggs, lightly beaten
vegetable oil, for greasing

TO FINISH
1¼ cups heavy cream
grated chocolate

1 Put the sugar and water into a small, heavy-bottomed saucepan and heat very gently, without stirring, until the sugar has dissolved. ⚠ Bring to a boil and boil rapidly until the syrup turns a rich caramel color. ⚠
2 Immediately remove from heat and plunge base of pan into a bowl of cold water until the sizzling stops. Pour the milk onto the caramel, ⚠ then return to low heat and leave, stirring occasionally, until caramel has dissolved. Set aside.
3 Preheat the oven to 350°. Lightly oil a 1¼-quart charlotte mold or soufflé dish, line the base with waxed paper, then oil the paper.
4 Spread the cut side of each cake with jam. Arrange, jam-side-up, in the prepared mold. Lightly beat the cream, and then the caramel milk into the eggs; strain into the mold and leave for 15 minutes.
5 Lay a piece of oiled waxed paper over the top of the pudding. Stand the mold in a small roasting pan and pour in enough cold water to come halfway up the sides of the mold. Carefully transfer to the oven and bake for about 2 hours, until the custard is set.
6 Lift the mold out of the pan. Cool for 30 minutes, then remove waxed covering and run a palette knife around the side of the pudding. Invert a serving plate on top of the mold. Hold mold and plate firmly and invert them. Do not remove mold. Refrigerate for at least 3 hours, or overnight.
7 To serve: Lift off mold, remove paper, then mop up liquid on plate. with paper towels. Beat the heavy cream until standing in soft peaks, then pipe over pudding. Decorate with grated chocolate.

Cook's Notes

⏱ **TIME**
1 hour preparation (including decoration), 2 hours baking, plus chilling.

⚠ **WATCHPOINTS**
Make sure every granule of sugar has dissolved or the syrup will crystallize.
Watch the caramel constantly as it can easily scorch.
Stand well back as the milk will splutter for 1-2 seconds.

● 620 calories per portion

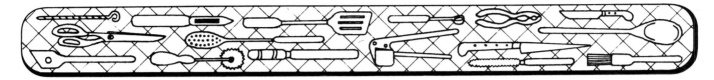

Ginger syllabub

SERVES 4

5 tablespoons Advocaat
3 tablespoons ginger marmalade
(see Cook's tip)
1¼ cups heavy cream
candied ginger or drained stem
ginger, cut into small pieces, to
decorate
crisp wafers, to serve

1 Mix the Advocaat and marmalade together in a small bowl.
2 Beat the cream until standing in soft peaks. Using a large metal spoon, fold the marmalade mixture into the cream.
3 Spoon the mixture into 4 stem-

Cook's Notes

TIME
10 minutes preparation, plus a minimum 30 minutes chilling time and a maximum of 2 hours.

COOK'S TIP
A jar of ginger marmalade is a useful pantry item, as it can be used to enliven both sweet and savory dishes. It makes a delicious filling for sponge cakes and 1 tablespoon is enough to pep up a beef casserole. Alternatively, try 1 tablespoon with cooked

rhubarb or in a rhubarb fool

! WATCHPOINTS
Do not beat the cream until standing in stiff peaks, or the syllabubs will be too solid.
Syllabubs are always chilled before serving so that the flavors can mingle, but do not leave any longer than the specified time or the mixture will separate.

● 425 calories per portion

med dishes, cover with plastic wrap and refrigerate for at least 30 minutes, or up to 2 hours.

4 Just before serving, decorate each syllabub with pieces of ginger. Serve chilled, with crisp wafers.

Cranberry brûlés

SERVES 4
½ lb cranberries (see Cook's tips)
5 tablespoons water
⅔ cup light brown sugar, or to taste
1½ teaspoons arrowroot

TOPPING
⅔ cup dairy sour cream (see Cook's tips)
2 tablespoons light brown sugar
large pinch of ground allspice

1 Put the cranberries and 4 tablespoons water into a heavy-bottomed saucepan. Cover and simmer gently for 5 minutes, then stir in ⅔ cup light brown sugar and cook for a further 3-4 minutes.
2 Blend the arrowroot with the remaining water and stir into the cranberry mixture. Bring to a boil and simmer for 1-2 minutes until thickened and no longer cloudy, stirring constantly.
3 Cool the cranberry mixture for 30 minutes, then taste and stir in more sugar if liked. Divide the mixture equally between 4 ramekins or other small flameproof dishes.
4 Preheat the broiler to high.

5 Spread the dairy sour cream over the cranberry mixture, almost to the edges. Mix the sugar and allspice and sprinkle evenly on top of the cream.
6 Place under the broiler for a few seconds, until the sugar is melted and bubbling. Remove immediately from the heat, leave to settle for 1-2 minutes, then serve hot. Alternatively, serve chilled (see Variation).

Marbled lime soufflé

SERVES 6
4 limes
1 rounded tablespoon (1 envelope)
   unflavored gelatin
6 tablespoons water
4 large eggs, separated
1 cup superfine sugar
1¼ cups heavy cream
few drops of green food coloring
unsalted pistachio nuts, blanched
   and chopped, to decorate (see
   Economy)

1 Prepare a 1¾-quart (6½-inch) ovenproof soufflé dish: Cut a 23 × 10 inch strip of aluminum foil or waxed paper. Fold in half lengthwise. Wrap the strip of aluminum foil around the dish so it stands above the rim and secure with masking tape. Lightly oil inside of collar, above rim of dish.
2 Finely grate the rind from 3 limes;

squeeze the juice from all the limes and measure out about ½ cup for the soufflé.
3 Sprinkle the gelatin over the water in a flameproof bowl. Leave to soak for 5 minutes until spongy, then set the bowl over a pan of simmering water and heat gently for 1-2 minutes until gelatin has dissolved, stirring occasionally. Remove gelatin liquid from heat and leave to cool slightly.
4 Meanwhile, put the egg yolks into a bowl with ¾ cup superfine sugar, the lime rind and reserved juice. Using an electric mixer, beat until very pale, thick and creamy.
5 Beat in the gelatin. Leave the mixture for 5-10 minutes, beating occasionally, until it is beginning to thicken.
6 In a clean, dry bowl, beat the egg whites until standing in stiff peaks. Beat in the remaining sugar, 1 tablespoon at a time, and continue beating until meringue is firm and glossy.
7 Meanwhile, beat the cream until standing in soft peaks.

8 Fold the whipped cream into the lime mixture, then gently fold in the meringue. Put half the mixture into another bowl and tint pale green with food coloring.
9 Put alternate spoonfuls of the 2 mixtures into prepared dish. Level the surface carefully, then chill for 4 hours, until set.
10 Remove tape from collar, then carefully peel away from soufflé with the aid of a round-bladed knife. Press chopped nuts around the sides of the soufflé. Serve as soon as possible.

Crêpe Alaska

SERVES 4
1 cup all-purpose flour
1½ teaspoons baking powder
¼ teaspoon salt
2 egg yolks
1 tablespoon superfine sugar
1 tablespoon vegetable oil
¾ cup milk
extra vegetable oil, for frying

FILLING
¾ cup apricot jam
1 tablespoon brandy or orange-
   flavored liqueur (see Economy)
1 can (about 1 lb) pineapple pieces,
   drained

MERINGUE
2 egg whites
½ cup superfine sugar
1 tablespoon flaked almonds

1 Preheat the oven to 425°.
2 Sift the flour, baking powder and salt into a bowl. Add the egg yolks, sugar, oil and milk and beat until just smoothly blended.
3 Brush a-6 inch heavy-bottomed skillet lightly with oil; place over moderately high heat. Remove from the heat and pour in about 2 tablespoons batter. Using the back of the spoon, spread the batter to the sides of the pan.
4 Return to the heat and cook until the bubbles burst on top. Loosen with a spatula, then turn the crêpe over and cook on the other side for a further 20-30 seconds, until browned. Lift onto waxed paper and keep warm.
5 Continue making crêpes, interleaving them with waxed paper, until you have about 7. Stir the batter frequently and grease the pan with more oil as necessary.
6 Warm the jam with the brandy in a small pan. Reserve 1 crêpe; spread the rest with warmed jam.
7 Place 1 crêpe, jam side up, on an ovenproof serving plate and top with a few pineapple pieces. Cover with another crêpe, jam side up. Continue layering in this way, ending with the reserved plain crêpe on top.
8 Make the meringue: In a clean, dry bowl, beat the egg whites until stiff, then beat in the sugar, 1 tablespoon at a time.
9 Swirl the meringue over the top and sides of crepe stack, taking it right down on to the plate. Sprinkle with the almonds. Bake immediately in the oven for 10 minutes, or until the meringue is tinged with brown and the nuts are golden. Serve at once, cut into wedges.

Cook's Notes

TIME
This spectacular dessert takes about 50 minutes to prepare (including 10 minutes baking time).

ECONOMY
Use syrup from the can of pineapple instead of the brandy or liqueur.

● 575 calories per portion

Raspberry soufflés

SERVES 4

1 cup raspberry purée
  (see Cook's tip)
1 tablespoon unflavored gelatin
3 tablespoons cold water
4 large eggs, separated
½ cup superfine sugar
1¼ cups heavy cream
vegetable oil, for greasing
crushed ratafias, extra superfine
  sugar and fresh hulled
  raspberries, to finish

1 Secure paper collars around 4 straight-sided, ¾-cup ramekins (see Preparation). Reserve 4 tablespoons of the purée.

2 Sprinkle the gelatin over the water in a cup; leave until spongy, then stand the cup in a bowl of very hot water until the gelatin is completely dissolved.

3 Meanwhile, beat the egg yolks and sugar together in a flameproof bowl over barely simmering water until thick and pale.

4 Remove from the heat. Beat in the dissolved gelatin and the remaining raspberry purée. Turn into a clean large bowl, cover and chill, stirring occasionally, until on the point of setting.

5 Beat 1 cup of the cream until it forms soft peaks. Using clean beaters, beat the egg whites until standing in soft peaks. Fold the cream and egg whites into the raspberry mixture. Divide between the prepared dishes, cover lightly and chill for about 2 hours, until set.

6 Remove the masking tape from paper collars; then gently peel away from the soufflés with the aid of a round-bladed knife. Press crushed ratafias around the sides.

7 Sweeten the reserve purée with superfine sugar, to taste. Spread 1 tablespoon purée over the top of each soufflé.

8 Beat the remaining cream with 2 teaspoons superfine sugar until standing in soft peaks. Decorate the top of each soufflé with raspberries, ratafias and piped cream.

Cook's Notes

TIME
50 minutes, plus chilling and setting.

COOK'S TIP
Work about 1-1¼ lb fresh or thawed frozen raspberries through a strainer or purée in a blender, then strain.

PREPARATION
The collars enable you to overfill the dish so that, when they are removed, the soufflés appear "risen."
  Measure the depth and circumference of the dishes with string. Cut 4 strips of double thickness waxed paper, 1 inch longer and 1 inch deeper. Wrap 1 strip tightly around each dish and secure with masking tape. Lightly oil inside of paper, above rim.

● 505 calories per portion

Hot coffee soufflés

SERVES 4
3 tablespoons butter or margarine
¼ cup all-purpose flour
⅔ cup milk
3 eggs, separated
2 tablespoons superfine sugar
2 teaspoons coffee extract
melted butter, for greasing

SAUCE
¾ cup hot strong black coffee
1½-2 tablespoons sugar
1½ teaspoons arrowroot
1 tablespoon water
1-2 tablespoons Tia Maria

1 Preheat the oven to 350°. Brush the insides of four individual soufflé dishes with melted butter, then stand them on a cookie sheet.
2 Melt the butter in a fairly large saucepan, sprinkle in the flour and stir over low heat for 1-2 minutes until straw-colored. Remove from the heat and gradually stir in the milk. Return to the heat and simmer, stirring, until very thick and smooth. [!]
3 Remove from the heat, allow to cool for a few minutes, stir in the sugar and coffee extract. Then beat in the egg yolks one at a time.
4 In a clean, dry bowl, beat the egg whites until they stand in stiff peaks. Using a large metal spoon, lightly but thoroughly fold egg whites into the coffee mixture. [!]
5 Spoon into dishes. Mark a circle with a knife in the top of each soufflé. Bake in the oven, above center, for 25-30 minutes until risen well above the rims of the dishes and browned on top.
6 Meanwhile, make the sauce: Pour the hot coffee into a small pan and then stir in 1½ tablespoons sugar. Blend the arrowroot with the water, add to the sweetened coffee and simmer gently, stirring, until thickened and no longer cloudy. Remove from the heat and flavor with Tia Maria and more sugar, if liked. Keep hot. Serve the soufflés *immediately* after they are cooked, with a little of the sauce poured over them and the rest passed around separately in a serving jug.

Baked mincemeat soufflé

SERVES 4-6

1 cup mincemeat
6 tablespoons dry wine
2 tablespoons brandy (optional)
¼ cup blanched almonds, chopped
4 large eggs, separated
pinch of salt
¼ teaspoon grated lemon or orange rind
2 tablespoons all-purpose flour
⅓ cup superfine sugar
confectioners' sugar, to dredge

1 Preheat the oven to 350°.
2 Put the mincemeat, wine, brandy (if using) and the blanched almonds into a saucepan and heat the mixture through gently.
3 Meanwhile, put the egg yolks, salt and lemon rind in a bowl and beat together lightly. Add the flour and continue beating until the mixture is pale and thick.
4 Beat the egg whites in a separate bowl until frothy. [!] Gradually beat in the superfine sugar and beat until the mixture forms soft peaks. Fold thoroughly into the egg yolk mixture with a metal spoon.
5 Pour the heated mincemeat mixture into a shallow ovenproof dish. Carefully spread the soufflé mixture on top.
6 Bake in the oven for about 15 minutes or until the topping is puffed up and golden brown.
7 Sift confectioners' sugar thickly over the top and serve at once.

Cook's Notes

TIME
Preparing 20 minutes, cooking 15 minutes.

WATCHPOINT
If using the same mixer or beater for both egg yolk and egg white mixtures, wash and dry them thoroughly after beating the egg yolks. If there is any egg yolk mixture or grease on the mixer or beaters, the egg whites will not thicken.

FOR CHILDREN
Omit the brandy and substitute apple juice for the wine.

● 325 calories per portion

ICE CREAMS AND SHERBETS

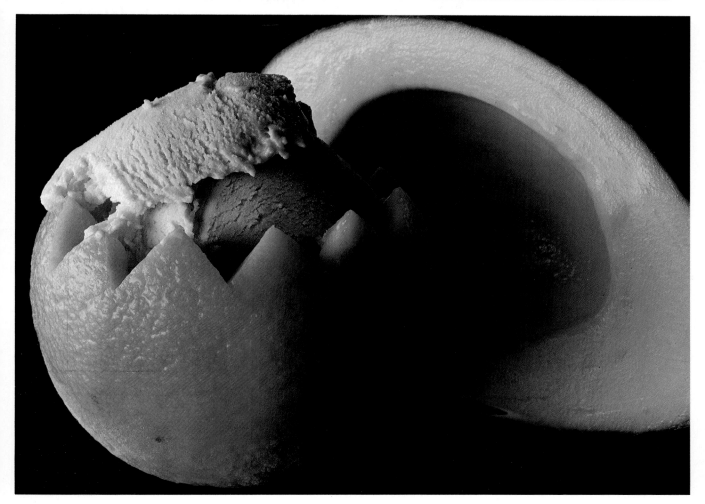

Avocado ice cream

SERVES 6-8
2 ripe avocados
2 eggs
⅓ cup superfine sugar
1¼ cups light cream
finely grated rind and juice of
**   1 large orange**
1¼ cups heavy cream

1 Put the eggs and sugar into a bowl and beat together with a wooden spoon until thick and creamy.
2 Pour the light cream into a small saucepan and heat gently until almost boiling then immediately remove from the heat and pour onto the egg mixture, stirring vigorously. Leave the custard to cool.
3 Halve, pit and peel the avocados, then roughly chop the flesh. Purée with the orange rind and juice in a blender.
4 In a large bowl, beat the heavy cream until it forms soft peaks. Using a large metal spoon, fold in the avocado purée and the custard.
5 Turn into a large freezerproof container, cover and freeze until the mixture is frozen 1 inch around the edges. Scrape the mixture into a bowl and beat until smooth, then return to the container, cover and freeze until firm.
6 Transfer to the main part of the refrigerator about 30 minutes before serving to soften.

Mixed fruit ice

SERVES 4-6

1 can (about 6 oz) evaporated milk,
  chilled (see Watchpoint)
½ cup confectioners' sugar, sifted
2 bananas
juice of 2 lemons
1 can (about 13 oz) crushed
  pineapple
1 jar (about 6 oz) maraschino
  cherries, drained and halved with
  2 tablespoons syrup reserved

1 Pour the milk into a large bowl
and beat until thick and frothy, then
beat in the confectioners' sugar.
2 Peel and mash the bananas with
the lemon juice, then stir into the
milk mixture together with the
pineapple and its syrup.
3 Set aside a few cherries for
decoration; stir the rest into the fruit
and milk mixture together with the
reserved syrup.

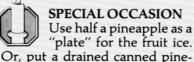
TIME
15 minutes preparation,
10 hours freezing and
30 minutes softening time.

COOK'S TIP
If using the freezing
compartment of the re-
frigerator, turn it to its lowest
setting 1 hour beforehand.
Remember to return it to the
original setting afterwards.

SPECIAL OCCASION
Use half a pineapple as a
"plate" for the fruit ice.
Or, put a drained canned pineapple ring on 4-6 individual
plates and top with scoops of
the ice mixture.

WATCHPOINT
The milk must be
chilled for at least 3
hours, or it will not beat to a
thick consistency.

FREEZING
Prepare up to the end of
stage 4, then cover,
label and freeze for up to 6
weeks. To serve: Follow stage 5.

● 280 calories per portion

4 Pour the mixture into a rigid
plastic container and freeze uncovered (see Cook's tip), for about 2
hours, until frozen around the
edges. Loosen the frozen mixture
with a fork and stir through the
whole mixture. Cover and return to
the freezer for a further 8 hours, or
overnight, until firm. ✳
5 To serve: Transfer the container
to the main part of the refrigerator
for about 30 minutes until softened,
then scoop into dishes and decorate
with reserved cherries.

Iced passion fruit dessert

SERVES 4

½ cup passion fruit pulp (see Preparation)
⅔ cup strawberry yogurt (see Variations)
1 teaspoon unflavored gelatin
½ cup water
3 tablespoons superfine sugar
2 egg whites

1 Put the passion fruit pulp into a large bowl with the yogurt and stir well until evenly blended.

2 Sprinkle the gelatin over the water in a flameproof bowl and leave to soak for 5 minutes, then stand bowl in a pan of gently simmering water for 1-2 minutes until the gelatin has completely dissolved, stirring occasionally.

3 Cool the gelatin slightly, then pour onto passion fruit mixture, stirring vigorously all the time to blend. Add the sugar and stir until dissolved.

4 Pour the mixture into a 1-quart metal or other freezerproof container. Leave, uncovered, in the freezer or freezing compartment of the refrigerator for 45-60 minutes until the mixture is frozen around the edges.

5 In an clean, dry bowl, beat egg whites until standing in stiff peaks. Turn passion fruit mixture into a large bowl and beat until smooth and creamy, then fold in egg whites with a large metal spoon.

6 Return mixture to the container, cover tightly and freeze for a further 4 hours or until firm.

7 About 45 minutes before serving, transfer the mixture to the main part of the refrigerator to soften slightly. To serve: Carefully scoop into individual glasses.

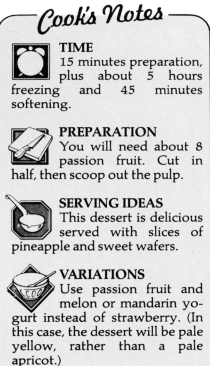

Cook's Notes

TIME
15 minutes preparation, plus about 5 hours freezing and 45 minutes softening.

PREPARATION
You will need about 8 passion fruit. Cut in half, then scoop out the pulp.

SERVING IDEAS
This dessert is delicious served with slices of pineapple and sweet wafers.

VARIATIONS
Use passion fruit and melon or mandarin yogurt instead of strawberry. (In this case, the dessert will be pale yellow, rather than a pale apricot.)

FREEZING
Seal the container, label and return to freezer for up to 6 weeks. To serve the passion fruit dessert: See stage 7.

● 95 calories per portion

Brown bread ice cream

SERVES 4

1 cup fresh whole wheat
   bread crumbs
2 tablespoons sugar
2 large eggs, separated
¼ cup light brown sugar (see
   Cook's tips)
⅔ cup heavy cream, whipped
   until in soft peaks
1 tablespoon coffee and chicory
   extract, or dark rum

1 Preheat the broiler to high. Mix the bread crumbs and sugar together; spread over the base of a small cookie sheet and toast under the broiler for about 5 minutes, turning occasionally, until golden and crunchy.
2 Turn the crunchy crumbs onto a plate and leave to cool completely, then crush coarsely with the back of a wooden spoon.
3 Beat the egg yolks with a fork until well blended, then set aside.
4 In a spotlessly clean and dry large bowl, beat egg whites until stiff. Beat in brown sugar, 1 tablespoon at a time. Using a large metal spoon, fold in the egg yolks, whipped cream, crushed bread crumbs and coffee and chicory.
5 Turn the mixture into a 1¼-quart metal container and cover securely with foil. Freeze (see Cook's tips) for 2 hours, stirring lightly every 30 minutes, [!] then leave for a further 2 hours, or until firm. ✳
6 Let the ice cream stand at room temperature for about 5 minutes, to soften slightly, before serving.

Cook's Notes

TIME
5 minutes toasting plus cooling time for the bread crumbs, then 30-40 minutes preparation and about 4 hours freezing time.

COOK'S TIPS
Light brown sugar gives a lovely pale coffee color, but superfine sugar can be used for a whiter ice cream. Sift light brown sugar if it is lumpy.

To make the ice cream in the freezing compartment of the refrigerator: Turn the temperature to the lowest setting and chill the container 1 hour beforehand.

SERVING IDEAS
Scoop into dessert bowls or stemmed glasses and top with fan wafers, or serve as an accompaniment to poached or canned fruit.

FREEZING
Overwrap, then return to the freezer and store for up to 3 months.

WATCHPOINT
The ice cream mixture should be lightly stirred and turned over at regular times during the first 2 hours or the crumbs will sink.

● 320 calories per portion

Lime ice box pudding

SERVES 10
grated rind of 2 limes
juice of 3 limes
3 eggs, separated
½ cup superfine sugar
2 cups heavy cream
8 plain sweet wafers, crushed
fresh lime slices, to decorate

1 Line the base of an 8½ × 4½ × 2½ inches loaf pan with waxed paper.
2 Put the egg yolks in a large flameproof bowl over a pan half full of gently simmering water. Using a rotary or hand-held electric mixer, slowly beat in the sugar until pale and thick. Remove from heat and stir in lime rind and juice.
3 Beat the cream until standing in soft peaks and fold into the lime mixture.

4 In a clean, dry bowl and using clean beaters, beat the egg whites until standing in soft peaks. Using a large metal spoon, fold the egg whites into the lime mixture.
5 Sprinkle a thin layer of wafer crumbs over the base of the pan. Carefully pour in the lime mixture and top with a layer of the remaining wafer crumbs.
6 Cover with foil, then place in the

freezer compartment of the refrigerator or in the freezer and freeze for about 8 hours, or overnight, until firm.
7 To serve (see Cook's tip): Uncover the pan, then run a palette knife around the edges of the pudding to loosen it. Turn out onto a flat serving plate and remove the waxed paper. Decorate the pudding with slices of lime and serve at once.

Cook's Notes

TIME
Preparation takes 40 minutes, plus about 8 hours freezing time.

COOK'S TIP
If you do not want to serve all the pudding at once, cut off as many slices as you need, then wrap the (undecorated) surplus in foil and return it to the freezer for up to 1 month.

WATCHPOINT
Make sure that the egg yolks and sugar are really thick before removing from the heat.

FREEZING
Freeze at the end of stage 6. Overwrap and return to the freezer for up to 1 month.

● 365 calories per portion

Cherries jubilee

SERVES 4

1 can (about 1 lb) pitted black cherries, drained, with syrup reserved
¼ cup brandy
2 teaspoons arrowroot
2 tablespoons water
large pinch of cinnamon
4 portions vanilla ice cream, to serve

1 Pour the brandy into a cup and stand in a pan or bowl of hot water to warm through gently.

2 In a small bowl, blend the arrow-root to a smooth paste with the water.

3 Pour the reserved cherry syrup into a saucepan. Add the cinnamon, then bring to a boil and boil briskly for 4 minutes, until reduced by one-quarter.

4 Remove pan from the heat [!] and stir in the arrowroot mixture. Return to the heat, bring back to a boil and cook, stirring, until the mixture thickens and clears.

5 Add the cherries to the pan and simmer gently for 1-2 minutes.

6 Meanwhile, put the ice cream into 4 dessert bowls.

7 Turn off the heat under the pan. Pour the warmed brandy over the cherries and immediately set light to it. [!] Let the flames die down completely, then spoon the cherries over the ice cream. Serve at once.

Cook's Notes

TIME
Preparation and cooking take 15-20 minutes.

WATCHPOINTS
Remove the pan from the heat immediately, or the cherry sauce will burn.

Hold the match just above the sides of the pan and stand well back since the flames will shoot high for a few seconds.

●210 calories per portion

Tutti frutti ice cream

SERVES 4
⅔ cup heavy cream
2 cups vanilla pudding, cooled and
    beaten until smooth
¼ cup candied cherries, chopped
1 tablespoon cut mixed peel
2 tablespoons seedless or golden
    raisins
1 tablespoon chocolate morsels
¼ cup chopped mixed nuts
    (optional)
fan-shaped wafers, to serve

1 Beat the cream until just thickened, then stir in the pudding and mix until evenly combined. Turn the mixture into a shallow 1-quart freezerproof container. Freeze uncovered (see Cook's tips) for about 1 hour, or until frozen around the edges and slushy in the center.
2 Scrape the mixture into a bowl and beat well with a wooden spoon or hand-held electric mixer. Stir in the cherries, peel, raisins, chocolate and nuts, if using, making sure they are evenly distributed (see Economy). Return the mixture to the container, cover and freeze for a further 2 hours, or until solid. ✳

3 Transfer the ice cream to the main part of the refrigerator for about 2 hours to soften slightly (see Cook's tips). Scoop into individual glass dishes and serve at once, with fan (or other shaped) wafers to give a texture contrast.

Cook's Notes

TIME
15 minutes preparation and about 3 hours freezing, plus softening time.

COOK'S TIPS
To shorten freezing time, refrigerate the pudding 2 hours in advance.
    If using the freezing compartment of the refrigerator, turn it to its coldest setting 1 hour before making the ice cream. Return it to the original setting afterwards.
    If you are in a hurry, soften the ice cream for 30 minutes at room temperature.

FREEZING
The ice cream can be stored in the freezer for up to 2 months.

FOR CHILDREN
Scoop the ice cream into cones and press half a chocolate flake into the top.

ECONOMY
Beat 1 egg white until standing in soft peaks and fold into the mixture after adding the fruit and chocolate. This gives a greater volume.

● 405 calories per portion

Watermelon frappé

SERVES 4
1 watermelon (about 3 lb), seeded, pared and cut into cubes (see Cook's tips)
½ cup superfine sugar
finely grated rind and juice of 1 large orange
finely grated rind of ½ lemon
1 tablespoon lemon juice

1 Purée watermelon, in batches, in a blender, or crush to a pulp with a potato masher, then work the pulp through a strainer.

2 Put the sugar into a large bowl with the orange and lemon rind. Slowly stir in the orange and lemon juice. Add the watermelon purée, a little at a time, stirring constantly to dissolve the sugar.

3 Pour the mixture into a 1¼-quart rigid plastic container and freeze, uncovered, for about 3 hours, or until the mixture is slushy (see Cook's tips).

4 Turn the mixture into a large bowl and beat to break up large icy crystals. Return to the container, cover and freeze for a further 2-3 hours, until firm.

5 Transfer to the main part of the refrigerator and leave for 1-1½ hours, until softened. Mash the ice briefly with a fork to break up large lumps, then spoon into dishes and serve at once before it begins to melt (see Serving ideas).

Cook's Notes

 TIME
20 minutes preparation, plus freezing and softening time.

 **DID YOU KNOW**
Frappé means iced in French, and aptly describes this cooling dessert with its granular, icy texture.

FREEZING
Overwrap the container, then return to the freezer for up to 2 months. To serve see stage 5.

● 160 calories per portion

 COOK'S TIPS
The easiest way to remove the seeds is to scrape them out with a fork.

If making the ice in the freezing compartment of the refrigerator, turn it to the lowest setting for 1 hour beforehand. Return to the original setting afterwards.

SERVING IDEAS
This refreshing ice is an ideal dessert after a rich main course. Spoon it into stemmed glass dishes and provide long-handled spoons for easy eating.

Sicilian orange cassata

SERVES 6-8

⅔ cup orange juice
10 mini sponge cakes
¾ lb Ricotta cheese (see Buying guide)
½ cup superfine sugar
½ cup cut mixed peel
2 squares (2 oz) semi-sweet chocolate, broken up into small pieces
finely grated rind of 1 orange
3 teaspoons medium sherry
vegetable oil, for greasing

TO DECORATE
⅔ cup heavy cream
3 orange slices, halved

1 Brush a 1¼-quart bombe mold or pudding basin very lightly with oil. Pour the orange juice into a shallow bowl.

2 Using three-quarters of the trifle sponge cakes, dip one side of each into the orange juice and use to line completely the sides and base of the mold with the darker sugar-coated sides facing inwards (see Preparation).

3 Place all the Ricotta cheese in a large bowl and stir in the remaining ingredients, mixing well. Spoon into the prepared mold and level the surface. If necessary, trim the ends of the sponge cakes level with the top of the filling.

4 Dip the remaining sponge cakes in the orange juice and use to cover the top of the cassata. Cover and refrigerate overnight.

5 Uncover, then carefully run a palette knife down the sides of the sponge lining to loosen. Invert a serving plate on top of the mold. Hold the plate and mold firmly and invert, giving a sharp shake halfway around. Carefully remove the mold from the cassata.

6 To decorate: Beat the cream until standing in stiff peaks, then spoon into a pastry bag fitted with a star nozzle. Pipe cream decoratively around base of the cassata, then pipe a ring on top. Arrange the halved orange slices overlapping on top of the ring of cream and serve at once or refrigerate for up to 1 hour before serving.

Cook's Notes

TIME
30-40 minutes to make cassata, plus chilling overnight and 10 minutes for decorating.

PREPARATION
To line the mold with trifle sponge cakes:

Press a soaked sponge cake into center of base, then press the rest against the sides.

DID YOU KNOW
This is a version of the famous Sicilian sponge cake that is traditionally served at weddings to celebrate the start of a new life.

BUYING GUIDE
Ricotta is made from the whey of cow's milk and is a smooth, mild cheese. It is always sold fresh and is available from Italian delicatessens or the delicatessen counters of some large supermarkets. If it is unavailable, use curd or cottage cheese instead but pass through a strainer before using.

● 520 calories per portion

Grapefruit ice

SERVES 4
grated rind and juice of 2 grapefruit
½ cup superfine sugar
1¼ cups water
2 grapefruit slices, quartered, to decorate

1 Place the sugar and water in a saucepan and heat gently until the sugar has dissolved, then bring to a boil and boil for about 5 minutes, without stirring, until a thick syrup is formed.
2 Remove the syrup from the heat and leave until completely cold.
3 Add the grapefruit rind and juice to the cold syrup and pour into a 1¼-quart shallow freezerproof pan or ice cube tray without the divisions. Freeze in the freezer

compartment of a refrigerator or in the freezer for about 30 minutes (see Cook's tip) until slushy.
4 Remove from the freezer and stir well with a metal spoon until evenly blended.
5 Return to the freezer for 30 minutes, then stir again. Repeat this process once more, then cover and freeze for at least 8 hours.
6 To serve: Stir the mixture well, to break up any large pieces of ice, then spoon into glasses or small dishes. Decorate each portion with quartered grapefruit slices. Serve at once (see Serving ideas).

Pear wine sherbet

SERVES 4
4 firm dessert pears, pared, cored and sliced (see Buying guide)
⅔ cup white wine (see Buying guide)
⅓ cup superfine sugar
strip of lemon rind
maraschino cherries, to decorate

1 Put wine, sugar and rind in a saucepan and stir over low heat until the sugar has dissolved. Bring to a boil, add the pears, then cover the pan and poach the pears gently for about 5 minutes, or until opaque. Remove the pan from the heat and set aside to cool.

2 Discard the lemon rind, reserve a few pear slices for decoration, then purée the cold mixture in a blender or press it through a strainer.

3 Pour into a freezer container, cover and freeze for several hours until firm (see Cook's tips).

4 Remove from the freezer and turn into a large bowl. ☐ Break the sherbet up with a fork, then beat it well until slushy.

5 Spoon the mixture back into its freezer container, cover and return to the freezer for a further 3-4 hours until firm.

6 Remove the sherbet from the freezer and allow it to soften at room temperature for about 15 minutes. Then spoon it into individual glasses and serve decorated with pear slices and maraschino cherries.

Cook's Notes

TIME
Preparation takes only about 20 minutes, but remember to allow several hours for freezing time.

FREEZING
The sherbet can be stored in the freezer for up to 2 months.

BUYING GUIDE
Choose firm pears such as Conference or Comice for this sherbet. Avoid Williams which will be too soft.

It is worth choosing a good wine, or the flavor of the finished sherbet will be disappointing. Choose sweet or dry according to your taste.

! **WATCHPOINT**
If the sherbet is too firm to mash, let it soften slightly at room temperature.

COOK'S TIPS
To make the sherbet in the freezing compartment of an ordinary refrigerator, use a pre-chilled shallow metal tray for freezing the sherbet and turn the refrigerator down to its coldest setting at least 1 hour before you start making the sherbet. This will help speed up the freezing process.

VARIATION
Decorate the sherbet with a few sprigs of fresh mint in season.

● 140 calories per portion

Mint sherbet

SERVES 4

1 cup fresh mint leaves (see Buying
    guide)
2 cups water
½ cup superfine sugar
thinly pared rind and juice of
    2 lemons
few drops of green food coloring
1 egg white
sprigs of mint, to decorate

1 Pour the water into a heavy-bottomed saucepan. Add the sugar and lemon rind and stir over low heat until the sugar has dissolved, then bring to a boil and simmer, without stirring, for 5 minutes.

2 Remove the syrup from the heat, stir in the lemon juice and mint leaves and leave to cool completely.

3 Strain the syrup into a 1-quart freezerproof container. Stir in the coloring, then cover and freeze (see Cook's tips) for about 3 hours, or until the mixture is frozen about ½ inch around the edges and slushy in the center.

4 Turn the mint mixture into a large bowl and mash well with a fork (see Cook's tips). In a clean, dry bowl, beat the egg white until standing in stiff peaks. Beat the mint mixture to break up large lumps, then beat in the egg white about a third at a time and continue beating until evenly incorporated.

5 Return the mixture to the container, cover and freeze for a further 3 hours, or until firm.

6 To serve: Allow the sherbet to soften for 5 minutes at room temperature, then scoop into stemmed glasses. Decorate with a sprig of mint and serve at once.

Tea sherbet

SERVES 8
10½ teaspoons China tea (see Buying guide)
⅔ cup superfine sugar
2½ cups boiling water
juice of 2 lemons
4 egg whites

1 Put the tea into a large flameproof bowl with the sugar. Pour over the boiling water and stir until the sugar has dissolved, then cover and leave to stand for 1 hour.

2 Strain the tea through a very fine strainer into a jug. Stir in the lemon juice, then pour into a 1¼-quart metal loaf pan or other freezerproof container. Cover tightly with foil and freeze in the freezer (or freezing compartment of refrigerator turned to its coldest setting) for 2½ hours, or until half-frozen and slushy.

3 Remove from the freezer, turn into a bowl and mash with a fork to break up the ice crystals, then beat briefly until smooth. Return to container, cover and freeze for a further 2 hours, or until firm.

4 In a clean, dry bowl, beat egg whites until standing in soft peaks.

5 Remove the tea ice from freezer, turn into a large bowl and break up with a fork as before, mashing well. Beat the ice until smooth, then slowly beat in the egg whites. Return the mixture to the container, cover and freeze for a further 4 hours, until firm. ❊

6 To serve: Remove from the freezer and soften at room temperature for 20-30 minutes. Scoop or spoon into small serving dishes. Serve at once (see Serving ideas).

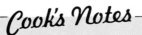

Cook's Notes

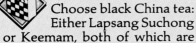

TIME
10-15 minutes preparation, plus 1 hour standing and about 8½ hours freezing, plus softening time.

BUYING GUIDE
Choose black China tea: Either Lapsang Suchong or Keemam, both of which are available from good supermarkets and specialist food stores. Do not use Indian or other teas, they are too strong.

❊ **FREEZING**
Seal the container, label and return to the freezer for up to 3 months. Soften and serve as in stage 6.

SERVING IDEAS
The subtle, slightly bitter, flavor of this sherbet is best complemented with a sweet fruit such as strawberries or raspberries. Candied fruit or rose petals would make a pretty decoration.

● 80 calories per portion

Lemon layer sponge

SERVES 4
3 large eggs, separated
3 tablespoons all-purpose flour
3 tablespoons superfine sugar
¾ cup milk
2 tablespoons butter, melted
grated rind and juice of 1 lemon
confectioners' sugar, to dredge
light cream, to serve

1 Preheat the oven to 325°.
2 Place the egg yolks, flour, super-fine sugar, milk, butter, lemon juice and rind in a large bowl and beat until smoothly blended.
3 In a clean dry bowl, and using clean beaters, beat the egg whites until stiff. Gently but thoroughly fold them into the lemon mixture, using a large metal spoon.
4 Spoon the mixture into a buttered 1¼-quart baking dish standing in a roasting pan. Pour enough hot water into the pan to come about 1 inch up the side of the dish (see Preparation).
5 Bake the sponge in the oven for about 1 hour until risen, golden, and just firm to the touch. Remove the dish from the pan. Sift confectioners' sugar thickly over the top of the sponge. Serve warm, with cream.

Cook's Notes

TIME
About 15 minutes to prepare and 1 hour to bake.

PREPARATION
Standing the dish in a pan of hot water for baking helps keep the sponge deliciously soft and moist.
During baking, the mixture separates into layers: A light sponge on top and a rich custard sauce underneath.

● 210 calories per portion

Creamy blackcurrant cheesecake

MAKES 8-10 SLICES
7 tablespoons butter
¼ cup superfine sugar
½ lb shortbread cookies, finely crushed
butter, for greasing

FILLING AND TOPPING
1 lb cream cheese (see Buying guide)
¾ cup superfine sugar
3 eggs, separated
finely grated rind of ½ lemon
few drops of vanilla
⅔ cup heavy cream
5 teaspoons unflavored gelatin
5 tablespoons water
1 can (about 14 oz) blackcurrant pie filling
lemon twists (optional)

1 Grease a deep, 9-inch round cake pan with a loose base.
2 Put the butter and sugar into a small, heavy-bottomed saucepan and stir over low heat until melted. Remove from the heat and stir in the cookie crumbs, then press the mixture evenly over the base of the prepared pan. Refrigerate.
3 Put the cheese into a large bowl and beat until softened. Beat in ⅓ cup sugar, the egg yolks, lemon rind, vanilla and cream.
4 Sprinkle the gelatin over the water in a flameproof bowl. Leave to soak for 5 minutes until spongy, then stand the bowl in a pan of barely simmering water for 1-2 minutes, stirring occasionally, until the gelatin has dissolved.
5 Allow the gelatin to cool slightly, then beat it into the cheese mixture. Leave in a cool place for about 15 minutes, until on point of setting.
6 In a clean, dry bowl, beat the egg whites until standing in stiff peaks, then gradually beat in the remaining sugar. Fold the meringue into the cheese mixture.
7 Turn filling into prepared pan and level the surface. Cover and chill for at least 3 hours, until set.
8 To serve: Loosen cake with a palette knife, then remove sides of pan. Spread pie filling over the top. Add lemon twists, if liked.

Cook's Notes

TIME
1 hour preparation, plus 3 hours setting and about 5 minutes for finishing.

BUYING GUIDE
Philadelphia (or an equivalent supermarket brand) gives best results and won't turn grainy.

● 665 calories per slice

Date and walnut baked apples

SERVES 4

4 large cooking apples (see Buying guide)
6 tablespoons natural unsweetened apple juice
whipped heavy cream, to serve

FILLING

⅓ cup dates, pitted and coarsely chopped
2 tablespoons shelled walnuts, chopped
2 tablespoons dark brown sugar
½ teaspoon cinnamon

1 Preheat the oven to 350°.
2 Using an apple corer or a small sharp knife, remove the core from each apple. Score the skin around the middle of each apple with a sharp knife (see Cook's tip).
3 Make the filling: Mix together the dates, walnuts, sugar and cinnamon in a bowl. Use to fill cavities, pressing down firmly with the back of a teaspoon.
4 Place in an ovenproof dish, then pour apple juice around apples.
5 Bake in oven for 50-60 minutes, basting occasionally with the apple juice, until the apples are soft when pierced through the center with a sharp knife.
6 Serve at once, accompanied by whipped heavy cream.

Cook's Notes

TIME
15 minutes preparation; 50-60 minutes cooking.

VARIATION
Replace the dates with chopped figs.

COOK'S TIP
Scoring the apples will prevent the skins from exploding during baking.

BUYING GUIDE
Choose Winesap apples, each weighing about ½ lb.

● 175 calories per portion

Magic chocolate pudding

SERVES 4
¾ cup all-purpose flour
1 teaspoon baking powder
2 tablespoons cocoa powder
pinch of salt
1 cup butter or margarine, softened
½ cup superfine sugar
½ teaspoon vanilla
2 eggs, lightly beaten
1-2 tablespoons milk
butter, for greasing

SAUCE
½ cup light brown sugar
2 tablespoons cocoa powder
1¼ cups boiling water

1 Preheat the oven to 375°. Lightly grease a 1¾-quart fairly deep ovenproof pie dish.
2 Sift flour and baking powder into a bowl with cocoa powder and salt, then set aside.
3 Beat the butter and superfine sugar together until pale and fluffy, then beat in the vanilla. Beat in the eggs, a little at a time, adding 1 tablespoon of the flour mixture with the last few additions of egg. Gradually stir in the remaining flour mixture and mix well, then add enough milk to give a smooth dropping consistency.
4 Spoon the mixture into the prepared dish, spread it evenly.
5 Make the sauce: Mix together the brown sugar and cocoa powder, then gradually blend in the water, stirring vigorously to avoid lumps. Pour the sauce over the mixture in the pie dish (see Cook's tip).
6 Bake the pudding in the oven for about 35-40 minutes, or until the pudding is well risen and browned and the chocolate sauce beneath is syrupy. Serve while hot. (See Serving ideas).

Cook's Notes

TIME
15 minutes preparation and 40 minutes baking.

COOK'S TIP
This quick and easy pudding, which is very popular with children, has the added bonus of an "instant" chocolate sauce that cooks with the mixture in the oven. Do not worry if the mixture looks unpromising when you pour over the sauce: During baking it rises above the sauce.

SERVING IDEAS
The pudding is rich enough to eat as it is, but if you are feeling really indulgent, serve it with ice cream or whipped cream.

SPECIAL OCCASION
Use dark rum instead of milk. Stir in ¼ cup chopped walnuts or blanched almonds at the end of stage 3.

● 520 calories per portion

Queen of puddings

SERVES 4
1 cup fresh white bread crumbs
2 tablespoons sugar
grated rind of ½ lemon
2 cups milk
1 tablespoon butter or margarine
2 egg yolks
5 tablespoons lemon curd
butter or margarine, for greasing

MERINGUE
2 egg whites
⅓ cup superfine sugar

1 Mix the bread crumbs, sugar and lemon rind together in a bowl. In a small saucepan, bring the milk and butter almost to a boil, then remove from the heat and pour over the crumb mixture. Stir well, then leave to soak for 10-15 minutes.

2 Meanwhile, preheat the oven to 350°. Grease a 1-quart ovenproof pie dish.

3 Beat the egg yolks into the milky crumbs, then spoon the mixture into the dish and spread it evenly. Bake in the oven for 35-40 minutes, until just set in the center. !

4 Remove the dish from the oven and spread the lemon curd over the pudding. In a spotlessly clean and dry bowl, beat the egg whites until standing in stiff peaks. Reserve 2-3 teaspoons of the superfine sugar; beat the remaining sugar into the egg whites, 1 tablespoon at a time, and continue beating until the meringue is stiff and glossy. Spread it over the pudding, then form into peaks (see Preparation) and sprinkle over the reserved sugar.

5 Return the dish to the oven and bake for 10-15 minutes, until the surface of the meringue is crisp and lightly browned.

6 Serve the pudding at once, straight from the dish.

Tropical crumble

SERVES 4-6

4 oranges, pared and chopped
4 fresh apricots, pitted and
　chopped or 8 canned apricot
　halves, chopped
2 large bananas, peeled and sliced
¼ lb fresh pineapple,
　chopped, or canned pineapple
　chunks
light cream or ice cream, to serve

TOPPING

½ cup all-purpose flour
½ teaspoon ground ginger
⅓ cup rolled oats
¼ cup desiccated coconut
⅔ cup dark brown sugar
5 tablespoons butter, melted.

1 Preheat the oven to 350°.
2 First make the topping: Sift the flour and ginger into a mixing bowl. Add the oats, coconut and sugar and mix together. Stir in the melted butter.
3 Put all the fruit into a deep oven-proof dish, turning the banana slices in the juice from the oranges to prevent them from discoloring.
4 Sprinkle the topping evenly over the fruit and press down gently to level the surface.
5 Bake for about 40 minutes or until the fruit mixture is bubbling up around the edge of the topping. Serve hot with light cream or, if preferred, ice cream.

Cook's Notes

TIME
The preparation of the fruit and the crumble topping will take about 20 minutes. The cooking time is about 40 minutes.

COOK'S TIP
If using canned pineapple, try to find a can that has unsweetened syrup, because the topping mixture for the crumble is itself very sweet.

VARIATIONS
Use other fruits such as apple or rhubarb with the same crumble topping. If you use dried fruit allow an extra 3 hours soaking time.

● 510 calories per portion

Bread and butter pudding

SERVES 4

4 medium thick slices white bread,
 crusts removed
3 tablespoons butter
⅓ cup golden raisins
2 tablespoons superfine sugar
2 large eggs
1¼ cups milk
¼ teaspoon ground nutmeg

1 Butter the bread well on one side. Cut each slice into 4.

2 Layer bread, buttered side up, in a well-greased 1¼-quart ovenproof dish, sprinkling raisins and sugar between each layer and on top of the last layer.

3 Beat the eggs and milk together and strain over the bread. Leave to stand in a cool place for 30 minutes.

4 Preheat the oven to 350°.

5 Sprinkle the nutmeg over the pudding and bake in the oven for 25-30 minutes until set and golden brown. Serve hot.

Cook's Notes

 TIME
Preparation 10 minutes, cooking time 30 minutes, but allow another 30 minutes soaking time.

ECONOMY
This is an excellent way of using up stale white or whole wheat bread.

● 665 calories per portion

Sherry trifle

SERVES 4-6
**2 sponge layers, cut in half
 horizontally**
⅓ cup raspberry jam
¼ cup medium sherry
**1 can (about 14 oz) raspberries,
 drained with syrup reserved**
3 large eggs
2 tablespoons superfine sugar
2½ cups milk
1 teaspoon vanilla
**1¼ cups heavy whipping
 cream**
candied cherries, halved
a little angelica, to finish

1 Spread the sponges with the jam, then sandwich together again. Cut into 1 inch pieces and arrange in the base of a glass serving bowl.
2 Stir the sherry into the reserved raspberry syrup, then pour over the sponges. Scatter the raspberries over the top.

3 Beat the eggs and sugar lightly together in a large bowl (see Cook's tip). Heat the milk until almost boiling in a small saucepan, then pour onto the egg and sugar mixture, beating constantly.
4 Strain the mixture into a heavy-bottomed pan. ⚠ Cook over low heat for 10-15 minutes, ⚠ stirring constantly with a wooden spoon, until the custard is thick enough to coat the back of the spoon. Remove from the heat, stir in the vanilla and leave to cool for 10 minutes.
5 Pour the custard over the raspberries and sponges and leave to cool completely. Cover and refrigerate for 3-4 hours, or overnight.
6 Beat the cream until it forms soft peaks. Spread one-third of the cream over the custard and mark the surface with a fork or small spatula, if liked. Put the remaining cream into a pastry bag fitted with a large star nozzle. Pipe a border of cream and a lattice on the trifle, then decorate with cherries and angelica. Serve at once, or cover and refrigerate for 2-3 hours.

Cook's Notes

TIME
1 hour preparation, plus cooling and chilling.

WATCHPOINTS
A heavy-bottomed pan is essential, or the custard will overheat and the eggs will scramble. Do not be impatient and attempt to hurry the custard by raising the heat, or it will turn lumpy.

VARIATIONS
Use another fruit, such as strawberries or apricots, and a jam of the same flavor.

COOK'S TIP
If you're hesitant about making an egg custard mix 1 teaspoon cornstarch with the superfine sugar, then beat in the eggs.

● 775 calories per portion

Nutty apple crumble

SERVES 4

3 large dessert apples (total weight about 1 lb)
⅓ cup golden raisins
¼ cup light brown sugar
2 tablespoons water

CRUMBLE TOPPING
1 cup whole wheat flour
1 teaspoon ground allspice
½ cup chilled butter or margarine, cubed [!]
½ cup walnuts, roughly chopped
¼-⅓ cup light brown sugar, according to taste

1 Preheat the oven to 375°.
2 Make the crumble topping: Put the flour in a mixing bowl with the allspice. Stir well to mix. Add the butter and cut it in with a round-bladed knife, then cut in the pieces until the mixture resembles coarse bread crumbs. Stir in the walnuts and sugar to taste, then set aside.
3 Pare, core and slice the apples (see Cook's tip) and layer them with the raisins and the sugar in a well-buttered 1¾-quart ovenproof dish. Sprinkle over the water.
4 Sprinkle the crumble mixture over the apples and press down lightly to level the surface.
5 Bake in the oven for 40-50 minutes or until the crumble topping is crisp and golden and the apples are tender. Serve hot or warm.

Cook's Notes

TIME
Preparation 15 minutes, cooking time 50 minutes.

SERVING IDEAS
This sweet dessert is best served with a sharp-tasting plain yogurt, rather than custard or cream.

! WATCHPOINT
Make sure the butter is well chilled or it will be impossible to rub in. Do not overwork the mixture or it will become sticky and doughy and impossible to work with.

COOK'S TIP
Slice the apples thinly so they will be cooked at the same time as the topping.

VARIATION
Use green apples and the full amount of sugar for the topping.

● 560 calories per portion

Jam soufflé omelet

MAKES 2, TO SERVE 4
6 eggs
2 tablespoons superfine sugar
few drops of vanilla
3 tablespoons butter
6-8 tablespoons jam, warmed
¼ cup confectioners' sugar, to dredge

1 Make the first omelet: Separate 3 of the eggs, placing the whites in a clean, dry bowl. Beat the egg whites until standing in soft peaks. In a separate bowl, beat the egg yolks with half the sugar and 1-2 drops vanilla.
2 Preheat the broiler to high.
3 Melt half the butter in an omelet pan or skillet with a base diameter of 8 inches. [!] Meanwhile, quickly fold the beaten egg yolks into the egg whites with a large metal spoon.
4 As soon as the butter is foaming, pour in the egg mixture and turn down the heat to low. Cook the omelet, without stirring, [!] for

Cook's Notes

TIME
Each omelet takes about 10 minutes to prepare and cook.

WATCHPOINTS
The size of the pan is important: If it is too small the omelet will be too thick to fold; if it is too large the omelet will be disappointingly thin.
If stirred, the omelet will lose its light, fluffy texture.

COOK'S TIP
If you only need to serve 2 people, make just 1 omelet, but if serving 4, do not try to keep the first omelet hot while cooking the second one. Pick an occasion when it does not matter if everyone is served at one time. To cut down the time between servings beat the second batch of egg whites while the first omelet is cooking.

DID YOU KNOW
This type of sweet omelet is traditionally decorated with a criss-cross pattern, made by placing heated metal skewers on top of the folded omelet until the confectioners' sugar is caramelized, as shown in the photograph.

● 340 calories per portion

2-3 minutes, until the underside is set and golden. Then place the pan under the broiler for 2-3 minutes, until the top of the omelet is golden brown.
5 Spread half the warmed jam over one-half of the omelet. Using a large palette knife or spatula, fold the omelet in half to enclose jam.
6 Slide the omelet onto a warmed dish and sift half the confectioners' sugar over the top. Cut across in half and serve at once.
7 Use the remaining ingredients to made the second omelet in the same way (see Cook's tip).

Orange castles

SERVES 4
1 package (about ¼ lb) orange flavored gelatin
1 cup boiling water
¾ cup cold water
8 oz cream cheese

TO DECORATE
about ½ cup desiccated coconut
1 can (about 11 oz) mandarin orange segments, drained
"leaves" of angelica

1 Put the gelatin in a jug, add 1 cup boiling water and stir until dissolved. Then gradually mix in the ¾ cup cold water.
2 Refrigerate the gelatin until beginning to set around the edges. Beat the cream cheese until smooth then gradually beat in the setting gelatin.

3 Rinse out four ⅔ cup molds with water (see Cook's tips). Divide the gelatin mixture between the prepared molds, cover with plastic wrap and refrigerate for 1-2 hours, until set.
4 Unmold the gelatins, one at a time: Run a round-bladed knife around the sides of the gelatin to loosen it. Dip the base of the mold in a bowl of hot water for 2-3 seconds, then invert a dampened dessert plate on top. Hold the mold and plate firmly and invert them, giving a sharp shake halfway around (see Cook's tips). Lift off the mold.
5 Sprinkle the coconut over the gelatins, covering the tops and as much of the sides as possible. Using the tip of a round-bladed knife, lift the loose coconut from the plates and gently press it onto the sides of the gelatins.
6 Arrange mandarin orange segments on the top and around the base of each gelatin, then decorate with "leaves" of angelica. Serve at once, or refrigerate for up to 2 hours.

Cook's Notes

TIME
30 minutes preparation (including decorating), plus setting time.

COOK'S TIPS
You can reduce setting time by chilling the dessert for 1 hour beforehand.
Empty plastic yogurt, cream or salad cartons make ideal molds for this dessert if you do not have individual castle gelatin or dariole molds.
The gelatins can be difficult to turn out; you may need to repeat dipping and shaking.

SPECIAL OCCASION
Turn gelatins out onto glass dishes. Sprinkle mandarins around base of gelatins with orange liqueur.

● 235 calories per gelatin

Iced chocolate boxes

MAKES 6

1 pint block chocolate ice cream (see Watchpoint)
24 peppermint chocolates (see Buying guide)
⅔ cup heavy cream
1 can (about ¾ lb) mandarin orange segments, drained
6 small sprigs fresh mint, to decorate (optional)

1 Cut the ice cream into 6 equal cubes and place on a freezerproof plate. Press 1 chocolate onto 4 sides of each cube leaving the top and bottom plain. Return to the freezer, or freezing compartment of the refrigerator while you prepare the cream.

2 Beat the cream until thick, but not stiff, then put into a pastry bag fitted with a large star nozzle (see Cook's tip).
3 Remove the chocolate boxes from the freezer and pipe the cream on the top of each box. Top with mandarin orange segments and a sprig of mint, if liked. Place on chilled, individual serving plates and serve immediately, before the ice cream melts.

Cook's Notes

TIME
Preparation takes only 15 minutes.

WATCHPOINT
Be sure to buy block ice cream; the soft-scoop variety is not suitable.

BUYING GUIDE
Wafer-thin plain chocolates with peppermint fondant cream centers are best; they are sold in ½ lb boxes, each containing about 26.

COOKS' TIP
Instead of piping the cream, you can pile it on top of each box with a spoon.

FREEZING
Prepare the boxes up to the end of stage 1; open freeze, then place in a single layer in a rigid container. Cover and return to the freezer for up to 1 month. Use straight from the freezer; decorate and serve.

● 300 calories per portion

Raisin semolina

SERVES 4-6
2½ cups milk
¼ cup semolina
¼ cup seedless raisins
1 egg, beaten
¼ cup soft brown sugar
½ teaspoon cinnamon
1 tablespoon butter or margarine,
   shaved into flakes
melted butter or margarine,
   for greasing

1 Brush the inside of a 2½-cup flameproof dish with butter.
2 Pour the milk into a heavy-bottomed saucepan and heat gently until just below boiling point. Sprinkle in the semolina and stir until the mixture comes to a boil. Add the raisins, then reduce the heat and cook gently for 15 minutes, stirring frequently.
3 Preheat the broiler to high.
4 Remove the pan from the heat.

Allow the semolina mixture to cool slightly, then beat in the egg, a little at a time. ⚠ Return the pan to low heat and cook, stirring, for 1 minute.
5 Turn the semolina mixture into the prepared dish and level the surface. Mix the sugar with the cinnamon and sprinkle over the surface of the semolina, then dot with the butter.
6 Place under the broiler for 2-3 minutes, until the sugar is melted and bubbling. ⚠ Serve hot or cold, straight from the dish.

Cook's Notes

TIME
Preparation and cooking take about 25 minutes.

WATCHPOINTS
Beat the egg into the mixture quickly, otherwise it will start to set.
   Watch the topping constantly; once the sugar starts to color it darkens very rapidly.

SERVING IDEAS
Divide the cooked semolina between 4-6 ramekin dishes. Add the sugar topping and butter and caramelize. Just before serving, top with whipped cream.

DID YOU KNOW
Semolina is made from the grains of durum wheat. It is a handy pantry item for savory as well as sweet dishes but, once opened, it goes stale very quickly and should be used within 3 months.

COOK'S TIP
If more convenient, you can finish the semolina in the oven, preheated to 375°. It will take about 10 minutes for the sugar to caramelize.

● 255 calories per portion

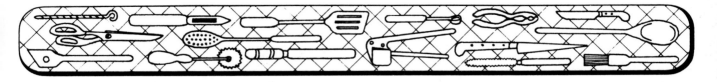

Treacle tart

SERVES 4-6

1 package (about 9 oz) pie crust
  sticks, prepared
1 cup dark corn syrup (see Cook's
  tips)
1½ cups white bread crumbs, made
  from stale bread
grated rind and juice of ½ lemon
heavy cream or custard, to serve
  (optional)

1 Preheat the oven to 400°.
2 Roll out the pastry thinly on a
lightly floured surface and use to
line an 8-inch loose-bottomed flan
dish. Trim the edges and reserve the
trimmings. Prick the pastry base
with a fork and refrigerate.
3 To make the filling: Put the syrup,
bread crumbs, lemon rind and juice
into a small saucepan and heat
gently, stirring, until the ingredients

are thoroughly combined. ⚠ Leave
to cool before spooning into the
prepared pastry case.
4 Roll out the reserved pastry
trimmings and cut into long, ¼-
inch wide strips. Use to decorate
the top of the tart in a lattice pattern,
moistening the ends of the lattice

strips and pressing them firmly
against the edge of the pastry case
so they do not come loose during
baking.
5 Bake in the oven for about 25
minutes or until the pastry is golden
and the filling is just set. Serve warm
or cold with cream or custard.

Cook's Notes

⏰ TIME
Preparation 20 minutes,
cooking time 25 minutes.

👨‍🍳 COOK'S TIPS
To measure the corn
syrup, first warm the
corn syrup container in a bowl
of hot water so that the syrup
flows freely. This is a traditional,
popular British recipe which is
normally made with golden
syrup, but sometimes black
treacle is used.

● 460 calories per portion

❗ WATCHPOINT
Do not allow the mix-
ture to boil or it will resemble toffee.

🥄 VARIATION
Make tart on a 9-inch
pie plate and decorate
with a sunflower edge as shown
in the photograph: Cut the
pastry edge into 1-inch strips,
fold the strips diagonally in half
and press down firmly. Glaze
the edge by brushing with egg
yolk which has been beaten
with a little milk.

Banana fan flambé

SERVES 4

4 large bananas, cut into fans (see Preparation)
¼ cup rum
juice of 1½ oranges
¼ teaspoon cinnamon
large pinch of freshly ground nutmeg
6 tablespoons butter
little lightly beaten egg white
4 tablespoons light brown sugar
vanilla ice cream or whipped cream, to serve

1 Pour the rum into a cup and stand in a pan or bowl of hot water to warm through gently. In a separate cup, mix the orange juice with the cinnamon and nutmeg.

2 Melt the butter in a large, heavy-bottomed skillet over low heat. Lightly brush fans with egg white, then add them to the pan and cook gently for about 5 minutes, turning once, until golden brown on both sides. [!] Sprinkle over the sugar.

3 Pour in the spiced orange juice and heat through gently. Turn off the heat. Pour the warmed rum over the bananas and immediately set light to it. [!] Let the flames die completely, then divide the fans and sauce between 4 warmed individual dishes and serve with ice cream.

242

Gooseberry fool

SERVES 4

1 pint gooseberries, topped and
    tailed if fresh (see Preparation),
    thawed and well drained if frozen
    (see Watchpoints)
2 tablespoons water
¼ cup superfine sugar
2 cups vanilla pudding, cooled
few drops of green food coloring
⅔ cup plain yogurt
4 teaspoons colored sugar crystals
    (optional)

1 Put the gooseberries into a heavy-bottomed saucepan with the water. Cover and cook over moderate heat for about 8 minutes, until soft.
2 Press the gooseberries through a strainer, or cool slightly, then purée in a blender and strain the purée to remove seeds. Sweeten to taste with superfine sugar, then leave to cool completely.
3 Stir the purée into the pudding until evenly blended, then add enough coloring to tint the fool pale green. Cover and refrigerate for 1-2 hours, if liked.
4 Divide the fool between 4 dessert glasses or bowls. Spoon a little yogurt carefully onto each portion.
5 Just before serving, scatter the yogurt with sugar crystals if liked.
⚠ Serve at room temperature or, chilled.

Cook's Notes

TIME
25 minutes preparation, plus cooling and chilling time.

WATCHPOINT

If using thawed gooseberries, drain them on paper towels before cooking otherwise the purée will be too watery.
Sugar crystals will dissolve if added more than 5 minutes before serving.

SERVING IDEAS
This smooth, light dessert needs to be served with crisp cookies for texture contrast.

STORAGE
Prepare up to the end of stage 3; cover with plastic wrap and refrigerate for up to 24 hours.

PREPARATION
Use a small, sharp stainless steel knife to trim off the small fibrous stalks and "tails" from fresh gooseberries. This is called "topping and tailing."

● 200 calories per portion

Flaky rice sundae

SERVES 4
2½ cups milk
½ cup flaked rice (see Buying guide)
2 tablespoons sugar
few drops of vanilla

TOPPING
1 tablespoon butter or margarine
1 tablespoon corn syrup
1 cup corn flakes or rice crispies

1 Pour the milk into a medium heavy-bottomed saucepan. Bring slowly to simmering point over low heat, then sprinkle in the flaked rice. Simmer gently, stirring frequently, for 15-20 minutes, until the rice is tender and thickened. ⚠
2 Remove from the heat and stir in the sugar and vanilla, to taste. Cool slightly, then spoon into 4 dessert dishes. Leave to cool completely.
3 Make the topping: Melt the butter with the syrup in a saucepan over low heat. Remove from the heat, add the corn flakes and stir gently with a large metal spoon until evenly coated.
4 Spoon the topping over the sundaes. ⚠ Leave to set about 30 minutes before serving.

Cook's Notes

 TIME
35 minutes preparation, plus cooling time.

BUYING GUIDE
You can buy white and brown rice flakes. The brown variety, which are sold in health food stores, have a pleasant "nutty" flavor and more food value.

! WATCHPOINTS
The milk should only simmer gently, otherwise it will evaporate and the pudding will be too thick.
The topping sticks together and hardens as it cools, so it must be divided between the dishes while still warm.

SERVING IDEAS
This easy-to-make milk pudding with its tempting crisp, sweet topping can also be served hot. Spoon the pudding into the dishes, but do not cool; make and add the topping, then serve at once.

 VARIATIONS
Try this topping over other milk puddings (canned, if liked), such as sago or semolina.

● 240 calories per portion

QUICK 'N' EASY COOKING

This is the section for the cook who never has enough time. All the dishes can be prepared and cooked in under an hour, giving you an infinite variety of meals for snacks, brunch, lunch and supper. There are salads and vegetables, soups and snacks, rice 'n' pasta and egg 'n' cheese dishes. There is also a selection of recipes for those main meals when you just haven't much time or guests arrive unexpectedly. Try making the delicious *Country goulash*, or tasty *Baconburgers*, which children will love. Appetizing and filling sandwiches are also included for those quick lunches or the late-night impromptu snack.

SALADS AND VEGETABLES

Mushroom and Stilton salad

SERVES 4
¼ lb button mushrooms, chopped
1 cup grated Stilton cheese
½ cup shelled walnut halves
4 large lettuce leaves
2 tomatoes, quartered

VINAIGRETTE DRESSING
1 tablespoon white wine vinegar
2 teaspoons lemon juice
3 tablespoons vegetable oil
1 teaspoon dried mixed herbs (optional)
about ½ teaspoon sugar
salt and freshly ground black pepper

1 Mix the mushrooms and Stilton cheese together in a bowl, forking them through gently until thoroughly combined. Cover and refrigerate for at least 1 hour.
2 Meanwhile, make the vinaigrette dressing: In a bowl mix together the vinegar, lemon juice and oil. Add the dried herbs, if using, and sugar to taste. Season with salt and freshly ground black pepper.
3 Reserve 8 walnut halves to garnish and chop the remainder roughly. Mix with the mushrooms and Stilton cheese.
4 Spoon a little of the dressing into the mixture and fork through gently until well combined.
5 Arrange the lettuce leaves on 4 individual serving plates. Carefully spoon a quarter of the mushroom and Stilton cheese mixture onto the

top of each of the lettuce leaves.
6 Garnish each serving with 2 walnut halves and 2 tomato quarters. Hand the remaining vinaigrette dressing separately.

Cook's Notes

TIME
The salad takes about 15 minutes to prepare but allow time for chilling the mushrooms and the Stilton.

SERVING IDEAS
This salad is very rich, but very tasty. Serve it with warm granary toast or rolls for a supper or lunch dish.

● 315 calories per portion

Tropical salad

SERVES 4-6

¾ cup pasta shells
2 grapefruit, peeled and segmented
2 oranges, peeled and segmented
2 large dessert apples, diced
3 celery stalks, finely chopped
¼ lb Italian salami, roughly
    chopped
1 tablespoon chopped chives
¼ cup salted cashew nuts

DRESSING

¼ cup thick mayonnaise
2 tablespoons fresh orange juice
finely grated rind and juice of 1
    lemon
2 tablespoons rosehip syrup
salt and freshly ground black
    pepper

TO GARNISH

slices of unpeeled orange
watercress

1 Bring a pan of salted water to a boil and cook the pasta for about 10 minutes or until just tender. Rinse in cold water and drain well.

2 Turn the pasta into a large bowl and stir in the prepared fruit, celery and salami. Mix thoroughly.

3 To make the dressing: Mix together the mayonnaise, orange juice, lemon rind and juice and the rosehip syrup. Beat with a fork until thoroughly combined. Season with salt and pepper.

4 Toss the salad and dressing well together, then turn into a salad bowl and sprinkle over the chives and cashews.

5 Serve garnished with slices of unpeeled orange and watercress.

Cook's Notes

TIME
Preparation of this salad takes 20 minutes plus 10 minutes to cook the pasta.

SERVING IDEAS
This makes a refreshing summer lunch.

● 430 calories per portion

Tuna salad

SERVES 4
1 can (about 7 oz) tuna, drained and flaked
1 crisp lettuce (see Buying guide)
1 can (3 oz) pimientos, drained
1 can (about 1 lb) red kidney beans, drained
1½ cups black olives, pitted
1 onion, sliced into rings

DRESSING
3 tablespoons olive oil
1 tablespoon wine vinegar
½ teaspoon dry mustard
pinch of sugar
1 clove garlic, crushed (optional)
salt and freshly ground black pepper

1 Make the dressing: Put all the dressing ingredients into a screw-top jar with salt and pepper to taste. Shake thoroughly to mix, then chill in the refrigerator until ready to use.
2 Line the sides of a large salad bowl with the outside leaves of the lettuce, discarding any damaged leaves.
3 Cut the pimientos into strips.
4 Shred the remaining lettuce (see Preparation) and combine it with the flaked tuna, kidney beans, pimiento and olives. Place in the center of the salad bowl.
5 Place the sliced onion decoratively on top of the prepared tuna salad to garnish.
6 Pour the dressing over the salad, but do not toss it or you will spoil its appearance, then serve at once. [!]

Cook's Notes

TIME
Preparation takes 10 minutes.

BUYING GUIDE
A small iceberg lettuce is the best kind for this recipe.

WATCHPOINT
Do not dress the salad until just before serving or it will become soggy.

VARIATIONS
Use canned butter or white haricot beans instead of the kidney beans. Add sliced hard-cooked egg for extra nourishment and color.

SERVING IDEAS
Serve with hot French bread and/or potato salad.

PREPARATION
To shred lettuce:

1 *Pile several lettuce leaves on top of each other with the stem ends at right angles to you.*

2 *Roll up the leaves, rolling away from you, then slice the roll into thin strips.*

● 305 calories per portion

Harvest ham salad

SERVES 4

½ lb cooked ham, diced
2½ cups water
salt
¾ cup fresh peas (shelled weight)
½ lb zucchini, sliced diagonally into ½-inch lengths
2 tablespoons thick mayonnaise
¼ cup plain yogurt
½ teaspoon dry mustard
freshly ground black pepper
½ lb white cabbage, finely shredded
chopped chives, to garnish

1 Bring the water to a boil in a saucepan, add salt to taste, then the peas. Bring back to a boil, then lower the heat, cover and simmer 3 minutes.

2 Add the sliced zucchini to the pan, cover again and simmer further 4-5 minutes until the vegetables are just tender. Drain, rinse under cold running water, then spread out on paper towels to cool and drain thoroughly.

3 In a large bowl, mix the mayonnaise, yogurt and mustard with salt and pepper to taste. Fold in the cabbage, ham, peas and zucchini.

4 Turn the mixture into a serving dish and garnish with chopped chives. Serve at once or place ungarnished in a covered container and refrigerate overnight, then garnish just before serving.

Cook's Notes

TIME
Total preparation time is about 20 minutes.

VARIATIONS
Frozen peas can be used, but need less cooking time. Put them into the boiling water with the zucchini.

Other cooked meats can be used in place of ham. Try chicken, salami or smoked continental sausage.

SERVING IDEAS
Serve with French or fresh pita bread.

● 210 calories per portion

Chef's layered salad

SERVES 4
8 lettuce leaves, shredded
4 hard-cooked eggs, sliced
4 tomatoes, sliced
about ½ lb boneless cooked chicken, diced (see Economy)
¼ small cucumber (about 2 inch), unpared and thinly sliced
1 large carrot, grated
1 cup grated Cheddar or Edam cheese

DRESSING
¼ cup olive oil
1 tablespoon cider vinegar
salt and freshly ground black pepper

1 Arrange the shredded lettuce in the base of a large glass bowl (see Serving ideas).

2 Arrange the sliced eggs on the lettuce and then sliced tomatoes in a third layer over the eggs.

3 Place the diced chicken on top, then add layers of cucumber, carrot and finally grated cheese. When you arrange the cheese, leave a 1-inch border of carrot showing around the edge.

4 Make the dressing: Mix the oil and vinegar together and season to taste with salt and pepper. Pour evenly over the salad and serve.

Cook's Notes

TIME
Preparation, including hard-cooking and cooling the eggs, takes 45 minutes.

COOK'S TIP
The salad can be prepared in advance and covered with plastic wrap, and the dressing mixed and stored in a screw-top jar, to be added at the last minute.

ECONOMY
Buy chicken thighs and roast them in foil. This will be far less expensive than buying a whole chicken. Five thighs will yield about ½ lb chicken meat.

SERVING IDEAS
Be sure to make the salad in a glass bowl, to display the layers to best effect. Vary the arrangement of the layers as you wish.

This substantial main-course salad makes a complete meal served either with potato salad or with thinly sliced whole wheat bread and butter.

● 430 calories per portion

Eggplant and pasta bake

SERVES 4

2 cans (about 14¾ oz) eggplants in
   sunflower seed oil (see Buying
   guide)
2 tablespoons vegetable oil
1 large onion, chopped
1 red pepper, seeded and
   chopped
1 teaspoon dried mixed herbs
large pinch of ground cinnamon
   (see Cook's tips)
salt and freshly ground black pepper
1½ cups whole wheat short-cut
   macaroni, (see Variation)

TOPPING
2 eggs
1¼ cups plain yogurt
½ cup grated mature Cheddar
   cheese
paprika, for sprinkling

1 Preheat the oven to 400°.
2 Heat the oil in a heavy-based
saucepan. Add the onion and red
pepper and cook gently, stirring
frequently, about 10 minutes until
the vegetables are softened. Stir
in the eggplants and their oil,
herbs, cinnamon and salt and
pepper to taste. Cover and keep
warm.
3 While the vegetables are cooking, bring a large pan of salted water
to a boil. Add the macaroni and stir
once. Bring the water back to a boil
and cook for 9-11 minutes, until the
macaroni is just tender.
4 Drain the macaroni thoroughly,
then stir into the eggplant mixture.
Check the seasoning, then turn into
a 2½-3 pint baking or gratin dish
and level the surface.
5 Make the topping: Whisk the
eggs into the yogurt, then stir in the
cheese and salt and pepper to taste.
Pour over the eggplant mixture
and sprinkle with paprika according
to taste.
6 Bake in the oven about 40
minutes, until the topping is set and
browned (see Cook's tips). Serve
hot, straight from the casserole.

Cook's Notes

TIME
30 minutes preparation
plus about 40 minutes
baking time.

BUYING GUIDE
Canned eggplants, av-
ailable in delicatessens
and large supermarkets, are a
useful buy when the fresh ones
are not available.

● 700 calories per portion

VARIATION
Use white macaroni in-
stead of whole wheat
but remember that it needs less
time to cook.

COOK'S TIPS
Cinnamon adds a hint
of spice to the mixture,
without making it "sweet".
   The casserole can be left in the
oven, with heat turned off, for
20-30 minutes without spoiling.

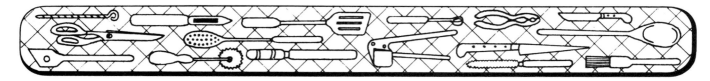

Paprika potatoes

SERVES 4
1½ lb potatoes
salt
2 tablespoons vegetable oil
1 medium onion, sliced
1 teaspoon paprika
1¼ cups chicken broth
**½ teaspoon caraway seeds
(optional)**
**1 large tomato, peeled and
chopped**
freshly ground black pepper
3 tablespoons dairy sour cream
extra paprika, to garnish

1 Boil the potatoes in salted water until they are beginning to soften — about 7 minutes. Drain and cut into ¼-inch slices.
2 Heat the oil in a large saucepan and cook the onion over moderate heat about 4 minutes, or until it is just beginning to turn light brown. Add the paprika, chicken broth, caraway seeds, if using, tomato and pepper. Stir well and add the potatoes, stirring carefully.
3 Bring slowly to a boil, cover the pan and simmer for 20-25 minutes. The potatoes should have absorbed most of the liquid.
4 Pour over the dairy sour cream and allow just to heat through. Turn onto a warmed serving dish. Sprinkle with a little extra paprika to garnish.

Cook's Notes

TIME
This dish takes 45 minutes to make.

? DID YOU KNOW
Caraway seeds have an aniseed taste which imparts a very definite flavor to food.

● 265 calories per portion

Sunshine supper

SERVES 4

1 large eggplant
salt
4 tablespoons olive oil
1 clove garlic, crushed (optional)
1 onion, chopped
1 green pepper, seeded and finely
  chopped
1 can (about 14 oz) tomatoes,
  chopped (see Economy)
¼ cup red wine
2 teaspoons tomato paste
½ teaspoon sugar
1 teaspoon dried basil
freshly ground black pepper
1 cup ribbon noodles (see Buying
  guide)
6 slices processed cheese
3 tablespoons grated Parmesan
  cheese
melted butter, for greasing

1 Wipe the eggplant with a damp cloth and trim off the stem. Slice the eggplant into ¼-inch thick slices and put them in a colander in layers, sprinkling salt between each layer. Cover with a plate and place a heavy weight on top. Leave for about 1 hour to draw out the bitter juices then rinse the slices and pat dry on paper towels.
2 Preheat the oven to 350°.
3 Heat 1 tablespoon of the oil in a saucepan, add the garlic, if using, the onion and green pepper and cook gently for about 5 minutes until the onion is soft and lightly colored. Stir in tomatoes with juices, wine and tomato paste. Bring to boil, stir in the sugar and basil and season with salt and pepper to taste. Let the sauce boil gently to reduce and thicken.
4 Meanwhile, bring a pan of salted water to a boil and add 1 teaspoon of oil. Cook the noodles for 10-12 minutes until just tender then drain thoroughly.
5 Heat the remaining oil in a skillet, add the eggplant slices and cook gently until they are lightly colored on both sides. Remove with a slotted spoon and drain on paper towels.
6 Grease an ovenproof dish with melted butter and spread a third of the tomato sauce over the bottom.

Put half the noodles on top, followed by half the eggplant slices and half the processed cheese. Cover with another third of the tomato sauce and then the remaining noodles, eggplant slices and processed cheese. Spread the remaining tomato sauce over the cheese slices and sprinkle the Parmesan cheese on top.
7 Cook in the oven for about 20 minutes, until heated through. Serve immediately straight from the dish.

Cook's Notes

TIME
Draining the eggplant takes 1 hour; allow another 20-25 minutes for the rest of the preparation. Cooking takes 20 minutes.

BUYING GUIDE
Look for green noodles available in most supermarkets; they are particularly suitable for this dish.

● 355 calories per portion

SERVING IDEAS
This delicious supper dish needs only a salad accompaniment to make it a complete meal.

ECONOMY
Use fresh tomatoes for the sauce when they are plentiful and low in price — you will need ¾ lb. Peel and chop them and add to the onion and green pepper with a little extra wine.

Creamed leek pastry

SERVES 4

1½ lb leeks, finely sliced
½ cup butter
1 sheet (½ 17 oz package) frozen
   puff pastry, thawed
1 small egg
salt
freshly grated nutmeg
3 tablespoons light cream
freshly ground black pepper

1 Preheat the oven to 400°.
2 Melt the butter in a large saucepan and add the leeks, stir and cover. Cook over very gentle heat for about 15 minutes, stirring occasionally until leeks are soft. ⚠
3 Meanwhile, roll out the pastry on a lightly floured surface to a 12 × 10-inch rectangle. Fold the pastry in half lengthwise so that it measures 12 × 5 inches. Lightly roll over the pastry to expel any air bubbles.

Cook's Notes

TIME
Preparation is about 10 minutes, cooking time 15 minutes for the leeks and 20 minutes for the pastry.

COOK'S TIP
If the pastry has risen unevenly, gently prick it to let the air escape and it will sink and become flat.

WATCHPOINT
Be careful not to let the leeks burn — cook them on the lowest possible heat.

SERVING IDEAS
Serve as an appetizer or a snack, with a tomato and cucumber salad.
   Make individual portions by cutting the long strip of pastry into four pieces before cooking.

VARIATIONS
Instead of leeks use grated or finely chopped carrots with ginger, or cabbage finely chopped with cinnamon added.

● 630 calories per portion

4 Press the edges of the pastry together well. Prick with a fork all over. Place the pastry strip on a dampened cookie sheet and bake in the oven for 10 minutes.
5 Beat the egg lightly with a pinch of salt. Remove the pastry from the oven and brush with the egg, pressing the pastry down gently as you brush. Return to the oven for a further 10 minutes until golden.
6 Add a little nutmeg to the cooked leeks, stir in the cream and season to taste with salt and pepper. Keep the leeks warm, but do not boil.
7 Carefully lift the pastry from the cookie sheet and place on a serving plate (see Cook's tip). Spoon the leek mixture on top of the pastry and serve at once.

Lentil layer pie

SERVES 4
¾ cup split red lentils (see Buying guide)
1 large onion, chopped
¼ teaspoon dried basil
¼ teaspoon dried thyme
1 can (about 8 oz) tomatoes
2 cups beef broth
salt and freshly ground black pepper
2 tablespoons butter or margarine
1 cup fresh white bread crumbs
4 large hard-cooked eggs, sliced
butter, for greasing

1 Preheat the oven to 375° and grease a shallow baking dish.
2 Put the lentils, onion, herbs, tomatoes and broth into a pan. Season with salt and pepper and bring to a boil. Lower the heat and cook gently 15-20 minutes, stirring occasionally until the lentils are just tender. The liquid will not be completely absorbed.
3 Meanwhile, melt the butter in a separate pan, remove from the heat and stir in the bread crumbs. Season with salt and pepper.
4 Cover the base of the prepared dish with a layer of the lentil mixture then top with a layer of sliced eggs. Continue these layers until all the ingredients are used, finishing with a layer of lentils.
5 Sprinkle the bread crumbs over the top and bake near the top of the oven for 25-30 minutes until the crumbs are browned. Serve at once, straight from the dish.

Cook's Notes

TIME
This layered pie takes only about 1 hour to prepare and cook.

BUYING GUIDE
Be sure to buy the small split red lentils for this dish—they need no pre-soaking.

SERVING IDEAS
For a satisfying supper dish, serve the pie with a green salad and "quickie"
garlic bread: Spread slices of French bread with softened butter mixed with garlic salt and finely chopped parsley, then wrap in foil and heat in a 375° oven for 7 minutes.

VARIATION
Layer the lentils with chopped or ground meat instead of, or as well as, the hard-cooked eggs.

● 260 calories per portion

Herby beans with eggs

SERVES 4

½ lb fresh or frozen sliced green or string beans (see Cook's tip)
½ lb fresh or frozen broad beans
½ lb fresh or frozen peas
salt
4 large eggs, hard-cooked and quartered

SAUCE

2 tablespoons butter or margarine
¼ cup all-purpose flour
2 cups milk
2 tablespoons chopped fresh parsley
2 tablespoons chopped fresh tarragon or 1½ teaspoons dried tarragon
2 teaspoons lemon juice
freshly ground black pepper

1 Bring a large saucepan of salted water to a boil. Then add the fresh or frozen vegetables and cook steadily for 10-15 minutes until just tender.

2 Meanwhile, make the sauce: Melt the butter in a small saucepan, sprinkle in the flour and stir over low heat for 1-2 minutes until straw-colored. Remove from the heat and gradually stir in the milk. Add the parsley and tarragon, return to the heat and simmer, stirring, until thickened and smooth. Stir in the lemon juice, and season to taste with salt and pepper.

3 Drain the vegetables. Reserve one-third of the sauce and mix the rest into the vegetables. Heat through, very gently, transfer to a warmed serving dish and keep warm.

4 Heat the remaining sauce in the same pan. When it is very hot but not boiling, arrange the eggs on the vegetables and drizzle the hot sauce over them. Serve at once straight from the dish.

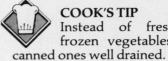

Cauliflower polonaise

SERVES 4
1 cauliflower

DRESSING
3 tablespoons vegetable oil
1 tablespoon wine vinegar
½ teaspoon dry mustard
salt and freshly ground black pepper

TO GARNISH
2 large eggs, hard-cooked
¼ cup butter or margarine
2 tablespoons dried white bread crumbs
chopped parsley

1 To make the dressing: Combine all the ingredients in a screw-top jar with salt and pepper to taste.

2 Put the cauliflower in boiling salted water and cook thoroughly for about 10-20 minutes, until the stalk is just tender when pierced with a knife. Drain thoroughly and then keep warm.

3 Make the garnish: Separate the yolks from the whites of the eggs. Chop whites finely, sieve yolks.

4 Melt the butter in a skillet, add the bread crumbs and cook over brisk heat, stirring, until golden brown and crisp. $\boxed{!}$

5 Transfer cauliflower to a serving dish. Shake the dressing well to mix and pour it over. Carefully turn the cauliflower in the dressing, so it is evenly coated. Spoon the fried bread crumbs evenly over the cauliflower, then arrange the chopped egg white and sieved yolk decoratively on top. Sprinkle with parsley and serve at once.

Brussels sprouts and Stilton

SERVES 4

½ lb Brussels sprouts, shredded
1 can (about 7 oz) pimientos, drained and sliced
½ lb Stilton cheese, diced
4 celery stalks, sliced
2 green dessert apples, cored and chopped

DRESSING
6 tablespoons vegetable oil
2 tablespoons cider vinegar or white wine vinegar
1 teaspoon dry mustard
1 tablespoon chopped chives or scallion tops
salt and freshly ground black pepper

1 Make the dressing: Combine the oil, vinegar, mustard and 2 teaspoons of the chives in a screw-top jar. Season with salt and pepper, then shake well to mix.

2 Put the Brussels sprouts in a large bowl. Pour in half the dressing and toss to coat thoroughly. Set aside for 5 minutes.

3 Put the pimientos, cheese, celery and apple into the bowl and toss in the remaining dressing until all the ingredients are thoroughly coated.

4 Serve at once, garnished with the remaining chives.

Cook's Notes

TIME
Preparation time for this unusual salad is about 30 minutes.

SERVING IDEAS
Serve as a light lunch or supper dish with slices of crusty French bread.

VARIATIONS
Shredded raw spinach or any well-flavored cabbage can be used instead of the sprouts.

Use other firm blue cheeses such as Danish Blue.

● 530 calories per portion

SOUPS AND SNACKS

Vegetable soup

SERVES 4
½ lb frozen mixed
  vegetables
2 cups boiling chicken broth
3 tablespoons butter or margarine
1 medium onion, chopped
⅓ cup all-purpose flour
2 cups warm milk
1 tablespoon tomato paste
salt and freshly ground black pepper

CROUTONS
¼ cup vegetable oil
4 slices day-old bread, crusts
  removed, cut into small cubes

1 Pour the broth into a saucepan. Add the frozen vegetables and cook gently for 8 minutes.

2 Melt the butter in a heavy-bottomed saucepan over moderate heat. When the foam subsides, add the onion and cook until golden.

3 Sprinkle in the flour and stir over low heat 2 minutes until straw-colored. Remove from the heat and gradually stir in the milk, then return to the heat and simmer, stirring with a wooden spoon until the mixture is thick and smooth. Stir in the tomato paste.

4 Add the mixture to the broth and vegetables, and season with salt and pepper to taste. Stir well and cook gently for 15 minutes, stirring occasionally.

5 To prepare the croutons: Heat the oil in a skillet over moderate heat until very hot. Cook the bread cubes until golden brown. Remove from the pan and drain on paper towels.

6 Reserve 2 tablespoons vegetables, then blend the remaining ingredients in a blender or rub them through a strainer. Return to the pan, taste and adjust seasoning and heat through until boiling.

7 Pour the soup into heated individual bowls, then stir in the reserved vegetables. Hand the croutons around separately.

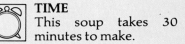

Corned beef soup

SERVES 6

1 can (about 7 oz) corned beef, diced
2 tablespoons vegetable oil
2 large onions, chopped
½ lb carrots, cut into ¼-inch
    dice
1½ lb potatoes, cut into ½-inch
    dice
3¾ cups hot beef broth
salt and freshly ground black pepper
chopped fresh parsley to garnish

1 Heat the oil in a pan and cook the onions gently for 5 minutes until soft and lightly colored. Add the carrots and potatoes and cook gently, stirring, for a further 3 minutes.
2 Pour in the broth and bring to a boil. Cover and simmer for 10 minutes until the carrots and potatoes are just tender.
3 Add the corned beef and season to taste with salt and pepper. Simmer gently, uncovered, for a further 5 minutes (see Cook's tip). Serve at once, sprinkled with a little parsley.

Cook's Notes

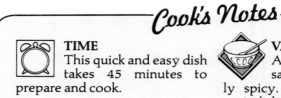

TIME
This quick and easy dish takes 45 minutes to prepare and cook.

COOK'S TIP
For a thicker, smoother soup, strain or purée in a blender with a little cream or milk. Reheat before serving.

VARIATIONS
A dash of hot-pepper sauce makes it slightly spicy. Try sprinkling with grated cheese before adding the parsley. Rutabagas are a good alternative to carrots, and they make an equally filling dish.

● 235 calories per portion

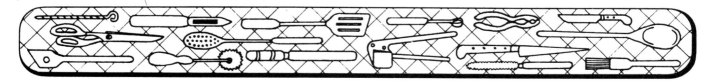

Carrot and parsley soup

SERVES 4
1 lb carrots, sliced
2 tablespoons freshly chopped
   parsley
2 tablespoons butter
1 onion, finely chopped
2½ cups chicken broth (see
   Cook's tip)
1¼ cups milk
salt and freshly ground black pepper

1 Melt the butter in a large saucepan. Add the carrots and onion and cook gently, covered, for 15 minutes, stirring occasionally until softened but not browned.
2 Pour in the chicken broth and bring to a boil, then lower the heat and simmer gently, covered, for a further 20 minutes.

3 Allow to cool slightly, then press the soup through a strainer or work in a blender until smooth.
4 Return the puréed soup to the rinsed-out pan and stir in the milk and parsley. Season to taste with salt and freshly ground black pepper. Heat the soup through very gently for about 5-6 minutes.
5 Pour the soup into 4 warmed individual soup bowls and serve at once (see serving ideas).

Cook's Notes

TIME
Total preparation time is 20 minutes. Cooking takes about 40 minutes.

COOK'S TIP
This soup is best made with a subtle, delicately flavored homemade broth.

SERVING IDEAS
Garnish each serving with cheese and mustard toast: Cut half a loaf of French bread into 8 slices. Toast one side of each slice under the broiler, then spread untoasted sides with butter and a little prepared mustard. Top each slice with grated Cheddar cheese and toast until cheese is bubbling. Place a slice on top of each bowl of soup and hand remaining bread separately.

VARIATION
For a really creamy soup, stir 2-3 tablespoons light cream into the soup just before serving.

● 135 calories per portion

Mushroom soup with dumplings

SERVES 4

½ lb flat mushrooms, finely
    chopped
1 can (about 10 oz) condensed
    bouillon
3 cups cold water
1 onion, finely chopped
bouquet garni
salt and freshly ground black pepper
chopped fresh parsley, to garnish

DUMPLINGS

¾ cup all-purpose flour
1 teaspoon baking powder
1½ tablespoons shortening suet
½ teaspoon salt
1-2 tablespoons finely chopped
    fresh parsley
2-3 tablespoons cold water

1 Put the bouillon into a saucepan and stir in the water. Add the chopped mushrooms, onion, and bouquet garni and season to taste with salt and pepper. ⚠ Bring to a boil, then lower the heat, cover and simmer 10 minutes, stirring occasionally.

2 Meanwhile, sift flour, baking powder and salt. Add parsley and shortening and cut in finely. Mix to a soft, not sticky dough with the cold water. Shape into 12-16 balls with hands.

3 Drop the dumplings into the soup, bring back to a boil, then lower the heat again and simmer for a further 15 minutes until the dumplings are cooked through.

4 To serve: Remove the bouquet garni and pour the soup into warmed individual soup bowls. Add a few dumplings to each bowl, then sprinkle with a little chopped parsley, if wished.

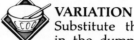

Tomato rice soup

SERVES 4

1 lb fresh tomatoes, chopped
1 can (about 14 oz) tomatoes
1 tablespoon tomato paste
⅔ cup water
salt and freshly ground black pepper
¼ cup long-grain rice
2 tablespoons medium sherry
  (optional, see Variation)
1 tablespoon finely chopped parsley,
  to garnish

1 Put all the ingredients except the rice, sherry, if using, and parsley into a large saucepan. Bring to a boil, stirring, then lower the heat, cover and simmer for 30 minutes.

2 Pass the contents of the saucepan through a strainer, or leave to cool slightly, then purée in a blender and strain (see Cook's tip).

3 Pour the strained tomato purée back into the rinsed-out pan and bring back to a boil. Stir in the rice, lower the heat, cover and simmer for about 15 minutes or until the rice is tender.

4 Stir in the sherry, if using, taste and adjust seasoning, then pour into warmed individual soup bowls. Sprinkle with parsley and serve at once.

Cook's Notes

TIME
Preparation and cooking take about 1 hour.

VARIATION
Use 2 tablespoons light cream instead of the sherry, and swirl a little into each bowl just before sprinkling with parsley.

SERVING IDEAS
Serve with hot whole wheat rolls.

COOK'S TIP
It is essential to strain the tomato mixture, to remove the seeds and skins.

● 80 calories per portion

Tasty meat triangles

SERVES 4
¾ lb lean ground beef (see Buying guide)
good pinch of cayenne
salt
8 small triangular portions processed cheese (see Buying guide)
2 eggs
3 cups day-old bread crumbs
vegetable oil, for deep frying

1 Put the beef in a bowl and mix in the cayenne and salt to taste.
2 Divide into 8 portions and put on a clean board. Then, using a small spatula or your fingers, flatten each one into a triangular shape about 4 inches on each side.
3 Press a cheese portion into the center of each beef triangle. Mold and seal the beef evenly and completely around the cheese, being very careful to cover the corners. [!]
4 Beat the egg in a shallow bowl and spread out the bread crumbs on a large flat plate. Dip each triangle into the egg and then into the bread crumbs, pressing firmly to coat evenly. Repeat a second time with each triangle.
5 Pour enough oil into a deep-fat fryer to come halfway up the sides of the triangles and heat to 350°, or until a day-old bread cube will brown in 60 seconds.
6 Using a slotted spoon, lower half the triangles into the hot oil and deep-fry for about 7 minutes until well browned.
7 Drain on paper towels and keep warm while cooking the second batch. Serve as soon as they are all cooked.

Cook's Notes

TIME
Total preparation and cooking time 30-40 minutes from start to finish.

BUYING GUIDE
Buy very lean ground beef so that it does not shrink during cooking.
Processed cheese triangles are available in different flavors, individually wrapped in flat round boxes.

WATCHPOINT
It is important to seal the cheese well inside the beef to prevent it leaking out as it melts during cooking.

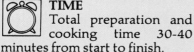
VARIATION
Instead of processed cheese portions, use small cubes of cheese and shape the beef into balls. Any soft melting cheese, such as mozzarella, would be suitable.

SERVING IDEAS
Serve with lettuce, broiled whole tomatoes and fried onion or with boiled rice, whole kernel corn or peas and tomato sauce. For parties, make bite-size triangles or balls and serve them hot with a chutney-flavored dip. You can double or triple the quantities when catering for large numbers.

● 385 calories per portion

Ham fritters with fried bananas

SERVES 4

⅓ lb cooked ham, ground
3 eggs, beaten
1 cup fresh bread crumbs
½ cup milk
freshly ground black pepper
6 tablespoons butter
4 bananas
parsley sprigs, to garnish

1 In a bowl, beat together the ham, eggs and bread crumbs.
2 Put the milk in a small saucepan and bring to a boil. Stir the milk into the ham mixture. Season to taste with pepper then mix all the ingredients together very thoroughly.
3 Melt 1 tablespoon butter in a large skillet over moderate heat. When the butter is hot and foaming, spoon tablespoonsfuls of half the mixture into the pan. Cook for 1-2 minutes until well browned, then turn them over using a spatula and cook for a further 1-2 minutes. Drain on paper towels and keep the mixture warm while you prepare the next batch.
4 Melt another tablespoon butter and cook the other half of the mixture in the same way. Drain on paper towels and keep warm.
5 Lower the heat and melt the remaining butter in the same pan. Peel the bananas and cut each in half lengthwise. Cook gently in the butter for 3-4 minutes, shaking the pan so that the butter coats all the bananas thoroughly.
6 Arrange the fritters on a warmed serving dish and put the bananas around them. Garnish with sprigs of parsley.

Sausage twists

SERVES 4
8 large pork sausages
½ sheet (¼ 17 oz package) frozen puff pastry, thawed
1 tablespoon tomato catsup

1 In a large non-stick skillet, gently cook the sausages for about 5 minutes, without adding any extra fat to the pan, or heat the broiler to low and broil them. Do not allow the sausages to become too brown (see Cook's tip). Remove from the heat and leave to cool.

2 Preheat the oven to 400°.
3 On a floured surface, roll out the pastry very thinly to a rectangle 10 × 8 inches. Trim the edges straight and cut into 8 equal sized rectangles.
4 Spread a little tomato catsup over the rectangles and then place a sausage, on the catsup, diagonally across the pastry. To make the "twist": Lift the bottom right-hand corner of the pastry and wrap in a band over the sausage. Press it onto the pastry underneath the sausage to seal it (see Preparation). Make the rest and place on a dampened cookie sheet seam-side down.
5 Bake in the oven 25-30 minutes until browned. Lift from the sheet with a spatula. Serve hot.

Cook's Notes

TIME
Preparation, including pre-cooking the sausages, takes about 20 minutes. Cooking in the oven takes 30 minutes.

COOK'S TIP
The sausages must be pre-cooked to remove some of the fat before they are baked in the oven.

PREPARATION
To make the sausage twists:

1 Place the sausage, on the catsup, diagonally across the pastry rectangle as shown.

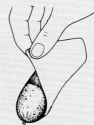

2 Lift bottom right-hand corner of pastry and fold over sausage to seal.

VARIATIONS
Use mustard or Worcesterhire sauce in place of tomato catsup. Or use a herby pastry by rolling the pastry out, sprinkling it with 1 teaspoon herbs, folding and rolling the pastry out again. These variations are less suitable for children.

CHILDREN
Children will enjoy the sausage twists by themselves, or served with canned spaghetti in tomato sauce or baked beans.

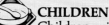

● 520 calories per portion

Beefburger parcels

MAKES 6

6 fresh or frozen hamburgers
2 sheets (¾ 17 oz package) frozen
   puff pastry, thawed
⅓ lb smooth pâté (see Buying
   guide)
1 egg, lightly beaten

1 Preheat the oven to 425°.
2 Cook or broil the hamburgers according to package directions. Drain well on paper towels, then set aside to cool for 5-10 minutes. ⚠
3 Roll out both sheets of pastry on a floured surface to a 14-inch square then, using a saucer, cut into 6 rounds so that each is about 1½ inches larger all around than the cooked hamburger. Reserve the pastry trimmings.
4 Spread a quarter of the pâté on top

Cook's Notes

TIME
Preparation time, including cooking and cooling the hamburgers is 20 minutes; baking in the oven is 15-20 minutes.

WATCHPOINTS
It is important to drain and cool the hamburgers before placing on the pastry or the pastry will melt.
If the edges are not completely sealed, the pâté may leak out.

VARIATIONS
Replace the pâté with horseradish sauce and sliced tomatoes. Alternatively, top each hamburger with a ring of pineapple or green pepper.

BUYING GUIDE
Use a can of liver pâté for this recipe, or choose a smooth pâté from a delicatessen counter.

● 608 calories per portion

of each hamburger and place pâté side down on the pastry rounds. Brush the pastry edges with water and draw them together over the meat to form a neat parcel. Seal the edges carefully. ⚠
5 Dampen a cookie sheet and place the parcels on it with their seams underneath.

6 Make leaves from the pastry trimmings, brush them underneath with water and place them on top of the parcels. Brush the pastry all over with beaten egg, make 2 slits in the top of each for the steam to escape and bake in the oven for 15-20 minutes until golden and well risen. Serve hot.

Cheese and chicken pockets

SERVES 4

½ lb Gruyère cheese, cut into thin
    strips
½ lb cooked chicken, thinly sliced
    (see Buying guide)
4 pita breads
1 small green pepper, seeded and
    sliced into thin rings
2 large firm tomatoes, thinly sliced
salt and freshly ground black pepper
3 tablespoons mango chutney

1 Preheat the oven to 400°. Cut out
8 squares of foil each large enough
to enclose half a pita.
2 Cut each pita bread in half
crosswise and ease the pockets open
with a knife, taking care not to
pierce the sides of the bread.
3 Divide the ingredients for the
filling into 8, then hold each pita
pocket open with one hand and,
with the other, layer the ingredients
into the pockets in the following
order: Green pepper, cheese, tomato
and chicken. Sprinkle each layer
with a little salt and pepper, then
spread the chicken with chutney.

4 Place each filled pocket, chicken
layer uppermost, on a square of foil,
and wrap securely in a parcel. Put
the parcels on 1 or 2 cookie sheets,
and heat through in the oven for
about 20 minutes. Serve at once.

Cook's Notes

TIME
Preparation takes about
30 minutes. Heating
through takes 20 minutes.

SERVING IDEAS
These tasty chicken
pockets can be heated
on a barbecue instead of in the
oven. They are best eaten with
fingers so provide each person
with a plate and a paper napkin.

VARIATIONS
Try using cooked lamb,
beef, ham or turkey in-
stead of chicken. Another good
melting cheese, such as mozzarella, can be used instead of the
Gruyère.

 WATCHPOINT
The order in which the
pitas are filled is important. If tomato is put next to the
bread, the bread will become
soggy.

 BUYING GUIDE
Sliced, pressed rolled
chicken, available from
supermarkets and delicatessens,
is ideal for this recipe and saves
preparation time.

● 570 calories per portion

Grilled corned beef on buns

SERVES 4

1 can (about 12 oz) corned beef
2 tablespoons pickle relish
1 tablespoon mild mustard
6 tablespoons mayonnaise
freshly ground black pepper
4 soft buns, cut in half
1½ cups grated Swiss or sharp
   Cheddar cheese
8 tomato slices, to garnish

1 Preheat the broiler to moderate.
2 Mash the corned beef with the relish, mustard and mayonnaise until smooth. Taste and season with a little pepper.
3 Spread the cut surfaces of the buns evenly all over with the corned beef mixture.
4 Broil gently for 4-5 minutes or until the corned beef mixture begins to brown.
5 Sprinkle the cheese over the top. Return to the heat and broil for a further 3-4 minutes or until the cheese has melted and is browned. Serve hot, garnished with tomato.

Cook's Notes

TIME
Preparation takes 10 minutes. Cooking time is 8-10 minutes.

COOK'S TIP
The corned beef mixture may be kept, covered, in the refrigerator for 3-4 days, and is ideal for snacks or impromptu meals.

● 645 calories per portion

269

Eggs Benedict

SERVES 4
4 eggs
4 bacon slices
2 English muffins (See Buying
   guide)
2 tablespoons butter, for spreading

SAUCE
2 teaspoons lemon juice
2 teaspoons wine vinegar
½ cup butter
2 egg yolks
few drops of hot-pepper sauce
salt and freshly ground black pepper
paprika, to finish

1 Preheat the oven to 225°. Preheat the broiler to moderate.

2 Broil the bacon slices for about 8 minutes, turning once, until cooked through. Cut the slices in half and keep them warm in the oven.

3 Slit the muffins in half horizontally, turn broiler to high and toast the muffins lightly on both sides. Spread the cut side of each muffin thinly with butter, top each one with 2 bacon halves and return to the oven.

4 Heat a large skillet of water just to simmering point (see Cook's tips).

5 Make the sauce: Put the lemon juice and vinegar in a small saucepan and bring to a boil. ⚠ Melt the butter in a separate pan until it is sizzling, but do not let it start to brown. ⚠

6 Warm the goblet of the blender (see Cook's tips) by filling it with very hot water. Tip the water out and put the lemon juice and vinegar into the goblet together with the egg yolks and the hot-pepper sauce. Season well with salt and pepper. Blend for a few seconds.

7 With the motor switched on, gradually pour the melted butter in a very thin stream through the hole in lid of blender. The sauce will thicken as the butter is added.

8 Pour the sauce into an ovenproof bowl standing over a pan of gently simmering water. Keep hot while poaching the eggs, stirring from time to time.

9 Cook the eggs by breaking them one by one into a cup and slipping them into the skillet of just simmering water for 3-4 minutes, until set. Remove them with a slotted spoon if using a skillet or by running round the outside of each egg with a round-bladed knife if using a poacher. Slip a poached egg onto each half muffin.

10 Transfer the egg-topped muffins to warmed plates. Spoon a little sauce over each, sprinkle with paprika and serve at once.

Cook's Notes

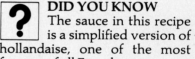

TIME
Preparation and cooking take about 30 minutes.

COOK'S TIPS
If you have one, you can use an egg poacher for this recipe; you do not need to prepare it until end of stage 8.

You really do need a blender to make this a quick and easy recipe. Made in the traditional way in a double boiler it takes much longer.

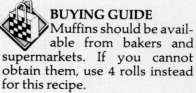

WATCHPOINTS
The vinegar and lemon juice mixture evaporates quickly, so watch it carefully.

Butter browns very quickly, so also needs careful watching.

DID YOU KNOW
The sauce in this recipe is a simplified version of hollandaise, one of the most famous of all French sauces.

BUYING GUIDE
Muffins should be available from bakers and supermarkets. If you cannot obtain them, use 4 rolls instead for this recipe.

● 465 calories per portion

Tuna strudel

SERVES 4

1 can (about 7 oz) tuna, drained
6 stuffed green olives, chopped
1 hard cooked egg, chopped
2 tablespoons light cream
2 tablespoons finely chopped fresh
    parsley
salt and freshly ground black pepper
1 sheet (½ 17 oz package) frozen puff
    pastry, thawed
beaten egg yolk, for brushing
lightly beaten egg white, to glaze

1 Preheat the oven to 400°.
2 Put the tuna into a bowl with the olives, hard-cooked egg, cream and parsley. Season to taste with salt and pepper and mix thoroughly with a fork.
3 Roll out the pastry on a floured surface into a thin rectangle about 15 × 11 inches; trim edges.

4 Spread the tuna mixture over the pastry leaving a pastry border all around of about ½ inch. Starting at a long edge roll up the pastry. Brush the opposite long edge with beaten egg yolk and press down firmly so that it sticks. Gently press the roll to flatten its shape slightly. Tuck the ends in, brushing with egg yolk so that they stick. ⚠
5 Dampen a cookie sheet and carefully transfer pastry roll to it. ⚠ Brush over with beaten egg white.
6 Bake 20 minutes or until pastry is cooked through and golden. Serve hot or cold, cut into slices.

Sherried cod

SERVES 4

1 lb cod fillets, skinned and cut into
   1-inch cubes
2 tablespoons all-purpose flour
½ teaspoon dried thyme
salt and freshly ground black pepper
¼ cup butter or margarine
2 tablespoons vegetable oil
½ red pepper and ½ green pepper,
   seeded and cut into narrow strips
   1½ inches long
1 onion, finely chopped
¼ lb button mushrooms,
   sliced
2-3 tablespoons dry sherry
⅔ cup dairy sour cream

1 Mix the flour and thyme on a large plate and season with salt and pepper. Dip the fish pieces in the seasoned flour, turning until well coated, then set aside.

2 Melt half the butter and oil in a saucepan, add the peppers and onion and cook over moderate heat for 5 minutes, stirring. Add the mushrooms and cook, stirring, for a further 2 minutes. Keep warm.

3 Melt the remaining butter and oil in a large skillet, add the fish pieces and cook over moderate heat for about 4 minutes until just cooked, turning once.

4 Pour over the sherry, allow to bubble, then stir in dairy sour cream, turning the fish very gently. Arrange on a serving plate, spoon over the pepper mixture and serve at once (see Serving ideas).

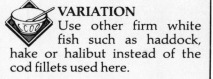

Fruity chicken pie

SERVES 4-6

¾ lb boneless cooked
   chicken, cut into bite-sized
   pieces
4 tablespoons butter or margarine
1 onion, chopped
1 cooking apple, pared, quartered
   and sliced
2 teaspoons curry powder
¼ cup all-purpose flour
1¼ cups chicken broth
¼ lb mushrooms, sliced
salt and freshly ground black pepper
3 tomatoes, peeled and roughly
   chopped
1 sheet (½ 17 oz package) frozen puff
   pastry, thawed
beaten egg, to glaze

1 Preheat the oven to 425°.
2 Melt the butter in a large skillet, add the onion and cook for 5 minutes until soft and lightly colored. Add the apple and curry powder and cook gently for another 5 minutes. Sprinkle in the flour and stir until blended. Gradually stir in the broth and simmer, stirring, until thick and smooth.
3 Stir in the chicken pieces and mushrooms and season with salt and pepper to taste. Cook for a further 5 minutes, then stir in the chopped tomatoes. Pour the mixture into a large pie plate or ovenproof dish.
4 Roll out the pastry on a floured surface to a shape slightly larger than the top of the pie plate. Cut off a strip of pastry all around edge.
5 Brush the rim of the plate with water and press the strip of pastry on the rim. Brush the strip with a little more water, then place the large piece of pastry on top. Press to seal, then knock up and flute.
6 Make decorations with the pastry trimmings, brush the undersides with water and arrange on top of the pie. Brush the pastry all over with the beaten egg and make a small hole in the center of the pie. Bake in the oven for 30 minutes until golden. Serve at once.

Cook's Notes

TIME
Preparation 40 minutes, cooking 30 minutes.

VARIATIONS
Turkey makes a delicious alternative to chicken. A chopped green pepper may be used instead of the sliced mushrooms.

SERVING IDEAS
Serve with a creamy potato purée and a fresh green vegetable such as broccoli, or with French bread and a green salad. For special occasions, pop the pie plate into a paper frill to serve.

●535 calories per portion

Chicken and yoghurt curry

SERVES 4
2 large chicken breasts, each weighing ½ lb, skinned and cut into ½-inch pieces
2 tablespoons butter or margarine
1 tablespoon vegetable or olive oil
1 large onion, chopped
1 clove garlic, crushed (optional)
1½ teaspoons ground ginger
2 teaspoons garam masala (see Variations)
⅔ cup chicken broth
⅔ cup plain yogurt
½ cucumber, cut into ½-inch pieces
⅓ cup roasted salted peanuts (see Watchpoint)
coriander or parsley sprigs, to garnish

1 Heat the butter and oil in a large skillet, add the onion and garlic, if using, and cook gently for 5 minutes until soft and lightly colored. Stir in

TIME
This dish takes only 30-40 minutes to prepare and cook.

VARIATIONS
To make your own garam masala for this recipe use 1 teaspoon ground cumin, ½ teaspoon ground chili powder, ½ teaspoon ground turmeric and a large pinch of cinnamon. Mix well together.
  Replace the cucumber with 2 thinly sliced zucchini, added to the pan with the chicken.

SERVING IDEAS
Serve with halved pita bread, lightly toasted on both sides, and a selection of chutneys or pickles, such as mango chutney and lime pickle. Sliced bananas sprinkled with lemon juice make a good side dish to offset the hot curry.

WATCHPOINT
Roasted salted peanuts give a good flavor to this curry so do not add extra salt or it will be too salty.

● 305 calories per portion

the spices and cook for a further 2 minutes.
2 Add the chicken and cook over moderate heat until sealed on all sides. Mix in the broth, bring to a boil, then lower the heat and simmer, uncovered, for 20 minutes or until the chicken is cooked.
3 Turn the heat to very low, then stir the yogurt into the pan. Heat gently until warmed through, stirring constantly. Remove from the heat and mix in the cucumber.
4 Divide the mixture equally between 4 small bowls and sprinkle a few peanuts on top of each. Garnish with coriander or parsley sprigs and serve at once.

Apricot barbecue chicken

SERVES 4

12 chicken drumsticks, each weighing ¼ lb, skinned
toasted almonds, to garnish (optional)

BARBECUE SAUCE
1 can (about 14 oz) apricots
2 tablespoons malt vinegar
2 tablespoons light soy sauce
1 clove garlic, crushed (optional)
1-inch piece fresh root ginger, peeled and crushed
pinch of dried tarragon (optional)
salt and freshly ground black pepper

1 Preheat the oven to 400°.

2 Make the sauce: Put the apricots and their syrup into the goblet of a blender, add the remaining sauce ingredients with salt and pepper to taste and work for a few seconds to a rough purée.

3 Turn the apricot mixture into a saucepan and bring to a boil. Boil, stirring, for 2-3 minutes until it thickens to a coating consistency.

4 Fill a roasting pan to a depth of ½-inch with cold water and set a rack over the pan (see Cook's tip). Arrange the drumsticks on the rack and brush thickly with half the sauce. Cook in the oven, on the shelf above center, for 40-45 minutes until the juices run clear when the thickest part of the drumstick is pierced with a fine skewer. Turn the drumsticks over once or twice during cooking time and brush with the remaining sauce.

5 Transfer drumsticks to a serving platter and spoon over any sauce and juices which have collected in the pan. Garnish with the toasted almonds, if using, and serve.

Cook's Notes

 TIME
Preparing and cooking take about 1 hour.

VARIATIONS
Use ¾ lb fresh ripe apricots instead of canned. Simmer the peeled, halved and pitted apricots with 1¼ cups water and ⅓ cup sugar for 10-15 minutes then follow the recipe.

Use sauce to baste chicken drumsticks. Broiled, on an outdoor barbecue, they make tasty finger food.

COOK'S TIP
Water in the roasting pan helps to keep any sauce that drips through the rack from spitting and burning and spoiling the dish.

● 300 calories per portion

Turkey toss

SERVES 4

⅔ lb boned, cooked turkey, diced (see Economy)
1 cup Basmati rice (see Buying guide)
2 tablespoons butter or margarine
1¼ cups boiling water
2 tablespoons turkey dripping or vegetable oil (see Economy)
1 onion, finely chopped
2 celery stalks, sliced
1 clove garlic, crushed (optional)
¼ lb frozen peas, cooked
1 green pepper, seeded and diced
2 tablespoons currants
1 can (about 7 oz) pimientos, drained and sliced
1-2 tablespoons soy sauce
salt and freshly ground black pepper
a few bay leaves, to garnish

1 Rinse the rice thoroughly in several changes of cold water. Place in a pan with the butter and boiling water and bring rapidly to a boil. Lower the heat, cover with a tight-fitting lid and simmer very gently for 10 minutes, or until all the liquid has evaporated and the rice is just tender.

2 Meanwhile, heat the dripping in a large skillet or wok. Add the onion, celery and garlic, if using, and cook gently for 5 minutes until the onion is soft and lightly colored.

3 Add the rice, cooked peas, turkey, green pepper, currants and half the pimiento. Cook over moderate heat, stirring frequently, until heated all through.

4 Stir in the soy sauce and season with salt and pepper to taste.

5 Transfer to a warmed serving dish, garnish with the remaining pimiento slices and a few bay leaves, and serve at once while still piping hot.

Pork turnovers

SERVES 4

8 cured pork loin steaks, trimmed of all visible fat (see Buying guide)
freshly ground black pepper
2 sheets (1 17 oz package) frozen puff pastry, thawed
1 egg yolk
1 tablespoon cold water

STUFFING
¾ cup dry white bread crumbs
3 tablespoons finely chopped fresh parsley
1 tablespoon grated or very finely chopped onion
finely grated rind of 1 lemon
2 teaspoons lemon juice
½ teaspoon ground ginger
1½ teaspoons mild curry powder
pinch of cayenne
3-4 tablespoons melted butter
celery salt or salt

1 Put the pork steaks between 2 sheets of waxed paper and beat with a rolling pin until ¼-inch thick. Season the steaks on both sides with pepper.

2 Mix together all the stuffing ingredients, except the melted butter and salt. Add enough melted butter to bind the mixture and season to taste with celery salt and pepper.

3 Preheat the oven to 425°.

4 Spread the stuffing mixture on 4 of the steaks, to within ½-inch of the edges. Cover with the remaining steaks, to make sandwiches with stuffing filling.

5 Cut sheets of pastry into 2 equal pieces and roll out each piece on a floured surface to an even 10-inch square. Trim the edges of each square. Mix the egg yolk with the cold water and brush the pastry squares with a little of this mixture, making sure you brush right to the edges of the squares.

6 Place a pork "sandwich" on one-half of each square, fold the pastry over and press the edges together to seal. Trim the edges to a semi-circular shape, leaving about a ¾-inch pastry border around the pork. Seal edges, knock up and flute.

Cut 3 small slits in the top of each turnover with a sharp knife.

7 With a fish slice, transfer the turnovers to a dampened baking sheet and brush them all over with the remaining egg yolk mixture. Bake in oven for 20-25 minutes, until deep golden brown. Serve hot.

Cook's Notes

TIME
Preparation takes 30-40 minutes, cooking in the oven 20-25 minutes.

BUYING GUIDE
Cured pork loin steaks are very easily available from large supermarkets. They are an excellent buy as they are tender and lean, with very little waste. Or buy a 1½ lb boneless pork loin joint and cut it into 8 pieces.

SERVING IDEAS
Serve these tasty stuffed pork turnovers with a mixed green salad tossed in an oil and vinegar dressing.

● 685 calories per portion

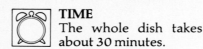

Pork chops in apple sauce

SERVES 4

4 medium pork chops, each
  weighing ⅓-½ lb
3 tablespoons all-purpose flour
salt and freshly ground black
  pepper
pinch of ground mace (optional)
¼ cup butter

SAUCE

8 scallions, trimmed and thinly
  sliced
⅔ cup unsweetened apple juice
1 teaspoon tomato paste
4 thin slices lemon, or 2 teaspoons
  concentrated lime juice
1 tablespoon light cream
  (optional)

1 Trim the meat, discarding any skin or fat.

2 Put the flour into a waxed or plastic bag and season with salt and pepper and a pinch of ground mace, if using. Toss the chops in the seasoned flour one at a time until they are thoroughly coated and dry. Put on one side.

3 Melt the butter in a large skillet over moderate heat. When it stops foaming, add the chops and cook them gently for 8 minutes. Turn each one over very carefully, taking care not to pierce the meat, and cook for a further 5 minutes or until they are cooked through and well browned.

4 Using a slotted spoon remove the meat from the pan and transfer it to a warmed serving dish. Cover the dish with foil and then keep it warm while the apple sauce is being prepared.

5 Add the chopped onions to the fat remaining in the pan. Stir well and cook, stirring occasionally, for 3 minutes. Pour in the apple juice, stir in the tomato paste and bring rapidly to a boil, stirring all the time. Add the lemon slices or lime juice and boil for 1 minute. Taste the sauce and season with salt and pepper. If the sauce is a little too sharp, stir in the cream.

6 Pour the sauce over the pork and heat the dish through for a further 5 minutes. Serve at once. ✳

TIME
The whole dish takes about 30 minutes.

SERVING IDEAS
Serve with buttered pasta shells, boiled rice or new potatoes plus a crisp green vegetable such as sprouts.

COOK'S TIP
When adding the apple juice to the juices and fat in the pan, use a flat-edged wooden spoon so that you can scrape all the delicious brown pieces from the pan. Their flavor will make all the difference to the sauce.

SPECIAL OCCASION
Replace the juice with dry white wine, or with half dry sherry and half water.
For a real celebration, substitute sliced pork tenderloin.

FREEZING
Place in one or more aluminum or similar containers, seal, label and freeze. Store for up to 6 months. To serve, reheat thoroughly, either from frozen or after thawing. Add a tablespoon of broth, juice or water if the sauce is too thick.

● 530 calories per portion

Bacon burgers

SERVES 4
½ lb cooked bacon
salt
¾ lb potatoes
1 small onion
1 tablespoon tomato paste
freshly ground black pepper
1 egg, beaten
¼ cup vegetable oil
4 buns or rolls, halved horizontally
4 canned pineapple rings, well
   drained

1 Bring a pan of salted water to a boil and cook the potatoes for about 20 minutes or until tender.
2 Meanwhile, grind the cooked bacon and onion.
3 Drain the cooked potatoes very thoroughly ⚠ and mash them.
4 Mix the potato, bacon, onion and tomato paste together in a bowl. Season with pepper and add enough beaten egg to bind the mixture together. ⚠

5 Divide the mixture into 4 and shape each portion into a flat round 3 inches in diameter. ❋
6 Preheat the broiler to high.
7 Heat the oil in a skillet, add the burgers and cook for 5-7 minutes on each side until golden.
8 Meanwhile, lightly toast the cut sides of each of the bun halves.
9 Remove the burgers from the skillet, place on the bottom halves of the buns and keep warm. Cook the pineapple rings for 1 minute on each side and place on top of the burgers. Replace the bun lids and serve the burgers at once.

Cook's Notes

TIME
Preparation and cooking takes 45-50 minutes.

VARIATIONS
These burgers can be made with cooked ground chicken or corned beef instead of the bacon.

WATCHPOINTS
Make sure that the potatoes are very well drained before mashing or they will make the mixture too moist.
  Add just enough egg to bind the mixture. If too much is added the burgers will become soft and difficult to handle.

FOR CHILDREN
Children may prefer this served as a main meal without the pineapple ring and bun. Serve the burgers instead with spaghetti in tomato sauce.

FREEZING
Open freeze the burgers on a tray and then pack in plastic bags and seal, label and return to freezer. Store for up to 3 months. To serve: Thaw at room temperature for 1-2 hours and then continue from step 6 of the recipe.

● 430 calories per portion

Streaky pork with mandarin sauce

SERVES 4

1 lb lean belly of pork
   slices, bones and excess fat
   removed, and cut in half across
   (see Buying guide)
1 tablespoon vegetable oil
1 large onion, sliced
1 can (about 11 oz) mandarin orange
   segments, drained with juice
   reserved
about ⅔ cup chicken broth
¼ teaspoon ground ginger
1 tablespoon lemon juice or vinegar
1 green pepper, seeded and
   chopped
salt and freshly ground black pepper
1 tablespoon cornstarch
2 tablespoons water

1 Heat the oil in a large skillet. Add the pork and cook over moderate heat for 5 minutes turning, until brown on both sides.

2 Add the onion to the skillet and cook a further 5 minutes until the onion is soft. Pour off excess fat from the pan.

3 Make up the reserved fruit juice to 1¼ cups with the chicken broth and pour into the skillet. Add the ginger, lemon juice and green pepper and season to taste with salt and pepper. Bring to a boil, then lower the heat, cover, and simmer for 30-40 minutes until the pork is cooked (the juices run clear when the meat is pierced with a skewer).

4 Remove from the heat (see Cook's tip). Blend the cornstarch with the water, then stir in a little of the liquid from the skillet. Pour back into the skillet, and bring to a boil, stirring constantly, then simmer for 3 minutes until the liquid is thick and has a smooth consistency. [!] Add the mandarin orange segments and stir carefully to coat in sauce.

5 Turn into a warmed serving dish and serve at once.

Cook's Notes

TIME
Preparation takes 20 minutes; cooking takes about 40 minutes.

BUYING GUIDE
Belly of pork is sold in supermarkets cut into slices. If not easily available in your supermarket ask for the slices in the butcher's department.

WATCHPOINT
The sauce should be of a coating consistency. If it gets too thick, however, add some remaining chicken broth.

COOK'S TIP
Belly of pork is a fatty meat. If liked, blot the surface of the sauce with some paper towels to remove the excess fat at this stage.

VARIATION
Use a can (about 8 oz) of pineapple pieces instead of the mandarins.

SERVING IDEAS
For a delicious supper dish, serve with plain boiled rice and a mixed salad.

● 380 calories per portion

Beef and bean crumble

SERVES 4
1 lb lean ground beef
2 tablespoons butter or margarine
1 onion, chopped
2 carrots, coarsely grated
2 celery stalks, finely chopped
⅔ cup beef broth
⅔ cup tomato paste
½ teaspoon dried oregano
salt and freshly ground black pepper
1 can (about 1 lb) baked beans in
   tomato sauce

CRUMBLE TOPPING
1 cup rolled oats
1 cup all-purpose flour
½ teaspoon dried oregano
½ cup finely grated Cheddar
   cheese
3 tablespoons butter, melted

1 Preheat the oven to 400°. Melt the butter in a large saucepan, add the onion, carrot and celery and cook gently for 5 minutes until the onion is soft and lightly colored. Add the ground beef and cook over moderate heat for 3-4 minutes until browned.
2 Add the broth to the pan with the tomato paste, oregano and salt and pepper to taste, and simmer, uncovered, for 10 minutes, stirring.
3 Meanwhile, make the crumble topping: Mix the oats in a small bowl with the flour, oregano and grated cheese. Add ¼ teaspoon salt, then season well with pepper. Stir in the melted butter.
4 Stir the baked beans into beef mixture and heat through, then transfer the mixture to a 2-quart ovenproof dish. Sprinkle the crumble mixture over the top.
5 Bake in the oven for 30 minutes, until the topping is golden brown. Serve hot, straight from the dish.

Spaghetti with meat balls

SERVES 4
¾ lb spaghetti
3 tablespoons vegetable oil
1 onion, chopped
1 clove garlic, crushed (optional)
1 can (about 14 oz) tomatoes
½ cup hot chicken broth
1 tablespoon tomato paste
¼ teaspoon dried thyme
1 teaspoon dried oregano
salt and freshly ground black pepper
1 lb ground beef
2 tablespoons chopped fresh
    parsley
a knob of butter, for tossing
grated Parmesan cheese (optional)

1 Heat 1 tablespoon oil in a large saucepan, add the onion and garlic, if using, and cook gently for 5 minutes until soft and lightly colored. Add the tomatoes with their liquid, the broth, tomato paste, thyme and half the oregano. Season to taste with salt and pepper. Bring to a boil, cover and simmer for 30-40 minutes.

2 Meanwhile, in a bowl mix the beef with the remaining oregano and the parsley and season well with salt and pepper. Shape into 32 balls.

3 Heat the rest of the oil in a skillet over moderate heat and cook the meat balls on all sides for 6-8 minutes until golden brown. Drain on paper towels and keep warm.

4 Bring a pan of salted water to a boil and cook the spaghetti for about 10 minutes until *al dente* (tender, yet firm to the bite).

5 Meanwhile, strain the tomato sauce, or purée in a blender. Return to the pan to reheat, adding a little water if the sauce is too thick. Stir in the meat balls and then transfer to a warmed serving dish.

6 Drain the pasta thoroughly and toss in butter. Transfer to warmed individual serving bowls. Spoon 8 meat balls and a quarter of the sauce over each spaghetti serving. Serve at once, with cheese, if liked.

Cook's Notes

TIME
This dish takes about 1 hour to prepare and cook.

SERVING IDEAS
This dish makes a substantial lunch on its own. For dinner, serve with some crusty white bread and a crisp green salad.

VARIATION
Instead of the broth use the same quantity of red wine and perhaps drink the rest with the meal!

● 685 calories per portion

Country goulash

SERVES 4
2 onions, sliced
2 tablespoons vegetable oil
2 carrots, sliced
2 celery stalks, sliced
2 zucchini, sliced
1 green pepper, seeded and diced
½ cup mushrooms, sliced
1 lb hard white cabbage, finely
    shredded
1 can (about 14 oz) tomatoes
1 tablespoon tomato paste
1 teaspoon lemon juice
1¼ cups water
4½ teaspoons paprika
1 tablespoon caraway seeds
salt and freshly ground black
    pepper
½ cup dairy sour cream

Cook's Notes

TIME
Preparation and cooking the goulash take about 55 minutes.

SERVING IDEAS
Serve as a vegetarian meal with hot whole wheat rolls. Or serve as an accompaniment to hot pastrami.

COOK'S TIP
The paprika loses color when exposed to strong light. Store it in a cool, dark place to preserve the bright red color which adds greatly to the distinctive appearance and taste of this dish.

● 235 calories per portion

1 Heat the oil in a large saucepan, add the onions, carrots and celery and cook for about 5 minutes until soft and lightly colored.

2 Add zucchini, green pepper, mushrooms and white cabbage and cook over moderate heat for 10 minutes, stirring occasionally to prevent the vegetables sticking to the saucepan.

3 Stir in the tomatoes with their juices, the tomato paste, lemon juice and water. Sprinkle in the paprika and caraway seeds and season well with salt and pepper.

4 Cover the pan and simmer for 20 minutes or until the vegetables are just tender. Taste and add more seasoning if necessary.

5 Transfer the goulash to a hot serving dish and spoon over the dairy sour cream. Serve at once.

Lamb and apricot salad

SERVES 4

¾ lb cooked lamb, diced
1 can (about 14 oz) apricot halves,
    drained and chopped
⅔ cup thick mayonnaise
¼ cup plain yogurt
1 tablespoon clear honey
2 teaspoons finely grated lemon
    rind
½ teaspoon cinnamon
salt and freshly ground black
    pepper
¾ lb potatoes, boiled and roughly
    chopped
1 small lettuce
¼ cup toasted slivered almonds

1 Put the mayonnaise in a large
bowl and stir in the yogurt, honey,
lemon rind and cinnamon. Season to
taste with salt and pepper, then
cover and refrigerate for 30 minutes
(see Cook's tip).
2 Mix together the lamb, potatoes
and apricots and gently fold into the
mayonnaise mixture.
3 Arrange the lettuce leaves in a
bowl or shallow dish. Spoon the
salad into the center and sprinkle the
almonds over the top. Serve the
salad at once.

Cook's Notes

TIME
Preparation is about 10
minutes, but allow 30
minutes for chilling.

VARIATIONS
Use canned mandarins
or pineapple instead of
the apricots, and chicken, ham
or tongue instead of the lamb.
Substitute 1 cup cooked rice for
the boiled potatoes. If cooking
the rice especially for this dish,
you will need ⅓ cup uncooked
rice.

COOK'S TIP
Chilling the mayon-
naise mixture improves
the flavor but is not essential.

● 575 calories per portion

Lamb and pasta medley

SERVES 4
1 lb ground raw lamb
2 tablespoons olive oil
1 onion, chopped
1 green pepper, seeded and chopped
2 zucchini, finely chopped
1 can (about 14 oz) tomatoes
1¼ cups water
2 cups pasta shapes
½ teaspoon dried basil
½ teaspoon dried thyme
salt and freshly ground black pepper
¼ lb mushrooms, sliced

1 Heat the oil in a saucepan and cook the onion, green pepper and zucchini gently for 2-3 minutes until they are beginning to soften.
2 Add the lamb, turn the heat to high and cook until the meat is evenly browned, stirring with a wooden spoon to remove any lumps. Pour off any excess fat.
3 Stir in the tomatoes with their juice and the water, breaking up the tomatoes with the spoon. Bring to a boil, stirring frequently.

4 Add the pasta, herbs and salt and pepper to taste and mix well. Cover the pan and simmer the lamb and pasta for 15 minutes.
5 Stir in mushrooms and simmer, uncovered, for 10 minutes. Serve the lamb and pasta medley at once (see Serving ideas and Variations).

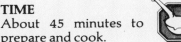

Cook's Notes

TIME
About 45 minutes to prepare and cook.

VARIATIONS
Instead of pasta shapes, use any type of pasta from the pantry. Break up spaghetti into small pieces.

Ground beef can be used as an alternative to the lamb.

Dried mixed herbs may be used instead of the dried basil and thyme.

SERVING IDEAS
This dish needs no accompaniment as it is a meal in itself, but grated hard cheese such as Parmesan or sharp Cheddar may be served separately for sprinkling.

ECONOMY
Use left-over cooked lamb, chopped finely, and omit all of stage 2.

● 570 calories per portion

Maytime flan

SERVES 4
**1 stick (½ 11 oz pie crust sticks)
prepared as directed**

FILLING
**1⅓ cups cottage cheese with
chives
3 eggs
2 tablespoons butter
¼ lb button mushrooms,
sliced
½ teaspoon dried thyme
salt and freshly ground black pepper
1 tomato, thinly sliced**

1 Preheat the oven to 400°.
2 Roll out the pastry on a lightly floured surface and use to line a 7-inch loose-bottomed flan ring standing on a cookie sheet. Prick the pastry with a fork, line with waxed paper and fill with dried beans. Bake blind in the oven for 10 minutes.
3 Meanwhile, make the filling: Put the cottage cheese into a bowl with the eggs and beat together with a fork until well mixed.
4 Melt the butter in a small saucepan, add the mushrooms and cook gently for 2 minutes, stirring. Drain well, then add the mushrooms to the cottage cheese mixture. Stir in the thyme and season to taste with salt and pepper.
5 Remove the waxed paper and beans from the pastry case, pour in the cottage cheese mixture and arrange the tomato slices around the edge. Return to the oven and bake for 35 minutes until the filling is golden brown and set.
6 Leave to stand for 5-10 minutes. Remove sides of ring and place the flan on a serving plate. Serve while still warm or leave until cold.

Cook's Notes

TIME
Preparation and cooking take 50-55 minutes.

SERVING IDEAS
Serve the flan with white wine and salad.

VARIATION
This flan can be made with homemade whole wheat pastry. Use half whole wheat flour and half all-purpose flour if wished.

●385 calories per portion

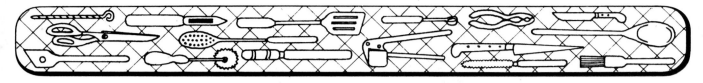

Pan pizza

SERVES 2-4

1 can (about 8 oz) tomatoes, drained and chopped
1 teaspoon dried marjoram
freshly ground black pepper
1 tablespoon vegetable oil
¼ lb mozzarella cheese, sliced
1 can (about 1¾ oz) anchovy fillets in oil, drained and soaked in milk for 20 minutes

DOUGH BASE

1 cup all-purpose flour
1 teaspoon baking powder
pinch of salt
2 tablespoons butter
3 tablespoons water

1 Mix the tomatoes and marjoram together and season with pepper.

2 Make the dough: Sift flour and salt in a bowl and cut in the butter. Bind with the water.
3 Heat the oil in an 8-inch skillet. Roll the dough out lightly to fit the skillet base and put it into the skillet. Cook the pizza over moderate heat for 4 minutes, then turn it over and

cook the other side for about 3-4 minutes.
4 Spread the tomato and herb mixture over the cooked dough. Cover with cheese; top with anchovies.
5 Preheat the broiler to high.
6 Place the skillet under the broiler to brown the pizza. Serve hot.

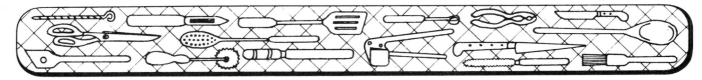

Salmon in puff pastry

SERVES 4

1 can (about 7½ oz) red salmon (see Buying guide), drained and flaked, skin and bones discarded
¼ cup long-grain rice
salt
2 hard-cooked eggs, chopped
2 tablespoons chopped parsley or chopped chives
¼ cup butter or margarine, melted
2 tablespoons tomato catsup
freshly ground black pepper
1 sheet (½ 17 oz package) frozen puff pastry, thawed
1 small egg, beaten

1 Preheat the oven to 425°.
2 Rinse the rice thoroughly under cold running water, then cook in a saucepan of boiling salted water for 12 minutes. Drain and rinse again under cold running water to separate the grains.
3 Put the salmon in a large bowl with the rice, hard-cooked eggs, parsley, melted butter, tomato catsup and salt and pepper to taste. Fold gently to mix, taking care not to break up the pieces of salmon and egg.
4 Roll out the pastry on a floured surface to a rectangle about 14 × 10 inches. Transfer to a dampened cookie sheet.
5 Place the salmon and rice mixture in the center of the pastry, spreading it out evenly. Dampen the edges of the pastry and press them together over the top of the filling. Crimp the edges and make 3-4 cuts each side.
6 Brush the pastry all over with beaten egg, then bake in the oven for about 40 minutes until golden brown. ☐ Serve hot or cold.

Seafood quickie

SERVES 4

4 tomatoes, peeled and sliced
1 lb cod or other white fish fillets,
    skinned and thawed if frozen (see
    Buying guide)
¼ lb shelled and deveined shrimp,
    thawed if frozen
1 can (10 oz) condensed cream of
    asparagus soup
1 tablespoon butter
¼ cup vegetable oil
3 slices white bread, crusts removed
    and cut into triangles or fish
    shapes
extra tomato slices or small can
    asparagus tips, to garnish
    (optional)

1 Preheat the oven to 375°.
2 Place the sliced tomatoes in the bottom of a 1½-quart shallow oven-proof dish and arrange the fish on top (see Preparation). Sprinkle the shrimp evenly over the surface of the fish and pour the can of condensed asparagus soup over the top.

3 Cover the dish with a lid or foil and bake in the oven for 35 minutes. Remove the lid or foil, then continue to cook in the oven, uncovered, for a further 10-15 minutes, until the fish pieces are cooked through (see Cook's tip).

4 Meanwhile, melt the butter with the oil in a skillet. When sizzling, add the bread shapes and cook over high heat for 2-3 minutes, turning once until golden brown on each side. Drain on paper towels.

5 Arrange the fried bread shapes around the edge of the fish in the dish, then garnish with tomato slices, if liked. Serve at once, straight from the dish.

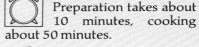

Cook's Notes

TIME
Preparation takes about 10 minutes, cooking about 50 minutes.

BUYING GUIDE
Almost any kind of white fish can be used in this recipe. Choose from cod, tilefish, flounder, or the more economical whiting or coley.

PREPARATION
Cut the fish fillets to fit evenly into the dish in a single layer.

COOK'S TIP
The fish takes longer to cook in the soup than if poached in milk and water.

● 375 calories per portion

Mackerel pilaff

SERVES 4

2 mackerel, each weighing about 1 lb
  (see Variations)
2 tablespoons butter or
  margarine
1 onion, chopped
1 red pepper, seeded and cut into ¼-
  inch strips
1 cup brown rice
4½ cups boiling chicken broth
salt and freshly ground black pepper
¼ cup whole blanched almonds or
  salted peanuts
⅓ lb zucchini, cut into ¼-inch slices
parsley sprigs and lemon slices, to
  garnish (optional)

1 Melt the butter in a heavy-bottomed saucepan. Add the onion and red pepper and cook gently for 5 minutes until the onion is soft and lightly colored.

2 Stir in the rice and cook for 1 minute. Remove from the heat and stir in the broth. Season with salt and pepper, return to a boil then simmer, covered, for 30-40 minutes until the rice is tender and nearly all the liquid has been absorbed. Check the pan during cooking and add more boiling broth or water if necessary.

3 Preheat the broiler to high. Cover the broiler rack with foil.

4 Spread the almonds out on foil and toast under the broiler until golden on all sides turning constantly. Remove from broiler and leave to cool.

5 Broil the mackerel for 10-12 minutes on each side, or until the flesh flakes easily.

6 Meanwhile, bring a pan of salted water to a boil and cook the zucchini for 3-4 minutes until just tender. ⚠ Drain well.

7 Flake the mackerel flesh into large pieces with a fork, removing all the skin and bones.

8 Drain any liquid from the rice and carefully fork in the zucchini and fish. Heat through for a few seconds then taste and adjust seasoning.

9 Spoon onto a large serving platter, and sprinkle over the toasted almonds. Garnish with parsley sprigs and lemon slices, if liked, and serve hot or cold.

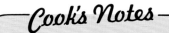

🕐 TIME
Preparation takes 25 minutes, cooking time 35 minutes.

🍲 VARIATIONS
Herrings or smoked mackerel can be used for this recipe. If the fish is already cooked, broil it for only 1 minute on each side to heat it through.

White rice can be used in place of brown, but allow 15-20 minutes less cooking time.

⚠ WATCHPOINT
Take care not to overcook the zucchini. They should be just firm when pierced with a knife.

● 520 calories per portion

Spicy sausage macaroni

SERVES 6

1 lb chorizo sausages (see Buying guide)
salt
¾ lb elbow macaroni
1 tablespoon shortening
1 small onion, finely chopped
2 cans (about 8 oz each) tomato or mushroom spaghetti sauce
1 teaspoon dried oregano (optional)
freshly ground black pepper
1½ cups grated mild Cheddar cheese
butter for greasing

1 Bring a large saucepan of salted water to a boil. Meanwhile, skin the sausages.

2 Preheat the oven to 350°. Drop the macaroni into the boiling water and cook according to package directions until just tender. ⚠ Drain thoroughly.

3 While the macaroni is cooking, melt the shortening in a large skillet, add the sausages and cook, turning, until brown on all sides. Remove the sausages from the pan, drain on paper towels and set aside.

4 Add the onion to the pan and cook gently, stirring often, until it is soft and golden. Remove from the pan with a slotted spoon and pour away the fat left in the pan.

5 Cut the sausages into ½-inch pieces. Return to the pan with the onion, spaghetti sauce and oregano, if using. Season carefully with salt and pepper. Bring the contents of the pan to simmering point.

6 Lightly grease a 2-quart casserole. Form separate layers of macaroni, sausage and sauce, and one-third of the cheese. Repeat these layers once, then finish with a layer of macaroni. Sprinkle the top with the remaining one-third of the grated cheese, making sure all the macaroni is covered. ⚠

7 Bake in the oven for about 30 minutes, until the topping is golden and the macaroni heated through.

Pasta and ham supper

SERVES 4
½ lb pasta shells
salt
2 teaspoons vegetable oil
2 cans (about 10 oz each) condensed
   chicken soup
⅓ lb Parma ham (see Economy),
   fat removed and cut into
   thin strips
½ lb frozen peas, thawed
2 egg yolks (see Economy)
2 tablespoons chopped chives or
   chopped fresh parsley
freshly ground black pepper

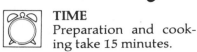

1 Preheat the oven to 225°. Bring a saucepan of salted water to a boil, add the vegetable oil and cook the pasta for about 12 minutes, or until it is just soft. Drain well and turn into a warmed serving dish. Cover and keep warm in the oven.

2 While the pasta is cooking, heat the chicken soup in a saucepan. Add the ham strips and the peas. Heat until the soup is just bubbling.
3 Beat the egg yolks into the contents of the pan and warm

through very gently without boiling. Stir in half the chives and season to taste with pepper. Spoon the sauce over the pasta and sprinkle with the remaining chives. Serve at once.

Cannelloni
with tuna

SERVES 4-6

12 cannelloni tubes (see Buying
    guide)
¼ cup butter or margarine
½ cup all-purpose flour
2¼ cups milk
1 can (about 7 oz) tuna, drained and
    flaked
¼ lb frozen petits pois (see Buying
    guide)
salt and freshly ground black pepper
1 tablespoon tomato paste
generous pinch of paprika
½ cup finely grated sharp Cheddar
    cheese
2 tablespoons grated Parmesan
    cheese
butter or margarine for greasing

1 Preheat the oven to 400°. Grease
a shallow ovenproof dish.
2 Make the filling: Melt the
butter in a saucepan, sprinkle in the
flour and stir over low heat for 1-2
minutes until straw-colored. Remove from the heat and gradually
stir in 1¼ cups of the milk. Return to
the heat and simmer, stirring, until
thick and smooth. Remove from the
heat.
3 Spoon half the sauce into a bowl,
then fold in the tuna and peas with
salt and pepper to taste.
4 With a small teaspoon, or a
piping bag fitted with a large plain
nozzle, fill the cannelloni with the
filling mixture, pushing it well into
the tubes.
5 Over low heat, gradually stir the
remaining milk into the reserved
sauce in the pan. Beat vigorously
until smooth, then add the tomato
paste, paprika and salt and pepper to
taste, then simmer for a few minutes
until thickened.
6 Cover the bottom of the prepared
dish with a little of the hot sauce,
then arrange the cannelloni on top,
separating each one with a little
sauce. Cover with the remaining
sauce. Mix the cheeses together,

then sprinkle over the top.
7 Bake in the oven for 30-35
minutes until the sauce is bubbling

at the edges and the cannelloni are
cooked through. Serve hot, straight
from the dish.

Cook's Notes

TIME
Preparation takes 40
minutes, baking 30-35
minutes.

VARIATION
Use ¼ lb cooked ham
or Italian salami, finely
chopped, instead of the tuna.

BUYING GUIDE
Be sure to buy cannel-
loni that does not need
pre-cooking. Directions are
printed on the package.
    Petits pois are the smallest

variety of frozen peas available,
and are, therefore, the most
suitable for filling cannelloni
tubes. If difficult to obtain, use
ordinary frozen peas.

DID YOU KNOW
Cannelloni is a favorite
dish in Italy; the filling
often includes veal, ham, curd
cheese or spinach.

SERVING IDEAS
Serve the cannelloni
with a mixed salad.

● 530 calories per portion

Spaghetti with olives

SERVES 4
¾ lb spaghetti
⅔ cup olive oil (see Cook's
   tip)
1 onion, finely chopped
1 green pepper, seeded and thinly
   sliced
4 tomatoes, peeled and chopped
salt and freshly ground black pepper
¼ lb pitted black olives, halved (see
   Buying guide)
⅓ cup grated Parmesan cheese, to
   finish

1 Heat the oil in a large skillet with a lid. Add the onion, green pepper and tomatoes, with salt and pepper to taste, then cover the pan and cook over moderate heat for 20 minutes, stirring from time to time.
2 Add the olives to the tomato and pepper mixture in the skillet and cook gently for 5 minutes.

3 Meanwhile, bring a large saucepan of salted water to a boil and cook the spaghetti for about 10 minutes, until *al dente* (tender yet firm to the bite). Drain well.

4 Add the drained spaghetti to the skillet and turn gently to coat evenly with the sauce. Transfer to a warmed serving dish and serve, sprinkled with Parmesan cheese.

Cook's Notes

TIME
Preparation takes about 15 minutes. Cooking takes 25 minutes.

COOK'S TIP
It is essential to use olive oil for this dish, to insure the sauce has the right flavor and a consistency just to coat the spaghetti.

BUYING GUIDE
There are many different varieties of olive, some very large, some very small. They are available pickled in brine in jars, or loose from delicatessens. Choose medium-sized olives for this recipe.

VARIATION
2 large celery stalks, thinly sliced, could replace the pepper: the flavor of celery combines very well with olives too.

DID YOU KNOW
Olives grow profusely in Mediterranean countries, especially in France, Italy, Spain and Greece. Black olives, which are fully ripe when picked, are often used in the cooking of these countries. Green olives, which are picked unripe, are most often used for garnishing rather than cooking.

● 810 calories per portion

Creamy rigatoni

SERVES 4
1 lb rigatoni (see Buying
    guide)
salt
1 tablespoon vegetable oil
⅔ cup butter
¼ lb button mushrooms,
    sliced
½ cup light cream
2 egg yolks
¾ cup grated Parmesan cheese
pinch of ground nutmeg
freshly ground black pepper
¼ lb frozen peas, cooked

1 Bring a large saucepan of salted water to a boil. Add the rigatoni and oil, lower the heat and simmer for about 12 minutes until just tender.

2 Meanwhile, melt 2 tablespoons butter in a skillet. Add the mushrooms and cook over moderate heat until just tender. Set aside.

3 Make the sauce: Melt the remaining butter in a large saucepan. Remove from the heat and set aside. In a bowl, quickly mix the cream, egg yolks and Parmesan with the nutmeg. Season with salt and plenty of pepper. Add this mixture to the melted butter in the pan and stir well.

4 When the rigatoni is nearly cooked, set the saucepan with the sauce mixture over very low heat to warm it through slightly. [!]

5 Drain the cooked rigatoni, add to the cream sauce with the peas and the mushrooms and stir continuously for a few seconds, then pile into warmed individual serving dishes and serve at once.

Cook's Notes

 TIME
Preparation time is about 10 minutes, total cooking time 15 minutes.

WATCHPOINT
When heating the cream mixture, watch it very carefully so that the eggs do not begin to scramble.

 SERVING IDEAS
Serve with a tossed green salad, and offer extra Parmesan for sprinkling over the pasta just before eating.

VARIATION
Use ¼ lb chopped cooked ham in place of, or in addition to the peas.

BUYING GUIDE
Rigatoni, a pasta that looks like large, ribbed macaroni, is available from delicatessens and some supermarkets. If it is difficult to obtain, use ordinary elbow macaroni instead.

● 870 calories per portion

Creamy mushroom noodles

SERVES 4

¾ lb noodles (see
   Variation)
salt
1 tablespoon vegetable oil
½ lb bacon slices
½ lb button mushrooms, very thinly
   sliced
½ cup milk
3 eggs
½ cup heavy cream
¾ cup grated Cheddar cheese
2 tablespoons chopped parsley
¼ lb cooked ham, diced
freshly ground black pepper
3 tablespoons butter
2 tablespoons freshly grated
   Parmesan cheese
   (optional)

1 Bring a large saucepan of salted water to a boil. Add the oil and drop in the noodles. Bring back to a boil and cook according to package directions, until just tender, (see Cook's tip). Drain and rinse with boiling water to remove the excess starch.

2 Meanwhile, preheat the broiler to high. Broil the bacon until really crisp. Drain on paper towels, then cut into small strips and keep warm.

3 Put the mushrooms and milk in a saucepan and simmer for 3 minutes. Drain the mushrooms and keep warm. Reserve half the milk.

4 Beat the eggs, cream and the reserved milk together. Stir in the grated Cheddar cheese, half the parsley, the ham and salt and pepper to taste.

5 Melt the butter in a large saucepan, add the drained noodles, and toss over very gentle heat, to heat through.

6 Stir the cream and egg mixture into the noodles, and toss quickly until they are well coated and the ingredients well mixed. Stir in the mushrooms.

7 Turn the noodles into a warmed serving dish. Scatter the bacon, the remaining parsley and Parmesan, if using, on top. Serve at once.

Englishman's paella

SERVES 4

1 jar (about 5 oz) mussels in vinegar,
    drained
1 can (about 4 oz) sardines, drained
2 tablespoons vegetable oil
2 onions, chopped
1 cup long-grain rice
1 can (about 14 oz) tomatoes
2½ cups chicken broth
2 cloves garlic, crushed (optional)
1 bay leaf
½ teaspoon ground turmeric
¼ teaspoon cinnamon
¼ lb green beans, cut into ¼-inch
    lengths
salt and freshly ground black pepper

Cook's Notes

TIME
Preparation and cook-ing take a total of about 50 minutes.

VARIATION
Substitute canned ma-ckerel or pilchards for the sardines.

SERVING IDEAS
Serve on its own garnished with bay leaves, coriander and lemon. For a more substantial meal, serve with crusty bread and a salad.

● 410 calories per portion

1 Heat the oil in a large skillet, add the onions and cook gently for about 10 minutes until browned. Stir in the rice and cook until the oil is absorbed, about 2 minutes.

2 Add the tomatoes and their juices, the broth, garlic, if using, bay leaf, turmeric, cinnamon, and the beans. Season to taste with salt and pepper and bring to boil, stirring. Lower the heat, cover pan and simmer for 20-25 minutes until the rice is tender and most of the liquid has been absorbed.

3 Cut sardines into pieces, add to skillet with mussels and herrings, and heat through for 3-4 minutes. Serve straight from the pan, piping hot.

Chicken biriani

SERVES 4-6

¾ lb cooked chicken, cut into
   cubes
4 tablespoons butter
1 cup long-grain rice
2 tablespoons Madras curry
   powder
⅓ cup seedless raisins
16 black peppercorns
¼ teaspoon salt
1 chicken bouillon cube
3¾ cups hot water
1 large onion, quartered
¼ cup flaked almonds
1 hard-cooked egg, quartered
   lengthwise, to garnish

1 Melt 2 tablespoons butter in a heavy-bottomed saucepan and cook the rice over moderate heat for about 1 minute, until the rice is only just beginning to brown on all sides.

Cook's Notes

TIME
This tasty dish takes only about 25 minutes to prepare and cook.

SERVING IDEAS
Serve accompanied by mango chutney and a side dish of plain yogurt mixed with chopped fresh mint.

DID YOU KNOW
Birianis are normally finished by drizzling saffron water or food coloring over them so that some of the grains of rice turn a golden yellow to contrast vividly with those that remain white.

● 520 calories per portion

2 Lower the heat, add half the curry powder and stir well. Reserve a few raisins and add the rest to the pan with the peppercorns and salt.

3 Crumble the bouillon cube into the water, stir to dissolve and add to the rice mixture. Cover the pan and cook gently for about 10 minutes until the rice is almost cooked but there is still some liquid left in the bottom of the pan.

4 Meanwhile, melt the remaining butter in a skillet and add the chicken and onion. Cook gently for about 2 minutes, turning the chicken and onion frequently.

5 Add the remaining curry powder and cook quickly, stirring well, until the chicken is brown and well coated in spices while the onion stays crisp.

6 Add the chicken mixture to the rice. Reserve a few almonds and stir into the pan. Cook gently until all the remaining liquid is absorbed. Serve at once, garnished with the reserved raisins and almonds and the hard-cooked egg quarters.

Farmhouse chicken and rice

SERVES 4-6

¾ lb boneless cooked chicken meat, skin removed and cut into bite-sized pieces
2 tablespoons butter or margarine
1 large onion, chopped
2 celery stalks, chopped
2 carrots, sliced
¼ lb Chinese cabbage or summer cabbage, shredded
1 can (about 14 oz) tomatoes, drained and chopped (see Cook's tips)
1½ cups cooked long-grain rice (see Cook's tips)
1 can (about 7 oz) whole kernel corn, drained
salt and freshly ground black pepper
1 tablespoon chopped parsley
½ cup grated sharp Cheddar cheese

1 Melt the butter in a large saucepan, add the onion, celery, carrots and Chinese cabbage and cook for about 10 minutes or until the vegetables are just tender, stirring occasionally.

2 Stir in the chicken, tomatoes, rice and corn and season to taste with salt and pepper. Cover and cook gently for a further 10 minutes or until piping hot.

3 Add the parsley and cheese and stir until the cheese has melted. Transfer to a warmed serving dish and serve at once.

Cook's Notes

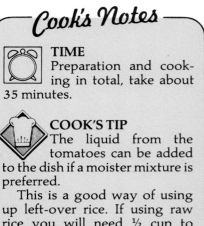

TIME
Preparation and cooking in total, take about 35 minutes.

COOK'S TIP
The liquid from the tomatoes can be added to the dish if a moister mixture is preferred.

This is a good way of using up left-over rice. If using raw rice you will need ½ cup to make the amount required for the dish.

● 405 calories per portion

Kabanos risotto

SERVES 4

2 tablespoons vegetable oil
1 onion, finely chopped
1 small green pepper, seeded and finely chopped
1 can (about 14 oz) tomatoes
1 teaspoon paprika
½ teaspoon sugar
salt and freshly ground black pepper
⅓ lb kabanos sausages, cut into ½-inch slices (see Buying guide)
1½ cups cooked long-grain rice (see Cook's tip)
2 tablespoons chopped parsley, to garnish

1 Heat the oil in a saucepan and cook the onion and the pepper over moderate heat for 3 minutes until soft and lightly browned.

2 Add the tomatoes and their juice, paprika, sugar, and salt and pepper to taste. Bring to a boil, breaking up the tomatoes with a wooden spoon and simmer, uncovered, for about 10 minutes, stirring the tomato sauce from time to time.

3 Add the kabanos and rice to the sauce, stir well and simmer for a further 5 minutes or until piping hot all the way through.

4 Serve immediately in a warmed serving dish, garnished with the chopped parsley.

Cook's Notes

TIME
Preparing and cooking take 30 minutes.

BUYING GUIDE
Kabanos, a Polish pork sausage, is available in delicatessens — 2 sausages should provide the amount needed. If unavailable, use some pepperoni or chorizos.

VARIATION
Add ¼ lb frozen peas with the tomatoes.

COOK'S TIP
This is a good way of using up left-over rice. If using raw rice, you will need ½ cup at stage 1.

● 375 calories per portion

Chicken and Zucchini salad

SERVES 4

¾ lb boneless cooked chicken meat, cut into bite-sized pieces
1 cup long-grain rice
2 tablespoons vegetable oil
¾ lb zucchini, thickly sliced
2 teaspoons curry powder
1½ tablespoons lemon juice
salt and freshly ground black pepper
2 tablespoons thick mayonnaise
2 bananas

1 Bring a pan of salted water to a boil and cook the rice for 12-15 minutes until just tender. Rinse well under cold running water to separate the grains. Drain well and set aside for 30 minutes until cold.

2 Meanwhile, heat half the oil in a skillet and cook zucchini and curry powder briskly for about 4-5 minutes, turning, until golden and cooked through. Remove from pan with a slotted spoon and drain.

3 Put 1 tablespoon of the lemon juice and the remaining oil in a large serving bowl, season to taste with salt and pepper and mix well. Stir in the cold rice and zucchini.

4 Put mayonnaise into a separate bowl. Add the cooked chicken pieces and stir them into the mayonnaise until well coated.

5 Fold the chicken into the rice mixture until evenly distributed. Peel and slice the bananas and arrange on top, then sprinkle with the remaining lemon juice. Serve at once (see Serving ideas).

Quick beef curry

SERVES 4

1 lb lean ground beef
1 large onion, chopped
1 clove garlic, crushed (optional)
1 tablespoon curry powder (see Did you know)
¼ teaspoon ground ginger
¼ teaspoon ground cumin
1 dessert apple, pared and grated
2 tablespoons golden or seedless raisins
1 can (about 10 oz) condensed beef broth
salt and freshly ground black pepper
¼ lb mushrooms, quartered

1 Place the beef, onion and garlic in a saucepan and cook over moderate heat until the beef is well browned, stirring constantly to break up lumps.

2 Stir in the spices and cook for 2 minutes, then stir in the apple, raisins and the beef broth. Season to taste with salt and pepper.

3 Bring to a boil, then simmer gently for 5 minutes.

4 Stir in the mushrooms and simmer a further 10 minutes. Taste and adjust seasoning. Serve at once.

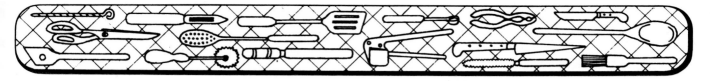

Savory rice mountain

SERVES 4
1 cup cooked long-grain rice (see Cook's tip)
1 can (about ¾ lb) luncheon meat, diced
2 hard-cooked eggs, chopped
1 can (7 oz) whole kernel corn, drained
¼ lb frozen peas, cooked
3 tablespoons thick mayonnaise
salt and freshly ground black pepper
vegetable oil, for greasing

TO SERVE
2 tablespoons chopped chives
grated carrot
extra mayonnaise

1 Brush the inside of a 1¼-quart jelly mold or pudding bowl with vegetable oil. Set aside.
2 In a large bowl, toss the rice,

luncheon meat, eggs, corn and peas. Mix in the mayonnaise and season with salt and pepper.
3 Spoon the rice into the prepared mold and then press down firmly. Cover with a plate and weight down. Refrigerate at least 1 hour.
4 Remove the weight and plate

from the mold and invert a serving plate on top. Holding mold and plate firmly together, turn them over, then carefully lift off the mold to release the rice. Arrange chives on top and grated carrot around the rice mountain and hand a bowl of mayonnaise separately.

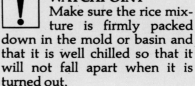

TIME
This dish, ideal for using up leftovers, takes less than 10 minutes to prepare plus 1 hour chilling in mold.

COOK'S TIP
Rice triples in weight when it is cooked so use ⅓ cup raw rice to give the required amount of cooked rice.

VARIATIONS
Left-over cooked vegetables such as carrots and beans can be chopped and

added to the rice mixture to give colour and added flavor.

Use ⅓ lb smoked mackerel or one 7 oz can of tuna instead of the luncheon meat.

WATCHPOINT
Make sure the rice mixture is firmly packed down in the mold or basin and that it is well chilled so that it will not fall apart when it is turned out.

● 660 calories per portion

EGG 'N' CHEESE DISHES

Celery soufflé

SERVES 4
1 can (about 10 oz) condensed celery soup
3 celery stalks, chopped
3 egg yolks
pinch of nutmeg
salt and freshly ground black pepper
4 egg whites
1 tablespoon grated Parmesan cheese
butter, for greasing

1 Preheat the oven to 350°. Grease a 2-quart soufflé or ovenproof dish.
2 Pour the celery soup into a saucepan and warm through gently. Stir in the celery.
3 Remove the soup from the heat and stir in the egg yolks and nutmeg. Season to taste with salt and freshly ground black pepper.
4 In a clean, dry bowl beat the egg whites until they are standing in stiff peaks.
5 Using a metal spoon, fold a spoonful of the egg whites into celery mixture and then fold in the remainder of the egg whites.
6 Pour the mixture into the prepared dish and bake in the oven for 40 minutes.
7 Carefully slide the oven shelf out a little way, sprinkle the grated Parmesan over the soufflé and return it to the oven for a further 5 minutes. Serve at once.

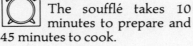

TIME
The soufflé takes 10 minutes to prepare and 45 minutes to cook.

VARIATIONS
Use can of condensed mushroom soup and some sliced fresh mushrooms instead of the celery soup and celery. Cheddar cheese can be used instead of Parmesan, or the cheese can be omitted altogether, if you prefer.

COOK'S TIP
Reserve the spare egg yolk and add it to a sauce for a savory dish to give it extra richness.

● 150 calories per portion

Ham and egg cobbler

SERVES 4-6

BISCUIT TOPPING
1 cup plus 2 tablespoons all purpose flour
1 cup plus 2 tablespoons whole wheat flour
2 teaspoons baking powder
½ teaspoon dry mustard
½ teaspoon salt
1 tablespoon chopped parsley
pinch of dried sage
3 tablespoons shortening
1 egg, beaten
½ cup milk

FILLING
3 tablespoons butter or margarine
1 large onion, finely chopped
3 tablespoons all-purpose flour
½ teaspoon dry mustard
2 cups milk
¾ lb lean cooked ham, diced
4 eggs hard-cooked and chopped
¾ lb potatoes, boiled and cut
2 tablespoons chopped parsley
salt and freshly ground black pepper

1 Preheat the oven to 400°. Melt the butter in a saucepan, add the onion, cover and cook very gently for about 10 minutes, until soft but not colored.

2 Meanwhile, make the biscuit topping: Mix the flours, baking powder, dry mustard and salt in a large bowl. Stir in the herbs. Using two knives, cut the shortening into the dry ingredients until the mixture resembles bread crumbs. Make a well in the center, pour in the egg and milk and stir with a fork until all the dry ingredients are drawn into the liquid to form a soft dough.

3 Knead the dough lightly on a floured surface, then roll out to a thickness of ½-inch. Cut into rounds with a floured 2-inch cookie cutter. Set the dough rounds aside while you prepare the filling.

4 Sprinkle the flour and dry mustard for the filling into the onion mixture over the heat. Stir over low heat for 1-2 minutes, then remove from the heat and gradually stir in the milk. Return to the heat and simmer, stirring, until thick and smooth.

5 Remove the sauce from the heat and lightly stir in the ham, eggs, potatoes and parsley. Add salt and pepper to taste. Transfer the mixture to a 1½-quart ovenproof dish and arrange the rounds of dough on top. Bake the cobbler in the oven for 25 minutes or until the topping is risen and golden brown, and the filling is heated through. Serve hot, straight from the dish.

Cook's Notes

TIME
Preparation, including cooking the eggs and potatoes and making the topping and sauce, takes about 30 minutes. Cooking in the oven takes 25 minutes.

DID YOU KNOW
Cobbler is a term used to describe a fruit pie with a biscuit topping. The dough, which is always made with baking powder, is often cut into round "cobble" shapes, hence the name.

● 810 calories per portion

Leek and bacon flan

SERVES 4

1 stick (½ 11 oz package pie crust
   sticks) prepared as directed
3 tablespoons butter or margarine
1 lb leeks, sliced
3 large slices lean bacon, cut into ½-
   inch strips
1½ teaspoons all-purpose flour
1½ teaspoons paprika
1 teaspoon lemon juice
¼ cup milk
salt and freshly ground black
   pepper
2 eggs, beaten

1 Preheat the oven to 400°.
2 Roll out the pastry on a floured
surface and use to line an 8-inch flan
dish. ❋ Prick the base with a fork.
Place a large circle of waxed paper
or foil in the case, weight it down
with dried beans and bake blind in
the oven for 10 minutes. Remove

the dried beans and waxed paper
then return to the oven for 10-15
minutes until crisp and lightly
colored.
3 Meanwhile, prepare the filling:
Melt the butter in a saucepan, add
the leeks, cover and cook gently for
about 10 minutes until soft.
4 Place the bacon in a skillet and
cook it gently in its own fat for
about 10 minutes until colored. Set
aside.
5 When the leeks have softened,
sprinkle in the flour and paprika and
cook for 1-2 minutes stirring.
Gradually blend in the lemon juice
and milk and bring to a boil, stirring.
Add salt and pepper to taste
(remembering that the bacon will be
salty), then remove from the heat
and stir in the eggs.
6 When the flan case is cooked,
lower the oven temperature to
350°. Spread the bacon pieces
over the base of the prepared
case, then pour the leek mixture
over the top. Return to the oven
and bake for 20-25 minutes. Serve
warm.

Cook's Notes

TIME
Total preparation and
cooking is 50 minutes.

COOK'S TIP
If using a ceramic flan
dish, place it on a metal
cookie sheet to improve heat
conduction.

VARIATIONS
Use 1½ teaspoons of
curry powder in place
of the paprika.

FREEZING
Bake the flan in a foil
dish, then cool quickly.
Cover, seal, label and freeze.
Store for up to 3 months. To
serve: Uncover and thaw for 3
hours at room temperature,
then reheat in a 350° oven for
15 minutes.

● 415 calories per portion

Scrambled eggs and onions

SERVES 4
6 eggs
3 tablespoons milk
salt and freshly ground black pepper
¼ cup butter or margarine
1 tablespoon vegetable oil
4 onions, thinly sliced
2 tablespoons chopped chives
8 slices of French bread, toasted,
   to serve

1 Beat the eggs in a bowl with the milk; season with salt and pepper.
2 Heat the butter and oil in a skillet, add the onions and cook gently for about 20 minutes or until golden (see Cook's tips).
3 Add the egg mixture and cook over low heat, stirring constantly until the eggs are just set but not dry (see Cook's tips). Taste and adjust seasoning.
4 Pile on slices of French bread, sprinkle over chives and serve.

Cook's Notes

TIME
Preparation and cooking take 15 minutes.

VARIATIONS
Vary the flavor by adding a little freshly grated nutmeg or a pinch of paprika, or a mixture of chopped fresh herbs instead of the chives.

COOK'S TIPS
Take care not to let the onions become brown or they will impart a bitter flavor which will spoil the finished dish.

Do not overcook the eggs — they taste best when left a little runny.

● 270 calories per portion

Spanish vegetable omelet

SERVES 4

**1 lb potatoes, cut into ½-inch dice
(see Cook's tip)**
salt
**⅓ lb fresh green beans or ¼ lb
frozen green beans**
2 tablespoons vegetable oil
1 onion, chopped
1 red pepper, seeded and diced
7 eggs, beaten
**2 tablespoons finely chopped fresh
parsley**
½ teaspoon paprika
freshly ground black pepper
**a little extra finely chopped fresh
parsley, to garnish**

1 Bring a pan of salted water to a boil and cook the potatoes for about 5 minutes, until just tender but not mushy. Drain, refresh in cold water and drain again. Put the potatoes in a large bowl.
2 If using fresh beans, bring a pan of salted water to a boil and cook them for about 8 minutes until tender but still crisp. If using frozen beans, cook for about 5 minutes. Drain, refresh in cold water and drain again. Cut the beans into 1-1½ inch lengths and add to the potatoes in the bowl.

3 Heat the oil in a large non-stick skillet, add the onion and red pepper and cook gently for about 5 minutes, stirring occasionally, until softened but not colored. Remove the onion and pepper from the pan with a slotted spoon, draining all the oil back into the pan, and add to the potatoes and beans.
4 Add the beaten eggs, parsley and paprika to the vegetables in the bowl and stir lightly together. Season to taste with salt and pepper.
5 Reheat the oil in the pan over low heat and pour in the omelet mixture.

Level out the vegetables and leave to cook very gently for 15-20 minutes, until the bottom is set but the top is still creamy. Meanwhile, preheat the broiler to high.
6 Set the skillet under the broiler at the lowest position from the heat for 2-3 minutes, until the top of the omelet is set and light golden. Loosen the omelet from the pan with a round-bladed knife, then with a spatula slide it carefully onto a large plate. Sprinkle lightly with chopped parsley and leave to cool slightly. Serve the omelet cut into wedges.

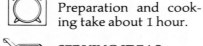
Cook's Notes

TIME
Preparation and cooking take about 1 hour.

SERVING IDEAS
Serve the omelet warm or cold, on its own for a snack, or with French bread and salad for a lunch or supper dish. Alternatively, try slipping wedges of the hot omelet into lightly toasted pita bread pockets, adding slices of cucumber or tomato.

VARIATIONS
Use peas or broad beans instead of green beans, or replace half the potato with diced carrot. Use 8 scallions, trimmed and cut into ¼-inch slices, in place of ordinary onion, and finely chopped fresh mint makes a refreshing alternative to parsley. Add ¼ cup left-over cooked chicken, ham or sausage, finely chopped, to the recipe for extra flavor and nourishment.

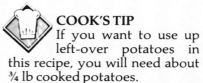
COOK'S TIP
If you want to use up left-over potatoes in this recipe, you will need about ¾ lb cooked potatoes.

● 315 calories per portion

Creole eggs

SERVES 4

8 eggs
1 tablespoon vegetable oil
2 onions, sliced
1 small green pepper, seeded and
  sliced
2 tablespoons cornstarch
2 cups milk
4 tomatoes, peeled and quartered
salt and freshly ground black pepper
pinch of cayenne (optional)
2 tablespoons chopped fresh
  parsley
onion and green pepper rings, to
  garnish

1 Heat the oil in a large saucepan, add the onions and green pepper and cook gently for 5 minutes until the onions are soft and lightly colored.
2 Put the cornstarch into a bowl and mix with a little of the milk to form a smooth paste. Mix in the remaining milk and stir into the vegetables. Bring slowly to a boil, stirring, then when the mixture thickens, add the tomatoes with salt, pepper and cayenne, if using, to taste.
3 Lower the heat, cover the pan and simmer for about 10 minutes, stirring from time to time.
4 Meanwhile, hard-cook the eggs, remove their shells and halve the eggs lengthwise. Arrange the halves in a single layer on the base of a warmed serving dish.
5 Pour the sauce over the eggs, sprinkle with chopped parsley and garnish with rings of onion and green pepper. Serve at once.

Cook's Notes

TIME
This easy dish takes about 25 minutes to prepare and cook.

DID YOU KNOW
Dishes using a combination of tomatoes and peppers are a popular feature of Creole cookery in the southern United States.

● 275 calories per portion

Eggs in a nest

SERVES 4

8 eggs

2 tablespoons butter or margarine

¼ lb sliced bacon, cut into strips

¼ cup all-purpose flour

1¼ cups milk

1 can (about 10 oz) whole kernel corn, drained

1 teaspoon Worcestershire sauce

salt and freshly ground black pepper

1 small package potato chips, crushed

1 tablespoon chopped fresh parsley

1 Put the eggs into a saucepan, cover with cold water and bring to a boil. Simmer for 5 minutes.

2 Meanwhile, preheat the broiler to high.

3 Run cold water over the eggs [!] and remove shells. Put the eggs into a bowl, cover with warm water and set aside until needed.

4 Melt the butter in a small skillet, add the bacon and cook for 4-5 minutes until lightly browned. Sprinkle in the flour and stir over low heat for 1-2 minutes. Remove from the heat and gradually stir in the milk. Return to the heat and simmer, stirring, until the mixture is thick and smooth.

5 Stir the whole kernel corn and the Worcestershire sauce into the bacon sauce. Taste and season with salt, if necessary, and pepper.

6 Spread the corn mixture in an ovenproof serving dish, dry the eggs on paper towels and arrange them in the corn. Sprinkle over the crushed chips. Put the dish under the broiler for a few minutes to warm the chips. Sprinkle parsley over the top and serve at once.

Cheese puff

SERVES 4

1 cup coarsely grated Swiss or
   Gouda cheese
2 sheets (1 17 oz package) frozen
   puff pastry, thawed
½ cup all-purpose flour
⅔ cup milk
2 tablespoons butter or margarine,
   cut into small pieces
2 large eggs, beaten
3 tablespoons heavy cream
cayenne
nutmeg
salt and freshly ground black pepper
beaten egg, to seal and glaze

Cook's Notes

TIME
Preparation 30 minutes,
baking 40 minutes.

COOK'S TIP
If the sauce is too thick,
thin with a little more
cream. If too runny, chill in the
refrigerator until thickened.

FREEZING
Prepare up to the end of
stage 8, open freeze raw
on a cookie sheet, then wrap in
foil and freeze for 3 months.
Bake from frozen, uncovered,
allowing an extra 10 minutes.

VARIATIONS
For a meaty version,
add ¼ cup diced ham or
broiled bacon to the cheese
sauce; for a cheesier flavor,
add ¼ cup diced blue cheese
(such as Stilton, Danish Blue,
Gorgonzola).

SERVING IDEAS
Eat hot for supper cut
into thick slices with
either hot vegetables or a salad.
Or serve cut into small squares
for a snack to eat with drinks.

● 680 calories per portion

---

1 Preheat the oven to 450°.
2 Put the flour in a saucepan and mix it to a smooth paste with some of the milk. Stir in the remaining milk gradually until smooth, then add the butter.
3 Place the pan over moderate heat and beat until the sauce is almost at boiling point (it may look lumpy at this stage). Remove the pan from the heat and beat until smooth.
4 Beat in the eggs a little at a time, then return to the heat and bring to a boil, stirring all the time. Cook until the sauce is very thick and holds its shape.

5 Remove from the heat and leave to cool slightly, then stir in the cheese and cream with a pinch of cayenne and nutmeg, and salt and pepper to taste. To prevent a skin forming on top, press a piece of plastic wrap or damp waxed paper onto the surface of the sauce, then leave to cool.
6 Roll out sheet of the pastry on a floured board to about a 12 × 7-inch rectangle, ⅛-inch thick. Trim the edges square, then place the pastry on a dampened cookie sheet.
7 Spread the cheese sauce over the pastry, leaving a 1½-inch margin around the edge. Turn in this pastry border to partially cover the cheese filling. Roll out the remaining pastry to a rectangle the same size as the first and trim the edges square. Brush all around the edge with water or beaten egg, then place on top of the first rectangle, pressing the edges together firmly to seal. Knock up the edges with the back of a knife, then flute.
8 Brush the top with more beaten egg, then slash across at 1-inch intervals with a sharp knife. ✳
9 Bake in the oven for 20 minutes, then cover the pastry with foil or waxed paper to prevent it becoming too brown. Lower the heat to 400° and continue baking in the oven for a further 30 minutes.
10 Slide onto a wire rack, sprinkle lightly with cayenne, if liked, then leave to cool for 5 minutes before serving.

Cheese fondue

SERVES 4

½ lb Gouda or Swiss cheese, finely grated
½ lb sharp Cheddar cheese, finely grated
1 clove garlic (optional)
1¼ cups dry white wine
1 tablespoon all-purpose flour
1 teaspoon kirsch (optional)
pinch of nutmeg
salt and freshly ground black pepper

TO SERVE

selection of raw crisp vegetables (celery stalks, cauliflower flowerets, carrot sticks)
French bread, cut into cubes

1 Halve garlic, if using and rub cut surfaces on inside of a heavy-bottomed fondue pan or saucepan.
2 Pour the wine into the pan and heat until it starts to boil.
3 Put the flour in a plastic bag, add the cheeses, and shake.
4 Turn the heat to low and slowly add the cheese to the wine, stirring.
5 Add the kirsch, if using, and nutmeg, salt and pepper to taste, then cook for 10-15 minutes on the lowest possible heat to allow the fondue flavors to develop. [!]
6 To serve: Place fondue pan over spirit burner, or pour fondue into warmed individual soup bowls. Serve at once, using forks to dip crisp vegetables and cubes of bread into the fondue.

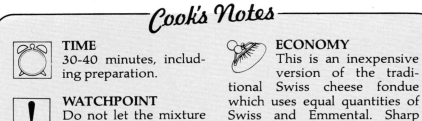

Cook's Notes

TIME
30-40 minutes, including preparation.

WATCHPOINT
Do not let the mixture become too hot during cooking or the cheese will become stringy.

ECONOMY
This is an inexpensive version of the traditional Swiss cheese fondue which uses equal quantities of Swiss and Emmental. Sharp Cheddar is more economical.

● 275 calories per portion

Cheese and apple pie

SERVES 4-6
3 sticks (¾ 22 oz package) pie crust
   sticks prepared as directed
1 lb tart dessert apples
juice of ½ lemon
¼ cup firmly packed dark brown
   sugar
½ teaspoon cinnamon
2 tablespoons golden raisins
¾ cup grated Cheddar cheese
milk and dark brown sugar, for
   glazing

1 Preheat the oven to 400°.
2 Roll out half the pastry on a
floured surface and use to line an 8-
inch pie plate.
3 Core, pare and thinly slice apples.
Arrange half the slices on the pastry;
sprinkle at once with half the lemon
juice and half each of the sugar,
cinnamon and raisins. Top with the
remaining apple slices, followed by
the remaining lemon juice, sugar,
cinnamon and raisins.
4 Sprinkle the grated cheese evenly
over the top of the apples. Brush
around the edges of the pastry with
milk, then roll out the remainder of
the pastry and cover the apples and
cheese. Trim around the edge of the
plate with a sharp knife.
5 Press the edges of the pastry
together firmly, then knock up with
back of a knife and scallop or flute to
make an attractive finish.
6 Roll out the pastry trimmings and
cut out leaves or diamonds to
decorate the top of the pie. Brush
with a little milk and fix on top.

7 Brush the top of the pie with milk
and sprinkle with a little dark brown
sugar. Bake the pie in the oven for
about 20 minutes, turning the pie
once so that it browns evenly.
8 Reduce the oven temperature to
350° and cook the pie for a further
20 minutes or so, [!] until the
apples feel tender when pricked
with a fine skewer. Serve warm or
cold.

Cook's Notes

TIME
Preparation takes about
20 minutes, cooking 40
minutes.

SERVING IDEAS
This pie makes a per-
fect cut-and-come-again
sweet snack, by itself or with a
wedge of cheese. It can be eaten
warm or cold.

You could also serve the pie
for a family snack, or with cream
as a dessert.

WATCHPOINT
If the pastry becomes
too brown before the
pie filling is cooked, cover the
top with foil.

FREEZING
The cooked pie can be
successfully frozen. Let
it cool completely, then open
freeze on the pie plate. When
solid, carefully remove from the
plate and pack in a rigid
container (cooked frozen pastry
is very fragile and tends to
crumble easily). Seal, label and
return to the freezer for up to 6
months. To serve: Place the
frozen pie, uncovered, into a
preheated 425° oven. Bake for
20 minutes, reduce the oven
temperature to 350° and bake
for a further 20 minutes until
warm through.

● 615 calories per portion

Cheese and ham rolls

SERVES 4
8 slices cheese, processed or
**   Gouda**
8 slices cooked ham
1 cup cottage cheese
freshly ground black pepper
1 tablespoon chopped parsley or
**   chopped chives**

TOMATO SAUCE
1 tablespoon butter
1 tablespoon vegetable oil
1 small onion, finely chopped
1 clove garlic, crushed
1 can (about 14 oz) tomatoes
1 teaspoon sugar
1 bay leaf
1 teaspoon chopped parsley
**   or basil**
salt and freshly ground black
**   pepper**

1 Preheat the oven to 400°.
2 To make the sauce: Melt the butter with the oil in a saucepan and lightly cook the onion and crushed garlic until soft. Add all the remaining ingredients, breaking up the tomatoes if necessary. Bring to a boil, then lower the heat, cover the pan and simmer for 30 minutes. Adjust seasoning if necessary.
3 Meanwhile, place a slice of cheese on each piece of ham. Season the cottage cheese with pepper, stir in the parsley or chives and divide evenly between the ham and cheese slices. Roll up and place in a single layer in an ovenproof dish, with the seams underneath. Pour the tomato sauce over the ham slices and place in the oven for 10 minutes until bubbly on top. For a crisper topping, scatter a little grated cheese mixed with a few bread crumbs over the top before baking.

Cook's Notes

TIME
Preparation and cooking 55 minutes.

SERVING IDEAS
Cook in individual gratin dishes and serve with French bread and a side salad for supper.

● 400 calories per portion

VARIATION
Place the rolls on a bed of spinach and coat with a cheese sauce.

FREEZING
The tomato sauce can be poured into trays for freezing and then packed in freezer bags. Thaw in a pan over low heat.

Cheesy vegetable curry

SERVES 4

⅓ lb sharp Cheddar cheese, cut into ½-inch cubes
3 tablespoons butter or margarine
1 large onion, chopped
1 small green pepper, seeded and cut into strips
2 small carrots, halved lengthwise and thinly sliced
4 small or 2 large zucchini, halved lengthwise and cut into ½-inch slices
1 large cooking apple, pared, cored and cut into ¾-inch dice
2 teaspoons curry powder
3 tablespoons all-purpose flour
2½ cups chicken broth
2 tablespoons golden raisins
salt
2 tablespoons mango chutney, chopped

1 Melt the butter in a saucepan, add the onion, green pepper and carrots and cook gently for 3-4 minutes, stirring, until the onions are soft but not colored. Add the zucchini, apple and curry powder and cook for 2 minutes, stirring.
2 Sprinkle in the flour, cook for 1-2 minutes, stirring, then gradually blend in the broth. Bring to a boil, stirring, then add the raisins and salt to taste. Lower the heat, cover the pan and simmer for 5 minutes.
3 Add the mango chutney, then stir in the cubed cheese. ☐! Serve at once in an attractive bowl.

Cheese and tomato loaf

SERVES 4
¾ lb sharp Cheddar cheese, grated
   (see Buying guide)
1 lb firm tomatoes, very finely
   chopped
8 large pickles, finely chopped
6 scallions, finely chopped
2 teaspoons plain yogurt
1 teaspoon Dijon-style mustard
1 tablespoon chopped fresh parsley
salt and freshly ground black pepper
melted butter or margarine, for
   greasing

TO GARNISH
1 tomato, sliced
2 large or 4 cocktail pickles, sliced
sprigs of parsley

1 Brush an 8½ × 4½ × 2½-inch
loaf pan with the melted butter or
margarine.

2 Put all the loaf ingredients in a
large bowl with salt and pepper
to taste and mix together until
thoroughly combined.
3 Spoon the mixture into the
prepared loaf pan, press down and

cover with waxed paper and weight
down. Chill overnight.
4 Drain off liquid, then turn out loaf
onto a serving dish and garnish with
tomato and pickle slices and sprigs
of parsley.

Cook's Notes

TIME
This loaf only takes
about 10 minutes to
prepare, but remember to allow
for chilling overnight.

VARIATIONS
Ordinary Cheddar can
be used for a less
expensive, milder-tasting loaf.
Try one of the flavored
Cheddars with mixed herbs or
pickled onions for a different
flavor.
   Instead of yogurt, use mayonnaise, dairy sour cream or
heavy cream.

SERVING IDEAS
For a snack, cut into
slices with fresh bread
and butter and a mixed salad or
a salad of sliced beets and
chicory. If you are short of time,
do not chill, simply spoon the
mixture onto a bed of shredded
lettuce. For an appetizer to serve
6 people, serve with crisp toast.

BUYING GUIDE
The sharp type of
Cheddar gives a good
cheese flavor to the dish.

● 400 calories per portion

SANDWICHES

Spicy club sandwich

MAKES 4
¼ lb cooked chicken, chopped into
   bite-sized pieces
4 lean bacon slices
2 teaspoons mild curry powder
¼ cup mayonnaise
8 slices whole wheat bread
4 slices white bread
4 tablespoons butter, softened
4 small lettuce leaves
16 thin slices cucumber
2 tomatoes, sliced
chopped fresh parsley (optional)

1 Preheat the broiler to moderate. In a bowl, stir the curry powder into the mayonnaise and mix in the chicken. Lightly broil the bacon, drain well on paper towels and keep warm.
2 With a very sharp knife, remove the crusts from the bread and trim the slices to exactly the same size. Butter both sides of the white, and one side of the whole wheat slices. Spread the chicken mixture equally over 4 slices of the whole wheat bread. Top with the white bread slices.
3 Put a lettuce leaf and 4 slices of cucumber on each sandwich. Top with remaining brown bread slices.
4 Finally top each sandwich with tomato slices, a bacon slice and chopped parsley, if using.

Cook's Notes

TIME
Preparation takes about 30 minutes.

VARIATIONS
Cold cooked pork or canned tuna could be substituted for chicken.

SERVING IDEAS
You may find it easier to eat these double-decker sandwiches with a knife and fork.

● 505 calories per portion

Chicken and banana double deckers

SERVES 4

⅓ lb boneless cooked chicken
1 tablespoon vegetable oil
1 small onion, chopped
1-2 teaspoons curry powder
2 tablespoons thick
   mayonnaise
juice of 1 lemon
1 tablespoon golden raisins
butter, for spreading
8 slices whole wheat bread, crusts
   removed
4 slices white bread, crusts removed
8 teaspoons mango chutney
2 bananas
4 teaspoons shredded coconut

1 Heat the oil in a small pan, add the onion and cook gently for 5 minutes until soft and lightly colored. Sprinkle over curry powder (see Cook's tips) and cook for 2 minutes.

2 Put the chicken and the onion mixture into a blender. Add the mayonnaise and 2 teaspoons lemon juice and blend for 1-2 minutes (see Cook's tips). Transfer to a bowl.
3 Stir the raisins into the chicken mixture until well blended.
4 Spread butter on one side of all the slices of bread. Lay 4 whole wheat slices, buttered side up, on a board. Divide the chicken mixture between them, spreading it evenly.

Top with slices of white bread, buttered side down.
5 Spread the mango chutney over the top of the white bread slices. Slice the bananas evenly. Put the banana slices on top of the chutney and brush with the remaining lemon juice. Sprinkle over the coconut and top with remaining whole wheat bread slices, buttered side down.
6 Cut sandwiches in quarters and arrange on a serving plate.

Cook's Notes

TIME
20-30 minutes for preparation.

COOK'S TIPS
The amount of curry powder you use will depend on how strong a curry flavor you like.

If you do not have a blender, chop the chicken finely, then put the onion mixture into a bowl and mix in the mayonnaise, lemon juice and chicken stirring well to combine all the ingredients.

SERVING IDEAS
These sandwiches make a tasty snack on their own, or serve a tomato and onion salad with them.

● 620 calories per portion

Fried sardine sandwiches

SERVES 4
1 can (about 4 oz) sardines in oil, drained
2 large eggs, hard-cooked and chopped
2 tablespoons chopped chives or finely chopped scallions
freshly ground black pepper
⅓ cup butter or margarine, softened
grated rind of 1 lemon
1 tablespoon lemon juice
generous pinch of paprika
8 thin slices bread, crusts removed

1 Mash the sardines until smooth, then mix in the chopped eggs, chives and plenty of pepper.
2 Using a wooden spoon, beat the butter in a separate bowl until light and creamy, then beat in the lemon rind, lemon juice and paprika.
3 Spread the bread slices on 1 side with the lemon-flavored butter. ⚠ Turn 4 of the slices over, and spread evenly with the sardine mixture. Top with the remaining 4 slices of bread, butter side facing upwards.
4 Set a large skillet over fairly high heat and leave it for about 30 seconds to heat through (see Cook's tip). Put the sardine sandwiches into the pan and press them down gently with a spatula.
5 Cook the sandwiches for about 3 minutes until golden brown, then carefully turn them over, using a spatula, and cook for a further 3 minutes until golden brown. Serve at once.

Cook's Notes

 TIME
Preparation takes about 20 minutes, including hard-cooking the eggs. Cooking the sandwiches takes about 6 minutes.

VARIATION
Mix the mashed sardines with peeled, chopped tomatoes or peeled, diced cucumber instead of the egg.

! WATCHPOINT
Make sure you spread the butter right to the edges of the slices of bread. This insures an even, golden-brown finish.

 COOK'S TIP
No fat for cooking is needed, as the sandwiches are spread on the outside with the butter.

SERVING IDEAS
These sandwiches are best eaten with a knife and fork.
Or cut each sandwich into 4 triangles with a sharp knife, and serve the triangles skewered with toothpicks and a garnish of tiny lemon wedges or lemon twists.

● 350 calories per portion

Baked ham and tomato sandwiches

SERVES 4

8 slices smoked ham
3-4 large tomatoes, sliced
6 tablespoons mayonnaise
1 tablespoon Dijon-style mustard
½ teaspoon Worcestershire sauce
½ teaspoon soy sauce
3 scallions, finely chopped
½ cup grated sharp Cheddar
   cheese
salt and freshly ground black pepper
½ lb loaf of French bread

1 Preheat the oven to 400°.
2 In a bowl mix together the mayonnaise, mustard, Worcestershire sauce, soy sauce, scallions (reserving a little to garnish), cheese and salt and pepper to taste.
3 Cut the French bread in half across, then cut each half open horizontally. Cut off the rounded ends so that you have 4 rectangular pieces of bread.
4 Spread the cheese mixture over the cut surfaces of the bread. Lay 2 ham slices on each piece of bread, then top with tomato slices. Season with salt and pepper.
5 Wrap each open sandwich in a piece of foil and arrange them side by side on a cookie sheet.
6 Bake for 30 minutes or until the cheese mixture is melted and bubbling. Serve hot, garnished with the reserved scallion.

Cook's Notes

TIME
Preparation and cooking take 45 minutes.

VARIATION
Substitute any other strong-flavored cheese, that you can find for Cheddar, or use a mixture of cheeses.

COOK'S TIP
If liked, these sandwiches may be prepared ahead of time and kept, wrapped in their foil, in the refrigerator. In this case, increase the cooking time by 10-15 minutes.

●670 calories per portion

Melted Mozzarella sandwiches

SERVES 4

8 large slices white bread
4 tablespoons butter, softened
freshly ground black pepper
Worcestershire sauce
¼ lb mozzarella cheese (see
Buying guide)
3 eggs, beaten
vegetable oil, for cooking
parsley sprigs, to garnish

1 Spread the bread with the butter and cut off the crusts (see Cook's tip) with a sharp knife. [!] Season 4 of the bread slices with pepper and a few drops of Worcestershire sauce.

2 Cut the mozzarella into thin slices and arrange them in a single layer on the seasoned bread, leaving a ¼-inch margin all round the edge of the bread.

3 Top with the remaining 4 bread slices. Press the edges firmly together.

4 Put beaten eggs on a plate and dip in each sandwich to coat thoroughly all over. Make sure that the edges are well covered with egg so that they are sealed.

5 Pour enough vegetable oil into a large skillet to come to a depth of ¼-inch. Heat the oil gently until a bread crust sizzles and turns golden brown when it is dropped into the hot oil.

6 Cook the sandwiches 2 at a time for 3-4 minutes on each side until golden brown.

7 Drain very thoroughly on paper towels. Keep the sandwiches warm while cooking the remaining sandwiches. Serve at once, garnished with parsley sprigs.

Cook's Notes

TIME
The sandwiches take about 15 minutes to prepare and cook.

DID YOU KNOW
In Italy these sandwiches are called mozzarella in *carrozza* (a small covered carriage).

COOK'S TIP
Use a little of the removed bread crust to test the temperature of the oil.

WATCHPOINT
It is important that the bread slices are exactly the same size so that they can be sealed neatly.

BUYING GUIDE
Mozzarella cheese has outstanding melting qualities. If you can, buy an individually packed mozzarella cheese from an Italian delicatessen; a single cheese will weigh about ¼ lb.

● 365 calories per portion

Sandwiches in batter

MAKES 4 SANDWICHES
8 lean bacon slices
2 tablespoons butter, softened
8 large, thin slices bread,
 crusts removed
2 bananas

BATTER
½ cup all-purpose flour
pinch of salt
pepper
2 large eggs, separated
¼ cup water
vegetable oil, for cooking

1 Preheat the broiler to high. Broil the bacon on both sides until crisp, then drain on paper towels.
2 While the bacon is broiling, butter the bread and then just before ready to use, mash the bananas well with a fork. [!]
3 Spread the mashed banana over 4 slices of bread, dividing it equally between them. Cut the broiled bacon slices in half and arrange 4 halves on each banana-topped slice of bread. Top with the remaining bread slices and press down well.
4 Make the batter: Sift the flour into a large bowl with the salt and pepper. Make a well in the center. Beat the egg yolks with the water and pour into the well, gradually drawing the flour into the liquid with a wooden spoon. When all the liquid is incorporated, beat well to make a smooth batter.
5 Beat the egg whites until stiff but not dry, then fold into the batter. [!]
6 Dip the sandwiches into the batter, insuring that they are thoroughly and evenly coated on all sides.
7 Pour enough oil into a large skillet to cover the base and heat over moderate to high heat, until sizzling. Add the batter-coated sandwiches and cook until crisp and golden brown on both sides, turning once with a spatula.
8 Drain the cooked sandwiches on paper towels and serve at once.

Cook's Notes

 TIME
Preparation and cooking takes about 25 minutes.

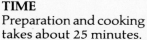 **VARIATIONS**
Instead of the bananas, substitute 8 pitted, sliced prunes.

 FOR CHILDREN
Children will enjoy the sandwiches spread with yeast extract or peanut butter.

! **WATCHPOINTS**
Bananas discolor very quickly once peeled, so mash them only just before using.

Do not add the beaten egg whites until just before you intend to use the batter. Once the egg whites are added the batter will collapse if it is not used immediately.

● 530 calories each

Triple meat sandwiches

SERVES 4
8 large slices white bread
8 large slices whole wheat bread
½ cup butter or margarine
¼ lb liver sausage
4 small dill pickles, chopped
1 teaspoon A-1 sauce
salt and freshly ground black pepper
4 lettuce heart leaves
¼ lb luncheon meat slices
½ teaspoon mustard
½ cup raw beansprouts (see Buying
    guide)
¼ cup thinly sliced peaches
¼ lb salami slices
2 tomatoes, sliced
1½ tablespoons pickle relish
watercress

TO GARNISH
12 cocktail onions (see Buying
    guide)
parsley sprigs

1 Spread the 8 white and 4 of the whole wheat bread slices with 6 tablespoons butter.
2 Put the liver sausage in a bowl, add the remaining 2 tablespoons butter and mix with a fork to make a smooth spread. Mix in the chopped pickles and A-1 sauce and season to

Cook's Notes

TIME
Preparation takes about 30 minutes.

COOK'S TIP
The uncut decker sandwiches can be wrapped in plastic wrap and refrigerated for up to 6 hours, then cut into squares and left at room temperature for 20 minutes before serving.

VARIATIONS
Mashed corned beef can be used instead of liver sausage, and sliced cooked ham instead of luncheon meat. Coleslaw and pineapple chunks can be substituted for the beansprouts and peaches.

BUYING GUIDE
Fresh beansprouts are now readily available from supermarkets, packed in boxes. Do not use canned beansprouts, as they are not crunchy.
    You can buy jars of different colored cocktail onions, which would make an especially attractive garnish.

SERVING IDEAS
For a lunch or supper snack, serve the sandwiches with a knife and fork. The sandwiches are satisfying by themselves, or may be served with a selection of salads for a more filling meal.

● 800 calories per portion

taste with salt and pepper. Spread the mixture over the remaining 4 slices of whole wheat bread. Lay a lettuce leaf on each slice and season with salt and pepper. Cover each with a slice of white bread, buttered side up.
3 Arrange the luncheon meat slices on top and spread with the mustard. Top each sandwich with beansprouts and peach slices. Cover with the remaining whole wheat bread slices, buttered side up.

4 Lay the salami and tomato slices on top and season lightly with salt and pepper. Top each sandwich with relish and watercress.
5 Cover the sandwiches with the remaining white bread slices, buttered side down, and press down firmly (see Cook's tip).
6 Thread the cocktail onions and parsley sprigs alternately onto 4 toothpicks and spear a stick securely into each Triple meat decker sandwich.

Crusty steak sandwiches

SERVES 4
4 slices thin-cut sirloin steak, each weighing about ¼ lb (see Buying guide)
1 tablespoon vegetable oil
salt and freshly ground black pepper
4 large slices whole wheat bread
1 tablespoon mustard
1 egg, beaten
¼ cup finely grated Cheddar cheese
¼ cup butter or margarine

1 Brush the steaks with a little oil and sprinkle with salt and pepper.
2 Spread the bread on 1 side only with the mustard. Dip the other side of the bread into the beaten egg, then into the grated cheese.
3 Preheat the broiler to high.

4 Melt the butter in a large skillet, add the slices of bread, mustard side down, and cook over gentle heat for about 5 minutes until golden brown and crisp (see Cook's tip). Remove from the pan with a spatula and drain well on paper towels. Cut each slice of bread diagonally in half and keep them hot.
5 Broil the steaks for 1 minute on each side for a rare steak, 2-3 minutes for medium to well-done steak.
6 When the steaks are broiled to your liking, place each between 2 triangles of cooked bread with the cheese on the inside.
7 Serve the steaks on a warmed serving dish with the meat juices from the broiler pan poured over.

Cook's Notes

 TIME
Preparation and cooking take 20 minutes.

 COOK'S TIP
The cheese on the non-fried side melts and holds the sandwiches together.

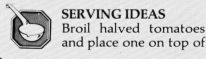 **SERVING IDEAS**
Broil halved tomatoes and place one on top of each sandwich or garnish with lettuce leaves.

 **BUYING GUIDE**
Thin-cut sirloin steaks are available in packs from most supermarkets and also from freezer centers. If using frozen steaks cook them for an extra few minutes.

● 475 calories per portion

VEGETABLE DISHES

Vegetables are so versatile, they can add goodness and color as accompaniments to a normal meal with meat, or they can be made into tasty and nutritious main courses in their own right. Here you will find a varied mixture of appetizers, soups, salads, main dishes and accompanying dishes plus some more spicy vegetable dishes like *Cauliflower creole* or *Vegetable biriani* to add more interest to a special meal.

This section is ideal for vegetarians who want to try more exciting recipes, or for people who just love the taste and texture of vegetables and salads.

APPETIZERS

Spring rolls

MAKES 6

10 oz beansprouts
8 scallions, cut into matchstick
    strips
1 red pepper, seeded, quartered and
    thinly sliced
1 cup thinly sliced
    mushrooms
3 tablespoons vegetable oil
1 slice fresh ginger root,
    finely chopped
1 tablespoon soy sauce
1 tablespoon dry sherry
freshly ground black pepper
vegetable oil, for deep frying
scallion tassels, to garnish

PASTRY

2 cups all-purpose flour
½ teaspoon salt
½ cup warm water

1 Make the pastry: Sift the flour and salt into a bowl, then make a well in the center and pour in the water. Mix with a wooden spoon until well blended, then knead well until the dough is soft and pliable. Wrap in plastic wrap and put in the refrigerator 30 minutes to chill.

2 Heat the oil in a large skillet or wok and add the beansprouts, the scallions and red pepper, mushrooms and ginger. Cook briskly, stirring, for 2 minutes, then add the soy sauce, sherry, and pepper to taste. Cook 1 further minute and remove from the heat.

3 Roll out the pastry on a lightly floured surface as thinly as possible to a neat rectangle, about 18 × 12 inches. Cut the pastry into six 6 inch squares.

4 Place 2 tablespoons of the vegetable mixture in the center of each pastry square. Fold in the sides, brush with a little water then carefully roll up. Dampen underside of pastry ends and press to seal.

5 Heat the oil in a deep-fat frier to 375° or until a stale bread cube browns in 50 seconds.

7 Using a slotted spoon lower 3 rolls into the oil and fry for about 5 minutes until crisp and golden. Remove with a slotted spoon and drain. Keep all the spring rolls warm while cooking the remainder (see Cook's tip).

Cook's Notes

TIME
1 hour to prepare, including chilling time, then 10 minutes cooking.

COOK'S TIP
The rolls may be made a few hours in advance, allowed to cool, then reheated in a 325° oven just before serving.

● 230 calories per roll

Egg and lettuce rolls

MAKES ABOUT 20
5 large crisp lettuce leaves (see Buying guide)
3 hard-cooked eggs, roughly chopped
2 tablespoons butter or margarine softened
¼ cup crumbled Danish Blue cheese

1 Cut off a thin slice from the stalk end of each lettuce leaf to remove the thickest part of the stalk. Wash and gently pat dry on paper towels. Set aside.

2 Make the filling: Put the eggs into a bowl with the butter and the cheese. Mash with a fork to form a smooth paste, adding a little more butter if the mixture is too stiff to blend.

3 Place 1 lettuce leaf on a work surface and spoon 1 tablespoon of the egg mixture into the center. Gently spread the mixture over the lettuce leaf right up to the edges. Starting at the trimmed end, tightly roll up the leaf to enclose the egg mixture. Wrap firmly in plastic wrap immediately after rolling.

4 Spread, roll and wrap the remaining lettuce leaves in the same way and refrigerate overnight.

5 To serve: Unwrap the rolls and cut with a sharp knife into 1-inch lengths. Serve at once.

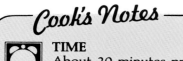

Cook's Notes

TIME
About 20 minutes preparation, plus overnight chilling.

BUYING GUIDE
Choose a romaine or iceberg lettuce for this recipe.

VARIATIONS
For a milder flavor, use a cream cheese instead of blue cheese and season with salt and pepper and a little paprika.

Alternatively, replace the blue cheese with anchovy paste, available in tubes and jars from delicatessens and specialty food stores.

SERVING IDEAS
Serve as a summery appetizer, garnished with tomatoe wedges and cucumber slices. these rolls also make delicate accompaniments for cocktails — arrange attractively on a serving platter and garnish with tomato or sprigs of watercress and parsley for a pretty effect.

● 25 calories per roll

Spinach surprise

SERVES 4

1 lb fresh spinach or ½ lb frozen chopped spinach
salt
¼ cup butter or margarine
1 onion, finely chopped
¼ cup all-purpose flour
⅔ cup milk
good pinch of freshly ground nutmeg
freshly ground black pepper
4 eggs, separated
1 tablespoon grated Parmesan cheese
butter, for greasing

1 If using fresh spinach, wash very thoroughly and remove the stems and central midribs. Place the spinach in a saucepan with only the water that clings to the leaves, and sprinkle with salt. Cover and cook over moderate heat for about 10 minutes, until the spinach is cooked, stirring occasionally. If using frozen spinach, cook according to package directions.

2 Drain the spinach well in a strainer, pressing out all the excess water. Chop the spinach, if using fresh. Grease a 1½ quart soufflé dish.

Preheat oven to 375°.

3 Melt the butter in a large saucepan, add the onion and cook over low heat for about 5 minutes until soft and lightly colored. Sprinkle in the flour and stir over low heat for 1-2 minutes until straw-colored. Remove from the heat and gradually stir in the milk. Return to moderate, heat and simmer, stirring, until thick.

4 Stir in the chopped spinach and grated nutmeg and season well with salt and pepper. Simmer over gentle heat 2 minutes.

5 Remove from the heat. Beat the egg yolks and beat them into the spinach mixture.

6 Beat the egg whites until they are just standing in soft peaks then fold gently into the spinach mixture with a metal spoon. ▨

7 Pour the mixture into the greased soufflé dish and sprinkle the top evenly with the grated Parmesan cheese. Bake in oven about 30-40 minutes until risen and lightly browned on the top. It should be firm to the touch on the outside, and not wobbly if gently shaken, but still moist in the center. Serve at once straight from the dish.

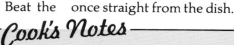

Cook's Notes

TIME
Preparation takes about 30 minutes cooking 30-40 minutes.

SERVING IDEAS
This spinach dish is very versatile: serve as a light lunch or supper or as an appetizer. Or try it as a vegetable accompaniment: it goes very well with veal dishes.

For individual soufflés, bake in four 1¼ cup greased custard cups for 20-30 minutes, or eight ½ cup greased custard cups for 15-20 minutes.

WATCHPOINT
Do not overbeat the egg whites. It is easier to fold in the whites if you first beat 1-2 tablespoons of beaten whites into the spinach mixture to slacken it. Carefully fold in the whites so as not to lose the trapped air.

VARIATION
For a more substantial main-course dish, add ½ cup finely chopped cooked ham or chicken.

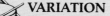

● 250 calories per portion

Mushroom puffs and cheese sauce

SERVES 4
12 cup mushrooms (see Buying guide)
1 sheet (½ of 17 oz package) frozen puff pastry, thawed
1 tablespoon butter
½ teaspoon dried marjoram
freshly ground black pepper
1 egg, lightly beaten

CHEESE SAUCE
1 oz blue cheese
⅔ cup plain yogurt
2 scallions, finely sliced
salt and freshly ground black pepper

1 Trim the mushroom stems level with the caps, then chop the stems finely and reserve.
2 Roll out the pastry thinly on a lightly floured surface. Then, using a 3-inch fluted cookie cutter, cut out 24 pastry rounds.
3 Place one mushroom, stem side up, on each of 12 pastry circles. Put a small knob of butter, a pinch of marjoram and a sprinkling of pepper on each mushroom.
4 Brush the edges of each mushroom-topped pastry circle with beaten egg, then place a second circle of pastry on top. Bring together the pastry edges, pressing well to seal. Crimp the edges.
5 Dampen 2 cookie sheets and transfer the puffs to them. Cover the puffs with plastic wrap and refrigerate 15 minutes.
6 Preheat the oven to 425°.
7 Meanwhile, make the cheese sauce: Crumble the cheese into a serving bowl, add a little yogurt and mix together with a fork until fairly smooth. Stir in the remaining yogurt, reserved mushroom stems and half the scallions. Sprinkle the remaining scallions on top of the sauce, cover with plastic wrap and refrigerate.
8 Brush the tops of the puffs with the remaining beaten egg, then bake in the oven 10-15 minutes until well-risen and golden brown.
9 Pile the hot puffs onto a warm serving plate and serve with the chilled sauce handed separately (see Serving ideas).

Cook's Notes

TIME
Preparing the puffs takes 15-20 minutes. Allow 15 minutes chilling and 10-15 minutes baking. Making the sauce takes 5 minutes.

SERVING IDEAS
These mushroom puffs make an ideal appetizer to a meal. Allow 3 puffs per person and serve on plates garnished with celery or scallion tassels and, if liked, sliced raw mushrooms, and small lettuce leaves.

BUYING GUIDE
Cultivated cup mushrooms are larger than button mushrooms: their caps have begun to open. Choose mushrooms about 1¼ inches wide, so the caps will hold the butter and be the right size for the pastry rounds.
Buy a 17 oz package of ready-made frozen puff pastry and use 1 sheet for this recipe. Keep the remaining sheet frozen for another use.

● 340 calories per portion

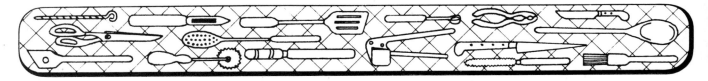

Grapefruit and celery salad

SERVES 4
2 large grapefruits
2 heads celery
4 teaspoons chopped fresh mint
2 tablespoons seedless raisins
4 sprigs mint, to garnish

DRESSING
⅔ cup plain yogurt, chilled
1 tablespoon olive oil
1 tablespoon orange juice
salt
freshly ground black pepper

1 Cut each grapefruit in half, into a waterlily shape (see Preparation). Scoop out the flesh, using a curved grapefruit knife. (Alternatively run a small sharp knife between the flesh and the peel, taking care not to pierce the peel, then remove the flesh). Reserve the shells in the refrigerator.
2 Discard the pith, membranes and pits and put the grapefruit flesh into a bowl.
3 Remove and discard the outer stalks of the celery, leaving the tender, yellowy "hearts" (see Economy). Cut the celery hearts into ¼-inch slices.
4 Add the sliced celery to the bowl, together with the chopped mint and raisins. Toss well.

5 Make the dressing: Stir together the yogurt, olive oil and orange juice and season to taste with salt and pepper.
6 Add the dressing to the salad, toss well and pile the salad into the grapefruit shells. Refrigerate the filled shells 30 minutes. Garnish the salad with mint sprigs and serve (see Cook's tip).

Cook's Notes

 TIME
Preparation takes about 40 minutes.

COOK'S TIP
The shells may be stored and re-used in another dish: wash, pat dry and store for a few days covered in the refrigerator or wrap them and freeze.

ECONOMY
Reserve the outer stalks and leaves of the celery for stock or soup.

PREPARATION
To cut the grapefruits into waterlilies:

Insert knife at an angle through side into center. Make second cut to form v-shape. Continue all round the grapefruit and pull apart.

● 100 calories per portion

Vegetable samosas

MAKES 12

¾ lb potatoes, diced
½ lb package frozen mixed
 vegetables
1 tablespoon vegetable oil
1 onion, finely chopped
1 tablespoon curry powder
6 tablespoons water
salt and freshly ground black pepper
vegetable oil, for deep frying

PASTRY
1½ cups all-purpose flour
salt
2 tablespoons butter or margarine,
 diced
about 4 tablespoons water

1 Make the pastry: sift the flour and salt into a bowl. Add the butter and cut it into the flour slowly until the whole mixture resembles fine bread crumbs. Then mix in just enough water to make a soft elastic dough. Wrap dough in plastic wrap and refrigerate 30 minutes.

2 Meanwhile, make the filling: Heat the oil in a saucepan, add the onion and fry gently 5 minutes until soft and lightly colored.

3 Stir in the curry powder, then add the potatoes and cook further 1-2 minutes.

4 Add the mixed vegetables, water and salt and pepper to taste. Bring to a boil, stirring all the time Lower the heat slightly, cover and simmer for 15-20 minutes, stirring occasionally, until all the vegetables are tender. Allow to cool slightly.

5 Divide the dough into 12 pieces and roll out each piece on a floured surface to a 4-inch square.

6 Place 1 tablespoon filling in the center of each square. Brush the edges of the pastry with water and bring over one corner to form a triangle. Press the sides together and crimp. ✳

7 Heat the oil in a deep-fat frier with a basket to 350°, or until a day-old bread cube browns in 60 seconds. Put 3 samosas into the basket, then lower into the oil and cook 2 minutes or until the pastry bubbles and turns golden. Drain on paper towels and keep warm while cooking the remaining samosas in the same way. Serve at once.

Cook's Notes

TIME
Samosas take about 35 minutes preparation and cooking, plus 30 minutes chilling time.

FREEZING
Freeze the samosas before cooking: Open freeze until solid, then pack into a rigid container or polythene bag. Seal, label and return to the freezer for up to 3 months. To serve: Deep-fry from frozen for about 3-4 minutes.

SERVING IDEAS
Samosas are a favorite Indian snack. Serve them as an appetizer to an Indian meal with mango chutney, or with a tasty sauce made by blending plain yogurt with mint, finely chopped cucumber, salt and freshly ground black pepper to taste.

● 155 calories per samosa

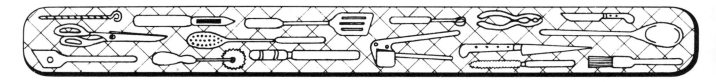

Stuffed green peppers

SERVES 4
4 green peppers (see Buying guide)
⅔ cup long-grain rice
1 small onion, chopped
3 tablespoons vegetable oil
2 tablespoons tomato paste
5 tablespoons water
½ cup slivered almonds
⅓ cup golden raisins
2 teaspoons dried oregano
grated rind of 1 orange
salt and freshly ground black pepper

1 Preheat oven to 350°.
2 Bring a large saucepan of water to the boil, add the rice, bring back to boil and cook about 15 minutes until the rice is tender.
3 Meanwhile, slice the tops off the peppers and reserve them. Carefully seed the peppers.
4 Drain the rice thoroughly, rinse under cold running water and then drain again.
5 In a bowl, thoroughly mix the rice together with all the remaining ingredients, reserving 2 tablespoons of oil and 2 tablespoons of the water.
6 Fill the peppers with the stuffing mixture, packing it in well but taking care not to break the peppers.
7 Put the peppers into a casserole in which they will stand together closely but comfortably (see Cook's tip). Replace the tops.

8 Mix together the reserved oil and water and drizzle it over the peppers.

9 Cover the dish and bake 25 minutes. Uncover and bake 25 minutes. Serve hot, warm or cold.

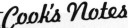
Cook's Notes

TIME
Preparation takes about 30 minutes, including cooking the rice. Cooking in the oven takes 50 minutes.

BUYING GUIDE
Buy firm, squat peppers as they stand up better in the dish and the stuffing will not fall out.

COOK'S TIP
If necessary, put a little crumpled foil between the peppers to keep them upright and remove it before serving.

VARIATION
Red peppers could be used instead of green or use 2 of each.

SERVING IDEAS
These make a filling first course on their own or with a tomato sauce, served with hot garlic or pita bread. They are especially good served warm. They could also be served as a tasty supper dish.

● 325 calories per portion

Vegetable kabobs

SERVES 4

3 small zucchini, cut into 1½-inch
    slices
12 whole baby white onions
salt
12 whole small mushrooms
8 tomatoes, halved
8 small bay leaves
¼ cup butter or margarine,
    melted
vegetable oil, for greasing

MARINADE
6 tablespoons vegetable oil
1 tablespoon lemon juice
1 small onion, finely chopped
2 tablespoons chopped fresh
    parsley
1 clove garlic, crushed (optional)
salt and freshly ground black pepper

1 Bring a saucepan of salted water
to a boil, add the zucchini slices
and white onions and boil gently for
1 minute. Drain and immediately
plunge the vegetables into cold
water to prevent them cooking
further. Drain vegetables well again
and pat dry with paper towels.
2 Divide the zucchini slices, onions,
mushrooms, tomatoes and bay
leaves into 4 equal
portions and

thread them onto 4 greased metal
kabob skewers, alternating the
shapes and colors as much as
possible. Lay the skewers in a
shallow dish.
3 To make the marinade: Put all the
ingredients in a screw-top jar with
salt and pepper to taste. Shake well
to mix. Pour the marinade over the
vegetable kabobs and leave them in
a cool place for about 2 hours,
turning them occasionally to coat
the vegetables evenly.
4 Preheat broiler to moderate. Lift
the kabobs from the marinade and
allow any excess dressing to drain
off. Brush the vegetables with the
melted butter. Broil the kabobs
about 8 minutes, turning them
frequently to brown the vegetables
evenly. Serve at once, while hot.

Cook's Notes

TIME
Preparation takes about
25 minutes, marinating
2 hours, cooking 8 minutes.

SERVING IDEAS
Serve on a bed of herb-
flavored rice.

● 230 calories per portion

Mixed vegetable croquettes

MAKES 16
2 onions, very finely chopped
6 celery stalks, very finely chopped
2 carrots, grated
1½ cups very finely chopped mushrooms
1 tablespoon vegetable oil
1 tablespoon smooth peanut butter
½ cup unsalted peanuts, ground or very finely chopped
1½ cups fresh whole wheat bread crumbs
pinch of dried mixed herbs
salt and freshly ground black pepper
2 eggs, beaten
¾ cup dried bread crumbs (see Economy)
vegetable oil, for deep-frying

1 Heat the oil in a large saucepan, add the onions and celery and cook gently 5 minutes. Do not allow the vegetables to brown.
2 Add the carrots and mushrooms to the pan and continue cooking a further 5 minutes, stirring from time to time.
3 Remove from the heat, then stir in the peanut butter until well combined. Add the peanuts, whole wheat bread crumbs, herbs and salt and pepper to taste. Mix well and bind with half the beaten eggs. Leave until cool enough to handle.
4 Meanwhile, pour the remaining beaten eggs into a shallow bowl or onto a plate. Place the dried bread crumbs on a separate plate, ready to coat the croquettes.
5 When the mixture is cool, divide it into 16 portions and shape them into croquettes. Dip each croquette in the beaten eggs, then roll in the bread crumbs until thoroughly coated.
6 Pour enough vegetable oil into a deep-fat frier to come to a depth of 1½ inches. Heat the oil to 350° or until a 1-inch stale bread cube browns in 60 seconds. Lower in the croquettes and deep-fry 3 minutes, or until golden brown (see Cook's tip). Drain the croquettes very thoroughly on paper towels and serve hot.

CHRIS KNAGGS

Cook's Notes

TIME
Preparation of the croquette mixture, cooling and shaping take about 40 minutes. Heating the oil and deep-frying take about 10 minutes.

ECONOMY
Dried bread crumbs are available commercially in packages and drums, but it is easy, and more economical, to make them at home. Save crusts or stale bread. Cut the bread into pieces and dry it out in a very cool oven or place in the oven as it cools down after cooking the main meal of the day: this method may require repeating 2 or 3 times. When the bread is dry and golden brown, crush it with a rolling pin or process in a blender. Store the crumbs in a screw-top jar.

VARIATIONS
Experiment with different coatings for the croquettes. Try flavoring the dried bread crumbs with a little curry powder or paprika, or use finely crushed cornflakes or potato chips (plain or flavored) as a tasty substitute for the dried breadcrumbs.

COOK'S TIP
If you do not have a deep-fat frier, you can shallow-fry the croquettes. Heat oil to a depth of about 1-inch in a large, deep skillet and cook the croquettes over moderate heat for 10 minutes until golden brown. Turn the croquettes over once during cooking so that the croquettes are evenly browned on both sides.

● 125 calories per croquette

Herby dip with cheese crackers

SERVES 4

1 cup grated mild cheese
½ cup sweet butter, softened
1 tablespoon chopped chives
1 tablespoon finely chopped fresh fennel leaves or mint
1 tablespoon finely chopped fresh parsley
¼ teaspoon paprika
¼ teaspoon caraway seeds
4 tablespoons milk
salt and freshly ground black pepper

CHEESE CRACKERS

½ cup butter, softened
1 cup grated sharp Cheddar cheese
1 cup whole wheat flour
2 tablespoons sesame seeds
butter, for greasing

Cook's Notes

TIME
30 minutes to prepare and cook the crackers 15 minutes to make the dip.

SERVING IDEAS
Serve as an unusual appetizer at a dinner party or, accompanied by a vege-table soup, as a quick supper dish. Alternatively, cut out the crackers with tiny petits fours cutters or cut into small straws and serve at a drinks party.
 The crackers may be served while still slightly warm.

● 685 calories per portion

1 Make the crackers: Preheat oven to 400° and lightly grease a cookie sheet. Sift the flour.
2 In a large bowl, beat the butter until pale and creamy, then beat in the cheese. Add the flour a little at a time, beating thoroughly after each addition, to form a stiff dough.
3 Sprinkle the sesame seeds on a lightly floured work surface and roll out the dough, until it is about ⅛-inch thick. Cut the dough into about 12 rounds using a lightly floured 3-inch cookie cutter.
4 Using a spatula, transfer the rounds to the prepared cookie sheet, spacing them apart, then bake 5-8 minutes until golden.
5 Remove from the oven, allow to settle 1-2 minutes, then transfer to a wire rack and allow to cool.
6 Meanwhile, make the dip: Put the grated mild cheese into a bowl with the butter, herbs, paprika, caraway seeds and milk. Beat until blended and creamy, then season to taste with salt and pepper.
7 Spoon the mixture into a small serving dish, smooth over the surface and serve with the crackers.

Spicy bean pâté

SERVES 4
1 can (about 1 lb) red kidney beans
1 clove garlic, crushed (optional)
1 tablespoon tomato paste
1 teaspoon Worcestershire sauce
1 teaspoon lemon juice
few drops of hot-pepper sauce
salt and freshly ground black pepper
parsley sprigs, to garnish

1 Drain the beans, reserving the liquid from the can.
2 Put all the ingredients into a blender and blend to a smooth paste; it will be flecked with pieces of bean skin. Alternatively, place all the ingredients in a bowl, pound them with the end of a rolling pin, then mash thoroughly with a fork. If the mixture becomes too thick, add 2-3 tablespoons of the reserved liquid from the can.
3 Taste and adjust seasoning.

4 Pack the pâté into 4 small custard cups or individual dishes and carefully smooth the surface of each with a small knife. Serve the pâté cold or chilled, garnished with parsley sprigs.

Cook's Notes

TIME
Preparation of this pâté takes 15 minutes.

COOK'S TIP
The pâté may be prepared up to 2 days before then stored in the refrigerator.

BUYING GUIDE
Different canned pulses can be a very handy pantry shelf standby. They can be used for many quick-to-make dips and sauces.

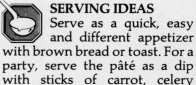
SERVING IDEAS
Serve as a quick, easy and different appetizer with brown bread or toast. For a party, serve the pâté as a dip with sticks of carrot, celery stalks and sliced cucumber, or spread it on cocktail crackers.

● 65 calories per portion

Avocado dip

SERVES 4-6
2 ripe avocados (see Buying guide)
juice of 1 lemon
1 clove garlic, crushed (optional)
4 tomatoes, skinned, seeded and
finely chopped
1 small onion, finely chopped
4 tablespoons finely chopped celery
2—3 tablespoons olive oil
1 tablespoon chopped fresh parsley
salt and freshly ground black pepper

1 Cut the avocados in half lengthwise (see Cook's tip), remove the seeds then scoop out the flesh with a teaspoon. Put the flesh in a bowl and mash it with a wooden spoon.
2 Add the lemon juice, garlic, if using, tomatoes, onion and celery.
3 Stir in enough olive oil to make a soft, smooth mixture, then add the chopped parsley and season with salt and pepper to taste.
4 Transfer the dip to a serving bowl, cover with plastic wrap and chill in the refrigerator about 30 minutes. Serve chilled.

Cook's Notes

TIME
This dip takes 20 minutes preparation, then 30 minutes chilling.

BUYING GUIDE
Avocados are ripe when the flesh at the rounded end yields slightly when gently pressed. Reject any avocados that are hard or very soft or have blotched, dry skins.

COOK'S TIPS
When cutting the avocado, use a stainless steel knife to prevent the avocado flesh from coloring at the beginning.

SERVING IDEAS
Serve with a selection of small crackers, potato chips or crisp raw vegetables.

● 325 calories per portion

Lima bean dip with crudités

SERVES 8
½ cup dried lima beans, soaked in cold water overnight (see Cook's tips)
4-6 tablespoons good-quality olive oil
1 tablespoon red wine vinegar
1 clove garlic, crushed (optional)
salt and freshly ground black pepper

CRUDITES
1 small cauliflower, broken into flowerets
1 cucumber, cut into sticks
2 celery stalks, cut into sticks
2 carrots, cut into sticks
1 small green pepper, seeded and cut into strips
1 small red pepper, seeded and cut into strips
bunch of radishes

1 Drain the beans and rinse thoroughly under cold running water. Put them in a large saucepan, cover with fresh cold water and bring to a boil. Lower the heat, half cover with a lid and simmer about 1¼ hours or until the beans are tender. Add more water to the pan during the cooking time if necessary.

2 Drain the beans, reserving the cooking liquid. Put the beans in a blender with 4 tablespoons oil, the vinegar, garlic, if using, a little salt and pepper and 4 tablespoons of the reserved cooking liquid. Blend until thick and smooth, adding a little more liquid if the mixture is too thick.

3 Taste and adjust seasoning, then spoon the mixture into a small bowl and fork over the top; or heap the mixture up in the center of a large flat serving plate.

4 Serve the crudités in a shallow basket or salad bowl, or stand the bowl of dip in the center of a large plate and arrange the crudités around the edge of the plate. If you like, drizzle 2 tablespoons oil over the top of the dip just before serving (see Did you know). Serve at room temperature or refrigerate about 1 hour before serving and serve the dip chilled.

Cook's Notes

TIME
Cooking the dried beans takes 1¼ hours and preparing the dip then takes 30 minutes.

COOK'S TIPS
If you do not have time to soak the beans in cold water overnight, you can cut down the soaking time considerably by using hot water. Put the beans in a large saucepan, cover with cold water and bring to the boil. Drain and repeat, then remove from the heat and leave to soak in the hot water 2 hours.

To save even more time, you could use 1 can (about 1 lb) cannellini beans, which are precooked. The whole dip can then be made within 30 minutes.

PRESSURE COOKING
Dried lima beans can be cooked in a pressure cooker. Soak and rinse as in recipe, then cook at high (H) pressure 20 minutes.

SERVING IDEAS
The lima bean dip makes an appetizer for 8 or a filling salad meal for 4.

FREEZING
The dip freezes well, either in the dish from which it will be served or in a rigid container. Store for up to 3 months and allow 2 hours thawing at room temperature before serving.

DID YOU KNOW
Finishing off the dip with extra oil drizzled on top is usual in Middle Eastern countries, where dips and pâtés made from pulses are very popular. If you do not like too oily a taste, this can be easily omitted.

● 225 calories per portion

SOUPS

Brussels soup

SERVES 4
1 lb Brussels sprouts
1 tablespoon vegetable oil
1 small onion, chopped
2 tablespoons medium sherry
    (optional)
3 cups chicken broth
freshly grated nutmeg
salt and ground black pepper

1 Heat the oil in a saucepan, add the onion and fry gently for 5 minutes until soft and lightly colored.
2 Stir in the sherry, if using, then add the broth. Bring to a boil, add the sprouts, a pinch of nutmeg and salt and pepper to taste. Lower the heat slightly, cover and simmer about 30 minutes.
3 Pass the soup through a strainer, or leave to cool slightly, then purée in a blender. Return the soup to the rinsed pan and heat through.
4 Taste and adjust seasoning, then pour immediately into warmed individual soup bowls. Sprinkle each serving with a pinch of nutmeg and serve (see Special occasion).

Cook's Notes

TIME
Preparation and cooking only take about 40 minutes.

SPECIAL OCCASION
Swirl a little light cream into the soup immediately before serving. Alternatively, serve with fried bread croutons or crumbled crisply fried fatty bacon.

 FREEZING
Cool the soup and pour into a rigid container. Seal, label and freeze for up to 4 months. To serve: Reheat from frozen in a heavy-based pan, stirring frequently to prevent sticking. Taste and adjust seasoning before pouring into warmed soup bowls.

● 75 calories per portion

Cream of chestnut soup

SERVES 4-6
1½ lb fresh chestnuts
5 cups chicken broth
1 bay leaf
2 onions, sliced
about ⅔ cup milk
1 egg yolk
⅔ cup heavy cream
pinch of freshly grated nutmeg
salt and freshly ground black pepper
1-2 teaspoons sugar

1 Nick the chestnuts with a sharp knife, then place in a saucepan and cover with cold water. Gradually bring to a boil and simmer 10 minutes.

2 Remove the pan from the heat, then take out the chestnuts, a few at a time (see Cook's tip). Remove both the outside and inside skins.

3 Put the peeled chestnuts into a large pan together with the chicken broth, bay leaf and onions. Bring to a boil, then lower the heat, cover and simmer gently 1½ hours.

4 Remove the bay leaf, then press the soup through a strainer or work in a blender.

5 Return the soup to the rinsed-out pan and gradually stir in enough milk to make it a smooth consistency. Heat through gently. Blend the egg yolk and cream in a bowl. Remove the pan from the heat and stir in the egg and cream. Reheat but do not boil. [!]

6 Add the nutmeg, and season to taste with salt and pepper. Add the sugar, a little at a time, to taste. Pour into warmed individual soup bowls and serve at once.

Cook's Notes

 TIME
Preparation takes 45-60 minutes (peeling the chestnuts is a lengthy process). Cooking 1½ hours, blending and finishing the soup, 15 minutes.

SERVING IDEAS
This is a substantial soup, ideal to serve on cold days with chunky slices of bread and butter and wedges of cheese.

COOK'S TIP
Keeping the chestnuts in hot water makes them easier to peel. If they are drained the skins toughen.

WATCHPOINT
Take care not to boil the soup at this stage as the egg and cream may overheat and curdle, and spoil the appearance of the dish.

● 460 calories per portion

Lentil and lemon soup

SERVES 4
½ cup split red lentils
1 tablespoon butter or margarine
2 celery stalks, chopped
1 medium onion, finely chopped
1 quart boiling water
2 chicken bouillon cubes
grated rind and juice of 1 lemon
¼ teaspoon ground cumin
(optional)
salt and freshly ground black pepper
1 red pepper, seeded and thinly
sliced into rings

TO GARNISH
1 lemon, thinly sliced
chopped chives (optional)

1 Melt the butter in a saucepan, add the celery and onion, then cover and cook gently 4 minutes.
2 Remove the pan from the heat, then stir in the lentils and water, with bouillon cubes. Add the lemon rind and juice, and the cumin, if using. Season to taste with salt and pepper. Cover and simmer over very gentle heat 30 minutes.
3 Add the sliced pepper to the pan, cover and cook a further 30 minutes. Taste and adjust seasoning. ✳
4 Pour the soup into warmed serving bowls, float the lemon slices on top, then sprinkle over the chives, if using. Serve at once.

Cook's Notes

TIME
Preparation 20 minutes; cooking takes 65 minutes.

FREEZING
Cool quickly, then freeze without the lemon and chives in a rigid polythene container or freezer bag (do not use foil containers, or the acid in the soup may react against the foil). Seal, label and freeze for up to 6 months. Thaw at room temperature, then reheat until bubbling, adding a little more water if necessary.

SERVING IDEAS
Warm crusty rolls are ideal to serve with this soup. For a luxurious touch, top each serving with 1 tablespoon dairy sour cream.

VARIATIONS
For a lentil and orange soup, use 2 small oranges instead of lemons.
If chives are unavailable, use chopped scallion tops or parsley, if using another garnish as well as the lemon.

● 135 calories per portion

Cream of potato soup

SERVES 4
1 lb old potatoes, diced
¼ cup butter
2 large onions, finely chopped
2 cups milk
2 cups vegetable or chicken broth
salt and freshly ground black
    pepper
4 tablespoons light cream
chopped chives or parsley, to
    garnish

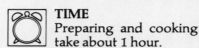

1 Melt the butter in a large pan and, when the foam has subsided, add the potatoes and onions and cook gently about 5 minutes until the vegetables are soft. Stir frequently to prevent any of the potato dice or chopped onion from sticking to the bottom of the pan.
2 Add the milk and broth (see Cook's tip), season to taste with salt and pepper and bring to a boil. Lower heat and simmer 30 minutes, stirring occasionally, until the potatoes are tender.
3 Allow the mixture to cool a little, then work through a strainer or purée in an electric blender.
4 Return the soup to the rinsed-out pan and reheat. Taste and adjust the seasoning, if necessary, and stir in cream just before serving. [!] Pour into a large tureen, or ladle into individual soup bowls, garnish with the chopped chives or parsley and serve at once (see Serving ideas).

Green bean soup

SERVES 4
1 lb frozen cut green beans
    (see Buying guide)
3 cups chicken broth
1 small onion, chopped
bay leaf
parsley sprig
about ½ teaspoon Worcestershire
    sauce
salt and freshly ground black pepper

BEURRE MANIE (kneaded butter)
1 tablespoon all-purpose flour
1 tablespoon butter

TO GARNISH
6 black olives, pitted and finely
    chopped
1 hard-cooked egg, finely chopped

1 Pour the broth into a pan, bring to a boil and add the beans, onion, bay leaf and parsley. Bring back to a boil, then lower the heat, cover and simmer about 15 minutes until the beans are soft.

2 Discard the bay leaf and parsley. Allow the soup to cool slightly, then work in a blender until smooth. Return to the rinsed-out pan and set over low heat.

3 Make the beurre manié: Blend the flour and butter together with a spatula to make a paste, then cut the paste into pea-sized pieces. Beat the pieces into the soup and bring to the boil. Add Worcestershire sauce and salt and pepper to taste. Simmer for a further minute, then remove from heat.

4 Pour the soup into a warmed tureen or 4 individual soup bowls. Mix together the olives and egg, sprinkle over the soup and serve at once (see Serving ideas).

Chunky soy vegetable soup

SERVES 4

½ cup soybeans, soaked in cold water overnight (see Watchpoint)
1 tablespoon vegetable oil
1 large onion, sliced
2 leeks, thickly sliced
1 carrot, thickly sliced
2 celery stalks, thickly sliced
1 small turnip, cubed
3 cups chicken broth
1 tablespoon lemon juice
2 tablespoons tomato paste
1-2 teaspoons dried mixed herbs
¼ lb zucchini, thickly sliced
a few tender cabbage or spinach leaves, finely shredded or chopped
salt and freshly ground black pepper
2 teaspoons toasted sesame seeds, to garnish (optional)

1 Drain the soaked beans, then put into a saucepan and cover with fresh cold water. Bring to a boil and boil 10 minutes, then lower heat, cover and carefully simmer about 1½ hours.
2 After the beans have been cooking 1 hour 20 minutes, heat the oil in a separate large saucepan. Add the sliced onion and cook very gently 2-3 minutes until brown. Add the leeks, carrots, celery and turnips and cook, stirring, a further 2 minutes.
3 Stir in the chicken broth, lemon juice, tomato paste and the dried mixed herbs.
4 Drain the beans and add to the pan. Bring to a boil, then lower the heat slightly, cover the pan and then keep simmering gently for about 1 hour.
5 Add the zucchini and cabbage and continue to cook a further 15 minutes or until the vegetables and beans are tender. Season to taste with salt and pepper.
6 Pour into warmed individual soup bowls and garnish with a sprinkling of sesame seeds, if liked. Serve the soup at once.

Jerusalem artichoke soup

SERVES 4-6

2 lb Jerusalem artichokes (see Preparation)
1 tablespoon butter or margarine
2 onions, chopped
2½ cups milk
2 cups chicken broth
salt and freshly ground black pepper
chopped fresh parsley

1 Melt the butter in a large saucepan, add the onions and cook gently for 5 minutes until soft and lightly colored.
2 Add the artichokes to the pan, together with the milk, broth and salt and pepper to taste.
3 Bring to a boil, [!] reduce the heat slightly, cover and simmer about 30 minutes, until the artichokes are soft.
4 Leave to cool slightly, then work in a blender or food processor until smooth. Or work through a vegetable mill.

5 Return the soup to the rinsed-out pan and reheat gently. Taste and adjust seasoning, then pour into warmed individual soup bowls. Serve at once, garnished with chopped parsley.

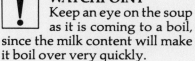

Sunshine soup

SERVES 4
2 lb pumpkin, seeded and
    cut into 1-inch cubes
    (see Variation)
salt
3 tablespoons butter
1 large onion, finely chopped
2 tomatoes, peeled and chopped
1 teaspoon chopped chives
¼ teaspoon freshly grated nutmeg
1 tablespoon shredded coconut
2½ cups chicken broth
freshly ground black pepper
1¼ cups light cream
paprika, to garnish

1 Put the pumpkin into a saucepan,
add enough water just to cover and
a good pinch of salt. Bring to a boil,
then lower the heat slightly and
simmer 15 minutes. Drain well.

2 Melt the butter in a saucepan, add
the onion and cook gently 5 minutes until soft and lightly colored.
3 Add the pumpkin, tomatoes,
chives, nutmeg and coconut and
cook gently a further 5 minutes.
4 Pour in the broth, season with salt
and pepper to taste and bring to a
boil. Lower the heat slightly, cover
and simmer about 30 minutes.
5 Remove the pan from the heat,
allow to cool slightly, then purée in
a blender. ✳ Then stir in half of the
cream.
6 Pour the soup into warmed soup
bowls, then swirl in the remaining
cream and sprinkle with paprika.
Serve at once.

Cook's Notes

TIME
10 minutes preparation,
55 minutes cooking
including simmering pumpkin.

FREEZING
Pour the purée into a
rigid container, leaving
headspace. Cool quickly, then
seal, label and freeze for up to 3
months. To serve: Thaw at
room temperature for about 4
hours, then heat through and
add the cream and paprika.

VARIATION
If you are unable to buy
pumpkin, carrots are a
very good substitute and they
do not need precooking.

SERVING IDEAS
This soup is good either
hot or cold. Serve with
crusty whole wheat bread and
chunks of Cheddar cheese for a
light supper.

● 185 calories per portion

Carrot soup
with egg and rice

SERVES 4-8

1½ lb new carrots, thinly sliced
2 tablespoons butter or margarine
2½ cups chicken broth
1 teaspoon sugar
salt and freshly ground black
    pepper
⅔ cup milk
½ cup cooked rice (see
    Cook's tips)
4 eggs at room temperature (see
    Cook's tips)
2 scallions, finely chopped
⅔ cup light cream

1 Melt the butter in a saucepan, add the carrots and cook gently 2-3 minutes to soften slightly.
2 Add the chicken broth and sugar and season to taste with salt and pepper. Bring to a boil, then lower the heat and simmer, uncovered, 30 minutes or until the carrots are very tender.
3 Remove the pan from the heat and allow mixture to cool slightly, then pour it into the goblet of a blender and work for a few seconds until smooth. Return the purée to the rinsed-out pan and stir in the milk and cooked rice. Taste and adjust the seasoning, if necessary.
4 Heat the soup gently until hot but not boiling, then break in the eggs and poach them for about 8 minutes or until they are firm enough to be lifted out with a slotted spoon.
5 Spoon an egg into each of 4 warmed soup bowls and pour over the soup. Sprinkle over the scallions, swirl in the cream and serve the soup at once.

Cook's Notes

TIME
Preparation takes 15 minutes, cooking takes about 50 minutes.

SERVING IDEAS
This is a fairly substantial soup, so serve with a light accompaniment such as Melba toast or a selection of crispbreads.

COOK'S TIPS
If cooking raw rice for this dish, you will need 2 tablespoons to provide ½ cup of cooked rice.
Remove the eggs from the refrigerator 1 hour before using: cold eggs will require a longer time to set.

● 155 calories per portion

Creamy mushroom soup

SERVES 4
½ lb small mushrooms (see Buying guide)
¼ cup butter
2 tablespoons all-purpose flour
2½ cups milk
⅓ cup cream cheese with chives
2 teaspoons lemon juice
salt and freshly ground black pepper
1 tablespoon chopped chives, to garnish

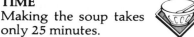
1 Finely chop the mushrooms, reserving 2-3 whole ones for the garnish. Melt half the butter in a skillet. Add the chopped mushrooms and cook gently about 5 minutes until soft. Set aside.

2 Melt the remaining butter in a large saucepan, sprinkle in flour and stir over low heat 1-2 minutes until it is straw-colored. Remove from the heat and gradually stir in milk. Return to the heat and simmer, stirring, until the mixture is thick and smooth.

3 Remove from the heat, add the cheese a little at a time and stir until melted. Stir in the mushrooms, their juices and the lemon juice. Season to taste. Return to heat and simmer 2-3 minutes. !

4 Pour into 4 warmed soup bowls. Float a few slices of mushrooms on top of each serving. Sprinkle lightly with chives and serve at once.

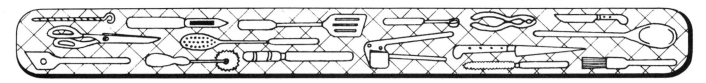

Chilled pea and bean soup

SERVES 4
**1½ lb peas, shelled, and 6 of the
best pods reserved (see
Cook's tip)**
1 lb lima beans, shelled
2 tablespoons butter or margarine
1 large onion, finely chopped
4 cups chicken broth
1 sprig fresh mint
salt and freshly ground black pepper
⅔ cup plain yogurt
¼ teaspoon curry paste
1 clove garlic, crushed (optional)
4 small mint sprigs, to garnish

1 Melt the butter in a skillet.
Add the onion, and fry gently 5
minutes, until soft and lightly
colored.

2 Pour in the broth and bring to a
boil, then add the peas, reserved
pods, beans, mint sprig and salt and
pepper to taste. Lower the heat,
cover and simmer 20 minutes.

3 Remove the pods and mint sprig,
leave the soup to cool slightly, then
work in a blender or food processor
until smooth. Or work through the
medium blade of a vegetable mill.
Leave until completely cold.

4 Mix the yogurt in a bowl with
the curry paste and garlic, if using,
then beat in about 6 tablespoons of
the soup until smooth. Stir the

yogurt mixture into the soup,
making sure that it is well mixed in.
Refrigerate for at least 30 minutes.

5 To serve: Pour the soup into 4
chilled individual soup bowls and
float a mint sprig on top of each.

Cook's Notes

TIME
Preparation and cook-
ing take 70 minutes, but
allow extra time for cooling and
chilling.

VARIATIONS
Frozen peas and beans
may be used. In this
case, you will need ¾ lb of
peas and ½ lb of beans. Do
not thaw them before cooking.

To serve the soup hot, make
up to the end of stage 3, but do
not cool. Pour into a saucepan,
heat gently without boiling,
then stir in the yogurt mixture.
Garnish with chopped mint.

FREEZING
Pour the cooled soup in
to a rigid container,
seal, label and freeze for 6-8
weeks. To serve: thaw for 6-8
hours in the refrigerator,

stirring occasionally. If too
thick, stir in a little cold milk.

COOK'S TIP
Pea pods have a
deliciously strong pea
taste. They are too fibrous and
stringy to be included in a soup,
but if added during the first part
of cooking and them removed,
they will add extra flavor.

● 150 calories per portion

SALADS

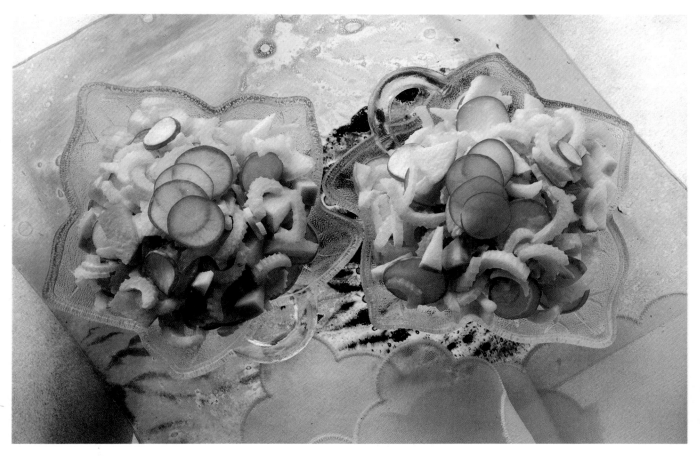

Celery and radish salad

SERVES 4
1 crisp dessert apple
1 small head celery, finely chopped
½ lb radishes, thinly sliced (see Buying guide)
salt and freshly ground black pepper

DRESSING
¼ cup ricotta cheese
4 tablespoons dairy sour cream
2 tablespoons cider vinegar
1 teaspoon firmly packed light brown sugar
1 clove garlic, crushed (optional)

1 Make the dressing: Put the cheese into a large bowl and beat until softened. Gradually beat in the sour cream and vinegar, then the sugar and garlic, if using.
2 Core and finely chop (but do not pare) the apple. Add to the dressing with the celery and half the radishes. Mix well, and season.

3 Transfer the salad to a serving bowl and arrange the remaining radishes on top in an attractive pattern. Serve as soon as possible, at room temperature.

Cook's Notes

 TIME
Preparation takes 25 minutes.

VARIATIONS
Cream cheese may be used instead of the ricotta and plain yogurt instead of dairy sour cream.

BUYING GUIDE
The average bunch of radishes available from vegetable stores weighs about ¼ lb so you will need 2 bunches for this recipe.

 SERVING IDEAS
This salad goes perfectly with a quiche for lunch, or with cold chicken or turkey. It also makes an attractive appetizer salad as shown in the photograph, served with Melba toast and butter.

DID YOU KNOW
Celery is rich in mineral salts, vitamins and iron, and is one of the best vegetables for slimmers.

● 70 calories per portion

Cauliflower salad with sultanas

SERVES 6

1 cauliflower, broken into flowerets
1 lb baby white onions (see
   Preparation)
salt
1 cup white wine
½ cup water
5 tablespoons olive oil
2 tablespoons wine vinegar
3 tomatoes, peeled, seeded and
   chopped
3 tablespoons golden raisins
1 teaspoon firmly packed light
   brown sugar
½ teaspoon dried thyme
½ teaspoon ground coriander
freshly ground black pepper

1 Bring 2 pans of salted water to the boil and blanch the cauliflower and the onion separately 5 minutes. Drain both together in a strainer, then rinse under cold running water to refresh. Drain the vegetables again.

2 Put the remaining ingredients in a large pan with salt to taste and a generous sprinkling of black pepper. Stir well to mix, bring to the boil and boil 5 minutes.

3 Lower the heat, add the cauliflower and onions and simmer a further 8 minutes. !

4 Using a slotted spoon, transfer the vegetables to a serving dish. Bring the sauce left in the pan to the boil and boil 5 minutes to reduce slightly. Pour the sauce over the vegetables and leave until cold. Serve at room temperature.

Cook's Notes

TIME
Preparation 10 minutes, cooking about 20 minutes, but allow time for cooling the salad before serving.

WATCHPOINT
Be careful not to overcook the cauliflower flowerets. Test with the point of a knife during cooking to check that they are still crisp.

PREPARATION
Cut off the ends of the onions and remove the skins: keep the onions whole.

SERVING IDEAS
This is an ideal dish for an appetizer as it can be prepared in advance. Serve with warm bread.

● 175 calories per portion

Crunchy mixed salad

SERVES 4
¼ **large cucumber**
10 oz beansprouts (see Buying guide)
6 oz green grapes
1 small onion, thinly sliced

DRESSING
2 oz mild Cheddar cheese
2 tablespoons vegetable oil
1 tablespoon white wine vinegar
½ teaspoon Dijon-style mustard
¼ teaspoon sugar
salt and freshly ground black pepper

1 Pare the cucumber, cut it in half lengthwise, then scoop out the pits (see Preparation and Cook's tip). Cut into matchstick strips about 2-inches long and pat dry on paper towels.
2 Wash the beansprouts well under cold running water and drain well on paper towels.

3 Cut the grapes in half, or quarter them if large, and remove the pits with the point of a sharp knife.
4 Make the dressing: Crumble the cheese finely into a large bowl. Beat in the oil, vinegar, mustard, sugar and salt and pepper to taste.

5 Add the cucumber, beansprouts, onions and grapes to the dressing and toss well to combine. Cover and leave to stand 10 minutes to allow the flavors to blend.
6 Just before serving, toss the salad to gather up the juices.

Cook's Notes

TIME
Preparation takes about 40 minutes including standing time.

PREPARATION
To remove the pits from the cucumber:

Scoop out the pits from each half with a teaspoon.

SERVING IDEAS
The salad goes well with canned fish such as tuna or mackerel.

BUYING GUIDE
Beansprouts are often sold in supermarkets in 10 oz packages. Eat beansprouts within 2 days of buying to ensure freshness.

COOK'S TIP
Removing the cucumber pits helps to reduce the moisture which can dilute salad dressing.

● 155 calories per portion

Waldorf salad

SERVES 4
1 lb crisp dessert apples
  (see Buying guide)
2 tablespoons lemon juice
1 teaspoon sugar
⅔ cup thick mayonnaise
½ head of celery,
  chopped
½ cup shelled walnuts, chopped
  (see Economy)
1 Bibb lettuce, leaves separated
  (optional)

1 Quarter and core the apples but do not pare them, cut into neat dice and put into a bowl. Add the lemon juice and toss well to prevent coloration.

2 Stir in the sugar and 1 tablespoon of the mayonnaise. Mix until the apple is well coated, then leave in a cool place until ready to serve.

3 Just before serving, add the remaining mayonnaise, celery and walnuts and toss well together.

4 Place the prepared apple mixture in a bowl lined, if liked, with lettuce leaves. Serve at once.

Cook's Notes

TIME
15 minutes advance preparation, then 5 minutes preparation before serving.

BUYING GUIDE
To add color to the salad, select red-skinned apples or buy half red and half green.

SERVING IDEAS
Serve as an accompaniment to cold meats or as part of a buffet selection. For a more decorative finish, add a border of thinly-sliced apples sprinkled with lemon juice, and garnish with a few whole walnuts.

DID YOU KNOW
This salad is so-called because it was first created by the chef of the Waldorf-Astoria Hotel in New York City.

ECONOMY
Buy packages of broken walnuts or walnut pieces; they are always less expensive than whole nuts.

SPECIAL OCCASION
Replace half the mayonnaise with lightly whipped cream and gently fold together until blended. If liked, add a little tomato paste.

● 355 calories per portion

Piquant zucchini salad

SERVES 4

4 large zucchini, trimmed
1 small red pepper, seeded and finely
  chopped
1-2 tablespoons drained capers
1 tablespoon finely chopped fresh
  parsley
1 lettuce, leaves separated, to serve

DRESSING
2 tablespoons vegetable oil
1 tablespoon lemon juice
pinch of superfine sugar
pinch of dry mustard
salt and freshly ground black pepper

1 Quarter the zucchini lengthwise,
then cut them into ½-inch slices.

Put them in a bowl with the red
pepper, capers and parsley and mix
together with a metal spoon (see
Cook's tips).
2 Put the dressing ingredients in a
small bowl with salt and pepper to
taste, and beat together with a fork.
Pour the dressing over the zucchini

mixture and stir with a metal spoon
until evenly coated.
3 To serve: Line 4 individual salad
bowls with the lettuce leaves, then
pile the zucchini mixture in the
center of each lettuce-lined bowl
just before the salads are to be
served (see Cook's tips).

Tomato and mozzarella salad

SERVES 6

1 lb firm ripe tomatoes, cut into ¼-inch slices

2 tablespoons chopped fresh parsley

2 tablespoons chopped fresh basil or ½ teaspoon dried basil

pinch of sugar

salt and freshly ground black pepper

6 oz mozzarella cheese, cut into ¼-inch slices (see Did you know)

3 tablespoons black olives

4 tablespoons olive oil

1 Arrange the tomato slices in an overlapping circular pattern around a flat serving dish. Sprinkle over the herbs and sugar and season with salt and pepper to taste. Cover the dish loosely with foil and chill in the refrigerator 30 minutes.

2 Remove the foil and arrange the cheese slices in the center of the tomatoes. scatter the olives over.

3 Just before serving, pour over the olive oil and, using a fork, gently lift up the tomato slices so that the oil drains through to them. Serve at once.

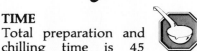

Cook's Notes

TIME
Total preparation and chilling time is 45 minutes.

DID YOU KNOW
Mozzarella cheese comes from southern Italy. Originally made from buffalo milk, but nowadays usually made with cow's milk, it is mild and moist, with a very definite flavor. It is available from specialty food stores.

SERVING IDEAS
This classic Italian tomato salad, which is dressed with oil alone, and not the more usual oil and vinegar dressing, makes a good accompaniment to roast and broiled meats. Serve it with pork chops or steak or, for a change, with roast or broiled chicken. Well chilled, it also makes a refreshing, easy-to-prepare first course.

● 205 calories per portion

Chinese beansprout salad

SERVES 4
½ large cucumber, pared
½ lb beansprouts
2 oz turnip greens, stems removed
  and finely shredded
¼ cup roasted peanuts
salt and freshly ground black pepper

DRESSING
2 oz Danish Blue cheese
6 tablespoons vegetable oil
2 tablespoons wine vinegar
a little milk (optional)

1 Cut the cucumber into 1½-inch lengths, then cut these lengthwise into thin sticks. Place in a salad bowl with the beansprouts.
2 Add the turnip greens and mix all the vegetables together.
3 Make the dressing: Crumble the blue cheese into a bowl and mash with a fork. Add the oil a little at a time, mixing it into the cheese with the fork to form a paste. Mix in the vinegar and add a little milk if the mixture seems too thick for a

dressing (see Cook's tips).
4 Just before serving, add the peanuts to the salad and pour over the dressing. ⚠ Toss until all the ingre-

dients are thoroughly coated in the dressing, then add salt and pepper to taste. Serve at once while the beansprouts and nuts are crunchy.

Cook's Notes

 TIME
Preparation takes about 20 minutes.

VARIATIONS
Try using any one of the other blue cheeses available in supermarkets, such as Stilton.

SERVING IDEAS
Serve as a side dish with beef casseroles, hot roast lamb or broiled white fish.
  Alternatively, serve as a first course in individual bowls, topped with garlic-flavored croutons (small cubes of bread fried in oil to which 2 crushed garlic cloves have been added).

 COOK'S TIPS
If you have a blender or food processor, put all the ingredients in the machine

together and work until smooth.
  You can prepare the salad ingredients and dressing separately, several hours in advance of serving. Store in covered plastic containers in the refrigerator and combine together with peanuts just before serving.

SPECIAL OCCASION
If you are feeling extravagant, for a dinner party or special occasion, use the French blue cheese, Roquefort, available from delicatessens and specialty food stores.

WATCHPOINT
Add the peanuts at the last minute, just before you dress the salad, so that they do not lose their crunchiness.

● 345 calories per portion

Crisp and crunchy salad

SERVES 4

6 oz white cabbage, coarsely
    shredded
6 oz red cabbage, finely
    shredded
1 large carrot, finely grated
2 celery stalks, chopped
1 small green pepper, seeded and
    finely chopped
4 oz fresh beansprouts (optional,
    see Buying guide)
½ cup salted peanuts

DRESSING

4 oz blue cheese
⅔ cup olive oil
3 tablespoons wine vinegar
½ teaspoon made English mustard
2 tablespoons chopped chives
salt and freshly ground black pepper

1 Put the cabbage in a large salad
bowl (use a glass one, if possible)
with the carrot, celery, green pepper
and beansprouts, if using.

2 Make the dressing: Using a fork,
mash the cheese in a small bowl.
When it is smooth, add the olive oil
a little at a time, and continue
mixing until creamy.
3 Add the vinegar and mix in until
combined, then stir in the mustard
and chives, and salt and pepper to
taste.
4 Just before serving, add the
peanuts to the salad in the bowl,
then pour over the dressing and stir
well to mix. ⚠ Serve as soon as
possible.

Cook's Notes

TIME
This salad takes 30
minutes to prepare.

COOK'S TIP
Try to shred the 2 cab-
bages to different thick-
nesses. The different textures
add interest to the salad.

WATCHPOINT
Do not add the peanuts
until just before you
mix in the dressing otherwise
they will become soft.

VARIATIONS
Add or subtract the in-
gredients according to
what you have available. Keep a
balance of colors and crisp
ingredients. Use any of the
cheeses such as Danish Blue
or Stilton.

SERVING IDEAS
Serve as a main course
for a healthy lunch —
there is plenty of protein in the
nuts and cheese to balance all
the vegetables.

BUYING GUIDE
Buy fresh beansprouts,
if they are available,
and use the same day. Canned
beansprouts are unsuitable as
they are not crisp.

● 600 calories per portion

Pea and bean salad

SERVES 4
¾ lb peas (weighed in the pod),
   shelled, or ¾ cup frozen peas
⅓ cup dried red kidney beans,
   soaked overnight, or 1 can (about
   8 oz) red kidney beans
1 lb lima beans (weighed in the
   pod), shelled, or ¼ lb frozen
   lima beans
salt
1 small red pepper, seeded and finely
   chopped
1 small green pepper, seeded and
   finely chopped
1 bunch scallions, finely
   chopped
2 tablespoons chopped parsley

FRENCH DRESSING
3 tablespoons olive oil
1 tablespoon lemon juice
1 tablespoon white wine or wine
   vinegar
1 teaspoon mild Dijon-style mustard
1 teaspoon superfine sugar
freshly ground black pepper

1 Drain the soaked kidney beans,
cook in boiling water about 1 hour
until tender (see Cook's tips), then
drain and cool slightly. If using
canned beans, drain off the liquid
from the can, then rinse the beans
thoroughly under cold running
water.
2 Cook the fresh lima beans and
peas in separate pans of boiling
salted water until just tender (5-7
minutes). If using frozen beans and
peas, cook according to package
directions. Drain and cool slightly.
3 Mix together the beans, peas, red
and green peppers, scallions and
chopped parsley in a bowl.
4 To make the French dressing:
Place all the ingredients in a screw-
top jar with salt and pepper to taste.
Replace the lid firmly and shake well
to mix.
5 Pour the French dressing over the
bean mixture and toss well until all
the vegetables are thoroughly
coated. Taste and adjust seasoning.
Cover the bowl with plastic wrap,
then refrigerate about 2 hours.
Transfer to a salad bowl before
serving.

Cook's Notes

TIME
Soak red kidney beans
overnight then cook 1
hour. Preparation of the other
vegetables 20-30 minutes, and
cooking about 5-7 minutes.
Chill salad for at least 2 hours.

COOK'S TIPS
The kidney beans *must*
boil vigorously for a
good 10 minutes, and then
simmer for the rest of the
cooking time. Do not add salt to
the cooking water; it toughens
the skins.

SERVING IDEAS
This makes a delicious
snack lunch on its own
with whole wheat rolls. It goes
well with all cold meat,
particularly beef, and makes a
colorful addition to a buffet
spread. Serve it, too, as part of a
vegetarian meal.

PRESSURE COOKING
The kidney beans will
cook in 20 minutes in a
pressure cooker at high pressure.

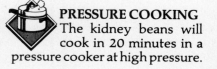

● 195 calories per portion

Avocado and grapefruit salad

SERVES 4
2 small avocados
1 small grapefruit
2 dessert apples
1 small lettuce, separated into
    leaves

DRESSING
1 tablespoon clear honey
2 tablespoons cider vinegar
6 tablespoons olive oil
salt and freshly ground black pepper

1 To make the dressing: Mix together the honey, vinegar and olive oil in a bowl. Beat with a fork until the dressing is thick and all the ingredients are thoroughly combined. Season to taste.
2 Peel the grapefruit. Hold it over a bowl to catch the juice and, using a

small, sharp knife, trim away any white pith. Divide the grapefruit into sections and remove the pips. Stir the sections into the dressing.
3 Halve the avocados lengthwise, remove the seeds and pare. Slice the flesh and add immediately to the dressing. [!] Toss thoroughly.
4 Quarter and core the apples. Slice them thinly and toss them in the dressing. Taste and adjust seasoning. Arrange the lettuce leaves in a salad bowl, pile the salad in the center and serve at once.

Brussels sprouts and date salad

SERVES 6
1 lb Brussels sprouts
½ lb carrots, grated
⅔ cup chopped pitted dates

DRESSING
⅔ cup plain yogurt, chilled
2 tablespoons mayonnaise
2 tablespoons fresh orange juice
salt and freshly ground black pepper
2 tablespoons chopped chives

TO SERVE
2 heads Belgian endive or 1 lettuce
   heart, trimmed and separated into
   leaves
¼ cup walnut halves (optional)

1 Trim the sprouts, discarding any tough or colored outer leaves. Wash and drain them thoroughly, tossing them in a clean dish cloth or on paper towels.

2 Shred the sprouts with a sharp knife, then place in a large mixing bowl with the grated carrots and dates. Mix well to combine.

3 To make the dressing: Beat together the yogurt, mayonnaise and orange juice. Add salt and pepper to taste, then stir in the chives.

4 Pour the dressing over the vegetables and mix well. Taste and adjust seasoning. Cover and refrigerate about 1 hour, or longer.

5 To serve: Line a deep serving bowl with the endive or lettuce leaves, then spoon the chilled salad into the center, piling it up in a mound. Garnish with walnuts, if using.

Gazpacho salad

SERVES 4

¾ lb tomatoes, peeled and thinly
    sliced

½ large cucumber, pared and thinly
    sliced

1 medium onion, thinly sliced

1 medium red pepper, seeded and
    thinly sliced

1 medium green pepper, seeded and
    thinly sliced

salt, freshly ground black pepper
    and sugar

10 tablespoons white or brown
    bread crumbs

8 tablespoons French dressing (see
    Cook's tips)

TO SERVE

10 black olives

1 tablespoon chopped parsley

1 Prepare the tomatoes, cucumber,
onion and peppers as indicated
above. Plunge the peppers in boiling water for 30 seconds (to blanch),
and then immerse them immediately
in cold water (to refresh them).

2 In a glass bowl, put a layer of
cucumber, followed by a layer of
tomatoes and a sprinkling of sugar,
a layer of onion and a layer of mixed
red and green peppers. Season with
salt and pepper and sprinkle over 2
tablespoons bread crumbs and 2
tablespoons French dressing.

3 Continue these layers, finishing
with a layer of 4 tablespoons bread
crumbs. Cover these with French
dressing so that they are well
soaked, then cover the bowl with
plastic wrap and refrigerate for 2-3
hours before actually serving.

Cook's Notes

TIME
The preparation of the
salad should take no
longer than 20 minutes, but
remember you should allow 2-3
hours chilling time in the
refrigerator before the gazpacho salad is ready to serve.

COOK'S TIPS
This is a salad version
of the better known
gazpacho soup. A French dressing well-flavored with garlic is
really essential. Mix together 6
tablespoons olive oil and 2
tablespoons wine vinegar (or
lemon juice) and season with
freshly ground black pepper.
Crush a garlic clove with salt
using the blade of a small knife,
and blend it into the dressing.
(Use only half a clove if your
family prefers a mild garlic
flavor). Vegetables are blanched
for a variety of reasons — to
soften them before further
cooking, to retain color, to get
rid of a bitter flavor. Refreshing
immediately in cold water stops
any further cooking.

SERVING IDEAS
The salad goes particu-
larly well with plain
broiled or barbecued meat. It is
also a good accompaniment to
simple, fried hamburgers.

● 185 calories per portion

Leek and potato pie

SERVES 4
1 lb leeks
salt
1½ lb potatoes
3 tablespoons butter or margarine
2 tablespoons all-purpose flour
1¼ cups warm milk
pinch of freshly grated nutmeg
freshly ground black pepper
½ cup grated Cheddar cheese
butter, for greasing

1 Trim the leeks, discarding most of the dark green part (see Economy). Slice thickly and wash under cold running water until completely clean. Cook in boiling salted water 8-10 minutes or until almost tender. Drain thoroughly, reserving the broth.
2 At the same time, cook the potatoes in boiling salted water about 20-25 minutes or until tender. Drain.
3 While the vegetables are cooking, make sauce: Melt 2 tablespoons of butter gently in a small saucepan, sprinkle in the flour and stir over a low heat 2 minutes until straw-colored. Remove from the heat and gradually stir in all but 2 tablespoons of the milk, then return to the heat and simmer, stirring, until thick and smooth. Measure out about ⅔ cup of the leek broth (see Economy); stir gradually into white sauce. Bring back to a boil, stirring constantly, then add the nutmeg and salt and pepper to taste. Remove the pan from the heat.
4 Preheat the oven to 375°.
5 Slice one-third of the potatoes, stir them gently into the leeks and turn into the base of a greased 5 cup ovenproof dish. Pour on the sauce; carefully turn vegetables with a fork, to coat thoroughly.
6 Add remaining butter and milk to the rest of the potatoes, season with pepper, then mash them until smooth. Beat in half the

cheese with a wooden spoon. Taste and adjust seasoning.
7 Spread the mashed potato over the vegetables, then sprinkle on the

rest of the cheese. Stand the dish on a cookie sheet and bake in the oven 20-25 minutes, or until the topping is golden brown. Serve hot.

Cook's Notes

TIME
Preparation 35-45 minutes, cooking in the oven 20-25 minutes.

SERVING IDEAS
Serve with fried or boiled bacon or any cold cooked meat.

ECONOMY
Reserve the green parts of the leeks and remaining leek broth and use for soup.
Leeks give excellent flavor to a vegetable soup. Remember to wash trimmings thoroughly.

● 390 calories per portion

Vegetable pie

SERVES 4-6
1 cup all-purpose flour
salt
¼ cup butter or margarine, diced
½ cup grated Cheddar cheese
about 4 teaspoons chilled water
beaten egg or milk, for glazing

FILLING
1 lb potatoes, diced
3 carrots, sliced
3 leeks, cut into ½-inch slices
1 tablespoon chopped fresh parsley
freshly ground black pepper
2 tablespoons butter or margarine
2 tablespoons all-purpose flour
1¼ cups vegetable or chicken
    broth

1 Make the pastry: Sift the flour and a pinch of salt into a bowl. Add the butter and cut it into the flour until all the mixture resembles fine crumbs.
2 Mix in the grated cheese and just enough cold water to draw the mixture together to a firm dough. Wrap in plastic wrap and refrigerate 30 minutes.
3 Preheat the oven to 350°. Meanwhile, make the filling: Cook the potatoes and carrots in boiling salted water 10 minutes. Drain thoroughly, then place vegetables in 3¾ cup pie dish with leeks, mixing them well together. Sprinkle with the pastry and salt and pepper to taste. Set aside.
4 Melt the butter in a clean saucepan, sprinkle in the flour and stir over a low heat 1-2 minutes until straw-colored. Gradually stir in the broth, then bring to a boil and simmer, stirring, until thick and smooth. Pour over the vegetables.
5 Roll out the pastry on a floured surface to a shape slightly larger than the top of the pie dish. Cut off a long strip of pastry all around the edge. Reserve this and other trimmings. Brush the rim of the pie dish with water, then press the narrow strip of pastry all around the rim. Brush the strip with a little more water, then place the large piece of pastry on top. Press to seal, then trim, knock up and crimp the edge of the pie.
6 Make decorations from the trimmings, brush the undersides with water and place on top of the pie. Brush the pastry lid with a little beaten egg, and make a hole in the center. Bake in the oven 40-45 minutes until the pastry is golden brown and the vegetables are tender. Serve at once.

Cook's Notes

TIME
1½ hours preparation and cooking time, including chilling the cheese shortcrust pastry.

VARIATIONS
The vegetables may be replaced by whatever is in season.
Instead of the cheese pastry crust, use 1 sheet (½ of 17 oz package) frozen puff pastry.

● 425 calories per portion

Zucchini bake

SERVES 4-6
1 lb small zucchini, cut into
1-inch lengths (see
Buying guide)
2 tablespoons butter or margarine
1 onion, chopped
salt
3 eggs, beaten
¾ cup grated Cheddar cheese
⅔ cup milk
2 tablespoons chopped fresh
parsley
good pinch of freshly grated
nutmeg
freshly ground black pepper
butter, for greasing

1 Preheat the oven to 350° and grease an 8½-inch flan dish, about 1½-inches deep, with the butter.

2 Melt the butter in a skillet, add the onion and cook gently 10 minutes until browned. Remove the pan from the heat and cool.
3 meanwhile, bring a saucepan of lightly salted water to a boil. Add the zucchini and simmer for 5 minutes. Drain thoroughly and then set aside.
4 Mix the eggs, cheese, milk, parsley and nutmeg together in a bowl. Season to taste with salt and pepper then stir in the onion.
5 Stand the pieces of zucchini upright in the flan dish, then carefully spoon in the egg mixture, making sure it is evenly distributed.
6 Bake the custard in the oven about 40 minutes until it is set and the top is golden brown. Leave to stand for about 10 minutes before serving, cut into wedges.

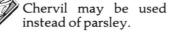

Cook's Notes

TIME
The custard takes 20 minutes to prepare and 40 minutes to cook.

VARIATION
Chervil may be used instead of parsley.

SERVING IDEAS
This custard makes an unusual vegetable accompaniment to plainly broiled meat. You may find that because of the large amount of zucchini used you will not need an additional vegetable.

BUYING GUIDE
Buy the smallest zucchini you can find — there should be 6-9 to 1 lb.

● 230 calories per portion

Vegetable crumble

SERVES 4
2 leeks, cut into ½-inch slices (see
   Preparation)
2 tablespoons olive oil or
   sunflower oil
2 large carrots, thickly sliced
1 small red pepper, seeded
   and diced
1 lb zucchini, cut into ½-inch
   slices
1 can (about 14 oz) tomatoes
½ teaspoon dried basil
salt and freshly ground black pepper
about ½ cup pine nuts (see Buying
   guide)
2 teaspoons wine vinegar

CRUMBLE TOPPING
1 cup all-purpose or whole wheat
   flour
¼ teaspoon salt
3 tablespoons butter, diced
½ cup grated fresh Parmesan
   cheese, (see Buying guide)

1 Heat the oil in a large saucepan,
add the leeks and carrots and cook
over moderate heat 5 minutes.

stirring. Add the red pepper and
cook 5 minutes, then add the
zucchini and cook a further 5
minutes, stirring constantly.
2 Add the tomatoes and their juices
to the pan with the basil and salt
and pepper to taste. Bring to a boil,
then lower the heat, cover and
simmer 10 minutes.
3 Meanwhile, preheat the oven to
400° and then make the crumble:
Sift the flour and salt into a bowl.

Add the butter and cut slowly into
the flour until all the mixture
resembles fine bread crumbs. Stir in
most of the Parmesan, and then add
pepper to taste.
4 Add the pine nuts and vinegar
to vegetables, then transfer to a
1½ quart casserole. Sprinkle the
crumble evenly over vegetables,
then top with remaining Parmesan.
5 Bake in the oven about 40
minutes, until golden.

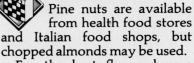

Cook's Notes

TIME
Preparation time 30-40
minutes, then about 40
minutes baking.

PREPARATION
Wash the leeks, then
slice them and put into
a strainer. Rinse again under
cold running water, to remove
any remaining grit and dirt.

BUYING GUIDE
Pine nuts are available
from health food stores
and Italian food shops, but
chopped almonds may be used.
  For the best flavor, buy a

whole piece of Parmesan and
grate it yourself at home when
needed. Tightly wrapped in
plastic wrap it will keep its
flavor for several weeks in the
refrigerator. Special graters for
this hard cheese can be bought
from some kitchen and hardware shops.
  If you do not want to go to
the trouble of grating the cheese
yourself, buy freshly grated
Parmesan from an Italian
delicatessen; do not buy packages or tubs of grated Parmesan
from a supermarket for this dish.

● 390 calories per portion

Vegetable fried rice

SERVES 4
1⅓ cups long-grain rice
salt
½ lb carrots, diced
1 parsnip, diced
1 small turnip, diced
2 tablespoons vegetable oil
1 large onion, chopped
1 clove garlic, crushed (optional)
½ cup sliced mushrooms
2 large tomatoes, peeled and sliced
⅓ cup frozen peas, thawed
freshly ground black pepper
2 eggs, lightly beaten
1 tablespoon chopped fresh parsley
grated Parmesan cheese, to serve

1 Bring a large saucepan of salted water to a boil, add the rice and cover. Lower the heat and simmer 10 minutes, or until the rice is just tender.
2 Meanwhile, bring another pan of salted water to the boil. Add the carrots, parsnip and turnip and cover. Lower the heat and cook about 8-10 minutes, or until all the

Cook's Notes

TIME
This dish will take about 35 minutes to make.

VARIATIONS
Small, partly-cooked cauliflower flowerets or broccoli make tasty alternatives to the root vegetables used here — and their shape adds a pleasant variation, too.
Make the dish even more substantial by adding about ½ cup chopped, cooked ham or cooked chicken at the beginning of stage 5.

FREEZING
Cool completely and pack into a rigid container. Seal, label and freeze for up to 2 months. To serve: Allow to thaw overnight in the refrigerator. Reheat very gently and stir in the eggs just before serving.

SERVING IDEAS
This dish makes an excellent accompaniment to meat dishes. Or serve with tomato sauce on its own.

● 410 calories per portion

vegetables are barely tender.
3 Drain the cooked root vegetables and reserve. Drain the rice in a strainer and rinse well under hot running water to separate the grains. Drain again.
4 Heat the oil in a large non-stick saucepan, add the onion and garlic, if using, and cook gently 5 minutes, or until the onion is soft and lightly colored.
5 Add the drained root vegetables to the pan, together with the mushrooms, tomatoes, peas and rice. Stir well and season to taste with salt and plenty of pepper. Cover the pan and cook over very low heat 10 minutes. ✳
6 Stir in the eggs and gently turn the mixture so that the egg cooks. Remove from the heat and turn into a warmed serving dish. Garnish with the parsley and serve at once with the Parmesan cheese.

Potato pizza

SERVES 4
1 cup self-rising flour
salt
¼ cup butter or margarine
1 cup cold mashed potatoes
vegetable oil, for greasing

TOPPING
1 tablespoon vegetable oil
1 large onion, sliced
1 red pepper, seeded and sliced
1 clove garlic (optional)
   (optional
1 cup sliced small mushrooms
pinch of oregano
2 teaspoons vinegar
freshly ground black pepper
1 tablespoon tomato paste
6 oz Cheddar cheese, sliced

1 Preheat the oven to 450°. Oil a large cookie sheet.

2 Make the base: Sift the flour and salt into a large bowl. Add the butter and cut it in until all the mixture resembles bread crumbs, then add the mashed potatoes and knead the mixture lightly until smooth.

3 Press the dough into a 10-inch round and refrigerate.

4 Meanwhile, make the topping: Heat the oil in a skillet, add the onion, red pepper and garlic, if using, and cook gently 5 minutes or until the onion is soft and lightly colored. Remove the pan from the heat and stir in the mushrooms, oregano, vinegar and salt and pepper to taste.

5 Place the potato base on the cookie sheet and spread the tomato paste over it, then top with the onion mixture. Arrange the cheese slices over the top.

6 Bake in the oven 25-30 minutes or until the base is firm and the cheese is golden brown.

Red summer flan

SERVES 4-6

½ lb red peppers, seeded and cut
    into thin slices
¾ lb tomatoes, thinly sliced
2 tablespoons vegetable oil
4 cloves garlic, crushed
½ cup fresh white bread crumbs
½ teaspoon dried basil
salt and freshly ground black pepper
1 teaspoon sugar

PASTRY

1½ cups all-purpose flour
pinch of salt
¼ cup butter, diced
2 tablespoons shortening, diced
½ cup finely grated Cheddar cheese
½ teaspoon dried mixed herbs
2 tablespoons cold water
lightly beaten egg white, to seal

1 Preheat the oven to 400°.
2 Make the pastry: Sift the flour and
salt into a bowl. Add the butter
and fat and cut in until the mixture resembles fine bread crumbs.
Stir in the grated cheese and herbs,
then add the cold water and mix to
a fairly firm dough.
3 Turn the dough out onto a lightly
floured surface and roll out thinly.
Use to line a 8-9 inch flan ring, set
on a cookie sheet, prick the base
with a fork. Place a large circle of
waxed paper or foil in the pie shell
and weight it down with baking
beans. Bake 10 minutes.
4 Remove the paper or foil lining
and beans, brush the inside of the
pie shell with beaten egg white,
then return the pastry to the oven a
further 5 minutes. Remove from the
oven and set aside.
5 Make the filling: Heat the oil in a
skillet, add the peppers and cook
gently 5 minutes until beginning to
soften. Add the garlic and continue
to cook until soft and lightly
colored. Set aside.
6 Put the bread crumbs in a bowl
with the basil and salt and pepper
to taste. Mix well.
7 Spread the peppers over the base
of the pie shell, then cover with the
tomto slices. Sprinkle with sugar,
then finish with a layer of the bread
crumb mixture.
8 Bake in the oven 30-35 minutes
until the tomatoes are tender and
the pastry is golden.
9 Serve the flan hot or cold.

Cook's Notes

TIME
35 minutes to prepare
and bake the pie shell;
about 50 minutes to finish.

SERVING IDEAS
This colorful flan
makes a satisfying
lunch or supper dish. Serve hot
with a fresh green vegetable
and new potatoes, or serve cold
with a mixed green salad.

VARIATION
To cut down on
preparation time, use
about ½ lb of pie crust
sticks.
Canned peppers may be used
instead of fresh peppers—there
is no need to cook them, simply
drain, slice and stir into the
cooked garlic.

● 395 calories per slice

Spinach fried with mushrooms

SERVES 4
¼ cup butter
1 lb spinach, stems and large midribs removed, shredded (see Watchpoint)
2 cups sliced mushrooms
½ teaspoon freshly grated nutmeg
salt and freshly ground black pepper
4 tablespoons dairy sour cream

1 Melt the butter in a heavy saucepan or flameproof casserole. Add the spinach, sliced mushrooms and nutmeg and season to taste with salt and pepper. Cover the pan and cook over a very low heat 8-10 minutes until the vegetables are just cooked. Stir frequently during this time to ensure even cooking.

2 Transfer the vegetables to a warmed serving dish and drizzle dairy sour cream over top in an attractive pattern. Serve at once while still hot.

Cook's Notes

 TIME
Preparation and cooking take 20-25 minutes.

 **VARIATIONS**
Light cream may be used as a substitute for dairy sour cream. Alternatively, to make the dish less expensive, omit the cream altogether and sprinkle with lemon juice before serving.

SERVING IDEAS
Serve this quickly made dish as a vegetable accompaniment for 4, or as a light lunch dish for 2-3 people.

! WATCHPOINT
It is important to drain the spinach thoroughly and then to pat it dry.

● 145 calories per portion

Leek and tomato casserole

SERVES 4-6

2 large leeks, trimmed, washed and cut into 1 inch pieces (see Preparation)
2 large onions, cut into eighths
1 can (about 14 oz) tomatoes
1 tablespoon chopped parsley
1 bay leaf
2 cloves garlic, crushed (optional)
1 teaspoon salt
freshly ground black pepper
⅔ cup chicken or vegetable broth
4 tablespoons vegetable oil
1 tablespoon lemon juice
pinch of dried thyme

1 Preheat the oven to 350°.
2 Put all the ingredients into a large bowl and mix well. Turn into a large ovenproof dish or casserole, cover and cook in the oven 1½-2 hours, until tender. Serve hot.

Cook's Notes

TIME
Preparation of vegetables 15 minutes, cooking time in the oven 1½-2 hours.

ECONOMY
Save fuel by cooking this dish with something else on the shelf below.

SERVING IDEAS
Serve this easy-to-make vegetable dish on its own or with roast beef or pork.

VARIATION
When tomatoes are cheap and plentiful, use fresh instead of canned, in which case you may need a little extra broth. Peel them before mixing with other ingredients.

PREPARATION
Top and tails leeks; slit them down almost to base. Fan out under cold running water to rinse off all dirt.

● 175 calories per portion

Soy burgers

SERVES 4
¾ cup soybeans
2 tablespoons vegetable oil
1 onion, finely chopped
1 small carrot, grated
1 small green pepper, seeded and
   chopped
1 tablespoon tomato paste
1 teaspoon dried mixed herbs
salt
freshly ground black pepper
1 egg, beaten
1 tablespoon water
dried bread crumbs, for coating
vegetable oil, for frying

1 Put the beans into a bowl, cover with plenty of cold water and leave to soak overnight. Drain the soaked beans and put them into a saucepan; cover with cold water.
2 Bring the beans to a boil, then lower the heat and simmer over very gentle heat 3 hours until tender, topping up with more water if necessary. Transfer to a strainer and drain thoroughly. ✳
3 Heat the oil in a skillet and gently cook the onion and carrot 5 minutes, until the onion is soft and lightly colored. Add the green pepper and cook a further 5 minutes, or until the vegetables are just tender.
4 Add the beans, tomato paste and herbs to the pan, mashing the beans with a spoon to make the mixture hold together. Season with salt and pepper to taste.
5 Divide the mixture into 8 and shape each piece into a neat, flat circle. Beat egg and water together in a shallow bowl and spread the bread crumbs out on a plate. Dip the burgers first into the beaten egg mixture, then into the dried bread crumbs, making sure they are well coated.
6 Heat the vegetable oil in a large skillet, add 4 burgers and cook over moderately high heat 3 minutes on each side until crisp and browned. Remove with a slotted spoon, place on a serving platter, and keep warm. Cook the remaining burgers in the same way and serve at once.

Cook's Notes

TIME
Allow for the overnight soaking of the beans, followed by 3 hours cooking. Preparation and cooking then take about 30 minutes.

PRESSURE COOKING
Soybeans can be cooked in a pressure-cooker. Soak and rinse as in the recipe, then cook at high (H) pressure for 1 hour.

FREEZING
Drained, cooked soy-beans can be frozen in plastic bags for use. Soy bean burgers can be frozen before cooking: open-freeze until solid, then pack in a rigid container, separating the layers with foil. Seal, label and return to the freezer for up to 2 months. To serve: Cook from frozen.

SERVING IDEAS
Serve the burgers with mashed potatoes or French fries and parsley sauce; or with chutney and soft rolls.

DID YOU KNOW
Soybeans are one of the richest sources of protein, described in China as "meat without bones".

● 360 calories per portion

Creamy spring vegetables

SERVES 4

1 small onion, sliced
2 large scallions cut into ½-inch
  slices
2 carrots, cut into ½-inch slices
¼ cup butter
1¼ cups hot chicken broth
pinch of superfine sugar
salt and freshly ground black
  pepper
½ lb lima beans
  (shelled weight)
1½ cups shelled peas
1 teaspoon cornstarch
6 tablespoons heavy cream
1 tablespoon chopped fresh parsley,
  to garnish (optional)

1 Melt the butter in a saucepan, add the sliced onion and scallions and cook over moderate heat 2 minutes. Add the sliced carrots and cook a further 2 minutes, stirring to coat thoroughly.

TIME
Preparation, if using fresh vegetables, takes 20-25 minutes. Cooking the Creamy spring vegetables takes about 35 minutes.

SERVING IDEAS
This dish is delicious with roast or broiled chicken, pork, lamb or veal. It is also very good as a light lunch or supper dish, simply served with boiled rice, tiny new potatoes or whole wheat rolls.

VARIATIONS
When fresh lima beans and peas are not in season, use frozen ones. Add them to the pan after the carrots have been cooking 10 minutes, then cook 8-10 minutes or according to package directions.
Add ½-1 teaspoon curry powder to the cornstarch when making the sauce to give a mild spiciness to the dish.

● 295 calories per portion

2 Pour the hot broth into the pan, add the sugar and salt and pepper to taste, then bring to a boil. Lower the heat, cover and simmer gently 10 minutes. Add the lima beans and simmer a further 5 minutes. Add the peas and continue simmering another 10 minutes, until all the vegetables are tender.
3 Put the cornstarch into a small bowl and stir in 1 tablespoon of the hot vegetable broth from the pan. Stir to make a smooth paste, then pour back into the pan. Stir the contents of the pan over a low heat about 4-5 minutes, until the sauce thickens and clears. Stir in the cream and allow just to heat through.
4 Turn the vegetables with the sauce into a warmed serving dish. Sprinkle with parsley, if liked, and serve at once.

Cheesy cabbage pan-flan

SERVES 4

2 lb potatoes, quartered
salt
1 lb green cabbage, cored and shredded
1½ cups grated sharp Cheddar cheese (see Buying guide)
1 large egg, beaten
freshly ground black pepper
6—8 scallions, chopped
2 tablespoons shortening

1 Cook the potatoes in boiling salted water about 20 minutes or until tender.
2 Meanwhile, cook the cabbage in boiling salted water 5 minutes. Drain thoroughly.
3 Drain the potatoes well, then return them to the saucepan. Dry out over gentle heat, then mash with 1 cup of cheese, the beaten egg and plenty of salt and pepper. Stir in the cabbage and scallions.
4 Melt shortening in a large skillet over high heat and swirl it around to cover the base and sides. Add the potato and cabbage mixture and spread it out evenly. Cook 3 minutes or until underside is golden (see Cook's tip).

5 Sprinkle with the remaining cheese, then put under a moderate broiler about 5 minutes, until the top is golden brown. Serve at once straight from pan cut in wedges.

Cook's Notes

TIME
Total preparation and cooking time is about 30 minutes.

COOK'S TIP
To see if the underside of the dish is golden brown, gently lift up the edge with a spatula. The center will become brown before the outside, so take care not to let the center become burnt.

VARIATIONS
Traditionally this dish is made with left-over mashed potato and cooked Brussels sprouts. If you prefer the stronger flavor of sprouts, then use these instead of the cabbage. A dash of Worcestershire sauce is a good complement to the cheese. Add it when mashing the potatoes and, if liked, mix a few drops in with the grated cheese for the topping.

SERVING IDEAS
Serve as a vegetable with sausages, bacon, chops, etc., or add chopped left-over cooked meat such as ham or bacon to the cheesy cabbage pan-flan to make a more substantial dish.

BUYING GUIDE
Canadian Cheddar cheese has just the right amount of flavor to give a "kick" to the potatoes and cabbage.

● 510 calories per portion

Potato and radish crunch

SERVES 4

1 lb new potatoes (see
  Buying guide)
salt
¼ cup butter
3 thick slices white bread,
  crusts removed and cut
  into ½-inch dice
2-inch piece of cucumber, diced
6 radishes, thinly sliced
1 tablespoon dry roasted
  peanuts
1 teaspoon chopped chives
freshly ground black pepper
4 tablespoons dairy sour cream

1 Boil a saucepan of salted water
and cook the potatoes 15-20
minutes until just tender. ⚠ Drain
well and, when cool enough to
handle, cut into ½-inch dice. Leave
to cool completely.

2 To make the croutons: Melt the
butter in a skillet. When it is sizzling,
add the diced bread and cook
gently, turning as necessary, until
golden. Drain well on paper towels.
Leave to cool completely.

3 Place the diced potato, fried
croûtons, cucumber, radishes, peanuts and chives into a bowl. Season
to taste with salt and pepper. Add
dairy sour cream and mix gently. ⚠
Serve at once.

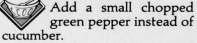

Cook's Notes

TIME
Preparation, including
cooking the potatoes
and frying the croutons, takes
about 30 minutes. Allow 30
minutes for cooling. Preparing
the salad takes 5 minutes.

BUYING GUIDE
Choose a firm type of
potato such as the red
or white new potatoes which
will not break up during
cooking.

WATCHPOINT
Watch the potatoes
carefully: they should
be cooked through but still firm.
If overcooked, they will break
up instead of cutting into neat
dice.

Mix gently so that the ingredients are thoroughly coated in
dairy sour cream but remain
separate.

VARIATIONS
Add a small chopped
green pepper instead of
cucumber.
Omit the peanuts and
sprinkle the top of the salad
with toasted, slivered almonds.

● 310 calories per portion

Potato 'n' tomato gratin

SERVES 4
1½ lb firm potatoes, sliced
salt
1¼ cups milk
1 cup grated Cheddar cheese

TOMATO SAUCE
3 tablespoons butter or margarine
1 medium onion, sliced
1 tablespoon all-purpose flour
1 can (about 14 oz) tomatoes
½ teaspoon sugar
1 teaspoon dried oregano
salt and freshly ground black pepper

1 Make sauce: Melt 2 tablespoons butter in a small saucepan, add the onion and cook gently 3 minutes, stirring occasionally. Do not allow the onion to brown. Sprinkle in the flour and cook 2 minutes, stirring constantly.

2 Add the tomatoes with their juice to the pan, stir in the sugar and oregano and season with salt and pepper to taste. Simmer 20 minutes until the tomato sauce has thickened, stirring occasionally.

3 Meanwhile, put the potatoes in a saucepan with the milk and ½ teaspoon salt. Bring slowly to a boil, then lower the heat and simmer uncovered 10-12 minutes. The potatoes should be tender when pierced with a fine skewer, but not beginning to break up. ⚠ Drain thoroughly.

4 Grease the inside of a shallow 3¾-4 cup flameproof dish with remaining butter, then arrange the potatoes in overlapping circles over the base.

5 Heat broiler to moderate. Taste and adjust seasoning of the tomato sauce. Pour over the potatoes ✳ and sprinkle the cheese over the top. Place the dish under broiler until the cheese topping is golden brown and bubbling. ✳ Serve the gratin very hot, straight from the dish.

Cook's Notes

TIME
Preparation 10 minutes. Boiling the potatoes, preparing sauce and browning takes 25 minutes.

FREEZING
You can freeze the dish completely assembled, or without the cheese topping. Thaw at room temperature before broiling. Alternatively, cook it in the oven straight from the freezer: heat the oven to 375° and cook the dish 35-40 minutes or until the topping is golden brown.

WATCHPOINT
Make sure that you cut the potatoes into even, thick slices and be careful not to overcook them as well. The dish would be very unattractive if made with squashy, moist potatoes. They must be in whole slices and still slightly firm.

VARIATION
Leeks, cooked till just tender and thoroughly drained, could be successfully used instead of the potatoes.

● 400 calories per portion

Bulgur wheat casserole

SERVES 4
8 oz bulgur wheat (see Did you know)
¼ cup butter or margarine
1 tablespoon vegetable oil
1 large onion, finely chopped
2 large leeks, thinly sliced
2 large carrots, diced
1 small red pepper, seeded and diced
1¼ cups boiling water
2 tomatoes, peeled and chopped
⅓ cup seedless raisins
1 cup diced Cheddar cheese
salt and freshly ground black pepper

1 Melt half the butter with the oil in a large saucepan. Add the onion, leeks, carrots and red pepper, cover and cook gently about 20 minutes.

2 Meanwhile, melt the remaining butter in a large saucepan. Add the bulgur wheat and stir until the grains are thoroughly coated with butter. Stir in the boiling water, cover and place over gentle heat. Cook 10 minutes until the water has been absorbed.

3 Using a fork, gently mix the cooked vegetables into the bulgur wheat. Lightly stir in the tomatoes, raisins and cheese and fork through until the cheese is melted. Season to taste with salt and pepper. Transfer to a warmed serving dish and serve at once.

Cabbage gratin

SERVES 4

1 green cabbage, weighing approximately 1 lb, coarsely shredded
1 teaspoon salt
6 juniper berries, crushed (optional)
2 tablespoons butter
2 tablespoons all-purpose flour
⅔ cup milk
⅔ cup light cream
pinch of white pepper
pinch of cayenne pepper
½ teaspoon freshly grated nutmeg
3 tablespoons fresh bread crumbs
¼ cup grated Cheddar or Monterey Jack cheese
extra 1 tablespoon butter

1 Preheat the oven to 375°.
2 Cook the cabbage until just tender, but still crisp, in boiling salted water. Drain thoroughly and mix in the juniper berries, if used.
3 Make a thick creamy sauce with the butter, flour, milk and cream mixed (see Preparation). Add salt, peppers and nutmeg, then taste and adjust seasoning; the sauce should be very highly flavored.
4 Stir the cabbage into the sauce and pour into a buttered ovenproof dish.
5 Mix together the bread crumbs and grated cheese. Sprinkle over the cabbage and sauce and top with flecks of butter.
6 Cook about 15 minutes and then increase oven temperature to 425°. Cook a further 10 minutes, until the cheese has melted and the top is crisp and bubbling.

Cook's Notes

 TIME
Preparation 20 minutes, cooking 20-25 minutes.

SERVING IDEAS
Add peeled, chopped tomatoes to the sauce and scatter some crispy, fried bacon bits on top to make a complete supper dish.
Serve as an accompaniment to broiled or roast meat.

PREPARATION
To make the sauce: Melt the butter in a small saucepan, sprinkle in the flour and stir over a low heat 1-2 minutes until straw-colored. Remove from the heat and gradually stir in the milk and cream. Return to the heat and simmer, stirring, until thick and smooth.

 **VARIATIONS**
Substitute cauliflower for cabbage to make the classic dish, cauliflower cheese. If you like your vegetable gratin really cheesy, add ¼ cup more cheese to the sauce. Mixing a little mustard into the white sauce in Stage 3 makes it a bit more tangy (you will need about ¼-½ teaspoon).

● 225 calories per portion

ACCOMPANYING DISHES

Creamy rutabaga bake

SERVES 4

2 lb rutabaga, cut into 1½-inch pieces
3 tablespoons butter or margarine
salt and freshly ground black pepper
freshly grated nutmeg
1 bunch scallions, chopped
2 tablespoons light cream
3–4 tablespoons fresh white bread crumbs
vegetable oil, for greasing

1 Preheat the oven to 375°. Lightly grease an ovenproof dish or casserole.
2 Put rutabaga in a large saucepan with just enough cold water to cover. Bring to a boil, then lower the heat. Cover, simmer 20 minutes or until tender, then drain.
3 Mash the rutabaga with 2 table-spoons butter; season. Stir in nutmeg, scallions and cream.
4 Put rutabaga mixture into the greased dish, smooth the top and sprinkle evenly with the bread crumbs. Dot with the remaining butter. Bake 40 minutes, until golden on top. Serve hot.

Stir-fried celery

SERVES 4

1 head celery, stalks cut into ½-inch
    diagonal slices
1-2 tablespoons vegetable oil
3 scallions, thinly sliced
salt and freshly ground black pepper
2 tablespoons slivered almonds
2 tablespoons dry sherry
1 teaspoon soy sauce
1 teaspoon tomato paste
½ teaspoon superfine sugar
¼ teaspoon ground ginger

1 Heat the oil in a large skillet. Add
the sliced celery and scallions and
season with salt and pepper. Stir-fry
over moderate heat 5-7 minutes,
until the celery has lost its raw taste
but is still crunchy (see Cook's tip).
Add the almonds and stir-fry 1
minute.
2 Mix together the remaining
ingredients, pour into the pan and
stir-fry 2 minutes. Serve at once.

Cook's Notes

TIME
Preparation takes 15
minutes, cooking 10
minutes.

SERVING IDEAS
Serve stir-fried celery as
part of a Chinese meal
that you have prepared yourself
or bought from a takeaway. It
goes well with almost any meat
or fish dish, or with a savory flan
or a vegetarian dish such as
macaroni cheese.

VARIATIONS
If you do not have any
dry sherry, you can use
vermouth or white wine
instead.

COOK'S TIP
Use a wooden spoon or
spatula to stir-fry,
keeping the ingredients on the
move all the time, so that they
cook evenly.

● 85 calories per portion

Cheesy eggplant bake

SERVES 4
2 eggplants
salt
½ cup vegetable oil
6 oz Swiss or mozzarella cheese,
  very thinly sliced
  (see Economy)
1 egg
1 can (about 8 oz) tomatoes
½ onion, finely chopped
1 tablespoon tomato paste
1 tablespoon water
salt and freshly ground black pepper
butter for greasing
1 large tomato, sliced

1 Cut the eggplants into about ¼-inch slices and put them in a strainer in layers, sprinkling salt between each layer. Cover with a plate and place a heavy weight on top. Leave about 1 hour to draw out the bitter juices, then rinse the slices under cold running water and pat dry on paper towels.

2 Preheat the oven to 350°. Grease a shallow baking dish.

3 Pour enough of the oil into a large skillet to cover the base. Heat the oil, put a layer of eggplant slices in the pan and cook 3-4 minutes on each side, turning once, until golden brown on both sides. Remove from the pan and drain on paper towels. Continue in the same way until all the eggplant slices are browned.

4 Place layers of eggplant and cheese alternatively in prepared dish, finishing with a layer of cheese on top.

5 Put the egg, canned tomatoes, onion, tomato paste and water in a blender and blend until smooth. Season with a little salt and pepper, then pour over the eggplants and the cheese. Arrange the tomato slices on top.

6 Bake, uncovered 25 minutes, until heated through and bubbling. Serve straight from the dish.

Cook's Notes

TIME
Once the eggplants are drained, preparation will take about 30 minutes, baking the dish in the oven takes 25 minutes.

ECONOMY
While the Swiss or mozzarella cheese gives the best flavor to this dish, a less expensive sharp Cheddar cheese can be used as a substitute quite successfully.

SERVING IDEAS
Serve this dish with plenty of warm, fresh bread and a green salad as a vegetarian meal.

●405 calories per portion

Creamed lemon spinach

SERVES 4

1½ lb fresh spinach leaves
1 teaspoon salt
2 tablespoons butter
1 tablespoon all-purpose flour
⅔ cup heavy cream
grated rind and juice of ½ lemon
freshly ground black pepper
pinch of freshly grated nutmeg
2 hard-cooked eggs, yolks and
    whites separated and finely
    chopped, to garnish

1 If using fresh spinach, thoroughly wash it in several changes of cold water to remove all the grit. Remove the stems and midribs and discard. Put the spinach in a large saucepan with just the water that clings to the leaves after washing. [!] Sprinkle over the salt.
2 Cook the spinach over moderate heat about 15 minutes, stirring occasionally with a wooden spoon. Turn the cooked spinach into a strainer and drain thoroughly, pressing the spinach with a large spoon or a saucer to extract as much moisture as possible.
3 Melt the butter in the rinsed-out pan, sprinkle in the flour and stir over moderate heat 3 minutes. Remove from heat, pour in the cream, and when it is completely blended, add the lemon rind and juice. [!] Season to taste with salt, pepper and nutmeg. Stir the spinach into the cream sauce and return to very low heat, just to heat through. [!]
4 Turn the spinach into a heated serving dish and arrange the chopped hard-cooked eggs in rows over the top. Serve at once.

Cook's Notes

 TIME
Preparation, if using fresh spinach, takes about 15 minutes. Cooking takes about 20 minutes.

 WATCHPOINTS
It is best to cook spinach in its own juices—added water only makes it soggy.

Do not add lemon juice until butter, flour and cream are well blended. Otherwise, the acid will curdle the cream.

On no account allow the cream sauce to boil when heating through, or it will curdle.

BUYING GUIDE
If fresh spinach is not available, use 2 packages (10 oz each) frozen cut leaf spinach, thawed and all moisture pressed out. Stir into the sauce and cook 5 minutes.

● 295 calories per portion

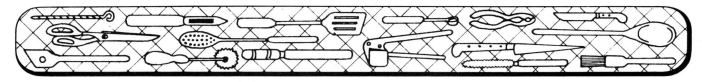

Carrots in orange juice

SERVES 4
1½ lb small carrots, thinly sliced
finely grated rind of ½ orange
juice of 1 orange
2 tablespoons butter or
margarine
1 teaspoon light brown sugar
½ teaspoon salt
freshly ground black pepper

TO GARNISH
twist of orange (see Preparation)
sprig of parsley

1 Put the sliced carrots in a saucepan with the orange rind and juice, butter, sugar, salt and pepper to taste. Add enough cold water to cover the carrots.
2 Bring to a boil over high heat, then simmer very gently, uncovered, over the lowest possible heat 40-45 minutes, until the carrots are just tender.

3 Increase the heat and boil the carrots 4-5 minutes until the amount of cooking liquid has reduced to a few tablespoonfuls. ⏱
4 Transfer the carrots to a warmed serving dish and pour over the remaining cooking liquid. Garnish in one corner with the twist of orange and the sprig of parsley. Serve at once.

Cook's Notes

TIME
20 minutes preparation, then 45-50 minutes cooking.

VARIATION
Use the finely grated rind of 1 lemon and 2 tablespoons lemon juice in place of the orange rind and juice.

SERVING IDEAS
This dish makes a refreshing accompaniment to any chicken, beef or lamb dish.

WATCHPOINT
The carrots are boiled for the last 4-5 minutes of cooking to evaporate the water and give the remaining cooking liquid a more concentrated flavor. This is known in cookery terms as "reduction". Be careful that you do not reduce the liquid too far, or the little that remains will burn on the base of the pan.

PREPARATION
To make a twist of orange to garnish the carrots, cut a thin slice from the halved orange before you grate it. Cut through the orange slice to the center, then twist each half in opposite directions. Keep covered with plastic wrap until required.

● 100 calories per portion

Peperonata

SERVES 4

4 red or green peppers, seeded and
  cut into thin strips
2 tablespoons butter
2 tablespoons vegetable oil
1 onion, chopped
8 large tomatoes, peeled and
  chopped (see Preparation)
1 clove garlic, crushed
pinch of sugar
salt and freshly ground black pepper

1 Heat the butter in a saucepan with
the oil. Add the peppers and onion
and cook gently 5 minutes until the
onion is soft and lightly colored.
Cover the pan with a lid and
continue frying gently until the
peppers are soft.

2 Add the tomatoes, garlic, sugar
and salt and pepper to taste. Stir
gently.
3 Cover and simmer over a very
low heat, stirring from time to time,
25-30 minutes, or until the mixture
is soft and the tomato juices have
evaporated.
4 Spoon the mixture into a warmed
serving dish and either serve hot or
allow to cool and serve cold, but not
chilled.

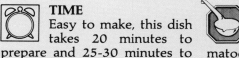

Cook's Notes

TIME
Easy to make, this dish
takes 20 minutes to
prepare and 25-30 minutes to
cook.

PREPARATION
It is important to peel
the tomatoes: put them
in a bowl, cover with boiling
water and leave 1 minute.
Remove with a slotted spoon,
plunge into a bowl of cold
water, then peel off the skins
with a sharp knife.

SERVING IDEAS
This versatile casserole
of peppers and to-
matoes can be served hot with
broiled meat or fish, or cold as a
side salad or starter.

DID YOU KNOW
This dish originates
from Italy, where
peppers and tomatoes grow in
abundance. An Italian cook
would use olive oil for frying.

● 150 calories per portion

Peas portugaise

SERVES 4

3 cups frozen peas
2 tablespoons vegetable oil
1 medium onion, finely chopped
1 clove garlic, crushed (optional)
2 teaspoons paprika
1 can (about 14 oz) tomatoes (see Variation)
1 teaspoon superfine sugar
celery salt and freshly ground black pepper

1 Heat the oil in a saucepan, add the onion and garlic, if using, and cook over moderate heat 3-4 minutes, stirring occasionally, until the onion is soft but not colored. Stir in the paprika and cook a further 2 minutes, then stir in the tomatoes with their juice, the sugar, celery salt and pepper to taste. Bring to a boil, lower the heat and simmer, uncovered, for about 10 minutes or until the tomato sauce is reduced to a thick purée.

2 Meanwhile, cook the peas in a small quantity of boiling salted water, according to package directions. Drain well.

3 Turn the peas into a warmed serving dish. Taste and adjust the seasoning of the tomato sauce, then spoon it over the peas and fork through lightly so that the sauce can run through the peas to flavor them. Serve the peas at once, while very hot.

Cook's Notes

TIME
Total preparation and cooking time is 15-20 minutes.

COOK'S TIP
The tomato sauce can be made separately and used with other vegetables.

SERVING IDEAS
The dish may be garnished with small points of toasted or fried bread.

VARIATION
When tomatoes are cheap and plentiful, use 1 lb fresh tomatoes instead of canned.

FREEZING
The tomato sauce can be frozen in a rigid container or plastic bag for up to 2 months. To serve: Reheat from frozen in a heavy-based saucepan, stirring frequently.

● 145 calories per portion

Baked potatoes with apple

SERVES 4

**4 large potatoes, about ½ lb each
(see Buying guide)**
½ medium green apple
2 tablespoons butter or margarine
1 large onion, finely chopped
**4 sage leaves, chopped, or 1
teaspoon dried sage**
½ teaspoon dry mustard
salt
butter, for greasing

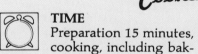
TIME
Preparation 15 minutes, cooking, including baking potatoes, 1¾ hours.

SERVING IDEAS
These potatoes are especially good served with pork or ham.

For a snack meal, top each potato with ¼ cup of grated Cheddar cheese and broil under moderate heat until the cheese is golden brown.

BUYING GUIDE
Idaho or russet potatoes are best for baking.

CHILDREN
The apple-baked potatoes would make a nutritious light meal for children. As young children might find the flavor of sage and mustard too strong, it would be advisable to omit these ingredients.

● 280 calories per portion

1 Preheat the oven to 400°.
2 Scrub the potatoes and with a fork prick each one in 2 places on both sides. Bake the potatoes in the oven 1½ hours.
3 Remove the potatoes from the oven (leaving the oven on), allow to cool slightly, then cut each one in half lengthwise. Scoop the cooked potato into a bowl, leaving the shells intact. Mash the potato well.

Pare, core and finely chop the apple.
4 Melt the butter in a small skillet add the onion and cook gently until it begins to soften, stirring occasionally. Stir in the apple and cook a further 2-3 minutes, until soft.
5 Stir the apple and onion mixture into the mashed potato. Add the sage, mustard and a little salt. Mix thoroughly.

6 Spoon the mixture back into the potato shells and make criss-cross patterns on the top with a fork for a decorative finish.
7 Put the potato shells in a greased shallow ovenproof dish and return to the oven. Bake 15 minutes until the tops are browned. Serve piping hot. Alternatively, top the potatoes with grated cheese (see Serving ideas).

Cabbage and lemon sauce

SERVES 4-6
1 large green cabbage, finely sliced
salt

SAUCE
4 teaspoons butter or margarine
1½ tablespoons all-purpose
flour
1¼ cups warm milk
grated rind and juice of 1 large
lemon
freshly grated nutmeg
freshly ground black pepper
lemon slices and 2 teaspoons chives,
to garnish (see Variations)

1 Bring a saucepan of salted water to a boil.
2 Meanwhile, make the sauce: Melt the butter in a separate saucepan, sprinkle in the flour and stir over a low heat 1-2 minutes until straw-colored. Remove from the heat and gradually stir in the milk. Return to heat; or simmer, stirring, until thickened and smooth.
3 Plunge the cabbage into the boiling water and boil gently 5 minutes, stirring frequently.
4 Stir the lemon rind and juice into the sauce, then season to taste with nutmeg, and plenty of salt and pepper (see Cook's tip).
5 Drain the cabbage well, then return to the rinsed-out pan. Pour in the sauce, then toss over gentle heat until the cabbage is lightly coated in the sauce. [!]
6 Turn into a warmed serving dish. Garnish with the lemon slices and chives and serve at once.

Cook's Notes

TIME
Preparation 10 minutes, cooking 10 minutes.

COOK'S TIP
The sauce needs plenty of salt to bring out the lemon flavor.

WATCHPOINT
It is essential that the cabbage is tossed quickly in the sauce, so that it still has a "bite" to it. Do not overcook it at this stage, or the finished dish will be soggy.

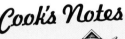

VARIATIONS
If chives are not available, use finely chopped scallion tops instead. Or use fresh tarragon if available.

SERVING IDEAS
The lemon sauce makes this a delicious accompaniment to poached, broiled or fried white fish.
It is also good with a joint of roast lamb or broiled lamb chops or cutlets.

● 125 calories per portion

Snow peas with water chestnuts

SERVES 4

½ lb snow peas (see Buying guide)
2 tablespoons vegetable oil
4 scallions, cut into 2-inch lengths
1 can (about 8 oz) water chestnuts, drained and sliced
2 tablespoons soy sauce
½ teaspoon sugar
4 tablespoons chicken broth
salt and freshly ground black pepper

1 Top and tail the snow peas and, if necessary, remove any strings from the pod sides.
2 Heat the oil in a wok or a large skillet, add the scallions, snow peas and water chestnuts and stir until the vegetables are coated with oil.
3 Add the soy sauce, sugar and chicken broth and stir-fry over moderate heat about 5 minutes, stirring constantly, until the vegetables are hot but still crisp.
4 Season to taste with salt and pepper, turn into a warmed serving dish and serve at once.

Cook's Notes

TIME
15 minutes preparation and cooking.

SERVING IDEAS
Serve as part of a Chinese meal with a beef dish or crispy roast duck.

BUYING GUIDE
Snow peas tend to be quite expensive, but are well worth buying occasionally for their delicate flavor.
If fresh snow peas are not available, buy them frozen from freezer centers.

VARIATION
Use about 1 cup sliced mushrooms instead of the water chestnuts.

● 100 calories per portion

Brussels sprouts country style

SERVES 4
1½ lb Brussels sprouts
salt
1 tablespoon vegetable oil
1 large onion, sliced
1 green pepper, seeded and chopped
1 lb tomatoes
½ teaspoon dried basil
freshly ground black pepper

1 Trim the sprouts. Wash them thoroughly and cut a cross in the base of each one.
2 Cook the sprouts in boiling salted water until just tender (about 10-12 minutes). [!] Drain well.
3 Meanwhile, heat the oil in a skillet over moderate heat. Fry the onion and green pepper until the pepper is soft and the onion brown.
4 Peel the tomatoes and chop them roughly (see Preparation).
5 Add the sprouts, tomatoes and basil to the pan and heat through. Season well with black pepper and serve immediately.

Cook's Notes

TIME
Preparation of vegetables will take 20 minutes. Cook Brussels sprouts and soften onion and peppers 10-15 minutes. Heat through about 10 minutes.

WATCHPOINT
Never overcook sprouts or they will color and become soggy.

SERVING IDEAS
Serve with any savory dish, from an omelet to a roast.
To turn Brussels sprouts country style into a supper dish, add slices of bacon to the onion and pepper mixture.

SPECIAL OCCASION
Add ½ cup dairy sour cream to the Brussels sprouts country-style. Stir in well before serving.

● 95 calories per portion

PREPARATION
Tomatoes can be peeled easily as shown below.

1 *Cover the tomatoes with boiling water and leave 1 minute, then plunge into cold water.*

2 *Remove with a fork and use a sharp knife to take away the skin which will peel off easily.*

Creamed onions

SERVES 4-6
1½ lb onions
salt
⅔ cup dairy sour cream
freshly ground black pepper
paprika
2 tablespoons butter or margarine
4 tablespoons day-old white bread
    crumbs (see Cook's tip)
1 tablespoon chopped fresh parsley
2 hard-cooked eggs
parsley, to garnish

Cook's Notes

TIME
Preparation takes 30-40 minutes, cooking in the oven 15 minutes.

COOK'S TIP
Use day-old, not absolutely fresh, bread crumbs to ensure that they cook crisply.

PREPARATION
Use a serrated knife to slice the onions — they tend to be slippery.

WATCHPOINT
Watch the bread crumbs carefully, since they brown very easily.

SERVING IDEAS
Serve with lamb, instead of onion sauce.

ECONOMY
For a slightly less expensive version, use white sauce instead of cream.

● 215 calories per portion

1 Cook the onions in boiling salted water 15-20 minutes. Drain them thoroughly, reserving 1 tablespoon of the cooking liquid. Leave the onions to cool slightly, then pat them dry with paper towels.

2 Preheat the oven to 350°.

3 Put the onions on a board and slice them (see Preparation). Arrange the sliced onions in an ovenproof dish.

4 Beat dairy sour cream with the reserved onion liquid and season with salt, pepper and paprika to taste. Pour the cream over the onions in the dish.

5 Melt the butter in a small skillet, add the bread crumbs and cook about 5 minutes over moderate heat, stirring frequently, until they are golden and crisp. [!]

6 Remove the pan from the heat and stir in the parsley. Chop 1 hard-cooked egg and stir it into the fried crumb mixture. Spoon the mixture evenly over the onions.

7 Bake in the oven 15 minutes. Meanwhile, slice the remaining hard-cooked egg.

8 Arrange the egg slices in a row along the top of the dish. Sprinkle with paprika, garnish with parsley and serve at once.

Farmhouse lentils

SERVES 4

1 cup split red lentils
1 tablespoon vegetable oil
1 large onion, thinly sliced
3¾ cups chicken broth
1 lb potatoes, cut into even-sized
   chunks
4 tomatoes, peeled, quartered and
   seeded
½ teaspoon dried marjoram or
   thyme
½ teaspoon paprika
salt and freshly ground black
   pepper
¾ cup frozen peas
1 cup thinly sliced small mushrooms

1 Heat the oil in a large saucepan, add the onion and cook over moderate heat about 3-4 minutes, stirring occasionally.
2 Add the broth to the pan and bring to a boil. Add the lentils, potatoes, tomatoes, herbs, paprika and salt and pepper to taste. Stir well then cover and simmer 20 minutes, stirring occasionally. !
3 Add the frozen peas and mushrooms to the pan, cover and simmer a further 5-10 minutes, stirring occasionally, until the lentils are soft and the potatoes are cooked.
4 To serve: Taste and adjust seasoning, then transfer to a warmed shallow dish. Serve hot.

Cook's Notes

TIME
Preparation 10 minutes, cooking 30-45 minutes.

WATCHPOINT
It is important to stir the simmering mixture from time to time, to prevent it sticking to the base of the pan as it cooks.

SERVING IDEAS
This dish would go very well with bacon or ham, or plump sausages — especially herb-flavored ones.

 ●355 calories per portion

Green beans
provençal

SERVES 4
**1 package (about ¾ lb) frozen green
  beans**
1 tablespoon vegetable oil
1 medium onion, chopped
1 large clove garlic, crushed
½ lb tomatoes, peeled and chopped
1 teaspoon dried basil
**salt and freshly ground black
  pepper**

1 Heat the oil in a heavy-based saucepan. Add the onion and garlic and cook gently 10-15 minutes, or until the onion is soft.

2 Add the tomatoes, plus the basil

—— *Cook's Notes* ——

TIME
Total preparation and cooking, 30 minutes.

VARIATIONS
Use fresh green beans in season, or perhaps fresh zucchini.

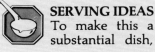

SERVING IDEAS
To make this a more substantial dish, place

the cooked mixture in a buttered ovenproof dish, top with a mixture of ¾ cup of grated Cheddar cheese and 1 cup fresh bread crumbs, then place on a high shelf in a hot oven 425° for 15-20 minutes until the top is well browned. Serve hot for a light lunch or supper dish.

● 65 calories per portion

and salt and pepper to taste, then simmer over moderate heat, uncovered, 10 minutes, stirring occasionally.

3 Meanwhile, cook the beans according to package directions in

boiling salted water until they are tender but still crisp to the bite. Drain thoroughly.

4 Stir the beans into the tomato mixture, then taste and adjust seasoning. Serve hot.

New potatoes with wine

SERVES 4

1½ lb new potatoes, scrubbed
2 tablespoons butter
½ small can anchovies, drained, soaked in milk for 20 minutes, then drained and chopped
1 tablespoon finely chopped fresh mint, chives or parsley
salt and freshly ground black pepper
⅔ cup dry white wine
1 tablespoon finely grated Parmesan cheese

1 Preheat the oven to 375° and grease a shallow ovenproof dish with half of the butter.
2 Bring the potatoes to a boil in salted water, lower the heat and cook 12-15 minutes or until barely tender. Drain and leave until cool enough to handle.
3 Slice the potatoes into the prepared dish, sprinkling each layer with anchovies, mint, chives or parsley and salt and pepper to taste.
4 Pour the wine over the top, then sprinkle evenly with Parmesan cheese and then finally dot the potatoes with the remaining butter.
5 Bake above center of the oven for about 30 minutes or until the potatoes are cooked through and the top is crisp and golden brown. Serve at once, straight from the dish (see Serving ideas).

Cook's Notes

TIME
This dish only takes about 1 hour to make.

ECONOMY
Cook the potatoes in this style when the oven is already in use for other dishes, for example, when roasting meat or poultry (see Serving ideas) or baking.

WATCHPOINT
Anchovies are salty, so only a very light seasoning of salt is necessary.

SERVING IDEAS
A deliciously different way of cooking new potatoes, this dish can be served as a light meal with crisply broiled bacon or topped with poached eggs, or as an unusual and tasty vegetable accompaniment to roast meat and poultry.

Because this dish includes anchovies, it is also particularly suitable for serving with a main course of fish.

● 220 calories per portion

SPICY VEGETABLES

Curried cauliflower salad

SERVES 4
1 medium cauliflower, broken into bite-sized flowerets
2 medium dessert apples
2 medium carrots, coarsely grated
½ cup golden raisins

DRESSING
1 tablespoon vegetable oil
10 scallions, trimmed and finely chopped
2 teaspoons hot curry powder
6 tablespoons mayonnaise
1 tablespoon lemon juice
salt and freshly ground black pepper

1 To make the dressing: Heat the oil in a skillet, add scallions and cook over gentle heat until they begin to brown. Stir in the curry powder and cook 1-2 minutes, then remove from the heat and leave to cool slightly. Stir in the mayonnaise and lemon juice, then season to taste with salt and pepper.

2 Plunge the cauliflower into a saucepan of boiling salted water, then blanch by boiling 2 minutes (see Cook's tip). Drain and immediately refresh under cold running water. Drain the cauliflower flowerets thoroughly again, then put them into a large bowl.

3 Core and dice the apples, but do not pare them. Add to the cauliflower with the carrots and raisins, then fold gently to mix, being careful not to break up the cauliflower. Add the dressing and gently toss the vegetables in it, turning them over lightly with a fork, to coat them evenly.

4 Pile the salad into a serving bowl. Cover tightly with plastic wrap and chill the salad in the refrigerator for at least 2 hours. Remove the salad from the refrigerator 10 minutes before serving.

Cook's Notes

TIME
Preparation, including making the dressing, takes 30 minutes. Allow at least 2 hours for chilling the salad.

SERVING IDEAS
This is a versatile salad which can be served with any cold meal, or as part of a buffet. It would make a tasty part of an hors d'oeuvre selection, or it could be served on its own as an appetizer.

VARIATION
Use 1 medium onion, finely chopped, if scallions are not available.

COOK'S TIP
Blanching the cauliflower slightly lessens its strong flavor, and flowerets remain quite crisp. However, if you want a very crunchy salad, use the cauliflower raw.

● 280 calories per portion

Spicy potato sticks

SERVES
1 lb even-sized potatoes
salt
2 cloves garlic, crushed
1 small onion, finely chopped
1 teaspoon ground cumin
1 teaspoon ground turmeric
½ teaspoon chili powder
2 tablespoons water
vegetable oil, for frying

1 Boil the potatoes in salted water 5 minutes. Drain in a strainer then rinse under cold running water until cool enough to handle. Pat dry on paper towels.

2 Cut the potatoes into ¼-inch thick slices, then cut each slice lengthwise into ⅛-inch wide sticks. Set aside.

3 Put the garlic with the onion, spices, 1 teaspoon salt and the water into a blender and blend until the mixture is very smooth.

4 Heat 1 tablespoon oil in a large skillet add the spice mixture and cook gently 5 minutes, stirring often. Remove from heat.

5 Fill a large heavy-based skillet to a depth of ½-inch with oil and heat until stale bread cube browns in 50 seconds.

6 Cook a batch of the potato sticks in the oil until golden. [!] Remove with a slotted spoon and drain on paper towels. Cook the rest.

7 While cooking the last batch, return the pan of spice mixture to low heat and heat through.

8 Add the potato sticks to the spice mixture and toss to coat well.

9 Turn the sticks into a warmed serving dish and serve at once.

Cook's Notes

 TIME
Preparation and cooking take about 20 minutes in total.

COOK'S TIP
This is a mildly spicy dish — for a hotter taste, increase the amount of chili powder slightly.

SERVING IDEAS
These tasty potato sticks are excellent for brightening up plain dishes such as roast or broiled chicken or lamb. Alternatively, they make a delicious addition to an Indian meal.

For a dash of color, garnish with fresh coriander sprigs.

WATCHPOINT
During cooking, move the potato sticks occasionally with a spatula to prevent them from sticking, but be very gentle or they will break up. There is no need to turn the sticks in this depth of oil.

● 195 calories per portion

Indonesian salads

SERVES 4
¼ lb beansprouts
1 can (about 8 oz) pineapple rings
    (see Buying guide)
3-inch length of cucumber,
    diced
1 dessert apple
juice of ½ lemon

SAUCE
2 tablespoons smooth peanut butter
2 teaspoons soy sauce
juice of ½ lemon

1 Divide the beansprouts between
4 serving plates.
2 Drain the pineapple, reserving
the juice, and chop finely. Put in a
bowl and set aside.
3 Make the sauce: Put the peanut
butter in a bowl and beat in the soy
sauce and lemon juice to form a
thick cream. Add about 2 tablespoons of the reserved pineapple
juice. Set aside.
4 Mix the cucumber into the
chopped pineapple. Core and dice
the apple, toss in the lemon juice
and add to the pineapple mixture.
Immediately divide this mixture
between the 4 plates, piling it onto
the beansprouts.
5 Pour the sauce over each salad
and serve at once.

Cook's Notes

TIME
This quickly prepared
dish only takes about
15 minutes to make.

BUYING GUIDE
If you are watching
your weight, look out
for pineapple rings in natural
fruit juice. These do not have
any added sugar and so the
calorie count will be lower.

SERVING IDEAS
Serve this tasty and re-
freshing salad as a appe-
tizer or as an accompaniment.

● 85 calories per portion

Okra
Mediterranean-style

SERVES 4

1 lb okra (see Buying guide and
    Preparation)
4 tablespoons vegetable oil
1 large onion, chopped
1 lb tomatoes, peeled and quartered
1 clove garlic, crushed
1 teaspoon ground coriander
salt and freshly ground black
    pepper
coriander leaves, to garnish

1 Heat the oil in a large saucepan,
add onion and cook 5 minutes.
2 Add the okra to the pan, stir to
coat well with the oil, then add the
tomatoes, garlic and coriander. Stir
well to mix, then season to taste.
3 Bring to a boil, then lower the
heat slightly, cover and simmer 30
minutes until okra is tender. Serve
garnished with coriander.

Cook's Notes

 TIME
Preparation and cook-
ing take about 40 min-
utes in total.

 SERVING IDEAS
This dish is a natural accompaniment to broiled
lamb chops or kabobs. It is also
delicious served with either
plain boiled or fried rice as a
main course.

 BUYING GUIDE
Okra can be bought at
Asian, Greek and West
Indian food shops, as well as
specialty food stores and large
supermarkets.

Canned okra is also available
and may be used in this recipe,
but the flavor and texture will
not be as good.

● 165 calories per portion

PREPARATION
To prepare the okra for
this dish:

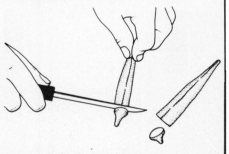

*Cut ends off the okra and remove
any blemishes with a sharp knife. It
is not necessary to pare the okra
before they are cooked.*

VARIATION
Replace the fresh toma-
toes with 1 can (about
14 oz) tomatoes, but use only
half the canned juice, otherwise
the dish will be watery.

Noodles Chinese-style

SERVES 4

¼ lb Chinese egg noodles (see Buying guide)

salt

2 tablespoons vegetable oil

6 scallions, sliced

1 tablespoon grated fresh root ginger

1 lb Chinese cabbage, cut into ½-inch thick slices

½ cup chopped lean cooked ham (see Economy)

¼ lb beansprouts

1 tablespoon soy sauce (see Buying guide)

4 tablespoons chicken broth, dry sherry or water

freshly ground black pepper

1 Bring a large saucepan of salted water to a boil. Add the noodles bring back to a boil and cook about 3 minutes or according to package directions, until just tender. Drain and set aside.

Cook's Notes

TIME
10 minutes preparation, 10 minutes cooking.

ECONOMY
Any left-over lean cooked meat can be substituted for the ham.

SERVING IDEAS
This Chinese-style dish is particularly good served as a vegetable accompaniment to broiled or fried fish, chops or chicken.

To serve as a quick, economical light lunch or supper dish, double the quantities. If liked, add extra ingredients such as sliced mushrooms or cooked peeled shrimp.

BUYING GUIDE
Thin Chinese egg noodles are available at supermarkets and specialty stores, but if difficult to obtain, Italian spaghetti or egg noodles can be used instead. These will need longer initial cooking in water — follow package directions.

Some supermarkets may have a choice of soy sauces — choose the lighter type for this dish.

● 230 calories per portion

2 Heat the oil in a wok or large skillet add the scallions and ginger and cook gently 2 minutes, stirring constantly.

3 Add the Chinese cabbage to pan with the chopped ham. Cook a further 2 minutes, stirring the mixture constantly.

4 Add the drained noodles, together with the beansprouts, soy sauce, broth and salt and pepper to taste. Increase the heat to moderate and stir-fry about 5 minutes until the vegetables are tender but still crisp and most of the liquid in the pan has evaporated.

5 Taste and adjust seasoning. Turn into a warmed serving dish.

Stir-fried beans and beansprouts

SERVES 4

½ lb small French beans, left whole
 (see Buying guide)
2 tablespoons vegetable oil
1 onion, sliced
4 tablespoons water
1 tablespoon light soy sauce
1 tablespoon lemon juice
salt and freshly ground black pepper
½ cup sliced mushrooms (see
 Buying guide)
½ lb beansprouts

1 Heat the oil in a wok or large heavy-based pan. Cook the onion 2 minutes, then add the beans and stir-fry 1 minute.

2 Add the water, soy sauce, lemon juice and season to taste with salt and pepper. Cook 5 minutes, tossing the beans in the liquid until it has evaporated.

3 Add the mushrooms and stir constantly until they are tender. Add beansprouts and stir-fry a further 2 minutes until the beansprouts are heated through and just tender, but still crisp. Transfer to a warmed serving dish and serve at once (see Serving ideas).

Cook's Notes

TIME
Preparation time is 5 minutes and cooking time about 10 minutes.

SERVING IDEAS
This crunchy dish makes an excellent accompaniment to roast or broiled meats, particularly steaks and chops.

BUYING GUIDE
Small, thin French beans are best for stir-frying and they will give the crunchiest result.
Choose small mushrooms for this recipe — they make an attractive addition and will give the dish a lighter color.

● 85 calories per portion

Chinese lettuce parcels

SERVES 6
6 large crisp lettuce leaves (see Preparation)
2 tablespoons vegetable oil
4 scallions, finely chopped
1 teaspoon ground ginger
1 celery stalk, finely chopped
¾ cup finely chopped mushrooms
2 oz canned water chestnuts, drained and finely sliced
1 cup cooked long-grain rice
¾ cup frozen peas, cooked and drained
1½ tablespoons soy sauce
1 egg, beaten
extra soy sauce, to serve

1 Heat the oil in a wok or large skillet. Add the scallions and ginger and cook gently 2-3 minutes until soft.
2 Add the celery, mushrooms and water chestnuts and cook a further 5 minutes.
3 Stir in the rice, peas and soy sauce. Remove the pan from the heat and stir in the egg.
4 Lay the lettuce leaves out flat on a work surface. Put about 2 generous tablespoons of the mixture at the base of each lettuce leaf. Fold the leaf around the mixture and roll up to form neat parcels. Secure with toothpicks, if necessary.
5 Place the parcels in a steamer. If you do not have a steamer, use a metal strainer which fits neatly inside a saucepan (the base must not touch the water). Fill the pan with boiling water, place the parcels in the strainer and place the strainer in the pan. Cover with foil or lid of steamer and steam 5 minutes.
6 Remove the toothpicks from the parcels, if using, then place the parcels on a warmed serving dish. Serve at once, with extra soy sauce handed separately.

Cauliflower creole

SERVES 4
1 cauliflower
1 tablespoon vegetable oil
1 large onion, chopped
1 clove garlic, crushed (optional)
1 can (about 14 oz) tomatoes
salt
2 tablespoons butter or margarine
1 large green pepper, seeded and
    chopped
½-1 teaspoon hot-pepper sauce
freshly ground black pepper

1 Heat the oil in a large saucepan, add the onion and garlic, if using, and cook 2-3 minutes until just tender.
2 Stir in the tomatoes, breaking them up against the sides of the pan with a wooden spoon. Cover and simmer gently 20-30 minutes.
3 Meanwhile, bring a pan of salted water to boil, plunge the cauliflower head down in it and cook about 20 minutes ⚠ until just tender. Preheat the oven to 250°. Drain the cauliflower well, place on a warmed serving dish and keep hot in the oven.
4 Add the butter and green pepper to the tomato sauce, stir well and simmer 5 minutes. Season to taste with hot-pepper sauce and salt and pepper.
5 Pour a little of the sauce over the cauliflower, leaving some of the white flower showing. Pour the remaining sauce round the sides.

Cook's Notes

TIME
Preparation takes 10 minutes, cooking about 35 minutes.

VARIATION
Add a little Worcestershire sauce instead of hot-pepper, for a different, less hot flavor.

SERVING IDEAS
Serve the cauliflower with plainly cooked but not too bland meat: it would go well with fried liver and bacon.

WATCHPOINT
It is important not to overcook the cauliflower: it should be just tender. Cooking time will vary according to size.

DID YOU KNOW
Hot-pepper sauce is a sauce that is made of spirit vinegar, red pepper and salt. Use sparingly to give a piquant flavor — too much would prove very fiery.

● 115 calories per portion

DON LAST

Sweet and sour Brussels sprouts

SERVES 4

1¼ lb fresh Brussels sprouts (see Buying guide), or 1 package (1 lb) frozen sprouts
¼ cup butter or margarine
1 medium onion, finely chopped
2 dessert apples
2 tablespoons seedless raisins
3 tablespoons lemon juice (see Cook's tip)
3 tablespoons clear honey
salt and freshly ground black pepper

1 Cook the sprouts in boiling salted water about 10-15 minutes until just tender. If using frozen sprouts cook according to package directions.
2 Meanwhile, melt the butter in a saucepan, add the onion and cook gently until soft but not colored. Pare, core and chop the apples fairly coarsely, then add to the onion with the raisins and stir well. Season well with salt and pepper.
3 Mix together the lemon juice and honey and pour into a pitcher.
4 When the sprouts are cooked, drain well, add to onion mixture and stir well to mix. Transfer to a serving bowl, pour over the sauce and serve.

Cook's Notes

TIME
Total preparation and cooking time, if using fresh sprouts, is 25 minutes.

VARIATIONS
Broccoli may be substituted for Brussels sprouts and any crisp dessert apple such as a Granny Smith, Jonathan or Red Delicious may be used.

COOK'S TIP

The average lemon yields 2 tablespoons of juice, so for this recipe you will need 1½ lemons.

BUYING GUIDE
When buying Brussels sprouts, choose ones which are small, compact and a good green color with no signs of yellowing. If buying sprouts packed in a package from a supermarket, make sure there are no signs of mold on them.

SERVING IDEAS
You can serve this unusual dish of Brussels sprouts in place of ordinary boiled sprouts with roast or broiled meats.

● 190 calories per portion

Oriental vegetable fritters

SERVES 4

1 large cauliflower, broken into bite-sized flowerets
2 bunches large scallions, trimmed and halved lengthwise
1 lb carrots, halved lengthwise and cut into 2½-inch lengths
vegetable oil, for deep-frying

BATTER

1 cup all-purpose flour
¼ teaspoon baking soda
¼ teaspoon salt
¼ teaspoon ground ginger
1 egg yolk
¾ cup cold water

DIPPING SAUCE

3 tablespoons tomato paste
1½ tablespoons soy sauce
1½ tablespoons clear honey
4 tablespoons chicken broth

1 Make the dipping sauce: Stir together the ingredients for the sauce, then divide the mixture between 4 custard cups or small dishes. Set aside.

2 Make the batter: Sift the flour, baking soda, salt and ginger into a bowl. Beat the egg yolk with the cold water and gradually add to the flour, stirring with a wooden spoon, to make a smooth thin batter.

3 Preheat the oven to 250°. Heat the oil in a deep-fat frier to 375° or until a cube of bread browns in about 50 seconds.

4 Dip the vegetable pieces a few at a time into the batter. Transfer them to the hot oil with a slotted spoon and deep-fry for about 3 minutes or until golden brown, turning once with the spoon. Remove from the pan with the slotted spoon and drain well on paper towels. [!] Arrange on a warmed large serving platter and keep warm in the oven while frying the remaining vegetables pieces in the same way.

5 Serve the fritters as soon as they are all cooked: Provide each person with a bowl of sauce so that they can dip their vegetables into it.

Cook's Notes

TIME
10-15 minutes preparation, then 30-40 minutes cooking.

WATCHPOINT
Use plenty of paper towels to drain the fritters, so that they are not excessively oily.

VARIATIONS
Delicious alternatives are thickly sliced zucchini, wide strips of green and red pepper, eggplant slices, whole small mushrooms and whole or halved French beans.

DID YOU KNOW
These fritters are a version of the Japanese tempura – vegetables deep fried in a batter. Tempura batter is different from other fritter batters because it contains no oil or butter and must be used immediately.

• 400 calories per portion

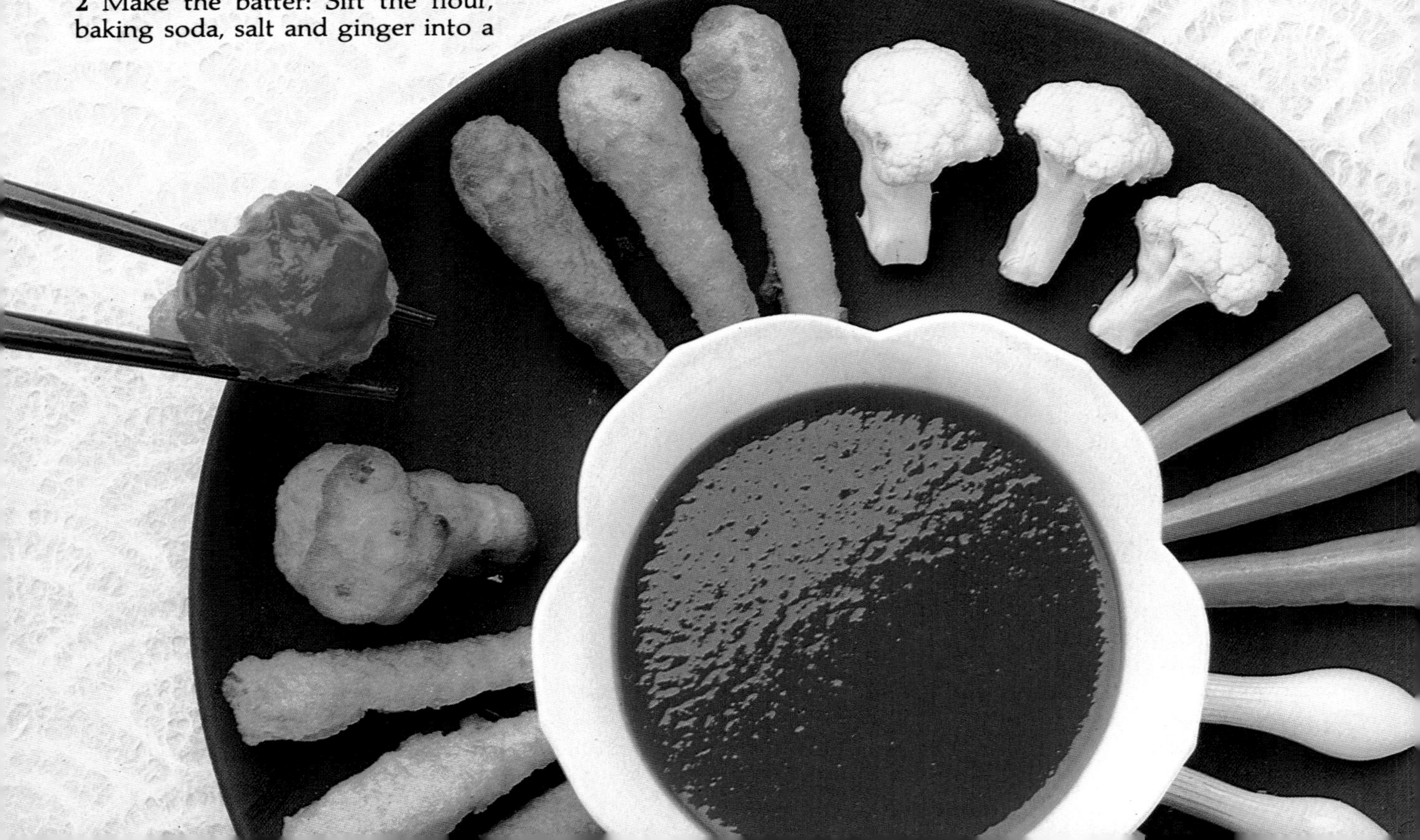

Vegetable biriani

SERVES 4-6
2 tablespoons vegetable oil
1 large onion, chopped
2 cloves garlic, crushed (optional)
2 teaspoons hot curry powder
½ teaspoon ground cinnamon
½ teaspoon ground ginger
2 cups water
1 tablespoon tomato paste
1 large carrot, diced
2 teaspoons salt
1 cup long-grain rice
½ cup seedless raisins
½ lb sliced runner or French beans, fresh or frozen
1 cup frozen peas

1 Heat the oil in a large saucepan. Add the onion and garlic, if using, and cook gently about 10 minutes until the onion is soft but not browned, stirring frequently.

TIME
Preparation and cooking take about 45 minutes.

WATCHPOINT
Try not to lift the lid of the pan during the cooking and do not stir unless absolutely necessary: this way the rice will be tender and fluffy. Heat must be low at this stage.

COOK'S TIP
If using frozen beans, cook them straight from the freezer, without thawing.

DID YOU KNOW
Biriani is an Indian rice dish usually served as an accompaniment to a main-course curry, although sometimes it has meat, fish or poultry added to it and is served with a curry sauce, in which case it becomes a main course in its own right. If you like the flavor of curry, you can serve this biriani as a vegetable accompaniment to any main-course meat or fish dish.

● 365 calories per portion

2 Add the spices to the pan, stir well and cook a further 2 minutes.
3 Add the water, tomato paste, carrot and salt. Bring to a boil.
4 Add the rice, raisins and fresh or frozen beans, and stir well (see Cook's tip).
5 Lower the heat, cover the pan tightly and simmer very gently 20 minutes, without stirring. ☐
6 Gently fork in the frozen peas, cover the pan and simmer very gently a further 5 minutes. Taste and adjust seasoning. Pile the biriani into a warmed serving dish and serve hot.

Sambols

SERVES 5-6
½ lb tomatoes, peeled and
   chopped
2 tablespoons coconut milk, water
   and desiccated coconut
1 green chili, seeded and sliced
1 large onion, sliced
juice of ½ lemon (see Cook's tip)
salt
½ cucumber, thinly sliced
⅔ cup shredded coconut
2 tablespoons hot water
pinch of chili powder

1 Make the tomato sambol: Put the
tomatoes into a bowl and stir in half
the coconut milk, half the chili and
one-third of the onion. Mix well,
then add ½ teaspoon lemon juice
and season to taste with salt.

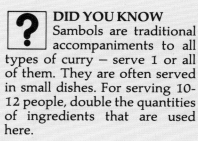
2 Make the cucumber sambol:
Arrange the cucumber slices in a
shallow dish and sprinkle with salt.
Leave for 30 minutes.
3 Meanwhile, make the coconut
sambol: Put coconut in bowl,
pour over hot water and leave 15
minutes. Stir in chili powder, one
third of onion and ½ teaspoon

lemon juice. Season with salt.
4 Rinse and pat the cucumber dry
and transfer to a bowl. Mix in the
remaining coconut milk, lemon
juice and almost all remaining green
chili and onion. Season with salt.
5 Transfer sambols to individual
dishes; garnish with onion and chili
rings and more chili powder.

PARTY COOKING

Entertaining family and friends can be fun; but it can also involve a great deal of time and expense. But it need not be so, "Party Cooking" shows you how entertaining can be economic and fun for the busy cook. There is a full three-course menu for each meal with detailed planners on when to prepare each course. Each meal is attractively illustrated in full color so that you can see the finished effect. Menus have been planned with an international flair – treat your friends to a Mexican evening, for example. Those special occasions like a romantic Valentine's dinner for two or entertaining friends at a New Year's party are also catered for. A more formal cocktail party menu is also included, as are special birthday and party meals just for the kids.

If you really need to cook to a strict budget or are in a hurry, several menus on this theme have been included – try the *Cheap and cheerful supper* or the *Meal in under an hour*.

MEXICAN EVENING

Throw an exciting buffet party centered around two savory dishes that are made with tortillas, the famous Mexican crêpes: Chicken enchiladas and Beef tacos. Start with a tequila cocktail, and finish with a pineapple pudding to complete the exotic flavor.

Flour tortillas

MAKES 12
2 cups all-purpose flour
1 teaspoon salt
1 teaspoon baking powder
1 tablespoon shortening, diced
¾ cup water

1 Sift the flour, salt and baking powder into a bowl. Add the fat and cut it slowly and carefully into the flour until the mixture resembles fine bread crumbs. Mix in the water to form a stiff dough.

2 Divide the dough into 12 pieces and shape into balls. Roll each ball out thinly on a lightly floured surface to form 4-inch rounds.

3 Put an ungreased heavy-based skillet over moderate heat until hot, then add a dough round and cook 2 minutes on each side until lightly flecked with brown. Wrap tortilla in a dish towel. ⚠

4 Fry remaining rounds adding them to the dish towel as they are cooked (see Cook's tip).

Chicken enchiladas

SERVES 6
12 warm tortillas
1 lb boneless cooked chicken, shredded (see Buying guide)
vegetable oil, for frying
½ cup grated Parmesan cheese

SAUCE
1 can (about 4 oz) jalapeño peppers, (see Buying guide)
1 small onion, roughly chopped
1 can (about 14 oz) tomatoes
2 tablespoons vegetable oil
1 large egg
1 cup heavy cream
salt
about 2 tablespoons chicken broth

1 Make the sauce: Rinse the peppers under cold running water, pat dry, then chop roughly. Purée the peppers, onion and tomatoes in their juice in a blender until smooth.

2 Heat the oil in a skillet, add the purée and cook over moderate heat, stirring constantly 3 minutes. Remove pan from the heat.

3 Beat the egg with cream, and salt to taste.

4 Gradually stir the cream mixture into the cooked purée. Return the pan to low heat and cook, stirring, 1 minute. If sauce is too thick, thin slightly with chicken broth. Remove from heat; set aside.

5 Put the shredded chicken into a bowl and stir in 2-3 tablespoons of the sauce to moisten it. Set aside.

6 Preheat the oven to 350°.

7 Fill a heavy-based skillet with oil to a depth of ½-inch and heat over moderate heat. When the oil is sizzling, add a tortilla and fry for a few seconds on each side. Lift out with tongs and dip into the sauce, which should still be warm.

8 Place the sauce-coated tortilla in a shallow ovenproof dish, about 12 × 8 inches. Put a spoonful of the chicken mixture onto the tortilla, then fold in half.

9 Cook, dip and fill the remaining tortillas in same way, arranging them neatly in the dish. Pour over the remaining sauce, then sprinkle with cheese.

10 Bake 20 minutes.

Beef tacos

SERVES 6
12 warm tortillas

BEEF FILLING
1 lb lean ground beef
2 tablespoons vegetable oil
1 onion, finely chopped
1 clove garlic, crushed
1 can (about 8 oz) tomatoes
2 teaspoons chili powder
½ teaspoon ground cumin
½ teaspoon dried oregano
salt

1 Make the beef filling: Heat the oil in a skillet, add the onion and cook gently 5 minutes until soft and lightly colored. Add the garlic and continue to cook about a further 2 minutes.

2 Add the beef and cook briskly, stirring with a wooden spoon to remove lumps, about 5 minutes until the meat is evenly browned.

3 Stir in the tomatoes with their juice, the chili powder, cumin, oregano and salt to taste. Bring to a boil, then lower the heat and simmer, stirring, about 20 minutes until the meat is cooked.

4 To serve: spoon a little beef filling into the tortilla, then fold over and eat with your fingers (see Serving ideas).

Cook's Notes

Flour tortillas

TIME
The tortillas take 1 hour to make in total.

WATCHPOINT
Keep the tortillas warm in a dish towel, so that they remain soft and pliable and do not crack when folded.

COOK'S TIP
These tortillas can be made up to 45 minutes in advance: wrap them, still in the dish towel, in foil and keep warm in an oven heated to 225°.

DID YOU KNOW
Tortillas of this type are very popular in northern Mexico where they are known as *Tortillas de harina del norte*. The other kind of tortillas famous to Mexico use a special flour, *masa harina*, which is made from boiled maize. Traditionally they are cooked on an ungreased griddle called a *comal*.

● 80 calories per tortilla

Chicken enchiladas

TIME
About 1 hour to prepare and cook.

BUYING GUIDE
2 lb cooked chicken yields about 1 lb meat. Jalapeño peppers are sold in larger supermarkets.

● 580 calories per portion

Beef tacos

TIME
The beef filling takes 35 minutes to make.

SERVING IDEAS
Provide side bowls of shredded lettuce, grated cheese, guacamole (avocado dip), finely chopped onion and bottled taco sauce or any other hot chili sauce. Each person can then add a little of each to the beef filling before folding.
    As an appetizer, serve tortilla chips, if wished, to dip into the taco sauce.

● 340 calories per portion

Acapulco pineapple pudding

SERVES 6

½ lb pound or white cake
3 tablespoons apricot jelly
1¼ cups dairy sour cream
½ cup slivered almonds,
  toasted

PINEAPPLE SAUCE
1 can (about 13 oz) crushed
  pineapple
¾ cup sugar
½ cup ground almonds
4 egg yolks, lightly beaten
generous pinch of ground cinnamon
½ cup dry sherry

1 Make the sauce: Put the pineapple with its juice in a saucepan with the sugar, almonds, egg yolks, cinnamon and half the sherry. Stir with a wooden spoon until the ingredients are well mixed.

2 Place the pan over very low heat and cook, stirring constantly, about 5 minutes or until the sauce has thickened. Set aside to cool about 15 minutes.

3 Meanwhile, split the cake into three layers, then spread cut cake into fingers with the apricot jelly.

4 Arrange half the sponge cakes, jelly side up, in a glass serving dish large enough to hold the cakes in a single layer.

5 Sprinkle with half the remaining sherry, then spread half the pineapple sauce over the top. Repeat these layers once more, using the remaining sponges, sherry and sauce. Refrigerate 2-3 hours.

6 Remove the pudding from the refrigerator and spread dairy sour cream over the top. Sprinkle the surface with the toasted almonds and serve at once.

CHINESE MEAL

For an exotic change, try making a Chinese meal – it will provide an interesting break from the more usual diet and eating traditions. The ginger-flavored fried shrimp appetizer has to be eaten with the fingers to be enjoyed, while the glazed pork is fun to eat with chopsticks. The meal ends on a light refreshing note with delicately flavored fruit salad.

Gingered deep-fried shrimp

SERVES 6
1 lb large shrimp
(see Buying guide)
vegetable oil, for frying

BATTER
½ cup all-purpose flour
¼ teaspoon salt
1 egg
⅔ cup water
1 teaspoon chopped root ginger
¼ teaspoon freshly ground black
pepper

1 Peel the shrimp, then make a shallow cut down the center back of each shrimp and gently scrape away the black vein with the point of a knife. Rinse well, then pat dry.
2 Make the batter: Sift the flour with the salt into a bowl and make a well in the center. Beat the egg with the water, pour into the well and, using a wire whisk, gradually draw the flour into the liquid. When all the flour is incorporated, beat well, then beat in the ginger and pepper.
3 Fill a skillet with oil to a depth of ¾-inch and put over moderate heat. When the oil is on the point of smoking, dip a few shrimp in the batter: coat well with batter, then drop into the hot oil.
4 Cook the shrimp for 1 minute on each side, until the batter turns golden brown. Transfer with a slotted spoon to a serving platter; keep hot while cooking the rest.
5 Serve hot, accompanied by dips (see Serving ideas).

Marinated roast pork

SERVES 6
3 lb pork tenderloin, cut into 6-inch
lengths
3 tablespoons sunflower or
groundnut oil
3 tablespoons honey
shredded lettuce, to garnish

MARINADE
5 tablespoons soy sauce
3 tablespoons medium-dry sherry
1½ tablespoons brown sugar
2 cloves garlic, crushed
½ teaspoon freshly ground black
pepper
½ teaspoon salt
½ teaspoon mixed dried sage and
thyme
¼ teaspoon ground cinnamon

1 Place the pork lengths in a single layer in a deep dish.
2 Make the marinade: Beat the marinade ingredients together until thoroughly combined.
3 Pour the marinade over the pork and leave to marinate at least 2½ hours, turning occasionally.
4 Preheat the oven to 425°. Remove the pork from the marinade with a slotted spoon, reserving the marinade. Place the pork on a rack in a roasting pan.
5 Roast the pork in the oven 15 minutes, then remove from the oven and reduce the oven temperature to 350°. Brush the pork with the reserved marinade and the oil to coat thoroughly, then return to the oven a further 10 minutes.

6 Just before the end of the cooking time, warm the honey in a small pan over low heat. Remove the pork from the oven, brush with the warmed honey, then return to the oven to roast a further 5 minutes.
7 Cut the pork crosswise into ¼-inch thick slices. Serve hot, garnished with shredded lettuce.

Fried rice

SERVES 6
2¼ cups long-grain rice, boiled
5 tablespoons vegetable oil
1 large onion, chopped
⅓ cup frozen peas
½ green pepper, seeded and diced
1 cup shredded lettuce
1 tablespoon soy sauce
salt and freshly ground black
pepper

1 Heat 3 tablespoons of the oil in a large skillet, add the onion and cook gently 5 minutes until soft and lightly colored.
2 Add the peas, green pepper and lettuce, stir 1 minute, then push to the side of the pan.
3 Pour the remaining oil into the center of the pan, heat gently, then add the rice and cook 1 minute, stirring. Draw the vegetables from the sides of the pan into the rice and stir together.
4 Stir in the soy sauce, then add salt and pepper to taste. Remove the pan from the heat and continue to stir for a further minute off the heat. Transfer to a warmed dish.

Cook's Notes

Gingered deep-fried shrimp

TIME
Preparation and cooking take 30 minutes.

BUYING GUIDE
The king-sized shrimp suitable for this dish may be fresh or frozen (thaw before peeling), and can be of various species. Shrimp deteriorate quickly so use as soon as thawed.

SERVING IDEAS
Spicy dips are an essential accompaniment to the prawns: for *Soy-tomato dip*, mix together equal quantities of tomato catsup and soy sauce. To spice it up, add a dash of chili sauce.
For *Soy-mustard dip*, mix 1 part English mustard with 2 parts soy sauce.

● 105 calories per portion

Marinated roast pork

TIME
2½ hours marinating, 30 minutes cooking.

● 420 calories per portion

Fried rice

TIME
20 minutes for boiling rice, then 15 minutes.

● 330 calories per portion

Oriental fruit salad

SERVES 6
1 small honeydew
  melon
1 can (about 11 oz) mandarins,
  drained
¼ cup medium-dry
  sherry
1 can (about 1 lb) lychees

1 Cut the melon in half and scoop out the pits. Cut the flesh into balls using a melon baller, then put in a glass bowl.
2 Add the drained mandarins and sherry to the melon, then pour the lychees, together with their juice, into the bowl.
3 Stir the fruit gently, cover and refrigerate 2 hours before serving.

Cook's Notes

TIME
This delicately-flavored fruit salad only takes 15 minutes preparation, plus chilling time.

VARIATION
Use fresh mandarins and lychees when in season and substitute the canned lychee juice with a sugar syrup: Dissolve ¼ cup sugar in ⅔ cup water, add the sherry, then boil the syrup mixture for 2-3 minutes. Leave the syrup to cool completely before mixing with the fruit.

The sherry in the salad may be replaced by dry white wine, or, for added zing, by an orange liqueur, such as Cointreau.

● 110 calories per portion

COUNTDOWN
In the afternoon
●Marinate the pork for the Marinated roast pork.
●Boil the rice for the Fried rice.
●Make the Oriental fruit salad and refrigerate.
1½ hours before
●Prepare the vegetables for the Fried rice.
●Peel the shrimp and refrigerate.
●Make the accompanying dips for the Gingered deep-fried shrimp.
45 minutes before
●Heat the oven.
●Make the batter for the shrimp.
30 minutes before
●Start roasting the pork.
●Fry the shrimp; keep hot.
15 minutes before
●Reduce the oven temperature, baste the pork and continue to roast.
●Make the Fried rice.
5 minutes before
●Baste the pork with honey; continue to roast. Slice before serving.

CARIBBEAN-STYLE DINNER

The colorful atmosphere of the Caribbean is captured in this exciting menu for six. The flavors that are the very essence of West Indian cookery feature strongly in every dish, and the choice of three sensational cocktails really makes the meal!

Piña colada

MAKES 6 LONG DRINKS
3 cups unsweetened pineapple juice
1¼ cups canned coconut cream (see Buying guide)
1½ cups white or golden rum
plenty of crushed ice

1 Quarter fill a pitcher with ice, add one-third of the ingredients and mix briskly. Or blend for 2-4 seconds in a blender.

2 Pour into 2 chilled glasses and serve at once. Mix up 2 more batches with the remaining ingredients.

Caribbean blues

MAKES 6 SHORT DRINKS
1½ cups vodka
⅓ cup blue Curaçao
⅓ cup dry vermouth
plenty of crushed ice, to serve

1 Put all the ingredients, except the ice, in a large pitcher and mix well.
2 Fill 6 chilled cocktail glasses with crushed ice, pour the cocktail over the ice and serve at once.

Planter's punch

MAKES 6 LONG DRINKS
1½ cups dark rum
¾ cup lemon juice
4 teaspoons grenadine
1¼ cups orange juice
1¼ cups pineapple juice
few dashes of Angostura bitters
plenty of crushed ice, to serve

TO GARNISH
6 orange slices
6 lemon slices
6 cocktail cherries

1 Put all the ingredients, except the ice, in a large pitcher and stir well.
2 Fill 6 large glasses with crushed ice and pour the punch over the ice. Garnish each glass with an orange and lemon slice and a cherry.

Piña colada

TIME
20 minutes preparation in total.

BUYING GUIDE
Canned coconut cream is available in some large supermarkets, but if you find it difficult to obtain, use a 6 oz block creamed coconut and dissolve it in about 1¼ cups hot water. Creamed coconut is available from most supermarkets, and shops specializing in Indian food.

? DID YOU KNOW
The name piña colada means soaked pineapple in Spanish.

● 365 calories per glass

Caribbean blues

TIME
5-10 minutes preparation in total.

COOK'S TIP
To make crushed ice: Crush ice cubes in a strong blender or in a food processor. If you do not have either, place the ice in a strong plastic bag, squeeze out the air and tie firmly. Place the bag on a folded dish towel and beat with a rolling pin until the ice is reduced to fragments.

● 160 calories per glass

Planter's punch

TIME
5 minutes preparation in total.

● 170 calories per glass

West Indian fish patties

SERVES 6
½ lb cod fillets
1 tablespoon wine vinegar
1¼ cups cold water
1 tablespoon vegetable oil
½ small onion, chopped
¼ red pepper, seeded and chopped
2 tablespoons chopped parsley
2 tablespoons canned chopped
　tomatoes
juice of ½ lemon
3 dashes hot-pepper sauce
salt and freshly ground black
　pepper
1½ sheets (¾ of 17 oz package)
　frozen puff pastry, thawed
1 egg white, lightly beaten

1 Put the fish in a heavy pan with the vinegar and water, bring just to a boil, then lower the heat slightly and simmer gently 10 minutes.
2 Drain the fish and, when cool enough to handle, skin, bone and flake the flesh.
3 Heat the oil in a pan, add the onion and cook gently 5 minutes until soft and lightly colored. Add the red pepper and parsley and cook a further 5 minutes.
4 Add the flaked fish, together with tomatoes, lemon juice, pepper sauce, salt and a generous sprinkling of pepper. Simmer, uncovered, stirring occasionally, a further 10-12 minutes until most of the liquid has evaporated. Transfer to a bowl, taste, adjust seasoning and leave to cool.
5 Roll out the pastry: the large sheet to a 16 × 8 inch rectangle and the small sheet to an 8 inch square.
6 Preheat the oven to 425°.
7 Cut the pastry into twelve 4-inch squares. Place a portion of the fish mixture in the center of each square, then lightly dampen the pastry edges with cold water and fold each square into a triangle. Press the edges together, then crimp with a fork to seal well.
8 Arrange the patties well apart on 2 cookie sheets and brush the surfaces with egg white, then prick each patty with a fork 2-3 times. Bake in the oven about 20 minutes until golden brown.

Pork roast with rum

SERVES 6
4½ lb pork loin on the bone
1 teaspoon salt
1 teaspoon ground ginger
½ teaspoon freshly ground
　black pepper
½ teaspoon ground cloves
3 cloves garlic, crushed
3 bay leaves
2½ cups chicken broth
¾ cup dark rum
⅔ cup firmly packed light brown
　sugar
4 tablespoons lime juice
1 tablespoon all-purpose flour

1 Using a very sharp knife, score the skin of the pork fairly deeply, almost through to the fat, in a diamond pattern.
2 Preheat oven to 325°.
3 Pound the salt, ginger, pepper, cloves and garlic to a paste in a mortar and pestle. Rub the paste well into the scored surface of the pork; place bay leaves on top.
4 Pour about ⅔ cup of the broth into a roasting pan, together with one-third of the rum. Put the meat, skin-side up, on a rack in the pan and roast in the oven 1 hour.
5 Meanwhile, mix the brown sugar, lime juice and remaining rum in a bowl.
6 Remove the meat from the oven and baste with the sugar and lime mixture. Return the meat to the

oven and continue to roast a further 1¼ hours. Add more broth to the pan during this time, if the liquid appears to be drying out.

7 Transfer the meat to a warmed serving platter and discard the bay leaves. Keep the meat hot.

8 Pour off the liquid from the roasting pan into a jug, skim off the excess fat and return 1 tablespoon to the roasting pan Place the pan on top of the cooker and sprinkle in the flour. Stir over low heat 1 minute, then stir in the remaining broth and the reserved cooking liquid. Simmer, stirring constantly, until the sauce has thickened. Season to taste with salt and pepper, transfer to a warmed sauceboat and hand separately.

Coconut soufflé

SERVES 6

1½ cups canned coconut cream (see Buying guide)
6 eggs, separated
⅓ cup superfine sugar
1½ envelopes unflavored gelatin
4 tablespoons cold water
2 limes (see Preparation)
1 cup unsweetened shredded coconut

1 Put the coconut cream into a pan and gently bring almost to simmering point. Remove from the heat and set aside.
2 Put the egg yolks and sugar in a heatproof bowl that will fit over a pan of water. Beat together until thick and pale, then stir in the warmed coconut cream until thoroughly mixed in.
3 Set the bowl over a pan of barely simmering water and cook, stirring constantly, about 10 minutes until the mixture is smooth and slightly thickened. Remove the bowl from the heat.
4 Sprinkle the gelatin over the water in a heatproof bowl. Leave to soak 5 minutes until spongy, then stand the bowl in the pan of gently simmering water 1-2 minutes, stirring occasionally, until the gelatin has dissolved.
5 Beat the gelatin into the coconut cream mixture, together with the lime rind and most of the shredded coconut. Allow the mixture to cool about 30 minutes.
6 Meanwhile, secure a paper collar carefully around an 3¾-4 cup capacity soufflé dish.

7 In a spotlessly clean dry bowl, beat the egg whites until they stand in stiff peaks, then fold into the cooled coconut cream mixture. Transfer to the prepared soufflé dish and refrigerate at least 3 hours
8 Meanwhile, brown the remaining shredded coconut: put the coconut on a foil-covered broiler pan and toast under a fairly hot broiler 2 minutes, turning constantly, until evenly browned.
9 Carefully remove the paper collar from the soufflé, then, using a spatula, press the toasted coconut onto the sides. Decorate the top with lime slices.

Cook's Notes

TIME
Preparation takes 1 hour, plus 30 minutes cooling and at least 3 hours chilling.

BUYING GUIDE
If canned coconut cream is difficult to obtain, use 4½ oz block creamed coconut dissolved in about 1 cup hot water.

PREPARATION
Finely grate the rind from 1½ limes, then cut the remaining half into very thin slices for decorating.

● 680 calories per portion

FRENCH DINNER PARTY

Style and elegance are the hallmarks of French cookery, and here is a superb menu that captures these qualities. The three distinguished dishes include mouthwatering Garlic mushrooms, Dijon lamb noisettes in a gloriously creamy sauce and a fruity Currant sherbet — a selection of dishes that any French chef would be proud to serve. Bon appétit!

The day before
● Make the Currant sherbet.
In the morning
● Prepare the Garlic mushrooms.
1 hour before
● Start the Dijon lamb noisettes.
40 minutes before
● Put the lamb dish in the oven.
20 minutes before
● Fry the Garlic mushrooms.
Just before the main course
● Remove the Currant sherbet from the refrigerator to soften.
● Make the mustard sauce, pour over the lamb and shallots.

Garlic mushrooms

SERVES 4
24 cup-shaped mushrooms (see Buying guide)
½ cup sweet butter, softened
2 cloves garlic, crushed
1 tablespoon finely chopped fresh tarragon, or 1½ teaspoons dried tarragon
finely grated rind of ½ lemon
freshly ground black pepper
2 eggs
¾ cup dried white bread crumbs
vegetable oil, for deep-frying
lemon wedges, to garnish

1 Carefully remove the mushroom stems and then chop up the stems finely.
2 Beat the butter with the mushroom stems, garlic, tarragon, lemon rind and pepper to taste, then spoon into the cavities of the mushroom caps. Sandwich the mushrooms together in pairs and secure with toothpicks.
3 Lightly beat the eggs in a bowl and spread the bread crumbs out on a plate. Dip each mushroom pair, first in the egg, then roll in the bread crumbs. Repeat once more, then refrigerate at least 1 hour.
4 Heat the oil in a deep-fat frier to 375° or until a stale bread cube browns in 50 seconds. Cook a few of the mushrooms about 5 minutes until golden brown. Drain on paper towels and keep hot in the oven while frying the rest.
5 To serve: Remove the toothpicks and serve at once.

Dijon lamb noisettes

SERVES 4
4 boneless lamb chops, each about 1½-inches thick
2 tablespoons vegetable oil
1 tablespoon butter
12 baby white onions
½ cup white wine
salt and freshly ground black pepper
bouquet garni
2 egg yolks
⅔ cup heavy cream
about 2 tablespoons Dijon-style mustard (see Buying guide)
1 bunch fresh herbs, to garnish (optional)

1 Preheat the oven to 375°.
2 Form the chops into neat rounds and secure with string.
3 Heat the oil and butter in a large skillet, add the lamb and cook briskly about 2 minutes on each side until browned. Transfer the lamb to a small roasting pan.
4 Add the onions to the fat remaining in the pan and cook gently 10 minutes until browned. Transfer to a lamb pan with a slotted spoon.
5 Pour the wine into the pan and bring to a boil, scraping up all the sediment from the base of the pan. Season to taste with salt and pepper, then pour over the lamb. Add the bouquet garni, cover with foil or a lid and bake in oven for 1 hour.
6 In a bowl, mix together the egg yolks, cream and 2 tablespoons of the mustard. Set aside.
7 Using a slotted spoon, transfer the cooked lamb and the onions to a serving dish and keep warm.
8 Discard the bouquet garni and strain the cooking liquid into a small, heavy-based saucepan. Boil briskly until the liquid is reduced by about half.
9 Pour a little of the hot cooking liquid into the egg yolk mixture, stirring vigorously all the time, then pour this mixture back into the pan. Heat through, stirring constantly, until thick and on the point of boiling. ☐! Taste and adjust the seasoning, if necessary.
10 To serve: Pour over lamb and garnish with herbs, if liked.

Garlic mushrooms

TIME
About 45 minutes preparation, plus at least 1 hour chilling, then about 20 minutes cooking.

BUYING GUIDE
Buy the medium-sized cultivated mushrooms for this recipe, rather than the small or large, flat open varieties. The mushrooms must have cups deep enough to hold the filling.

● 380 calories per portion

Dijon lamb noisettes
TIME
Preparation takes about 30 minutes. Total cooking time is about 1 hour 10 minutes.

WATCHPOINT
Do not let the sauce boil or it may curdle and the mustard will turn bitter.

BUYING GUIDE
Dijon mustard, from the area of Burgundy south east of Paris, is available at most good supermarkets and specialty stores. Made from brown mustard seeds, it is a smooth mustard with a distinctive flavor. Dijon is also available with green peppercorns added — *moutarde au poivre vert*. Or, use a herb mustard based on Dijon mustard.

SERVING IDEAS
Serve with plainly boiled potatoes tossed in chopped parsley, if liked, plus broccoli or snow peas. For a really authentic flavor, serve a light, red French wine to complement the food — a Bordeaux wine (claret) would be the perfect choice.

If wished, follow the French custom of serving a tossed green salad or selection of cheese after the main course.

● 660 calories per portion

Currant sherbet

SERVES 4
½ lb fresh or frozen currants,
    without stems
½ cup sugar
1¼ cups water, plus
    2 tablespoons
2 teaspoons lemon juice
½ teaspoon unflavored gelatin
1 egg white

1 Put the sugar and the ½ cup water in a heavy-based pan and heat gently until the sugar has dissolved. Boil 10 minutes until syrupy, then remove from the heat and set aside to cool.

2 Put the currants in a pan with the lemon juice and heat gently about 10 minutes until softened. Allow to cool slightly, then purée in a blender. Press the puréed currants through a sieve into a bowl to remove seeds and skin.

3 Sprinkle the gelatin over the 2 tablespoons water in a heatproof bowl and leave to soak 5 minutes until spongy. Stand the bowl in a pan of gently simmering water and heat gently 1-2 minutes stirring occasionally until the gelatin has dissolved. Stir the gelatin into the cooled sugar syrup.

4 Stir the sugar syrup into the currant purée and mix well. Turn into a rigid container and freeze, uncovered, (see Cook's tip) about 3 hours until the mixture is firm around the edges.

5 Remove the currant mixture from the freezer and break up with a fork. Beat the egg white until it stands in stiff peaks, then fold into the currant mixture. ❄ Cover and freeze overnight, until solid.

6 To serve: Stand at room temperature about 30 minutes until the sherbet is soft enough to scoop into individual glasses.

SANGRIA EVENING

Conjure up an exotic, festive atmosphere at any time of year with a Sangria party. The delicious wine cup Sangria is a perfect accompaniment to food with a Spanish flavor — crunchy raw vegetables with a creamy dip. The Mediterranean Chicken catalan, and Spanish caramel custards with the sunny taste of orange.

To help create the informal atmosphere typical of a meal eaten in Spain, hand round the crudités before you and your guests sit down at the dinner table.

Sangria

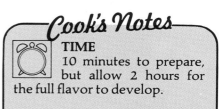

SERVES 6
1½ quarts sweet red Spanish wine
5 fresh peaches, thinly sliced, or 1 can (about 14 oz) sliced peaches, drained
juice of 1 lemon
4 tablespoons brandy (optional)
1 dessert apple
1 lemon
2½ cups soda water
ice cubes

1 Put the peaches in a pitcher or glass bowl. Add the wine, lemon juice and brandy and allow to soak about 2 hours.
2 Just before serving, slice the apple and lemon thinly and add to pitcher with soda water and ice cubes.

Cook's Notes

TIME
10 minutes to prepare, but allow 2 hours for the full flavor to develop.

● 240 calories per portion

Crudités and dip

CRUDITES

SERVES 6
6 carrots
6 celery stalks
6 small or 3 large tomatoes
½ cucumber
8 radishes (optional)
1 small cauliflower

1 Top and tail, wash and pare the carrots. Cut into thin sticks.
2 Wash celery and cut into sticks.
3 Cut large tomatoes into quarters, leave small ones whole.
4 Cut the tails off the cucumber and pare it if you prefer. Divide into 2 both lengthwise and widthwise. Cut each piece into 4 long strips.
5 Wash, top and tail the radishes.
6 Wash, the cauliflower. Cut off the base then separate the head into flowerets.
7 Arrange the crudités in groups around the edge of a tray, shallow basket or dish, leaving room for the dip in the center.

COTTAGE CHEESE AND YOGHURT DIP

SERVES 6
1 cup cottage cheese
2 tablespoons plain yogurt
2 scallions or ½ onion
1 dill pickle, finely chopped
salt and freshly ground black pepper
dash hot-pepper sauce (optional)

1 Strain or blend the cottage cheese until smooth.
2 Add the yogurt and mix well.
3 Wash and trim the scallions. Chop finely and add to mixture.
4 Add finely chopped pickle.
5 Season to taste and add hot-pepper sauce, if using.
6 Give a final mixing. Transfer to a serving bowl and place in center of crudités.

Cook's Notes

TIME
Allow 45 minutes to prepare the vegetables and make the dip.

COOK'S TIP
Save time by preparing the dip in a blender. Blend all the ingredients except the onions and pickles. Add these at the end and switch on for about 2 seconds so that they are only partially chopped.

● 40 calories per portion

WATCHPOINT
If vegetables are prepared in advance store them in a plastic box or in the salad drawer of the refrigerator to avoid wilting.

VARIATIONS
Use different varieties of vegetables such as red or green peppers, raw small mushrooms or small French beans.

● 45 calories per portion

Chicken catalan

SERVES 6

6 small chicken breasts, skinned
6 tablespoons olive oil
3 medium onions, thinly sliced
2 cloves garlic, crushed
2 cups long-grain rice
1-2 tablespoons tomato paste
pinch of saffron threads (see Steps)
  or few drops of yellow food
  coloring
5 cups boiling chicken broth
1 teaspoon paprika
salt and freshly ground black pepper
¼ lb Spanish chorizo sausage or
  other firm garlic sausage
  (optional), cut into large chunks
1 green pepper, seeded and sliced
  into rings
1 red pepper, seeded and sliced into
  rings
¾ cup stuffed olives
chopped parsley, to garnish

1 Heat half the oil in a large flame-proof casserole. Cook the chicken breasts over moderate heat until golden brown in color and half cooked through (about 7 minutes each side).
2 Reserve chicken pieces and keep them warm.
3 Add 1 tablespoon more oil to the casserole. Cook the onions over low heat 2 minutes until transparent but not brown.
4 Add the garlic, the remaining oil and the rice. Stir for a few minutes with a wooden spoon until the rice starts to color.
5 Meanwhile, stir the tomato paste and coloring, if used, into the boiling broth.
6 Stir broth, with saffron liquid, if used, into the rice mixture, add paprika and salt and pepper to taste, then bring to a boil, stirring constantly.
7 Add the chicken to the casserole with the sausage and peppers, pressing them all well down into the rice.

8 Lower the heat, cover and simmer about 30 minutes or until the rice is just tender, stirring occasionally with a wooden spoon. Be careful not to overcook the rice so that it becomes mushy.
9 Add the olives to the rice and heat through for a few minutes. Taste and adjust seasoning.
10 Transfer to a large warmed serving dish. Sprinkle the chopped parsley over the top to garnish and serve at once.

Cook's Notes

TIME
10-15 minutes for preparation plus 1 hour cooking.

ECONOMY
Chicken breasts are meaty and convenient to use, because they are sold boned or partially boned, but they do tend to be rather expensive. Ordinary chicken pieces are not so expensive as breasts, and they can be used just as well but will need to be cooked for about 10 minutes on each side in stage 1. (You could even buy a whole chicken and joint it yourself.) If you prefer not to have awkward-looking bones in the finished dish, it is quite simple to remove the bones before the chicken is cooked.

DID YOU KNOW
Saffron is an immensely popular spice in Spain where it is used for coloring rice (it has hardly any taste). It was introduced to the Spaniards by the Arabs, and has for centuries been used as a coloring agent, especially in Arab and Eastern cooking. It is used in this recipe to give the rice a bright, golden-yellow color, but as it is so expensive, we have suggested yellow food coloring as a cheaper alternative. If you have ground turmeric this can also be used, but it has a more distinctive flavor than saffron. Saffron threads and turmeric are available from delicatessens, good supermarkets and specialty food stores.

BUYING GUIDE
Spanish chorizo sausages can be obtained at most good delicatessens, and are easily recognizable by their bright red appearance. They are made from pure pork flavored with pimiento (hot red pepper), and so are hot and spicy. If you find them difficult to obtain, use any continental-type cured sausage with a spicy flavor.

● 605 calories per portion

 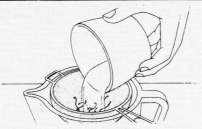 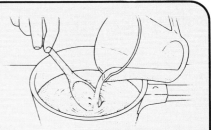

Spanish caramel custards

SERVES 6

CUSTARD
1 orange
2½ cups milk
4 eggs
⅓ cup superfine sugar

CARAMEL
6 tablespoons granulated sugar
6 tablespoons water

1 Preheat the oven to 300°.
2 Wash and dry the orange, then pare off rind with a vegetable parer.
3 Place the orange rind and milk in a saucepan and allow to infuse over low heat. This means bringing the milk to a boil slowly and allowing it to stand 10 minutes.
4 Beat the eggs and sugar together in a bowl and strain over the milk. Beat lightly to mix.
5 Half fill a roasting pan with warm water and place in the oven.
6 To make the caramel: Put the sugar and water in a saucepan. Heat slowly until the sugar has dissolved, then boil steadily without stirring until the sugar turns a pale golden brown. [!]
7 Pour caramel into individual custard cups or a 6-inch diameter soufflé dish. Leave about 2 minutes to set.
8 Remove roasting pan from the oven.
9 Strain the egg and milk mixture onto the caramel in the dishes and place in the roasting pan. Replace in the oven and cook until the custard is set — about 40 minutes to an hour.
10 Cool at least 3 hours, then chill in the refrigerator.
11 Remove the pith from the orange with a sharp knife and divide the flesh into sections.
12 Turn the custards onto a plate and arrange the orange sections on top or around the plate.

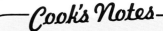

Cook's Notes

TIME
The custards take about 30 minutes to prepare and 1 hour to cook. Remember to allow at least 4 hours afterwards for the custards to cool and for chilling.

COOK'S TIP
Always use a heavy-based saucepan for making caramel as it will give an even spread of heat and help prevent burning.

WATCHPOINT
Do not take your eyes off the caramel once it begins to turn brown as it burns very easily.

● 215 calories per portion

MEDITERRANEAN MEAL

Transport your guests to the sunny shores of the Mediterranean with this continental-style menu. Small onion tarts provide a tempting appetizer, before the magnificent Provençal fish stew. And, to finish, sophisticated fruit salad captures all the sunshine flavor of the meal.

Genoese onion tarts

SERVES 6
1 sheet (½ of 17 oz package) frozen puff pastry, thawed
1 can (2 oz) anchovy fillets (see Preparation)
12 black olives, halved and pitted

FILLING
1 lb onions, finely chopped
2 tablespoons butter or margarine
1 tablespoon olive oil
4 fatty bacon slices, chopped
1 teaspoon dried mixed herbs
½ teaspoon Dijon-style mustard
1 egg, beaten
2 tablespoons milk
salt and freshly ground black pepper

1 Make the filling: Heat the butter and oil in a skillet, add the bacon and cook over moderate heat 7-8 minutes. Remove the bacon from the pan with a slotted spoon and set aside. Remove the pan from heat and cool 10 minutes.
2 Add the onions to the fat remaining in the pan and cook very gently 15 minutes until they are soft and lightly colored.
3 Preheat the oven to 425°.
4 Meanwhile, dampen 6 individual 3-inch tart pans. Roll out the pastry very thinly on a lightly floured surface and cut out 6 rounds with a 3½ inch plain cookie cutter. Use to line tart pans and then prick base of each pie shell with a fork.
5 Add the herbs to the onions in the pan, together with the mustard, egg and milk. Mix well together, then season with salt and pepper.
6 Divide the filling between the tart shells, spread evenly and garnish with a cross made of anchovy strips and 4 olive halves.
7 Bake in the oven for about 25-30 minutes until the pastry is crisp and the filling is browned on top. Remove the tarts from the oven then carefully transfer them to a platter and serve while still warm.

Provencal fish stew

SERVES 6
2-2½ lb mixed fish fillets, skinned and cut into 2 inch pieces (see Buying guide)
6 tablespoons olive oil
2 large cloves garlic, crushed
1 sprig fresh fennel
bouquet garni
1-2 strips orange rind
1¼ cups dry white wine
salt and freshly ground black pepper
2 onions, thinly sliced
2 celery stalks, sliced
4 tomatoes, peeled, seeded and chopped
2 tablespoons tomato paste
5 cups fish broth or water
pinch of ground saffron (optional)
⅔ cup peeled shrimp, thawed if frozen
few cooked mussels, shelled
6 slices French bread, to serve
chopped parsley, to garnish

ROUILLE SAUCE
1 slice bread, crusts removed, soaked in water
1 chili, seeded and chopped
3 cloves garlic, crushed
1 egg yolk
⅔ cup olive oil

1 Place the fish in a large dish. Add 2 tablespoons olive oil, the garlic, fennel, bouquet garni and orange rind, then pour in the wine. Season well with salt and pepper, cover and leave to marinate at room temperature about 1 hour, stirring occasionally.
2 Heat 2 tablespoons of the olive oil in a large, heavy-based skillet or flameproof casserole, then add the onions and celery and cook gently 5 minutes until onions are soft and lightly colored then stir in the chopped tomatoes and the tomato paste and cook a further 2 minutes, stirring constantly with a wooden spoon.
3 Drain the fish and add the marinade to the pan. Stir in the fish broth and sprinkle in the ground saffron, if using. Bring to a boil, then simmer 20 minutes.
4 Meanwhile make the sauce: Squeeze the bread dry and put it into a bowl with the chili, garlic, egg yolk and a pinch of salt. Beat together with a little of the oil until well blended. Gradually beat in the remaining oil and season to taste with salt and pepper. Transfer the sauce to a serving bowl, cover with plastic wrap and set aside until it is required.
5 Discard the fennel, bouquet garni and orange rind from the drained fish, then add the marinated fish pieces and any remaining juices to the pan. Bring to a boil and then simmer, uncovered, about 15 minutes.
6 Add the shrimp and mussels. Simmer a further 5 minutes or until the fish is still in pieces but flakes easily when it is tested with a fork.
7 Meanwhile, cook the French bread in the remaining 2 tablespoons of oil until crisp.
8 To serve: Taste the stew and adjust seasoning, if necessary. Transfer to large, individual soup plates, sprinkle with parsley and serve at once. Serve the fried French bread and rouille sauce separately (see Serving ideas).

Cook's Notes

Genoese onion tart

 TIME
35 minutes preparation;
25-30 minutes cooking.

 PREPARATION
Drain the anchovies
then soak in milk 20
minutes. Drain again and cut
into 12 even-sized strips.

● 280 calories per portion

Provençal fish stew

 TIME
Preparation 30 minutes
plus marinating; cook-
ing about 50 minutes.

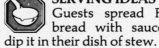 **SERVING IDEAS**
Guests spread French
bread with sauce and
dip it in their dish of stew.

● 570 calories per portion

 DID YOU KNOW
This is a simplified ver-
sion of the classic
Provençal fish stew known as
bouillabaisse. Rouille sauce is a
traditional accompaniment.

BUYING GUIDE
Buy as wide a variety of
fish as possible. Choose
from cod, halibut, whiting,
mackerel or flounder.

Riviera fruit salad

SERVES 6
2 cups heavy cream
4 teaspoons Strega liqueur (see Did
you know and Variations)
1 cup strawberries
2 bananas
2 dessert apples
1 cup green grapes, halved and
pitted

CARAMEL SAUCE
1 cup superfine sugar
8 tablespoons water

1 Make the caramel sauce: Put the superfine sugar in a heavy-based saucepan together with 2 tablespoons water. Heat very gently, until the sugar has dissolved. Bring to a boil and boil rapidly without stirring, until the syrup turns a rich caramel color. [!]
2 Remove from the heat and add the remaining water, 1 tablespoon at a time, taking care as it will splutter when the water is added to the very hot caramel. Stir well together, returning to the heat if necessary, until well blended. Set aside to cool about 2½ hours.
3 Beat the cream until standing in soft peaks, then fold in the liqueur (see Cook's tip). Divide between 6 individual shallow glass dishes, about 5 inches in diameter, and smooth over top with a knife. Cover and refrigerate at least 1-2 hours.
4 Just before serving, slice the strawberries, slice the bananas, then core and slice the apples. Arrange, with the grapes, in neat rows on top of the chilled cream and carefully coat with the caramel sauce. Serve the fruit salad at once.

Cook's Notes

TIME
45 minutes preparation, plus cooling the syrup and chilling the cream, then 10 minutes finishing the salad.

DID YOU KNOW
Strega is a sweet, citrus liqueur from Italy.

VARIATIONS
Use different varieties of fruit or liqueur to taste — apricot- or cherry-flavored liqueurs are both suitable.

COOK'S TIP
Sugar is not added to the cream — the caramel sauce sweetens the dish.

WATCHPOINT
It is important not to stir the syrup while it is boiling as this may crystallize the sugar. Watch the caramel carefully — if it is too dark, it will taste strong and rather bitter.

● 525 calories per portion

NEW YEAR'S PARTY

Celebrate New Year's Eve with a flourish. Start the evening with drinks accompanied by Finnan haddie tarts, then launch into a full-flavored Scotch beef casserole. End the meal in spirited style with Drambuie creams.

Finnan haddie tarts

MAKES 24 TARTS
13 oz Pie Crust Sticks
1¼ lb finnan haddie
1 teaspoon ground mace
2 bay leaves, crumbled
freshly grated nutmeg
freshly ground black pepper
milk
2 tablespoons butter
1 tablespoon all-purpose flour
1 egg yolk, beaten
salt and freshly ground black
    pepper
pinch of cayenne pepper
grated Parmesan cheese

1 Preheat the oven to 375°.
2 Roll out the pastry on a lightly floured surface and cut out 24 circles with a 3-inch fluted cookie cutter. Use to line 24 tart pans and prick the base of each with a fork.
3 Line shells with foil and weight down with baking beans. Bake blind in the oven 10-15 minutes. Remove the foil and beans and set aside to cool.
4 Meanwhile, put the finnan haddie in a large saucepan with the mace, bay leaves, and a generous sprinkling of nutmeg and black pepper. Add enough milk to cover the fish, then poach gently about 15 minutes or until it flakes easily with a fork.
5 Using a slotted spoon, transfer the fish to a plate, then strain the cooking liquid. Make up the cooking liquid to 1¼ cups with milk and reserve.
6 Remove the skin and bones from the fish, then transfer to a bowl and mash extremely thoroughly with a fork.
7 Melt the butter in a small saucepan, sprinkle in the flour and stir over a low heat 1-2 minutes until straw-colored. Remove from the heat and gradually stir in the reserved milky cooking liquid. Return to the heat and, stirring constantly, simmer until thick and smooth.
8 Add 1 beaten egg yolk and the mashed fish, stirring well to mix thoroughly. Taste and adjust seasoning, adding more salt, pepper and nutmeg if necessary.
9 Preheat the broiler to high. Carefully remove the tart shells from the pans, put on a large flameproof serving dish and divide the fish mixture between the shells. Sprinkle each one with a pinch of cayenne and a little Parmesan cheese.
10 Put under broiler 3-4 minutes until the cheese is melted and the tops of the tarts bubbly and golden. Serve at once.

Scotch beef casserole

SERVES 12
5 lb chuck steak, cut into 1 inch
    cubes (see Buying guide)
3 tablespoons olive oil
¼ cup butter
3 Bermuda onions, thinly sliced
2 tablespoons all-purpose flour
1½ lb tomatoes, peeled
2½ cups beef broth
salt and freshly ground black
    pepper
1 lb small mushrooms
1 tablespoon red currant jelly
2 teaspoons Dijon-style mustard

MARINADE
2½ cups medium red wine
3 tablespoons olive oil
3 cloves garlic, crushed
1 teaspoon juniper berries, crushed
3 bay leaves
2 sprigs fresh thyme, or ¾ teaspoon
    dried thyme
1 teaspoon ground caraway seeds

1 Mix the marinade ingredients together. Put the beef cubes in a large bowl and pour the marinade over them. Stir well to mix, then cover and marinate overnight.
2 Drain the meat, reserving the marinade. Remove the bay leaves and sprigs of thyme from the drained meat, then pat dry.
3 Heat the oil and butter in a large deep flameproof casserole. Add enough meat to cover the base of the pan and cook briskly 3-4 minutes until brown on all sides. Remove the meat with a slotted spoon, set aside. Cook remaining meat in batches.
4 Add the onions to the pan and cook gently 5 minutes until soft and lightly colored. Return the meat to the pan, sprinkle over the flour and cook, stirring, a further 5 minutes.
5 Add the tomatoes, broth and reserved marinade to the casserole with salt and pepper to taste. Bring to a boil, then lower the heat, cover and simmer 2-2½ hours.
6 Add the mushrooms to the casserole and simmer for 5 minutes.
7 Add the red currant jelly and mustard to the pan and simmer a further 10 minutes, stirring occasionally. Taste and adjust seasoning, if necessary. Serve hot.

COUNTDOWN
The day before
● Marinate meat for casserole.
In the morning
● Make and bake blind the tart shells for the Finnan haddie tarts.
● Toast the oatmeal for the creams.
3½ hours before
● Start cooking the casserole.
1 hour before
● Make the filling for the tarts.
30 minutes before
● Make the Drambuie creams.
15 minutes before
● Add mushrooms to casserole.
10 minutes before
● Complete the casserole.
● Fill the tarts and broil them.

Cook's Notes

Finnan haddie tarts

 TIME
30 minutes preparation,
50 minutes cooking.

● 100 calories per tart

Scotch beef casserole

TIME
30 minutes preparation,
plus 12 hours marinating, then 3-3½ hours cooking.

BUYING GUIDE
Chuck steak will give the best flavor to this dish, but any other type of beef will be quite adequate.

VARIATION
For a different, more "gamey", flavor, try using stewing venison. It is very rich so decrease the amount to 4½ lb.

SERVING IDEAS
Serve with generous helpings of mashed rutabagas mixed with mashed potatoes and butter and seasoned generously with freshly ground black pepper and salt — it is a delicious way to mop up the rich sauce of the casserole.

● 480 calories per portion

Drambuie creams

SERVES 12
4 cups heavy cream
½ cup fine oatmeal
½ cup confectioners' sugar
4 tablespoons Drambuie

1 Preheat broiler to moderate.
2 Spread the oatmeal out in a thin layer on a cookie sheet, and broil 3-4 minutes, turning once, until lightly toasted. Remove and leave to stand until completely cold.
3 Pour the cream into a large bowl and beat until it stands in soft peaks. [!]
4 Add the cold oatmeal, sugar and Drambuie and stir until thoroughly mixed.
5 Spoon into individual glasses or custard cups and chill in the refrigerator 30 minutes before serving.

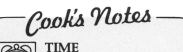

 TIME
8-10 minutes preparation, plus, cooling time and 30 minutes chilling.

! **WATCHPOINT**
Be careful not to beat the cream too stiffly otherwise the dessert may become too thick when the other ingredients are added.

 DID YOU KNOW
This is an unusual adaptation of the famous Scottish drink Atholl Brose, which is made from Scotch whisky, cream and oatmeal.

Drambuie is a famous Scottish liqueur, based on the finest Scotch whisky. The name Drambuie is derived from the Gaelic *an dram buideach:* "the drink that satisfies". The secret recipe is alleged to have been give to the Mackinnon family by Bonnie Prince Charlie in return for saving his life.

● 365 calories per portion

VALENTINE'S DINNER

Valentine's day is traditionally a day for romance, so this year why not whet the appetite with a delicious dinner just for two. The dishes chosen – avocados, stuffed trout and a creamy heart-shaped dessert – have a seductive delicacy about them that sets the tone for a romantic and very intimate evening.

Avocado special

SERVES 2
1 large ripe avocado
juice of ½ lemon
¼ cup thick-type mayonnaise
1 slice cooked ham, finely chopped
1 tablespoon chopped chives
¼ teaspoon Dijon-style mustard
salt and freshly ground black
    pepper

TO GARNISH
lettuce leaves
tomato flesh, cut into heart shapes
    (see Preparation)

1 Cut the avocado in half lengthwise and remove the seed. Scoop out the flesh with a teaspoon, leaving a thin lining of flesh on the inside of the shells.
2 Put the flesh in a bowl, sprinkle over the lemon juice, then beat until smooth. Add the mayonnaise, ham, chives and mustard, mix well and season to taste with salt and pepper.
3 Pile the mixture back into the avocado shells.
4 Line 2 individual plates with lettuce leaves, and arrange the filled avocados on the lined plates. Garnish the avocados with the tomato shapes and serve at once.

Trout with mushroom stuffing

SERVES 2
2 fresh or frozen trout, each
    weighing about 1 lb (see
    Preparation)
⅓ cup butter
1 small onion, finely chopped
2 cups finely chopped mushrooms
juice of ½ lemon
1 tablespoon chopped fresh parsley
½ cup fresh white bread crumbs
salt and freshly ground black
    pepper

TO GARNISH
sliced stuffed olives
parsley sprigs
4 lemon wedges

1 Preheat the oven to 375°.
2 Melt 2 tablespoons of butter in a skillet, add the onion and cook gently for about 5 minutes until soft and lightly colored.
3 Add the mushrooms to the onion with the lemon juice and cook gently 5 minutes until the mushrooms are soft and all the liquid has evaporated.
4 Remove the pan from the heat and stir in the parsley and bread crumbs. Season to taste with salt and pepper and allow to cool.

5 Fill each trout with mushroom stuffing, then close openings with 2-3 wooden toothpicks.
6 Put the remaining butter into a shallow ovenproof dish large enough to hold the trout side-by-side. Place the dish in the oven for a few minutes until the butter melts. Remove from the oven.
7 Place the stuffed trout in the dish and turn them in the melted butter until they are well coated. Sprinkle with salt and pepper to taste.
8 Bake the trout, uncovered, 25-30 minutes until the flesh flakes easily when tested with a fork. Baste frequently during cooking.
9 Transfer trout to a hot serving plate, remove the toothpicks and garnish attractively with sliced olives and parsley sprigs. Serve at once, with lemon wedges.

COUNTDOWN
The day before
● Make the *Coeurs à la crème* and refrigerate overnight.
1¾ hours before
● Fill the Trout with mushroom stuffing and make the garnishes.
1 hour before
● Sprinkle the soft fruit with sugar for *Coeurs.*
30 minutes before
● Preheat oven and put in trout.
● Prepare the Avocado special.
Just before the dessert
● Unmold *Coeurs* and decorate.

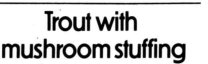

Cook's Notes

Avocado special
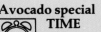
TIME
This appetizer takes 20 minutes to make.

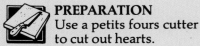
PREPARATION
Use a petits fours cutter to cut out hearts.

● 420 calories per portion

Trout with mushroom stuffing
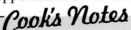
TIME
About 30 minutes preparation, and 25-30 minutes cooking.

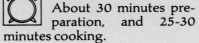
PREPARATION
Fresh trout should be gutted, rinsed under cold running water and patted inside and out with paper towels. Your fishmonger will gut them for you, if asked.

SERVING IDEAS
Serve with sauté potatoes and tender, young peas (*petits pois*).

● 605 calories per portion

Coeurs à la crème

SERVES 2
½ cup cream cheese
1 tablespoon superfine sugar
finely grated rind of ½ lemon
⅔ cup heavy cream
1 egg white
2 cups fresh or frozen small
    strawberries or raspberries
extra superfine sugar

1 Line 2 *coeurs à la crème* molds (see Buying guide) with large squares of wet cheesecloth. ⬚ Allow the cheesecloth to hang over the sides.
2 Pass the cream cheese through a nylon sieve into a bowl, add the sugar and lemon rind and beat well until very soft.
3 Beat 4 tablespoons of the cream until it forms soft peaks, then mix into the cheese mixture.
4 Beat the egg white in a clean, dry bowl until it stands in stiff peaks. Fold 1 tablespoon of the egg white into the cheese mixture to lighten it, then fold in the rest.
5 Spoon the cheese mixture into the prepared molds and smooth the

Cook's Notes

TIME
20 minutes to make, plus chilling overnight.

BUYING GUIDE
The tiny heart-shaped molds made especially for *Coeurs à la crème* can be bought from any good kitchen equipment store or china store. Each mold has a raised base, with small holes in it, to enable the cheese and cream mixture to drain during refrigeration.
    Alternatively, use custard cups — drain the mixture overnight in a strainer placed over a bowl, then spoon the mixture into the custard cups before serving the dessert.

WATCHPOINT
Make sure that the cheesecloth is wet when lining molds: this makes the job much easier and also helps prevent the cheese mixture from sticking.

COOK'S TIP
Use fresh fruit when possible in preference to frozen fruit when serving this dessert.

DID YOU KNOW
Literally translated, the title of this classic French dessert is heart of cream.

● 490 calories per portion

tops. Fold the overhanging pieces of cheesecloth over the cheese mixture to enclose it completely. Put the molds on a flat plate and refrigerate them overnight.
6 About 1 hour before serving, sprinkle the strawberries with sugar to sweeten.
7 To serve: Remove the molds from the refrigerator and unwrap the

tops. Place a small serving plate on top of each mold, then carefully invert the plate and mold together. Shake gently, unmold, then carefully remove the cheesecloth.
8 Decorate with some of the fruit then pour over the remaining unwhipped cream. Put the remaining fruit in the empty molds and serve separately.

EASTER WEEKEND

Pretty, colorful eggs, whether to eat or to exchange, and the family gathering for a leisurely weekend meal, are what make Easter such an enjoyable occasion. Attractively marbled cooked eggs will make breakfast a special treat and the festively decorated eggs, which can be made in advance, may be passed round later on. For the main meal, a fruity appetizer, stuffed lamb and a triumphant meringue-topped dessert will appeal to both young and old. So start preparing for a wonderful Easter.

Marbled eggs

SERVES 6
6 large eggs
2 teaspoons each of green, red and blue food colorings (see Watchpoints)
12 slices white or brown bread, crusts removed
butter, for spreading
2-3 tablespoons sesame seeds

1 Preheat the broiler to high.
2 Put 2 eggs in each of 3 small saucepans and cover the eggs with water. Add 2 teaspoons of one of the food colorings to each pan and stir well. Bring the water to a boil and boil the eggs 2 minutes.
3 Meanwhile, toast the bread slices on one side only. Remove from the broiler and butter the untoasted sides, then sprinkle generously with sesame seeds. Set aside.
4 Remove the eggs from the water with a slotted spoon and, holding them in an oven glove, gently tap the shells all over with the back of a teaspoon, until they are cracked and crazed. ⚠
5 Return the eggs to their pans, ⚠ bring back to a boil and boil for a further 1-2 minutes for soft eggs or 6-8 minutes for hard-cooked eggs.
6 Meanwhile, toast the sesame-coated sides of the bread until golden brown. Cut the toast into fingers or small points.
7 Drain the eggs and rinse under cold running water, then carefully remove the shells. Serve at once, with the sesame seed toast.

Chocolate eggs

MAKES 6
6 large eggs
24 squares (1½ lb) semisweet chocolate

DECORATIONS
a little lightly beaten egg white
about 1 cup confectioners' sugar, sifted
few drops of food coloring
sugar flowers or other decorations

1 Using a small skewer or a large darning needle, very carefully pierce a small hole in both ends of the eggshells. Enlarge one hole in each egg to about ¼ inch wide. Hold eggs over a bowl and blow out the contents through the larger of the holes.
2 Wash the eggs well in cold water, shaking out any remaining contents and put back in the egg box to drain and dry about 30 minutes.
3 Meanwhile, make a large and a small bag from greaseproof paper, without cutting off the ends.
4 When the eggshells are dry, place a small piece of sticky tape over each of the smaller holes.
5 Put the chocolate in a heatproof bowl over a pan of barely simmering water. Heat gently until melted, stirring occasionally, then pour into the large pastry bag.
6 Cut a small hole in the end of the bag and pipe the chocolate into the eggshells. Stand the eggs, sticky tape end downwards, back in the egg box. Allow the chocolate to settle for a few minutes, then top up with a little more chocolate, if necessary. Refrigerate the eggs in the box overnight until set.
7 When the eggs are set, crack them gently, then carefully peel off shells.
8 To decorate: Stand each egg in a glass. Add a little of the beaten egg white to the sugar and beat until the frosting forms stiff peaks, beating in more egg or sugar, if needed. Dot frosting onto the undersides of the decorations and fix in attractive designs to each egg (see Variations). Add a few drops of food coloring to remaining frosting, if liked, then use to fill the small pastry bag. Cut a small hole in the end and pipe leaves or other designs onto eggs.
9 Leave about 1 hour until set completely. Tie a small ribbon around each egg, fixing with a little frosting if necessary.

Cook's Notes

Marbled eggs
TIME
Preparing and cooking the eggs and toast take about 20 minutes.

⚠ **WATCHPOINTS**
It is very important to use only edible food colorings to tint the eggs.
Tap the shells very gently to avoid damaging the eggs.
Remember to put the eggs back in the same color water.

 VARIATIONS
Try creating your own designs on shells of hard-cooked eggs. Use eggs with pale shells and draw or paint on patterns or face with felt-tip pens, water or oil paints.
The eggs can also be boiled in food coloring to give color to the shell itself. To create patterns, cut out shapes from masking tape, stick them onto the eggs before boiling in colored water, then peel the tape away after boiling.

● 400 calories per serving

Chocolate eggs
TIME
Making the chocolate eggs takes about 40 minutes, plus setting overnight. Decorating the eggs takes about 30 minutes, plus setting time.

STORAGE
The decorated eggs can be made up to 1 week in advance, if stored in an airtight container in a cool dry place.

VARIATIONS
Here is a chance for the equipped cake decorator to be really creative. Use 2 cups confectioners' sugar and 1 large egg white to make frosting. Divide into bowls and add a few drops of food coloring to each. Using a petal tip, pipe your own flowers such as pretty daffodils onto waxed paper, then peel off and fix onto the eggs.

● 755 calories per serving

435

Melon and orange appetizers

SERVES 6
1 small honeydew melon
3 oranges
1 teaspoon chopped fresh mint,
   or ¼ teaspoon dried mint
2-3 teaspoons superfine sugar
6 mint sprigs or matchstick
   strips of blanched orange rind
   to garnish

1 Cut the melon in half and scoop out the pits. Cut the flesh into balls with a melon baller and put into a bowl, together with the melon juice (see Variations).
2 Squeeze the juice from half an orange and add to the melon balls. Pare the remaining half orange and the 2 whole oranges over a bowl to catch the juices. Use a fine serrated knife and a sawing action so that the rind is removed together with the pith. Section the oranges and discard the pits and membranes from between the sections.
3 Add the orange sections and juice to the melon with the mint. Sweeten to taste with sugar and mix lightly together.
4 Divide the melon and orange mixture between 6 individual glass dishes and garnish each portion with a sprig of mint.
5 Cover and refrigerate up to 1 hour before serving.

Lamb with walnut stuffing

SERVES 6
3-3½ lb leg of lamb, boned (see
   Buying guide)
½ lb sausagemeat
1 cup finely chopped shelled
   walnuts
2 tablespoons chopped fresh
   parsley
¼ teaspoon freshly grated nutmeg
1 teaspoon dried rosemary
salt and freshly ground black pepper
fresh parsley, to garnish

1 Preheat the oven to 400°.
2 Put the sausagemeat in a bowl together with the walnuts, parsley, nutmeg and half the rosemary. Season to taste and mix well.
3 Pack the stuffing into the boned cavity of the lamb, then secure with a trussing needle and fine string or meat skewers.
4 Place the lamb, fat side up, on a rack in a roasting pan and sprinkle with the remaining rosemary and salt and pepper to taste. Cover with foil. Roast in the oven 30 minutes, then lower the heat to 325° and roast a further 1½ hours. Remove the foil for the final 30 minutes of roasting.
5 Transfer to a serving platter, remove the string or skewers and serve, carved into slices and garnished with parsley.

Cook's Notes

Melon and orange appetizers

 TIME
Preparation time is about 15 minutes, chilling time 1 hour.

 VARIATIONS
Instead of cutting the melon flesh into balls, thickly pare off the rind and cut the melon into cubes.
   Use mandarins or satsumas in place of oranges — use 4 if they are small.
   Add 1 tablespoon toasted almonds for extra crunch.

● 55 calories per portion

Lamb with walnut stuffing

 TIME
30 minutes preparation, cooking 2 hours.

BUYING GUIDE
Ask your butcher to bone the leg of lamb: it is essential to order in advance, especially at Easter time.

SERVING IDEAS
Serve with a selection of buttered carrots, turnips and new potatoes, and hand round mint jelly.

● 520 calories per portion

Princess dessert

SERVES 6
2 tablespoons butter
2 cups whole wheat bread crumbs
finely grated rind of ½ lemon
2 cups milk
3 eggs, separated
3 tablespoons black cherry jelly
scant 1 cup firmly packed light
    brown sugar

1 Preheat the oven to 325°. Generously grease a 1 quart ovenproof dish with butter.
2 Mix the bread crumbs with the lemon rind, milk and egg yolks. Pour into the greased dish and dot with the remaining butter.
3 Bake in the oven about 40 minutes or until the mixture is set. Remove from oven (see Cook's tip).
4 Put the jelly in a small saucepan, heat gently until melted, then drizzle over bread crumb mixture.
5 In clean, dry bowl, beat the egg whites until they stand in stiff peaks. Beat in the sugar, 1 tablespoon at a time, beating thoroughly after each addition. Pile on top of jelly and return to the oven about 20 minutes or until the surface of the meringue is crisp and lightly browned. Serve the pudding at once.

Cook's Notes

TIME
Preparation 20 minutes, cooking 1 hour.

SERVING IDEAS
Serve the dessert with light cream.

COOK'S TIP
For convenience, bake the bread crumb base before cooking the lamb. When the lamb is cooked, return the pudding to the oven with jelly and meringue topping and cook just 10 minutes. Turn off oven and finish cooking as the oven cools 30-40 minutes.

● 280 calories per portion

MIDSUMMER NIGHTS DINNER

Conjure up your own midsummer night's dream with an elegant dinner-party menu that takes full advantage of all that's fresh and good in summer. Glowing with soft summer colors, our heady meal starts with a delicate asparagus soup and is followed by a sumptuous vision of cucumbered salmon. Frosted fruit and rose petals provide a fantasy finish.

Chilled asparagus soup

SERVES 8
1 lb fresh asparagus, cut into 2-inch lengths (see Buying guide)
1 chicken bouillon cube
salt and freshly ground white pepper
½ cup light cream
juice of 2 limes

TO GARNISH
8 whole unpeeled shrimp
8 thin fresh slices of lime, cut through to the center
about 3 tablespoons light cream

1 Bring a large pan of cold water to a boil, add the asparagus pieces and cook about 15 minutes until soft. Remove the asparagus with a slotted spoon and put in the goblet of a blender.
2 Rapidly boil the liquid left in the pan 5 minutes, then measure out 5 cups. Add bouillon cube to the measured liquid and stir until dissolved. Leave the liquid to cool slightly.
3 Add a little of the broth to the asparagus in the blender and blend until smooth.
4 Pour the asparagus purée into a large bowl, gradually stir in the remaining broth and season to taste with salt and pepper. ⚠
5 Stir in cream, blend thoroughly, then gradually add the lime juice. Cover the bowl of soup with plastic wrap and refrigerate 2 hours until well chilled.
6 To serve: Pour the soup into 8 chilled individual soup bowls and hook 1 shrimp and a lime slice over the side of each bowl. Swirl 1 teaspoon of cream into each bowl of soup, and serve at once.

Salmon with fennel mayonnaise

SERVES 8
4 lb fresh salmon, cleaned and trimmed with head and tail left on (see Buying guide)
1½ quarts water
¾ cup dry white wine
1 small onion, finely sliced
1 lemon slice
2 sprigs fresh fennel
1 parsley sprig
1 bay leaf
6 whole black peppercorns
generous pinch of salt

FENNEL MAYONNAISE
⅔ cup thick-type mayonnaise
4 tablespoons chopped fresh fennel
1 teaspoon Pernod (see Did you know)

TO GARNISH
1 slice stuffed olive (optional)
1 large unpeeled cucumber, thinly sliced
8 small lettuce leaves
finely chopped fresh fennel
sprigs fresh fennel

1 Pour the water and wine into a large saucepan, then add the onion, lemon slice, fennel, parsley, bay leaf, peppercorns and salt. Bring to boil, then lower heat and simmer 30 minutes. Cool then strain.
2 Put the salmon into a fish kettle or a large roasting pan and pour over the strained broth. Bring to boil, then turn to the lowest possible heat, cover and simmer gently 20 minutes until the fish flakes with a fork. Remove the pan from heat and leave fish, still covered, to cool in the liquid overnight.

3 Make the fennel mayonnaise: Put the mayonnaise in a bowl with the fennel and Pernod and mix well together. Cover and refrigerate.
4 When the fish is completely cold, dampen a sheet of waxed paper with water. Remove the fish carefully from the cooking liquid with 2 fish slices, then transfer to the dampened waxed paper.
5 Using the tip of a round-bladed knife, carefully peel off and discard the skin.
6 Roll the fish gently over and remove the skin from the other side, then gently scrape away any bones along sides of fish. Transfer fish to a long serving platter.
7 Garnish the salmon: Place the olive slice over the eye, if liked, then completely cover the side of the fish with cucumber slices (see Preparation). Arrange remaining thin cucumber slices around the edge. Arrange the lettuce along one edge of the salmon, and spoon the fennel mayonnaise into the center of each leaf. Sprinkle the mayonnaise with chopped fennel, then garnish the edge of the dish with fresh fennel sprigs.

COUNTDOWN
The day before
● Cook the salmon and leave to cool overnight.
● Prepare frosted grapes and rose petals and leave to set overnight.
2¾ hours before
● Make the chilled asparagus soup and refrigerate.
2 hours before
● Make the fennel mayonnaise. Skin the salmon and garnish.
● Frost the strawberries.
Just before the meal
● Pour the soup into individual soup bowls and garnish.
Just before the dessert
● Assemble the frosted fruit and rose petals on a dish.

Chilled asparagus soup

 TIME
35 minutes to make, plus 2 hours chilling.

 WATCHPOINT
The bouillon cube adds a certain amount of salt to the liquid so be careful when seasoning.

 BUYING GUIDE
Buy the thin green asparagus for this soup or, if available, the kind sold as *sprue* — very thin stalks not regarded good enough for eating whole. They are just as delicious for soup — and much less expensive than the graded varieties of asparagus spears.

● 55 calories per portion

Salmon with fennel mayonnaise

TIME
1½ hours preparation, including cooking the salmon; then overnight cooling, plus 20 minutes finishing.

PREPARATION
Start arranging the cucumber slices at the tail end and overlap them so that they resemble fish scales.

BUYING GUIDE
Salmon usually weighs between 5 and 10 lb; it is often difficult to obtain a small salmon so be sure to order your salmon in advance to avoid disappointment. It is highly perishable, so use at once.

DID YOU KNOW
Pernod is a French aniseed-tasting drink and is available in miniature-sized bottles. When water is added to Pernod, it turns quite white and cloudy.

● 450 calories per portion

Frosted fruit and rose petals

SERVES 8
large pink rose petals (see Watchpoint)
2 egg whites
½ cup superfine sugar
32 green pitted grapes, separated into small bunches
16 whole fresh strawberries, stems still attached

1 Lightly beat the egg whites in a bowl and spread the sugar onto a flat plate.
2 Frost the rose petals: Holding each by tweezers, dip first into the egg white, then sprinkle with the sugar, to coat both sides thoroughly. Spread out in a single layer on a plate, and leave to dry overnight.
3 Frost the green grapes: Holding each fruit by its stem, dip first into lightly beaten egg white, then roll in the sugar. Place on a large flat plate, making sure they do not touch each other, and leave to dry overnight.
4 Two hours before serving, repeat process with the strawberries.
5 To serve: Pile the strawberries and grapes carefully into a pyramid on a flat dish, then arrange the rose petals on top.

Cook's Notes

TIME
30 minutes for frosting the rose petals and fruit, plus drying time.

WATCHPOINT
Do not pick rose petals that have been sprayed with chemicals. Use unblemished petals and wash them carefully but gently before frosting. Hold each at base with a pair of tweezers and quickly dip in very cold water, gently pat dry with paper towels.

SERVING IDEAS
These sophisticated frosted fruits and petals are delicious served with lemon sherbet, or with tea sherbet.

● 65 calories per portion

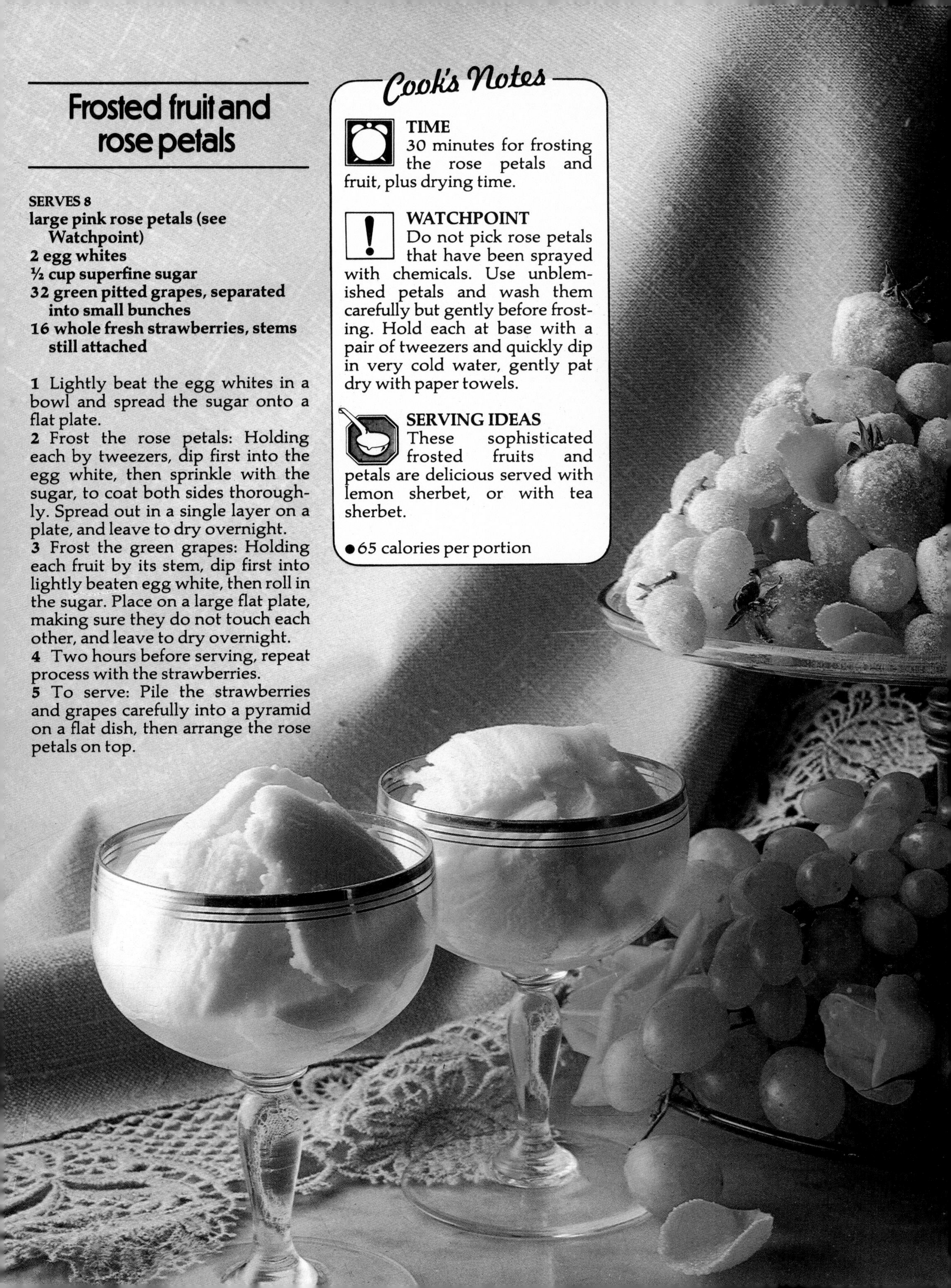

HALLOWE'EN PARTY

The pumpkins, apples and jacket potatoes in this menu are all traditional Hallowe'en fare, which are sure to be popular with children and adults alike. To add to the fun there is for the adults a vivid witches' brew. For the kids, serve milk shakes.

Witches' brew

MAKES 30 GLASSES
2½ cups dry vermouth
⅔ cup lime cordial
⅔ cup crème de menthe
1½ quarts soda water
Angostura bitters, to taste (optional)
about 24 ice cubes
3 limes, thinly sliced

1 Crush the ice cubes (see Cook's tips) and place in a pitcher or punch bowl.
2 Stir in the vermouth, lime cordial and crème de menthe, then the soda water. Mix well and add Angostura bitters to taste, if liked.
3 Float slices of lime on top; serve.

Lamb and pumpkin casserole

SERVES 12
3 lb boneless lamb, trimmed of fat and cut 1 inch cubes (see Buying guide)
2 lb pumpkin, pared and cut into ½ inch cubes
4 tablespoons vegetable oil
2 large onions, chopped
4 cloves garlic, crushed
1 can (about 14 oz) tomatoes
2½ cups beef broth
1 teaspoon dried oregano
salt
freshly ground black pepper
¾ lb chorizo sausages, sliced (see Buying guide)
2 cans (about 14 oz each) chick-peas
sprigs of parsley, to garnish

1 Heat the oil in a large flameproof casserole, add the lamb (in batches if necessary) and cook over brisk heat until evenly browned on all sides. Remove the casserole from the heat and transfer the browned meat with a slotted spoon to a large plate. Set aside.
2 Return casserole to the heat. Lower the heat, add the onions and garlic and cook gently 5 minutes until the onions are soft and lightly colored.
3 Add the tomatoes with their juice, the broth, oregano and salt and pepper to taste. Bring to a boil, return the meat with its juices to the casserole, then add the chorizos. Stir well, lower the heat slightly, then cover and simmer gently 30 minutes.
4 Add the pumpkin cubes to the casserole together with the chick-peas and their canned liquid. ❋ Cover, bring back to a boil, then reduce the heat slightly and simmer gently a further 30 minutes.
5 Skim off any excess fat from the surface and taste and adjust seasoning if necessary.
6 Garnish with sprigs of fresh parsley and serve at once, straight from the casserole.

West country potatoes

SERVES 12
12 even-sized potatoes, scrubbed
vegetable oil, for brushing
salt
½ lb herbed cheese (with chives and onion) (see Buying guide)

1 Preheat the oven to 425°.
2 Prick the potatoes well with a fork, then brush each one with a very little oil.
3 Sprinkle the potatoes with salt and place in the oven, directly on the shelves. Bake about 1 hour or until they feel soft in the center when pierced with a skewer.
4 Just before serving, cut the cheese into 24 thin slices. Make 2 slits in each potato and put a slice of cheese in each slit. Serve at once while the potatoes are still hot.

Cook's Notes

Witches' brew

TIME
Preparation takes about 5 minutes.

COOK'S TIPS
Crush the ice in a strong blender, or in a food processor. If you do not have either, place the ice in a strong polythene bag, squeeze out the air and tie firmly. Beat with a wooden mallet or rolling pin.

VARIATION
Add a little green food coloring if you prefer a darker green drink.

● 35 calories per glass

Lamb and pumpkin casserole
TIME
30 minutes preparation, 1 hour cooking.

FREEZING
After adding the pumpkin and chick-peas, cook 15 minutes only. Cool quickly, lift off and discard any excess solidified fat, then pack into rigid container. Seal, label and freeze for up to 3 months. To serve: Thaw overnight in the refrigerator, then turn into a casserole and simmer about 20 minutes or until heated through.

BUYING GUIDE
Frozen joints of boneless lamb, such as shoulder, can be found in most supermarkets.
Spanish chorizos are sold cooked and uncooked: either type can be used for this casserole, but the cooked type is the most commonly available. If you have difficulty buying chorizos, use kabanos or a similar type of strong-flavored sausage.

● 520 calories per portion

West Country potatoes
TIME
5 minutes preparation, 1 hour cooking.

BUYING GUIDE
If you have difficulty in buying the cheese, use plain Cheddar and sprinkle with finely chopped chives or chopped onions.

● 245 calories per portion

Caramel-topped apples

SERVES 12

6 crisp dessert apples
**2½ cups dairy sour
    cream**
⅓ cup superfine sugar
**finely grated rind and juice of 3
    oranges**
**matchstick strips of orange rind, to
    decorate**

CARAMEL CHIPS
½ cup granulated sugar
⅔ cup water
vegetable oil, for greasing

1 Make the caramel chips: Grease a cookie sheet and put the sugar and water into a small, heavy-based saucepan. Heat gently, without stirring, until the sugar has dissolved, then bring to a boil and boil 5 minutes, until the syrup turns a deep golden color. ⚠

2 Immediately remove from the heat and plunge the base of the pan into a bowl of iced water. ⚠ Leave for a few seconds until the sizzling stops, then remove pan from water.

3 Pour the syrup immediately onto the greased cookie sheet to make a thin layer. Allow it to become completely cold.

4 Meanwhile, pour dairy sour cream into a large bowl and stir in sugar. Add orange rind and juice.

5 Core and slice the apples, mix into sour cream, then turn into a large, shallow serving dish. Cover and refrigerate until ready to serve.

6 Crack the set caramel with a rolling pin to form fine chips and sprinkle over the apple mixture (see Cook's tip). Top with orange rind.

Cook's Notes

  TIME
20 minutes preparation, plus setting time for the caramel.

WATCHPOINTS
Watch the syrup constantly and be sure to remove it from the heat immediately it turns a deep golden color.

Plunging the pan into cold water stops the cooking: take care that no water splashes into the syrup, otherwise it will split.

COOK'S TIP
Do not sprinkle the chips over the dessert until just before serving, otherwise the caramel will become soft and melt into the mixture.

STORAGE
The caramel chips will keep in a dry, airtight container for a day or two, but after that they will become sticky.

● 205 calories per portion.

TEENAGE PARTY

The key to keeping a crowd of young teenagers happy is to provide heaps of hearty, unfussy food that they can tuck into with gusto. An authentic Italian lasagne, accompanied by garlic bread, is the perfect 'come-and-grab-it' style food. Served with an exciting-looking punch and rounded off with ice cream topped with hot sauces, this party is sure to be a winner!

Italian wine cup

MAKES ABOUT 60 GLASSES
About 2½ quarts Italian red wine
(see Variations)
1 quart ginger ale
2 quarts lemonade or soda
water
3 lemons, thinly sliced
2 oranges, thinly sliced
2 red-skinned apples
fresh mint sprigs
crushed ice

1 Put the wine, ginger ale and lemonade into a large bowl.
2 Add the sliced lemons and oranges. Leave the punch to stand 1 hour.
3 Just before serving, core and thinly slice the apples. Add to the punch with the mint sprigs and the crushed ice.
4 To serve: Ladle into pitchers together with some of the fruit, then pour into glasses.

Garlic bread

SERVES 10-12
3 long French loaves
1½ cups butter, softened
6 cloves garlic, crushed
4 tablespoons chopped parsley
(optional)

1 Preheat the oven to 375°.
2 Beat the butter until creamy, then beat in the garlic and parsley, if using, until well mixed.
3 Cut each loaf diagonally into slices, about 2 inches thick, slicing to the base of the loaf but not cutting through it.
4 Spread the cut surfaces of the bread with the butter, then reform into a loaf shape. ❋ Wrap each loaf firmly in foil and place on a cookie sheet join side up.
5 Bake in the oven 15 minutes. Open the foil and bake a further 5 minutes to crisp the bread.
6 Remove the garlic bread from oven and serve it at once, straight from the foil.

Lasagne al forno

SERVES 10-12
1½ lb green lasagne (see Buying guide)
3 tablespoons olive oil
3 large onions, chopped
4 cloves garlic, chopped
3-3½ lb lean ground beef
2 cans (about 14 oz each) tomatoes
4 tablespoons tomato paste
1¼ cups Italian red wine
3 cups sliced mushrooms (optional)
2 teaspoons dried basil
salt and freshly ground black pepper
¾ cup grated Parmesan cheese
butter, for greasing

SAUCE
⅓ cup butter
¾ cup all-purpose flour
3¾ cups milk
freshly grated nutmeg

1 Heat the oil in large heavy-based skillet, add onions and garlic and cook gently 5 minutes.
2 Add the meat, turn the heat to high and fry until the meat is evenly browned, stirring with a wooden spoon to remove any lumps. Add the tomatoes with their juice, the tomato paste, wine, mushrooms, if using, basil and salt and pepper to taste. Bring to a boil, stirring well, cover and cook 30 minutes.
3 Preheat the oven to 375° and grease a rectangular ovenproof dish about 15 × 10 inches.
4 Make sauce: Melt butter in a pan, sprinkle in the flour and stir over low heat 1-2 minutes until straw-colored. Remove from the heat and gradually stir in all the milk. Return pan to the heat and simmer, stirring, until thick and smooth. Remove from the heat and season to taste with nutmeg, salt and pepper.
5 Spread one-third of the meat mixture in the bottom of the prepared dish. Place one-third of the lasagne on top in an overlapping layer, then spread over one-third of the white sauce. Repeat these layers twice more, ending with a layer of sauce.
6 Sprinkle with grated Parmesan cheese and bake in the oven about 45 minutes.

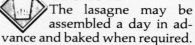

Hot-topped ice cream

SERVES 20
4 quarts vanilla ice cream

CHOCOLATE SAUCE
9 squares (9 oz) semisweet
** chocolate**
¼ cup butter, softened
4 tablespoons milk
4 tablespoons clear honey
1 teaspoon vanilla

BUTTERSCOTCH SAUCE
¾ cup butter
1 cup firmly packed light brown sugar
2 tablespoons light corn syrup

RASPBERRY SAUCE
6 tablespoons raspberry jelly
juice of 1 lemon
2 teaspoons cornstarch
⅔ cup water
150 ml/¼ pint water

1 Make the chocolate sauce: Put the chocolate pieces in a small heavy-based saucepan. Beat in the butter, milk and honey and heat gently until the chocolate has melted. Add the vanilla (see Cook's tips).

2 Make the butterscotch sauce: Put all the ingredients in a heavy-based saucepan and heat gently until the sugar has dissolved. Bring to a boil and cook over high heat 3-4 minutes until the mixture is golden brown and thick (see Cook's tips).

3 Make the raspberry sauce: Put the jelly with the lemon juice in a heavy-based saucepan. Blend the cornstarch with 1 tablespoon of the water, then gradually stir in the remaining water. Stir into the jelly.

4 Heat gently until jelly has melted, bring to a boil and cook 2-3 minutes until the mixture is thick. Strain, return to the pan and heat through gently 2 minutes (see Cook's tips).

5 To serve: Pour the hot sauces into individual warmed pitchers; serve at once with the ice cream.

FAMILY PICNIC

A picnic by the sea is a great way to entertain the family, as long as the food is well planned. We have devised a picnic for six that can be made in advance and is easy to serve: we suggest a savory selection of pasties, ham rolls and chicken drumsticks, all of which are easy to eat with your fingers and can be neatly packed. The Banana creams for dessert are ready-made in sandproof containers, and are accompanied by crunchy shortbread fingers.

Tuna puff pasties

SERVES 6
2 cans (about 7 oz each) tuna, drained and flaked
1 tablespoon vegetable oil
1 onion, finely chopped
3 hard-cooked eggs, chopped
2 potatoes, boiled and diced
3 tablespoons tomato catsup
1 teaspoon dried mixed herbs
grated rind of 1 lemon
2 eggs, beaten
1 clove garlic (optional)
dash of Worcestershire sauce (optional)
salt and freshly ground black pepper
1½ sheets (¾ of 17 oz package) frozen puff pastry, thawed

1 Heat the oil in a skillet, add the onion and cook gently 5 minutes until soft and lightly colored. Transfer with a slotted spoon to a bowl.
2 Add the tuna to the bowl [!] together with the hard-cooked eggs, potatoes, tomato catsup, herbs, lemon rind, half the beaten egg, garlic and Worcestershire sauce, if using. Season with salt and pepper to taste and mix well.
3 Preheat the oven to 425°.
4 Roll out the pastry on a lightly floured surface: the larger sheet to an oblong 15 × 10 inches and the smaller sheet to an oblong 10 × 5 inches; cut into 6 × 7½-inch pieces.
5 Spoon a portion of the tuna and egg mixture onto the center of each piece of pastry. Brush the edges of each piece of pastry with water, then draw up the 2 long sides to meet over the filling. Firmly seal the edges together and crimp. Press the short sides together to seal them,

making a neat parcel. Repeat this process with the remaining pastry pieces.
6 Place the 6 parcels on a dampened cookie sheet and brush them with the remaining beaten egg. Bake in the oven 15-20 minutes until the pastry is golden brown and the underside is dry. Carefully transfer to a wire rack and leave to cool.

Herby chicken drumsticks

SERVES 6
6 chicken drumsticks
¾ cup dried white bread crumbs (see Preparation)
1 teaspoon dried rosemary
1 teaspoon dried thyme
1 teaspoon dried marjoram
salt and freshly ground black pepper
2 tablespoons all-purpose flour
2 eggs, beaten
2 tablespoons milk
2 tablespoons vegetable oil
¼ cup butter

1 Mix together the bread crumbs and herbs in a bowl and season well with salt and pepper. Place the flour in a plastic bag.
2 Put the beaten eggs in a shallow bowl and stir in the milk and a drop of oil. Put the bread crumb mixture on a plate. Shake each drumstick in the bag of flour to coat, then dip first into the egg mixture and then into the bread crumbs.
3 Heat the oil and butter in a large skillet over moderate heat. When the butter foams, add the drumsticks and cook gently about 20 minutes until cooked through and golden brown on all sides.
4 Remove the drumsticks, drain on paper towels and cool.

Ham rolls

SERVES 6
12 thin slices cooked ham
1 cup smooth liver pâté
3 tablespoons medium-dry sherry
2 tablespoons light cream
salt and freshly ground black pepper

1 Put the pâté in a bowl and mash it lightly with a fork.
2 Add the sherry and cream and mash well into the pâté until the mixture is smooth. Season with salt and pepper to taste.
3 Divide the mixture between the 12 slices of ham, spreading it evenly over each slice with a knife.
4 Carefully roll up each slice of ham as tightly as possible and secure with a toothpick.

Cook's Notes

Tuna puff pasties

 TIME
40 minutes preparation, 15-20 minutes cooking, plus cooling time.

! **WATCHPOINT**
Make sure as much oil as possible is drained from the tuna or it will seep through the pastry during cooking.

 SERVING IDEAS
Serve these unusual pasties with crisp salad ingredients — sticks of carrot, celery and cucumber, or whole radishes and scallions — accompanied by a pot of mayonnaise. A plain green salad and sliced tomatoes packed in rigid containers also make excellent additions.

● 550 calories per portion

Herby chicken drumsticks

TIME
10 minutes preparation, 20 minutes cooking, plus cooling time.

PREPARATION
It is easy and economical to make your own bread crumbs. Put pieces of stale bread in a low oven until dry and lightly colored. Crush the pieces with a rolling pin or crush in a blender, to produce crumbs. Store in a screw-top jar.

● 210 calories per portion

Ham rolls

TIME
These simple rolls only take 15 minutes preparation.

VARIATIONS
Cream cheese mixed with a little tomato catsup and Worcestershire sauce makes a good alternative filling.

● 200 calories per portion

449

Orange shortbread fingers

SERVES 6
1¼ cups all-purpose flour
⅓ cup ground rice
pinch of salt
½ cup butter, softened
¼ cup superfine sugar
grated rind of 1 small orange
butter, for greasing
superfine sugar, to decorate

1 Preheat the oven to 325° and lightly grease a cookie sheet.
2 Sift the flour, ground rice and salt onto a piece of waxed paper. Using a wooden spoon, beat the butter in a bowl until creamy, then beat in the sugar and orange rind until thoroughly combined.
3 Gradually work the sifted flour mixture into the butter mixture, using a wooden spoon at first and finishing by gathering the dough into a ball with your hands. !
4 Roll the dough out on a floured surface to an 8-inch square about ½-inch thick, patting the shortbread into shape with your fingers to give a neat edge.
5 With a fish slice, carefully lift the shortbread onto the greased cookie sheet and prick all over with a fork.

Bake in the oven 25 minutes until lightly colored. Immediately cut in half lengthwise, then cut into fingers.
6 Cool for 10 minutes on the cookie sheet until firm, then transfer to a wire rack to cool completely. Sprinkle with superfine sugar if wished.

Banana creams

SERVES 6
4 bananas
1 can (about 2 cups) evaporated milk
2 teaspoons sugar
juice of 1 lemon

1 Slice 3 bananas and put in a blender with the evaporated milk, sugar and lemon juice. Blend until thick and smooth. Alternatively, mash the sliced bananas with a fork until they form a smooth pulp, then beat in the remaining ingredients.
2 Divide the banana cream among 6 plastic containers (see Serving ideas) and refrigerate.
3 Just before serving, cut the remaining banana into diagonal slices and arrange on top of each portion. Serve the creams in the plastic containers.

CHILDREN'S BIRTHDAY PARTY

Give a children's fancy-dress birthday party with an "animal" theme. Animal-shaped cheese crackers are good fun, and for those who like savories there are also sausages and bacon rolls stuck into a 'caterpillar' made from a cucumber. For an impressive centerpiece make our colorful butterfly cake, decorated with feather frosting.

The day before
- Make the animal crackers.
- Make the cake.

On the day
In the morning:
- Assemble and frost cake.

2 hours before
- Decorate the cake with sugar-coated chocolate buttons and add the liquorice "antennae".

1 hour before
- Prepare the cucumber and begin to cook the sausages and bacon and pineapple rolls.

Cucumber caterpillar

SERVES 12
1 large cucumber, preferably slightly curved
2 candied cherries
1 lb cocktail sausages (see Cook's tips)
6 slices fatty bacon, cut in half crosswise
1 can (about 8 oz) pineapple pieces, drained

1 Cutting at a slant, slice off the thicker end of the cucumber. To make the eyes: Spear each cherry on to the end of half a toothpick; press sticks in cut end of cucumber.
2 At the other end, with a sharp knife, make a few small cuts across the cucumber, about ⅛ inch apart, for the "tail".
3 Preheat the broiler to high.
4 Prick the sausages with a fork and cook over gentle heat until they are golden brown on all sides.
5 Meanwhile, wrap each half bacon slice around a piece of pineapple and secure with a wooden toothpick. Broil the bacon and pineapple rolls 3-4 minutes until the bacon is crisp. Drain on paper towels.

6 Drain the sausages and spear a toothpick into each one. Stick the sausages in a ridge down the center of the cucumber and the bacon rolls on either side and serve at once (see Cook's tips).

Animal cheese crackers

MAKES 50
2 cups all-purpose flour
pinch of salt
¼ teaspoon dry mustard
½ cup butter or margarine
¾ cup finely grated sharp Cheddar cheese, (see Watchpoint)
1 egg yolk
2 tablespoons water
little milk, for glazing
sesame seeds and/or poppy seeds
butter, for greasing

1 Sift the flour, salt and mustard powder into a large bowl. Rub in the butter until mixture resembles fine bread crumbs, then add the cheese. Mix in the egg yolk and water with a knife, then gather up the pastry in your hands to make a firm dough.
2 Turn the dough onto a lightly floured surface and knead briefly until smooth. Place in a plastic bag and leave to rest in the refrigerator 30 minutes.
3 Heat the oven to 400° and grease 2 cookie sheets.
4 Roll out the pastry on a floured surface until it is about ⅛ inch thick. Using different-shaped animal cookie cutters, cut out shapes and place on the greased cookie sheets spacing them apart to allow for them spreading during baking. Brush all over with milk. Using a skewer or point of a knife, make holes for the eyes, mouths, noses, etc.
5 Decorate the crackers with sesame seeds and/or poppy seeds.
6 Bake in the oven, in 2 batches 15-20 minutes each until golden brown. Remove from the oven, allow to settle 1-2 minutes, then place on a wire rack and leave to cool before serving.

Cook's Notes

Cucumber caterpillar

TIME
Preparation time is about 30 minutes, cooking time about 10 minutes.

COOK'S TIPS
If you have difficulty buying cocktail sausages, buy thin ones and cut each in half by twisting skin in the middle then cutting it.
If you wish, keep the cucumber warm for 30 minutes in a 225° oven.

- 180 calories per portion

Animal cheese crackers

TIME
30 minutes preparation, 30-40 minutes cooking, plus resting and cooling time.

WATCHPOINT
Use a sharp Cheddar cheese or the crackers will lack flavor.

STORAGE
These crackers will keep for 1 week in an airtight container in a cool, dry place.

- 35 calories per cracker

Butterfly birthday cake

MAKES 24 SLICES
2 cups self-rising flour
2 teaspoons baking powder
1 cup soft butter
1 cup superfine sugar
grated rind of 2 oranges
4 large eggs
butter, for greasing

FILLING AND DECORATION
¾ cup apricot jelly
½ cup flaked coconut
2 cups confectioners' sugar
2-3 tablespoons water
brown food coloring

TO FINISH
12-inch square of heavy cardboard,
    covered in foil
3 chocolate flake bars
candles and candle-holders
3 small packages of sugar-coated
    chocolate buttons
2 liquorice ropes

1 Preheat oven to 325°. Grease a deep 9-inch square cake pan. Line the sides and base of the pan with waxed paper, then grease.
2 Sift the flour and baking powder into a large bowl. Add the butter, sugar, orange rind and eggs. Mix well, then beat with a wooden spoon 2-3 minutes, or with a hand-held electric beater 1 minute, until blended and glossy.
3 Turn the mixture into the prepared pan and level the surface, then make a slight hollow in the center. Bake in the oven about 65 minutes, until the top of the cake is golden and springy to the touch.

4 Cool the cake in the pan for 5 minutes, then turn out onto a wire rack and peel off the lining paper. Leave the cake upside down to cool completely.
5 Trim the cake to level it off, if necessary. Slice the cold cake in half horizontally and sandwich together with 5 tablespoons of the apricot jelly. Cut the cake in half diagonally to make 2 triangles, then trim off the triangle tips opposite the cut edge.

6 Strain all but 1 tablespoon of the remaining jelly into a small, heavy-based saucepan and stir over low heat until melted. Brush the sides of the cakes, except the trimmed corners, with some melted jelly.
7 Spread a thick layer of coconut on a large plate. Press jelly coated sides of cake into the coconut one at a time until evenly coated. (Add more coconut to plate if needed.)
8 Brush the trimmed corner of each cake with melted jelly. Place the 2 pieces of cake on the cake-board, with the trimmed corners almost touching to make a butterfly shape. Place the chocolate flakes in the gap, one on top of another, then push the 2 "wings" together.
9 Make the frosting (see Cook's tips): Sift the sugar into a bowl, then beat in enough water to give a thick coating consistency.

10 Put 2 tablespoons of frosting into a small bowl. Add several drops of brown food coloring, mix well, to make a fairly dark frosting. Spoon frosting into a small pastry bag fitted with a writing tip.
11 Brush the top of the cakes with remaining melted jelly. Spread the white frosting smoothly and evenly over the top with a knife. Immediately [!] pipe parallel lines of brown frosting down the "wings."

12 Draw a skewer through the brown lines to give a "feather" effect.

13 Neaten edges, removing surplus frosting; arrange the candles in their holders on top. Leave to set.
14 Two hours before the party, melt the remaining tablespoon jelly. Brush jelly on each chocolate button and stick them round the edges of the cake. Stick in 2 pieces of liquorice for the "antennae" and curl them round slightly.

Cook's Notes

TIME
20 minutes preparation, 65 minutes baking, plus cooling time. Shaping and decorating take about 1 hour.

COOK'S TIPS
Very fresh cake is difficult to cut and frost neatly, so bake the cake a day before decorating.

You can assemble and frost cake on the evening before the party, but not before, otherwise frosting will dry out and crack.

[!] WATCHPOINT
Speed is essential: the frosting must not start to set before "feathering".

● 265 calories per slice.

BURGER AND PIZZA PARTY

Create a relaxed atmosphere for family and friends, and cater for all ages from 4 to 50 plus, with a burger and pizza party. Featuring food that is both popular and easy to make, the menu also includes an unusual chocolate fondue which will add to the fun and informality. For outsize appetites you can double up on the quantities given here.

THE DAY BEFORE
● Make the tomato sauce for the pizzas, cover and refrigerate.
● Make the pizza dough and put into refrigerator to rise slowly overnight.
● Prepare and shape the burgers. Cover and refrigerate.
● Make the syrup for the fruit cup.
● Wash salad ingredients, wrap and refrigerate; make salad dressings and store in the refrigerator.
ON THE DAY
● Prepare ingredients for the pizza toppings and cake for the fondue.
JUST BEFORE THE PARTY
Remove pizza dough from the refrigerator, allow it to return to room temperature then knead again.
● Assemble the salads, but do not dress them.
● Prepare the fruit dips and the chocolate for the fondue.
PARTY TIME
● Finish making the fruit cup.
● Cook and serve the burgers.
● Complete and bake the pizzas.
● Dress the salads.

Beefburgers

MAKES 12 BURGERS
1½ lb chuck steak (see Buying guide)
1 large onion
2 cups fresh bread crumbs
salt and freshly ground black pepper
1 egg, beaten
2 tablespoons beef broth or water

TO SERVE
6 tablespoons vegetable oil
6 onions, sliced
12 burger buns
1 Bibb lettuce, separated into leaves
tomato slices

1 To make the burgers: Grind the meat finely by passing it through the mincer twice. Grind the onion.
2 Put the ground meat, onion and bread crumbs into a bowl and season with salt and pepper. Add the egg and broth and mix together with your hands until combined.
3 Divide the mixture into 12. On a floured board, shape each piece into a neat, flat 4-inch circle.
4 Line a cookie sheet or tray with plastic wrap, place the shaped burgers on top, then cover with plastic wrap. Refrigerate until required.
5 To serve: Heat 2 tablespoons oil in a large skillet, add the onion slices and fry gently until soft and lightly browned. Removed with a slotted spoon and drain on paper towels.
6 Preheat the oven to 250° then put the burger buns in the oven to warm while cooking the burgers. Keep the fried onions warm in the oven at the same time.
7 Heat 2 tablespoons oil in each of 2 large skillets. Put 6 burgers in each pan and cook gently about 5 minutes on each side, or until lightly browned and cooked.
8 Cut open the warm burger buns and fill each with a lettuce leaf, a burger, a slice of tomato and some fried onions. Serve at once.

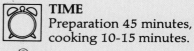

Cook's Notes

TIME
Preparation 45 minutes, cooking 10-15 minutes.

BUYING GUIDE
Alternatively, buy best-quality ground beef for the burgers, although the burger will have more flavor if you grind your own beef.

FREEZING
Open freeze, pack in a plastic bag, seal, label and freeze. Store up to 2 months. To serve: Cook from frozen as in recipe.

SERVING IDEAS
Wrap each cooked burger in a paper napkin. Serve with a selection of pickles, relishes, and mustards.

● 305 calories per portion

Lemon and apple cup

MAKES ABOUT 2 QUARTS
thinly pared rind and strained juice
of 2 lemons
1¼ cups sugar
2½ cups cold water
1 red skinned dessert apple
1 orange
1 lemon
1 quart apple juice or white wine,
chilled (see Cook's tip)
2½ cups fizzy lemonade,
chilled
mint leaves, to serve (optional)

1 Put the lemon rind and sugar into a saucepan with the water. Heat gently until sugar has dissolved, then bring to a boil and boil 3 minutes. Remove from the heat, cover and leave to stand at least 3 hours, preferably overnight.
2 Just before serving, strain the lemon syrup into a chilled serving bowl. Stir in the lemon juice.

3 Quarter and core the apple, but do not pare, then slice it thinly and add to the lemon syrup. Thinly slice the orange and lemon (including the rind) and add to the syrup. Pour the apple juice and lemonade into the bowl and stir well. Decorate with mint leaves if liked; serve at once.

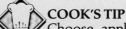

Cook's Notes

TIME
Preparation time 15 minutes, cooking time 5 minutes, but allow at least 3 hours standing time for the flavor of the lemon syrup to develop.

VARIATION
If fresh mint is out of season, soak 1 teaspoon dried mint in boiling water, drain and add to the cup before serving.

COOK'S TIP
Choose apple juice or white wine for the cup according to the age and preferences of your guests.

● 145 calories per serving

Party pizzas

SERVES 12

PIZZA DOUGH
4 cups all-purpose flour
1 teaspoon salt
¼ cup butter or margarine
1 package active dried yeast
1 teaspoon sugar
1¼ cups tepid water
vegetable oil, for brushing and
    drizzling

TOMATO SAUCE
2 tablespoons olive or
    vegetable oil
3 medium onions, finely chopped
1 can (about 1¾ lb) tomatoes
2 tablespoons tomato paste
1 tablespoon dried mixed herbs
2 beef bouillon cubes
salt and freshly ground black pepper

TOPPINGS
¾ lb mozzarella cheese, thinly
    sliced
¼ lb thinly sliced salami, rinds
    removed, cut into strips
¼ lb cooked ham, cut into strips
1 cup thinly sliced small
    mushrooms
1 red pepper, seeded and thinly
    sliced
1 green pepper, seeded and thinly
    sliced
4 teaspoons capers
1 large onion, chopped
    (optional)
2 cans (about 2 oz each) anchovy
    fillets, drained
24 black olives

1 First make the tomato sauce: Heat the oil in a large saucepan. Add the onions and cook gently 5 minutes or until soft but not colored. Stir in the tomatoes with their juice, the tomato paste and the herbs. Crumble in bouillon cubes. Break up the tomatoes with a wooden spoon, then add salt and pepper to taste. Bring to a boil, stirring all the time. Reduce the heat to low, partially cover the pan and simmer about 1 hour. Cool.

2 Next make the pizza dough (see Cook's tips): Mix the yeast and sugar in a bowl and then add ¼ cup of tepid water. Leave for 10 minutes until frothy. Sift flour and salt into a large bowl. Rub in the butter then make a well in the center of the flour and stir in the yeast mixture and the tepid water. Mix the ingredients together thoroughly to form a stiff dough.

3 Turn the dough onto a very lightly floured surface, then knead 10 minutes until smooth and elastic. Alternatively, knead it in an electric mixer, using a dough hook, 3 minutes. Put the dough back into the bowl, cover with plastic wrap or a clean dish towel and leave in a warm place for about 1 hour or until the dough has more than doubled in size.

4 Preheat oven to 400°. Lightly brush two 12-inch round ovenproof plates or two 14 × 12 inch oblong cookie sheets with vegetable oil (see Cook's tips).

5 Turn the risen dough onto a lightly floured surface, punch down then knead for a minute. Cut dough in half and form each half into a ball. Coat with oiled plastic wrap and leave to stand for 10 minutes.

6 Roll each piece of dough out to a round or an oblong to fit the prepared plates or cookie sheets. Place dough in position and press out firmly until it fits neatly. Finally carefully pinch up the edge of dough to make a neat raised rim.

7 Brush the dough with a little more oil, then spread with tomato sauce. Cover with the cheese to within ¼-inch from the edge. Arrange the salami, ham, mushrooms, peppers, capers, onion, if using, on top, in separate sections or mixed together (see Serving ideas). Divide off the sections with anchovy fillets and place black olives in each section.

8 Drizzle a little oil over the surface, then bake in the oven about 25 minutes, or until the cheese is bubbling and golden. Cut the pizza into sections and serve at once accompanied by a varied selection of salads.

Cook's Notes

TIME
Preparation time is 1½ hours, including rising time. Cooking time is about 25 minutes.

COOK'S TIPS
To save time you can use three packages ready pizza dough mix to make the pizza base. Cook according to package directions.

Choose cookie sheets with sides to contain the pizza dough neatly and stop it spreading.

SERVING IDEAS
Invite party guests into the kitchen to select their own toppings which can be arranged in separate sections.

FREEZING
Open freeze after stage 7, seal in plastic bags, label and freeze. Store up to 3 months. To serve: Cook from frozen at 425° about 30 minutes.

● 375 calories per portion

Chocolate fondue

SERVES 12

14 squares (14 oz) semisweet chocolate, broken into small pieces
1¼ cups heavy cream
6 tablespoons sweet sherry
¼ cup sweet butter

DIPPERS
2 × 8-inch sponge cake layers
apricot jelly, for spreading
4 large bananas
2 tablespoons lemon juice
2 large dessert apples
1 can (about 1 lb) sliced peaches in syrup, well drained

1 First prepare the dippers: Slice the cake in half horizontally and sandwich with apricot jelly. Cut into neat 1-inch cubes. Peel the bananas, cut into slices ½-inch thick and toss in 1 tablespoon lemon juice. Quarter, core and slice the apples and toss in the remaining lemon juice. Leave peach slices whole, or cut into chunks if large. ⊡

2 Arrange in separate bowls.

3 Put the chocolate into a heavy-based fondue pan or small saucepan and add the cream and sherry.

4 Just before serving, gently heat the chocolate, cream and sherry together until the chocolate melts, stirring all the time. Continue until almost, but not quite boiling. ⊡ Stir in the butter until melted.

5 Place the pan over a small spirit burner on the table. Arrange the bowls of cake and fruit around the fondue, along with fondue or ordinary forks for spearing the cake and fruit before they are dipped in.

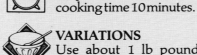

SUNDAY LUNCH FOR SIX

Sunday lunch is traditionally a time when the whole family sits down for a meal together. Even if you have little time for cooking during the week, it is worth treating Sunday lunch as a special occasion and making an extra effort, particularly if you have guests as well as the family.

If you have any spare time, you can begin the preparations the day before, to ease your workload next morning. Use the countdown below to help you time both cooking operations and the serving of the meal to perfection.

The day before
Thaw the puff pastry overnight so that you can make the dumplings in the morning.
Thaw the shrimp overnight if using frozen.

On Sunday morning
Make the grapefruit cocktails and then refrigerate.

Pare the potatoes and keep them in water to prevent browning. Pare the apples and onion. Keep the apples in salted water to prevent browning and wrap onion in plastic wrap. Prepare the other vegetables you have chosen for the meal.
11.00 Prepare the pork for cooking in its roasting pan and put in the oven for the time required.
11.45 Prepare the fruit filling and roll out and cut the pastry. Make the dumplings and put on a cookie sheet.
12.10 Drain the potatoes, dry them with a clean cloth and coat in oil. Slice the onion and apples, place them around the pork and put the potatoes on top. Pour over the apple juice and return the roasting pan to the oven (see Recipe).
12.30 Cook the other vegetables. Make gravy in your usual way (you can also use the thin cooking juices under the pork). Drain vegetables when they are ready and put them in warm serving dishes. Cover and keep hot.
1.00 Serve the first course.
1.15 or 1.30 Reduce oven and bake the dumplings.

Grapefruit and shrimp cocktail

SERVES 6
3 small grapefruit
1 cup peeled shrimp
1 tablespoon chopped parsley
5 tablespoons mayonnaise
salt
pinch of cayenne pepper (optional)
3 lettuce leaves, finely shredded
1 teaspoon ground ginger (optional)
parsley to garnish

1 Halve the grapefruit, vandyking the edges: To do this use a sharp knife to cut V-shapes all round, cutting right through to the center of the grapefruit. Separate the halves and remove the flesh, discarding all the white pith. Reserve the shells.
2 Separate the grapefruit flesh from the pith and the membranes.
3 Drain the grapefruit flesh and shrimp well, then mix them with the parsley and mayonnaise. Add salt and cayenne pepper to taste.
4 Line each reserved grapefruit shell with lettuce, then divide the shrimp mixture equally between them and place each on a small plate.
5 Cover and chill at least 30 minutes before serving.
6 Sprinkle on ground ginger, if using, and garnish with parsley.

Cook's Notes

TIME
Preparation time 20 minutes. Allow at least 30 minutes chilling time.

COOK'S TIP
Use a good commercial mayonnaise — a homemade one may separate.

● 120 calories per portion

Apple roast pork

SERVES 6
3 lb boneless pork joint
salt
3 tablespoons vegetable oil
2 sprigs fresh rosemary, or 2
  teaspoons dried rosemary
3 lb potatoes, thickly cut
2 dessert apples
1 medium onion, thinly sliced
¾ cup apple juice
freshly ground black pepper

1 Preheat the oven to 350°. Weigh the joint of pork and calculate the exact cooking time, allowing 25 minutes per 1 lb plus an extra 25 minutes.

2 Check that the butcher has scored the skin of the pork to make crackling. If he has not, do this yourself with a sharp knife (see Preparation).

3 Wipe the pork dry. Sprinkle the skin with salt and rub it lightly with ½ tablespoon oil.

4 Put the rosemary sprigs in a roasting pan or sprinkle in the dried herbs. Place the pork on top.

5 Roast the joint in the oven about 1¾ hours, or according to the calculated cooking time per weight.

6 About 1¼ hours before the end of the cooking time, put the potatoes in a bowl with the remaining oil and shake well to coat. Pare, core and slice the apples.

7 Remove the pork from the oven, scatter the apple and onion around the joint, then place the potato pieces on top of them. Pour in the apple juice. Sprinkle with salt and pepper.

8 Return the pan to the oven and continue roasting a further 30 minutes.

9 Turn up the oven to 500°, and then cook a further 30 minutes. The pork crackling should be crisp and the potatoes golden.

10 Place the pork on a warmed carving dish and arrange the apple, onion and potato around the pork or, for easier carving, in a separate dish. Serve at once.

Cook's Notes

TIME
Preparation time is 5 minutes. Exact cooking time will depend on the size of the joint, but will be approximately 1¾ hours for the weight recommended here.

If the meat is cooked before you are ready, turn down the oven and keep the roast warm.

SERVING IDEAS
Shredded red cabbage baked in the oven with sliced cooking apple, onion, chicken broth and a dash of vinegar is a good sharp accompaniment to the richness of the roast pork and crackling.

Serve dry white wine as a drink with the meal to complement the flavors of the food.

PREPARATION
Scoring pork: Using a very sharp knife, make parallel cuts in the pork skin about ½-inch apart. Make sure that you cut right through the skin, to the thin layer of fat beneath the skin.

Crush dried rosemary well, to avoid any sharp spikes.

● 1110 calories per portion

Appleberry dumplings

SERVES 6
6 dessert apples
1 can (about 1 lb) blackberries,
 drained
juice of ½ lemon
1 package (17 oz) frozen puff pastry,
 thawed
1 large egg, beaten
superfine sugar
cream to serve (optional)

1 Preheat the oven to 425°.
2 Pare the apples and core carefully with an apple corer or vegetable parer. Brush with lemon juice.
3 Roll out the pastry on a lightly floured surface and trim to a 12 × 8 inch rectangle, then cut into 6 squares.
4 Pat the apples dry with paper towels. Place an apple on each square of pastry, then divide the drained blackberries equally between the apples, pressing them into the apple cavities.
5 Brush the pastry edges with some of the beaten egg, then wrap each apple loosely but completely sealing the joins firmly. ⚠
6 Place the dumplings, seam-side down on a dampened cookie sheet. Roll out the pastry trimmings and use to make leaves. Brush with cold water and place on top of the dumplings. Brush each one with the remaining egg and sprinkle with the sugar. ⚠ Make a small hole in the top of each dumpling to allow steam to escape during baking.
7 Bake in the oven 15 minutes then reduce to 350° and cook for a further 10 minutes until the apples are tender when pierced with a skewer. Serve with cream.

Cook's Notes

TIME
Preparation and cooking can be completed in 50 minutes.

VARIATIONS
When in season, use fresh blackberries. Also try using blackberry jelly.

WATCHPOINT
While cooking, the apples expand. It is therefore essential to wrap them *loosely* in the pastry or it will break open.
To help prevent the pastry bursting open, make sure the joins are well sealed with egg.

COOK'S TIP
Serve the dumplings straight from the oven. If they are allowed to cool, the apple shrinks back and looks rather sad when you cut through the pastry.

● 490 calories per portion

CHEAP AND CHEERFUL SUPPER

Here is a menu that conjures up a colorful and tasty meal for six without breaking the bank! The appetizer uses inexpensive seasonal vegetables served with an unusual hot dip, while the main course, an economical version of a traditional paella, is filling and substantial. A frothy citrus dessert is the perfect foil for the richer taste of the main course.

Cook's Notes

Smoky dip with vegetables

TIME
20 minutes to prepare the vegetables and 10-15 minutes to cook the dip.

ECONOMY
The tomato juice may be used in the Mock paella, if wished - add at stage 1 with the tomatoes.

COOK'S TIP
To ensure that the sauce is really smooth, put it back into the blender for a few seconds at this stage.

VARIATION
For a slightly more spicy dip, add a few drops of hot-pepper sauce.

● 135 calories per portion

Mock paella

TIME
15 minutes preparation, 35-40 minutes cooking.

SERVING IDEAS
The dish is a meal in itself, but serve with a green salad, if liked.

VARIATIONS
The ingredients can be varied according to taste and what stores you have to hand. For instance, try using left-over chicken or pork instead of the luncheon meat. Add a jar of drained mussels if your budget can stretch to it. A small can of whole kernel corn makes an interesting addition, too.

● 705 calories per portion

Smoky dip with vegetables

SERVES 6
¼ lb small mushrooms
1 large green pepper, seeded and cut into thin strips
4 carrots, cut into thin strips
1 cauliflower, broken into flowerets
1 bunch scallions

DIP
1 can (about 8 oz) tomatoes
⅔ cup milk
2 tablespoons butter or margarine
2 tablespoons all-purpose flour
1 teaspoon Dijon-style mustard
½-1 teaspoon chili powder
1 cup grated smoked cheese
black pepper

1 Make the dip: Drain the tomatoes (see Economy) and blend with the milk in a blender until smooth.
2 Melt the butter in a pan, sprinkle in the flour. Then add the mustard and chili powder to taste, and stir over low heat 1-2 minutes. Remove from the heat and gradually stir in the tomato and milk mixture. Return to the heat and simmer, stirring, until thick.
3 Add the grated cheese and stir over low heat until the cheese has melted (see Cook's tip).
4 Season to taste with pepper, transfer to a small serving bowl and place in the center of a large plate. Arrange the vegetables around the dip and serve while dip is warm.

Mock paella

SERVES 6

3 kabanos sausages, chopped into
  ½-inch lengths
1 can (about 11 oz) luncheon meat,
  cut into ½-inch dice
2 tablespoons vegetable oil
1 large onion, chopped
1 large red pepper, seeded and
  chopped
2 cloves garlic, crushed
  (optional)
6 oz smoked fatty bacon slices,
  chopped
3 tomatoes, peeled and chopped
1 teaspoon ground turmeric
1⅔ cups long-grain rice, rinsed
1½ cups frozen peas
2½-3 cups chicken broth
2 bay leaves
salt and freshly ground black
  pepper
1 can (about 7 oz) shrimp, drained
lemon wedges, to garnish

1 Heat the oil in a large skillet, add the onion, red pepper and garlic, if using, and cook gently 5 minutes until the onion is soft and lightly colored. Add the bacon and continue to cook for 3 minutes, then add the tomatoes and cook a further 5 minutes.

2 Add the chopped kabanos and luncheon meat and continue to cook, stirring, a further 2 minutes.

3 Stir in the turmeric, rice and frozen peas. Add about 2½ cups of the chicken broth, stir well and add the bay leaves. Season with salt and pepper to taste and simmer gently 20-25 minutes, stirring occasionally until the rice is tender and the liquid has been absorbed. Stir in the remaining broth, a little at a time, during cooking if the paella begins to look dry and the rice is not quite cooked.

4 Add the shrimp and stir until they are heated through. Discard the bay leaves, transfer the paella to a warmed serving dish and serve at once, garnished with lemon wedges.

Citrus snow

SERVES 6
1 small orange
1 lemon
1 lime
1¼ cups cold water
1 envelope unflavored
   gelatin
½ cup sugar
3 egg whites (see Economy)
candied orange and lemon slices, to
   decorate

1 Pour the cold water into a small saucepan and sprinkle in the gelatin. Leave to soak about 5 minutes.

2 Meanwhile, using a vegetable parer, thinly pare the rind from the orange, lemon and lime. Add to the spongy gelatin with the sugar.

3 Over low heat stir the mixture with a metal spoon until the sugar and gelatin have both dissolved. [!] Remove from the heat and leave to stand about 10 minutes.

4 Meanwhile, squeeze the juice from the orange, lemon and lime.

5 Put the gelatin mixture through a nylon strainer into a large bowl and add the squeezed fruit juices. Stir well, then refrigerate about 45 minutes, stirring occasionally, [!] until the mixture begins to thicken and turn syrupy.

6 Add the egg whites and beat until very thick (see Cook's tip). Turn into individual glasses and refrigerate for 3 hours.

7 Decorate the tops with candied orange and lemon slices just before serving up.

COUNTDOWN
In the morning
●Prepare the vegetables for the Smoky dip and refrigerate: Put the green pepper, cauliflower and scallions in a plastic bag, the carrots in a bowl of iced water and mushrooms in a covered bowl.
4 hours before
●Make Citrus snow; refrigerate.
1 hour before
●Make the Mock paella up to the end of stage 2.

15 minutes before
●Make the Smoky dip.
●Add the turmeric, rice, peas, broth and seasoning to the paella and simmer.
Just before the meal
●Transfer the dip to a serving dish and surround with the vegetables.
Just before the main course
●Stir the shrimp into the paella, garnish and serve.
Just before the dessert
●Decorate the Citrus snow.

Cook's Notes

 TIME
25 minutes preparation, plus thickening and chilling time.

COOK'S TIP
Beating with an electric beater will take about 10 minutes. Do not be tempted to skimp on this operation; the mixture should be really fluffy and thick.

 ECONOMY
If you do not want to use the left-over egg yolks straightaway, you can freeze them. Decide whether you want them for a sweet or savory dish and beat ¼ teaspoon sugar or salt into them. Pour into a small rigid container and freeze up to 6 months with salt and 8 months with sugar. Use as soon as thawed.

VARIATION
Use 3 lemons instead of the mixed fruits.

 WATCHPOINTS
Do not allow the mixture to boil.
The mixture must be stirred occasionally to prevent it from setting at the base.

●90 calories per portion

FREEZER DINNER

Make the most of your freezer with this delicious three-course meal! Scallops in tomato sauce, Orange chicken casserole and Frozen raspberry favorite, can be cooked in advance and stored in the freezer until required, leaving you free on the day to enjoy your own dinner party.

Scallops in tomato sauce

SERVES 6
12 cleaned scallops, fresh or frozen (see Cook's tips)
½ cup white wine or apple juice
½ cup water
1 bay leaf
10 peppercorns

SAUCE
1 small onion, finely chopped
1 small clove garlic, finely chopped (optional)
1 tablespoon olive oil or vegetable oil
1 lb tomatoes, peeled and chopped
pinch of sugar
2 teaspoons chopped fresh basil (optional)
1 teaspoon dried oregano
pinch of dried thyme
salt and freshly ground black pepper

TO GARNISH
¼ cup butter or margarine
1 lb potatoes, cooked and mashed
2-3 tablespoons warm milk

TO SERVE
2 tablespoons butter
2-3 tablespoons fine bread crumbs
1-2 tablespoons chopped fresh parsley

1 Bring the wine and water to a boil in a shallow pan with the bay leaf and peppercorns. Put in the scallops, cover the pan, and remove from the heat immediately, leaving the scallops in the liquid. ⚠
2 Preheat the oven to 400°.
3 To make the sauce: Heat the oil in a pan, add onion and garlic, if using, and cook gently until soft and lightly colored. Add the tomatoes, sugar, herbs and salt and pepper to taste, then strain in the liquid from the scallops. Bring to a boil, then lower the heat and simmer about 15 minutes until sauce is thick and almost all liquid has evaporated.

4 Slice the scallops, stir them into the sauce, then taste and adjust seasoning. Spoon into individual ovenproof dishes or scallop shells.
5 To prepare the garnish: Beat the butter into the mashed potato and add enough warm milk to give a smooth creamy mixture, stiff enough to pipe. Spoon into a pastry bag fitted with a plain or star tip, then pipe a decorative border around each dish.
6 Allow the scallops to cool completely. Open-freeze until solid, then wrap and seal in plastic wrap and label and return to the freezer.
7 To serve: Unwrap and reheat from frozen in a 375° oven about 15 minutes. Remove from the oven, dot with the butter and sprinkle with the bread crumbs. Return to the oven a further 15 minutes or until the topping is golden brown. Serve at once, sprinkled with parsley.

COUNTDOWN
3 months before
● Make the chicken casserole and freeze. Make the ice cream mixture and the raspberry sauce and freeze.

1 month before
● Prepare the scallops and freeze.

The day before
● Take the chicken casserole out of the freezer and allow to thaw overnight at room temperature.

4 hours before
● Take the raspberry sauce out of the freezer.

30 minutes before
● Take the scallops out of the freezer and thaw in the oven.

Immediately before serving
● Take the ice cream mixture out of the freezer. Decorate and pour sauce into a pitcher.

Cook's Notes

TIME
Total preparation time before freezing is about 40 minutes. (Can be stored in the freezer for up to 1 month.) The scallops then take about 30 minutes to thaw and finish before serving.

COOK'S TIPS
If using fresh scallops, reserve 6 of the deepest shells for serving. Frozen scallops are available off the shell in large supermarkets, freezer centers and high-class fishmongers. Shells can be bought separately at fishmongers and specially kitchen stores. They can be kept and used again.

If using frozen scallops, there is no need to thaw them. Add them to the hot wine liquid while still frozen, but bring the liquid back to a boil before removing from heat.

WATCHPOINT
Like all shellfish, scallops need very little cooking or they will become tough. The standing time in the hot liquid plus the browning in the oven is sufficient to cook them through.

● 300 calories per portion

Orange chicken casserole

SERVES 6

6 chicken pieces
2 tablespoons all-purpose flour
salt and freshly ground black
    pepper
¼ cup butter or margarine
1 tablespoon vegetable oil
1¼ cups dry white wine
⅔ cup orange juice
½ teaspoon ground coriander
½ teaspoon dried tarragon or
    chervil

TO SERVE

⅔ cup heavy cream
2 large oranges, peeled and
    sliced
⅓ cup pitted black olives,
    halved

1 Put the flour in a plastic bag and season with salt and pepper. Wipe the chicken pieces dry with paper towels, place in the bag and shake until they are well coated.

2 Melt the butter with the oil in a large flameproof casserole and cook the chicken until golden.

3 Pour the wine and orange juice into the casserole and add the coriander, tarragon and salt and pepper to taste. Cover and simmer over a low heat about 45 minutes, or until the chicken is cooked.

4 Transfer chicken and sauce to a rigid container, leaving headspace. Cool quickly, seal, label and freeze.

5 To serve: Thaw in container overnight in the refrigerator, or 4-5 hours at room temperature. Turn into a flameproof casserole and reheat gently until bubbling, stirring occasionally, then cover and cook 10 minutes. Remove the chicken from the sauce with a slotted spoon, place in a warmed serving dish and keep hot. Boil the sauce until reduced, stir in the cream and adjust seasoning.

6 Pour the sauce over the chicken. Cut the orange slices in half, then arrange a few on the chicken and remainder around the dish. Scatter over olives and serve at once.

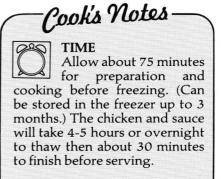

Cook's Notes

TIME
Allow about 75 minutes for preparation and cooking before freezing. (Can be stored in the freezer up to 3 months.) The chicken and sauce will take 4-5 hours or overnight to thaw then about 30 minutes to finish before serving.

● 490 calories per portion

Frozen raspberry favorite

SERVES 6
1¼ cups heavy cream
3 tablespoons kirsch or medium
   sweet sherry
8 ready-made meringue shells
   (see Buying guide), roughly
   broken
½ cup confectioners' sugar,
   sifted
1 lb fresh or frozen raspberries,
   thawed (see Variation)
vegetable oil, for greasing

TO SERVE
½ cup fresh or frozen raspberries,
   thawed

1 Brush the inside of an 8½ × 4½
× 2½ inches loaf pan with oil and
place in the bottom of the refrigerator to chill for 1 hour.
2 Beat the cream until it forms soft

peaks, then add the kirsch and beat
again until thickened.
3 Fold in the meringue pieces with
a metal spoon and 1 tablespoon of
the confectioners' sugar.
4 Turn the mixture into the chilled
pan, cover with foil, seal, label and
freeze.
5 Prepare the raspberry sauce:
Press the raspberries through a
sieve into a bowl, or work in a
blender. Stir in the sugar and mix
well. Pour into a rigid container,
seal, label and freeze.
6 To serve: Thaw the raspberry
sauce about 2-4 hours at room
temperature. Just before serving,
remove the ice cream from the
freezer and remove wrappings. Dip
the base of the pan into hot water 1-
2 seconds, then invert a serving
platter on top. Quickly invert the
pan onto the platter, giving a sharp
shake halfway round. Pour a little of
the sauce over the mold, decorate
with raspberries and serve at once.
Pour the remaining sauce into a
pitcher and hand separately.

MEAL IN UNDER AN HOUR

Friends are coming round for dinner at short notice! Don't panic, just follow this super-quick, super-delicious menu: the ingredients are uncomplicated and the meal can be on the table in under an hour. Open with a light egg appetizer, follow with steaks in a luscious vermouth sauce, and end with Peach flambé – your guests will think you've spent hours in the kitchen!

Egg mayonnaise appetizer

SERVES 4
6 large eggs, at room temperature
6 tablespoons thick-type
  mayonnaise (see Variation)
2 teaspoons lemon juice
¼ teaspoon dry mustard
salt and freshly ground black pepper

GARNISH
4 lettuce leaves
paprika

1 Put the eggs in a saucepan and cover with water. Bring to a boil then lower the heat and simmer gently 8-10 minutes. Drain off water and hold the pan under cold running water to cool the eggs quickly. As soon as the eggs are cool enough to handle, tap each one once against a hard surface to crack the shell, then cool (see Cook's tip).

2 Put the mayonnaise in a bowl and stir in the lemon juice, mustard and salt and pepper to taste.

3 Remove the shells from the cold eggs, then slice the eggs. Reserve 8 slices and chop the rest. Mix the chopped egg into the mayonnaise.

4 Arrange the lettuce leaves on individual serving plates and spoon the egg mixture onto them. Garnish each portion with 2 egg slices and sprinkle with paprika.

Steak with vermouth sauce

SERVES 4
4 beef steaks (see Buying guide)
freshly ground black pepper
2 tablespoons butter or margarine
1 tablespoon vegetable oil
sprigs of watercress, to garnish

SAUCE
2 tablespoons butter
⅔ cup red vermouth
½ teaspoon French grainy mustard
salt

1 Sprinkle the steaks with pepper on both sides.
2 Heat the butter and oil in a large skillet add the steaks and cook over brisk heat until browned on both sides, turning once. Remove

the steaks from the pan with a slotted spoon, arrange on a warmed serving platter and keep hot.
3 Make the sauce: Melt the butter in the pan over moderate heat. When it begins to froth, stir in the vermouth, mustard and salt and pepper to taste. Boil quickly until the liquid has become slightly syrupy.
4 Pour the sauce immediately over the steaks, garnish with watercress and serve at once.

Cook's Notes

Egg mayonnaise appetizer

TIME
35 minutes to cook and cool the eggs, then 10 minutes preparation.

COOK'S TIP
Cracking the shell will prevent a dark rim forming around the yolk.

VARIATION
Homemade mayonnaise made with olive oil will give a richer flavor to the dish.

SERVING IDEAS
The egg mayonnaise can also be served on points of buttered brown bread. Garnish with chopped walnuts and watercress. Or, serve it in stemmed glasses on shredded lettuce, layered with well-drained chopped tomato and cucumber.

● 280 calories per portion

Steak with vermouth sauce

TIME
10 minutes preparation and cooking time in total.

BUYING GUIDE
For best results, buy rump or sirloin steaks, cut about ¼-inch or so thick. Less expensive alternatives, sold in supermarkets, are flash-fry steaks — lean beef which has been tenderized – or minute steaks — the name often given to thin slices of sirloin.

SERVING IDEAS
Serve the steaks with small potatoes baked in their jackets, a frozen vegetable and baked tomatoes. Alternatively, serve with garlic bread and a fresh green salad, tossed in a dressing.

DID YOU KNOW
Vermouth is a wine-based drink to which alcohol and herbs have been added. The herb flavor makes it ideal for cooking. Available in both dry and sweet forms, it is sold under various well-known trade names. For cooking, the sweeter red vermouth goes well with steak, while the drier white marries well with chicken and fish.

● 455 calories per portion

COUNTDOWN

50 minutes before
● Put the potatoes in the oven (see Serving ideas) or prepare the garlic bread and green salad.
● Put the eggs onto boil for the Egg mayonnaise appetizer, and prepare the mayonnaise mixture; cover and refrigerate.

35 minutes before
● Drain the eggs, crack the shells, then leave to cool.
● Start making the Peach flambé: Dissolve the sugar in the butter, stir in the wine, add the peaches and remove the pan from the heat. Set aside until needed.

15 minutes before
● Bake the tomatoes, if using, or put the garlic bread in the oven.

10 minutes before
● Complete the Egg mayonnaise appetizer and refrigerate until needed.
● Put the frozen vegetables on to cook, if using.

Just before the main course
● Cook the steak, make the sauce, pour over the steak, garnish and serve.

Just before the dessert
● Warm the brandy, reheat the peaches, flambé and serve sprinkled with walnuts.

Peach flambé

SERVES 4
1 can (about 2 lb) peach halves
4 tablespoons brandy
¼ cup sweet butter
¼ cup superfine sugar
**⅓ cup medium-dry white
   wine**
**1 tablespoon finely chopped shelled
   walnuts**

1 Drain the peaches well (see Cook's tip).
2 Pour the brandy into a cup and stand in a pan or bowl of hot water to warm through gently.
3 Melt the butter in a large, heavy-based pan. Add the sugar and cook over low heat, stirring occasionally, until the sugar has dissolved.
4 Stir in the wine, bring the mixture to a gentle simmer and add the peaches. Turn the peaches several times in the liquid to heat through and absorb the flavor.
5 Remove the pan from the heat, poor the warmed brandy over the peaches and set alight..
6 Allow the flames to die down, spoon into individual bowls and sprinkle with the walnuts. Serve.

Cook's Notes

TIME
This special party dish takes just 15 minutes to prepare and serve.

! WATCHPOINT
Turn the peaches gently with a fish slice and a spatula so that they do not break up.

When lighting the brandy, stand well back and hold the match just above the side of the pan.

 SERVING IDEAS
Serve with whipped cream or ice cream and wafers or thin sweet cookies.

COOK'S TIP
The canned syrup is too sweet to be used in the flambé sauce. If stored, covered, in the refrigerator it will keep 2-3 days. Use it as the liquid for poaching fresh fruit.

● 400 calories per portion

BUDGET DINNER

A budget dinner need not mean a dull dinner. With a little forethought and imagination, some of the most delicious dishes can be made from the most economical of ingredients – and without spending hours in the kitchen. This menu of home-made soup, kabobs with rice and a barbecue sauce, and a meringue dessert is both economical and impressive.

Nearly all home-made soups are less expensive than bought ones, and also have infinitely better flavor. So impress your guests by making a soup such as creamy watercress, which is not only economical, but unobtainable from a package or can.

For the main course of the meal, show just what can be done with ground beef by making it into mouthwatering kabobs topped with a spicy sauce. Cut main course costs even further by choosing the best of the vegetables in season to accompany the kabobs. Budget desserts are often uninspiring, but not this Meringue dessert, an English dish which is a perfect all-year standby, most useful in the dark days of winter when there are few interesting and inexpensive fresh fruits in season.

When entertaining, it is always important, and polite, to know your guests' likes and dislikes. This is particularly so with budget food – many bargain buys are cheap simply because they are not popular! If you know what to buy, and how to prepare it – then your family and friends will be in for a pleasant surprise and a tasty treat.

Creamy watercress soup

SERVES 4
2 bunches watercress
1 medium onion, quartered
2½ cups well-flavored chicken broth (preferably homemade, see Economy)
1 teaspoon lemon juice
salt and freshly ground black pepper
2 tablespoons cornstarch
1¼ cups milk
pinch of freshly ground nutmeg

Cook's Notes

TIME
This soup takes 45 minutes to make.

VARIATION
Substitute 1 package (about 9 oz) frozen leaf or chopped spinach for watercress.

ECONOMY
To be even more economical, and improve the flavor, make your own broth from left-over chicken carcass.

COOK'S TIP
A quick way to blend cornstarch and milk without first making a paste is to whizz it for a few seconds in the blender, after puréeing the soup.

● 95 calories per portion

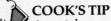

1 Put watercress into a saucepan, reserving a few sprigs for the garnish. Add the onion, chicken broth, lemon juice and salt and pepper to taste.
2 Bring to a boil, then lower the heat, cover the pan and simmer 30 minutes. Remove from the heat and leave to cool slightly.
3 Work the soup to a smooth purée in a blender or rub through a sieve.
4 Return the soup to the rinsed-out pan. Mix cornstarch to a paste with a little of the milk, then stir in the remaining milk. Stir this mixture slowly into the soup, then bring to a boil, stirring all the time. Simmer for 2 minutes.
5 Add the nutmeg, taste and adjust seasoning, then pour into warmed individual soup bowls. Serve piping hot, garnished with watercress sprigs.

Beefball and apricot kabobs

SERVES 4
1 lb lean ground beef
1 small onion, grated
½ cup fresh white bread crumbs
½ teaspoon ground ginger
¼ teaspoon dried thyme
½ teaspoon salt
¼ teaspoon freshly ground black pepper
1 egg, lightly beaten
6 slices fatty bacon, cut in half
6 large dried apricots, halved

BARBECUE SAUCE
3 tablespoons wine vinegar
2 tablespoons light brown sugar
2 tablespoons tomato catsup
2 tablespoons fruit chutney
2 teaspoons cornstarch
2 teaspoons soy sauce
1¼ cups water
salt and freshly ground black pepper

1 Preheat broiler to high.
2 Mix together the beef, onion, bread crumbs, ginger, thyme and salt and pepper. Add the egg, then mix with your hands until combined (see Cook's tip). Shape into 16 balls.
3 Wrap each bacon slice around each apricot half.
4 Thread the meatballs and apricots in bacon alternatively onto 4 skewers, allowing 4 meatballs and 3 apricots in bacon for each. ✳
5 Broil the kabobs 7-10 minutes, turning them over frequently until browned and cooked through. ⚠
6 Meanwhile, make the sauce: Put all the ingredients into a saucepan and bring to boil, stirring constantly. Boil 2 minutes.
7 Serve at once on a bed of rice, with the sauce poured over.

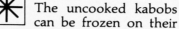

Cook's Notes

TIME
The kabobs take 35 minutes.

COOK'S TIP
Mixing the meat with your hands is quick and makes it easier to shape.

BUYING GUIDE
Make sure you buy really lean ground beef for this dish. Fatty ground beef will make the meatballs shrink and lose their shape when cooked, so it is a false economy.

WATCHPOINT
If the kabobs look as if they are going to burn, reduce the heat and continue to broil until they are cooked through. Remember to keep turning them frequently.

FREEZING
The uncooked kabobs can be frozen on their skewers for up to 1 month, wrapped individually in foil or plastic wrap. To use, unwrap and broil from frozen for about 15 minutes. Uncooked meatballs can be frozen individually, then packed together in a plastic bag or rigid container. They can then be used for quick family snacks and suppers since you can take out only as many as you need.

● 525 calories per portion

Meringue dessert

SERVES 4
6 oz pie crust sticks

FILLING
1¼ cups milk
grated rind of 1 lemon
1 cup fresh white bread crumbs
2 medium eggs, separated
¼ cup butter or margarine
½ cup superfine sugar
1 teaspoon vanilla
3 tablespoons raspberry jelly

1 Preheat the oven to 350°.
2 Roll out the dough on a floured board and use to line an 8 inch flan ring standing on a cookie sheet. Set aside to rest while you prepare the filling.
3 Bring the milk to a boil in a saucepan, remove from the heat, then add the lemon rind, bread crumbs, yolks, butter, ¼ cup sugar and the vanilla. Stir well with a wooden spoon until the bread crumbs have absorbed most of the milk. Leave to cool.
4 Spread jelly over the base of the uncooked pie shell, then pour all of the bread crumb mixture on top. ⚠
5 Bake in the oven 45 minutes until the filling is set, then carefully remove the flan ring.
6 Beat the egg whites until they stand in soft peaks. Fold in the remaining sugar with a metal spoon, then pile the meringue on top of the cooked pudding. ⚠
7 Return to the oven and bake a further 15 minutes, or until the meringue is browned. Transfer to a serving plate and serve either warm or cold.

Cook's Notes

TIME
Preparation time about 30 minutes, including time for making fresh pastry. Allow an extra 30 minutes for the pastry to chill before using. Baking time is 1 hour.

WATCHPOINTS
Take care when putting the pie in the oven with the uncooked filling; it is fairly runny and can easily spill over onto the cookie sheet.
Beat the egg whites for the meringue topping immediately before they are put on the pudding. If beaten in advance they will deflate, and become watery.
Make sure the meringue touches the pastry all round or it will shrink back during cooking and look unsightly.

COOK'S TIP
The quantities given here will produce at least 4 ample portions. Any leftover pudding is delicious cold.

● 535 calories per portion

COCKTAIL PARTY

Inviting a few friends round for drinks? Why not be adventurous – and serve cocktails? Choose one or two from the chart on page 476, offer them with our two sophisticated nibbles, and your evening is sure to be a wild success!

Mixing cocktails

The ingredients for cocktails are either stirred or shaken together. Traditionally, a cocktail shaker is used for shaking the ingredients, and many of these have built-in strainers, but rather than going to the expense of buying one especially for this occasion, you can easily improvise with a tight-lidded jar and a small strainer.

To shake a cocktail, put enough crushed ice into the shaker to cover the base to a depth of about 1 inch. Then add the ingredients, shake and strain into the glass.

Crushed ice is often a vital ingredient of the drink – to prepare the ice, either crush ice cubes in a strong blender or food processor, or put ice in a strong plastic bag and crush with a wooden mallet or rolling pin.

A proper cocktail measure is very helpful, but a standard measuring cup and spoon can be used if the ingredients are kept in the proportions given in the recipes. As a guide remember that a measure normally equals 2 tablespoons.

The proportions given on page 476 are for one serving only.

Hot cheese and crab dip

SERVES 12
1½ cups grated sharp Cheddar cheese
¼ cup butter or margarine
½ cup all-purpose flour
2 cups milk
1 tablespoon lemon juice
1 teaspoon Worcestershire sauce
1 teaspoon Dijon-style mustard
salt and freshly ground black pepper
2-3 tablespoons finely chopped canned pimiento
2-3 tablespoons finely chopped green pepper
6 black olives, pitted and finely chopped
4 tablespoons dry white wine
1 can (about 6 oz) crabmeat, drained and all cartilage removed

TO SERVE
small Melba toast squares
small cubes of French bread
small savory crackers

1 Melt the butter in a saucepan, sprinkle in the flour and stir over low heat 1-2 minutes until straw-colored. Remove from the heat and gradually stir in the milk. Return to the heat and simmer, stirring, until thick and smooth.

2 Remove from the heat and stir in the cheese until melted and smooth. Add the lemon juice, Worcestershire sauce, mustard and salt and pepper to taste and mix well.

3 Stir in the pimiento, green pepper, olives, wine and crabmeat, then heat through gently, stirring.

4 Pour into a warmed serving dish. Serve at once with small Melba toast squares, cubes of French bread and savory crackers (see Cook's tip).

Cook's Notes

TIME
10 minutes preparation;
10 minutes cooking.

COOK'S TIP
This dip is best if served piping hot. If possible, stand it on a warmed serving tray or hostess trolley.

● 160 calories per portion

Chili meat balls

MAKES 36-40
1 lb lean ground beef
2 tablespoons tomato catsup
2 tablespoons mild chili sauce
1 tablespoon Worcestershire sauce
1 cup cornflakes, finely crushed
½ cup canned evaporated milk
salt and freshly ground black pepper
vegetable oil, for greasing

DIPPING SAUCE
5 tablespoons tomato catsup
3 tablespoons mild chili sauce
1 tablespoon lemon juice
¾ teaspoon creamed horseradish
¾ teaspoon Worcestershire sauce
few drops of hot-pepper sauce

1 Preheat the oven to 400°. Grease 2 cookie sheets with oil.
2 Place the beef in a large bowl together with the tomato catsup, chili sauce, Worcestershire sauce, cornflakes and evaporated milk. Season with salt and pepper to taste, then mix well together with your fingers.
3 Shape the beef mixture into about 40 bite-sized meat balls (see Cook's tip) and arrange on the greased cookie sheets. Cook in the oven 15-20 minutes or until browned.
4 Meanwhile, make the sauce: Put the tomato catsup in a small serving bowl and stir in the rest of the sauce ingredients. Place the bowl of sauce in the center of a large platter.
5 Serve the meat balls on a warmed serving dish accompanied by the dipping sauce (see Serving ideas).

Cook's Notes

 TIME
The meat balls take about 10 minutes preparation, then 15-20 minutes cooking.

 COOK'S TIP
The meat balls should be about the same size as walnuts, so that they are easy to eat in one mouthful.

SERVING IDEAS
Provide wooden or colored plastic toothpicks so that the meat balls can be dipped into the sauce and eaten without difficulty.

● 130 calories per portion

COCKTAILS

COCKTAIL	INGREDIENTS	METHOD	TO SERVE
Gin-based:			
Boxcar	3 tablespoons gin 3 tablespoons Cointreau 1 teaspoon lime juice 1 egg white 1-2 dashes grenadine	Put all ingredients in shaker with crushed ice and shake well	First frost rim of champagne glass: dip glass into beaten egg white and then superfine sugar. Strain cocktail into glass
Gimlet	¼ cup gin 2 teaspoons sweetened lime juice	Put ingredients in shaker with crushed ice and shake well	Strain into old-fashioned type glass and add ice cubes
Martini	¼ cup gin 1-2 teaspoons dry vermouth	Stir ingredients together	Serve in chilled cocktail glass garnished with an olive or twist of lemon rind
Bourbon or whiskey-based:			
Horse's Neck	5 tablespoons whiskey few drops of lemon juice ginger ale	Stir whiskey and lemon juice together, then add ice cubes and fill glass with ginger ale	Serve in a highball glass garnished with a long spiral of lemon rind
Manhattan	5 tablespoons whiskey 2 tablespoons sweet vermouth	Stir ingredients together	Serve in cocktail glass garnished with maraschino cherry
Vodka-based:			
Black Russian	3 tablespoons vodka 1½ tablespoons coffee liqueur	Put ingredients in shaker with crushed ice and shake well	Strain into an old-fashioned type glass and add crushed ice.
Bloody Mary	3 tablespoons vodka 6 tablespoons tomato juice 1 tablespoon lemon juice dash of Worcestershire sauce few drops of hot-pepper sauce salt and black pepper	Put all ingredients in shaker with crushed ice and shake well. Strain and season to taste with salt and pepper	Serve in tall glass garnished with stick of cucumber and mint sprigs or lemon wedge
Harvey Wallbanger	2 tablespoons vodka orange juice 2 teaspoons galliano	Put vodka in glass, add ice cubes and fill with orange juice. Stir, then float galliano on top	Serve in tall glass
Rum-based:			
Between the sheets	2 tablespoons rum 2 tablespoons brandy 2 tablespoons Cointreau 1 teaspoon lemon juice	Put all ingredients in shaker with crushed ice and shake well	Strain into an old-fashioned type glass and add crushed ice
Daiquiri	¼ cup white rum 2 tablespoons lime juice 1 teaspoon sugar syrup	Put all ingredients in shaker with crushed ice and shake well	Strain into cocktail glass and add crushed ice
Tequila-based:			
Marguerita	¼ cup tequila 2 teaspoons Cointreau 1 tablespoon lime juice	Place all ingredients in shaker with crushed ice and shake well	Frost rim of cocktail glass: dip glass into lime juice and then salt. Strain cocktail into glass
Tequila Sunrise	¼ cup tequila ½ cup orange juice 2 teaspoons grenadine	Put tequila in glass, add ice cubes and fill glass with orange juice. Stir. Slowly pour in grenadine so it settles on bottom of glass	Serve in tall glass garnished with lemon slice. Stir cocktail before drinking

FESTIVE MEAL

This menu has been created to serve on that special festive occasion when traditional charm and flavor are appropriate. The meal begins with a melon and shrimp cocktail that is suitably light and refreshing before the main course of stuffed turkey which is half boned to make carving easier. The dessert is impressively flambéed with the added surprise of a fruity, creamy center. So, gather your friends and celebrate with our festive meal.

Melon and shrimp cocktail

SERVES 8

1 small honeydew melon, seeded and pared
2 tablespoons red wine vinegar
4 tablespoons vegetable oil
1 teaspoon Dijon-style mustard
1 tablespoon chopped fresh parsley
salt and freshly ground black pepper
1 large red dessert apple
3 celery stalks, thinly sliced
1½ cups peeled shrimp
8 unpeeled shrimp, to garnish

1 Put the vinegar, oil, mustard and parsley into a bowl. Season with salt and pepper. Beat well.
2 Cut the melon into small neat cubes. Quarter and core the apple but do not pare it, then cut the flesh into neat cubes.
3 Put the melon, celery, apple and shrimp into the dressing and mix lightly together. Spoon the melon and shrimp mixture into 6 serving glasses. Garnish and serve at once.

Festive turkey

SERVES 8

9 lb turkey, boned (see Buying guide and Preparation)
⅓ cup butter, softened
2 tablespoons all-purpose flour
2½ cups turkey broth, made from the giblets and bones
sliced red and green pepper, to garnish

STUFFING

1 tablespoon corn oil
1 large onion, finely chopped
1 small red pepper, seeded and chopped
1 small green pepper, seeded and chopped
1 cup chopped lean ham
3 cups fresh white bread crumbs
2 teaspoons dried mixed herbs
3 tablespoons chopped fresh parsley
1 lb pork sausagemeat
1 egg
salt and freshly ground black pepper

1 Make the stuffing: Heat the oil in a large skillet, add the onion and peppers and cook gently 5 minutes until the onion is soft and lightly colored. Cool completely.
2 Put the ham, bread crumbs, herbs, sausagemeat and egg into a large bowl. Add the onion and peppers and season well with salt and pepper. Mix thoroughly together.
3 Preheat the oven to 375°.
4 Lay the boned turkey out flat on a board, skin-side down, and tuck in the small pieces of wing. Then trim off the excess skin at the neck and season the turkey well with salt and pepper. Stuff the body cavity and upper part of the legs where the bone has gone (to stop legs collapsing during roasting). Bring the sides of the turkey neatly up and over the stuffing to enclose it completely.
5 Using a large trussing needle and fine string, neatly sew up the turkey along the backbone where it was cut, to seal in the stuffing.
6 Turn the turkey over so that it is breast side up again. Press into a neat shape and tie the legs tightly together. Spread the skin with the softened butter and season with salt and pepper.
7 Wrap tightly in foil, put in roasting pan and roast 2½ hours.
8 Remove the foil from the turkey and continue to roast 60 minutes until the turkey is tender and the juices run clear when the thickest part of the thigh is pierced with a skewer.
9 Transfer the turkey to a warmed serving platter and allow to stand at least 30 minutes to firm up before carving.
10 Meanwhile, make the gravy: Drain off all the fat from the roasting pan, leaving behind the turkey juices. Sprinkle in the flour and cook over low heat until lightly colored. Stir in the broth and bring to a boil, scraping up all the sediment from the base of the pan. Reduce the heat slightly and simmer gently for 10-15 minutes. Strain into a warmed sauceboat.
11 Just before serving, remove the string from the turkey and garnish with red and green pepper slices. To serve, carve into slices, cutting right across the bird. Remove the legs in the normal way.

Cook's Notes

Melon and shrimp cocktail

TIME
This light appetizer takes 20 minutes to prepare.

● 120 calories per portion

Festive turkey

TIME
2 hours preparation, then 3½ hours roasting.

PREPARATION
To bone the turkey, first cut off the parson's nose.

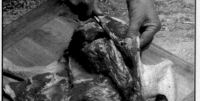

1 Place the turkey breast-side down and cut through skin all along backbone. Carefully scrape flesh away from carcass, close to ribs, cutting thighs and wings free.

2 To remove top leg bone and top wing bone, scrape flesh from all round bones, then break ball and socket joints and pull out top bones. Repeat on other side. Ease knife between skin and breastbone and lift out the carcass. Do not cut through breast skin.

BUYING GUIDE
Boning is fairly difficult but becomes easier with practice. Use a fresh turkey, as the skin of a frozen bird is more likely to break. You can ask your butcher to bone it, but give him plenty of advance warning.

● 820 calories per portion

Flambéed ice cream dessert

SERVES 8

¼ cup candied cherries
⅓ cup dried apricots
⅓ cup pitted dates
2 tablespoons golden raisins
2 tablespoons seedless raisins
2 tablespoons candied peel
6 tablespoons brandy
2 cups heavy cream
⅔ cup sifted confectioners' sugar
1 teaspoon vanilla

CHOCOLATE COATING
6 squares (6 oz) semisweet chocolate
  broken into small pieces
2 tablespoons water
2 tablespoons butter

1 Cut the cherries, apricots and dates into small pieces, then put them in a bowl with the raisins and peel.

2 Add half the brandy to fruits and mix well. Cover and leave to stand at least 2 hours, stirring occasionally, until the fruits have softened and absorbed all the alcohol.

3 Pour the cream into a bowl, add confectioners' sugar and vanilla and beat until the cream forms soft peaks. Fold in the soaked fruits.

4 Spoon the cream mixture into a 1 quart pudding bowl and smooth the top. Cover with plastic wrap and freeze 4-5 hours until frozen solid.

5 Remove from the freezer, then dip a spatula in hot water and run around the edge of the dessert. Place a round of foil on top of the pudding, turn out onto a small wire rack and return to the freezer while you are preparing the chocolate coating.

6 Put the chocolate, water and butter in a heatproof bowl. Set the bowl over a pan half full of simmering water and leave, stirring occasionally, until the chocolate is melted.

7 Remove the dessert from the freezer and place the rack over a plate. Pour the chocolate coating over the frozen pudding, smoothing it round the sides with a spatula to coat it completely — the chocolate does not have to be completely smooth. Return to the freezer until

chocolate hardens. ✳

8 Pour remaining brandy into a pan and heat through gently.

9 To serve: Remove the dessert from the freezer, peel off the foil round the base and place the pudding on a serving plate. Set light

to the warmed brandy and pour, flaming, over the dessert. Allow to flame until the chocolate starts to bubble round the base, then blow out the flames and serve.

COUNTDOWN
2 days before
● Make and freeze the Flambéed iced cream dessert.
The day before
● Bone the turkey and make the turkey broth.
In the morning
● Thaw the shrimp for the Melon and shrimp cocktail.
● Make the stuffing for the Festive turkey, stuff the turkey and sew up.
3½ hours before
● Roast the turkey.
20 minutes before
● Prepare the Melon and shrimp cocktail.
Just before the meal
● Transfer the turkey to a platter.
Just before the main course
● Make the gravy and carve turkey.
Just before the dessert
● Remove the pudding from the freezer, heat the brandy, ignite and pour over the pudding.

BARBECUE PARTY

A barbecue party is the perfect way to relax with friends on a warm summer's evening. Cooking in the open is a lot of fun, and so easy to organize – less washing up for you, and guests can join in with the cooking! Try our exotic selection of three spicy dishes using marinated pork, chicken and lamb from which guests can pick and choose. Accompany them with an unusual Coconut rice salad and finish with a refreshing Orange and lemon water-ice.

BARBECUE KNOW-HOW

Equipment: There are many portable barbecues which can be bought or hired, but you can improvise by building your own with bricks or using a container such as a garden refuse burner. All you really need is a hole for the draught to keep the fire burning and a grid (oven shelves are ideal).

Fuel: Always use charcoal for burning. This can be bought in bags from hardware stores, garden centers and some large supermarkets. Briquettes are more expensive than ordinary charcoal pieces, but they usually burn for longer and are, therefore, more economical in the long run – they are also less messy to use. You will also need a stock of firelighters.

Tools: Long-handled barbecue tool sets, which usually comprise tongs, a spatula and a two-pronged fork, are a must for easy handling of food – and for safety; they are widely available and inexpensive.

Other general utensils: You will need a brush for brushing oil or marinade onto the food to keep it moist during barbecuing, and prevent it sticking to the grid; long metal skewers for kabobs; a slotted spoon for removing meat from marinades and pot holders for protecting your hands and paper towels for mopping up.

Lighting the barbecue: Light the charcoal 45-60 minutes before you intend to cook. The simplest way to light the coals is to mound them up in a pyramid in the center of the barbecue and insert some fire-lighters in between the coals. Barbecue lighting fluid can also be used – it is very efficient; so too are special barbecue pokers, but these are expensive and only worth buying if you intend to do a lot of barbecuing. When the flames have subsided and the coals look gray or

glow red in the dark, you can start cooking. Always oil the grid before starting to cook.

Cooking: a constant eye must be kept on the food to make sure that it does not burn. For a party to serve

12 people such as this one, it is unlikely that all the meats will fit on the grid at the same time so the food will have to be cooked in batches — the idea of our menu is that guests can pick and choose from the selection of meats and cook their own at their leisure.

Since appetites will be stimulated in the open air, it is a good idea to serve lots of accompaniments with the barbecued meat. The rice dish we suggest is a good filler and the Indian flavor combines well with the spiciness of the meat. A selection of different salads would make a refreshing addition. Potatoes wrapped in foil and baked over the grid are delicious served with dairy sour cream, or try barbecuing parcels of vegetables, such as drained canned whole kernel corn or sliced mushrooms, mixed with a little butter.

A clever tip for creating an extra herby flavor, is to sprinkle the hot coals with mixed dried herbs.

COUNTDOWN
2-3 days before
● Make the Orange and lemon water-ice.

The day before
● Prepare the coconut and cook the rice for the Coconut rice salad.

4 hours before
● Prepare the 3 marinades.
● Put the chicken, pork and lamb in their marinades.

1 hour before
● Light the barbecue.
● Mix the dressing for rice salad.

15 minutes before
● Begin cooking on the barbecue.
● Mix together all the ingredients for the Coconut rice salad.

Just before serving
● Take water-ice out of the freezer.

Curried pork

SERVES 12

3 pork tenderloins, total weight about 2½ lb, trimmed and halved lengthwise (see Buying guide)

MARINADE
8 tablespoons vegetable oil
2 tablespoons curry powder
2 tablespoons tomato paste
1 large onion, finely chopped
salt and freshly ground black pepper

1 First make the marinade: Put the oil into a large bowl with the curry powder, tomato paste, onion and salt and pepper to taste. Mix well.
2 Cut each tenderloin half into bite-sized pieces.
3 Put the meat into the marinade and stir well to make sure each piece is well coated. Cover and leave to marinate in a cool place at least 3 hours.
4 Thread the pork pieces onto 12 oiled skewers, reserving any marinade left in the bowl.
5 To cook: Place the skewers on the oiled grid and barbecue about 10 minutes until cooked through, turning several times and brushing occasionally with any reserved marinade during cooking.

Chicken in yogurt and ginger

SERVES 12

12 boneless skinned chicken breasts, each weighing about 5 oz
vegetable oil, for brushing

MARINADE
1¼ cups plain yogurt
2 tablespoons finely chopped fresh root ginger (see Buying guide), or 2 teaspoons ground ginger
½ teaspoon ground cardamom
½ teaspoon cayenne pepper
2 tablespoons finely chopped fresh coriander or parsley
1 teaspoon salt
2 cloves garlic, crushed (optional)

1 Put all the marinade ingredients, including the garlic, if using, into a large bowl and then stir them all well to mix.
2 Pat the chicken breasts dry with paper towels, then place in the marinade, making sure they are well coated. Cover and leave to marinate in a cool place at least 3 hours.
3 To cook: Remove the chicken breasts from the marinade with a slotted spoon, place on the oiled grid and barbecue about 10 minutes until cooked through, turning several times. Brush occasionally with oil during cooking.

Spiced lamb

SERVES 12

12 lean lamb chops, each weighing about ¼ lb
vegetable oil, for brushing

DRY MARINADE
1 tablespoon finely chopped fresh root ginger, or 1 teaspoon ground ginger
2 cloves garlic, crushed (optional)
1 teaspoon ground cardamom
½ teaspoon ground cinnamon
1 teaspoon ground cumin
¼ teaspoon cayenne pepper
2 teaspoons ground turmeric
salt and freshly ground black pepper

1 First make the dry marinade: Mix the ginger and garlic, if using, in a shallow dish with all the spices and plenty of salt and pepper.
2 Place the lamb chops in the dish and turn them in the spice mixture to make sure each chop is well coated. Cover the dish and leave to marinate in a cool place for at least 3 hours.
3 To cook: Place the chops on the oiled grid and barbecue 10-15 minutes until cooked through, turning several times with tongs and a fork. Brush occasionally with oil during cooking.

Cook's Notes

Curried pork

TIME
15 minutes to prepare, then at least 3 hours to marinate, 10 minutes cooking.

BUYING GUIDE
Pork tenderloin is an expensive cut, but there is so little fat on it that it is not so uneconomical as it may seem at first. Each tenderloin weighs about ¾ lb.

● 235 calories per portion

Chicken in yogurt and ginger
TIME
20 minutes to prepare, then at least 3 hours to marinate, 10 minutes cooking.

BUYING GUIDE
You can buy fresh root ginger and coriander at some farm markets and larger supermarkets. Peel fresh ginger with a vegetable parer before chopping.

● 190 calories per portion

Spiced lamb

TIME
10 minutes to prepare, then at least 3 hours to marinate and 10-15 minutes cooking.

● 175 calories per portion

Coconut rice salad

SERVES 12
1 lb long-grain rice
salt
3 chicken bouillon cubes, crumbled
2 teaspoons cumin seeds
1 small coconut, broken open and flesh removed (see Preparation), or 1 package (about ½ lb) shredded coconut
4 tablespoons corn or vegetable oil
2 tablespoons red wine vinegar
3 tablespoons finely chopped fresh parsley
¼ teaspoon dry mustard
freshly ground black pepper
3 bananas
1 cup salted peanuts

1 Fill a large saucepan with salted water and add crumbled bouillon cubes. Bring to a boil, then add the rice and cumin seeds. Stir once to mix the ingredients together, then cover and simmer gently 20-25 minutes until the rice is tender.

2 Pour the cooked rice into a strainer and rinse well under cold running water. Leave to cool and drain well.

3 Meanwhile, grate the coconut flesh finely.

4 Put the oil in a large serving bowl with vinegar, parsley, mustard and pepper to taste. Mix well.

5 Just before serving: Pare the bananas and slice them directly into the dressing. Mix lightly. Add the rice, grated coconut and peanuts ⚠ and fork lightly together.

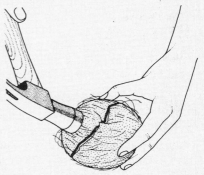

until it has frozen to a width of about 1 inch around the edge, then remove from the freezer and stir well with a large metal spoon until evenly blended. Return to the freezer and freeze a further 3 hours or until the water-ice is frozen to a firm mushy consistency, not completely hard. Stir with a metal spoon once every hour during this freezing process.

8 Fill the orange cases with the water-ice, mounding it up well on top. Replace the "lids", pressing them in at an angle. Return the oranges to the freezer for 1-2 hours or until the water-ice is frozen.

9 When ready to serve, remove the oranges from the freezer and place on small decorative plates or saucers. Serve at once.

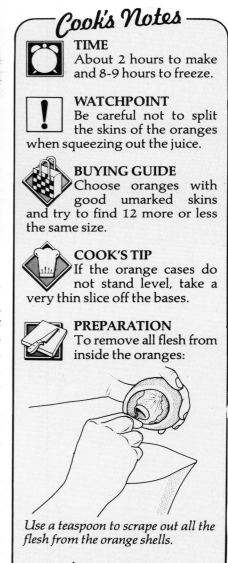

Cook's Notes

TIME
About 2 hours to make and 8-9 hours to freeze.

WATCHPOINT
Be careful not to split the skins of the oranges when squeezing out the juice.

BUYING GUIDE
Choose oranges with good umarked skins and try to find 12 more or less the same size.

COOK'S TIP
If the orange cases do not stand level, take a very thin slice off the bases.

PREPARATION
To remove all flesh from inside the oranges:

Use a teaspoon to scrape out all the flesh from the orange shells.

● 190 calories per portion

Orange and lemon water-ice

SERVES 12
12 oranges (see Buying guide)
8-9 lemons
1 cup water
2 cups sugar

1 Set the refrigerator or freezer at its coldest setting.
2 Wash the oranges and 3 of the lemons. With a vegetable parer, pare the rind from the 3 lemons thinly, then put them into a saucepan with the water and sugar. Stir over a low heat until the sugar has dissolved, then bring to a boil. Boil for 2 minutes, without stirring, remove from the heat, cover and leave the syrup to stand for 1 hour.
3 Squeeze all the lemons and measure out about 2 cups juice, making up the quantity with water if necessary. Cut the top third off each orange and carefully squeeze out the juice from the bottom two-thirds. ⚠ Strain both lemon and orange juices together – you should have about 6 cups.
4 Remove all the remaining flesh from the orange cases (see Preparation). Put the orange cases and "lids" on a tray (see Cook's tip) and put into the freezer.
5 Choose a very large bowl that will fit into the freezer compartment of a refrigerator or fast-freeze compartment of a freezer.
6 Pour the orange and lemon juice into the bowl then strain in the sugar syrup and stir well.
7 Freeze the juice for about 4 hours,

INDEX

A

Acapulco pineapple pudding 408
American chocolate pie 188
Appleberry dumplings 461
Apple(s)
    Appleberry dumplings 461
    and Avocado grill 75
    Baked, date and walnuts 230
    Baked potatoes, with 385
    Breast of lamb and, 116
    Caramel-topped 444
    and Cheese pie 313
    and Cider roast pork 460
    and Citrus flan 194
    Flummery 201
    Fruit kebobs 176
    Gingered fruit cocktails 175
    and Gooseberry amber 173
    Harvest pudding 172
    Lemons and, cup 455
    Nutty crumble 236
    Riviera fruit salad 427
    Roast pork 460
    Spicy crunch 186
    Stuffed veal chops 111
    Tropical salad 247
    Waldorf salad 353
Apricot(s)
    Barbecue chicken 275
    Beefball and, kebobs 471
    Honeyed whips 202
    and Lamb salad 284
    Tropical crumble 233
Asparagus
    Chilled soup 439
    Lamb and, casserole 121
Autumn soup 13
Avocado
    and Apple grill 75
    Dip 337
    Egg bake 71
    and Grapefruit salad 359
    Ice cream 215
    Mexican beef 106

B

Bacon
    Baconburgers 279
    Kebobs with peanut dip 80
    Leek and, flan 306
    and Liver hotpot 162
    and Onion crispies 78
    Sandwiches in batter 322
    Savoury fritters 84
Baked ham and tomato sandwiches
    320
Baked honey ribs 91
Baked mincemeat soufflé 214
Baked potatoes with apple 385
Baked stuffed peppers 40
Bananas
    Chicken double deckers 318
    Creams 450
    Fan flambé 242
    Fruit kebobs 176
    Ham fritters, with 265
    Mixed fruit ice 216
    and Plum compote 171
    Riviera fruit salad 427
    Spiced dumplings 168
    Tropical crumble 233
Barbecue 480
Bean(s)
    and Beef crumble 281
    Creamy spring vegetables 372
    Herby, with eggs 256
    and Pea salad 358
    and Pea soup chilled 349
    Spicy pâté 336
    Stir-fried, and beansprouts 398
Beef
    and Bean crumble 281
    Beefball and apricot kebobs 471
    Beefburger parcels 267
    Beefburgers 454
    Chilli meat balls 475
    Crusty steak sandwiches 324
    Curry 107
    Flemish beef casserole 105
    Goulash 109
    Marinade 428
    Marinated summer 102
    Meat terrine 29
    Mexican 106
    Pot roast brisket 104
    Quick curry 302
    Scotch, casserole 428
    Serbian 110
    Spaghetti with meat balls 282
    Steak and parsnip pie 101
    Steak with vermouth sauce 469
    Stilton steak 100
    Stir-fried, with cashews 108
    Tacos 407
    Tasty hamburgers 103
    Tasty meat triangles 264
Beefball and apricot kebobs 471
Beefburger parcels 267
Beefburgers 454
Beefy soup 11
Biriani, vegetable 403
Blackberry(ies)
    Appleberry dumplings 461
    Harvest pudding 172
Bread and butter pudding 234
Bread, pineapple 166
Breast of lamb and apple rounds
    116
Breton steaks 145
Brown bread ice cream 218
Brussels sprouts
    Country style 388
    and Date salad 360
    Soup 339
    and Stilton 258
    Sweet and sour 401
Bulgur wheat casserole 376
Butterfly birthday cake 453

C

Cabbage
    Crisp and crunchy salad 357
    Gratin 377
    and Lemon sauce 386
Cannelloni with tuna 293
Caramel
    Chips 444
    Rich mould 207
    Spanish custard 424
    Topped apples 444
Carrot
    Crudités with butter bean dip
    338
    Crudités and dip 421
    in Orange juice 382
    and Orange soup, chilled 23
    and Parsley soup 261
    Soup, with egg and rice 347
Casseroles and stews
    Beef goulash 109
    Bulgur wheat 376
    Chicken catalan 422
    Chicken paprikash 132
    Country goulash 283
    Duck 'n' beans 143
    Dynasty pork 97
    Flemish beef 105
    Lamb and asparagus 121
    Lamb and pumpkin 443
    Leek and tomato 370
    Mediterranean pork 88
    Mexican beef 106
    Orange chicken 466
    Pork and peas 99
    Pork ragoût 89
    Provençal fish 425
    Scotch beef 428
Cauliflower
    Creole 400

Crudités with butter bean dip
    338
Crudités and dip 421
Polonaise 257
Salad with sultanas 351
and Salami soufflés 67
Celery
    Crudités with butter bean dip
    338
    Crudités and dip 421
    and Grapefruit salad 330
    and Peanut soup 19
    and Radish salad 350
    Soufflé 304
    Stir-fried 379
    Stuffed trout 148
    Stuffing 148
Cheese
    and Apple pie 313
    Baked ham and tomato
      sandwiches 320
    Cheesy aubergine bake 380
    Cheesy bubble and squeak 373
    and Chicken pockets 268
    and Chive soufflé 68
    Coeurs à la crème 432
    Cottage cheese and ham cocottes
      56
    Cottage cheese pancakes 55
    Crab and cheese florentines 52
    Crackers 335, 452
    Crudités and dip 421
    Crunchy Camembert 57
    Dutch fondue 59
    Fruit and cheese kebobs 54
    Grilled corned beef baps 269
    Herby dip with cheese biscuits
      335
    Hot cheese and crab dip 474
    Maytime flan 286
    Melted Mozzarella sandwiches
      321
    Parsley cheese bites 58
    Puff 311
    Quick pâté mousse 33
    Salad kebobs 72
    Spinach and Brie puffs 73
    Stilton quiche 61
    Stuffed zucchini 70
    Three-tier pâté 28
    Tomato and basil flan 60
    and Tomato loaf 316
    Tomato and Mozzarella salad 355
Cheesecakes
    Chocolate 185
    Creamy blackcurrant 229
Cheesy eggplant bake 380
Cheesy cabbage pan-flan 373
Cheesy potato soup 20
Cheesy vegetable curry 315
Chef's layered salad 250
Cherry(ies)
    Chilled compote 167
    Cream slices 182
    Fruit flambé 174
    Jubilee 220
    Mixed fruit ice 216
Chicken
    Apricot barbecue 275
    and Banana double deckers 318
    Biriani 298
    Catalan 422
    Cheese and, pockets 268
    Crunchy salad 131
    Curried salad 82
    Curry 129
    Enchiladas 406
    Farmhouse, and rice 299
    Fritters 81
    Fruity pie 273
    Herby drumsticks 448
    Lasagne 133
    Liver and walnut pâté 15
    in Lychee sauce 127
    Marinade 482

Meat terrine 29
Orange casserole 466
Paprikash 132
Peanut drumsticks 83
Polka pie 134
Rosé 130
Spanish stuffed 128
Spicy club sandwich 317
and Yoghurt curry 274
in Yoghurt and ginger 482
and Zucchini salad 301
Chilled asparagus soup 439
Chilled carrot and orange soup 23
Chilled cherry compote 167
Chilled courgette and cheese soup
    22
Chilli meat balls 475
Chinese beansprout salad 356
Chinese egg rolls 64
Chinese lettuce parcels 399
Chinese-style liver 164
Chocolate
    American pie 188
    Cheesecake 185
    Coating, for ice cream 479
    Eclairs 181
    Eggs 435
    Fondue 458
    Iced boxes 239
    Magic pudding 231
    Mocha meringue 184
    Mousse special 206
Chunky soy vegetable soup 344
Citrus apple flan 194
Citrus snow 464
Cobbler
    Ham and eggs 305
    Liver 163
Cocktails, see also Drinks 476
Coconut rice salad 482
Coconut soufflé 416
Coeurs à la crème 432
Coffee mousse 198
Corn and tuna chowder 16
Corned beef
    Grilled baps 269
    Quick meat and potato soup 7
    Soup 260
Cottage cheese and ham cocottes
    56
Cottage cheese crepes 55
Cottage cheese and yoghurt dip
    421
Country goulash 283
Country stew 10
Coupe Jacques 177
Crab and cheese florentines 52
Crab-stuffed tomatoes 47
Crackers 335, 452
Cranberry brûlés 209
Cream of chestnut soup 340
Cream of potato soup 342
Creamed leek pastry 254
Creamed lemon spinach 381
Creamed onions 389
Creamy almond turkey 136
Creamy blackcurrant cheesecake
    229
Creamy cod appetizer 41
Creamy mushroom noodles 296
Creamy mushroom soup 348
Creamy pasta with tuna 46
Creamy rigatoni 295
Creamy rutabaga bake 378
Creamy spring vegetables 372
Creamy watercress soup 471
Creole eggs 309
Crepes
    Alaska 211
    Cottage Cheese 55
Crisp and crunchy salad 357
Croquettes, mixed vegetables 334
Crudités 53, 338, 421, 462
Crunchy Camembert 57
Crunchy chicken salad 131

Crunchy mixed salad 352
Crusty steak sandwiches 324
Cucumber
  Caterpillar 451
  Crudités with butter bean dip
    338
  Crudités and dip 421
  Crunchy mixed salad 352
  and Egg mousse 35
  Gazpacho salad 361
  and Stir-fried pork 90
  Stuffed salad 76
Currant(s)
  Creamy cheesecake 229
  Sherbet 419
Curried cauliflower salad 393
Curried chicken salad 82
Curried pork 482
Custard, courgette 364
Custard, Spanish caramel 424

D
Date rice 179
Date and walnut baked apples 230
Desserts, *see also* Ice cream and
    Soufflés
  Acapulco pineapple pudding 408
  American chocolate pie 188
  Apple flummery 201
  Appleberry dumplings 461
  Baked mincemeat soufflé 214
  Banana creams 450
  Banana fan flambé 242
  Bread and butter pudding 234
  Caramel-topped apples 444
  Cheese and apple pie 313
  Cherry cream slices 182
  Chilled cherry compote 167
  Chocolate cheesecake 185
  Chocolate éclairs 181
  Chocolate fondue 458
  Chocolate mousse special 20, 206
  Citrus apple flan 194
  Citrus snow 464
  Coconut soufflé 416
  Coeurs à la crème 432
  Coffee mousse 198

Coupe jacques 177
Cranberry brûles 209
Creamy blackcurrant cheesecake
  229
Date rice 179
Date and walnut baked apples
  230
Drambuie creams 430
Flaky rice sundaes 244
Frangipani tart 192
Fruit flambé 174
Fruit kebobs 176
Fruit mallow 200
Ginger cream refrigerator cake
  180
Ginger syllabub 208
Gingered fruit cocktails 175
Gooseberry and apple amber 173
Gooseberry fool 243
Grilled pineapple 178
Harvest pudding 172
Honeyed apricot whip 202
Hot coffee soufflés 213
Jam soufflé omelettes 237
Latticed gooseberry tart 196
Lemon layer sponge 228
Magic chocolate pudding 231
Mango spoon sweet 170
Marbled lime soufflé 210
Mediterranean rice dessert 197
Melon mousse 204
Mocha meringue 184
Nectarine tart 189
Nutty apple crumble 236
Orange jelly castles 238
Oranges in cointreau 169
Oriental fruit salad 411
Pancakes Alaska 211
Peach flambé 470
Pineapple bread pudding 166
Pineapple meringue pie 193
Plum and banana compote 171
Princess dessert 438
Queen of puddings 232
Raised plum pie 190
Raisin pie 191
Raisin semolina 240
Raspberry soufflés 212

Redcurrant jelly tart 187
Rhubarb and orange cream 199
Rich caramel mould 207
Riviera fruit salad 427
Sherry trifle 235
Spanish caramel custards 424
Spiced banana dumplings 168
Spicy apple crunch 186
Tangerine jelly 205
Treacle tart 241
Tropical crumble 233
Tropical flan 195
Devilled prawns and eggs 51
Dijon lamb noisettes 418
Dips
  Avocado 337
  Butter bean 338
  Cottage cheese and yoghurt 421
  Gingered aubergine 74
  Herby 335
  Hot cheese and crab 474
  Slimmers' crab dip 53
  Smoky 462
Drambuie creams 430
Drinks
  Between the sheets 476
  Black Russian 476
  Bloody Mary 476
  Boxcar 476
  Caribbean blues 412
  Daiquiri 476
  Gimlet 476
  Harvey Wallbanger 476
  Horse's neck 476
  Italian wine cup 446
  Lemon and apple cup 455
  Manhattan 476
  Marguerita 476
  Martini 476
  Pina colada 412
  Planter's punch 412
  Sangria 420
  Tequila sunrise 476
  Witches' brew 443
Duck
  'n' Beans 143
  Honey salad 142
  Roast, with grapes 141

Dutch fondue 59
Dynasty pork 97

E
Eclairs, chocolate 181
Egg(s), *see also* Meringue and
    Soufflé
  and Almond lamb 119
  and Avocado bake 71
  Carrot soup, and rice 347
  Chinese egg rolls 64
  Creole 309
  and Cucumber mousse 35
  and Devilled prawns 51
  Florentine 62
  Ham and, cobbler 305
  with Herby beans 256
  Jam soufflé omelettes 237
  and Lettuce pinwheels 327
  Marbled 435
  Mayonnaise appetizer 468
  Mocha meringue 184
  Mousse 66
  Mussel omelettes 50
  in a Nest 310
  Pâté 26
  Pineapple meringue pie 193
  in Potato nests 69
  Princess dessert 438
  Scrambled, and onions 307
  Spanish caramel custards 424
  Spanish vegetable omelette 308
  and Spinach nests 63
Eggplant(s)
  Cheesy bake 380
  Gingered dip 74
  and Pasta bake 251
  and Waffles 77
Enchiladas, chicken 406
Englishman's paella 297

F
Family fish pie 149
Farmhouse chicken and rice 299
Farmhouse lentils 390
Farmhouse turkey and ham pie 139
Fennel mayonnaise 439

Festive turkey 478
Finnan haddie tarts 428
Fish, *see also* Salmon, Shellfish, Tuna
  Baked stuffed kippers 40
  Breton steaks 145
  Celery stuffed trout 148
  Creamy cod appetizer 41
  Family fish pie 149
  Gratin 37
  Halibut special 147
  Herby kebobs 152
  Herring salad 45
  Kedgeree special 157
  Mackerel pilaff 290
  Mixed fish pâté 24
  Peanut flounder 146
  Provençal fish chowder 17
  Quick pilchard pâté 25
  Roes on toast 48
  Rolls 42
  Seafood macaroni bake 155
  Seafood and orange kebobs 158
  Seafood quickie 289
  Selsey soused herrings 43
  Sherried cod 272
  Smoked cod and spinach roll 153
  Smoked haddock tarts 428
  Smoked mackerel salad 39
  Spiced fried herrings 144
  Spicy fish 38
  Tilefish thermidor 151
  Trout with mushroom stuffing 431
  and Vegetable soup 15
  West Indian fish patties 414
Flan, *see* Quiche
Flounder, peanut 146
Flour tortillas 406
Fondue
  Cheese 312
  Chocolate 458
  Dutch 59
Frangipani tart 192
Frankfurter and vegetable soup 6
Fried rice 410
Fried sardine sandwiches 319
Fritter(s)
  Batter 412
  Ham, with fried bananas 265
  Oriental vegetable 402
  Savoury bacon 84
Frosted fruit and rose petals 441
Frozen macaroon mould 183
Frozen raspberry favourite 467
Fruit and cheese kebobs 54
Fruit flambé 174
Fruit kebobs 176
Fruit mallow 200
Fruity chicken pie 273
Fruity salad 57
Fruity stuffed pork chops 98

G

Garlic bread 446
Garlic mushrooms 418
Gazpacho salad 361
Genoese onion tarts 425
Ginger cream refrigerator cake 180
Ginger syllabub 208
Gingered eggplant dip 74
Gingered deep-fried shrimp 410
Gingered fruit cocktails 175
Gooseberry(ies)
  and Apple amber 173
  Fool 243
  Latticed tart 196
Grapefruit
  and Avocado salad 359
  and Celery salad 330
  Ice 224
  and Shrimp cocktail 458
Green bean soup 343
Green beans provençal 391
Grilled corned beef on buns 269

Grilled pineapple 178

H

Halibut special 147
Ham
  Baked tomato sandwiches 320
  and Cheese rolls 314
  and Cottage cheese cocottes 56
  and Egg cobbler 305
  Fritters with fried bananas 265
  Harvest salad 249
  and Pasta supper 292
  Rolls 449
  Saucy shrimp rolls 79
Hamburgers, tasty 103
Harvest ham salad 249
Harvest dessert 172
Hawaiian pork parcels 94
Herby beans with eggs 256
Herby chicken drumsticks 448
Herby dip with cheese crackers 335
Herby fish kebobs 152
Herring salad 45
Honey duck salad 142
Honeyed apricot whips 202
Hot cheese and crab dip 474
Hot coffee soufflés 213
Hot-topped ice cream 447

I

Ice cream
  Avocado 215
  Blackcurrant sorbet 419
  Brown bread 419
  Cherries jubilee 220
  Flambéed dessert 479
  Frozen macaroon mould 183
  Frozen raspberry favourite 467
  Grapefruit ice 224
  Hot-topped 447
  Iced chocolate boxes 239
  Iced passion fruit dessert 217
  Lime ice box pudding 219
  Mint sorbet 226
  Mixed fruit ice 216
  Orange and lemon water ice 484
  Pear wine sorbet 225
  Sicilian orange cassata 223
  Tea sorbet 227
  Tutti frutti 221
  Watermelon frappé 222
Iced chocolate boxes 239
Iced passion fruit dessert 217
Indonesian salads 395
Italian veal rolls 112

J

Jam soufflé omelets 237
Jerusalem artichoke soup 345

K

Kabanos risotto 300
Kebobs
  Bacon 80
  Fruit 176
  Fruit and cheese 54
  Herby fish 152
  Indian skewered lamb 120
  Salad 72
  Seafood and orange 158
  Vegetable 333
Kedgeree special 157
Kidney and orange simmer 159
Kidney and pork medley 160

L

Lamb
  and Apricot salad 284
  and Asparagus casserole 121
  Bake 125
  Breast, and apple rounds 116
  Chops and peppers 117
  Dijon noisettes 418
  Egg and almond, mince 119

Indian skewered 120
and Pasta medley 285
with Plums 123
Pot-roast leg 115
and Pumpkin casserole 443
Ratatouille 122
Roast, with zucchini sauce 118
Spiced 482
Spinach-stuffed lamb 126
Summer 124
with Walnut stuffing 436
Lasagne al forno 446
Latticed gooseberry tart 196
Leek(s)
and Bacon flan 306
and Barley soup 21
Creamed pastry 254
and potato pie 362
and Tomato casserole 370
Lemon
Citrus snow 464
Layer sponge 228
and Orange water-ice 484
Lentil layer pie 255
Lentil and lemon soup 340
Lentils, farmhouse 390
Lima bean dip with crudités 338
Lime
Citrus snow 464
Ice box pudding 219
Marbled soufflé 210
Liver and bacon hot pot 162
Liver cobbler 163
Liver loaf 161
Lychees
Chicken in sauce 127
Oriental fruit salad 411

M
Macaroni turkey 137
Mackerel pilaff 290
Magic chocolate pudding 231
Mango spoon sweet 170
Mango yoghurt foam 203
Marbled eggs 435
Marbled lime soufflés 210
Marinated pork chops 87
Marinated roast pork 410
Marinated summer beef 102
Maytime flan 286
Meat terrine 29
Mediterranean pork casserole 88
Mediterranean rice dessert 197
Melon(s)
Gingered fruit cocktail 175
Mousse 204
and Orange appetizer 436
Oriental fruit salad 411
and Shrimp cocktail 478
Melted Mozzarella sandwiches 321
Meringue
Dessert 473
Mocha 184
Pancake Alaska 211
Pineapple pie 193
Queen of puddings 232
Meringue dessert 473
Mexican beef 106
Mexican chilli soup 12
Mincemeat, baked soufflé 214
Mint sherbet 226
Mixed fish pâté 24
Mixed fruit ice 216
Mixed vegetable croquettes 334
Mocha meringue 184
Mock paella 463
Mushroom(s)
Creamy noodles 296
Creamy soup 348
Garlic 418
Puffs and cheese sauce 329
Soup with dumplings 262
Spinach fried with 369
and Stilton salad 246
Mussel omelet 50

Mussel and shrimp pie 156
Mussel soup 14

N
Nectarine tart 189
New potatoes with wine 392
Noodles Chinese-style 397
Nutty apple crumble 236

O
Offal
Chinese-style liver 164
Kidney and orange simmer 159
Kidney and pork medley 160
Liver and bacon hotpot 162
Liver cobbler 163
Liver loaf 161
Okra Mediterranean-style 396
Onion(s)
and Bacon crispies 78
Creamed 389
Creamy spring vegetables 372
Genoese tarts 425
Scrambled eggs and, 307
Vegetable kebobs 333
Orange(s)
Carrots, in juice 382
and Carrot soup, chilled 23
Chicken casserole 466
Citrus snow 464
in Cointreau 169
Gingered fruit cocktails 175
Castles 238
and Kidney simmer 159
and Lemon water-ice 484
Melon and, appetizers 436
and Rhubarb cream 199
and Seafood kebobs 158
Shortbread fingers 450
Oriental fruit salad 411
Oriental seafood salad 49
Oriental vegetable fritters 402

P
Pan pizza 287
Paprika potatoes 252
Parsley cheese bites 58
Parsnip, steak pie with 101
Party pizzas 456
Pasta
Cannelloni with tuna 293
Chicken lasagna 133
Creamy mushroom noodles 29
Creamy rigatoni 295
and Eggplant bake 251
and Ham supper 292
and Lamb medley 285
Lasagna al forno 446
Macaroni turkey 137
Salmon and macaroni layer 44
Seafood macaroni bake 155
Spaghetti with meat balls 282
Spaghetti with olives 294
Spicy sausage macaroni 291
with Tuna, Creamy 46
Pastry, shortcrust 368
Pâté puffs 30
Peach(es)
Flambé 470
Fruit flambé 174
Stuffed, for pork 93
Peanut drumsticks 83
Peanut flounder 146
Pear(s)
Fruit flambé 174
Pork and, 95
Wine sherbet 225
Pea(s)
and Bean salad 358
and Bean soup, chilled 349
Creamy spring vegetables 372
Herby beans with eggs 256
Pork and, 99

Portugaise 384
Soup with cheese toast 18
Pies, savoury
Chicken polka 134
Family fish 149
Farmhouse turkey and ham 139
Fruity chicken 273
Mussel and prawn 156
Pork turnovers 277
Steak and parsnip 101
Vegetable 362
Pineapple
Acapulco pudding 408
Bread 166
Cucumber caterpillar 451
Fruit flambé 174
Grilled 178
Hawaiian pork parcels 94
Mango spoon sweet 170
Meringue pie 193
Mixed fruit ice 216
Pancake Alaska 211
Tropical crumble 233
Tropical flan 195
Piquant courgette salad 354
Pizza
Pan 287
Party 456
Potato 367
Plum(s)
and Banana compote 171
Harvest pudding 172
Lamb with, 123
Raised pie 190
Pork
Apple roast 460
Baked honey ribs 91
Chops in apple sauce 278
Curried 482
Dynasty, stew 97
Fillet in puff pastry 92
Fruity stuffed chops 98
Hawaiian parcels 94
and Kidney medley 160
Marinated chops 87
Marinated roast, fillet 410
Meat terrine 29
Mediterranean casserole 88
and Pears 95
and Peas 99
Quick Portuguese 96
Ragoût 89
Roast, with peaches 93
Roast, with rum 414
Scallops with plums 86
Stir-fried, and cucumber 90
Streaky, with mandarin sauce 280
Turnovers 277
Pot roast brisket 104
Pot-roasted leg of lamb 115
Potato(es)
Baked with Apples 385
Corned beef soup 260
Cream soup 342
Creamy cod appetizer 41
Eggs in nests 69
Farmhouse lentils 390
and Leek pie 362
Marinated summer beef 102
Paprika 252
and Radish crunch 374
Spanish vegetable omelet 308
Spicy sticks 394
'n' Tomato gratin 375
Vegetable pie 363
West country 443
Princess dessert 438
Provencal fish chowder 17
Provencal fish stew 425
Puddings, see Desserts, Ice cream, Souffles
Pumpkin
Lamb and, casserole 443
Sunshine soup 346

Q
Queen of puddings 232
Quiche
Creamed leek pastry 254
Genoese onion tarts 425
Leek and bacon flan 306
Maytime flan 286
Red summer flan 368
Small corn quiches 65
Smoked haddock tarts 428
Stilton quiches 61
Tomato, cheese and basil flan 6(
Quick beef curry 302
Quick meat and potato soup 7
Quick pâté mousse 33
Quick pilchard pâté 25
Quick Portuguese pork 96
Quick tuna pâté 32

R
Radish
and Celery salad 350
and Potato crunch 374
Raised plum pie 190
Raisin pie 191
Raisin semolina 240
Raspberry(ies)
Frozen favourite 467
Sauce, for ice cream 183, 447
Sherry trifle 235
Soufflés 212
Red summer flan 368
Redcurrant jelly tart 187
Rhubarb and orange cream 199
Rice
Biriani, chicken 298
Biriani, vegetable 403
Chicken catalan 422
Coconut rice salad 482
Date rice 179
Englishman's paella 297
Flaky rice sundae 244
Fried 410
Kabanos risotto 300
Kedgeree special 157
Mackerel pilaff 290
Mediterranean dessert 197
Mock paella 463
Savoury rice dish 303
Tomato rice soup 263
Vegetable biriani 403
Vegetable, fried 366
Rich caramel mould 207
Riviera fruit salad 427
Roast duck with grapes 141
Roast lamb with zucchini sauce 188
Roes on toast 48
Rosé chicken 130
Rose petals, frosted 441

S
Salad(s)
Avocado and grapefruit 359
Brussels sprouts and date 360
Brussels sprouts and Stilton 258
Cauliflower with sultanas 351
Celery and radish 350
Chef's layered 250
Chicken and zucchini 301
Chinese beansprout 356
Crisp and crunchy 357
Crunchy chicken 131
Crunchy mixed 352
Curried cauliflower 393
Curried chicken 82
Gazpacho 361
Grapefruit and celery 330
Harvest ham 249
Herring 45
Honey duck 142
Indonesian 395
Kebobs 72
Lamb and apricot 284
Marinated summer beef 102

Mushroom and Stilton 246
Oriental seafood 49
Pea and bean 358
Piquant zucchini 354
Potato and radish crunch 374
Smoked mackerel 39
Squid 154
Stuffed cucumber 76
Tomato and Mozzarella 355
Tropical 247
Tuna 248
Waldorf 353
Salami and tomato soup 8
Salmon
  with Fennel mayonnaise 439
  and Macaroni layer 44
  Mousse 34
  Parcels 150
  in Puff pastry 288
  Spicy fish 38
Sambols 404
Samosas, vegetable 331
Sandwiches 322, 323
Sauces, savoury
  Barbecue 275, 471
  Cheese 79, 329
  Lemon 386
  Rouille 425
  Tomato, fresh 27, 465
  White 133
  Zucchini 118
Sauces, sweet
  Butterscotch 447
  Caramel 427
  Chocolate 447
  Raspberry 183, 447
Saucy ham and shrimp rolls 79
Sausage twists 266
Savory bacon fritters 84
Savory rice dish 303
Scallops in tomato sauce 465
Scotch beef casserole 428
Scrambled eggs and onions 307
Seafood macaroni bake 155
Seafood and orange kebobs 158
Seafood quiche 289
Selsey soused herrings 43
Semolina, raisin 240
Serbian beef 110
Shellfish
  Crab and cheese florentines 52
  Crab-stuffed tomatoes 47
  Creamy cod appetizer 41
  Devilled prawns and eggs 51
  Englishman's paella 297
  Gingered deep-fried shrimps 410
  Grapefruit and shrimp cocktail 459
  Hot cheese and crab dip 474
  Melon and shrimp cocktail 478
  Mock paella 463
  Mussel omelet 50
  Mussel and shrimp pie 156
  Mussel soup 14
  Orange and seafood kebobs 158
  Oriental seafood salad 49
  Saucy ham and prawn rolls 79
  Scallops in tomato sauce 465
  Seafood macaroni bake 155
  Seafood quiche 289
  Slimmers' crab dip with crudités 53
  Squid salad 154
Sherried cod 272
Sherry trifle 235
Shortbread, orange fingers 450
Sicilian orange cassata 223
Small corn quiches 65
Smoked fish and spinach roll 153
Smoked mackerel, dressed 39
Smoky dip with vegetables 462
Snow peas with water chestnuts 387
Soufflés, savory
  Cauliflower and salami 67

Celery 304
Cheese and chive 68
Spinach surprise 328
Soufflés, sweet
  Baked mincemeat 214
  Coconut 416
  Hot coffee 213
  Jam soufflé omelet 237
  Raspberry 212
Soup(s)
  Autumn 13
  Beefy 11
  Brussels 339
  Carrot and parsley 261
  Celery and peanut 19
  Cheesy potato 20
  Chilled asparagus 439
  Chilled carrot and orange 23
  Chilled pea and bean 349
  Chilled zucchini and cheese 22
  Chunky soya vegetable 344
  Corned beef 260
  Country 10
  Cream of chestnut 340
  Cream of potato soup 342
  Creamy mushroom 348
  Creamy watercress 471
  Fish and vegetable 6
  Frankfurter and vegetable 6
  Green bean soup 343
  Jerusalem artichoke soup 34, 345
  Leek and barley 21
  Lentil and lemon soup 341
  Mexican chilli 12
  Mushroom, with dumplings 26, 262
  Mussel 14
  Pea, with cheese toast 18
  Provençal fish chowder 17
  Quick meat and potato 7
  Salami and tomato 8
  Spinach and liver pâté 9
  Sunshine 346
  Sweetcorn and tuna chowder 16
  Tomato rice soup 263
  Vegetable 259
Soya burgers 371
Soya, chunky vegetable soup 344
Spaghetti with meat balls 282
Spaghetti with olives 294
Spanish caramel custards 424
Spanish stuffed chicken 128
Spanish vegetable omelet 308
Spiced banana dumplings 168
Spiced lamb 482
Spicy bean pâté 336
Spicy fish 38
Spicy sausage macaroni 291
Spinach
  and Brie puffs 73
  Crab and cheese florentines 52
  Creamed lemon 381
  Egg nests 63
  Eggs florentine 62
  Fried with mushrooms 369
  and Liver pâté soup 9
  and Smoked cod roll 153
  Stuffed lamb 126
  Stuffing 126
  Surprise 126
Spiced fried herrings 144
Spicy apple crunch 186
Spring rolls 326
Squid salad 154
Steak and parsnip pie 101
Steak with vermouth sauce 469
Stews, see casseroles
Stilton
  Brussels sprouts and, 258
  and Mushroom salad 246
  Quiche 61
  Salad dressing 357
  Steak 100
  Veal and walnuts 114

Stir-fried beans and beansprouts 398
Stir-fried celery 379
Stir-fried pork and cucumber 90
Strawberries, Riviera fruit salad 427
Streaky pork with mandarin sauce 280
Stuffed cucumber salad 76
Stuffed green peppers 332
Stuffed turkey drumsticks 140
Summer lamb 124
Sunshine supper 253
Swede, creamy bake 378
Sweet and sour Brussels sprouts 401

T
Tacos, beef 407
Tangerine jelly 205
Tasty hamburgers 103
Tasty meat triangles 264
Tea sherbet 227
Three-tier pâté 28
Tilefish thermidor 151
Tomato(s)
  Baked ham sandwiches 320
  Brussels sprouts country-style 388
  Cheese and basil flan 60
  and Cheese loaf 316
  Crab-stuffed 47
  Gazpacho salad 361
  Green beans provençal 391
  Leek and, casserole 370
  and Mozzarella salad 355
  Okra Mediterranean-style 396
  Peas portugaise 384
  Peperonata 383
  Potato gratin 375
  Red summer flan 368
  Rice soup 263
  and Salami soup 8
  Sambols 404
  and Zucchini mousse 36
Tortillas, flour 406
Treacle tart 240
Trifle, sherry 235
Tropical crumble 233
Tropical flan 195
Trout with mushroom stuffing 431
Tuna
  Cannelloni with, 293
  with Creamy pasta 46
  Puff pastries 448
  Quick pâté 32
  Salad 248
  Strudel 271
  and Sweetcorn chowder 16
Turkey
  in Breadcrumbs 138
  Creamy almond 136

Farmhouse ham pie 139
Macaroni 137
Parcels 135
Stuffed drumsticks 140
Toss 276

V
Veal
  Apple-stuffed chops 111
  Italian rolls 112
  Ratatouille 113
  with Stilton and walnuts 114
Vegetables
  Biriani 403
  Chunky soya soup 344
  Cheesy curry 315
  Country goulash 283
  Creamy spring 372
  Crudités 338, 421, 462
  Crumble 365
  and Fish soup 15
  and Frankfurter soup 6
  Fried rice 366
  Kebobs 333
  Oriental fritters 402
  Pie 363
  Samosas 331
  Soup 259
  Smoky dip with 462
  Spanish omelet 308
  Terrine 27

W
Waldorf salad 353
Watercress, creamy soup 471
Watermelon frappé 222
West country potatoes 443
West Indian fish patties 414

Y
Yoghurt
  Chicken curry, and 274
  Chicken and ginger, in 482
  Gingered eggplant dip 74
  Honeyed apricot whips 202
  Indian skewered lamb 120
  Mango foam 203
  Salad dressing 49, 330
  Slimmers' crab dip with crudités 53

Z
Zucchini
  and Cheese soup, chilled 22
  Cheese-stuffed 70
  Chicken and, salad 301
  Custard 364
  Harvest salad 249
  Piquant salad 354
  and Tomato mousse 36